ALTHEA

ALSO BY SALLY H. JACOBS

The Other Barack

ALTHEA

The Life of Tennis Champion
ALTHEA GIBSON

SALLY H. JACOBS

ST. MARTIN'S
PRESS
NEW YORK

First published in the United States by St. Martin's Press, an imprint of St. Martin's Publishing Group

ALTHEA. Copyright © 2023 by Sally H. Jacobs. All rights reserved. Printed in the United States of America. For information, address St. Martin's Publishing Group, 120 Broadway, New York, NY 10271.

www.stmartins.com

Designed by Steven Seighman

Library of Congress Cataloging-in-Publication Data

Names: Jacobs, Sally H., 1957– author.
Title: Althea: the life of tennis champion Althea Gibson / Sally H. Jacobs.
Description: First edition. | New York: St. Martin's Press, 2023. | Includes
    bibliographical references and index.
Identifiers: LCCN 2023015096 | ISBN 9781250246554 (hardcover) |
    ISBN 9781250246561 (ebook)
Subjects: LCSH: Gibson, Althea, 1927–2003. | African American women tennis
    players—Biography. | Women tennis players—United States—Biography. | Racism
    in sports—United States—History—20th century. | Discrimination in sports—
    United States—History—20th century.
Classification: LCC GV994.G53 J33 2023 | DDC 796.342092 [B]–dc23/eng/20230412
LC record available at https://lccn.loc.gov/2023015096

Our books may be purchased in bulk for promotional, educational, or business use.
Please contact your local bookseller or the Macmillan Corporate and Premium Sales
Department at 1-800-221-7945, extension 5442, or by email at
MacmillanSpecialMarkets@macmillan.com.

First Edition: 2023

10 9 8 7 6 5 4 3 2 1

For Dice

Contents

Preface

In the film *King Richard*, a drama about the tennis-playing Williams sisters and their father released in 2021, there is a fleeting moment in which the face of Althea Gibson appears. She gazes out from a black-and-white photograph stuck to the refrigerator as the Williams parents argue about which of them has contributed more to their daughters' success. Althea is smiling, a tennis racket gently clasped against her chest, as though amused at the couple's wrangling. After all, she knows better than anyone that it's she who deserves primary credit. If it weren't for her the Williams sisters likely wouldn't have become who they did.

Sixty-five years ago, Althea Gibson did the seemingly impossible. A skinny high school dropout bearing the scars of her father's beatings on her back, she served and lobbed her way from Harlem's mean streets to the lush green courts of Wimbledon to become the first Black woman to be the number-one tennis player in the world. Seven years later she rewrote history again when she broke the color barrier in women's golf and became the first Black member of the Ladies Professional Golf Association Tour in 1964.

Althea's achievements earned her a place in the then-fledgling pantheon of Black sports heroes who came before her, like boxer Jack Johnson and baseball icon Jackie Robinson. But the truth is that her undertaking was much harder than theirs. That Althea was a woman made her task infinitely more challenging. Unlike her male counterparts she had no models before her to lead the way, no teammates to support her, and an earning power that could not compare with that of the men. What's more, she was a woman of fluid sexual identity, which earned her the enmity of not only many in the white world who were inclined to reject her for her skin color alone but also some people in the Black community. That she appeared at times remote, even self-absorbed, scarred as she was by a childhood of neglect and physical abuse, kept some at a further distance. To others she was a heroine without compare. When Venus and Serena published a Black History Month newsletter in their high school years it was Althea who they put on the back cover.

Like many Black women of achievement in America's past, Althea's story has been largely ignored. To the bulk of those at the upper levels of the white-dominated world of tennis in her day, she was both an astonishing athlete who had to be recognized and a conundrum to be avoided. Nor did they come to feel much more warmly toward her with the passing of years. When the USTA named its new tennis stadium at Flushing Meadows in 1997 it chose the name of Arthur Ashe, a Black player who earned his number-one ranking nearly two decades after Althea. When the organization christened its national tennis complex nearly a decade later it chose the name of white tennis champion Billie Jean King. It was not until 2019 that Althea was honored with a granite bust at the complex, nestled in the shadow of the other two structures.

It is likely that few on the set of *King Richard*, other than the Williams family members, were aware of the identity of the woman in the photograph on the refrigerator. Even the set decorator who selected the picture and put it on the refrigerator admits that she had never heard of Althea Gibson before she began rooting through the history books for props. That she chose Althea's photo at all, she explained, was simply a reasoned guess. After all, there were few other high-ranking Black tennis players in the twentieth century to choose from, only a tiny handful of them women.

It is time now, at this long-delayed moment of racial reckoning, that Althea Gibson's story be told, time at long last that the chronic neglect that she endured in her final years be corrected. Over the past four years I have roamed widely in what was once Althea's world, from the swamps of Clarendon County, South Carolina, up the churning boulevards of Harlem, and onto the verdant grasses of the West Side and Wimbledon tennis clubs and beyond. Through it all I was aided by a great many of her closest friends and relatives as well as a good number of her tennis partners and opponents. Sadly, of the nearly 150 people I interviewed in the preparation of this book, more than a few of them have died.

Among those on that list who was perhaps the closest to Althea in her tennis years was Angela Buxton, her British doubles partner and lifelong tennis friend. During our many visits, the last of which occurred over dinner on the night before the unveiling of the statute of Althea at Flushing Meadows, Buxton agreed to try to find a long-lost five-page poem her mother had composed about her and Althea during the several days' buildup to their triumphant doubles match at Wimbledon in 1956. Six months after Angela found the poem covered in cobwebs in an old suitcase buried in her garage in England and had it sent to me along with a bundle of photographs, she passed away in August of 2020.

Another who is now gone is Frances Clayton Gray, a friend of Althea's in her post-tennis years who eventually became her caretaker and the formidable gatekeeper at the door of her East Orange apartment. After laboring for years to help preserve Althea's memory, she died in September of 2019. One more who passed away during the writing of this book was Billy Davis, Cosmopolitan Club star and half of an enormously talented tennis-playing pair of brothers who were raised not far from Althea. Both of them generously spent many hours explaining to me the Black tennis world of the 1950s and how the combative Althea found a place within it. Billy, who was the winner of eleven American Tennis Association national titles and worked as Althea's training partner and road manager during her exhibition tour, died at the end of 2021. Bob Davis, an ATA national champion and the first executive director of the Black Tennis Hall of Fame, met with me in his Bradenton, Florida, office and patiently fielded my many phone calls and emails for the four years that the book took to complete.

Long before there was Angela or the Davis brothers, there was the town of Silver, a one-store community in the heart of South Carolina named for the cofounder of the railroad that once steamed across the flat farmlands that unfurl below the Piedmont. It was there that Althea was born. It was also there that a man named Harold "Sunny" Billie, the proprietor of that lone store called Sunny's and a distant cousin of Althea's, outdid himself in his efforts to help me find precisely where that event occurred and what came afterward. Sunny, who also passed away during the evolution of this book, spent many of his days at the counter of the store that his grandfather opened in the 1950s and had a working knowledge of local genealogy that would put Ancestry.com to shame. One warm spring afternoon, Sunny, who lost his left leg to circulatory problems and was confined to a brilliant blue wheelchair, produced a truck with a U-Haul attached and wheeled himself onto the trailer, leaving room next to him for me and a couple of his cousins. Together, we bumped for hours across the fields that once belonged to Althea's great grandfather in search of her birthplace. One cousin was certain the site was near the river where he once carted moonshine with his father, while Sunny was confident that the location was several hundred yards in the opposite direction. Either way, we were about as close as you can get to where this book begins. It was the starting place of a life story that turned out to be as triumphant as it was pained, a tale of courage entwined with disappointment.

As many of Althea's era have passed away, a new generation now dominates the world of tennis. It is tempting to imagine how Althea Gibson might have fared in today's quite different cultural moment when Black female athletes are far more the norm. At the time I started working on this book in 2018 there were four Black tennis players listed among the top twenty of the Women's Tennis Association (WTA), or 20 percent. They included Naomi Osaka, Sloane Stephens, Serena Williams, and Madison Keys. Venus Williams was just a bit further down the ladder while Zina Garrison and Leslie Allen, who had reached a world ranking of number 4 and number 17, respectively, had retired. In perhaps the most notable reflection of the racial revolution in the sport, three years earlier Katrina Adams, doubles champion, became the first African American president and CEO of the United States Tennis Association. In Althea's day, while many Black female tennis players competed in the ATA tournaments, she was with few exceptions the lone Black player on USTA turf. Had she played in a later era, Althea would have found herself in good company and not an isolated maverick as she maneuvered a solitary hurdle-ridden course.

The increased number of players of color, of course, does not change everything for the better. In the fall of 2018, Serena Williams was made the subject of a cartoon in an Australian newspaper after her stunning defeat by Naomi Osaka at the U.S. Open. The cartoon depicted her in a childish rage, stomping furiously on her racket, with thick lips wide open and her hair askew. Many viewed it as a racist Jim-Crow-esque assault despite the artist's claim that it was intended solely as a reflection of Williams's temperamental behavior after the umpire had called several code violations.

Althea experienced something similar, although to markedly less fanfare. When she became the first Black to win the Paris International Indoor Tournament in 1956, one of her first major victories, one French newspaper cartoon portrayed her as a menacing figure with her racket raised threateningly over her head. The cartoonist exaggerated her features giving her bulging eyes and enlarged lips as well as a cap of tightly coiled hair. Amused, Althea sent a copy of the cartoon to her friend Ro back home and in an accompanying letter joked, "this one is good for a few giggles. (smile.)"

While race continues to percolate in press coverage of the sport, there has been some progress on other fronts that might have made life a little easier for Althea. Naomi Osaka ignited a long-simmering conversation about the mental health of athletes in the spring of 2021 when she announced that she would not participate in post-match news conferences at the French Open because the stressful encounters caused her significant anxiety and depression. After officials fined her for doing so, she quit the tournament, saying she didn't want to be a distraction. In the days to come, other tennis players, including Black athletes Sloane Stephens and Coco Gauff, began to speak out about the mental toll their careers exacted. Nearly two months later, four-time Olympic gold medal gymnast Simone Biles withdrew from the Olympic finals citing mental health stress. While not everyone was entirely empathetic with the athletes' views, the incidents clearly triggered a broader cultural appreciation of the stress under which professional athletes often live.

Althea could only dream of such support. Like Osaka and others, she often found the post-match scrum of inquiring reporters more than she could endure. When she declined several interviews and ignored photographers following her victory at Wimbledon in 1957, several Chicago reporters who had long been angry with her for refusing to publicly advocate more forcefully for the Black cause verbally attacked her in a manner unimaginable today. One reporter called her "as ungracious as a stubborn jackass" in his column, while another derided her as "so obsessed with herself . . . that she apparently speaks only to kings and queens." Althea, who had a difficult relationship with the press during periods of her tennis career, would likely have greatly appreciated the different tenor of the relationship between the media and today's athletes.

The Black press of the 1940s and 1950s was in many respects torn about how to regard Althea Gibson. On the one hand, she was a most highly valued barrier-breaking athlete, one of a small handful of "firsts" with the capacity to make inroads into white culture for her brothers and sisters. But for various reasons Althea chose not to be a racial champion of the fist-raising sort and she made not the slightest apology for doing so. As she wrote in her autobiography, "I am not a racially conscious person. I don't want to be. I see myself as just an individual. . . . I'm a tennis player, not a Negro tennis player. I have never set myself up as a champion of the Negro race." The Black press of the day, not surprisingly, fumed.

In today's polarized culture where the motto "If you're not with us, you're against us" often prevails, one can only imagine that Althea might have been canceled on Twitter and Facebook for her stance. And yet, in her later post-tennis years, as the activism of the 1960s came into play, Althea became somewhat more engaged in the cause. For years after she retired from professional tennis she worked on multiple fronts to train Black youth in the sport and paired with Arthur Ashe and others in fundraising efforts to increase opportunities for young athletes of color.

In the aftermath of George Floyd's brutal murder in 2020, a group of prominent Black tennis players took a stand. Outraged at the ongoing brutality inflicted upon African Americans, professional player Frances Tiafoe launched a video called *Racquets Down, Hands Up* in which a succession of the highest profile Black players, including Coco Gauff, Zina Garrison, and Serena Williams, do just that, laying their racquets on the ground and raising their hands in the air. While the film clip is culturally light-years removed from Althea's own experience, it is hard to believe that she would not have fully shared the sentiment expressed in the video.

And how would the participants in the video have regarded the Black player peering out from the photograph on the refrigerator in the *King Richard* film? How would the many other women of color now on the WTA rankings list view her? It would seem likely that every one of them might bow to Althea Gibson's image. After all, it was she who put tennis rackets in their hands.

1

The Promised Land

It was one of the most important and little-noticed events in American sports history.

It happened on a summer day in 1941 on a cramped clay tennis court at the Cosmopolitan Club in Harlem, a leader among a growing number of Negro tennis clubs in the country at the time whose members represented the elite echelons of Black society. At the far end of the court was a skinny thirteen-year-old girl wearing torn blue jeans and a formidable scowl. At the other end stood a one-armed tennis coach sporting his trademark green-visored cap. Watching from the stands were a couple of dozen men and women neatly turned out in pressed collared shirts and tailored floral dresses, who were taking a midday break to watch what they had been told was one of the most promising young players to come on the tennis scene. If she was as good as they said she was, the Cosmopolitan Club might just consider sponsoring her for major competitions.

They did *not* like what they saw. That girl wore a shoddy T-shirt, and her tangled black hair was an unruly mess. She was not at all the type sought by the Cosmopolitan, whose members prided themselves on pursuing the aristocratic sport of tennis. The way she strode brazenly around the court was just flat-out alarming to those watching from the stands who had expected a far more genteel approach to the game. Truth be told, they couldn't quite tell if she was a boy or a girl, the way she carried herself. Had they heard correctly that someone had actually called her Al? And was that really a *used* tennis racket in her hand, one well-heeled spectator perhaps sniffed to her neighbor.

They didn't know the half of it. Althea Gibson—yes, they were looking at a girl—was one of the toughest streetfighters in upper Harlem, the leader of the unofficial 146th Street gang, and the queen of the "snitchers," or petty thieves, known to ply their trade at the Bronx Terminal Market. Most days, she didn't bother to go to school at all, choosing instead to while away the afternoons in the theaters, watching what she called "the flickers," or roaming around the city. She'd learned her fighting skills from her father, Daniel, a stocky garage mechanic, who had taught her to box in brutal sessions that left her body badly bruised and her spirit sapped. Not surprisingly, Althea did her best to stay out of his way. Sometimes, when she didn't bother to come home for days at a time, her father would beat her with his belt until red welts appeared on her back, just to remind her who was boss. More than once, when she couldn't bear to go back to their cramped third-floor apartment and endure another one of his beatings, she passed the night dozing on a subway car, riding the train alone for the entire night, up and down the length of the city from Van Cortlandt Park to New Lots Avenue and then back again. For years, this pattern played out in a vicious circle that stained Althea's childhood, one not unlike that unfolding in many other tenements.

Althea had a rough side, without question, but she was also an astonishing athlete with a burning desire to win. When Buddy Walker, a Harlem saxophonist at the time, who worked a second job helping city police monitor children playing on the streets, happened to notice her impressive speed and aggressive athleticism, he bought her a pair of restrung rackets for five dollars apiece.[1] But when he and some of his friends urged her to try out tennis at the Cosmopolitan Club on 149th Street, Althea balked.

"What do I get out of it?" she asked.[2]

Althea wasn't at all sure she wanted to play such a sissy sport as tennis. It was a high-falutin' game played by the rich folks who cruised the streets in their fancy convertibles and sleek foreign roadsters. One boy she knew on the block actually hid his tennis racket in a suitcase so other kids wouldn't make fun of him when he walked to the public courts. Besides, all those lily-white clothes and the equipment cost money of which her family could only dream. But Althea was never one to turn her back on a challenge. Just a couple of days after Walker made his suggestion, she found herself standing on the Cosmopolitan Club court across from its venerated coach, Fred Johnson. A draftsman for a ship design firm, Johnson had lost his left arm in an industrial accident as a child and had gone on to become one of the most successful coaches on the Black tennis scene.[3] It took only a few minutes and half a dozen balls for the club members to make their decision. Never mind her unsettling demeanor, the girl was a formidable player with dazzling speed and an intimidating swing, precisely the sort of athlete they had been hoping for. They'd just presumed—well, hoped—that that athlete would be a boy.

"You only had to see her hit one ball to forget the blue jeans she first wore to the court," one club member told Ted Poston, a reporter for the *New York Post*.[4]

Impressed, the movers and shakers of the Cosmopolitan Club took up a collection to buy Althea a junior membership to the club that would provide her both regular lessons with Johnson and access to a Black society she had never before encountered. At the time, Black communities were known to put up funds to sponsor a member of their group who showed promise, just as an earlier generation in the days following slavery had pooled their very limited resources to secure education for the most able among them. After one member put up five dollars so the girl could get a new racket, Johnson contributed ten dollars from his own pocket and bought Althea a Dreadnought Driver tennis racket from Harry C. Lee & Company, famous for the enormous tennis racket suspended above its storefront down on Warren Street. Later that evening, the slender coach dropped in on Althea's parents in order to get approval to teach her tennis. The Gibson family had struggled for more than a decade since abandoning sharecropping in South Carolina to come up to Harlem, and it hadn't been easy putting food on the table for their five children. When Johnson showed up at the door and proposed his plan, Althea's mother had only one thing on her mind.

"How much money is there in it?" Annie Bell Gibson asked.[5]

Money was not the aim of the members of the Cosmopolitan Club. These prominent doctors, political figures, and professionals composed a leadership class dubbed "The Talented Tenth" by W. E. B. Du Bois, sociologist, historian, and one of the self-described Negro intellectual leaders at the forefront of the new thinking about race that had sparked the cultural explosion of the Harlem Renaissance in the 1920s. As part of that movement, club members were far more interested in the integration of their sport, which had proven infuriatingly resistant to Negro players. By the 1940s, though, fissures were beginning to appear in the monolith of the white American sports world. This was not to say that anything remotely resembling actual integration was occurring on the lush tennis courts that hosted the nation's highest-ranking tournaments. Tennis would remain one of the sporting world's most stubbornly unyielding holdouts to competitors of color until the late 1940s, when halfback Kenny Washington became the first Black player in the modern era to sign a contract with the National Football League in 1946, and Jackie Robinson broke the color barrier in baseball the following year when he signed with the Brooklyn Dodgers. In tennis, a handful of players of color were quietly allowed to compete in national tournaments during the decade, joined here and there by a celebrated white player or two who occasionally ventured onto a court populated by Black players.

Just one year before tomboy Althea showed up, the Cosmopolitan Club hosted an unprecedented interracial exhibition match between Jimmie McDaniel, a Xavier College junior and the reigning singles champion of the Negro American Tennis Association (ATA), and white tennis superstar Don Budge, who had become the first player to achieve a Grand Slam, winning Wimbledon and the national championships in Australia, France, and New York in 1938. The landmark and much-publicized event in 1940 drew an ebullient crowd of more than two thousand spectators who packed the Harlem courts, while others perched on the fire escapes and rooftops of adjacent buildings, hoping for a glimpse of the action. Although the redheaded Budge trounced McDaniel in straight sets, he graciously declared afterward that McDaniel was "a very good player," adding, "I'd say he'd rank with the first ten of our white players."[6] More important, the racial barrier in tennis had been at least symbolically cracked, which many hoped would lead to future interracial tournaments. Seen as a critical milestone, the event was largely regarded, as the *New York*

Amsterdam News put it, as "the most important sports and social event to hit Harlem in many years."[7]

For the ATA, the goal on the horizon was that Black players would eventually play in the exclusive white tournaments of the United States Lawn Tennis Association (USLTA.) The message was clear. Although the USLTA did not officially comment on the event, its executive committee "privately squirmed uneasily," according to Warren F. Kimball, a former member of the board of directors of what came to be called the United States Tennis Association (USTA) and author of a history of the organization, called *The United States Tennis Association: Raising the Game.*[8]

Althea Gibson, the brawling teenager in rumpled dungarees, was a far cry from the charming and mannered college man McDaniel. Taming the tempestuous young woman and molding her into a model representative of the Black tennis establishment was going to take some serious doing. The rangy young player knew little about the court etiquette of the elite, British-born sport of lawn tennis, and what she did know of it she often ignored. When tennis balls from other courts happened to come within her reach, she would belt them away randomly into the air. When Coach Johnson urged her to tone down her arrogant attitude or tried to teach her some court strategy, she generally turned a deaf ear. Although she grudgingly agreed to wear the prim white clothing often required to play the game, she could barely suppress her desire to leap across the net and assault her opponent. That's what she had done on the streets, after all.

"I remember thinking to myself that it was kind of like a matador going into the bull ring, beautifully dressed, bowing in all directions, following the fancy rules to the letter, and all the time having nothing in mind except sticking that sword into the bull's guts and killing him as dead as hell," she later wrote. "I probably picked up that notion from some movie I saw."[9]

Fortunately, the matador had the game to match her killer instinct. One year after she made her debut in front of the sophisticated Cosmopolitan crowd, Althea was entered in her first tournament, the ATA-sponsored New York State Open Championships, held at the same club. Not only did she win the girls' singles, but she beat a white girl, Nina Irwin, in the finals.

As it turned out, Althea was not only as good as Irwin, she thought smugly to herself; she was even better.[10] Althea also knew full well that many in the predominantly Black audience had been cheering not for her but for her more likable opponent. But it was she who was the winner, and so, a few weeks later, the club took up a collection to send Althea to the ATA National Girls' Championships at Lincoln University in Pennsylvania, one of the first Historically Black Colleges and Universities (HBCUs) in the nation. Even before she got onto the court, Althea was strutting about and challenging her opponent, Nana Davis, to make herself known so that the opponents could take stock of each other. As Davis later recalled it, "Althea was a very crude creature." When Davis defeated her in the girls' semifinals, Althea was furious and abruptly ran into the stands without saying a word, much less shaking hands. "Some kid had been laughing at her and she was going to throw him out," Davis said.[11] Tennis be damned, the matador was going to teach someone a lesson.

Integrating tennis, clearly, was going to be difficult. If Althea was already being criticized in Black tennis circles—and, indeed, a number of young players and Cosmo veterans were taken aback by her seemingly cocksure and aggressive style—it appeared nearly impossible that she could penetrate the well-barricaded doors to the white tennis kingdom. Althea, however, came from a people who knew hardship all too well. Generations of her family had confronted the most brutal and exacting conditions known to humankind. Now it was Althea's turn. To prepare herself, she might have looked back on four generations of her family line in order to find guidance. There, she would have found a certain enslaved African woman named Tiller, who just happened to be her great-great-grandmother.

Tiller's name was at the bottom of the 1849 handwritten list. It followed a dozen other items deemed more important by the estate accountants—like the mule, the one hundred bushels of corn, and the three head of cattle. They were all the estate property of the recently deceased Benjamin Walker, a prominent white businessman in the hardscrabble Sumter County, South Carolina, of the mid-nineteenth century and had been carefully catalogued by the accountants. But Althea Gibson's great-great-grandmother didn't come cheap, even if she was the last item on the estate accounting list.

Tiller was sold for $378, a pretty steep price for a fourteen-year-old enslaved girl just a few steps out of Africa. The accountants speculated that her relatively high price was because she was likely carrying the child of the man who had put the bid on her, Walker's son-in-law. After all, the other young people on the list cost around of $200, and one old woman had a price tag of just $13.12.[12] The young women were always getting pregnant by someone or other, as the bean counters saw it, and they didn't care one way or another, as long as the price was right. Walker had owned a vast amount of property, and his agents had plenty of work to do to wrap up his estate. If Benjamin Reese Gibson wanted to buy the teenager and take her back to his home in the sweeping cotton fields of Clarendon County, he was free to do so.

At some point before or after the sale, Tiller gave birth to Gibson's child, a boy she named January apparently because of the month in which he was born.[13] January entered the world fifteen years, give or take, before the signing of the Emancipation Proclamation that marked the first step toward bringing an end to slavery in the opening days of 1863. Although the act was limited in what it accomplished, and especially in the South, it eventually eliminated some barriers that might have kept a clever and enterprising Black man such as January from making something of himself.

During his eighty-five years, January Gibson lived on the fertile fields that unfurled to the west of the meandering Sammy Swamp, just a little over a daylong wagon ride from where the first shot of the Civil War was fired. He lived a somewhat remarkable life for the child of a slave. He started with empty pockets in his one pair of pants, a single pair of shoes, and a shirt. Every Saturday night, he would give his clothes to his wife, who would then wash them, along with his underwear, and dry them in front of the fire. Early the next morning, she'd iron the clothing, and the two of them would head to church. Afterward, January would set off to work in the fields.[14]

By the time he died in 1928, January Gibson had accumulated more than three hundred acres of property worth $6,000 and possessed a life insurance policy worth roughly $2,250, payable upon his death, as well as several hundred dollars in cash. All this was meticulously detailed in his 1928 will, complete with typed notations of outstanding debts and loans as well as an itemized accounting of who among his relatives should get precisely what. January, who apparently could neither read nor write, signed the documents with an *X*, under which someone routinely scribbled the words "his mark," presumably at his verbal request.[15] When January's body was lowered into his grave at the Mount Zero Missionary Baptist Church in Clarendon County, a church at which he had long served as a deacon, he could not have known that one of his greatest legacies lay gurgling on a blanket on the floor of his eldest son's nearby home. In time, that sturdy baby girl, his great-granddaughter, was going to help change America.

The social heart of January's universe was a tiny hamlet called Silver, not so much an actual town as a rural community punctuated by brooding swamps and waterways turned nearly black by the drip of tannic acid from the cypress and tupelo gum trees overhead. Everyone pretty much knew everyone else, and many of them were related in one way or another. Devastated by the turmoil of the Civil War, the county grappled with poverty and political chaos for more than a decade after the South's surrender. Toward the end of the century, however, the local economy was beginning to hum with lumberyards, gristmills, and cotton gins. Linking them all was a network of expanding train lines, one of which was the Charleston, Sumter and Northern Railroad, cofounded by John S. Silver, for whom the community was named. By 1890, Silver had a sawmill, a cotton gin, and its very own post office, which was located on the main street, just a short way down from one of the busiest stores in town. That store, the first of three to open in Silver, was owned by Althea's maternal grandfather, Charlie Washington.[16]

Washington was The Man. A stern individual of strong opinion, Uncle Charlie, as he was called by almost everyone, kept a close eye on the doings in his store, which had an impressive array of offerings. There were stylish secondhand dresses and shoes shipped by train down from Manhattan, beef butchered on-site, and an abundance of local vegetables and livestock. On Fridays, the train from Charleston pulled up in front of the store and delivered wooden boxes of freshwater fish packed in ice. Every morning, a pair of Washington's granddaughters lit the fireplace in the early morning and got to work frying the fish for sandwiches to be served to customers at a couple of tables at the rear of the store.

Like many prominent men of the day, Washington was a stalwart of the church. Although he didn't claim a specific house of worship as his own, he served as a visiting preacher at several churches throughout the county. Every Sunday found him clad in his best suit and a well-pressed tie, his pretty young wife on his arm. A man of many hats, Washington also leased a swath of former plantation lands from one of the dominant white landowners, land Althea's father would sweat over for several years.[17]

One of Washington's granddaughters, Agnes Washington James, whom he had raised since her infancy after her parents died, helped out with everything, from serving food to arranging store items. James well remembers unpacking the clothing as a child when it arrived neatly folded in boxes from New York. "They wasn't new," she recalls, "but they was nice." Her far more vivid memories are of sweltering days harvesting crops on her grandfather's land along with her sister, cousins, and a host of elders. In time, many of the next generation came down from the northern cities where they had been born to help out in the summers, including her own son. "My grandfather used to have trucks come down to the farm, and he would sell the stuff to them," James recalled. "They'd drive those trucks down—I think they'd come from New York—and we'd fill them up with vegetables. Oh, we used to work. Sun up and sun down. . . . Cotton, corn, you name it. Peas, beans, every kind of vegetable you can think of, Papa had."[18]

Washington's leased lands bordered on the hundreds of acres that January Gibson had accumulated over the past two decades, and the two men were well acquainted. Although roughly two decades apart in age, Washington and January Gibson had much in common. Gibson had served for forty-five years as the deacon of the Mount Zero Missionary Baptist Church, north of town. The seeds of that church were planted under the bush arbor near the murky waters of Mill Pond, on the James Tindal plantation, where slaves had regularly gathered before the Civil War. In the years afterward, Tindal gave the land to the group and donated a church building.[19] Like many other enterprising Black men of the day, the two neighbors were ardent believers in the importance of education for their community, whose residents, for more than one hundred years, had been prohibited under state law from writing down words. For generations of enslaved people and some poor whites, schooling had been sporadic, if available at all. At best, it was limited to a few months during the off-season. In the years following Reconstruction, it became apparent that not only did many of the impediments to Black progress remain firmly in place, but also a good number of whites actively opposed expanding education for Black people, especially in the South. Why kindle their ambitions and empower them to seize opportunities better left for others? Or, so the thinking went. And so it was that not a single Black person in South Carolina received a high school diploma until 1930, and even then, only 104 out of 5,646 diplomas awarded went to Black people.[20] In communities such as Clarendon County, where more than 35 percent of the Black citizens were illiterate when Althea was born, Black people began to work determinedly to initiate schools for their children.[21]

January Gibson was at the head of the pack. Education was just as important to him as the personal fortune he was carefully cultivating and perhaps more so. Like many other illiterate children of enslaved people, he recognized that literacy was not only crucial to the progress of Black people, but also one of the very few means available to escape the lingering yoke of slavery. Having sired eleven children and fifty-four grandchildren, January launched a personal crusade in his later years to establish proper schools for them and all the other Black children in the area.[22] That he apparently did not take steps to learn to read and write himself is an irony that some family members puzzle over to this day. At the end of 1906, January and several other Black men from county churches organized the Ministers, Deacons, and Laymen's Union for the specific purpose of building schools and churches for local Black residents. The local paper, *The Manning Times*, described the effort in a headline as "The Colored People of Clarendon at Work."[23] The organization was instrumental in opening several rural schools, and by the time Althea was born, in 1927, the residents of Silver had started negotiations to purchase the local Silver School, formerly used by whites, for $750. When the school eventually opened its door for Black students the following fall, it was able to remain open for a whopping seven months of the year.[24]

Charlie Washington's life also intersected, albeit indirectly, with what turned out to be one of the most critical developments in educational reform, not just locally but on a sweeping national scale. For a period of two years, Washington provided lodging in his home to a bold young pastor named Joseph Armstrong DeLaine and his wife. A slender man customarily clad in a worn black suit and vest, DeLaine had returned to the damp clay soil of his youth in the 1930s to serve as principal of the Silver School, where he remained for close to a decade. Deeply frustrated by the inequities in the segregated schooling of Black and white children made possible by the "separate but equal" doctrine sanctioned by the U.S. Supreme Court decades earlier, he led a petition drive of local Black people seeking educational services equal to those received by whites. In 1949, that petition culminated in the unthinkable: the group challenged the segregated system and brought a lawsuit against the Summerton School Board. Reprisal came fast and furious. DeLaine, his wife, and his nieces lost their jobs; his mailbox was jammed with threatening letters signed by the Ku Klux Klan; and his house was burned to the ground while the fire department stood by and watched the flames. Other petition signers, including at least one of Althea's cousins, were denied credit and barred from purchasing goods ranging from food to farm equipment. In the end, however, the Black petitioners prevailed in the case. Their lawsuit rose to the U.S. Supreme Court, where it was merged with several other legal actions to become the *Brown v. Board of Education of Topeka* court case that culminated in the landmark 1954 decision that brought an end to segregation in America, at least on paper.[25]

By the late 1920s, Gibson and Washington became connected on a much more personal level when two of their family members fell in love. Daniel Gibson, the eighteen-year-old son of January Gibson's eldest child, Junius, was a stocky young man of the earth with a thatch of luxuriant brown hair. Annie Bell Washington, Charlie Washington's boisterous daughter, also eighteen, was nearly Daniel's physical equal and entertained herself by taking rides on not just horses but hogs, cows, and whatever else happened through the barnyard. During their courtship, Gibson, who was known as "Dush," dutifully walked the one-mile distance to his beloved's home every Sunday night and finally won the beaming girl's hand in marriage. Despite the gloomy farming prospects that had already propelled a stream of locals to pack their bags and head north, the couple moved into Gibson's father's house and began their life together. Determined to succeed, Daniel Gibson got to work with his brother on a five-acre plot of his father-in-law's leased property.

Not long afterward, the product of their love was ushered into the world by a midwife on the unseasonably cool morning of August 25, 1927, an eight-pounder so sturdy that folks called her "a big fat one." The first of five children, she arrived in a crowded four-room cabin owned by her grandfather Junius Gibson and occupied by half a dozen of her aunts and uncles.[26] The baby girl was named Althea at the suggestion of her uncle, who was dating a girl with the same name. As Annie Bell Gibson later explained to a reporter, "He thought it was pretty sounding. I did, too."[27]

Beyond the bedroom window, vast fields of ivory cotton and nodding corn unfolded, land on which baby Althea's grandparents and now her parents and other family members had struggled to earn a living. At the time, South Carolina was in the grip of a severe financial crisis stemming from the overproduction of cotton and tobacco in the years following World War I and the loss of overseas markets at the war's end. Making matters far worse, an infestation by the boll weevil, a beetle originating in Mexico that feeds on cotton buds and flowers, coupled with a prolonged period of drought had radically reduced the value of the annual cotton crop yield. With large amounts of food having to be imported, and less income to spend on it, many poorer South Carolinians were reduced to a diet of pork and corn bread. In those difficult days of want, according to Walter Edgar's book *South Carolina: A History*, a widespread lament went, "Ten-cent cotton and forty-cent meat / How in hell can a poor man eat?"[28] Living conditions were grim. The state already had the dubious distinction of having some of the worst roads in the nation, many of which were either sand or dirt. Just 1 percent of Clarendon County's homes had electricity, while only slightly more claimed the luxury of running water.[29] By the end of the 1920s, the state's agricultural system was on the brink of collapse and its entire economic infrastructure teetered on the edge of ruin. More than half the state's banks had failed, and cash was almost impossible to come by. With the Depression lurking right around the corner, things were about to get much worse.

For families such as the Gibsons, the situation was demonstrably more difficult than for whites. While the end of slavery had eliminated some of the more horrific brutalities of enslaved life, such as the beatings, rapes, and forcible fracture of families, conditions were almost as grim as ever in some crucial aspects. This was arguably truer in Clarendon County than just about anywhere else in the nation.[30] Black folks there may have had something officially called freedom, and they outnumbered the white man by almost three to one, but they were still bound by rigid economic practices that strangled their hopes and left their children gaunt. One form of bondage had simply been substituted for another. Many Black citizens and some poor whites resorted to sharecropping, a system by which the white landowner permitted a tenant to work the land in return for supplies and a share of the crops ultimately harvested. At the end of the sweltering months of the harvest season, though, the landowner invariably called the shots, and usually to his own advantage. In times of economic duress such as the late 1920s, the sharecropper sometimes walked away from that season of hard labor in the fields empty-handed.

"When it come time to settle up, a lot of [the landowners] used to tell us, 'Well, we broke even this time. So, we'll just call it even right now, and you can start over next year,'" said Harold "Sunny" Billie, seventy-four, the one-legged owner of Sunny's Store, which was less than a mile from what was once January Gibson's property. "They used to give 'em a pack of meal and some meat, butt meat, and that was it. A lot of poor folks had to eat mush and meat, and peas and beans. People used to dry it all and just have dried beans and peas through the winter."[31]

In the late summer of 1927, the situation started getting even worse. On the day of Althea's birth, ominous clouds churned overhead, threatening rain, a harbinger of the violent storms and flooding that would plague the Carolina lowlands in the year ahead, dragging crop yields ever lower. The erratic wet weather would continue far into the following year. By the end of 1928, many households had abandoned cotton entirely. As scores of families migrated north to escape the storm belt of the lower states, the farmers who remained behind were compelled to man rowboats in order to harvest their corn.[32]

The turmoil visible in the skies overhead that day was even manifest on the paper of baby Althea's birth certificate. Whether it was the fault of an overexcited family member who failed to provide accurate information or of an exhausted midwife hungry for some breakfast will never be known. But Althea's birth certificate as recorded soon afterward was glaringly incorrect. It wasn't just her name that was inaccurate, but her gender as well. Instead of recording the birth of a girl named Althea, the record documented the birth of a boy named Alger. Althea's father was also given the incorrect name of "Duas." Almost three decades later, the information on Althea's birth certificate would be corrected at Daniel Gibson's request, for reasons that are unclear, but apparently no one paid any mind at the time it was recorded.[33]

Some three years after Althea's father began to work in the fields, the choking dust and burrowing boll weevils had done him in. By the end of the 1920s, cotton prices had plummeted, and the state's overall agricultural production had dropped even farther. In his third year, Daniel Gibson harvested a single bale and a half of cotton, which brought him a grand total of seventy-five dollars. "I worked three years for nothin'," he would later say.[34] So had lots of other folks. Sales at all three stores in little downtown Silver were down, and many of the pretty dresses on Charlie Washington's shelves were gathering dust. By 1930, the Silver post office would close up permanently, and soon the trains, with their deliveries of fresh fish, would come to a halt.

The previous summer, Annie Bell's sister Sally swung open a door of possible escape. In town for the funeral of one of their other sisters, Sally urged Annie Bell and her family to come north and join her in bustling Harlem. What's more, she was willing to take baby Althea with her when she went back home, to make the couple's relocation easier. The young Gibsons were well aware of the lure and promise of the streets of New York City, and not just from the images in mail-order catalogues. Over the past decade, Black residents throughout the South had begun to flee to the cities of the North and West, to Chicago and Baltimore and New York, in an unprecedented exodus of human beings that would come to be known as the

Great Migration. Over the course of six decades, some six million Black people would leave to escape the brutal caste system of the South known as Jim Crow, named for a nineteenth-century minstrel who satirized the Black race. They were escaping a system that denied them opportunity and education, that hanged them from trees, and that humiliated them at most every step. The North was now the Promised Land. There, Black people could speak their minds and make good money and dance at nightclubs with glittering marquees. There was electricity and indoor plumbing, even telephones and store shelves of abundance. Or, so they were told.

Of the multitude of Black writers who penned the story of Harlem in the early twentieth century, few put it as bluntly as Claude Brown, Althea's own first cousin, who, as a child, lived a few blocks away from her in Harlem. As he wrote in his landmark 1965 classic, *Manchild in the Promised Land*, "Going to New York was good-bye to the cotton fields, good-bye to 'Massa Charlie,' good-bye to the chain gang, and, most of all, good-bye to those sunup-to-sundown working hours. One no longer had to wait to get to heaven to lay his burden down; burdens could be laid down in New York."[35]

And so began an unparalleled march of mass humanity fueled by the rawest of hope. It kept on going, even into the 1970s. Sally Washington had left years before, while the going was still good. Althea's paternal aunt Ossie would head to Harlem in the mid-1930s with her husband. In time, Charlie's granddaughter Agnes James, like lots of young girls in town, would go up north monthly, to work as a domestic. Cleaning floors and washing windows was backbreaking work, to be sure, but it was better to be inside a shaded house than on the sweltering fields inhaling dust.

"We had a lady down in Silver, and she used to hire girls," James recalled. "That was her job, hiring girls to go to New York to work. When we got there, the white people would meet us at the bus station. . . . Most of them was Jewish."[36]

It was time, now, for two-year-old Althea to head to the promised land of Harlem. The plan was that her father would join her in New York as soon as he could pull together enough money for a train ticket. Then he'd get a job and send back home for the rest of the family. That the devastating economic blight of the Great Depression would descend on America within months was something none of them could have anticipated. Neither could they have foreseen that the Black mecca of Harlem about which they had heard so many exciting reports was soon to become something quite different. And so, the migration out of the South continued.

Not long after Althea arrived in New York City, her father followed as planned. With the money he had earned from selling that single bale and a half of cotton, he bought a cheap blue suit for $7.50 and a $25 train ticket. As the train churned along the northbound corridor, he regaled one of the porters with stories of the grueling hardship of farm life in South Carolina and the difficulties his family had experienced. When the train pulled into Pennsylvania Station, the amiable porter pointed out that the city was hard for a newcomer to navigate and offered to escort Gibson on the subway up to Harlem. All he had to do was pony up five dollars to cover the cost of the subway fare. Gibson agreed, only to find out weeks later that a subway ride cost just a nickel.

As they walked out onto the sidewalk of 125th Street, the porter tipped his cap. "Here you are, Mr. Gibson," he said. "This is Harlem."[37]

2

The Cosmo Club

Daniel Gibson took a long, hard look at his skinny twelve-year-old daughter a few feet away from him. They were standing on the trash-strewn rooftop of their Harlem tenement, the churning waters of the Harlem River several blocks east. Gibson, who prided himself on being able to knock another man out with a single blow, was sizing up his daughter's tender face, trying to settle on the best place to land his first punch.

"Put up your dukes," he commanded.[1]

And then he slammed his fist into her face. Al, as her father had nicknamed her, stumbled backward, momentarily off-balance. The girl, who was nearly her father's height even as a preteen, was a fighter, though, and she pulled herself back up in front of her father and punched him squarely in the jaw. The battle continued, the two of them maneuvering around each other in a violent, sweaty dance as Althea's brother Daniel Jr. watched nervously from the roof's edge. The sparring went on for more than an hour, as most of their bouts did.

Dush Gibson was a man ensnared, near powerless, in the choke hold of segregation and chronic unemployment during the Depression. He didn't hesitate to whip out the iron's power cord and use it on any of his five children who dared displease him. Al never cried when he beat her; she barely even winced. She just stared coldly back at him, and it drove him nuts.

"I was tough. I wasn't afraid of anybody, not even him," Althea would write years later. "He says himself that when he would whip me, I would never cry, not if it killed me. I would just sit there and look at him."[2]

In a way, this was precisely what her father wanted. While Gibson's intent was to punish his rogue daughter, who sometimes disappeared on the streets for days at a time, he also wanted to teach her how to fight. Harlem may have been a cultural mecca in the late 1930s, but it could still be a mean and punishing place. Even a girl—maybe *especially* a girl—needed to be prepared to defend herself, which is why Gibson bought his daughter a pair of boxing gloves. There was still another potential benefit to being able to box, and that was money. Professional women boxers were in the news, and some of them brought in a handsome gate. A couple of Black girls had appeared in a big-time boxing benefit down in Midtown not so long before. If Al were good enough to be a contender or even a world champion, her winnings could help support the family.

Sometimes, however, her father's punches had nothing to do with training. Once, when Althea returned home after living on the streets for a couple of nights, Dush went after her. "When I finally sashayed in, he just walked up to me and punched me right in the face and knocked me sprawling down the hall. I got right back up and punched him as hard as I could, right in the jaw, and we had a pretty good little fight going and we weren't fooling around either."[3]

Althea mostly stood her ground in their boxing matches, but other times, she tried to get away from him, especially after one of his particularly angry whippings, which left raw welts covering her back. Once, when she ran away from home after a beating, she was so afraid to return to their crowded third-floor apartment that she went to the police station instead and begged for help. The police let her hang around for an hour, but then they called her mother to come get her. When her mother, who was terrified of the police, didn't show up, a police officer was sent to the Gibsons' door. "Don't you want your daughter?" he asked. Althea got it good that night.[4]

So determined was Althea to steer clear of her father's punishing blows that she sometimes aimlessly wandered the streets for hours, anything but go home to those painful whippings. When subway workers kicked her off the train late at night, she retreated to building stoops and stairwells, where she'd curl up shivering on the cement and try to sleep. But, of course, the longer she stayed away from home, the worse the punishment would be when she returned.

"He would beat the"—Daniel Gibson Jr., known as "Bubba," indicated the expletive with a deep nod of his head—"out of her. Teach her a lesson. . . . Althea was improving more and more. The next thing you know, one day they went up there, and Althea tore him up. She'd beat the *H* outta him. And we all was happy. And then the lessons stopped. No more boxing lessons."[5]

When Althea came of age during the Depression, Harlem was in many respects a brutal battlefield, one on which even young children were left to survive as best they could. That overcrowding and poverty were chronic is an understatement. The stretch of land north of Central Park that was Harlem, bordered roughly by the Hudson and East rivers, contained more Black residents per square mile than any other spot on earth at the time.[6] Not only were truancy and disease widespread, but the city suffered a chronic shortage of recreational spaces where children could safely play, nowhere more severe than in Harlem. Childhood there was hazardous at best. For many children, gang membership was mandatory and drug and alcohol use not uncommon. Claude Brown, Althea's cousin, wrestled with alcoholism and street violence from age six until well into his later years. In his autobiographical novel, which details the horrors of childhood in Harlem, Brown writes that by the time the main character was nine years old, he had been "hit by a bus, thrown into the Harlem River (intentionally), hit by a car, severely beaten with a chain. And I had set the house afire." As one of the author's southern relatives put it succinctly, "New York was no place to raise a child."[7] After spending time in a juvenile detention center, Brown ultimately found his way out and became a successful writer and speaker. Althea would find a very different escape route.

Not that there wasn't fun of a certain sort to be had in Harlem. A chronic truant in her preteen years, Althea routinely hung out with a boy who was one of the toughest gang leaders around. There was no hanky-panky between them, though, as Althea explained in her autobiography. "We were what we called boon-coons, which in Harlem means block buddies, good friends."[8] They and other pals entertained themselves by shoplifting food, roasting their haul on open fires in abandoned lots, and fighting in the streets. Once she and a friend named Charlie scrounged together a bunch of discarded soda bottles and, with the money they got from the store returns, rented a bicycle for thirty-five cents to pedal the nearly twenty-five-mile distance to Coney Island, each of them taking turns sitting on the main bar while the other gripped the handlebars. When Althea wasn't proving her toughness with her fists, she often spent long days in the dark theaters absorbed by her beloved "flickers." All this instilled in her a golden rule that would prevail throughout her life: Winning was the only thing that counted. Not doing your best, not just doing well—only triumph. What she also learned as a child was that she was alone in that fight and in the world. In the end, she could depend only on herself. These were hard truths that would take some time to learn. The lessons began as soon as she set foot in New York.

The Harlem that the Gibsons arrived in was a place like no other in American history. It was not just a confluence of hopeful refugees such as themselves, although it was that, too. It was also ground zero for a state of human and racial self-expression that vibrated on the broad boulevards that stretched a couple of miles north from Central Park. This was no longer the old Harlem of the Dutch or even the Italians. By 1930, Harlem was now nothing less than "the Negro Capital of the World." The Negro population in the borough of Manhattan alone had skyrocketed to nearly a quarter of a million, a 500 percent increase since the turn of the century.[9] That churning universe was the nexus of an unparalleled outpouring of creative expression by Black artists known as the Harlem Renaissance, which lasted from roughly 1920 to 1935.

The bedrock of the Harlem Renaissance was a new concept of African American culture articulated in large part by Alain LeRoy Locke, a distinguished scholar and educator who was widely recognized as the spiritual father of what was dubbed the "New Negro" movement. The slender Locke, a familiar figure striding down Harlem's streets in his tailored suit with an umbrella clasped at his side, was a prime example of that "Talented Tenth" extolled by Du Bois, with whom Locke often disagreed, particularly regarding the role of art. Locke believed that it was crucial for the race to develop original forms of cultural expression—art, music, dance, and literature—in part to create a new sense of racial identity but also to dispel negative racial stereotypes entrenched in American culture. In 1925, Locke edited *The New Negro: An Interpretation*, a groundbreaking anthology of predominantly Black literature and poetry. An ardent champion of civil rights, Locke heralded the volume as "our spiritual Declaration of Independence." The book triggered an intellectual and cultural flowering that established Harlem as the mecca of Black America and drew many thousands of Black pilgrims.

Throughout the decade and into the 1930s, a rising generation of writers such as Langston Hughes, Zora Neale Hurston, and Countee Cullen gave voice to a wholly new vision and embrace of Black identity. Their aim, in part, was to undermine the deep-seated racism in American society. As writer and activist James Weldon Johnson wrote, "Nothing can go farther to destroy race prejudice than the recognition of the Negro as a creator and contributor to American civilization."[10]

The "New Negro" identity was something to be discussed, debated, and certainly celebrated by the Black residents of Harlem in ways as unique as they were unfettered. It was an identity that spilled out of living rooms and churches, restaurants and bars, and it generated a palpable kind of excitement. In few places was it more evident than the intersection of Lenox Avenue and 133rd Street, often called "Swing Street" and home to some of the most popular speakeasies and cabarets. There were glittering dance halls with mahogany floors and nightclubs with waiters on roller skates. In elegant salons, the rigid rules of gender evaporated as women in floor-length white furs mingled with drag queens in high heels, all of it scored to the electrifying rhythms of new forms of music known as jazz and the blues drifting through the streets in the hours long after midnight.

The evolving new culture of Harlem generated a hybrid dialect all its own, one that came in part from a Black slang rooted in the clay soil of the South and that came to be known as "Harlemese." Many artists who were part of the "New Negro" movement considered the expressive urban lexicon a valuable manifestation of the culture and wrote their own glossaries of the terms. In his 1928 debut novel, *The Walls of Jericho*, Harlem writer Rudolph Fisher, for example, included an introduction to contemporary

Harlemese in which he defined such popular terms as "dickty" (a high-class person), "ofay" (derogatory term for a white person), and "bring mud" (to fall below expectations, disappoint).[11] Whichever guide one used, outsiders visiting the Harlem nightclub circuit would have been wise to bone up on the lingo before pulling up a stool at the bar.

The cultural flowering of the Harlem Renaissance coincided with the dawning of a new era in professional Black sports. The first Black professional baseball leagues emerged in the 1920s and continued to expand in the late 1930s. In the same period, the first professional Black basketball team, the Commonwealth Big Five, was launched in Harlem in 1922. World-class boxer Sugar Ray Robinson moved to Harlem from Detroit in 1932 and, in later years, made headlines as much for his over-the-top lifestyle, which included a flashy flamingo-pink Cadillac and a personal entourage of assistants and beautiful women, as for his acclaimed performance in the ring. Another champion boxer, Beau Jack, moved to New York in 1942 and became known for the popular boxing gym he ran out of his Harlem basement.

While these figures were hugely popular among the average Harlemite and working person, many among the Harlem intelligentsia maintained a deliberate distance from spectator sports and popular culture, dismissing both as superficial.

To the elite leaders of the movement, sports and some aspects of popular music were regarded as superficial and even an impediment to their efforts to elevate the culture. The NAACP's magazine, *The Crisis*, which was edited by Du Bois himself, was so popular that it reached a circulation of one hundred thousand without ever having run a single story on baseball's enormously popular Negro Leagues, as David Anderson points out in his book, *The Culture of Sports in the Harlem Renaissance*.[12] For that, sports enthusiasts turned to the Black press, which along with the public widely celebrated Black athletes' accomplishments as critical steps in the march toward integration.[13] Some would use their sports analysis and detailed play-by-plays as a vehicle ultimately to make larger assessments about the state of race relations and to object to the fitful pace of racial progress in the early twentieth century.

For the Lockes and Du Boises of that New York hour, sports were too lowbrow to trouble with. Du Bois, for example, apparently wrote not a word in *The Crisis* about one of the landmark victories achieved by a Black athlete in the twentieth century when boxer Jack Johnson became the first Black to win the world heavyweight championship in 1908. Both the Black and white press went wild over the event, for varying reasons. Jack London, a celebrated white journalist and novelist who covered the fight for the *Call* newspaper of San Francisco, called the match-up a "hopeless slaughter . . . Johnson was too big, too able, too clever, too superb." Unhappy with the outcome, London demanded that another white fighter step forward and "remove that smile from Johnson's face."[14]

It would be six years before Du Bois wrote an arm's-length commentary, one that said virtually nothing about Johnson's stunning athletic achievement; Du Bois focused instead on the maelstrom of racism that subsequently embroiled the boxer. "Neither [Johnson] nor his race invented prize fighting or particularly like it," wrote Du Bois, expressing an opinion that many Black Americans might have disagreed with. "Why then this thrill of national disgust? Because Johnson is black."[15] It would take another generation before Black intellectuals embraced the powerful social significance of achievements on the playing field.

On their arrival in Harlem in 1930, the Gibsons found themselves thrust into the beating heart of it all. Sally Washington's apartment on 146th Street sat at the corner of Eighth Avenue, a stretch of street now known as Frederick Douglass Boulevard, one of the principal arteries of the churning Black cultural capital. A couple of blocks farther to the west were the elegant boulevards of Sugar Hill, so named for the "sweet life" there enjoyed by Harlem Renaissance luminaries and wealthy Black residents. Among its residents were Du Bois; Walter F. White, writer and executive secretary of the NAACP; heavyweight boxing champion Jack Johnson; and premier bandleader Duke Ellington. Head south a short distance on Seventh Avenue, and there was Smalls Paradise, the legendary basement nightclub where waiters twirled on roller skates while delivering drinks and where flashy limousines triple-parked outside as their owners danced the Charleston within.[16] At the time, Smalls had the distinction of being the only one of the dominant Harlem nightclubs to be owned by a Black person and to be integrated. Just a couple of blocks away was the highly popular Connie's Inn, a basement nightclub owned by a trio of immigrant bootleggers. Connie's featured Black entertainers and initially restricted its audience to white customers only. And down on 125th Street was the entertainment mecca the Apollo Theater, which showcased some of the greatest Black music and dance performances of the early twentieth century—and was soon to become one of Althea's favorite hangouts.

Dush Gibson was beside himself, thrilled to find his family at the heart of a world so very different from the punishing cotton fields of South Carolina, despite being ripped off by that porter the moment he arrived. What's more, he got a job right away, working as a handyman in a garage for ten dollars a week. Now, *that* was money.

"I didn't have nothin' to worry about no more," Gibson exclaimed. "I sent for my wife and we were in business."[17]

Gibson's growing family stayed at Aunt Sally's apartment, where things were comfortable and there was always plenty to eat. Sally worked as a domestic, but she was also a savvy businesswoman who sold bootleg whiskey and entertained male friends in the parlor, both trades prominent in Harlem at the time. As a toddler, Althea was introduced to whiskey when she happened upon a full jug of it on the kitchen table and downed every drop. The doctor who rushed to her bedside wasn't the last to empty her stomach of alcohol. Althea is not explicit in her autobiography about what Aunt Sally's visiting male friends, whom she calls "uncles," might have been seeking other than alcohol, although it seems possible that her aunt was working as a prostitute. Althea says only that the "uncles" and "some of the other men who came to see Aunt Sally, used to take me out with them for the afternoon and naturally they would always end up drinking whiskey. So would I."[18] On her return, it was her father who stuck his finger down her throat to make her vomit up the alcohol. "Daddy claims that I never used to get drunk but that when I got home he had to get all the whiskey out of me," Althea wrote in her autobiography. "I don't recommend this kind of childhood training."[19]

There were other family members close by, refugees from the South who had followed in their footsteps. Dush Gibson's sister Ossie, known as "Sweetie," and her husband moved to 145th Street, a short distance from Aunt Sally's, in the 1930s. In time, Junius Gibson, Daniel and Sweetie

Gibson's father, would join the household. A light-skinned man with slicked-back straight hair that reached below his neck and a tendency to go barefoot even on the city's litter-strewn streets, Junius Gibson prided himself on being able to sit in the front of segregated city buses down South; the drivers rarely realized he was Black.[20] More family members would follow in the years to come, and the Gibsons' house was often crowded with relatives.

The golden age of the Harlem Renaissance—the very phenomenon that drew many of them north—did not last, however. By the mid-1930s, that cultural explosion had collapsed, along with the stock market, at the onset of the Great Depression. As the lights went dark on the once-packed boulevards of Harlem, residents were hard-pressed either to find jobs or to pay their rent. Little, it seemed, had really changed in the lives of Black people at the time. Although many of the books and works of art produced during the celebrated Harlem Renaissance would become American classics, the decade-long effort to recast the image of Black people itself began to implode. The image of Harlem as an exotic and tantalizing playground was fast displaced by food pantries and homeless shelters as many of the famed nightclubs and juke joints shut their doors. The truth was that while the golden years in Harlem had given birth to a chapter of unique and unprecedented Black cultural expression, they had failed to create any real change in the brutal racial stratification that prevailed in the nation. Although the social workers, toiling along the streets beyond the bright lights of the commercial boulevards, had known it all along, had seen the suffering and want plaguing many Black families, their concerns were largely masked by the public exhibition that was the face of the Harlem Renaissance.[21]

That cultural outpouring had obscured the development of a ghetto of poverty and ill health that was a direct result of the massive influx of Black people during the Great Migration. Between 1910 and 1920, the Black population in New York City increased 66 percent. From 1920 to 1930, it surged 115 percent, bringing the population to 327,706. Of those who arrived in 1930 alone, 33,765 were from South Carolina.[22] White residents in Harlem, where the vast majority of Black migrants settled, fled by the thousands. In their wake, Harlem developed throughout the 1920s into a slum of chronic overcrowding, poverty, and sickness.

One of the primary problems plaguing residents was the exorbitant cost of living, a condition that resulted from the crush of newcomers look-ing for work coupled with unscrupulous landlords, both Black and white. Rents in Harlem, whose residents had few other options for where to live in Manhattan and were among the least able to pay, were easily 50 percent higher than elsewhere in the city.[23] Chronic overcrowding and the result-ing unsanitary living conditions soon led to a multitude of health problems, including spiraling rates of tuberculosis and infant and maternal mortality double those in other parts of Manhattan. One study of health conditions in Harlem in the mid-1920s found that the mortality rate for residents of Harlem in those years was 42 percent higher than those in the rest of the city.[24] As conditions steadily deteriorated, more than a few landlords gave up even pretending to provide maintenance services and instead allowed utilities to fail, stairs to collapse, and roofs to go unrepaired. Gradually, whole blocks of Harlem housing became unlivable as legions of rats and other vermin took over. Even the New Negro movement's founder, Alain Locke, conceded that the Harlem Renaissance he had fathered had come to a bitter end in the face of the stark conditions strangling Harlem. It was time, he said, for a reformation, one that would include both economic reconstruction and social reform.

"It is easier to dally over Black Bohemia or revel in the hardy survivals of Negro art and culture than to contemplate this dark Harlem of semi-starvation, mass exploitation and seething unrest," Locke wrote in an arti-cle titled "Harlem: Dark Weather Vane" for the magazine *Survey Graphic* in the summer of 1936. "But turn we must."[25]

Few events signified the demise of the hope that had fueled the Harlem Renaissance more than the arrest on March 19, 1935, of a teenage Puerto Rican boy in a Harlem department store for shoplifting a penknife. When a false rumor circulated that the boy had been killed by store employees, the streets erupted in a violent release of pent-up rage, the product of years of poverty, discrimination, and police violence. As night fell, thousands of Har-lemites rioted and looted white-owned stores. By the time police managed to bring the situation under control, three people were dead, two of them high school students, and hundreds injured. A detailed report about the event, drafted by the commission appointed by Mayor Fiorello La Guardia, con-cluded that the outburst had not been triggered by a couple of bad actors, as had been initially thought. Rather, the report, titled *The Complete Report of Mayor La Guardia's Commission on the Harlem Riot of March 19, 1935*, found that the rioting had been a spontaneous event driven by deep resentment over an "extraordinary record of discrimination against the Harlem Negro" in the area of employment. The riot had resulted from a continuous and chronic impoverishment that constituted "a denial of the fundamental rights of the people to a livelihood."[26] The report also pointed out that many Harlemites lived in dilapidated and filthy rentals that contributed to chronically high death rates. In its concluding chapter, the report cited the disgraceful physical condition of the Harlem schools and "the vicious environment that surrounds the schools all indicate the presence of a poverty-stricken and therefore helpless group of people in the community. One can almost trace the limits of the Negro community through the character of the school buildings. . . . Such an environment as Harlem is naturally a breeding place of juvenile and adult delinquency."[27]

Few knew that life better than Althea and her cousin Claude. A decade younger than Althea, Claude was routinely on the run from police and truant officers. So accustomed did he become to the beatings inflicted on him when he returned home that when his father pronounced, "Nigger, you got a ass whippin' comin," as Brown wrote in *Manchild in the Promised Land*, Brown barely nodded as his sisters, looking on, began to cry.[28] Brown's father one-upped Gibson's in the child abuse department; his tool of punishment was a razor strop, a thick strip of leather attached to a heavy metal coil. Like Althea, Brown had always considered the Harlem streets his home as a child, far more than his parents' apartment.

"I always thought of Harlem as home, but I never thought of Harlem as being in the house," he wrote. "To me, home was the streets. I suppose there were many people who felt that. If home was so miserable, the street was the place to be."[29]

Complicating matters, Althea faced a menace on her own street that was more formidable than any of those her cousin would run into. By a stroke of bad luck, the apartment the Gibsons wound up in after they moved out of Aunt Sally's was located on 143rd Street between Lenox and Seventh Avenue. According to a health survey completed shortly after they moved in, that very block was found to have an extraordinarily high rate of death from pulmonary tuberculosis, twice that of whites in Manhattan. Health officials aptly called it what it was: "the lung block."[30] Growing up on that plagued piece of real estate positioned Althea at ground zero of the health and economic ills that plagued Harlem in the 1930s. But the defiant adolescent in her torn blue jeans and short-cropped hair cared not at all, if she even knew.

What she cared about were the tastes and temptations that beckoned on the streets. Hanging out was what the hip kids did. There were sweets and packages of ice cream to be stolen from the five-and-ten, ripe pieces of fruit at corner markets, and yams roasting on an outdoor grill begging to be grabbed. There were freight cars filled with produce over at the Bronx Terminal Market—a "snitcher's heaven," as Althea thought of it. Sometimes, she and her pals managed to fill an entire basket with bananas and peaches and lettuce before anyone came running after them. Althea and her friends deliberately steered clear of the drug and drinking scene—they'd all heard the horror stories of reform school—and instead spent long afternoons in the darkened movie theaters or at the beloved Apollo Theater, which had an afternoon performance on Fridays. Who had time for the classroom or books? As Althea wrote years later, "I was a traveling girl, and I hated to go to school. What's more, I didn't like people telling me what to do. Take it from me, you can get in a lot of hot water thinking like that."[31]

Althea's ongoing clashes with authority as a child may have felt stressful, but her lawless ways earned her a formidable reputation on the streets. Even before she reached her teens, everyone knew not to mess with Al, in part because she rarely lost a fight. One of the first, and likely only, times she got beaten up on the streets happened when she was tossing pebbles at mailboxes and garbage cans as she wandered alone. A big girl approached her and demanded, "What, are you supposed to be tough or something?" When Althea ignored her, the girl punched her hard in the stomach and then walked away, leaving Althea gasping for breath on the pavement. She ran home in tears, but upon hearing the story, her father turned her around and ordered her to go back on the street immediately. "If you don't go back out there and find her and whip her, I'll whip the behind off you when you come home," he said.

For once, Althea did as she was told. As soon as she found the other girl, she went after her hard, pounding her repeatedly. "I beat the hell out of her," Althea wrote in her autobiography. "Every time I hit her in the belly and she doubled up with the pain, I straightened her up again with a punch in the face. I didn't show her any mercy, but I guarantee you one thing, she never bothered me again."[32]

Neither did the boys, after she beat up a member of the Sabers, one of the toughest boy gangs in the neighborhood. Althea was leaving her aunt Sally's place one afternoon when she noticed her uncle Junie, another refugee from South Carolina, lolling on the landing, recovering from a few too many drinks. Crouched in front of him, one of the Saber gang leaders was going through Uncle Junie's pockets, searching for cash. Althea shouted at the boy to stop, and as she helped her uncle back up the stairs, the Saber hurled a sharpened screwdriver at her. Althea threw up her fist and managed to stop the tool in flight, but the scar it left on her hand would remain with her for life, as would the memory of the bloody street battle that ensued. The two teenagers tore at each other up and down the length of 144th Street until a pair of adults finally pulled them apart.

Her performance impressed her brother Bubba. "She could beat the hell out of anybody in the block, including all of us," he told a reporter for the *New York Post* in a 1957 interview. "I remember once when she was about 13 that a guy six feet tall started playing the dozens (talking about her family) and she gave him a black eye. We never had no trouble out of that bully again."[33]

Althea found other kinds of competition that absorbed her almost as much as fighting, most of them having to do with a ball of some kind. Basketball was her favorite, but pretty much any kind of game would do. Badminton, volleyball, stickball, and bowling were high on her list. Early on, she opted to play against boys, who gave her stiffer competition than people of her own gender. Otherwise, when she and her girlfriends weren't at the "flickers," they practiced shooting hoops for Cokes or hot dogs in the park. Althea was also a standout forward on the Harlem girls' basketball team, the Mysterious Girls, and for several years she earned the distinction of being the fastest girl on a team that had some of the highest-scoring players in the country. The team was organized by Rev. Marsden Burnell, a religious man and a local activist, who urged the talented Althea to engage in several other sports, perhaps tennis someday. Sometimes, she even listened to him.

After their games, a few of the Mysterious Girls routinely headed down to the bowling alley for some late-night fun. One night, Althea and her pals noticed an attractive, square-jawed man with a honey-kissed smile playing with a loud group at the other end of the bowling alley. Inching closer to him, the girls realized that he was none other than *the* Sugar Ray Robinson, the undefeated lightweight boxer from Harlem who had scored a succession of wins over the past two years. Not so long ago, Robinson had stunned the packed grandstands at Madison Square Garden by vanquishing Bronx superstar Jake LaMotta by a unanimous decision, claiming his thirty-sixth professional victory. Althea, whose craving for competition seemed limitless, wasted no time. Introduced to Robinson by one of her friends who was acquainted with his then girlfriend, Althea put it to him straight: "So, you're Sugar Ray Robinson? Well, I can beat you bowling right now," she declared.[34]

It was the beginning of one of the most important relationships of Althea's life. Both Robinson and his soon-to-be wife, Edna Mae Holly, a Cotton Club dancer, took a liking to the girl and enjoyed having her around. Althea idolized them both. Many nights, she would show up unannounced on the couple's doorstep up on Saint Nicholas Avenue in the hope that they would invite her to spend the night. As they got to know one another better, she regularly traveled with Robinson's entourage to his training camp on Greenwood Lake, in upstate New York. Amused by teenage Althea's enthusiasm, Robinson sometimes let her drive his fancy car, despite her having no license. A music lover and drummer himself, he also bought her a saxophone for $125 from a local pawn shop, which she studiously played over the next decade and kept for the rest of her life. In time, Edna Mae in particular came to understand Althea's gnawing insecurity and her sometimes cool demeanor.

"She was unhappy; she had a gaunt build and she felt that she was the least good-looking girl she knew. She had insecurity and went into herself. She used to talk wild," Edna Mae said in a 1957 interview with *Time* magazine. "I tried to make her feel she could be something."[35]

When she was fifteen Althea received some medical information that further eroded her self-confidence. Doctors informed her, she would reveal to a reporter when in her fifties, that, for reasons that are unclear, she would never be able to have children. This fact ignited deep-seated feelings of inadequacy that simultaneously compelled her to personally withdraw while inspiring her to compete ever harder.

"Because of this I felt inadequate and withdrawn," Althea said in a 1984 interview. "I have always had this characteristic about me, of not letting myself really go with things and feeling negative." But competing in tennis compensated. She continued, "I became very adequate in sports. I felt a release from within myself when I was playing."[36]

With that, the appeal of the streets continued to be irresistible. As Althea began to stay away from home for ever-longer periods, sometimes disappearing for weeks at a time, her mother prowled the alleys until nearly dawn looking for her eldest daughter. Althea would later write of those searches, "She never had much chance of finding me. When I was really trying to hide out I never went near any of the playgrounds or gymnasiums or restaurants that I usually hung out at. I sneaked around to different friends' houses in the daytime, or sat all by myself in the movies, and then, if I didn't have any place lined up to sleep, I would just ride the subway all night. . . . At least it was a place to sit down."[37]

Although Althea managed to keep busy on the hardwood floors of the basketball courts and bowling alleys, most children of Manhattan found few outlets for sports and recreation at the time. In packed Harlem, with its teeming tenements and overrun apartment buildings, it was even worse. President Franklin Roosevelt's New Deal expanded urban recreational spaces when it got under way in 1933, but little of that effort reached the most crowded of Black ghettos. Black Harlem benefited hardly at all. Of the 255 new playgrounds built in New York City during the 1930s, only two were built in Black neighborhoods.[38] Even the fleet of new swimming pools constructed by Mayor La Guardia at the time offered little relief to sweltering residents of color, thanks to the tactics of Robert Moses, the controversial master designer of much of twentieth-century Manhattan.

Moses, characterized as a racist in Robert Caro's prizewinning biography *The Power Broker*, made sure that people of color were kept out of all but one of the ten community swimming pools he designed in the 1930s when he served as the city's park commissioner. His plan was that only the pool on 146th Street, in what was then called Colonial Park, a few blocks from the Gibsons, would be used by Black people and Puerto Ricans.[39] Moses feared that permitting them to mingle with whites would cause "fights and riots." He believed that "colored" people did not like cold water, and so, to keep them out of the other pools, he reportedly had the temperature of the water in them dropped by several degrees. "Well, they don't like cold water," he told one of his lawyers, according to Caro. "And we've found that that helps."[40] The strategy worked, according to Caro.

For the New York City Police, the shortage of pools and outdoor play space was far more than just inconvenient. As an ever-growing number of children resorted to playing in the streets, it was becoming lethal. With cars becoming more numerous on the streets of Manhattan in the early 1900s, children darting in and out of traffic were frequently injured or killed. In 1916, of the 664 people killed on the streets, 267, or nearly 41 percent, were children under the age of sixteen.[41]

Even before the number of street accidents began to rise, New York City Police Commissioner Arthur Woods took a stand. In 1914, when the number of child fatalities was beginning to rise, he helped initiate a program that closed off certain streets in the afternoons to provide safe space for children to play. The program, soon known as the Police Athletic League (PAL), grew rapidly, and by 1940, as many as 377 streets had been set aside for play alone.[42] The police provided each play street with equipment for games such as basketball, hopscotch, and paddle tennis, a sport akin to regular tennis but played with wooden paddles and a rubber ball on a much smaller court. Created by Rev. Frank Peer Beal before the turn of the century, the inexpensive and highly transportable game took off in popularity among New York City's children in the 1920s. When ten-year-old Althea Gibson walked out of her building one morning in 1937 to find 143rd Street shut off with wooden barricades and a paddle tennis court awaiting her, she was beside herself. Within months, she was not only the champion of the block, but had beaten her brother multiple times and almost all the boys who dared challenge her. In 1938, she was named the citywide paddle tennis champion, a title she would hold for the next four years, and the following year, she was presented with an award by Mayor

La Guardia. The only girl on the city's championship softball team and a pitcher to boot, she much preferred to compete against boys than to waste time on those wimpy girls, who couldn't even begin to give her a real fight.

A popular photo of a towering Althea dressed in a mannish black suit, a handkerchief tucked into her breast pocket, shows her at one of the award ceremonies standing next to none other than Beal himself. Al had found her sport on the streets of Harlem. Streaking across the court, her gangly adolescent body already displaying an impressive wingspan as she stretched to reach the ball, she was hard to miss. By now, Sugar Ray Robinson had introduced her to Buddy Walker, the saxophone player who would later connect her to some of his tennis friends; it was Walker whom Robinson asked to give Althea a hand in selecting a saxophone that he, Robinson, would buy for her.

"She was about twelve, not yet thirteen, when I first noticed her playing paddle tennis," Walker told Ted Poston, the *New York Post* reporter. "Her aggressive strokes and swift movement caught my attention immediately."[43]

When Walker's friends escorted Althea to the tony Cosmopolitan Club in upper Harlem, they swung open a door on a realm that she had never before encountered. Although just blocks away from the Gibsons' apartment, the club was a universe apart, with its cadre of professionals drawn from the country's emerging Black middle class. Proud to wear the crisp white tennis outfit—even if some among them couldn't play the sport particularly well—many were residents of Harlem's tony Sugar Hill neighborhood. The club's private coach, Fred Johnson, was one of the best instructors in the city as well as a champion on the Black ATA tennis circuit. Despite the loss of his left arm, the slender Johnson played a formidable, albeit unique, game of tennis. When he served, for example, he tucked one ball under his left armpit while balancing a second ball on his racket, which he grasped with his right hand. Somehow, he tossed the ball into the air off his racket and then slammed it across the net with surprising force. Always dressed immaculately in whites, the disciplined Johnson was a member of one of the first Negro tennis clubs, the Ideal Tennis Club in New York City, and had been awarded the trophy for the Nassau doubles championship in the Bahamas by the Prince of Wales before he became the king of England.[44]

In addition to coaching Althea, Johnson connected her to the Harry

C. Lee & Company tennis and golf shop, where he had purchased a new racket for her on the day they met. The store's vice president, Tommy Giangrande, was the son of Italian immigrants and believed firmly that tennis should be available to those other than just the wealthy who patronized the store and the sport. For years, he had donated rackets both new and used to Johnson, and he was an avid supporter of Althea's from early on. Not only did Giangrande give her rackets and introduce her to powerful people in New York tennis circles, but in years to come, Harry C. Lee would be the only sports outfitter to sponsor her as an amateur and the first to do so when she went pro. Althea, in return, invariably carried a clutch of the company's rackets close to her side, with the store's name highly visible on their covers.[45]

In the late summer of 1941, when Althea began taking regular lessons from Johnson, the rest of her life was in shambles. Unbeknownst to the Cosmopolitan members supporting her, she had dropped out of high school. Despite her protests, she had been transferred to the Yorkville Trade School after graduating from junior high, rather than being permitted to attend high school with her friends, as she had requested. While Althea was by her own account hardly a stellar student, it seems possible that her assignment may also have been the result of a common form of discrimination practiced by school authorities at the time. According to Mayor La Guardia's voluminous report on the causes of the Harlem Riot of 1935, few Black girls in the city were permitted to advance to high school because of a perceived deficiency in their training. This was no fault of their own, the report concluded, but rather "because the poorly equipped and crowded junior high schools of Harlem do not give them adequate preparation for entrance to a senior high school."[46] The report also found that educational advisers firmly believed that Black people had a limited capacity for academic pursuits. As a result, the majority of Black girls were directed to take vocational courses rather than advance to high school. That Althea was chronically truant likely did not help her case.

Such factors weren't the only things that compromised the Harlem students' experience. The report also noted that due to a chronic lack of recreational facilities in the schools, the students were compelled to use the streets for playgrounds. There, they were thrown into contact with "the vicious elements in the community." At least 25 percent of those students, the report noted in an effort to characterize the difficulties students faced, were also "retarded" and had apparently been inappropriately placed in the school.[47]

Almost a century later, such language seems as archaic as it is judgmental. Today, the term *retarded* is considered a form of hate speech. So, too, labeling members of the Harlem community as "vicious elements" might be seen from a present-day vantage point as failing to take into account the many complex factors that can lead to crime and homelessness. One might be tempted to conclude that the mayoral commission was composed of white bureaucrats with little understanding of the community, but it was anything but. In fact, the commission was deliberately biracial, composed of "both whites and Negroes, lawyers, preachers and civic and public servants," according to a published version of the report.[48] Among those Black members were Dr. E. Franklin Frazier, a prominent sociology professor at Howard University, who eventually served as the director of the studies used in the report; poet Countee Cullen; and A. Philip Randolph, president of the Brotherhood of Sleeping Car Porters.[49]

Whatever factors ultimately determined Althea's academic path— whether it was in part due to the attitudes of school administrators or to her own underwhelming academic performance—Althea found herself sitting in front of a sewing machine at the Yorkville Trade School. Quickly growing bored, she soon stopped showing up. Untethered by either school or a job, she began staying away from home for even longer periods of time. Her interests now had graduated to include shooting pool in smoky basements and listening to the jazz rhythms floating out of crowded bars. Ever more proficient on the saxophone, Althea was beginning to fantasize about a career as a nightclub singer or musician. Soon her days of absences stretched into weeks, but always there was the painful and sometimes bloody price to pay upon her return home.

"Naturally, the longer I would stay away the worse the beating I would get when I finally did go home," Althea wrote in her biography. "So I would just stay away longer the next time. It got so that my mother was afraid to let me out of the house for fear I wouldn't come back."[50]

Her mother was ultimately right. The next time Althea stayed away from home for an extended period, she decided not to return to 143rd Street for the inevitable beating. Instead, she knocked at the door of the New York Society for the Prevention of Cruelty to Children, which a friend had told her about. "I'm scared to go home," she told the head lady. "My father will whip me something awful."[51]

The organization, the first in the world devoted exclusively to child protection when it was created in 1875, agreed to take her in and gave her a bed with fresh white sheets. The next morning, however, the woman in charge telephoned her parents, just as the police had done. This time, her father showed up and marched her back home. Although Althea promised him earnestly that she would not run away again, her father silently unfurled his worn ironing power cord and went to work. And once again, Althea ran away.

"I went straight to the S.P.C.C. I told them that my father had whipped me bad, after he'd promised that he wouldn't, and I even skinned off my shirt and showed them the big red welts the strap had put on my back," Althea wrote in her biography. "They took me in again, and this time when Daddy came after me they asked me if I wanted to go back with him."[52]

Althea said no. Instead, she remained at the shelter for a while, thoroughly enjoying the food and living conditions, which were far more pleasant than those that existed at home. But in time, she began to chafe at the restrictions imposed on her coming and going, and with a deep sense of foreboding, she returned to 143rd Street. This time, however, her father kept his distance, and things remained peaceable, at least for a while.

Instead of going to school, Althea tried her hand at a series of jobs, none of which lasted very long. She worked as a counter girl at one of the Chock Full o' Nuts restaurants, as a messenger for a blueprinting company, as an elevator operator at the Dixie Hotel, and as a laborer at button and dress factories. One job had her cleaning the guts out of chickens at a butcher shop. Of them all, the only job she genuinely liked was working as a mail clerk at the New York School of Social Work, where she had a little office all her own and responsibilities that did not entail physical labor. It was the first job that had given her a sense of purpose and significance. It lasted for six months—until, one day, she decided to play hooky and go to the Paramount Theater in Times Square to see Sarah Vaughan, the great improvisational jazz singer and pianist. Perhaps most important, in Althea's view, Vaughan had won an amateur contest at the Apollo Theater, something she herself dreamed of doing. When Althea returned to work the next day and confessed to her boss where she had been the day before, she was let go from her job.

Now unemployed, fourteen-year-old Althea retreated to her comfort zone and returned to the place she and her cousin considered their "real" home, the streets. This time it was the city welfare department that approached her with concerns about her homelessness on the crime-ridden streets of Harlem. The social worker gave her a choice: she could either return to her parents' apartment or live in a furnished room in a private house they would select. All she had to do was check in with them weekly and pick up an allowance. It was either that or go to a reform school. Althea couldn't believe her good fortune. With no requirement to either work or attend school attached to the offer, she promptly accepted the room and moved in. Every now and then, she returned to her family's apartment and was surprised to learn that her parents were as pleased with the new arrangement as she was.

"They figured I was in good hands with the welfare ladies. I sure was; never better," she wrote.[53]

Years later, Althea defended her father's abusive behavior. That his regular beatings of at least one of his children could have landed him in prison, or that his singularly harsh treatment of her likely had lifelong psychological consequences, did not seem to figure in her assessment of his violent behavior. He was her daddy, after all. Just as important, it is likely that neither she nor the doctors or the Black press rallying behind her wanted any hint of domestic abuse to be a part of the public's understanding of the budding champion. Child abuse was a cliché component of Harlem family life at the time, along with absent fathers and alcohol abuse. As Althea was beginning her rise, it seemed there was an unspoken consensus among those who might have been aware of her father's brutality that it was best to keep such information out of sight.[54]

"If he had whipped me every day of my life from the time I was seven years old, I would have deserved it," she wrote shortly after she retired from tennis in 1958. "I gave him a whole lot of trouble. I don't hate him for anything today. In fact, I love him. I feel a lot of those whippings he gave me helped make me what I am today. Somebody had to knock a little sense into me, and it wasn't easy."[55]

Althea did her very best to hide her circumstances from the Cosmopolitan crowd, who surely would have disapproved. She did so for a couple of reasons. Tennis, that most exclusive and wimpiest of sports, was a pursuit that a hardened and streetwise tomboy like her would presumably have rejected. The more Althea learned about the game, though, the more it appealed to her, and not just because she was good at it. Tennis offered a potential escape, as one of her fellow players at the Cosmopolitan had figured out early on and that she would come to grasp as well. That player's name was Wilbert Davis, but everyone called him Billy. Long curious about what went on behind the Cosmopolitan Club's walls, the ten-year-old Davis was thrilled when he happened by its entrance one afternoon in 1940 and a player shouted out to him, asking him if he would be interested in working as a ball boy that afternoon. Davis promptly agreed, and when the first match came to an end, he was invited to hit a few balls. Like the slightly older Althea, Davis had a natural talent for the sport. Shortly afterward, he not only served as one of the ball boys for the historic interracial exhibition match in 1940 between Donald Budge and Jimmie McDaniel, but he was taking lessons from coach Fred Johnson. As he came to know some of the club members, he quickly realized that the situation offered him opportunities far more than sport.

"I grew up in Manhattan and lived in a predominantly Black environment. Tennis introduced me to a way of getting away from that environment," Davis explained in an interview. "In tennis, you meet the cream of the crop, teachers, doctors, lawyers, and professional Blacks who in their conversation would talk about productive things like getting a good education and the good things that would follow from living a certain kind of life and having ambition. I didn't want to be a porter or someone picking up dirt. I wanted to use my brain."

Davis, who won multiple boys' tennis titles, went on to become an eleven-time ATA national title winner as well as a training partner and road manager for Althea. He added, "Tennis is the type of sport that sort of frees you from the cage of adversity because of the kind of people you would meet."[56]

Tennis, if not the actual people who played it, was coming to have a similar appeal for Althea. What could have been farther from her own particular cage of adversity, the embattled sidewalks of 143rd Street and her father's lashing ironing cord, than the trim environs of the Cosmopolitan Club, where people in pristine white outfits played a genteel game rooted in Europe of eight centuries earlier? Could those people hold the keys to that very cage? By the 1940s, tennis had become popular among a certain echelon of the Black intelligentsia, the very sort Althea had stumbled into as a young girl. In its earliest days, however, the highly aristocratic sport would likely have been completely anathema to most any young person on Harlem's streets.

A game called *tennis*, requiring an expensive indoor court and played with the hand and, later, a glove, originated in France and Italy in the twelfth century. A kindred but quite different form of the sport, played outdoors with strung rackets, was officially introduced in England by Major Walter Clopton Wingfield in 1874. This new and much less costly version of the game, known as lawn tennis, exploded in popularity and, not long afterward, migrated across the ocean to a number of American cities. At the close of the nineteenth century, tennis was being played at the private homes of the wealthy or on the manicured courts of exclusive clubs such as the West Side Tennis Club in Queens, New York, and the Longwood Cricket Club in Boston. Because the sport required an investment in both apparel and equipment, and ideally some training by a professional, it remained largely the province of well-to-do whites. If there were some Black people who were intrigued by the new sport during the waning years of Reconstruction, the years that followed made its pursuit enormously difficult for them.

In the years after Reconstruction ended in 1877, overt racism and violence against Black citizens reached unprecedented heights in the United States as the progressive initiatives of the recent past were brutally dismantled. After suffering a history of enslavement, Black people were not only excluded from many aspects of white culture but were further persecuted as they were denied many basic civil rights and subjected to brutal forms of violence and even lynching by an evolving white terrorist group known as the Ku Klux Klan. As Jim Crow laws mandating segregation spread throughout the South, Black people were sometimes mocked in certain corners of the culture for their presumed intellectual deficiency and physical limitations. Even Nathaniel Currier and James Merritt Ives, the iconic New York printmakers best known for their images of a beatific American life, dipped their hands into the seething pot of racial defamation. Throughout the 1880s, Currier and Ives produced a scathing series of color lithographs known as *Darktown*, which depicted Black people as buffoonish incompetents unable to play sports or even engage in thoughtful conversation. In one set of prints, titled *Lawn Tennis at Darktown* (1885), Black players are depicted preparing to play the game formally dressed and equipped as white players would be, only to stumble into the net and drop their rackets in the next frame. Other prints depicted Black players fumbling on the baseball and football fields, unable even to keep their shoes tied. The *Darktown* series, among the best-selling items the company produced, was a grim reflection of racial views at the century's end.[57]

Faced with such overt hostility, Black people began to develop separate institutions as a means of survival. Tennis was no exception. By the end of the century, they had formed their own tennis clubs and had initiated a handful of interstate tennis tournaments, the first of which was held in Philadelphia in 1898 and included a group of clubs in the Northeast. By the early 1900s, there were several dozen private Black tennis clubs, such as the Ideal Tennis Club, the Chautauqua in Philadelphia, and the Chicago Prairie Tennis Club in Illinois. In 1915, the Colonial Tennis Club, tucked in between brick tenements at the corner of Convent Avenue and 149th Street in Harlem, opened its doors, and its quartet of courts was soon filled with the racket-wielding elite of New York's premier Black society. Several years later, the club changed its name to the Cosmopolitan Tennis Club. By 1916, with the number of Black tennis clubs growing steadily, a decision was made to bring them together into a single organization in the interest of promoting the sport among Black people nationwide. In November 1916, representatives from a dozen clubs met in Washington, D.C., to form the American Tennis Association, or the ATA, which would represent the interests of Black tennis for decades to come. The organization, which was open to all races, hoped to achieve its goal by not only holding tournaments but also cultivating junior players with potential.

The ATA held its first national tournament at Druid Hill Park in Baltimore, Maryland, in the summer of 1917, drawing competitors from thirty-three clubs. The event was so successful that the organization's future national tournaments were soon being staged on the grounds of Black colleges and universities, such as the Tuskegee Institute in Alabama and Wilberforce University in Ohio, where dormitories and courts were available to accommodate the large crowds. The events rapidly became popular social gatherings lasting several days and featuring cocktail parties, formal dinners, and fashion shows. In the early 1950s, the organization even launched a Miss ATA "popularity contest" among the most attractive young female members, in part to counter cultural discomfort with competitive female athletes who, some felt, violated prevailing notions of femininity.[58] The triumphant title winner was honored with a Miss ATA crown, often presented at the organization's annual ball.

For many prominent Black people, the ATA gatherings ranked among the most important happenings on the social calendar. Not surprisingly, the white press paid little attention to the ATA's events for decades after the association's inception, focusing instead on the white United States Lawn Tennis Association (USLTA), which had safeguarded the exclusivity of the sport since its founding in 1881. However, Black newspapers, which closely followed sports of all kinds, glowingly documented the Black tennis organization's events, right down to offering a who's who of the spectators in the bleachers, the models of the cars some of them drove there, and a detailed description of the ladies' more notable evening outfits and purses.

By the 1920s, two names had emerged as dominant players among the ranks of the ATA, demonstrating the enormous potential of Black tennis players. One was Reginald S. Weir, a varsity player at the City College of New York who along with his friend Gerald Norman Jr., a high school champion, paid the one dollar entrance fee in order to compete in the USLTA Junior Indoor Championships in Manhattan in 1929. Both their applications were accepted sight unseen, but when the two Black men showed up at the Seventh Regiment Armory and officials realized they were African American, they were turned away. Publicly challenged for doing so by the NAACP, the white tennis organization adamantly defended its action, saying that while it was making "no reflection upon the colored race," it believed that the practice of separate organizations to administer Black and white tennis should be continued.[59] Weir went on to become a physician at the Harlem Hospital in New York and won multiple titles in the ATA before breaking critical racial barriers in tennis. In 1948, on the basis of his success in those tournaments, he became the first Black player to be accepted by the USLTA to compete in the adult version of the very same national indoor championship from which he had been barred nineteen years earlier.[60]

Ora Washington of Philadelphia was another Black player who not only made headlines, but was also considered by many to be one of the nation's greatest female athletes of any color. A Virginia native, Washington moved as a child to Philadelphia in the early 1900s and soon became the ATA's reigning female champion, accumulating what was then a record of national championships: eight singles, twelve doubles, and three mixed doubles titles over the course of two decades. A muscular, powerfully built athlete with a square, chiseled jaw, "Queen Ora," as the Black press dubbed her, was known for her extraordinary foot speed and competitive drive. By the early 1930s, she was also the reigning center on the Philadelphia Tribune Girls, a premier Black women's basketball team. As with Weir's initial attempt, Washington's effort to test her skills in the white tennis arena were unsuccessful. Although she and others repeatedly asked the reigning white tennis champion, Helen Wills Moody, to play against Washington, Moody apparently did not respond to their requests, if she was ever even aware of them.[61]

A no-nonsense, plainspoken woman who worked as a housekeeper when not competing on a court, Washington came under criticism for being *too* competitive an athlete. Part of the concern was that her dominance was believed to have discouraged others from entering the sport and was thus damaging to Black tennis overall. There was also the larger concern that her masculine appearance and blunt demeanor did not conform to contemporary notions of appropriate femininity. Consistent with cultural stereotypes that frowned upon women who were too aggressive or even particularly competitive, both the Black and white press routinely lauded female players who were physically attractive and appropriately ladylike. The working-class Washington was not particularly either. Toward the end of her athletic career, it is believed that she was encouraged to retire so that other Black women would be emboldened to step forward.[62]

By the time Althea Gibson appeared on the Cosmopolitan courts in 1941, the mood in Black tennis was notably different from how it had been in Washington's day. Integration, while still the remotest of possibilities, had become at least conceivable. Washington never had a chance to compete against white players, so the rulers of Black tennis never pressed her to tone down her blunt, unladylike exterior, as they likely would have had she been playing on an integrated national stage. By the 1940s, however, the racial ground appeared to be shifting, and the physical appearance of Black athletes headed for center stage was at a premium. One of the several things that made the Cosmopolitan Club members hesitate at the prospect of championing Althea was her androgynous bearing.

At the time, homosexuality was frowned upon in American culture—even in prosperous corners of Harlem where queer culture had thrived during the Harlem Renaissance.

The giddy years of the 1920s had opened a door to homosexuality and to a kind of flamboyant sexual exhibitionism like never before. As Harvard University professor Henry Louis "Skip" Gates Jr. said in 1993, the Harlem Renaissance "was surely as gay as it was black, not that it was exclusively either of these."[63] More than a few of the prominent writers at the forefront of the movement—such as its patron saint Alain Locke and writers Langston Hughes and Countee Cullen—were believed to be homosexual or bisexual, even if they didn't publicly acknowledge it. This didn't mean that all elements of Black society embraced homosexuality, because they surely did not. In the late 1920s and early '30s, the emerging Black bourgeoisie was in some ways more culturally conservative than whites of similar status. Its members were determined to adhere to the mannered and gender norms of American society, lest they be dismissed as somehow of lower class. In the public sphere, homosexuality was often linked to degeneracy and disease, and lesbians were viewed as deviants.[64] By the 1940s, these attitudes had translated into a cultural expectation that female athletes should conform to ladylike behaviors, such as motherhood and childbearing, lest they be marginalized. For women, as Jennifer H. Lansbury writes in *A Spectacular Leap: Black Women Athletes in Twentieth-Century America*, "gender expectations were bound to class identity as well. Hitting the ball with too much power could result in masculine, working-class labels. In short, Black and white women alike who participated in sport were often scrutinized, questioned, challenged, qualified, and even ridiculed by white society."[65]

But Althea's talent was too formidable to ignore. With their eyes on the lily-white terrain of national tennis, Cosmopolitan Club members overlooked the more questionable aspects of Althea's situation, such as her delinquent status and masculine bearing and threw their support behind her. And yet, she would never receive the wholehearted embrace of the Black community in the way that baseball pioneer Jackie Robinson or boxer Sugar Ray Robinson did, in part because of her aloofness. Her personal style alone, considered crude by some, could be off-putting.

There was also the question of her uncertain sexuality. Althea never publicly declared herself a lesbian, and she was twice married to men from whom she eventually divorced. But from an early age, she had close relationships with women who were lesbians, and many of those who knew her well during her tennis- and golf-playing years were in no doubt that she preferred women to men. During her college years, talk of her propositioning female classmates was so widespread that some classmates hid in their rooms to escape her amorous advances. Many among the ATA suspected that Althea was bisexual or a lesbian. Robert Ryland, an ATA champion and the first Black professional tennis player, remembers walking into a dormitory at an ATA tournament in Florida in the early 1950s and finding Althea in bed with a woman. "One day somebody called her for her match. I went to get her and I jumped in the bed," Ryland said in an interview. "And her and her girlfriend threw me out."

Although Althea was apparently amused at Ryland's antic, he says he knew better than to inquire about her bedmate. "You don't mess with Althea," he added.[66]

The members of the Cosmopolitan Club were likely unaware of such things, but many were nonetheless privately uneasy about their pants-clad contender. More than a few would find themselves at odds with the tennis star in later years over her reluctance to vocally champion the Black cause, but in the 1940s and the early '50s, they were among her most ardent public supporters.

One of the most enthusiastic among them was club member Rhoda Smith, one of the first of a series of adopted "moms" on whom Althea would depend in the coming years. In all, Althea would grow attached to more than half a dozen mentors whom she called "Dad" or "Mama," apparently in attempt to compensate for her chronically absent biological parents. As the first of those surrogate parents, Smith was embraced by Althea with particular fervor. A native of Barbados who had long been active in New York tennis circles on behalf of both the New York Tennis Association and the ATA, Smith was also a former New York State tennis champion player herself in the 1930s. Not only did she win twenty-seven trophies in both singles and doubles, but, according to the *Pittsburgh Courier*, she also gained distinction in 1933 for being the first nationally known player of color to appear in shorts on the New York city tennis courts.[67] The stylish Smith had originally turned to tennis at the advice of her doctor after her three-year-old daughter died, and when Althea first appeared at the Cosmopolitan, Smith unhesitatingly took the teenager under her wing. The wealthy Harlemite even dared to walk bravely onto the court, shortly after she met Althea, to apparently become the first woman with whom the teenager ever played the game.

"She resented it because I was always trying to improve her ways," Smith told Poston, the *New York Post* reporter. "I had to keep saying 'Don't do this,' and 'Don't do that,' until she would cry out, 'You, Mrs. Smith, you're always (picking) on me.'"

One of the things that Smith tried to get Althea to do was to politely return stray tennis balls from adjacent courts, as is the custom, rather than batting them wildly into the air, as was Althea's custom. "But," Smith explained to Poston, "after all, [Althea] had played in the street all of her life and she didn't know any better."[68]

Smith stepped wholeheartedly into the role of surrogate mother. The first winter after they met, she escorted Althea to a downtown department store, where she bought the teenager a winter coat and some much-needed underwear. Some years later, Smith stayed up through the night sewing an outfit for Althea to wear in her first tournament final the following day. Althea, who was hardly known for her respectful or well-mannered ways as a young woman, clearly felt a deep attachment to the woman who mentored her in the early years of her tennis career and who accompanied her to most of her tournaments over the next decade. Her own biological parents were apparently absent from virtually all of them. Althea often spent a night or two at the handsome brick town house where Smith and her husband lived, on 154th Street in the Sugar Hill neighborhood, to prepare herself for the following day's tournament or simply to escape her father's wrath. In the later 1950s, she moved into the basement of the house for an extended period.[69]

Without Smith and the endorsement of the Cosmopolitan Club, it is unlikely that Althea would have been able to make her way into the top tier of tennis. Although the ATA had done much to develop the sport among a certain cadre of well-to-do Black players, it had made little progress in either nurturing a junior class of players or bringing down the racial barriers that prohibited its members from competing against more seasoned white players. It was hardly the organization's sole responsibility.

The truth was that competitive tennis required a level of coaching and experience, not to mention equipment, that was simply out of reach for many Black people of the day. In 1940, the *New York Age* published a five-part series called "Inside Tennis," designed to explain the sport and the role of the ATA. The *Chicago Defender*, one of several prominent Black newspapers that published versions of the series, nailed the issue in one of its headlines: "Finance a Big Problem for Most Tennis Players." In addition to the cost of a pair of rackets, the story continued, players needed to cover the expense of the white clothing and club or association membership that were considered crucial. Then there was the cost of tournament competition, which involved transportation, room, and board. Players who aspired to be first-rank would also need training by a professional coach, of which there were few among the Black ranks. Most players were apparently self-taught or instructed by colleagues. The series concluded with the hope that its list of expenses had not scared would-be players away. "What we want to do is to try to bring these expenses down so low, that the most humble in our land may be able to indulge in the greatest of all sports and we believe this is the ATA aim."[70]

One means to achieve that aim was through the financial sponsorship of talented players such as Althea. Another way to broaden the appeal of the sport was through the sponsorship of integrated exhibition matches, such as the much-celebrated 1940 encounter between Donald Budge and Jimmie McDaniel. Not altogether accidentally, that match coincided with a rumbling of racial discontent that would escalate throughout the 1940s. As the nation's economy began to recover from the Depression early in the decade, white citizens benefited from newly created jobs, particularly those in the defense industry, while Black people remained marginalized. That they were simultaneously being summoned to defend American democracy on the front lines of a looming Second World War made it even more infuriating. In early 1941, Black activists threatened a massive march on Washington in an effort to move the federal government to act against employment discrimination and to desegregate both the military and the defense industry. Although the military would not be desegregated for another seven years, President Franklin D. Roosevelt issued an executive order establishing the Fair Employment Practices Committee (FEPC) prohibiting discrimination in federal training programs and the nation's defense industry. The protest march was called off, but the seeds of racial ferment had been sown. That the hundreds of thousands of Black people who had migrated to the North as part of the Great Migration could finally exercise their right to vote, which they had been largely prohibited from doing in the Jim Crow South, would serve to fertilize those seeds.

With racial discontent continuing to smolder during World War II, the Carnegie Corporation of New York commissioned an analysis of race by Swedish economist Gunnar Myrdal. The voluminous 1944 study that resulted, titled *An American Dilemma: The Negro Problem and Modern Democracy*, identified a system of obstacles to Black participation in U.S. society that Myrdal found to be at odds with the principles of the nation's democracy. At its heart was the juxtaposition of America's cherished values of democracy and equality on the one hand and the harsh reality of racism on the other. Summoning Americans to live up to their democratic values,

Myrdal concluded in part that the "Negro problem" was, as one critique put it, in fact the "white man's problem." Cited a decade later in the landmark U.S. Supreme Court decision *Brown v. Board of Education*, Myrdal's observations laid the groundwork for the civil rights advances to come.[71]

Months after the study's release, the Cosmopolitan Club hosted another, even more controversial exhibition tennis match that highlighted both race and gender. The star attraction of the 1944 ATA Championships was a pair of the most prominent, and beautiful, white female players of the day, Alice Marble, the golden-haired world tennis champion, and Mary Hardwick, Britain's number-one female player. The plan was for the two women to participate in an exhibition match against each other, after which they would each be paired in a mixed doubles competition with a male ATA player—Marble with U.S. Army private Robert Ryland, who had been the winner of the Illinois State High School Tennis Singles Tournament in 1939, and Hardwick with Dr. Reginald Weir, by then a four-time ATA singles national champion. Invitations were sent to more than 150 tennis clubs, and the press drumroll announcing the event began weeks in advance.

In many parts of America, an event pairing Black and white players in this way would have been regarded as scandalous, particularly in the South. But this was Harlem, and the majority of the Black press celebrated the exhibition match as an indication of progress and a welcome harbinger of integration. Days before it began, Sam Lacy, sports columnist for the *Baltimore Afro-American*, declared that the match "will show to the world that colored and white athletes—their wide variance in economic levels notwithstanding—are able to play and mingle together with good results. . . . If only America would rouse itself; if only it were willing to open its eyes, the ATA could show it and the world at large an exhibition of true democracy at work."[72]

As the ATA Championships got under way on a sweltering afternoon before yet another packed audience, a visibly excited Bertram L. Baker, the ATA's executive secretary, declared, "This is democracy in action."[73]

It was also good tennis in action. Marble, a strong-willed woman and an outspoken Californian, was an intensely athletic player who rushed the net and smashed her returns in a manner unheard of in women's tennis at the time. Having won the U.S. women's national singles title four times in the late 1930s and in 1940, the Wimbledon women's singles in 1939, and countless doubles titles, Marble was considered one of the greatest female tennis players of her day. In 1939, she was named the Associated Press Female Athlete of the Year and appeared on the cover of *Life* magazine. Having turned pro in 1941, she now devoted a portion of her time to encouraging younger women players. Part of her mission in appearing at exhibition competitions was to scout out young talent.

Marble's striking career performance signaled a new era of women's tennis. While women at the time were largely discouraged from excessive exertion, for fear it might be bad for their health, Marble introduced a most vigorous and dominating model of play. Noting that she often wore shorts rather than the skirts or dresses more customarily worn by women players, more than a few reporters observed that Marble's style was just like that of a man. But no one was more impressed by her performance at the 1944 exhibition match than a skinny sixteen-year-old girl watching from the stands. Marble had easily defeated Hardwick in the singles that day and had also won the women's doubles with partner Frances Gittens and the mixed doubles with partner Robert Ryland. Here was a woman who was determined to win whether she was playing against a man or a woman.

"I can still remember saying to myself, 'Boy, would I like to be able to play tennis like that!'" Althea wrote in her autobiography. "Basically, of course, it was the aggressiveness behind her game that I liked. Watching her smack that effortless serve, and then follow it into the net and put the ball away with an overhead as good as any man's, I saw possibilities in the game of tennis that I had never seen before."[74]

If Marble and Hardwick's appearance on the Cosmopolitan courts was inspiring, so, too, were their hearty words of praise for their opponents' performance afterward. Sam Lacy of the *Baltimore Afro-American* took it all as an indication that Black tennis was coming into its own.

"Especially is this so when you have watched tennis progress, as I have, from a pat-pat, cream-puff stage to the slam-bang, explosive game it has lately become," he wrote in his column, Looking 'Em Over. The event, he concluded, served to "vindicate me in my satisfaction that we're coming, but fast—and without any help."[75]

In the final days of the tournament, Althea herself piqued some interest among the crowd. Two years after she had been beaten by Nana Davis at the National Girls' Championships in 1942, Althea turned the tables and trounced the same girl by a score of 6–1, 6–3. Those present at the event that day included not only Ora Washington, the onetime dominant Black female player, but also a serious-looking Virginia physician named Robert Johnson. A prominent figure in ATA circles, Johnson was ever on the lookout for budding junior tennis talent, and Althea had caught his eye. Even Marble had noticed the teen's "superior baseline play," as Lacy had described it in one of his columns. That evening, Marble met up with Robert Ryland and some others at a nearby Harlem bar. An outgoing woman who unabashedly enjoyed her liquor, she put a match to her cigarette and quizzed Ryland about that Gibson girl who had just won the girl's ATA National Championships. How good was she, really, Marble asked.

In the past, Ryland, a mannered Chicago native, had often been put off by Althea's roughshod ways. That girl was just a little too full of herself. But on the subject of her tennis, he had nothing but praise.

"I said, 'She's a great player,'" Ryland said. "'I think she's got what it takes.'"[76]

Marble took a drag on her cigarette and nodded. She would remember his words.

3

The Doctors

The final day of the American Tennis Association's Twenty-Ninth National Championships tournament at Wilberforce University in Ohio dawned under a near-cloudless azure sky. Coming at the end of a week of matches featuring the best of the Black organization's talent in the summer of 1946, the conclusion was attended by nearly three thousand well-turned-out spectators. A good number of them were just as exhausted as the players, and not just from sitting under a blistering sun in the jam-packed stands.

Like most national ATA events, this one had provided a relentless social schedule throughout the week. The previous night alone had featured several private cocktail parties followed by the elegant Tennis Ball in the gymnasium, capped by an unbuttoned bash in the school laundry hall, where the entrance fee was a fifth of scotch. The ATA officials at the door had each hauled in a couple of hundred dollars' worth of single malt by night's end, which, as one *Baltimore Afro-American* columnist archly put it, "is one reason why it takes more than knowing about tennis to be an ATA official."[1] The days before had seen a succession of picnics, brunches, and even a feast of steaks and corn on the cob at the state's legendary caves. Some attendees, who had traveled from far reaches of the country, joked that they barely had time for the tennis, there was so much else on the calendar. On this decisive final day of the tournament, the women spectators paraded into the stands in their absolute finest, closely observed by the gaggle of reporters in attendance.

An elegant Washington woman appeared in fox furs kissed with a touch of blue, her dark hair peeking out from beneath a naughty red hat. One of the university administrators showed up in black-and-white checks and a pair of red pumps, which, as Lula Jones Garrett, the *Baltimore Afro-American* reporter covering the event, observed, "did something special for her shock of white hair." But the hands-down prizewinner was the Los Angeles doyenne who, "in a beautiful state of undress, played up a prize-winning form in shorts, briefs and backlesses [*sic*] which were something to talk about as well as see."[2]

It was the beginning of the end of the event, and anything could still happen. The highlight of the day would be the concluding men's singles final, in which Jimmie McDaniel, the perennial favorite from Los Angeles, would attempt to win back the No. 1 standing he had surprisingly lost the year before. But first would come the women's singles final, pitting the petite Roumania Peters, the ATA doubles champion who had won the national women's singles title two years earlier, against the long-limbed Althea Gibson. A decade younger than her opponent, Althea had taken her first women's singles title at the New York State Tennis Association tournament at the Cosmopolitan Club just two weeks earlier. It was bound to be an epic battle.

As the crowd quieted in anticipation, Peters opened with an aggressive volley and a battery of her trademark cross-court shots, taking the first set 6–4. Althea fought back with a forceful net game and, despite hitting a series of erratic strokes, managed to keep her opponent on the run. Although compelled to battle repeatedly for the advantage, Althea nonetheless took the second set 9–7. After more than an hour's play, Peters was clearly tiring and appeared to wilt with exhaustion. But she suddenly revived and began to return her opponent's smashes with a sustained series of lobs that trapped Althea at the back of the court. Caught off guard by the older woman's clever tactic, Althea was visibly irked and struggled vainly to return the ball, her lips set in a tight line. Finally, exasperated, she abandoned any semblance of reserve and, as the raw street fighter within her took over, slammed the ball ruthlessly, and erratically, in return. Within minutes, the game slipped out of her control, and she lost the final set 6–3.

After an explosion of applause for Peters, the bleachers gradually began to empty as the well-heeled viewers headed to the next round of lunches and cocktails marking the tournament's end. Althea was left sitting by herself, slumped despondently over her racket. Two women dressed in elegant pastel skirts, both members of the ATA, which had paid Althea's expenses for the event, paused on their way out to glare pointedly at the girl in disgust. Tears began to slide down the nineteen-year-old's face.

"Maybe they thought they hadn't got their money's worth out of me because I had lost," Althea would write in her autobiography a decade later. "I remember one of them saying something to the effect that they were through with me, that they didn't think much of my attitude."[3]

It turned out that losing that match would be one of the best things that ever happened to her. Within minutes, a pair of trimly dressed men approached her. Althea straightened herself, bracing for a harsh critique. But the men, both doctors and talented tennis players, had something quite other than criticism on their minds. For the past few hours, the two had been scrutinizing Althea's game from high in the stands, hunched in concentration and whispering to each other. One was Dr. Hubert A. Eaton, a surgeon from Wilmington, North Carolina, who would become a national figure in the civil rights struggle in the coming decade. The other, Dr. Robert W. Johnson, a general practitioner from Lynchburg, Virginia, had earned his nickname "Whirlwind" owing to his astonishing speed on the football field in his college days. Soon his pioneering efforts on behalf of young Black tennis players would earn him another nickname: "the Godfather of Black Tennis." In addition to being medical colleagues and avid poker players, the two men were unofficial scouts for the ATA, agents of its long-range ambition of finding a singularly skilled Black player who might unlock the barricaded doors of the exclusive all-white United States Lawn Tennis Association. In an era when women's sports ran a pale second to men's, drafting a woman to break that rigid color barrier seemed highly unlikely. But what the doctors knew of Althea, coupled with the performance they had just witnessed—never mind that she had lost—bowled them over. Could Althea Gibson be the one they had been searching for all this time? Could this gangly, volatile, talented girl stride into the seemingly impenetrable fortress of the white sports establishment?

Eaton and Johnson were impressed by the teenager's speed on the court and her near-perfect eye-hand coordination. What she lacked was consistency and discipline, and she often seemed at the mercy of her emotions and an all-consuming desire to win. Both doctors had seen Althea in previous ATA tournaments. Eaton had noticed her the previous year, when she won the girls' national title, but her boyish appearance had left him puzzled about her gender, and he'd moved on. "She was such a tomboy in those days that I didn't know whether she was a boy or girl, with her hair straight back and wearing slacks. So I didn't pay much attention to her then."[4]

The doctors were well aware that Althea had dropped out of high school years earlier and was inclined toward wildness, neither of which was reassuring. Such conduct was nearly unthinkable to the pair of doctors, for whom discipline was a daily mantra as much as a way of life. Althea's athleticism was irresistible, though, even if she was going to take some serious smoothing out. Despite her fiery disposition, her inexperience and raw ambition suggested an openness to their guidance that more seasoned athletes were unlikely to possess. They decided to approach Althea with the proposal they'd been mulling over for the past couple of hours.

"How would you like to play at Forest Hills?" Johnson asked, referring to the national tournament in which no Black person had ever been permitted to compete.

"Go away, don't kid me now," Althea responded, crying even harder.[5]

The doctors weren't kidding in the slightest. Their proposal was as sweeping as it was unprecedented. Also unprecedented was the fact that each of the prosperous physicians had built a tennis court in his backyard equipped with a volleying machine, making them very likely the only Black players in their cities to have such a luxury. The proposal was this: Althea would live at Dr. Eaton's home in Wilmington, where it was warmer and the tennis season lasted longer, and would finish high school there while practicing with him in the afternoons. During the summer months, she would live at Johnson's home, in Lynchburg, and join him, along with a handful of other promising young Black players, on the summer tournament circuit. The doctors would cover all her expenses. While the two men's vision included lessons in how a young lady should conduct herself and the finer points of dinner table etiquette, they knew better than to say so early on. Johnson, who kept a dog-eared copy of Emily Post's *Etiquette* on a shelf above his bed, surely had a few choice chapters of the blue volume for Althea in mind, but for the moment, he kept this to himself.[6] Althea hesitated at their sweeping offer, tempted by the unconventional invitation but also wary of going to the Jim Crow South, about which she'd heard so many terrifying stories. She promised that she would think about it when she got back to Harlem.

Just two days earlier, a related development had absorbed the doctors' attention when controversy erupted at a press dinner pitting the ATA brass against a group of irate Black players. The dispute was triggered when ATA president Cleve L. Abbott, tennis and football coach at the Tuskegee Institute, declared that even high-ranking Black players were not yet prepared to compete against white opponents, infuriating the players' group that had been strongly lobbying to gain entrance into the white USLTA tournaments. The following day the group pointed out that the Black duo of Jimmie McDaniel and Lula Ballard had trounced the white couple Mary and Charles Hare in an interracial doubles exhibition match that very afternoon, and they accused the ATA executives of stalling and of being aloof and autocratic. Putting their frustration to paper, the players circulated a petition demanding that the ATA apply for membership in the USLTA and seek the entrance of two Black players in forthcoming white tournaments. As part of the players' effort to be admitted to nationwide tennis, they organized a separate group of their own and named the former men's champion Lloyd Scott president and Eaton secretary-treasurer.[7]

The disgruntled players could hardly have predicted that, at the tournament finals that followed, Eaton and Johnson would make a significant leap of faith toward precisely their goal in extending their offer to Althea. The standoff must have been highly awkward both for Eaton, a man far more inclined to negotiation than confrontation, and Johnson, who was already hosting a number of young players on his court while serving as the ATA's Middle Atlantic field secretary, but it would have been premature to make mention of their nascent plan. The issue appeared to have died down shortly afterward, and there was apparently no more press coverage of the matter. Nonetheless, the dispute presaged what would be years of tension and, in Johnson's case, outright conflict between the doctors and the ATA over how best to integrate tennis in general and how to get Althea through the tightly sealed door of the white tennis world in particular.

The players' petition nonetheless prompted some action. The following month, the ATA's executive secretary, Bertram Baker, and its assistant executive secretary, Arthur Francis, as well as ranking player Richard Cohen, met with the USLTA's president, Holcombe Ward, in New York and made their case for Black players to be permitted to play in some of its tournaments. In doing so, they were raising an issue that the organization had long managed to dodge. In 1922, the United States Lawn Tennis Association voted unanimously not to admit the all-Black Howard University as a member club. Deftly avoiding any engagement with the prickly topic of race, the association had long held the position that in order to play in its nationally sanctioned tournaments, a player had to be a member of one of its member clubs, and it was up to the clubs who could be admitted. Some of those clubs, particularly in the South, had language specifically barring Black players, while many in the North barred them more subtly.

Ward told the three Black men that "they were making a great mistake if they attempted to force the issue. I said that would merely antagonize people," as he later explained to his organization's executive committee.

At that committee meeting, in January 1947, members considered a suggestion from the ATA that a slot be reserved in the championships for the best "Negro" player. Lawrence Baker, the USLTA's first vice president, scoffed at the idea, saying, "I asked whether we ought to reserve a place for the best Chinese player and for the best Indian player." Later in the meeting, Baker dismissed the ATA request, saying, "They are not complaining of discrimination. They are asking for discrimination in their favor . . . I see no reason why we should legislate in a discriminatory fashion for some particular group simply because they happen to be colored people."

The executive committee agreed to take no action on the matter until, as the USLTA's Baker laid it out, "somebody comes up among the Negro players who shows clearly that he is entitled, by reason of his ability, to contest in our Championships. When we reach that point . . . I think we will have great difficulty in saying that that man cannot play."[8]

Meanwhile, a certain young woman struggled to make up her mind about the doctors' offer. She couldn't quite fathom who would go voluntarily into "this strange country where, according to what I'd heard, terrible things were done to Negroes just because they were Negroes, and nobody was ever punished for them . . . Harlem wasn't heaven but at least I knew I could take care of myself there."[9] Althea was accustomed to doing as she pleased, and that included taking whatever seat on the bus she chose or downing a hot dog at the counter of the 5–10–25 Cent Store on 125th Street. In the end, she listened to the advice of her buddy Sugar Ray Robinson, who told her she'd never get anywhere drifting from one job to another, especially without an education. Althea wrote to Eaton accepting the doctors' offer, which included the proviso that she resume her education, and it was agreed that she would take a train to Wilmington in a couple of weeks.[10]

Her departure from New York marked a significant shift in her relationship with her family. Although Althea would remain in contact with her parents in coming years, her journey south marked an end to a difficult childhood stained by neglect and abuse. Already she had distanced herself from her parents, as her decision to accept the doctors' offer was one she apparently made on her own, without serious consultation with either of them. Ill at ease with the unfamiliar tennis culture and lacking the funds to travel to Althea's tournaments even if they had wanted to go, her parents did not see her play tennis until late in 1956, when they apparently attended the U.S. National Championships at Forest Hills. In the years following their visit to Forest Hills, they made only rare appearances on the tennis circuit. So, too, they would be missing from many of the significant moments in their daughter's young adult life, including her graduation from both high school and college. Althea remained close to her mother and wrote to her regularly when she traveled, but she rarely returned home for more than a brief visit during the holidays until later years.

Her new life began in the first week of September 1946. Splurging with a few dollars she had saved, a nervous Althea headed in a taxicab by herself to the train station. With the saxophone Sugar Ray had given her slung around her neck and a pair of flimsy cardboard suitcases secured with belts grasped in her hands, she boarded the night train to Wilmington. A roll of dollar bills was pinned tightly inside her blouse with a large safety pin.

Every time the food vendor walked through the train car, Althea would peel off a bill and buy peanut butter crackers and milk. She traveled several hundred miles that night, but she wound up in a place so foreign that she might as well have crossed into a different continent.

To a little-traveled and poorly educated Black teenager, raised in a place where Black culture not only flourished but was celebrated and where the NAACP had headquartered its legal challenge to the laws that served as a bulwark to segregation, the reality of Wilmington, North Carolina, was beyond anything she could have imagined. Black and white residents lived separate and wholly unequal lives. Statewide, more than sixty Black people had been lynched between 1900 and 1943.[11] In Wilmington, as elsewhere in the South, schools were segregated by race, while signs over public water fountains, bathrooms, benches—public facilities of all kinds—dictated whether they could be used by "Whites Only" or "Colored Only." Although the city had benefited from a population boom during the war years due to its bustling shipyard, it remained utterly segregated. All the city's public facilities were segregated, and there was not a single Black person in the police department, fire department, city council, or board of county commissioners.[12] North Carolina, as a whole, experienced a surge of postwar energy and activism in the mid-1940s, but the picturesque city on the banks of the Cape Fear River remained geographically isolated and mired in racism.

Part of the reason for this lay in an episode of stunning racial violence that had set the city apart from the political progressivism emerging elsewhere in the state. In the years after Reconstruction, Wilmington, then North Carolina's largest city, had a majority-Black population and was widely touted as "the Mecca" to the many freed slaves who flocked there seeking work in the harbor trades. Black residents held many key jobs in the city and began to fill a variety of public offices, prompting a violent backlash by a coalition of ex-Confederates and white supremacists who had been seething with discontent since the end of the Civil War.

On November 10, 1898, two years after the U.S. Supreme Court's *Plessy v. Ferguson*, the landmark decision upholding "separate but equal" segregation, armed bands of white men numbering in the thousands roamed the city's streets slaughtering Black citizens and hurling some of their bodies into the Cape Fear River. While some families cowered in the city's Black cemetery, many of the city's most prominent Black figures were forced onto trains at gunpoint and warned never to return. Although there is no official count of the number of people killed during the massacre—an event obscured in or omitted from state history books for decades—some estimate that as many as three hundred died that day. At the bloody day's end, the extremists forced many city leaders to resign at gunpoint, in what stands as the only successful coup d'état in the nation's history. The event signaled a fervent embrace of Jim Crow racism and inspired similar brutal outbursts across the country.[13]

It would take the city decades to recover. Despite an influx of more progressive outsiders into Wilmington during World War II, memories of the searing racial violence of 1898 hung like a pall over the city, colored race relations during the first half of the twentieth century, and, some say, lingers to this day.

"In Wilmington, mythical visions of the plantation era, of Confederate glory, and the 'Revolution of 1898' still endowed many whites with the sense of a distinctive local identity, while racial fears haunted the imagination for both races," John L. Godwin, author of *Black Wilmington and the North Carolina Way*, wrote of the mid-1940s. "Since the war most North Carolinians thought of the existing relationship between the races, based as it was on the laws of segregation, as a fixed and established way of life."[14]

Bertha Todd, a Black woman who moved to Wilmington in 1952, remembers the terrifying whispers. "Local Blacks would whisper in your ear about how 'the whites killed a lot of us people, and they're buried in the cemeteries,'" recalled Todd, now in her nineties. A former librarian at the Wilmington Industrial High School, she remembers that "Blacks would not look at whites in the face when they were talking. They seemed very afraid, very subservient. I just felt I had gone back in time."[15]

When Althea stepped off the train in Wilmington—"nervous as a cat," as she later wrote—she stood anxious and alone on the platform. Waiting for her just outside the terminal was Eaton's chauffeur, standing in front of a gleaming blue Cadillac and holding the car door open for her. When she arrived at the Eatons' handsome two-story home on Orange Street shortly afterward, she was introduced to Eaton's wife, Celeste, their two young children, and Rachel, the maid. The doctor's new *en-tout-cas* tennis court, made of a kind of synthetic material designed to dry rapidly, and one of few private courts in the city, beckoned from just beyond a bank of windows on the far side of the house. Upstairs, the sheets on Althea's bed were starched. Celeste, a stylish woman and one of the city's leading social doyennes, winced when she saw Althea's tired skirt and threadbare shirt, but she quickly hugged the family's new addition and suggested she make herself some breakfast. Althea headed to the stove, and as she whipped up a feast for herself of five scrambled eggs, a dozen slices of bacon, and five pieces of toast, Eaton took a deep breath.

"As she consumed this mammoth meal with a huge glass of milk, I suddenly had doubts about my hasty decision to have Althea live with us," Eaton wrote in his autobiography. "I wondered if I could afford to feed this hungry young woman."[16]

Eaton, in fact, had little to worry about in that regard. The son of a doctor, he had been raised in Winston-Salem, a couple of hundred miles northwest of Wilmington, with its more conservative mind-set, and he was keenly sensitive to the harsh racial injustice that prevailed in the Jim Crow South. Having married the daughter of one of Wilmington's wealthiest, most eminent Black physicians, who was also one of the key founders of its Black hospital, Eaton arrived in Wilmington prepared to make his mark not just on the medical world but also on behalf of his race. A tall, slender man with an earnest demeanor, he would go on to become one of the city's most prominent civil rights leaders in the 1950s and '60s, filing lawsuits against both the county school system and the white-run local hospital, among others, while he repeatedly ran for public office.[17]

Eaton, who had also won multiple awards for both singles and doubles play while in college, was a ranking player in the ATA. In 1945, he built the tennis court behind his house, of which he wrote, "The balls were white, the court was green, and the color of the players varied."[18] Eaton first met Dr. Robert "Whirlwind" Johnson through a group of Black professionals in North Carolina, many of them doctors, who played tennis on Sunday afternoons at various courts around the state. For Johnson, the group provided an outlet for both his passion for the sport and his love of

THE DOCTORS • 61

entertaining, which he did frequently at the mirrored bar in his basement. The two men even shared another connection: the sister of Eaton's brother-in-law had worked in Johnson's Lynchburg medical clinic.

As a young man in the mid-1940s, Hubert Eaton was taking the first steps in the crusades that would define his professional life. In Althea, his two great passions, tennis and civil rights, converged. If the two doctors had anything to do with it, the rangy Harlem teenager with the ferocious serve was going to represent an opening salvo on the battlefield of integration. First, though, they had to teach her how to fold a napkin and use a knife and fork properly.

When she first arrived, the school dropout with the short-cropped hair was an alien creature in the Eatons' luxurious home, where the maid was summoned from the kitchen by a buzzer beneath the dining room table and the garage housed not just the blue Cadillac but a gray two-seater Oldsmobile. Although considerably warmer than her husband, Celeste Eaton was a refined woman, a member of the Black women's sorority Alpha Kappa Alpha, and a founder of the local chapter of the social organization known as The Links. She more than dressed the part. As reporter Lula Jones Garrett described "the feminine portion of the Hubert Eatons" attending the finals of ATA tournament in Wilberforce earlier in the summer, Celeste Eaton "topped her pink frock with pale cream serge and added dash with brown alligator accessories."[19] Althea was unlike anyone with whom Celeste had ever spent time, much less shared living quarters. Indeed, so disturbing did the Eaton family find Althea's table manners that they initially required her to eat in the kitchen. Eaton later explained in an interview that Althea "was underfed, and it took almost a year to fill her up properly."[20]

But if the Eatons were struggling a bit with their new houseguest's ways, so was Althea with theirs.

"It was the first real family life I had ever known," Althea wrote. "Nobody stayed out all night in that house, or decided to eat lunch in a dog wagon downtown instead of coming home for lunch with the family. And the rules that applied to the Eatons' own children applied to me, too. I even got an allowance every week, the same as they did, so I could see that the good came with the bad."[21]

Then there was the matter of her schooling. Given that Althea had dropped out of school right after completing junior high in New York, she was technically a nineteen-year-old high school freshman. When her transcript arrived on the desk of F. J. Rogers, the principal of Williston Industrial High School, two weeks after she arrived, he immediately telephoned Eaton. "Looking at her record," he observed tartly, "it seems she has spent more time in the flickers, as she calls the movies, than she has spent in school."[22] What's more, Rogers was concerned that Althea, being not only the oldest but the tallest in the freshman class, might find it difficult to connect with the other students and thus could develop emotional problems. Despite her poor grades, Althea was permitted to enter the sophomore class with the provision that Eaton keep on her to study hard.

The doctor was prepared to do that and immediately got to work with her, both on the court and off. He was well accustomed to long hours, having spent many years striving, as a Black man, to become a doctor, and he expected no less of his protégé. Every day, Eaton came home at 3 p.m. for dinner, a schedule that allowed him to return to his clinic at night to care for his Black patients who didn't have the luxury of leaving their day jobs to visit the doctor. In the hour or so before the afternoon meal was served, he'd play tennis with Althea, focusing on streamlining her erratic strokes and making her game less volatile. Eaton was a man of control, both in life and in sport, and his aim was to teach his young student how to harness her considerable powers. Strategy, he explained, is what determines the victor, more so than strength. Watch your opponent's feet, not her racket, he advised, for that will tell you where the ball will go. Always win the first game, if you can.

As Eaton got to know Althea's style of play, one thing continued to concern him, just as it had on the day he watched her lose at Wilberforce. Althea was dead set on *winning* and winning only. On the days that she managed to do so, she beamed. On the days that she lost, her face went blank and she spoke little for the rest of the day, drifting morosely around the house. Worried about the fire that lurked just below that flat expression, Eaton feared that when it came time to compete in public, Althea's emotions would undermine her, leading to another explosive, self-destructive display of the kind he and Johnson had already witnessed. Over time, however, he also came to admire her determination. Her behavior, he wrote, "was a mark of all champions. A true champion never wants to lose. Losing is not acceptable; winning is all that counts."[23]

Now firmly ensconced in her second-floor bedroom with its starched sheets and private bathroom, Althea struggled to adjust to a radically new life, one where things happened on schedule and the refrigerator was always full. Despite the daunting rules, she adopted the Eaton parents as her own—the latest in a succession of adults she would claim as surrogates—calling them "Mom" and "Dad." At school, things on the athletic front, not surprisingly, were working out well, if less so socially. Althea was the star forward on the basketball team and was soon named team captain; the team didn't lose a single game while she was there. More than a decade later, when making an appearance at the U.S. State Department in Washington, D.C., the agency that had sent her overseas on several goodwill tennis exhibition tours, Althea proudly noted that she had averaged twenty-two points per game while on the Williston team.[24] She also joined the school marching band and played her saxophone at the school's football games. Williston had no tennis team, so to fulfill her hunger for more athletic activity, she often headed to the school's playing fields and joined the boys' varsity baseball and football practices in the afternoons. The boys were entertained, for she could hurl a pass farther than the team's quarterback. But the girls mocked her mercilessly.

They whispered about her odd uniform of slacks and a T-shirt, so different from their own flounced skirts and pastel blouses. They giggled out loud when the choir instructor moved her to the tenor section because she sounded so much like a boy. When their towering classmate hit a home run on the baseball field and tore around the bases, they snickered among themselves that Althea played "just like a *man*." They weren't the first to speculate about Althea's apparent lesbian leanings—some among the Cosmo crowd had done so, too—and they wouldn't be the last. Back home, Althea might have paid no mind to such taunting, but down in the punishing South, lacking any real soul mate to whom she could complain, she raged to herself.

"They looked at me like I was a freak. I hated them for it," she later wrote. "I felt as though they ought to see that I didn't do the things they did because I didn't know how to, and that I showed off on the football field because throwing passes better than the varsity quarterback was a way for me to express myself, to show that there was something I was good at. It seemed sometimes as though nobody could understand me."[25]

Things at the Eaton home weren't much better, at least at the start. All the rules and the chores and the punctual meals were hard to get used to. Even the dinner table seating arrangement was unvarying: Eaton sat at one end of the table, Althea at the other end, in what might otherwise have been Celeste's place, while Celeste and her three-year-old daughter, Tina, sat on one side of the table and five-year-old Hubert Jr. sat on the other. That Althea was seated at the foot of the table seems to give some indication of her status within the family, but the children adored her nonetheless.

"All of a sudden, I had a big sister," Hubert Eaton Jr., who grew up to be a physician like his father, recalled in an interview. "We loved her. Althea would walk me to school in the mornings when I was little. When I got out of school later, I'd sometimes wait the half hour until she got out and we'd walk home together."[26]

Althea yearned for the freedom and delights of the urban streets that had been her home for so long, but Wilmington's byways felt alien and intimidating. Despite the bucolic appearance of the tree-lined boulevards and antebellum estates, Wilmington of 1946 was starkly divided. Those restaurants and stores that would serve Black customers were clustered on Castle Street, on the west side of the city, while a handful of "Jew-joints," businesses run by Jewish proprietors who would serve Black people, were scattered throughout town. The homes of the city's prominent Black residents were located largely on Red Cross Street, along with a handful of Black hair salons and coffee shops. More important for the movie-loving Althea, most Black people frequented the Ritz theater, on Fourth Street, although the city's classic theater, the Bijou, permitted them to sit in an upstairs balcony and provided them with after-hours shows.

Althea was aghast at Jim Crow laws that kept Black and white people divided or simply excluded Black people altogether. She hated the fact that even though she could buy a hot dog at the five-and-ten, she was required to eat it outside the store, or had to go upstairs at the Bijou because of the color of her skin. When the city bus driver ordered her to sit behind the red line toward the rear of the bus, Althea chose a seat as far forward, but still behind the line, and seethed for the entire ride.[27]

"She didn't like this business about segregation, being from New York. She didn't like that," recalled Eaton Jr. "We were southern Blacks, so we were used to that. We grew up with it. I knew that when you got on the bus you had that red line and everybody went behind the red line . . ."

But then she discovered Brown's Pool Hall, just a few blocks from the Eatons' home, a men-only establishment. One afternoon, while Eaton was still at work, Althea slipped out to Brown's, gleefully grasped a cue stick in her hands, and began to set up a rack and show her stuff. Within minutes, one of the hall regulars picked up the phone and dialed Eaton. "Doc, your girl's down here," the man said. "You better come and git her."

Eaton was shocked. That night, he carefully explained to Althea that southern girls didn't wear blue jeans around town, much less go around shooting pool at men-only clubs. Down south, he said, "ladies don't do that sort of thing. You just stay at home now."[28]

Even when she did just that, though, things went awry. One night when Hubert and Celeste Eaton were going out for dinner, they asked Althea to keep an eye on their two small children, whose bedrooms were on the first floor. Minutes after the couple left, the children got caught up in one of their favorite games—locking themselves in the downstairs bathroom with the key on the inside of the door. Althea begged them to come out, lying on the floor and cajoling Hubert Eaton Jr. to pass her the key, but the children only laughed even harder. Althea finally shrugged and climbed the stairs to her second-story bedroom. When the Eatons came home a couple of hours later, they found their two young children locked in the bathroom and Althea upstairs asleep. Both parents were furious that Althea had left the young children locked in a room on their own.

"I was just being devilish, you know, on purpose," Eaton Jr. confessed. "It was so fun to play with Althea. My mama came home and she raised hell, she was going to send [Althea] back to New York. Oh, she was so up-set."[29] Eaton had managed to take Althea out of Harlem, but how was he going to take Harlem out of Althea? Beside herself, Celeste insisted that Althea be sent back to New York immediately. Reluctantly, Eaton agreed, but when he told Althea the following afternoon that she would have to drop out of school and return to her parents, she begged him to reconsider. "Dad, please don't send me back. Let me talk to Mom. I swear to God I will never do such a stupid thing again." In the end, the couple agreed to give her one more chance.[30]

She blew that one, too. After all, how could anyone resist the handsome trumpeter in the jazz combo she'd been playing with at school? Truth be told, he had started it, making eyes at her in between musical arrangements, grinning across the drum set. Althea resisted. She tried hard to do what the doctor had asked of her, but self-restraint was a skill she knew not at all, much less had mastered. One night, when Dr. Eaton and his wife were out, Althea couldn't help but eye Eaton's mother's car sitting idle in the driveway, beckoning her away her from her homework until she could stand it no longer. Without a word to the children and their babysitter, who were elsewhere in the house, she snatched the car keys from the drawer where they were kept and took off. Never mind that she didn't have a driver's license.

Althea made a beeline for the trumpeter's house, beeped her horn until he came bounding out, and the two of them spent a half hour necking on the next block before she sped back to the Eaton home. Relieved that the couple was still out, Althea carefully parked the car in the exact same spot she had found it and returned to her bedroom, unaware that the babysitter had spied her through the window. Upon hearing the news the next morning, Eaton was livid.

"Althea," he barked, "did you take my mother's car out last night?"[31]

This time, however, the storm was diverted. Both adult Eatons recognized that the situation was just as challenging for Althea as it was for them, and in a way, both incidents bound them all together more as a family. Forgiven once again and finally feeling settled in her new home, Althea doubled down on her schoolwork, and as her grades began to improve, she and Celeste became increasingly close. By the time the high school prom rolled around, Celeste not only talked Althea into attending the event, but also got her to trade in her slacks for a flowing pink evening gown she had bought the teenager. When Althea headed out that night, her hair freshly coiffed at the beauty parlor, her escort at her side, both Eatons swelled with pride.

By then, the winter weather had moved on, and it was time to get back out on the tennis court in earnest. As the temperature rose, Althea spent most afternoons drilling with Eaton or with his volleying machine. On the weekends, Eaton sometimes paired her against local male players as he scrutinized the match closely from the sidelines. Althea rarely lost. By the end of the academic year, it was time for her to head to Dr. Johnson's for the summer months. Eaton packed up the Cadillac—the car he used for longer road trips, given that African Americans were prohibited from patronizing most hotels and restaurants along the route—with Althea's belongings, and the two of them drove the few hours to Dr. Johnson's home in Lynchburg, just days before the ATA's competitive summer circuit began.

Althea was eager to immerse herself in tennis, and she welcomed the change of scenery while adjusting to her summer mentor. At forty-seven, Johnson was seventeen years older than his Wilmington colleague, but the two men were similar in several respects. Both were hardworking doctors who went out of their way to provide the best care for the Black community. Each believed fervently in combating segregation through persistence and negotiation rather than confrontation. Men of means with stature in both Black and white society, they carried themselves with palpable pride and self-confidence. Neither smiled much.

They would also share the disconcerting distinction of being charged with murder. In Johnson's case, the charges stemmed from a 1942 disturbance at the Happy Land Lake Resort, just outside the city, after a young man attempted to crash a late-night dance there and was shot to death. Johnson, who leased the popular Black resort, and the club's manager were charged in the incident. In a handwritten statement to the court, Johnson explained that he shot a gun "up in the air" to scare the party-crashing young man and a couple of his friends, after which the manager shot several bullets toward the doorway. While Johnson was ultimately acquitted, and the manager was found guilty of involuntary manslaughter, the press accounts of the incident were followed word by word all over town.[32]

Eaton's case, which came years later, stemmed from an abortion he performed in 1963 on a thirty-year-old woman whom he said died from an allergic reaction to penicillin. The state's charge of second-degree murder was based primarily on the testimony of a physician at the white hospital in Wilmington, which at the time was under court order to integrate as a result of a lawsuit initiated by Eaton and two other Black doctors.[33] Some clearly viewed the charges as retribution for the court order. In the end, they were dismissed for lack of evidence. In his autobiography, Eaton describes the matter as one of a number of incidents of harassment he endured and noted that he had amassed a collection of state and national news stories about the event.[34]

In other ways, the doctors were exceedingly different. Eaton was largely a man of the mind, while the sturdy Johnson was a man of consuming physical force and virile appetites. At five foot ten, Johnson had been an athletic powerhouse in his years at Lincoln University, excelling at football and baseball. While captain of the football team, "Whirlwind" Johnson became known for his speed and deft footwork. Hungry for exercise in later years, he took up the game of tennis in earnest. Having come too late to the game to be the singles ace he'd hoped to be—he never made it to Eaton's level—he nonetheless had an uncanny ability to assess another player's potential and guide them in improving their game, which made him an exceptional coach.

Johnson was driven by a wide variety of interests. An avid outdoorsman, he hunted deer and raccoons with a couple of his prized Weimaraners or beagles at his side. He also kept a darkroom in his basement and personally cultivated an elaborate rose garden around his home. Johnson lived on a street of mixed race, where the prominent residents ranged from the local high school principal to the lauded Harlem Renaissance poet Anne Spencer, whose prestigious guest lists often included notables such as Langston Hughes, Booker T. Washington, and W. E. B. Du Bois. Johnson also pursued an active social life, but one that drew a different spectrum of acquaintances—including nationally known athletes, singers and performers such as Duke Ellington, photographer Gordon Parks Jr., and members of the Brooklyn Dodgers—to the elaborate blue-mirrored bar with red leatherette couches that furnished his basement. Many of his guests were gorgeous women, and Johnson's appetite for female companions was no secret. As Doug Smith, author of a biography of Johnson, *Whirlwind: The Godfather of Black Tennis*, wrote of the twice-divorced Johnson, "In a seemingly lifelong pursuit of beautiful women, Whirlwind was rarely slowed by the presence of wedding bands—on his finger or theirs."[35]

An aficionado of jazz and gospel music, Johnson also had an ear for a well-honed phrase. One of his favorite poems was Rudyard Kipling's "If," a lyrical ode to integrity and resilience in the face of adversity. It begins, "If you can keep your head when all about you / Are losing theirs and blaming it on you . . ." Johnson had his daughter memorize the poem, a few lines of which are etched across the players' entrance at Wimbledon's Centre Court. The oft-quoted lines there, taken from the second stanza, read, "If you can meet with Triumph and Disaster / And treat those two impostors just the same. . . ."

Like Eaton, Johnson was closely attuned to the shifting racial currents of the day, and in later years, he would become active on a number of civil rights fronts, playing a key role in integrating the local hospital and other institutions. When the celebrated halfback Kenny Washington and offensive end Woody Strode signed contracts with the Los Angeles Rams of the National Football League in the spring of 1946, the first Black players to sign with a national club in thirteen years, during which Black players were unofficially banned by NFL owners, Johnson took it as a sure sign that real change was coming. As his grandson Robert Johnson III recalls, "The thing that tipped everything was the day in 1946 when the NFL reintegrated. That is why he wound up approaching Althea Gibson. My grandad understood the minute the domino fell in the NFL, the rest of sports were coming next."[36]

By the time Althea climbed the steps to Johnson's trim brown-and-white house in Lynchburg in the summer of 1947, Johnson was developing the fundamentals of what would become the ATA's legendary Junior Development Program for promising young players, which would change the tone of American tennis, producing not just Grand Slam champion Arthur Ashe, but a couple dozen other Black players who would gain national prominence and help scores more players win college scholarships.

In the early 1940s, Johnson had begun inviting a handful of the most promising ATA junior players to spend time on his court during the summer months. In the fall of 1946, months before Althea arrived, Johnson had convinced the principal of the all-Black local Dunbar High School to allow him to establish a tennis team with half a dozen of its students.[37] It didn't matter that the school didn't have a court or that the students were prohibited from playing on the segregated municipal public courts. They would play on *his* clay court and follow *his* tennis training regimen and *his* code of conduct.

Some of the students found the experience daunting, to say the least. Geraldine Bennett Wood, one of the original members of the tennis team known as the Dunbar Six, remembers that when she initially shirked the balls speeding her way, Johnson had her stand on one side of the court and positioned his ball machine on the other side. When he flipped the On switch, dozens of balls began spraying through the air and pelting her.

"I was really scared the balls would hurt me, you know, but I stood there until all the balls came out," Wood recalled in an interview. "He had them hit me to let me know they wouldn't hurt me. . . . At first, I went in and said, 'Oh my goodness!' Any way I did it . . . they didn't hurt me at all. They weren't coming like that, that hard. I was just laughing at him in the end. I thought it was funny. From then on, I really did get into it."[38]

And so did the others. After training at "Dr. J's" for a while, the young players found they weren't just playing tennis; they were winning. Sometimes, when the students were waiting for Johnson to pull up in his big green Buick 225 to take them to a tournament, they hummed a little song they'd made up, using the rhythm of the popular Black spiritual "Good News! (Chariot's A-Comin')."

"We'd sing, 'Good news, Whirlwind's comin', / Good news, Whirlwind's comin', / Good news, we're gonna take all the trophies home, we're gonna take all the trophies home,'" crooned Lynchburg native Elmer Reid, seventy-five, who served as a ball boy for Althea and who, as a youth, participated in Johnson's summer program.[39]

Like his cherished Rudyard Kipling poem, Johnson's philosophy was strictly nonconfrontational. One of the cardinal rules in his code of conduct was to be respectful at all times. Players were never to question a call on the court or argue about *anything*. If the umpire called a ball out, the player was to hit the ball a foot inside the line the next time. There was to be no cursing, no racket throwing, no arguing of any kind, and if players showed disrespect or rudeness on the Lynchburg court, they were promptly put on a bus back home.

"We are going into a new world," Johnson often said.[40]

At the same time, he had no tolerance for certain racist behaviors in that new world. One thing that particularly infuriated him was when audience members shouted out the N-word at Black players on the court, as they often did in the 1940s and '50s. Sallie Elam, one of Johnson's students in later years, who went on to win multiple ATA and USLTA titles, and a former board member of the ATA, remembers describing such an experience to Johnson after the N-word had been shouted at her during a match.

"He said, 'Sallie, what is your name? Is nigger your name?'" Elam recalled. "I said, *Nooooooooo*. And he said, 'Well, then, why are you responding to something that is not your name? When someone calls you anything other than your name, you do not respond.' It was one of the best lessons he ever taught me."[41]

Weakness was also something Dr. J could not abide. Henry Kennedy Jr., one of Johnson's students in 1965 and now a retired federal judge in Washington, D.C., remembers competing in one of the ATA National Junior Championships on a sweltering summer day when the temperatures soared into the high nineties. His opponent was a skilled player, the only white competitor in the tournament, and the semifinals match had drawn a huge and enthusiastic crowd. Overwhelmed by the humidity and attention, Kennedy suddenly passed out from dehydration and collapsed on the court. Within seconds, Johnson had run out of the stands toward him with his black medical bag in hand, lowered the waist of the young man's shorts, and plunged a needle of what was apparently hydrating fluid into his rear end. As Kennedy regained consciousness, Johnson hissed icily, "Get up and win." Kennedy did.[42]

Johnson also had strong opinions about how Althea and the other players in his program should behave off the court as well, many of them culled from his worn copy of Emily Post's *Etiquette*, which he frequently shared at a dinner table laden with healthy food. Boys were to hold the door for women and help them into their chairs at the table. Hats were never permitted indoors. Girls were to wear skirts and *always* cross their legs when seated. Napkins went onto laps, and soup was always to be scooped away from the bowl first and then carefully delivered to the mouth. Soft drinks, candy, peanuts, and popcorn were forbidden. At the end of the day, showers were to be taken by all, and on the off chance that someone neglected to do so, Dr. J would come knocking on their door in the middle of the night and remind them. Although the code sometimes felt stern, and some of the northern-born students struggled to adapt, most realized it was the language on their passports to the new world. "You knew what the mission was, you knew what he wanted and what was required to be part of the team," explained Bob Davis, founder of the Panda Foundation, a children's tennis program in Bradenton, Florida, and an ATA national champion in the 1960s who spent two summers at Johnson's. "It was about our future."[43]

Johnson often used the dinner hour to remind his students to behave like ladies and gentlemen in any upcoming tournament and always to mind their table manners. If he sensed the slightest hint of attitude in a player, he would call them out in front of the others and might even send them home. At the end of the meal, the students did all the cleanup. In the end, Johnson's instructions all pretty much boiled down to one thing, as biographer Doug Smith, who spent a summer at Johnson's, wrote of his teacher: "Don't act crazy and give these white folks an excuse not to let you play or invite us back."[44]

Instruction continued on the court each day. Johnson was a busy doctor who headed to his office early in the morning, and so he left the players with a regimen from which they dared not deviate. First, the court was to be rolled, the kitchen cleaned up from breakfast, and the beds made. While two players warmed up on the court, the others tended to the outside chores. The grass was to be cut, the garden weeded, the boxwood trimmed, the dogs fed in their pen out back, and its concrete floor hosed down. If some initially resented being conscripted into domestic duty at the Johnson house, they soon realized it was a nonnegotiable part of the program.

Then came conditioning: twenty-five push-ups, fifty knee chest jumps, one hundred side straddle hops, weights, and a long run. On-court practice training followed. One hundred serves to the right court, one hundred serves to the left court. One hundred overheads, then one hundred cross-court forehands and backhands. The methodical Johnson believed firmly in practice, and his students rarely played actual games or matches with one another until he returned from work in the late afternoon. After plucking a weed or two from the rose bed, he would come out on the court in his white T-shirt and long white pants, racquet in hand, to assess what they had done during that day.

Johnson was a tennis equipment fanatic, and he eventually possessed almost every related device available. One of the most popular items among his students was the Tom Stow Stroke Developer, a metal arm attached to the wall about six feet off the ground and from which was suspended an elastic cord with an adjustable tennis ball anchored in the middle. Stow was a legendary California tennis coach who had worked not only with Grand Slam king Don Budge, but also Margaret duPont and Dorothy Knode. To perfect their strokes, Johnson's younger players were assigned to hit the ball repeatedly with a cut-off broom handle. There was also a ball machine of the kind that pelted Johnson's young student Geraldine Bennett Wood. While the doctor was at work, Althea practiced with a handful of handpicked college students and Johnson's son, Bobby Jr., with whom she squabbled over the equipment and many other things almost daily. Usually, Althea won.

Johnson only reinforced Althea's first-rank position in the household hierarchy, even at his son's expense. When she wanted to drive Dr. J around town to his appointments, he let her—a privilege he had not granted to Bobby Jr. Although Althea's room was on the third floor of the house, Johnson acquiesced to her request that she be able to shower in the basement, where the men did. Under Johnson's regime, what Althea wanted, she often got.

"He played favorites, and he sometimes could not see how that would affect another person like his own son," said Johnson III. "It was a reward thing, one of those carrots. You stick that carrot out there. Now here's another carrot. He was giving someone whatever little perks I can give you to make you keep going, climbing to the top. So be it."[45]

Lendward "Lenny" Simpson, who was coached by both Eaton and Johnson, boils the experience of being a Johnson student down to a fundamental truth. "He was very autocratic. There was no democracy," recalled Simpson, who grew up next to Dr. Eaton's home. "There was a pecking order among the kids. You had your orders, and you did what you were told. And when the doctor spoke, you listened."[46] Simpson turned out to be one of Dr. J's success stories: he went on to become the youngest Black male to make it into the main draw at the U.S. National Championships at Forest Hills, in 1964, and in later years, he founded the One Love Tennis program for at-risk youth, based in Eaton's former home.

Every summer, the schedule at Johnson's was pretty much the same, with the start of the season devoted to practice. By the beginning of July, the players were ready to compete, and a half dozen would pile into the big green Buick 225, which the kids had dubbed "the deuce and a quarter," and hit the tournament circuit. They were sometimes accompanied by a second car driven by Babe Jones, a talented Black tennis player who often came down from Baltimore in the summer. For Black drivers at the time, navigating the segregated South generally meant long spells on the highway with nowhere to stop for food or even gas, so, the two cars were invariably bulging with tennis gear, suitcases, and as much food as possible, some of it strapped to the roof.

Johnson's daughter, Carolyn "Waltee" Moore, who sometimes came along, helped prepare meals for the road trips. "Of course we couldn't stop at restaurants to go to the restroom or anything like that," she recalled. "So we would fix a big bag of sandwiches beforehand, chicken and that type thing, something that people could grab and eat . . . the players necessarily did have to relieve themselves in the woods but I am not sure how many times that was done. It had to be done."[47]

For Althea, who'd never traveled out of New York other than her train journey to Wilmington, the trips were a novel experience. "It was a revelation to me the first year we did it," she wrote of her first summer tour in 1947. "Dr. Johnson had a big Buick and he packed six or seven of us in it, with our bags stuffed in the trunk and in a big luggage rack bolted on the roof. We played in Washington, Philadelphia, New York and New Jersey, and then we all jammed into the car and headed for Kentucky."[48]

Althea's game had already benefited from the doctors' coaching. Her formidable serve was now deadly on target, and her aggressive rush to the net left some of her opponents flailing. By early August 1947, she had won tournaments in Virginia, North Carolina, New England, and Washington, D.C. At the Eastern Open Championships, held at the popular Shady Rest Country Club in Scotch Plains, New Jersey, the first Black-owned country club in the United States, she easily defeated Nana Davis 6–1, 6–0; Davis had routed her at her first big ATA tournament several years earlier.

By the time the thirtieth annual ATA Nationals rolled around at the Tuskegee Institute in Alabama at the end of August 1947, Althea's confidence was high, and she steeled herself for a rematch against Roumania Peters, the reigning women's champion who had trounced her at last year's tournament while Drs. Eaton and Johnson were watching. With Althea serving, Peters came on strong and won the first game. The two then battled it out, with Peters in the lead until Althea surged with energy and took the set 7–5. Appearing coolly confident as she streaked across the court, Althea wore out the weary Peters and triumphantly claimed the second set 6–0, as well as the championship. The victory marked a crucial juncture in her tennis career. Althea would go on to win the women's title every year for the next nine years, an unparalleled record that still stands today, making her the dominant female player in ATA history. Never again would she be beaten by a Black woman on the tennis court. The only shadow that fell that day was when she and Dr. J were defeated in three sets in the mixed doubles by Ora Washington and George Stewart, the Panamanian southpaw who had won the men's singles title. As it turned out, however, Dr. J and Althea were just finding their groove. Over the next eight years, the two of them would win every mixed-doubles championship but one, in 1951. The Black press exulted over Althea's triumph, and even the *The New York Times* nodded to her win, although it spelled her last name as "Gipson."[49]

Althea's ascendance to the pinnacle of Black women's tennis came just months after Jackie Robinson broke Major League Baseball's color barrier for the first time in the twentieth century when he signed with the Brooklyn Dodgers. Although Robinson is often credited with being the "First Negro" to play in the major leagues, catcher Moses Fleetwood Walker actually earned that distinction when he joined the short-lived American Association's Toledo Blue Stockings for a single season in 1884.[50] One year after Robinson, high jumper Alice Coachman would become the first

African American woman to win an Olympic gold medal. The barriers to Black individuals participation in American life remained formidable, but some, at least, were beginning to crumble. With her 1947 wins, Althea and her doctor mentors were digging into the steep uphill climb and setting their gaze firmly on the lush green lawns of Forest Hills, where the USLTA National Championships were held.

"For whatever it was worth, I was the best woman player in Negro tennis," Althea proudly wrote in her autobiography.[51]

Not everyone was thrilled by her performance, however. At the end of the tournament, Althea played an exhibition match against British player Mary Hardwick Hare, the Wimbledon veteran and former member of the Wightman Cup team who had competed in the 1944 exhibition match with Alice Marble at the Cosmopolitan Club three years earlier. Althea reportedly got "cute," paying too much attention to the crowd, and wound up giving Hare twenty-six points on errors and losing the match 6–4. Afterward, a female member of the ATA attempted to talk with Althea about her performance, but Althea spoke rudely to the woman, known as Miss Junior, and infuriated a prominent Black sportswriter who happened to overhear the exchange. In a blistering column in the *Chicago Defender*, columnist Fay Young admonished Althea for her rudeness, a harbinger of the sometimes-rocky relationship she would have with the Black press in the years to come.

"As a young woman, Miss Gibson has much to learn," the veteran sports columnist sniffed. "We were terribly sorry to see her get off on the wrong foot. But she did—not only with Miss Junior but with many others who found out about the incident."[52]

Johnson, who presumably was unaware of the incident, given that Althea was not banished but returned to his house, celebrated her singles title triumph at his popular Labor Day round-robin tournament, a hugely popular social event that marked the culmination of the ATA summer season and lasted for several days. The event took place in his elegant and elaborately decorated basement lounge, from which his students were barred for most of the year. Writer John McPhee once likened the place to "a small nightclub on a busy highway. The columns that support the floor above are encased in blue mirrors. . . . Glass doors, which are generally locked, close off a bar that is commercial in grandeur and is fully appointed and equipped."[53] The only time students were permitted to occupy the plush red leatherette furniture was when Johnson was showing a tennis film or giving a presentation. When it came time for one of his elaborate parties, though, the doors were swung open wide, and assorted prominent guests who had traveled from up and down the East Coast milled about beneath the mounted trophies of his hunting conquests.

The *Baltimore Afro-American*'s Lula Jones Garrett dropped in for the Labor Day event that summer and described the scene as a place "where the fabulous chromium and mirror bar of the chief host, Dr. Walter [*sic*] (Whirlwind) Johnson, is never closed during the four-day session . . . and where the crew . . . lounge on the side on long red and blue leather mats and sip tall frosted drinks while they match the invited players (and I do mean invited) for a flock of trophies."[54] Althea seemed to fit right in. In a photo accompanying Garrett's column, she beams from a table playing a penny card game with the men's champion George Stewart of Panama and half a dozen other young men and women.

At the season's end, Althea returned to live with the Eatons and resumed her work both on court and off. Meanwhile, a couple of hundred miles away, fissures were beginning to appear in the bedrock of the USLTA's unofficial policy of segregation. In March 1948, longtime ATA champion Reginald Weir became the first African American man to compete in a USLTA tournament when he played in the National Indoor Championships at the Seventh Regiment Armory in Manhattan. It was Weir who, nineteen years earlier, along with friend Gerald Norman Jr., had been denied entry to compete in the USLTA's Junior Indoor Championship tournament when the match officials saw the color of his skin. A popular New York physician, Weir had been unofficially playing in the Metropolitan and Eastern Indoor Championships for years, as he was a strong player and was well liked among a number of local USLTA members. So notable was Weir's admission in certain circles that sportswriter Harold Rosenthal ribbed the stolid tennis establishment in his story about the event in *American Lawn Tennis* magazine, writing, "The first Negro has played in an American tennis championship and, at this late date, there have been no reports of any worlds having split asunder as an aftermath. In New York, where this epochal event took place . . . subways still run on schedule, busses don't, and both are crowded as ever. . . . In short, life goes on just the same and what was regarded as an impossibility only twenty years ago is now an accomplished fact."[55]

Weir made a strong start at his first National Indoors and easily defeated his first-round opponent. But, unluckily matched against top-seeded player Billy Talbert in the second round, he lost 6–1, 6–1. Black journalists were nonetheless thrilled that Weir had been admitted to play, excitedly casting him as another sports "first" such as Jackie Robinson or Jack Johnson, the first Black world heavyweight boxing champ. In his write-up of the match, *New York Amsterdam News* reporter Joe Bostic declared that "the outcome is inconsequential to the greater result achieved in moving the cause of sports democracy a step ahead. For that, a salute to the trailblazing doctor."[56]

Alrick H. Man Jr., the head of the USLTA's National Indoor tournament committee, however, made it crystal clear that the decision to allow Weir to play was not intended to set a precedent. As Man told *The New York Times*, "This does not mean we are speaking officially for the USLTA or that we are establishing a precedent to be followed necessarily in other tournaments. It is simply a decision of this group." In a further reflection of the extent to which the tennis powers that be wanted to keep the whole thing quiet, Man added that Weir hoped "that no publicity would be given his entry and that he would probably withdraw if it caused any commotion."[57] Weir, whose relationship with the ATA had become strained in recent years, as his professional schedule often prevented him from appearing in the organization's tournaments, was more than happy to underplay what the USLTA surely knew would be a precedent-setting appearance.

Five months later, another crucial milestone was reached when ATA junior champion Oscar Johnson won the National Public Parks Junior Championships in Los Angeles, becoming the first Black player to win a national USLTA event. Still, the color barrier remained largely in place. When the eighteen-year-old Johnson tried to enter a white tournament later that year, in St. Louis, he was rejected when officials there saw the color of his skin. "Well, I'll be damned," the tournament director declared on seeing Johnson's name on the player list. "But you won't play here, boy." Only after pressure was brought to bear on the USLTA brass was he permitted to play.[58]

By the time she returned to the summer circuit in 1948, Althea was playing some of the best tennis of her life, easily trumping nearly every ATA opponent she encountered. In July, she won the women's singles at the Pennsylvania Open tennis tournament and at the National Capital tournament in Washington, D.C. In August, she made a clean sweep of the Eastern Tennis Championships at Shady Rest; the New York Tennis Association's thirtieth annual tournament at the Cosmopolitan Club; and the Southeastern Open tennis tournament in Durham, North Carolina. At the end of August, Johnson's crew climbed into the packed Buick followed by their second car and headed south toward the ATA Championships and the season's culmination at the Colored Normal Industrial Agricultural and Mechanical College of South Carolina (now South Carolina State University), in Orangeburg, South Carolina. The Black press was already bubbling with excitement in anticipation of Althea's defense of her national title.

"Miss Gibson is the representation of the graceful, gazelle-like racqueteer which American Tennis Association enthusiasts hoped for, but vainly, for many years," editorialized the *Pittsburgh Courier*. "Bringing to Dixie the greatest array of open singles titles ever owned at one time by any female star, the young lady seems launched upon an age of personal spread-eagling of the field that will dwarf even the dictatorial days of Ora Washington."[59]

Althea did not disappoint, easily defeating Nana Davis 6–3, 6–0—or, as columnist Joe Bostic of the *New York Amsterdam News* curiously put it, winning "the distaff diadem as she was expected to do."[60] Just about everyone in Johnson's group emerged from the event victorious. Althea and Johnson easily took the mixed doubles crown, their first national title, while Helen Mundy, fifteen, one of the original Dunbar Six, clinched the girls' junior title. Even Eaton and his partner, the left-handed George Stewart, turned back their opponents in the men's doubles in a grueling five-set match. It was a thrilling culmination to a summer of persistence and hard work. As the tournament's final ceremony drew to a close that evening, Johnson's group headed back to their cars at around 11 p.m., clasping their trophies and buzzing with chatter, eager to get on the road back to Lynchburg. Johnson and Babe Jones got behind the wheels of their respective cars and shifted into gear.

But the road home was not to be a smooth one. No sooner had Jones slipped behind the wheel than he realized that, in his excitement that day, he had neglected one of the Black motorist's cardinal rules: always fill up the gas tank before nightfall. In the segregated South, some gas station owners balked at filling a Black person's gas tank in broad daylight, much less after nightfall, when many "sundown towns" forbade Black motorists from driving through at all. Dr. J had repeatedly reminded Jones and the college students who sometimes drove the second car to keep the tank filled at all times. But here they were, on a sweltering Saturday night in South Carolina, the quivering gas gauge needle in Jones's car approaching empty.

"My grandad was livid," said Johnson III.

The two cars proceeded slowly along the dark roadway until they came upon a small mom-and-pop gas station and pulled up next to the pumps. Jones beeped his horn tentatively a few times before the owner burst out of the door clutching a shotgun aimed squarely at the car; Althea was sitting in the front seat.

"'Nigger,' the man screamed, 'get the hell out of here!'" Johnson's grandson recounted.[61]

After a frenzied exchange of charged words, Johnson and Jones drove the cars a few hundred yards up the road, turned off their engines, and grimly prepared to wait until daylight, when they hoped to be able to fill their tanks. Within hours, however, a young Black couple who knew the station owner happened by and explained to him that the passengers in the two cars were a group of scared young tennis players trying to get home, according to Helen Mundy's memoir.[62] The gas station owner reluctantly agreed to fill up their tanks, and the cars were soon back on the road heading to Virginia. Never again when they were on the road would Johnson or any of the team fail to replenish their tanks before nightfall.

Back in Wilmington in the fall of 1948, Althea struggled to balance the demands of tennis and school. Within months, she received astonishing news from ATA officials that made it almost impossible to focus on her books: the USLTA had indicated that it was open to her participation in the Eastern Indoor Championships, to be held at the 369th Regiment Armory in Harlem. All she had to do was apply. Althea was beside herself, as was the ATA. Not only would she be playing in her first all-white tournament, but the locale was in the heart of her old stomping grounds and just a few blocks from her childhood home.

Althea traveled to New York several months later, and on a raw spring afternoon in 1949, she became the first Black woman to participate in the Eastern Indoor Championships, widely celebrated by the Black media as another "first." Although the white media made only occasional mention of the color of the players, *American Lawn Tennis* magazine noted the event with enthusiasm under the headline "Negress Stars in Eastern." More than a few among the crowd of over seven hundred spectators, the magazine pointed out, had come specifically to watch the ATA star.[63]

Althea initially struggled with the unfamiliar indoor court, which she found slick, and she was visibly nervous as she headed into the quarterfinals, losing the first set to Sylvia Knowles of Newport 1–6. But she quickly pulled herself together. She displayed her usual aggressive game, rushing to the net and slamming overheads out of reach, and won the next two sets 6–3 and 8–6.

In the semifinals, she faced Betty Rosenquest, the No. 1 in the East. Althea came on strong out of the gate and almost took the first set, but Rosenquest stood her ground, consistently returning Althea's fierce forehands, and wound up winning 8–6, 6–0. Rosenquest, who went on to win the women's singles championship, praised Althea's performance afterward, saying she had "a big serve, a very aggressive game," and predicted that she would go far against the USLTA competition.[64]

On the strength of her performance, Althea, like Weir before her, was invited to compete in the USLTA's prestigious National Indoor Championships, a couple of weeks later. The Williston High School principal, a friend of Johnson's, granted her a few days off, so she could remain in New York, and a nervous Althea appeared before the well-heeled crowd at the Seventh Regiment Armory on Park Avenue, where Weir was also competing. As the tournament began, the *New York Amsterdam News* declared that the two Black players "stood on the threshold of racquet history."[65]

Althea neatly won her first two rounds, and as Weir advanced to the third round, the National Negro Press Association declared that both players had "moved nearer to tennis immortality."[66] Although Weir was defeated by twenty-year-old Pancho Gonzales, the match was a thrilling display of tennis that had the crowd cheering mightily for Weir, who was nearly twice the age of his opponent.[67]

Althea continued to play well, but in the quarterfinal round, she lost to the Californian Nancy Chaffee, seeded fourth in the tournament, 6–2, 6–3. Chaffee had a serve-and-volley game as aggressive as Althea's, and while Althea got in some spectacular forehands and net shots, she was visibly overmatched. Nonetheless, Althea was pleased, not just with her own performance, but with the warm welcome the other players gave her. In a style typical of her often-dispassionate, arm's-length discussion of race at the time, she later wrote in her autobiography, "I was made to feel right at home by the other girls. It wasn't just that they were polite; they were genuinely friendly, and believe me, like any Negro, I'm an expert at telling the difference. It was as though they realized how much of a strain I was under, and they wanted to do whatever they could to help."[68]

Such comments by Althea, not uncommon during her competitive years, were heard by some as an effort on her part to downplay the thorny topic of race. In time, they came to anger members of the Black press and others who felt that Althea had a responsibility to use her position as a sports her-oine in the late 1950s to address the issue of racial injustice. While the civil rights movement was just beginning to gain traction in that decade, there was a mounting belief in the Black community that public figures such as Althea not only had a responsibility to speak out but also owed it to the many Black individuals and institutions that had in large part had made their success possible—Althea just didn't happen to agree.

Althea, of course, not only knew all too well of the injustice and hardship her race endured, having encountered a barrage of racist attitudes and inci-dents throughout her life. But publicly, she would not fight it. It appears she felt that to speak out on the subject was one burden too many, as she boldly made her solo bid in the world of competitive sport. She was, after all, chal-lenging the barriers not just of race, but of gender and class. What's more, unlike the lionized Jackie Robinson, she had neither an embracing spouse nor a loving family awaiting her back home at the end of a rugged day. At a distance from her own family both physically and emotionally, Althea had little in the way of support. Instead, she was a guest at one of a series of foster homes throughout much of the late 1940s and early '50s, which surely added to the weighty burden on her angular shoulders. The truth was that all she really wanted to do was play tennis or, more precisely, win at tennis. When the increasingly fraught subjects of race and class were discussed more openly in years to come, she was more forthcoming, but as a young woman, she could not do it. As she began to scale the competitive ladder, any talk of the racist treatment she endured, either on the tennis circuit or in the punishing South, was strictly off the table. Let her success, as she often said, speak for her and for the potential of her race, rather than her raised fist.

Althea's supporters were jubilant over her performance in both matches, which boosted her to the top ranks of the nation's female players. The ATA's Arthur Francis seized the moment to point out that Negro tennis players were fully capable of conducting themselves in just as mannerly a fashion as whites, and he urged the USLTA to open the door wider to Negro players. Althea, he explained in a column in the *New York Age*, "is the very best woman player our race has produced, but she suffers from lack of proper competition against players equal or better than her. . . . The playing of both Dr. Weir and Miss Gibson, and their sportsmanship, and deportment, during the tournament, will surely pave the way for further invitations to our group by the USLTA."[69]

With Althea's successful performances in two white tournaments, Eaton and Johnson had achieved a historic milestone. The unruly teenager they had encountered wildly slamming tennis balls three years earlier had been transformed into a composed young woman and a national champion of formidable, and increasingly consistent, ability. What's more, by the early summer of 1949, she had graduated from Williston High School ranked tenth in her class and proudly sported a class ring paid for by Sugar Ray Robinson, who put up the fifteen dollars it cost. Althea accepted a basketball scholarship from Florida Agricultural and Mechanical College, in Tallahassee, and two days after graduation, she was headed even deeper into the forbidding South. The doctors, who would remain actively involved in her life in coming years, had delivered their prodigy to the door of the nation's preeminent tournament at Forest Hills. The trick now was how to open it.

4

"First Negro"

An incoming freshman arriving at the Florida Agricultural and Mechanical College (FAMC) in sleepy Tallahassee of 1949 would have found her new home a place steeped in tradition and a demanding code of decorum. A land-grant university founded in 1887 and one of four Black colleges in Florida at the time, the growing institution perched on one of the city's loftiest hills and shaded by a canopy of moss-draped oaks was determined to cultivate a cultured student body. The academic demands were the least of it.

The FAMC *Student Handbook* laid out the daunting ground rules. Freshman women were required to be back in their dorms by 7:30 p.m. and were prohibited from visiting the men's dormitory. Slacks and pedal pushers were permitted only under specially delineated circumstances. Mandatory chapel services were held twice a week, at which the women were to wear blue suits with crisp white blouses and black stockings, while the men wore dark suits and white shirts. Ironing done outside the laundry room was subject to a one-dollar fine for the first offense. Disciplinary action would be taken against any student for using profanity, exhibiting homosexuality (or even a *tendency* in that direction), or engaging in "any form of moral obtuseness and impropriety."[1]

Except, that is, in the case of Althea Gibson, better known on campus as "the Gib." The lanky tennis powerhouse, as students quickly learned, had special status, and not just because she was on a scholarship that covered her room, board, and tuition. When she arrived on campus that June, Althea was two months shy of her twenty-second birthday. Not only was she years older than most of the students, but her life had been vastly different from that experienced by the majority of them, who came predominantly from small towns throughout Florida. Althea was a city girl, with a rough mouth and manner to match. With her groundbreaking appearances at the USLTA-sanctioned indoor tournaments earlier in the spring, not to mention her impressive ATA record, she was a rising star in the Black media and was beginning to get notice in the white press. That FAMC had managed to lure her to its campus, despite offers from several other colleges, had been trumpeted by papers from New York to Florida. The *Tampa Tribune* even ran a mini biography of her, under the headline "Women Tennis Star Enrolled at State A&M," which provided a brief summary of her accomplishments to date.[2] It seemed notable that they even ran such a story on a single student indicating just how prominent she was.

Marion Jackson, sports columnist for the *Atlanta Daily World*, observed that the Florida college was making a bold bid for leadership in tennis, noting that "Althea Gibson has enrolled at Florida A. and M. and tennis has dominated news releases from the institution during recent weeks."[3]

Althea had been recruited by FAMC's renowned "Rattlers" football team coach and director of physical education, Alonzo "Jake" Gaither, who saw in her the kind of fiercely competitive athlete he most admired. Gaither, the son of a minister, was a stern tactician on the field, known for his pet phrase "I want my players mobile, agile and hostile,"[4] which might easily have described Althea. But he was also a man of heart who nurtured students from disadvantaged homes and went out of his way to help many forge a path to better post-college life. Like Eaton and Johnson, Gaither was a disciplined man, but when the unruly Althea arrived on campus early that summer, he knew to give her some latitude. And Althea, who thoroughly enjoyed her unique status and the independence it afforded her, seized it gladly.

"She was the only woman allowed to come into the men's dorm and use the rec room," said Charles "Trickshot" White, a basketball star who supervised the rec room in the early 1950s. "The guys were alarmed to even see a woman there, and then she started playing pool and beat them one, two, three. I tried to play Ping-Pong with her and couldn't even return the ball . . . Althea just didn't have the restrictions placed on her like other students. If she was late for lunch and the line was long, she'd just come in the front door instead of the side door like we were supposed to. It was like, 'Oh, yeah, that's Althea.'"[5]

Althea's years at FAMC marked her transition from a parochial amateur athlete to one of celebrated national prominence, whose name would be inextricably linked to that of Jackie Robinson and the growing list of African American athletes who had shattered the racial barrier in their sports. As her star rose steadily, however, she came under conflicting pressures that grew increasingly difficult to manage. While her mentors Johnson and Eaton, as well as her professors, strongly urged her to make her education a priority, determined that she graduate in the interest of her post-tennis days, the ambitious ATA executives pushed her hard to devote herself to competitive play, ever stressing her critical importance to the future of Black tennis. At times, these divergent interests erupted into outright conflict. Meanwhile, the press was keeping an unwavering eye on the promising tennis star. Althea grappled with all these competing demands as she struggled to determine for herself what was in her best interest.

Further complicating her thinking was the fact that she had mixed feelings about her college experience. Having arrived as an adult, she had already shed some of her unruly teenage ways. She took to her studies in earnest and, somewhat to her own surprise, even began assuming a role of some social leadership. Age, however, was just one of a number of factors that would separate her from her classmates. As the demands of her rising stature in the tennis world mounted, Althea was often on the road traveling to ATA and USLTA tournaments during the school year. While immersed in the college experience and deeply attached to Gaither, whom she called "Pop," she also chafed at the limited tennis opportunities available to her. The college had only four clay courts, and there was not a single player there who could give her the kind of demanding, high-level competition she needed to develop her game. More than once, she would consider dropping out in order to pursue her tennis career more aggressively, but in the end, she stayed put.

That decision was likely made easier by the singular status she enjoyed on campus. As usual, Althea called her own shots. Despite a prohibition against cigarettes and profanity, the Gib openly smoked her Marlboros in the dorm and made no effort to tailor her sometimes crude language, never mind that it made a number of her dorm mates cringe. The school's *Student Handbook*, which imposed limits predominantly on female students, forbade women from riding in cars off campus, but Althea came and went as she pleased, often in the company of some of the young men she met in Sampson Hall, the men's dorm that housed the pool table. There were nonetheless some things that even Althea wasn't permitted to do. Gaither allowed her to shoot hoops and play tennis with the men, and even toss a football around, but when she clamored to make the extra kick after a touchdown during a game, he drew the line.

"She thought it would be good publicity for her to make the kick, but Gaither said, 'No, no, no, I just can't do that,'" recalled White. "I mean, it was unheard of. Women just didn't play football at all then, but Althea did."[6]

Althea's masculine affect, coupled with the rumors about her ambiguous sexual orientation, set her even further apart from some female students. Sometimes, when she walked down the corridor of the freshman women's dormitory, students in their rooms hearing her deep voice mistook her for a man and quickly closed their doors. Indeed, Althea, according to several of her classmates, came on amorously to several young women on campus, and gossip about her was not uncommon. But, as usual, she didn't seem to mind what was being said about her.

"In the dorm, some girls would say, 'You know, Althea over there in the dorm, she a boy.' . . . A lot of girls would say she had approached them and this kind of thing. I said, 'Althea ain't never said nothing out of the way to me.' They all think she liked girls. That ain't true," recalled Elizabeth Swilley McElveen, known as "Swilley," a member of the class of 1953 and a forward on the basketball team with Althea, who lives in Fort Washington, Maryland. "I'd tell them, 'Y'all just saying that because the girl can compete with the boys.' . . . She was good at competing against the fellas. I think if she can beat them playing pool, she can beat them shooting at basketball, a lot of them. She can hit the baseball . . . I'd say, 'Y'all can hush that because there ain't nothing wrong with that girl.'"[7]

Some classmates, though, and particularly the girls who were living at home with their parents, stayed away from the towering city girl with the rough mouth. As Eva Clack Smith, now in her nineties, and a classmate raised in Tallahassee, puts it, "Althea was just different. There were things about her I did not like. The girls said you don't associate with her because she is gay. We called gay men and women 'punks.' It didn't happen to me, but there were a lot of stories."[8]

Althea's years in Tallahassee coincided with a crucial period in the college's development. When she arrived at FAMC in 1949, the school had embarked on a steady expansion both of its physical footprint and its academic programming. One of a number of Black universities noted for their extensive agricultural programs, it was perhaps best known for its acclaimed orange-and-green-clad marching band, called the Marching 100, and for its extensive athletic program, highlighted by its formidable Rattlers football team, which had flourished under Gaither. As African American soldiers returned from World War II eager to take advantage of the GI Bill, the college embarked on a period of sustained growth, its enrollment topping two thousand by the decade's end.

Those years were not without turbulence, however. Just weeks after Althea unpacked her bags, the school's president, William H. Gray Jr., who had awarded her the scholarship, resigned in the face of charges of financial mismanagement, leaving the college in a state of administrative chaos.[9] Gray's successor, Dr. George W. Gore, who held graduate degrees from both Harvard and Columbia Universities, would guide the school through a turbulent period of civil rights protest in the mid-1950s that was triggered in large part by the actions of three FAMC students. Gore was so keenly aware of the racket-wielding freshman on his campus that he praised Althea in his first address to the faculty and students at a spring assembly. FAMC, he said, must stand for quality just like Althea, whose very name "is a byword in America because she stands for quality. Whenever you excel[,] people respect you regardless of race, color or creed."[10] During Gore's tenure, the college continued to grow steadily, and in 1953, Althea's graduating year, it gained accreditation as a university, opening the way for the establishment of professional and graduate schools.

In the city of Tallahassee, the population was also growing steadily, but long-standing racist practices proved stubbornly resistant to change. Like many southern states, Florida embraced Jim Crow segregation with fervor, and despite its reputation for being less violent than other states below the Mason–Dixon line, it had the highest rate of lynchings per capita in the country between 1882 and 1930.[11] In its capital city, the center of the state's former slave trade and home to some of its wealthiest plantations, Black and white residents lived almost entirely separate lives in a society tightly controlled by a formidable white power structure. Black people were barred from white-owned restaurants and shops; banned from public buildings, beaches, and parks; and, according to several accounts, permitted to use only a single downtown public bathroom in the federal courthouse building.[12]

Many students in Althea's class had grown up in the city's racially stratified communities and well remembered bullying whites hissing the N-word at them on the streets and being either barred from the downtown department stores or permitted inside only to look at items, but prohibited from trying anything on. Often, Black parents would measure their children's feet with string, so they could size shoes inside the store. As was true throughout the South, Black students almost never got new school supplies, but had to make do with hand-me-downs from the white schools. Knowing this, some white children scrawled racist notes in the margins of their discarded textbooks—such things as "We're going to hang your daddy from a tree and your mama by her toes" or "[N-word], go to hell."[13] Carrie Meek, who graduated from FAMC in 1946 and went on to become the first Black member of Congress from Florida since Reconstruction, wrote in one memoir of having to chew off the tip of her pencil, as there were no sharpeners or other supplies in her school. Vastly eclipsing all this, one of her brothers was murdered by a white man over a grocery bill.

"Segregation was hell," Meek recounted in a memoir assembled by her deputy chief of staff. "You didn't feel whole, because you couldn't try on anything, you had to stay on your side of the street and you were shunned by white people and you knew they didn't want to be bothered by you. My parents always warned me, don't try anything, because in those days they were lynching black people."[14]

Such violence was hardly a thing of the past. Weeks after Althea arrived in Tallahassee, four young Black men were falsely accused of raping a seventeen-year-old white girl and assaulting her husband in Groveland,

Florida, several hours southeast of campus. One of the four young men fled on foot and was later shot hundreds of times while he slept under a tree. In the days afterward, a furious white mob went on a rampage, beating dozens of Black people and burning their homes to the ground. Following the hasty convictions of three of the young men—one of whom was sentenced to life in prison because he was only sixteen, while the other two were sentenced to death—Harry T. Moore, the executive secretary of the Florida NAACP, organized a defense campaign in what would become one of the highest-profile cases in the history of American civil rights.

Moore was a passionate and well-known advocate who spoke out against lynching and police brutality. As in Wilmington, North Carolina, Black citizens in Tallahassee and the surrounding counties adhered to a philosophy of accommodation and negotiation rather than the more confrontational style that would be adopted by a subsequent generation of civil rights leaders. Like other activists in the capital city, Moore worked tirelessly to combat discrimination within the system, largely through voter registration drives and court challenges. Such tactics infuriated white militants, who were known to respond with violence.

In the spring of 1951, the U.S. Supreme Court overturned two of the convictions in the Groveland case, saying the defendants had not been given a fair trial, and granted them a retrial. Florida newspapers generally fell in line with the decision but several ran the comments of Lake County sheriff Willis V. McCall, who was in charge of the initial arrests. McCall blamed the reversal on "subversive influences."

"The fact is that our U.S. Supreme Court let a few minority groups such as the NAACP (National Association for the Advancement of Colored People) and their eloquent and sensational lies . . . influence them to such a prejudiced extent that they saw fit to reverse one of the fairest and most impartial trials I have ever witnessed. It is shocking to think that our Supreme Court would bow to such subversive influences," McCall said.[15]

Several months after the court reversal McCall shot two of the young men while transporting them back to jail, killing one of them. He was eventually cleared of wrongdoing, however, when a federal grand jury found that he had been acting in self-defense when he shot the young men.[16]

McCall was not the only one who took issue with the Supreme Court decision calling for a retrial. At the end of 1951, Moore and his wife, Harriet, were killed on Christmas Night when a bomb went off in their home. Multiple investigations over the decades concluded that the Moores were likely murdered by several ranking Ku Klux Klan members, but no one was ever charged.[17]

In 2021, all four of the young men involved were exonerated after investigators were told about evidence suggesting that both the prosecutor and the judge overseeing the case at the time had been aware that no rape had occurred. Two years earlier, the four men, all of whom were by then dead, were pardoned by the Florida governor. The Florida state attorney who sought dismissal of the charges concluded that the case had been the result of a "complete breakdown of the criminal justice system."[18]

In part because of the city's harsh racial climate, FAMC students were largely required to stay on campus, where administrators made sure to keep them busy. There were on-campus movies, dances in the gym, and a Fountainette snack bar for meals. As was also true in Wilmington, Black life in Tallahassee was generally confined to a single area, called Frenchtown, known for its rocking nightclubs on Macomb Street, including the Red Bird Café, where Ray Charles and Cab Calloway performed. Nevertheless, male students, as well as the city-wise Althea, managed to venture into Frenchtown for a film at the Capital Theatre or a snack at the Five and Dime. Althea continued to play her saxophone and began tentatively exploring singing during her first two years of college, nabbing a lesson with early mentor Buddy Walker every time she returned to New York and even making appearances with his band at both the Hotel Theresa and Smalls Paradise in Harlem. Eventually she had to drop the lessons due to the demands both of her classes and of her busy extracurricular life.

Thanks to Coach Gaither, she also had a job on campus working as an assistant to the head of the women's physical education department, earning forty dollars a month, but she found few places to spend her cash.

"There was only one theater in town that would let Negroes in and that was the one that had nothing but second-run features," she wrote in her autobiography. "There was one off-campus eating place we were allowed to go at specified hours. You could get a bottle of beer there, or a drink, and there was a jukebox, although you couldn't dance."[19]

Althea, a physical education major, started taking classes in history and typewriting at FAMC just days after she graduated from high school, in order to get ahead academically. Coach Walter Austin also wanted her on campus playing tennis. Given the lack of on-campus tennis competition, she still found a way to push herself by practicing daily on the faster wooden surface of the gymnasium before breakfast and volleying with the male members of the tennis team. During the summer of 1949, Althea hit the road again, in the Buick with Johnson and the gang, to compete in several ATA tournaments. College, it turned out, hadn't hurt her tennis game. She trounced her old foe Nana Davis 6–0, 6–0, at both the New York Open at the Cosmopolitan Club and at the Eastern Open in Scotch Plains, New Jersey. For the third year, she took the national women's crown at the ATA Nationals at Wilberforce, Ohio, while she and Johnson took their second title in the mixed doubles. Althea was steadily gaining steam, and that summer, as the *Baltimore Afro-American* declared, she "continued her reign as queen of the nation's women players."[20]

In Tallahassee that fall, Althea got down to her studies in earnest. Keenly aware of her status as an older student, she grew more comfortable with her leadership role and even sometimes likened herself to an "aunt" overseeing the other students. She assumed the unlikely position of head of the judicial committee and earned a reputation for being a strict enforcer of the rules. She even took a role with the school chapter of New Homemakers of America, the Black version of Future Homemakers of America, addressing meetings from a podium draped with a poster reading, "Better Homes for a Better Nation," while sporting a dark suit with a starched white collar, neatly coiffed hair, and a pair of pointy spectacles.[21] During her second year, the young woman who once shoplifted at the Bronx Terminal Market and slept under public stairwells tied on the salmon-pink and apple-green colors of Alpha Kappa Alpha, the first Greek letter sorority for African American women.

As ever, sports dominated her life. Althea played on the men's golf team, led the women's basketball team to repeated victories, and often taught her classmates, male and female, on the tennis court. "All of us had to play against Althea. She'd serve the ball to us, and we'd have to try and return it. Then she'd show us how to hold the racket. I remember she stuck her chest out, she was so proud," recalled classmate Elizabeth Swilley McElveen. "If you could play against her and get a ball back or return her serve, you'd get an A in the class."[22]

Despite her stellar performance as a forward on the basketball court—her team won several district championships—Althea found the games tame. She chafed at rules of the day that restricted women players to using just half the court and limited them to a two-bounce dribble. For more challenging play, she routinely jumped into the men's softball and basketball practices and was a regular on the men's golf team. Her favorite place to flex her competitive muscle other than the tennis court, however, was in the basement of the men's dormitory Sampson Hall, where there wasn't just a pool table but also Ping-Pong and, often, an ongoing round of bid whist, a bridgelike card game that involved gambling. When she first started showing up there, male students flocked down the stairs to see the angular New York City girl who, word had it, could wield a cue stick better than Jackie Gleason. By the time freshman Brodes Hartley showed up a couple of years later, Althea's basement appearances had become popular sporting events.

"By then it was routine. She just came in, you know, the only girl who could shoot pool there because she had dispensation," said Col. Brodes Hartley Jr., then president of the school's student government and, in later life, CEO of Community Health of South Florida, in Miami. "She always drew a crowd. When she entered the dorm, the message would get out, and the guys would come just to watch her play. There were a few who could give her some competition, but not many. Mostly we just watched."[23]

Although Althea's basketball skills were clearly superior to those of many of her contemporaries, few of her classmates found her to be arrogant or presumptuous, as long as she was winning, that is. The Gib was just the Gib, an anomaly among them. As class president Col. James Wyatt recalls, "Althea was so far ahead of us. She was a bit apart, but it wasn't that she was distant. Althea was very approachable. We were just in awe of her. She was so many things that we were not."[24]

One of those things was being a bit of a wheeler-dealer. Althea may have been an enforcer of the rules in her new life, but that didn't mean she had to abide by them herself. Every week, students were required to attend a chapel service and listen to a guest speaker while wearing regulation attire and sitting in assigned seats, all of which most students dreaded. Edwina Martin, one of Althea's basketball teammates, and Althea cooked up the idea to charge students ten cents, sometimes more, for sitting in their seats for them, so they wouldn't have to attend. The two did a brisk business, despite threats from a couple of straight arrows who hinted that they might report them to the dean of students. When Althea growled at them and gave them her darkest menacing look, they backed off.

"On a good day we'd make five dollars, and five dollars in them days was like a million," Martin said, laughing.

Althea worked the deal both ways. Sometimes she'd pay other students to sit in her seat during a class, or she'd agree to tutor a younger student. If students grumbled about her terms, she'd let them have it.

"Althea didn't take no stuff, I guess is the way you say it," Martin added. "The kids were scared of her. She was so masculine. She wasn't a refined type like we girls were. If they said something she didn't like, she would curse them out in her big voice and use profanity. I mean, other girls liked her, but they were afraid of her."[25]

Althea's freshman roommate during her first semester was Helen Mundy, a member of Johnson's high school tennis team, the Dunbar Six, and a talented basketball and tennis player who had twice won the girl's ATA Championships. Like Althea, she had also received a FAMC scholarship with Johnson's help. Mundy had been in the Buick on that frightening night the previous summer, when the gas station owner in South Carolina pointed a gun at them. She was well accustomed to Althea's dominant ways, having spent several summers on the tournament circuit with Johnson's team. Mundy, however, had little more than sports in common with her older and more worldly roommate. For starters, they differed in their passionate feelings about grits—Mundy hated them, and Althea loved them. So, every morning, when a ladle-full of the boiled white porridge landed on their breakfast trays in the FAMC cafeteria, Althea would help herself to Mundy's portion.

Though Althea spent most of her time hanging out at the boy's dorm, when she was around the girl's dorm, smoking cigarettes in the hallway, Mundy found her a bit intimidating. Once, Althea even got into a fistfight with one of Mundy's closest friends.

"We were all just talking in the bedroom, and the next thing I know Althea and this other girl are fighting, I mean, fistfighting!" Mundy exclaimed. "I got one of them and another girl got one of them and we pulled them apart, and we said, 'You all are not going to get close to each other again because all of us are going to get kicked out of school.' You know, with her group Althea was fine. But she always had to be top dog."[26]

During her first semester, Althea wrote to Eaton a few times to tell him about her classes and the financial difficulties she had encountered as a result of the turmoil generated by the school president's resignation. Not only had she learned that she had to pay a $175 out-of-state fee, but the money she had earned on her job was being funneled into her scholarship account, meaning she was receiving nothing. She had turned to both Coach Gaither and Johnson for money in order to buy her books, but it wasn't enough to cover her expenses. Despondent, she wrote to Eaton in October and asked for money to buy a dictionary, a couple of her white uniform blouses, and some winter shirts.[27]

Just four months later, Althea was in decidedly better spirits. Her grades, she proudly wrote him, included three As, two Bs, and a C. Also boosting her spirits was the exciting news that she had been invited to compete again in the USLTA's Eastern Indoor tournament in New York. At the end of February, she was on a train headed back up north.[28]

As she had the previous year, Althea started out strong at the Eastern, which was held at the Kingsbridge Armory, easily overcoming several opponents and pushing into the finals. This time she sustained her strong performance and soundly defeated veteran player Millicent Hirsh Lang 6–3, 6–1, becoming the first African American to win the prominent event.

A couple of weeks, later she did less well in the USLTA's National Indoor tournament and was soundly defeated again by her old foe Nancy Chaffee 6–0, 6–2, this time in just forty minutes. Althea was visibly on edge, winning only two games in the two sets. Chaffee managed to break through Althea's powerful serve five times and easily outmaneuvered Althea's efforts to keep her on the backcourt as her steadier performance finally overcame her younger opponent, bringing the crowd to its feet.[29] Nonetheless, Althea's advancement to the finals and her win at the Eastern were viewed by many in the ATA and the Black press as evidence that she was qualified to compete at Forest Hills later in the summer.

The packed gallery at the Seventh Regiment Armory that day was due in large measure to a triumphant performance by former national turf court champion Don McNeill, the winner of the Indoor tennis crown a dozen years earlier, who had defeated Fred Kovaleski to take the title again. The tournament was notable also in that it marked another racial advance for Black players, reflecting the gradual easing of bars in sports nationwide. Dr. Reginald Weir had broken the barrier to this particular tournament in 1948, after which came Althea, and then three more Black players. By 1950, there were five in the draw for the first time: Althea; Weir, who was playing for his third year; Ubert C. Vincent, fifth in the ATA ranking; Desmond Margetson, an engineer and the New York University tennis team's former captain and No. 1 player, who would later be recognized for designing the indoor tennis bubble; and Vernon Morgan, former player for City College.

To her surprise, Althea found a triumphant welcome awaiting her back in Tallahassee. As she got off the train, she was met by the FAMC band, which burst into the school's alma mater as it led her back to her dormitory and a sign proclaiming, "Welcome Home, Althea!" There, the college's acting president, H. Manning Efferson, stepped forward to shake her hand in congratulations, as Althea beamed. Days later, the school paper, *The Famcean*, awarded her its "Orchid of the Month" for her achievement.

Althea, clearly, was pleased. Years later, she would point out in her autobiography, "You would have thought for sure I had won the tournament instead of losing it."[30] Still, she recognized that the exultant welcome she received was not just about her individual performance, but also the crucial milestone it represented in the crusade to integrate the seemingly impenetrable bastion of white tennis. Althea, it seemed, was going to be the next Black athlete to storm through the roadblocks to her race and take her place alongside such icons as sprinter Jesse Owens, high jumper and Olympic gold medalist Alice Coachman, and second baseman Jackie Robinson.

Althea was bursting to play, but she was unwilling to accept the larger mantle. Throughout her career, she would work furiously to play the absolute best tennis of which she was capable, but a racial pioneer she was not, and she did not hesitate to say so. That fact would earn her sharp disapproval among the Black press and even among some of her most ardent supporters.

"Obviously, they all felt that what I had done was important not just to me but to all Negroes," she noted in her autobiography. "I have never regarded myself as a crusader. . . . I don't consciously beat the drums for any special cause, not even the cause of the Negro in the United States, because I feel that our best chance to advance is to prove ourselves as individuals," she explained. "That way, when you are accepted, you are accepted voluntarily, because people appreciate you and respect you and want you, not because you have been shoved down their throats."[31]

It wasn't that Althea didn't care about the Black cause; it was that she couldn't, at least, not in the way expected of her. She had suffered a childhood of beatings, neglect, and intermittent violence on the street. At some point, perhaps during a cold night's sleep in a Harlem stairwell, or alone on a desolate subway car hurtling through the tunnels at night, she had confronted the knowledge that she was in this world alone. As an adult, she could take a swing at her father, stand up to a hostile white power structure skewed heavily against her, even square off with the male-dominated world of athletics of her day. But she could not shoulder the additional weight of the Black crusade for justice—at least not then, in the midst of her personal march toward excellence.

And yet, Althea couldn't help but be swept up in the current of change moving swiftly in just that direction. In a congratulatory letter he wrote her a couple of weeks after she returned, Eaton stressed not just the crucial point at which she had arrived in her own life, but also the enormous responsibility she had to her race. On her shoulders alone, the very future of Black tennis now rested, he declared. What's more, he added, she had the potential to become not only one of the greatest Black woman tennis players, but one of the greatest players of all times. All eyes would now be on her in the months to come.[32]

Eaton's was hardly a lone voice. In the weeks that followed Althea's performance at the two New York tournaments, members of the Black press hailed her in superlative terms as one of the most talented female tennis players in the country. An escalating drumbeat calling for her to be invited to play at Forest Hills at the end of the summer began to be heard across the country. As James L. Hicks put it bluntly in the *Baltimore Afro-American*, Althea's advancement to the finals "placed her in position to receive an invitation to compete in the United States Lawn Tennis Association matches at Forest Hills this summer—something no colored person has yet done. Officials of the USLTA are now faced squarely with inviting her to participate or being charged with discriminating against her because of her race."[33] When no offer had materialized a couple of weeks later, Hicks urged readers in another column to write the USLTA and demand that it "give the girl a chance!"[34] With an eye on the path to Forest Hills, the *Chicago Defender* editorialized that part of the reason that Althea did not win the National Indoor was because she "suddenly realized that she was a 'Negro first.' The pressure was terrific."[35] Shortly afterward, the paper published a lengthy interview with her, under the headline "Althea Gibson Looks Forward to Bid to Compete in National This Summer." The piece featured half a dozen photographs of her playing pool, practicing her saxophone, and bent over her homework. With an eye on Forest Hills, the story concluded, "to believe that she will be given the opportunity is not idealistic, for in all the darkness of the nights, past and present, in the night of the future—a star is shining."[36]

Althea was hardly the only civil rights milestone in the making in 1950. That spring, after years of balking, the American Bowling Congress voted to eliminate the prohibition against Black people playing in its annual tournaments and dropped the clause limiting membership to individuals of "the white male sex" from its constitution. Also, in May of that year, Gwendolyn Brooks of Chicago won the Pulitzer Prize for Poetry for her collection *Annie Allen*, the first African American to do so. Shortly afterward, the U.S. Supreme Court struck down barriers segregating Black people on railroad dining cars and at two state universities where it found they had been treated unfairly.

Nor were Althea's achievements being noticed in the Black press alone, as had so long been the case. In April 1950, *Life* magazine, a popular general interest publication known for its iconic photographs, published a piece on Althea featuring a photo of her in loose-fitting white T-shirt and shorts, her angular body curved in a powerful arc, about to slam a serve. Under the provocative title "New Tennis Threat," the magazine wrote, "With the slam-bang determination she once used fighting kids in Harlem, Althea Gibson, 22, fought through the National Women's Indoor Tennis Championships in New York before losing in the finals. . . . Her performance in the Indoors posed a question for tennis moguls: would she be the first Negro to play in the outdoor championships at Forest Hills next August?"[37]

ATA officials, led by executive secretary Bertram Baker and assistant executive secretary Arthur Francis, did everything in their power to make that happen. For years, the association had unsuccessfully lobbied the all-white USLTA to get players of color into its competitions. Buoyed by Althea's strong performances that spring and the surge of national media attention she was getting, however, they escalated their campaign. In June, representatives of the two organizations came together in the first of two private meetings in Manhattan, which were not revealed to the press until much later, to discuss the possibility of Althea's playing at Forest Hills. The ATA was proceeding with extreme caution, determined to ensure that they had a qualified player with whom to move ahead and that the USLTA was agreeable to it.

"We wanted to be sure we could offer a Negro player who would be worthy of such competition," Francis told the *New York Post* years later. "We would have waited another year or two if it had been necessary, but we were sure by 1950 that we had a proper candidate in Miss Gibson. So we initiated negotiations with the USLTA officials."[38]

At the next meeting, USLTA treasurer Dr. S. Ellsworth Davenport Jr. and Alrick Man Jr., chairman of the tournament committee, noted that there was no rule barring Black people from playing in their tournaments, but neither would they commit to inviting Althea. Instead, they dodged the issue, pointing out instead that the thirty-six-member national committee ultimately needed to get on board. They suggested that Althea compete in some Eastern grass tournaments over the summer, in order to bolster her qualifications, and suggested several tournaments that might be appropriate.[39]

As Althea returned to Wilmington at semester's end to concentrate on practice, Francis and Eaton embarked on a vigorous letter-writing campaign to the private clubs hosting the invitation-only USLTA tournaments leading up to Forest Hills that summer. Charles Hare, former British Davis Cup star and director of tennis sales for the Wilson Sporting Goods Company, had already offered to help get Althea an invitation to the National Clay Court Championships at Chicago's prestigious River Forest Tennis Club, one of the premier tournaments on the circuit. Hare was married to tennis champion Mary Hardwick, who had appeared with another prominent white female player, Alice Marble, in an interracial exhibition match at the Cosmopolitan Club in 1944 and defeated Althea in an ATA exhibition match in 1947. The Hares, dubbed "Mr. and Mrs. Tennis," were strong proponents of broadening participation in the sport and had conducted many tennis clinics and exhibitions for American servicemen during World War II.

The couple had followed Althea's tennis progress with interest, and that spring, they both stepped forward to help her. Then based in Chicago, Charles Hare sent Althea an entry form to the National Clay Courts Championships in May and urged her to fill it out and send it to the club's chairman of entries. He assured her that her application would be accepted and that she "would give a good account of yourself."[40] Several weeks later, Mary Hardwick sent her a follow-up letter saying that her entry had been accepted. She offered to practice with Althea when she arrived in Chicago, adding, "So keep in touch with me—either via Charles at the office or [on] my home phone. Good luck."[41]

Francis, meanwhile, was doing everything he could to ensure Althea's smooth passage onto the Forest Hills courts, including giving her a little coaching himself. In an April 1950 letter he wrote to her at FAMC, he outlined the multiprong initiatives under way on her behalf, including talking to Forest Hills officials. He concluded with the kind of reminder about her significance to her race that increasingly made her wince: "We are trying very hard to make you the woman 'Jackie Robinson' of tennis, and hope you can, and will do your part, in the way that Robinson did his for our racial group," Francis wrote.[42]

Weeks later, he wrote another letter, advising her that several publications, including the *American Lawn Tennis* magazine and the New York

Daily News, were planning to write stories about her in the near future. Asked by a *Daily News* representative about Althea's family background, Francis wrote, "We told him in a way that would not embarrass you nor them, that you were poor, that is your family cannot afford to maintain you in tennis and that your friends helps [sic] you along those lines. That the relationship between you and your family are O.K. Etc." The publications, he added, were trying to arrange for her to participate in some white tournaments and wanted to know when she would be getting out of school and how soon could she come to New York. In conclusion, Francis said that he and Bertram Baker were to meet with members of the USLTA the following week, ". . . so sit tight until you hear from me. In the meantime, send that information at once." Francis, who normally signed his letters to Althea formally, this time wrote, "With kindest regards from everyone, I am Sincerely yours, Arthur 'Daddy' Francis."[43]

Meanwhile, Francis and Eaton lobbied in tandem to elicit entry forms for Althea from a host of established white clubs. In his letters to the clubs in New Jersey and New York, Francis pointed out Althea's strong performance in the indoor tournaments in which she had played earlier in the year and her stellar record in the ATA matches. He also stressed that she had an excellent attitude, perhaps hoping to assuage any concerns among the well-mannered club officials over talk of Althea's sometimes unruly behavior. By the end of June, though, there had been no response. The doors to the country clubs, designed as exclusive preserves for a wealthy and predominantly WASP elite, were not going to open voluntarily, and the USLTA was apparently not going to press them. It was going to take a more formidable force.

The name of that force, as it turned out, was Alice Marble. By 1950, Marble was something of a grande dame of American women's tennis. In all, she had claimed a total of eighteen major championships in her storied career, including the women's singles title at Forest Hills in 1936 and 1938–40, the Wimbledon singles in 1939, and five other Wimbledon doubles and mixed doubles titles. Ranked among the world's top ten players five times during her career, she was the world's No. 1 female player in 1939. The attractive blond Californian was the first power player in women's tennis, stunning audiences with her searing serve, stinging volleys, and aggressive assaults at the net. Later star players such as Louise Brough, Margaret duPont, Margaret Smith Court, and Billie Jean King would model their games on hers. Often compared to male players of the day, Marble was once described by her pupil Billie Jean King as "a picture of unrestrained athleticism."[44] As an athlete, in short, Marble was not unlike Althea, who was dumbstruck by the older woman's aggressive game at the 1944 exhibition match in New York and her masculine rush-to-the-net strategy. The two women also shared a passion for singing—both sang briefly as professionals—and a somewhat inflated sense of their own vocal skills.

Marble was equally bold off the court as on. At the peak of her tennis career, during World War II, she accepted an assignment by U.S. Army intelligence to gather Nazi financial records held by a former lover in Switzerland. In her autobiography, *Courting Danger*, she gives a detailed description of her mission, complete with a dramatic and perilous nighttime escape in a stolen Mercedes carrying the photographed documents, a high-speed chase down a Swiss mountainside at night, and a surprise assault by a double agent, who pulled her car to the side of the road and shot Marble in the back. In the end, Marble was saved by a military intelligence officer as she lay bleeding in the snow, according to her telling. There is no documented verification of her vivid account, and some have raised questions about its veracity. But none has managed to disprove it, either.[45]

Marble, who also helped create the "Wonder Women of History" series for DC Comics, was a hard-drinking, cigarette-smoking, no-nonsense kind of woman who did not hesitate to speak out against what she considered to be injustice. Her regular column, "As I See It," in *American Lawn Tennis* magazine, enhanced her stature in the nation's dominant tennis circles. By the summer of 1950, Marble, who had long advocated the expansion of tennis beyond the country club set, had lost her patience with the evasive and dishonest behavior of the USLTA and its member clubs and decided to act. In July, the magazine carried an editorial by her called "A Vital Issue," which landed like a firebomb in the lap of the USLTA.

Marble opened by saying that, when on a lecture tour, she is no longer asked, "What do you think of Gussy's panties?"[46] She was referring to Gertrude Moran—known as "Gorgeous Gussie" in the media—a highly ranked player who triggered a rollicking scandal in the summer of 1949 when she appeared at Wimbledon wearing an outfit designed by Teddy

Tinling, the foremost and easily the boldest British fashion designer on the tennis circuit in the mid-twentieth century. Moran's outfit included elaborate lace-edged panties so shocking to some that club officials accused her of bringing "vulgarity and sin" onto the court, prompting questions from Parliament.[47] Instead, Marble wrote, "For every individual who still cares whether Gussy has lace on her drawers, there are three who want to know if Althea Gibson will be permitted to play in the Nationals this year."

Uncertain of the answer herself, Marble wrote that she had asked the question of a USLTA committee member. The answer was negative. Althea, the feeling was, had not adequately proven herself. Only by making a strong showing in the upcoming Eastern tournaments could she hope to get an invitation to play in the Nationals, Marble was told. Problem was, no one was inviting Althea to play in any of those tournaments. And there it was.

Althea, Marble wrote, "is over a very cunningly-wrought barrel, and I can only hope to loosen a few of its staves with one lone opinion." She continued:

> I think it's time we faced a few facts. If tennis is a game for ladies and gentlemen, it's also time we acted a little more like gentlepeople and less like sanctimonious hypocrites. If there is anything left in the name of sportsmanship, it's more than time to display what it means to us. If Althea Gibson represents a challenge to the present crop of women players, it's only fair that they should meet that challenge on the courts, where tennis is played. . . . The entrance of Negroes into national tennis is as inevitable as it has proven to be in baseball, in football, or in boxing; there is no denying so much talent. The committee at Forest Hills has the power to stifle the efforts of one Althea Gibson, who may or may not be the stuff of which champions are made, but eventually she will be succeeded by others of her race who have equal or superior ability. They will knock at the door as she has done.

Marble dug the knife in a little deeper. Her own fair skin, she pointed out, tanned heavily in the summer sun. Margaret duPont, another champion white player who ranked No. 1 in the world from 1947 to 1950 and ultimately won a total of thirty-seven Grand Slam titles, got freckles on her nose in the summer. The USLTA committee, Marble wrote bluntly, "would have felt pretty foolish saying, 'Alice Marble can't play because of that tan,' or 'We can't accept Margaret duPont; she gets freckles across her nose.' It's just as ridiculous to reject Althea Gibson on the same basis—and that's the truth of it. She is not being judged by the yardstick of ability but by the fact that her pigmentation is somewhat different."[48]

The bold editorial mushroomed into a USLTA nightmare. Not only had the magazine included a heartfelt endorsement of Marble's editorial, but it ran a highly empathetic profile of Althea, called "The Gibson Story," in the same issue. The piece cast her as a superior athlete and a demure, hardworking student who otherwise "enjoys tooting the saxophone or playing cards with her college friends." The accompanying photographs showed a bespectacled Althea bent intently over her schoolwork and grasping an armful of roses after the Indoor finals. The story concluded that Althea, "the greatest Negro woman tennis player in history," was a champion "who would like to stop defending for a while in order to do a little challenging."[49]

Marble's public accusation of racism had the dramatic impact that the ATA's nonconfrontational approach had failed to achieve. For starters, it triggered the Black press, which had already been calling for Althea to be invited to Forest Hills, to become even more vocal on the subject. "We hope that the USLTA will see the light and admit Miss Gibson and any others who can qualify with the requisite ability," the *Baltimore Afro-American* of Baltimore declared in an editorial titled "Justice on the Court." "This is no time to talk about color as a qualification in sports or anything else."[50] As Cal Jacox, columnist for the *New Journal and Guide*, put it, "The USLTA has come forth with a statement denying the existence of any racial restrictions at Forest Hills. . . . If this is so[,] Althea Gibson should experience no trouble having her entry approved whenever she submits it."[51]

Even members of the white press scrambled to get on board. In a strongly worded editorial titled "Justice and the Courts (Tennis)," *Life* magazine pointed out that Althea was "certainly a better player than many who are ordinarily invited to participate in the Nationals, and it is about time that the U.S. tennis fathers, who have been drawing a *de facto* color line at Forest Hills all these years, got over their ancient prejudices."[52]

Time magazine chimed in, too, albeit in a somewhat noncommittal manner. Under the heading "Ladies & Gentlemen . . ."—a nod to Marble's own language—the magazine pointed out that Negroes had never been invited to set foot on the Forest Hills courts. Without expressing a specific opinion of its own, the magazine quoted at length from Marble's "blistering guest editorial." It also ran a photograph of Althea taken by Gordon Parks, over the cutline, "Tennistar Gibson. An invitation soon?"[53]

The press, however, was not unanimous. Several columnists, both Black and white, objected that the campaign to get the nod for Althea to be allowed to play at Forest Hills impacted only a single player and failed to actually change the rules. As sportswriter Bill Mahoney of the leftist *Daily Compass* in New York correctly pointed out, "Waiving this formality for Althea Gibson is one thing, but allowing all Negro players their chance at the big time is another. . . . The truth is that until the USLTA admits people who can play tennis, regardless of their social and special belongings, it will be a thoroughly un-American and inhuman proposition. The resolution before the USLTA in August, if it is to mean something, should be that ability alone will determine qualification, and that the means must be found to achieve this. Until that happens, any action will be only patronizing."[54]

Overwhelmed by the mounting editorial assault, the USLTA blinked. Just two weeks after Marble's letter, Bertram Baker proudly announced that Althea had been invited to play at both the National Clay Court Championships at the tony River Forest Tennis Club in Chicago and the Eastern Grass Court Championships in South Orange, New Jersey, both prominent tournaments on the summer circuit. For the ATA, the long-sought-after invitations represented a major milestone in its effort to get a Black player into the white game. Althea's participation in the tournaments, the *Cleveland Call and Post* excitedly wrote, "marks a new epoch in this field of sports."[55] Forest Hills, it seemed, might be next.

Arthur Francis, who had spearheaded the letter-writing campaign to get Althea admitted to the tournaments, wrote a heartfelt note of thanks to James Dickey of the Eastern Lawn Tennis Association in an unctuous tone that characterized the Black organization's posture in negotiations.

"In these days of racial and religious restrictions it is very difficult to get people to think in terms of fairness, much more to act fairly, and your outstanding contribution of justice and fairness, your unafraid declaration that merit be recognized, as one of the important qualifications for an opportunity to play in your tournament, inspires us with the belief in the doctrine of the fatherhood of God and the brotherhood of man. Believe me when I say that members of my racial group, and of all groups who believe in fair play, will be everlastingly grateful to you and your colleagues."[56]

Not all tournament committees, however, were similarly swept up by the Marble wave. Francis had also written to the New Jersey State Championships seeking an entry form, but his letter was ignored. Allowing himself a bit of rare public pique, he wrote them a slightly different kind of letter: "We are somewhat surprised at the lack of common decency you have shown by not answering us. Whatever decision reached, or action taken by your body, can never be justified by your procrastination, evasion and absolute discourtesy to us in not answering," he wrote angrily. "You have exhibited the very thing that you apparently seemed to be afraid of in other people, snobbishness, prejudice and bad judgement."[57]

With the two major tournaments now on Althea's calendar, it was time to prepare in earnest. She headed to New York to practice with her old hitting friend Bill Davis and coach Fred Johnson. At a friend's suggestion, she called Sarah Palfrey Cooke, a highly ranked champion of the 1930s and '40s and one of Alice Marble's doubles partners, to ask about the possibility of their practicing together on the grass courts at Forest Hills. At first glance, Cooke appeared a somewhat unlikely person for Althea to approach. A Boston blue blood, she had learned the game as a child, at the exclusive Longwood Cricket Club in Chestnut Hill, Massachusetts, under the tutelage of Wightman Cup founder Hazel Hotchkiss Wightman. Cooke had twice won the women's singles title at Forest Hills, in 1941 and 1945, and ultimately claimed a total of eighteen major titles over her career. Of those, eleven were doubles titles, six of them won at Wimbledon and Forest Hills with Marble.[58] But Cooke, dubbed "the sweetheart of tennis" by veteran *The New York Times* sports reporter Allison Danzig and perennially admired in the media for her raven-haired good looks, had democratic views on the sport not unlike the Hares'. The author of two instructional tennis books, Cooke welcomed all players to the game, regardless of race or temperament, and had taught clinics for underserved youth and mentored many others.[59] She was also a contributor to several publications and TV programs. Following an interview with Althea during the indoor tournaments in the spring, Cooke had come away clearly impressed, not only by the odds that the younger woman had to contend with, but also with her aggressive, if somewhat erratic, game. In a later column in *Ebony* magazine, Cooke predicted that Althea's "strong serve which she could follow to the net would win her many points."[60]

Cooke was one of several high-profile white women tennis players who helped Althea. Over the years, Althea had been championed by multiple elements of the Black professional and sports communities and much of the Black press, the ATA, and the professional Black elites at the Cosmopolitan Club. But by the summer of 1950, as she inched slowly toward the iconic ivy-edged Tudor-style clubhouse at Forest Hills, and as her name became increasingly well known in the mainstream media, Althea had acquired a cadre of white supporters, many of them women. In addition to Marble and Hare, there was now Cooke, who practiced daily with Althea at the Cosmopolitan Club in the weeks leading up to the National Clay Court Championships and, later, at the West Side Tennis Club. Both Pauline Betz, another champion of the 1940s, and Gussie Moran of ruffled panties fame, once ranked No. 4 in the nation, also lent a practicing hand.

Affirmed by their support, as well as a private berth on the Pullman train to Chicago purchased by the ATA and a brand-new tennis suitcase contributed by the Cosmopolitan Club, Althea nervously headed to Chicago. Upon her appearance at the suburban River Forest Tennis Club, one of the most prestigious clubs in the country, anchored by an airy clubhouse designed by Frank Lloyd Wright, Althea found herself once again headlined in the local papers as a "First Negro," for she was the first person of color of any sex to play in the classic tournament. A profile of the club in *American Lawn Tennis* magazine described its complexion as having changed over the years, but the truth is that the color of its members had changed little since the club's founding in 1905 by a group of suburban tennis enthusiasts. In her first appearance at an outdoor USLTA-sponsored event, Althea met many of the top-notch women players she would face in coming years, several of them fresh back from competition at Wimbledon.

Playing against them, she did well. In her first round, she easily dominated the petite Mexican champion Mela Ramirez, driving her to the baseline with a series of blistering groundstrokes and beating her in straight sets 6–3, 6–1. Again, Althea felled her opponent easily in the second round, despite a shaky start. By the quarterfinals, she was squaring off with the seasoned veteran Doris Hart, the No. 1 seed and winner of the women's singles at the French Championships months before. Hart, a solemn competitor, had overcome a childhood knee infection that impaired her right leg and was known for a game more of finesse than force. In order to be competitive, she had developed a lethally effective strategy of drop shots and half volleys that forced her opponents to tear around the court, and by the early 1950s, she was on her way to becoming one of the best female players in both singles and doubles. In Chicago, Hart mowed down each of her opponents on the clay courts while barely extending herself and easily defeated Althea 6–2, 6–3, before going on to win the tournament. Although Althea and her partner, Laura Lou Jahn, then lost the semifinals of the women's doubles match 6–1, 6–1, the fact that Althea did as well as she did in the tournament left many in the Black press exultant.

"Her ability, and style of play which is hard-driving and sharp, have ticketed the student from Tallahassee as the star of the future," exclaimed the *Chicago Defender* shortly after the tournament. "It was predicted by one observer that she will be [the] women's clay courts single champion in the next two years."[61]

With the Eastern Grass Court Championships just a week away and the coveted Forest Hills tournament looming only a month beyond that, Althea's team stepped up their efforts. Dr. Johnson, who had been closely monitoring news accounts of her performance in Lynchburg, dispatched a Western Union telegram to his protégée outlining a few suggestions in much the same no-nonsense tone he used to instruct his juniors in how to hold a dinner fork properly or fold a cloth napkin. First off, he sternly advised her not to watch any other matches until she had completed her own, just as he routinely so instructed his players in the ATA tournaments. After she had played, he continued, she should watch all of them. Second, she should stay away from all social functions and instead, "Go home and rest. One of the reasons they don't want you to play at Forest Hills is because of the social functions. Pass these up to get to Forest Hills. Concentrate." He signed the letter, "Your partner, Dr. Johnson."[62]

Sarah Cooke was also watching the younger girl's game closely and had been impressed by Althea's acute sense of timing and her "huge cat-like strides" that enabled her to cover the court quickly. But she was also concerned that Althea had no experience on the fast grass courts of the sort at Forest Hills. Cooke placed a call to her old friend Ralph Gatcomb, president of the West Side Tennis Club, and asked if there would be any objection to her bringing Althea there to practice. In a response that seemed fashioned more for a magazine story than such a phone call, Gatcomb apparently said, "Of course not. This is America."[63]

That the much-talked-about dark-skinned girl from Harlem was heading out to practice her strokes at the venerated tennis capital of America further stoked the flames of anticipation in tennis circles of all colors. The *New York Herald Tribune* ran a photograph of a smiling Cooke and Althea kneeling on the court, side by side, their rackets in hand. The cutline underneath read, "EXPERT ADVICE: Althea Gibson, who may be the first Negro to play in the National tennis championships, gets some pointers . . ."[64]

On the same day that the photograph appeared, Althea "made history," as the *The New York Times* put it, on Court No. 1 at the Orange Lawn Tennis Club in South Orange, New Jersey, which was hosting the Eastern Lawn Tennis Association's Championships, one of the premier tournaments on the circuit. Althea was earning a place in the history books not just for being the "First Negro" to play in the grass court tournament, which she was, but also because she triumphed in her first match with a dazzling display of forceful serves and a commanding follow-up at net rarely seen in women's matches. With a small army of women serving as "linesmen" and another woman in the umpire's chair, Althea easily defeated veteran player Virginia Rice Johnson, one of the top players in the 1930s, 6–1, 6–3. Althea's hard-charging performance caught the eye of the *The New York Times*'s Danzig, who wrote of her "excellent showing" and noted that she follows her service to net, "as do few women, and no other player of her sex hits an overhead more emphatically." Althea, he added, "has a keen sense of position, is quick in her movements and varies her game with changes of pace, as she did in the second set. Miss Gibson has the equipment to be a very good tennis player once she has consolidated her game and acquired mastery over the speed she has at her call." And then, he added a not-so-subtle jab at the USLTA: "That can come only with experience and the opportunity to meet the best players in match competition."[65]

Danzig spoke a little too soon, for the following day, Althea bombed. Or, as he wrote succinctly, "Miss Gibson did not play well."[66] Althea's opponent was Californian Helen Pastall Perez, ranked No. 5 in the country. Perez had an even more powerful return than Althea. Caught off guard, and unsteady on a court moist from intermittent rains, Althea found her returns going astray and her usually powerful smashes erratic. In the end, she was routed 6–1, 6–1.

Her after-game performance was even worse. Althea reportedly refused to shake hands with Perez and annoyed some observers when she would not give autographs to several children who had been waiting patiently, saying, "I'm thirsty." With a glare at her opponent, Althea added, "I could have beaten her. I could have won that match."[67] Despite her loss and rude behavior, several Black papers nonetheless put a positive spin on her performance, an indication of how the hopes of so many were riding on her shoulders. The *Chicago Defender*, for example, observed that after her defeat, both newspaper writers and some in the audience were "making excuses" for the drubbing. "If anything predictions of future greatness for the slim New Yorker, were louder."[68]

Althea herself seemed to realize that her actions might not play well with USLTA committee members and meekly told a reporter, "I guess I just haven't had enough experience on grass," she said. "I hope I can redeem myself in the national singles championship at Forest Hills."[69]

If the outcome of her participation in the high-profile Eastern tournament in South Orange, New Jersey, left her future somewhat unclear, a different development emerged that week that seemed to hold more promise. ATA officials had arranged for Althea to stay during the tournament week at the home of a close-knit churchgoing Black family in nearby Montclair, New Jersey.[70] Althea had already met one of the daughters, named Rosemary Darben, at an ATA tournament at the Shady Hill Country Club. Three years older than Althea, Rosemary not only had the same lean, athletic build and had taken tennis lessons from Fred Johnson at the Cosmopolitan Club, but also had a similar sense of humor.

Althea took to the boisterous and welcoming Darben clan immediately, in part because the scene was so completely unlike her own home had been. Every night, the family sat down to a dinner that often included vegetables from the backyard garden and an occasional steak bought just for Althea. Afterward, there was invariably a game of pinochle or whist. The six children in the family took turns setting the table and were assigned weekly duties around the house, and in time, so was Althea. There were also touch football games and cookouts and silver napkin rings and abundant dinners after church services on Sunday, with homemade Parker House rolls lathered in jelly made from grapes plucked from the arbor out back. Althea called the Darben parents "Mama" and "Papa," about the fourth on her ever-growing list of parental substitutes and teachers of good manners following Eaton and Johnson. Both parents were active members of the St. Paul Baptist Church in Montclair, and every Sunday the entire family headed to services there, often taking Althea with them. Delighting over some of the food items that showed up on the table afterward, especially fresh vegetables like asparagus and mushrooms from a nearby farm, which were utterly foreign to her, Althea would proclaim, "Ooooooh, this is so good," recalled Rosemary Darben, now in her nineties and living in Red Bank, New Jersey. "What *is* this, Papa?"[71]

Althea and Rosemary had much in common, including a love of bowling and tennis as well as boisterous family gatherings. So close did the two of them become, so well attuned was their mutual athleticism, that they were routinely referred to as "Ro and Al." Once, Rosemary's teenage nephews challenged the two of them to a game of touch football, little realizing that the two women often participated in family football games in the backyard. The outcome? "We crushed 'em," Rosemary said.[72]

Althea also took a particular liking to the youngest of Rosemary's five siblings, a mild-mannered engineer named Will, who pursued her for years with love letters and gifts. As handsome as he was earnest, the six-foot, two-inch Will was the opposite of the hard-driving, uber-competitive Althea in many respects. Where he was accommodating and soft-spoken, she could be aggressive and stubborn. More than a few in their shared circle mused about the sexual orientation of each. As Rosemary's own niece Sandra Terry puts it, "He was feminine, she was masculine. That's what people said," said Terry. "My uncle was pensive, thoughtful. He was a gentle person. She would play flag football with the boys."[73] Yet, Althea and Will also had a great deal in common. Not only did they share a passion for music, but they also loved to stir up exotic mixed drinks together for their friends. On many an evening in the Darben home, Althea wound up crooning her beloved ballads as Will played the piano. Whatever the precise nature of their individual sexual preferences, or whether their pairing was initially intended to hide the fact that one, or even both, of them was gay, seemed irrelevant. The chemistry between them just worked, and over the years they grew intimately bonded.

Althea moved into the Darbens' home in part because there wasn't enough room for her in the Gibson family apartment on 143rd Street, but also because it was more fun. Soon after, she and Will, a World War II veteran and a production analyst with the Bendix Aviation Corporation, began to date. When Will began regularly picking her up from the airport on her return from tournaments and ferrying her around town, the press began to speculate that a wedding might be in the offing. It would be many years before such a story broke. For the most part, Althea spent her time at the Darbens with her new best friend, Ro, playing tennis, golf, and cards and listening to records.

"Althea's life and my life were totally different. I was the opposite of her life," said Rosemary Darben. "Althea was very selfish when she came to us, in that she thought of herself, more or less, because that's how she was raised. . . . She came into our house of love, as my mother and father were churchgoing, lovely people and they lived the Christian life. And Althea came in and saw this and she became softer."

As the years passed, Rosemary and Althea became ever closer. "I sort of was Althea's mentor. I taught her how to do certain things, because I was raised that way. She'd come in like a rough diamond to the family."[74] Later in her career, when she was traveling overseas on tour, Althea frequently penned her friend letters in which she described her hotel rooms and meals and occasionally poked fun at the media coverage of her.

It wasn't just the personal chemistry between the two young women and some other Darben family members that anchored Althea in the Montclair household on Pleasant Way. The Darben parents also recognized that their perennially hungry houseguest was an immensely talented athlete going up against barriers of class and race with little in the way of family or financial support. And so they took her in as one of their own.

"That's the way African American families were. They knew that if an African American was out being competitive among white people, they needed all the support they could get," said Sandra Terry. "They knew she needed to stay around a family, and so my grandparents took her in. As a matter of fact, she was closer to our family than her own family."[75]

After leaving the Darbens in early August 1950, Althea stopped in New York on her way back to Lynchburg, where she hoped to get in some more practice. For all the attention being paid to her matches that summer, two of the hardest sets she played in Manhattan received relatively little notice. At the New York Open at the Cosmopolitan Club, a hugely popular event that was as much a social happening as it was a tennis tournament, by fluke, Althea wound up paired in the second set against her beloved adoptive mama Rhoda Smith, who had taken care of her ever since she showed up on the Cosmopolitan court in blue jeans in 1941.

Smith was the Cosmopolitan Club veteran who had bought Althea some underwear and a winter coat long before others were paying much attention to her and who had welcomed her into her handsome home on 154th Street on multiple occasions. A seasoned athlete and a former New York State tennis champion now playing in the veterans' division, Smith had just recently returned to the regular women's division, which was how she had suddenly found herself across the net from the rising tennis juggernaut with whom she often sat at the breakfast table. Althea hit the ball gently toward her "mother" and was visibly distressed as Smith struggled to return it. "Mama, what are you doing?" Althea called. "Why play so hard?" At the end of the match, which Althea won 6–0, 6–0, the two women kissed on the court.[76] Althea went on to win not only the women's singles, for the third consecutive year, but also the mixed doubles with Dr. Johnson.

As Althea headed south a few days later, the future of her tennis career remained uncertain. The U.S. National Championship tournament was just a few weeks away, but the USLTA had given no indication of where it stood on her application to play at Forest Hills. At last, on August 15, the tight-lipped organization issued a terse statement acknowledging that it had received her form. They hadn't accepted it, but they had actually opened the envelope in which it had arrived! The press exulted over this tiny administrative development as anticipation smoldered with every inch of Althea's incremental march forward. Even white newspapers ran the wire story.

"Negro Woman's Entry Received by Net Group," declared the headline in the *Baltimore Sun*.[77]

Just what the association did next is unclear. In his book *The United States Tennis Association: Raising the Game*, historian Warren F. Kimball, who was a member of the USTA's board of directors for four years, notes that the organization's records in the first half of the twentieth century provide little mention of any discussion of race following a vote by its executive committee in 1922 not to admit Howard University as a member club. Even in 1948, when Reginald Weir was granted a waiver to play in the National Indoor Tournament, becoming the first Black player to do so, USLTA records of its executive committee and annual meetings make no mention of any discussion of the matter, despite the fact that the association had rejected his applications for two decades. As Kimball notes, "In fact there is no mention of Negroes, colored people, African Americans or anything of the like. . . . It was a nonevent."[78]

So, too, the association's records contain no reference to Althea or to the challenge to its all-white domain hovering at the door, according to Kimball, not even in the minutes of its two executive committee meetings in January and September 1950. Did they discuss it? "Absolutely," Kimball, history professor emeritus at Rutgers University, said in an interview. "But these are the kinds of decisions that are made in the cloakroom and not the boardroom, and there are no records of what happens in the cloakroom."[79]

In fact, the twenty-five-member executive committee apparently considered refusing Althea's application. Sidney Wood Jr., a member of the USLTA's executive committee in 1950 who astonishingly won the Wimbledon men's singles title in 1931 when his finalist opponent defaulted, wrote in his memoir, *The Wimbledon Final That Never Was*, that not only was

Althea's bid discussed, but that there was a "whispered motion" proposed at one of the committee's meetings to bar her from the Nationals. Furious that such a proposal was being put forward following "a star chamber get-together sustained by the customary double Manhattan aperitifs" among only a handful of the committee's members, with no discussion among the larger group, Wood, he writes, jumped to his feet to remind them of the state's antibias law. If the committee proceeded with such an action, he warned, it would show up in the headlines of every sports page in the country.[80] Whether or not Wood's somewhat self-aggrandizing account of the meeting indeed occurred in such a way, it seems more than likely that the committee members debated how best to handle the ticklish situation at hand.

In the meantime, Althea was trying hard to keep her mouth shut in order to avoid the bad press her comments had triggered in South Orange earlier that month. The pressure was taking its toll. Less than one week before the Nationals were scheduled to begin, Althea arrived by car at the ATA's annual tournament in Wilberforce, Ohio. Asked by a reporter if she thought she would be permitted to play at Forest Hills, Althea responded brusquely, "No comment."[81]

And then, at long last, seven days before the U.S. National Championships were to begin, a decision came down. Lawrence A. Baker, USLTA president, announced that Althea Gibson had been "accepted on her ability" and would be one of fifty-two women to play in the Tournament at West Side.[82] Whatever the outcome of her eventual performance there, Althea, who was just four days shy of her twenty-third birthday, had brought down one of the major barriers to Black athletes in American sports, forever inscribing in the history books her role as a racial pioneer, whether she liked it or not. Althea was elated at the opportunity to play, but she chose her words to reporters with newfound caution. "I think it is a very nice thing," she said. "I don't exactly know what my chances of winning are, but I'll do my best."[83]

The ATA's Bertram Baker was exultant. Hours after Althea easily played her way to the finals at Wilberforce, Baker gave a jubilant speech to a celebratory crowd there that included Eaton, Rhoda Smith, and many of the ATA brass. "The year 1950," Baker exclaimed emotionally, "will . . . go down in the history of the American Tennis Association as the beginning of a new era. . . . Many of us have worked untiringly for years to witness the day when our players would be accepted for competition in the National Championships of the USLTA. That day has come."[84]

Not everyone, however, was so pleased. Some ATA members, as well as ranking Black players, felt that the so-called milestone had done little to alter the Jim Crow club practices, but simply represented an exception for a lone player, just as they had argued back when Marble wrote her letter. The ATA, they felt, should have insisted on the elimination of the requirements that essentially barred them from the Nationals and, perhaps more important, the lower-level white tournaments that were essential to elevating the level of their game. Few put it as succinctly as Marion Jackson, sports editor for the *Atlanta Daily World*.

"Let's put the cold stiletto of reasoning into this trick play by the USLTA," he wrote under the headline "Althea Gibson, Pawn or Trailblazer?" "The lilywhite rules of the organization are still in effect. That is the by-laws which exclude Negroes haven't been changed. They have been ignored and suspended. . . . Next year—or two years hence—the barriers will be back up. The storm and fury over Miss Gibson will have abated. Jim Crow tennis will go on its way."

In a reflection of the frustration many in the Black community felt with the Black tennis organization, Jackson added, "The ATA has been self-perpetuating but not self-initiating. The fight for Miss Gibson's admission to the USLTA thereby is no real victory for the ATA. The group is merely riding the crest of a publicity bubble which it did nothing to inflate."[85]

What many critics apparently did not know was that a broader quota for Black participation in future U.S. National tournaments was already being informally discussed between the two organizations. In months to come it, would be revealed that the USLTA had made an unofficial agreement to accept into the Nationals up to five Black players handpicked by the ATA. Many thought the deal reeked of the ATA's timid negotiating stance and its arrogant presumption that it controlled Black players. A decade later, in a roundtable discussion sponsored by *Sport* magazine, ATA champion Bill Davis, Althea's old pal, lamented this selection system, which he described as "a major injustice."[86] That debate, though, would have to wait. For the moment, Althea needed to get back to New York.

Wilberforce tournament officials acted swiftly and moved the women's finals date up a day, to enable Althea to complete her last match. Anticipating the USLTA nod, the ATA had already convinced Rhoda Smith to cancel her summer trip to Europe in order to remain in the United States so that she could usher Althea to West Side for the big tournament. Hours after Althea claimed her fourth ATA women's singles title in 1950, trouncing Nana Davis yet again, Althea and Smith boarded the eastbound overnight train; they pulled into Manhattan the following morning.

On Monday, Althea got up early and packed a small bag of clothes to take to Forest Hills: white flannel shorts, a flannel shirt, tennis shoes, sweat socks, and a white knitted sweater made for her by some of the ATA ladies. Unlike most members of the elite club a dozen miles outside the city, Althea had no plush automobile or chauffeured sedan to whisk her to the courts. Instead, she and Smith headed to Sixth Avenue, where they would catch the subway and then an express train to Queens. They would walk the last three blocks to the West Side Tennis Club, the iconic capital of tennis in America. No Black player had ever competed there in a sanctioned tournament or been admitted to the club's membership list, nor would one become a member for nearly three more decades. It had been a long and difficult journey.

Now it was going to get harder.

5

The Other Gibson Girl

When Althea Gibson stepped onto the patio of the iconic Tudor-style clubhouse at the West Side Tennis Club, a pair of tennis rackets clasped tightly to her chest, she had arrived at the venerated mecca of tennis in America. Before her lay acres of green velvet grass courts, the playground not only of many of the sport's fabled champions, but also of a goodly number of bow-tied Manhattan power brokers. On the flagstone patio, shaded by trim blue-and-yellow awnings, members in tailored blazers and scalloped cotton shifts sipped frosted Rumbas as the nation's most prestigious tournament got under way.[1]

Lest there be any doubt about Althea's inferior status, club managers had assigned Court No. 23, the main court located directly in front of the clubhouse, to the curvaceous blond actress and sex symbol Ginger Rogers, known more for her ability to dance backward in stilettos than for any competitive athletic skills. Rogers was making her first, and only, celebrity appearance in the mixed doubles segment of the tournament, an event much trumpeted in the press. Although Althea's appearance had generated just as much interest, USLTA officials had dispatched her to Court No. 14, a remote court used largely for practice matches.

The press could not resist pairing the pert blond millionaire with the lanky "Harlem Negro Girl," as the headlines often described Althea. Months earlier, *Life* magazine had published photos of the two of them side by side—Althea, in tennis whites, dubbed a "New Tennis Threat," and a dancing Rogers, clad in sophisticated black, described as an "Oldtime Champ."[2] Outside the clubhouse, photographers posed them together, Althea in her conservative white flannels, Rogers in a snug midriff-baring shirt and pink socks.

Steeling herself before the explosion of flashbulbs, a nervous Althea headed to the distant court where she was to play what was the most significant match of her career to date. As one reporter put it, "No Negro player, man or woman, has ever set foot on one of these courts. . . . In many ways it's even a tougher personal jimcrow-busting assignment than was Jackie Robinson's when he first stepped out of the Brooklyn Dodger dugout. It's always tougher for a woman."[3]

Some members of the press believed that the club managers, whom Milton Gross of the *New York Post* dubbed "the staid and starchy puffballs running the tennis championships," had deliberately slighted Althea. Not only had she been assigned a court with limited seating, but news photographers were permitted to shoot their flashes off throughout the match, a violation of club tradition, potentially distracting Althea and her opponent in the critical opening points.[4]

"The excuse for all this is that Althea's historic appearance was virtually secreted on Court 14, as inaccessible a court as possible on which to stage her debut," Gross wrote. "While this seems a legitimate enough reason for allowing photogs to do what they are never allowed to do, say, in the stadium court, it is also a reflection of the persistent myopia with which the people who run tennis seem to be afflicted."[5]

Althea paid little mind to either the newsmen or the burgeoning crowd, which was four people deep at some points. Matched against British player Barbara N. Knapp, Althea took an offensive tack from the start and never backed off. Her face expressionless, as it often was in competition, she deployed her trademark overhead smash and relentlessly rushed to the net in an easy 6–2, 6–2 victory. Alice Marble was waiting for the triumphant Althea as she came off the court, and the two women walked side by side through the dense crowd toward the clubhouse. Exhilarated, Althea and Smith took the subway back to the city, where Althea tried to rest in anticipation of her next match the following day. She rose the next morning to find a photograph of herself dominating *The New York Times* coverage of the event.[6]

If the draw had gone in Althea's favor in the first round, it decidedly did not in the second. Her next opponent was America's No. 2 woman player, veteran Louise Brough, three-time Wimbledon champion and winner of the 1947 U.S. National Championships. Brough had also won multiple doubles titles with her longtime partner and close friend Margaret du-Pont, wife of millionaire William duPont Jr. Four years older than Althea, Brough was by far one of the most dominant female players of the day and was enjoying a particularly good year, which she had launched with a win in the women's singles at the Australian Open. An earnest competitor, Brough was known for her aggressive style and an acclaimed twist serve with topspin that often overwhelmed her opponents, especially on their backhand returns.[7] She was also known for her crisp, no-nonsense demeanor and humorless expression and many of the younger women on the circuit considered Brough a formidable figure best to be avoided off court.

Coincidentally, Althea and Brough shared the first name "Althea"—though Brough preferred to be called Louise—but the solemn Beverly Hills blond and the twenty-three-year-old college student who trounced the FAMC boys in pool had little else in common. If some among Althea's supporters suspected that the unbalanced draw was likely no accident but was, in fact, a deliberate attempt to ensure that the noxious young interloper would be swiftly vanquished and sent on her way, only a handful said so outright.[8]

Whether the pairing was the hand of fate or that of an ill-intentioned human being, it was clear that this was to be the match of the tournament, the formidable senior champion pitted against the inexperienced newcomer, the seasoned white insider squaring off with the rough-edged young Black woman with the astonishingly athletic playing style. This was the match that Althea, not to mention the many who had guided her along the way, had inched toward step by step over the past several years. This match was to be held on the club's grandstand court, and when the more than two thousand eager fans jammed the seats, Pinkerton guards sealed the gates. While some worried that Althea couldn't pull it off, and others were dearly hoping she wouldn't, few looking down from the stands couldn't help but be moved by the sight of the young player nervously pacing the court.

"I have sat in on many dramatic moments in sports, but few were more thrilling than Miss Gibson's performance against Miss Brough," said David Eisenberg, sports reporter for the *New York Journal-American*. "Not because great tennis was played. It wasn't. But because of the great try by this lonely, and nervous, colored girl, and because of the manner in which the elements robbed her of her great triumph."[9]

It was a match that would never be forgotten by those who witnessed it, not the least because Althea began so poorly. Unable to get her first service in play, she was repeatedly caught at mid-court by Brough's aggressive returns. Althea struggled determinedly to force Brough to the back of the court with her ferocious smash, but repeatedly overhit.[10] When Brough took the first set 6–1, some in the crowd made their opposition to Althea's presence abundantly clear, as Robert Minton wrote in his history of Forest Hills.

"There were those who did not conceal their hope that she would be beaten and that would be the end of such people at Forest Hills," Minton wrote.[11]

With the outcome of the match seeming all too clear after the first set, some viewers began to drift out of the stands to matches under way on other courts, such as the square-off in the stadium between Tony Trabert of Cincinnati and John Bromwich of Australia. Among those remaining was a small army of Althea's most avid supporters, who were watching anxiously. Drs. Johnson and Eaton sat together, exchanging observations about their student's performance, just as they had four years before, when they took her on after the ATA match in Ohio. There was also a large cluster of the Harlemites who had been instrumental in her launch. Sitting alongside the ever-loyal Rhoda Smith, identified in the press as "Miss Gibson's guardian," was sax player Buddy Walker, Cosmopolitan coach Fred Johnson, and ATA leaders Bertram Baker and Arthur Francis, all of whom had posed for a picture with Althea before the match began. Missing from the crowd were any members of Althea's family, according to *Baltimore Afro-American* columnist Sam Lacy. Althea had told Lacy that while her mother liked tennis, she wouldn't watch the tournament because "nerves wouldn't let her."[12]

As the second set got under way, Althea had clearly recovered her equilibrium. The first game, seemingly critical if Althea were to turn the tide, went to deuce time and again, but Brough managed to hold her serve.

Emboldened by her opponent's slowing pace, Althea grew steadily more forceful with her strokes, and her serve sliced sharply through a gathering wind. With games tied at 3–3, a now visibly tired Brough began to falter. Althea surged forward, breaking through the older woman's serve and then claiming the next two games to take the second set 6–3. As some members of the audience leaped to their feet, a ripple of excitement surged through the crowd with the realization that the gangly-legged New York City girl might actually manage to topple one of the world's greatest female players. So electrifying was the prospect of a potential upset that word went out over the club's loudspeakers, prompting many spectators to abandon their seats and rush toward the grandstand.

"At first, a lot of people didn't bother to watch the match because we all knew that Brough was going to win easily," recalled Barret Schleicher, a club member now in his nineties who was eighteen years old at the time. "But then we heard what was going on, and we went over and it was true, [Brough] had lost the second set. It was incredibly exciting. It had nothing to do with Black or white, it was that Brough was losing to an unknown. That's the kind of thing you go to these matches to see."[13]

As the skies overhead darkened ominously and the winds began to pick up, the third set began. Brough, who appeared to have recovered during the short break, promptly broke Althea's serve and took the first three games. But then Althea seized the momentum and began to play the kind of tennis that left some in the audience gaping. Artfully placing her lobs and following through with crushing overhead smashes, she claimed one game and then lost another. Hundreds of viewers, clearly rooting for Althea, began shouting and stamping their feet as the battling players inched forward, each claiming one critical game after another.

"It was apparent now that anything could happen, so strongly was Miss Gibson playing and so unreliable was Miss Brough's service," wrote *The New York Times*'s Danzig.[14]

But not everyone was so happy with the direction the match was taking. High up in the grandstand, a man abruptly stood up beneath the churning dark skies overhead and shouted at the players. What exactly he said is unclear, and neither press accounts nor the history books decisively clarify the matter. Bertram Baker, the ATA official, later said that he heard the man yell at Brough, "'Beat the nigger, beat the nigger.' I'll always remember it as the day the gods got angry," according to several published accounts.[15] Others reported that the heckler screamed, "Knock her out of there! Knock her out of there!"[16] Few among the mainstream white press, such as *The New York Times* or *Sports Illustrated*, mentioned the incident, apparently preferring to keep any hint of racial controversy at bay.

Whatever words were actually said, they spurred Althea to even more aggressive play, and she managed to claim two more games, bringing the score to 5–5. Pushing ahead with her brilliant service and a pair of forehand volleys, she claimed the next game. With the outcome now listing in Althea's favor, Brough pulled herself together. Running hard in the twelfth game to capture each successive lob, she evened the score at 6–6. The clouds, leaden with impending rain, hung ominously low as the winds churned through the grandstand and the rumble of boiling thunder caused many to tear their gaze from the game and glance briefly upward. Unfazed by the turbulence overhead, Althea pressed on to take three straight points and pulled into the lead, winning the thirteenth game and putting the score at 7–6.

And then the rain began, at first just a trickle, but soon a drenching downpour. Water began to seep into spectators' clothes as it slowly pooled on the walkways between courts. Debate began over whether to continue. Brough repeatedly asked to postpone until the next day, citing the dimming light. Althea, a single game away from a momentous conquest, knew she was within reach of victory and earnestly asked to keep on playing.

"Brough was a little cranky. She wasn't used to losing," recalls Schleicher. "There was a lot of discussion about whether it was dark enough to call, which is what Brough wanted, to have it called. . . . She didn't like losing to an unknown player."[17]

Scriptwriters might have prayed for what came next. Before a decision could be made, the heavens released a torrent of heavy rain while bolts of lightning ripped through the black sky. As spectators scurried for cover, a rogue bolt struck one of the stone eagles perched proudly atop the stadium and hurled it to the ground, where it shattered into dozens of pieces. The dramatic moment was surely, some would insist later, a profound message, a sign that the American way was finally changing and that the old order that had kept Black people on the outside was forever done with. That the violent manifestation of nature ultimately hurt the pioneering Black player on the court was a truth to be parsed by future historians and astrologists. The more literal-minded chalked it up to bad weather. Whatever it symbolized, the game was suspended and set to continue the following day.

That decision was, as Althea later wrote, the worst thing that could have happened for her. "It gave me the whole evening—and the next morning, too, for that matter—to think about the match," she wrote in her autobiography. "By the time I got through reading the morning newspapers I was a nervous wreck."[18]

When play resumed in the middle of the following day, the stage was set for a momentous finale. Five motion-picture cameras were trained on the court, with fifteen cameramen at the ready. Newsmen clustered at the fence, pads in hand, as the grandstand churned with an overflow crowd yet again. Althea, who rarely did well under pressure, was late to the game, apparently exercising a deliberate delaying strategy in an effort to unnerve her opponent, just as the great tennis champion Bill Tilden had done decades earlier. But in Althea's case, the technique appeared to backfire. By the time she showed up, the dozens of cameramen were bursting with expectation, and their flashbulbs exploded mercilessly, compounding Althea's obvious state of anxiety. Play began immediately, as the crowd grew quiet in anticipation.

It was over in just eleven minutes. Keenly aware that if she lost the opening game, her name would go down in history in a very different way from that to which she was accustomed, Brough hit with deliberate and forceful precision, swiftly bringing the score to 7–7. In the next two games, Althea double-faulted repeatedly, netted several shots, and generally failed to bring her play up to the previous day's level. As her final backhand soared off court, the match was called for Brough at 9–7. A battered Brough went on to lose the next round to Nancy Chaffee.

While Althea did not win the match, she scored a seismic victory for the history books in the eyes of many, particularly those of the Black media. "Althea Gibson's Amazing Tennis Thrills America" proclaimed the *New Journal and Guide*.[19] "Althea Did a Splendid Job," trumpeted the *New York Amsterdam News* on its front page, above a photo of a beaming Marble shaking Althea's hand after the match. The paper ran an accompanying story that gave a blow-by-blow account of the match and concluded, "It was generally conceded that Miss Brough was saved from defeat on Tuesday by the rain." Brough was quoted as saying, "The rain was probably the only thing that saved me. Althea was playing magnificently and my game had all but virtually collapsed. . . . She plays a beautiful game—all she needs is a little more experience."[20]

The *New York Herald Tribune* put it even more eloquently. In an editorial titled "Fine Achievement," the paper declared that Althea "did not come through the tournament with a crown of victory but she won something she can cherish throughout her life and which never can be taken away from her—the respect and admiration of all who saw her play this week at Forest Hills. She is a credit not only to the Negro race but to all good sportsmen and women who play and love the game of tennis."[21]

Eaton and Johnson were just as pleased. While they were disappointed that the match had been plucked from Althea's grasp, Eaton wrote in his autobiography, "Our overwhelming feeling was one of triumph. The fact that Althea Gibson, an American Negro, had played at Forest Hills was the important thing. Whether she won or lost was secondary to this accomplishment."[22]

Althea agreed with the sentiment that she would likely have won had it not been for the rainstorm. But she also felt that she had erred in playing a cautious game on the last day, rather than the more forceful one she had displayed in the earlier sets. Instead, she said in an interview after the match, "I decided to play it careful. I guess I'm too inexperienced to play it that way against a player like Miss Brough." As for the subject of race, the element that had made the event a riveting national story, Althea, as usual, demurred. That she was a Black woman breaking a national color barrier that had major implications for all of her race had never even entered her mind, or, so she said. "I just didn't think about it."[23]

Even among those who marveled at the young New Yorker's impressive performance, there were some who felt she had no place at the Nationals tournament. As one letter writer to a columnist at the *Atlanta Daily World* put it, "Althea Gibson is a whale of a tennis player . . . but in all frankness,

Miss Gibson had no business at Forest Hills this time even though she came within two points of licking Louise Brough."[24]

Regardless of Althea's own diffidence, the Black community seized on her accomplishment with glee. Whether she liked it or not, Althea's appearance at Forest Hills forever recast her both as an American and a Black athlete. However much she downplayed her role as a racial pioneer in the years to come, and she most adamantly did, she held a preeminent position within the Black civil rights movement. Eight years and eight Grand Slam titles later, Ed Fitzgerald, the eventual editor of her autobiography, ruminated on her status in the pages of a spring issue of the Sunday newspaper supplement *The American Weekly* as he considered the odds of her going professional, as some amateur players were beginning to do at the time. Althea, he wrote, "has neither the temperament nor the desire to play the role of a crusader. But she has had to carry the crusader's cross ever since the stuffy United States Lawn Tennis Association accepted her entry in the national championships in 1950. . . . Althea can never play only for herself; she carries the hopes of millions of others on her shoulders every time she goes into action."[25]

Two months after the Forest Hills match against Brough, Marble registered her own thoughts about the Forest Hills match in an open letter to Althea that appeared in her column in *American Lawn Tennis* magazine. Marble opened by telling her that while the seasoned Brough had rightfully won the Forest Hills match, Althea should be "a very proud girl. You made history in your own right, which is quite a burden of honor for twenty-three-year-old shoulders to carry, and you bore your responsibility well. You also played some remarkably good tennis." In addition, Marble offered a bit of explicit advice, saying that she had never seen "a combined service and forehand hit with better style and force than yours, unless it is that of Doris Hart." Althea's backhand, though, "could stand quite a bit of attention this winter; from where I sat, it did not look as sound as your other strokes."

Marble took some issue with what she described as the amazing number of managers and advisers who engulfed Althea when she arrived at Forest Hills, pointing out that a tournament committee member had been unable to reach her. Marble herself said she had been unable to reach

Althea after the two of them met for the first time before Althea's initial match. Somewhat sternly, Marble advised, "You don't need them, Althea. . . . They want to get into the act for their sakes, not for yours, now that you and a few others have done the necessary, heartbreaking work to make you a national contender. . . . I repeat, you don't need them. You don't need me. When you go out to play a match, not all the accumulated managers and advisors in the world can win it for you. Nobody but Althea Gibson will be on your side of the net."[26]

Back in Tallahassee again three months later, Althea wrote a lengthy response in an open letter in the magazine, thanking Marble profusely and apologizing for "the slurs you received and the friends you lost" as a result of her public endorsement. She then went on in a somewhat uncharacteristic manner to say that she did not mind having been beaten at Forest Hills because Brough was the far more experienced player. Brough, she added, "used her experience and confidence to out-think and out-play me. I agree Miss Brough had every right to win and I was pulling for her to win the tournament."

Had Althea Gibson, the ferocious combatant who never gave an inch, whether it be a game of whist or a national championship on the Williston High School basketball court, really been rooting for her opponent to beat her? It did not seem possible. Indeed, her oddly accommodating comment suggested that Althea, who had never in her life entered a contest of any kind that she was not dead set on winning, had been guided by a heavy editorial hand, likely that of an ATA official, in an effort to keep the race conversation nonconfrontational. Althea concluded cheerfully that she awaited with "hopeful anticipation for what 1951 might bring."[27]

ATA officials were already hard at work on that topic three months before she wrote those words. In the days between the Forest Hills tournament and her return to Tallahassee, Althea met with Bertram Baker and Hollis Dann, chairman of the USLTA's international exhibitions committee, at the Crossroads Restaurant on Forty-Second Street and Broadway. Baker had called the meeting to discuss the possibility of Althea's playing at Wimbledon in 1951. Conspicuously absent at the table were not only Eaton and Johnson, but any of the FAMC administrators who also had a stake in her doings in the coming year, a fact that would result in no little upheaval in later months. The two national tennis organizations, one Black and one white, had a shimmering star in their midst, and they were going to seize as much control of her orbit as they could. While Althea and the ATA had a common interest in her success, to be sure, the ATA fathers were far more concerned with the future of Black tennis in general than they were with Althea's particular road ahead or her personal well-being. It was just the kind of thing that Marble had warned her about in her fall letter.

The plan on the table was ambitious. In the spring, Althea was to leave school and embark on an extensive European tour, in order to gain experience before making her first appearance at Wimbledon. The oldest and most prestigious tennis tournament in the world, Wimbledon was a showcase of the sport's elite players, not to mention one of the premier events on the social calendar of the British royal family. In order to be prepared for that enormous undertaking, Althea would have to leave college early and travel first to Hamtramck, Michigan, to work with Jean Hoxie, legendary coach at Hamtramck High School and the city tennis director whose summer tennis camp had turned out dozens of teenage state and national title holders. A nurturing disciplinarian in her early fifties, the white Hoxie was cut from the same bolt of rugged cloth as both Dr. Johnson and coach Jake Gaither. Her favorite slogan was "I like 'em when they fight." Although the USLTA was clearly interested in Althea's next steps, as evidenced by one of their own being at the table, it still had no intention of paying her way at this point.[28]

Althea returned to school in the fall of 1950, now in her sophomore year, to find that her life was in many respects dominated by tennis more than ever. With a host of tournaments looming ahead of her the following spring, college officials had decided to place her in a single room to accommodate her busy travel schedule. In the aftermath of her much-publicized appearance at Forest Hills, she continued to be in enormous demand by the media, which made her status on campus soar even higher. Although she played tennis daily, she nonetheless suffered a post-tournament funk that left her disinterested in the sport, at least for a while. In a luncheon with State Department employees in 1959, Althea recalled, "I didn't have any enthusiasm for tennis at that time because . . . after getting into Forest

Hills and that disheartening defeat by Louise, I thought I was going to be the champ that year. But it eluded me. There goes the tennis ego again."[29]

Her bruised ego was likely to have been soothed by some of the widespread public attention she received that fall. In November, *Ebony*, a popular general-interest magazine launched in 1945 with the intention of focusing on "the zesty side of life" and the positive achievements of Black personalities, ran a six-page spread on Althea titled "Althea Gibson— Tomboyish Coed Startles Tennis World with Natural Ability on Court."[30] The piece included nearly a dozen photos of Althea signing autographs and executing graceful shots, and it cheerfully noted that "the quiet-spoken, poised young lady who is the Althea Gibson of today is a far cry from the harum-scarum, long-legged youngster from Harlem who first showed her athletic promise as a paddle tennis champion on the streets and playgrounds of New York City."[31]

Later that month, the Harlem YMCA presented her with its annual sports achievement award at the Century Club. Althea, her hair swept up in a stylishly coiffed do and wearing an enormous corsage on her lapel, accepted the award from Brooklyn Dodgers star Jackie Robinson, a member of the Harlem YMCA's Board of Managers. Also speaking at the event were Alice Marble and lawyer Edith Sampson, who had been appointed the first Black delegate to the United Nations days before Althea's Forest Hills appearance. Although nearly three decades apart in age, Althea and Sampson were not just "First Negroes," but "First Females," and their accomplishments that year were splashed across the front pages of the nation's Black newspapers, in some cases, side by side.[32]

The two also shared political views that infuriated some in the Black community. Selected for the UN post in order to strike back at mounting Communist propaganda deriding America's brutal and discriminatory treatment of Black people, Sampson was criticized for not taking a more aggressive stand against the nation's racist ways, just as Althea would be in coming years.[33]

At year's end, Althea did not earn a spot on the USLTA's list of the top twenty players, although she was placed in the Class A division of players and awarded "special recognition" for her performance that year. The Black media, however, gave her top billing in its roundup of the year's achievements. The *Baltimore Afro-American*, for one, published a star gallery of eighteen of the year's top Black athletes, including Sugar Ray Robinson, who had won yet another title; lightweight title holder Ike Williams, who had defended his title four times within five months that year; and sprinter Arthur Bragg, who won the national 100-meter crown. The only other woman in the array was sprinter Jean Patton, who had won the 100-meter race in the U.S. Championships.[34]

Whether she liked it or not, the twenty-three-year-old Althea was becoming an ever-more-popular figure among Black Americans. Increasingly, others positioned her at the forefront of the civil rights movement that was slowly building steam across the country. In the final days of 1950, Althea was awarded second place in an annual poll of leading Harlemites conducted by the *New York Amsterdam News*, trumped only by Judge Harold A. Stevens, who had been elected to the New York Court of General Sessions earlier in the year. Althea came in 106 votes ahead of U.S. congressman Adam Clayton Powell Jr., who was the first African American from New York to be elected to Congress and was a fierce combatant on behalf of civil rights.

The New Year began laden with both possibility and pressure. Wimbledon was just six months away, and Althea had much work to do to prepare for the event, while still maintaining a good academic standing. As ever, Eaton and Johnson were keeping a close eye on her, determined to ensure that her education remain a priority, while the ATA brass were hard at work to get her name on the international circuit leading up to Wimbledon. Althea worked hard to do both.

On the competitive front, her success continued. In February, Althea flew to Jamaica with forty-two USLTA players to compete in the second Caribbean Lawn Tennis Championships, in Montego Bay, where she was widely fêted across the island before play even began. The *Daily Gleaner* noted in a pre-event story that history was being written with the arrival of "Althea Gibson, the coloured American star," the first of her race to be part of a USLTA team, and four days later, the paper ran a large photo of the group being presented to the acting governor, the Hon. D. C. MacGillivray.[35]

Althea, who was a central attraction of the event, easily beat her first opponent, Edith Ann Sullivan of Massachusetts, 6–0, 6–4, at the Fairfield

Country Club, where she "hit with disguised ferocity, both off the ground and in the air," as one paper put it, and cruised her way through a second match to the finals.[36] Paired against Betty Rosenquest of New Jersey, who was ranked No. 12 in the United States, Althea was overconfident in the first set and made repeated errors, losing 5–7. By the third set, she had fine-tuned her game and managed to offset Rosenquest, a relentlessly steady hitter, with a series of lobs and a ferocious serve. Althea took the last two sets 6–4, 6–4, before an enthusiastic crowd that drew from all over the island, and thus captured her first international title.[37]

At the time of the tournament, the majority of Jamaicans were of Black or mixed heritage, and residents were clearly thrilled to host America's rising Black tennis star.[38] In fact, so often was Althea's race mentioned by local sports reporters covering the event that it prompted a tiff on the *Daily Gleaner*'s sports pages. Several days into the tournament, reader Vere Johns complained in a letter that such "over-emphasis on colour by coloured writers and commentators is ridiculous and indicative of a gross inferiority complex. I trust there will be no more of it."[39] The following week, local radio commentator Roy Lawrence responded with a letter explaining that he had mentioned Althea's race precisely because he felt "Jamaicans would take special pride" in her achievements. He concluded: "It would appear that if any one is suffering from an inferiority complex, it is Mr. Johns himself."[40]

Althea's foray into international competition culminated in a reception given for her at the Embassy Club in Montego Bay, which was attended by several local notables and the USLTA's Hollis Dann. Clad in a fashionable print dress, a departure from her habitual pants and shirt, Althea accepted several gifts, including a box of gourmet chocolates, an elegant clock, an evening bag, and a pair of Chinese slippers from David Yap, the 1947 all-Jamaica male singles tennis champion. With each congratulatory event, Althea was getting accustomed to her newfound celebratory status, a far cry from her old life on 143rd Street in Harlem.

While Althea's game was steadily improving, she continued to play inconsistently and often struggled to gain solid footing in the opening set of a match. Such inconsistency was on vivid display a couple of weeks later, at the National Indoor Championship tournament in New York, where she squared off for the third time against Nancy Chaffee. Althea easily won her first round and managed to take the second round from Marjorie Gladman, former captain of the Wightman Cup team, after a harrowing two-hour battle that saw the advantage shift dramatically from one side to the other. Paired next against Chaffee in the quarterfinals before a capacity crowd at the Seventh Regiment Armory, Althea played erratically there, too, making repeated errors in the first set, her serve wildly off target. She was trounced by Chaffee 6–1, 6–3, her third such defeat at the older woman's hand. Critics pounced on what they called Althea's "wild style" and predicted that her professional career was going to stall if she didn't get better control over her game.

"Miss Gibson looked lamentably erratic as she was pounded into the exits of the National indoor championship by Miss Chaffee. She couldn't do anything right," wrote one critic. The writer added, "Unless she learns to complement her powerful ground strokes and overhead smashes with steadiness, Althea Gibson isn't likely to realize any of her lofty tennis ambitions."[41]

Anxious about her performance, Althea got back on a plane and headed for Florida. This time she was going not to FAMC, but to the Good Neighbor tournament in Miami Beach. Not only was she the first Black person to play in that, or any mixed-race tournament in the racially stratified states below the Mason–Dixon line, but she also arrived at a particularly tumultuous time in the state's racial history. Her arrival coincided with the U.S. Supreme Court's decision overturning the two of the convictions in the high-profile case of the four Black Groveland men known as the Groveland Four, who were accused of raping a white woman.

News of developments in the case were stripped across the top of the state's daily newspapers. Although city fathers had begun to tout the "Magic City's" international flavor in the post–World War II years in an effort to broaden its tourist appeal, Miami adhered strictly to the Jim Crow separatism of the Deep South well into the 1950s. Long before that, its plush waterfront hotels prohibited their own Black employees from staying at the hotel and closely monitored their interactions with white guests.[42] Greater Miami was home to several small Black communities, but most Black people were confined to the northwestern part of the downtown, in an area known as Colored Town, later called Overtown. Under the strict terms of Ordinance 457, thousands of seasonal workers employed at the beach-front hotels, many of them Black, were required to register with the police and carry identification cards, while some Black city residents were barred from entering wealthy white neighborhoods, such as Coral Gables or Miami Beach, without passes until the mid-1960s.[43] At the Good Neighbor tournament, as at other public events, Black and white players were generally prohibited by Jim Crow laws from sitting together, and blocks of seats were set aside for patrons of color.

Althea was spared some of Miami's humiliating segregation laws that treated Black people as second-class citizens, in large part because of the efforts of tournament founder and director Eddie Herr, an irrepressible tennis enthusiast determined to create tennis opportunities for his teenage daughter. It was Herr, widely known as the "Mr. Tennis of South Florida," who not only invited Althea to participate in the tournament, but also secured her a room in the all-white Admiral Hotel on Miami Beach, where no Black person had ever stayed before; he even invited her to play tennis with his daughter.[44] Althea appreciated the gestures, but after a single night at the elegant Admiral, she moved to the Mary Elizabeth Hotel in Overtown, the treasured retreat of many high-profile Black people of the day, such as W. E. B. Du Bois, Adam Clayton Powell Jr., and Sugar Ray Robinson.

Of her first visit to Miami, Althea later wrote in her autobiography, "It was quite an experience. I felt as though I were on display, being studied through a microscope, every minute. . . . I was lonesome at the Admiral, all by myself. I'm an authority on what it feels like to be the only Negro in all-white surroundings, and I can assure you that it can be very lonely."[45]

Once again bearing the "First Negro" mantle, Althea made a good showing at the tournament, which had begun just a few years earlier and remained relatively low profile on the amateur circuit. She cruised easily through four matches before encountering top-seeded Betty Rosenquest in the final. Both women played a cautious game in the first set, weighted down by the heat. Then, the *Miami Herald* wrote, "Miss Gibson turned on her big guns and took the second set handily," winning the women's singles title 6–4, 6–2. She also won the mixed doubles championship with Miamian Tony Vincent, losing only the women's doubles paired with Herr's daughter, Suzanne.[46] In the stands, viewers of both races apparently ignored the "Colored Only" sign while enjoying Althea's performance, and together they "applauded the good plays and 'ohed' and 'ahed' at the missed shots," wrote the *Baltimore Afro-American*'s Lacy. "The players laughed with Althea, admired her hair-do, enthused over her strokes and even asked for advice. . . . The American Tennis Association champion was shown every courtesy to be found in the code of sports and sportsmanship."[47]

While many were thrilled at Althea's breaking yet another barrier, some among the Black press continued to grumble that her advances represented those of only one individual rather than the race as a whole. Marion Jackson of the *Atlanta Daily World* applauded Althea's participation in the tournament, saying that it "gave living evidence that net jimcrow [*sic*] even in the Deep South is cracking at the seams." He pointed out, nonetheless, that there had been no similar welcome for Black male players such as George Stewart of Orangeburg, South Carolina, or Reginald Weir of New York. Althea's trailblazing, Jackson continued, "is heartening, but as tennis, like golf, erected a 19th hole which taboos Negro males from luxurious club houses and the fraternalization [*sic*] which go along with these social conscious sports!!!!!"[48]

Jackson's observation was a reflection of what was becoming a heated and critical topic among Althea's supporters. The issue was, what was more important, Althea's future or that of Black tennis? Where, even, might the two intersect? While the ATA was pursuing an ambitious international tour for Althea that it felt would advance the race at large into the white tennis empire, Eaton and Johnson were not at all convinced that such a route was in their student's best interest. Clearly, both men had devoted much of their lives to issues related to the advancement of their race, but they were also determined that Althea complete her education.

In the spring of 1951, Althea seemed caught between those two conflicting points of view, increasingly drawn to the many attractions of the white tennis circuit, with its cocktail parties and high-profile events, but also mindful of the advice of her mentors.

The tension between these two conflicting aims boiled over shortly after she returned to the FAMC campus following the Miami tournament. In late March, the ATA's Bertram Baker wrote to Coach Gaither outlining the plan he had tentatively sketched out the previous September at the Manhattan meeting with Althea and the USLTA's Hollis Dann.

Notably, Baker did not include Eaton and Johnson in the letter, just as he had not included them or Gaither in the fall meeting. While the proposal called for Althea to leave school for a year and miss a full season of American tournaments, Baker explained that the proposed European tour would constitute a big step in developing Althea's game so that she might be prepared to compete at Forest Hills in 1952. Noting that the plan would also benefit the school and its athletic program in the long run, Baker asked if the college would be willing to make a financial contribution toward Althea's tour.[49]

Gaither was irked. If the college was expected to share the expenses of the proposal, he wrote back crisply, its representatives should have been invited to the New York meeting and had a say in its details. While he fully recognized all that Althea's achievements had done for FAMC, he stated that the school had also played its part for the community at large. The school, he concluded, would make no financial contribution to the proposed trip.[50]

On learning of the exchange, Johnson, not surprisingly, was even more annoyed than Gaither that the three of them had been excluded from the planning meeting, and he said as much. After four years of devoting themselves to Althea's personal and professional development, not to mention paying all her expenses, the doctors were being brushed aside in the ATA's rush to deploy her in the interests of Black tennis. More important, Johnson felt that their proposal was flatly ignoring what was in Althea's own best interest, which was to complete her college studies. The day would come, he well knew, when she would need to make a living. He wrote back to Baker, saying, "I told her [Gibson] that I did not approve of any tennis that would interfere with her scholastic work to such an extent that she would lose time out of school. That explains my attitude towards her future."[51]

Eaton agreed, for a couple of reasons. Like Johnson, he felt it wise that Althea remain in school in order to get her degree, but also because she needed to retain her amateur status. It would do her no good to risk alienating the USLTA, which was notoriously punishing for those players who flirted with turning professional in an effort to make money, barring them from their amateur tournaments if they were found to have done so. In addition, he wrote bluntly, she should be wary of those who were not guided first and foremost by her personal well-being. He advised her in a letter to be "very skeptical in going against the advice and decisions of those whom you must know are personally interested in you and your welfare." As a sort of compromise, he suggested that she cut down the time she spent in Detroit with Jean Hoxie and shorten the length of the European tour in order to minimize the impact the trip would have on her education. But Eaton acknowledged that it was Althea's decision to make.[52]

Anticipating long ago that the day would come when the three of them might not be in agreement, the doctors and Althea had decided that each of them would get a vote on the matter, with a majority ruling in such situations. But the truth was that, ultimately, Althea would make the decisions about her future. With the doctors in disagreement with the ATA, the decision in this case indeed now fell to her to make. For Althea, it wasn't just a decision about what she wanted to do, but a more complex judgment about what really was in her best interest and that of her tennis future. To whom should she listen? The wise doctors who had devoted years to her nurturing and development or the Black tennis organization that wanted to launch her into the international sphere, potentially bringing significant benefits both to her and to the race at large?[53]

"By this point the doctors had really become father figures for Althea, especially Eaton, and they really wanted what was best for her," said historian Jennifer H. Lansbury, author of *A Spectacular Leap: Black Women Athletes in Twentieth-Century America*. "But as she began to move into international competition, they were starting to lose their grip on that. Baker really wanted to pull the strings and say how things were going to go."[54]

The conflict between Althea's personal needs and the future of Black tennis was growing increasingly heated. So annoyed was Baker at the doctors' intransigence that he accused Johnson and Eaton of "doing the race a great injustice."[55]

The doctors weren't the only ones miffed at the ATA's domineering attitude regarding all things Althea. Alice Marble had also personally witnessed the multiple layers of handlers now surrounding the young tennis phenomenon whose case she had taken on. That spring, Marble wrote a letter to Bill Tilden, the towering prince of tennis in the 1920s and considered by many one of the greatest players of all times, expressing concern that Althea had become nearly unreachable. "I'm very gratified that you, too, see the spark that Althea Gibson has," she wrote. "Unfortunately, Bill, she has a thousand advisors and is so confused and bewildered that I doubt if she will make the grade. She has created a wall between herself and other people and one can't penetrate it. I'd love to help her, but she just won't be helped. She's much like a singer gifted with a beautiful natural voice but she doesn't know how the hell to use it."[56]

To a degree perhaps unknown to either Marble or the doctors, Althea, despite the generous liberties college administrators afforded her for her extensive travel, had long been chafing at the limitations that school put on her tennis life. Frustrated, she often turned to her latest father figure, Coach Gaither.

"I remember many afternoons when she would come into my office and argue about quitting school," Gaither told *Ebony* magazine in 1960. "She'd wind up running out into the hall and slamming the door. Then she would come back and say, 'Pop, are you mad with me?' 'No, honey,' I'd always tell her. 'I'm not mad with you.' She needed understanding."[57]

About the time that Baker and the doctors were having their go-round, word got out that Althea was thinking about quitting school. The Black press leaped on the news, treating it like a major sports development. Marion Jackson was among the first sportswriters to broadcast the item, leading his column in the *Atlanta Daily World* with the statement "Althea Gibson, the rising American woman tennis player, is quitting Florida A. & M. after this semester."[58] Several other Black newspapers subsequently ran a more detailed version of the news, explaining that Althea had confided in some of her friends that homework was impeding her progress as a tennis player. At the end of April, the *New York Amsterdam News* provided the additional information that Althea was to compete at Wimbledon the following month and had been invited to several preparatory tournaments elsewhere in Britain, suggesting that *that* might be the reason for her thoughts of dropping out of school.[59]

Althea put an end to the rumors in early May, explaining that she had no intention of withdrawing. "My relation here is most pleasant," she said of FAMC. "The academic requirements of me are the same as for other students. I want it that way."[60] With a final headline—"Althea Won't Quit Famcee"—the matter was put to rest.[61]

On her return to FAMC in the spring of 1951, Althea was delighted, and a bit stunned, to find an invitation to not just another white tournament, but *the* white tournament, the world's premier tennis event, the legendary tournament of international champions, where generations of players had humbly curtsied or bowed before the Queen and members of her family seated in the Royal Box. Althea would be the first African American to play in the storied event, but not the first person of color. That distinction went to Bertrand Milbourne Clark of Jamaica, the island's medical secretary and a renowned tennis champion in his own country, who lost in the first round in 1924 against Londoner Vincent Burr after five hard-fought sets. He again lost in the first round in 1930.[62]

Althea chose to accept the invitation, but she opted to go along with Eaton's suggestion and scale back the summer travel program. At her request, FAMC permitted her to take her exams two weeks early, enabling her to head to Detroit in May, where she would work with Hoxie for just a little over one week before heading to England. Gaither, who was as determined to see his young protégée succeed as were Eaton and Johnson, raised some cash from the physical education department for Althea's trip. He then gave the funds to Swilley McElveen, Althea's friend and a member of the basketball team, and asked her to help Althea prepare.

"Gaither just said, 'Get her ready for Wimbledon,'" said McElveen. "We didn't know anything about Wimbledon, we had no idea. The bulk of us didn't know anything about tennis, because there weren't many Blacks playing. We just knew she was going to be the only Black player there. That was exciting."[63]

McElveen and a few other girls accompanied Althea to the local Sears, Roebuck store, where they picked out a few white tennis dresses, a couple of pairs of shorts, and a new suitcase. As soon as she was done with her exams, Althea flew to Detroit, where a group of Black community members turned out to take care of her, while also raising money to cover the costs of her training and travel. While she was there, they sponsored a benefit, called "Althea Gibson Night," at the local Flame Show Bar, at which they raised $770. She was whisked from the airport to the elegant Gotham Hotel, another destination popular among prominent Black figures, where champion heavyweight boxer Joe Louis had not only reserved his personal suite for her, but later met the tennis star for breakfast to congratulate her on how well she was doing. He also promised to buy her a round-trip ticket to London, which he would have waiting for her at the New York airport.

Other members of the Black community now stepped forward to provide financial support as well. Earlier in the year, *New York Amsterdam News* sportswriter Joe Bostic launched a fundraising effort on behalf of Althea in his "Scoreboard" column, saying, "Come on Harlem, let's go. Let's substitute dollars for talk and insure a complete tournament circuit for Althea next year. Okay?"[64] When only a handful of donations had trickled into the ATA a month later, Bostic raised his voice with some irritation in another column, titled "What Are You Doing About the Althea Gibson Situation?"

"The issue is very simple," Bostic wrote. "Either we're for Althea and her gallant fight to win democracy in tennis or we don't give a damn. . . . This thing has reached the put up or shut up stage."[65]

Althea spent most of her time in Detroit at the elegant white-columned home of Jean Hoxie. A taskmaster and unlikely athletic coach, with her head of gray curls and matronly attire, Hoxie put Althea through two grueling three-hour training sessions a day, pairing her against her most talented male students. Explaining to a reporter that her star student's greatest fault was "that she never learned how to practice," Hoxie nonetheless predicted that "there's a brilliant future for her, if she can conquer her impatience."[66]

After a one-night stop in Manhattan to say goodbye to her family, Althea headed to Idlewild Airport in Queens, where she caught the Pan Am Clipper to London. As she soared over the Atlantic, Sam Lacy penned a column that extolled the magnificence of her achievement long before she even set foot on the hallowed Wimbledon grass court. The invitation to play on the patrician London tennis lawns alone, Lacy wrote, might be considered the highest achievement in Black sports history to date. The daughter of a car mechanic and product of Harlem's harsh streets, he added, "is currently preparing for the biggest undertaking of her life—and for that matter, the supreme ambition of every tennis player in the world."[67]

Upon landing, Althea was met with a media deluge celebrating the arrival of the Harlem-born tennis player whom reporters had dubbed the "New Gibson Girl," a play on artist Charles Dana Gibson's famed Gibson Girl of the late nineteenth and early twentieth century, an illustrated ideal of feminine perfection and elegance. Virtually every story referred to what appeared to be Althea's defining feature: the color of her skin. She was "coffee-coloured," "copper-coloured," plain old "coloured," "tan," the "First Negro," a "Negress," and more. Some British papers even mentioned her color twice in the same sentence, lest readers miss this astonishing bit of information. The *Daily Herald*, for example, announced the arrival of the tennis girl from Harlem beneath a photo of a grinning Althea, saying, "Coffee-coloured Althea Gibson from 143rd Street, Harlem, flew into London yesterday to be the first coloured girl to compete at Wimbledon." In case readers missed the point, the story concluded, "Althea is 23; America's coloured champion."[68]

Other publications, perhaps seeking to contextualize Althea, linked her to various Black athletes—"Like 'Sugar Ray,'" explained the headline in the *Belfast Telegraph*. The brief item read, "American coloured tennis champion Miss Althea Gibson, who is to compete at Wimbledon, has a punch—just like 'Sugar' Ray Robinson. That is the verdict of experts after watching her in action at Manchester yesterday."[69] In several cases, the description of Althea was reduced to color alone. "Coloured Player Impresses," read the headline over a story in the *Dundee Courier and Advertiser* of Manchester, which noted that the play of "the 23-year-old coloured student . . . was studied with interest." So exotic a creature was this "First Negress" that one paper noted with offensive awe that Althea even took a bath every day.[70]

As play got under way, attention at long last shifted to her tennis. In preparation for the Wimbledon Championships at the end of June 1951, Althea was scheduled to appear in three preceding tournaments. She debuted on the European circuit at the Northern Lawn Tennis Championships tournament in Manchester, several hours northwest of London, where she displayed little of the anxiety that often marred her opening games. Instead, she impressed the spectators with her powerful and consistent strokes. In the first round, she easily defeated Peggy Hodson 6–1, 6–1; time and again, Hodson stood helpless as Althea's powerful forehand drives streaked past her. In the second round, Althea did less well and made a number of nervous errors but still managed to beat her opponent 6–4, 6–4. By the semifinals, her anxiety seemed to overcome her as she managed to take only five games off her stern-faced opponent, American Doris Hart, the same number she had won when she and Hart first met, at the National Clay Court Championships in Chicago the previous summer. Althea was thrown by her opponent's strategic drop shots and fumbled her returns to surrender four straight games in the second set and lost the match 6–1, 6–4. It was hardly surprising. Hart was at peak performance and would go on to achieve a career high that year and be named the No. 1 female player in the world.[71]

Next stop was the Kent Lawn Tennis Tournament in Beckenham, England, where Althea displayed a similar pattern, this time easily winning her first three rounds before being beaten in the semifinals by her old foe Betty Rosenquest, whom she had trounced in Jamaica just months before. This time, Rosenquest was in complete control of her game, battling deep into both sets before winning 11–9, 7–5, in what the press dubbed the most grueling women's match of the grass court season to date.[72]

As Althea was swinging her way back toward London, a sixteen-year-old girl with reddish-blond hair and a forthright manner was closely following her progress in the daily newspapers. Her name was Angela Buxton, and she'd picked up tennis several years earlier, while living in Johannesburg, South Africa, where she and her family had gone to escape the bombing of London during World War II. Buxton had become familiar with people of color during her childhood years there, as she'd made a friend of a dark-skinned girl in her neighborhood, at least until she was forbidden to play with her. The white neighbors had informed Buxton's mother in no uncertain terms that white children in South Africa did not play with Black ones, and they certainly didn't want such a thing happening near their home. This was far from the only reason Buxton was drawn to Althea, though. Buxton was Jewish and more than once had felt rejected as an outcast, both in South Africa and at popular tennis clubs in England; more refusals were to come. She understood that the adjectives used to describe Althea's skin color were not merely descriptive. Mostly, though, Buxton's interest was piqued by the older girl's powerful game of tennis and her aggressive net play, which were unlike anything she had seen before.

On a warm afternoon in late June, Althea was due to play in the London Grass Court Championships at the elegant brick Queen's Club in West Kensington, an enormously popular pre-Wimbledon warm-up event that provided a glimpse of the competitions to come a little over a week later. Still wearing her school uniform, Buxton caught the bus after school and headed to the club, where she was also a member. As she approached Court No. 9, she noticed a crowd several people deep at the court's edge, and then she saw Althea. She had on shorts and a sleeveless vest atop a polo shirt—what some might consider men's clothing—and she was hitting the ball with a force that Buxton had not thought a woman even capable of, her face expressionless. Following her serve, Althea stormed toward the net, her angular form an arc of determination.

"I was stunned. I mean she didn't look like a female at all; she looked exactly like a man," Buxton recalled. "She hit the ball so hard, and then she charged up to the net. I thought, *I think I'd like to play like that someday.* I went right up to her after her first match and asked for her autograph, which she gave me. She entranced people because everything about her was so different."[73]

The term *different* was not high on the list of esteemed values at the exclusive All England Lawn Tennis and Croquet Club, which had hosted the venerable Wimbledon Championships, the world's fabled tennis tournament, since its beginnings in 1877. On the contrary, tradition is something of a moral imperative on the impeccable grass lawns, where the holy Centre Court is forever shadowed by the epic achievements of the world's greatest tennis players, including René Lacoste, Helen Wills, Don Budge, Bill Tilden, Alice Marble, and Fred Perry.

Indeed, in the leafy Wimbledon suburb southwest of London, certain rituals are sacrosanct. The signature staple on the afternoon tea menu is fresh strawberries and clotted cream—Elsanta strawberries only, please—as it has been since shortly after the tournament's inception. Until early in this century, officials and referees following tradition religiously wore the championship colors of purple and green as players bowed toward the Royal Box chockful of titled aristocrats.[74] So, too, the care and feeding, as well as the daily vacuuming, of the much-manicured green grass beneath the players' feet has long been a perennial topic of fascination, invariably scrutinized in the British coverage of the opening day of the Championships and its progressive condition carefully monitored throughout the tournament. Since 1930, the hundreds of balls used daily are refrigerated at courtside in order to maintain a consistent temperature and bounce.[75]

Wimbledon is as much a state of mind as it is a premier world sporting event. During the "dedicated fortnight" of play, as it is customarily called, thousands of fans make the annual pilgrimage to the packed site to be a part of the ritual summer spectacle. Some spend up to two nights in an interminable queue, camping out or cramped in their cars, in order to pay top dollar for a standing-room-only position. Wimbledon is, in short, as much the shimmering mecca of the sport of tennis as it is an unabashed paean to privilege, fuss, and excess. In June 1968, *The New Yorker*'s John McPhee penned a lengthy profile of the keeper of the then 930 square yards of lawn at Wimbledon, the craggy-featured Robert Twynam. The curator of the famed grass courts for forty-four years, Twynam frequently crawled across the immaculate green terrain examining individual blades of grass and, every day of the tennis fortnight, helped pull the Old Horse Roller across the courts, by hand, with four other men. Even when a match was in session, Twynam might leap to repair any court damage that occurred by filling it in with a mix of clay and grass, "which he sutures into place with matchsticks while the crowd and the competitors look on." Guiding McPhee through the exclusive Members' Enclosure, where straw parasols shaded white tables, Twynam nodded to a fountain pool stocked with lilies and goldfish. The goldfish were supplied by Harrods, the world's leading luxury department store, located in central London. "Nice goldfish," Twynam observed one day, "but expensive."[76]

In the seventy-four years since its inception, not a single African American had played there until the rainy morning of June 26, 1951, when Althea Gibson walked onto Centre Court in her white shorts and matching white shirt. Nor were there many of her race in the stands or nibbling on strawberries and cream. Ollie Stewart, the *Baltimore Afro-American*'s Paris correspondent covering the event, noted that as he wandered among the women dressed in their elegant best and the men sporting bowler hats and canes that day, "I didn't see a single child. And not until the second day did I see another colored person besides myself and Althea Gibson."[77]

Althea arrived at a moment widely recognized as a golden age of women's tennis, one dominated by a cadre of American women who had managed to keep playing the game during the tumultuous years of World War II, while their European counterparts had not. In the decade following the war, American players—including over a dozen dominant young female players such as Louise Brough, Margaret duPont, Doris Hart, and Maureen Connolly—introduced a more competitive, aggressive style that would come to characterize the sport. As British historian and vice president of the All England Lawn Tennis and Croquet Club John Barrett wrote in *Wimbledon: The Official History*, "The admirable professionalism, keen competitiveness and technical competence of this new breed of aggressive player set the standard for the rest of the world to follow."[78] The top women players were nonetheless a familial group. Some were intimate friends who had gone to school together and traveled the tournament circuit in pairs; others were more casual clusters of sporting buddies. When traveling the tennis circuit, they often attended the same cocktail parties in the evening or shared sleeping quarters at the homes of local hosts. *World Tennis* magazine regularly chronicled seminal events in players' lives, such as births, engagements, and hospitalizations, in its "Around the World" column, and featured photos of them gathered at elaborate dinners and festive cocktail parties in which Althea rarely appeared.

With her dark skin and overt aggression, Althea was cut from an entirely different cloth other "girls" found alien and abrasive. Some were flat-out rude to her, while others coolly ignored her. Emotionally inured after years of being subjected to incidents of racial abuse like name-calling and insults, Althea had developed a hard shell around herself that was at times difficult even for the well-intentioned to penetrate. Over the years, she would find an occasional tennis friend here and there, but those with whom she did connect were generally outsiders or loners much like her and young Buxton, who had asked for her autograph. For the most part, Althea was on her own.

The social isolation that Althea experienced in London, as well as the unrelenting press scrutiny, were leavened somewhat by several perks she

enjoyed there. On her arrival, she was pleased to find that the British sporting goods manufacturer Slazenger had left her a set of new tennis rackets
for use in the days ahead. Like the other players, she enjoyed a private car
that ferried her to the tennis club each day. Thanks to her old buddy Sugar
Ray, who bankrolled part of her trip, she was also able to indulge in a
steak dinner every other day and periodic visit to the flickers. Although
she steadfastly refused to tell reporters where she was staying, Althea acknowledged that she had found the time to do a bit of sightseeing and had
made a visit to the houses of Parliament.[79]

On the day of Althea's debut at Wimbledon, the heavens were once
again as uncooperative as they had been at Forest Hills the year before. A
chilly rain fell intermittently for much of the afternoon, delaying play and
heightening anticipation. Among her crowd of supporters in the damp
stands were photographer Gordon Parks and Robinson, who had recently arrived from Paris, where he had been training for some upcoming
bouts. The big attractions in the women's singles were defending champion Louise Brough, whose ability to retain her supremacy had been
thrown into question by a painful tennis elbow, and Doris Hart, third
seed and the sentimental favorite, who had twice made it to the finals
in previous years. Althea, who had lost to both women previously and
was unseeded, waited more than three hours for the skies to clear before
officials finally signaled that play could begin, reminding herself to stay
focused on the court.

"You're not going to look around. You're not going to listen to any calls
or remarks," she told herself. "All you are going to do is watch the tennis
ball."[80]

In the beginning, she did just that. Given a bye in the first round—
meaning that because of the random draw, she was permitted to automati-
cally advance to the next round without playing an opponent—Althea was
paired in the second round against Pat Ward, a solid British player whose
attractive appearance seemed to be of greater interest to the press than any
performance by Althea, identified as the "first negress ever to play in the
championships." Even when the visibly anxious Ward fell to the ground
during the match, she "still managed to typify the spirit of 'glamorous'
Wimbledon," the *Daily Mail* exclaimed.[81] In fact, Ward, also appearing on

Centre Court for the first time, was so nervous during the first set that she was unable to garner a single game, and Althea cruised to a 6–0 victory. Ward recovered in the second set and delivered a steady series of ground shots that derailed Althea before she managed to rally with her powerful serve. Althea finally took the match 6–0, 2–6, 6–4. Among those in the stands watching the play was the historian John Barrett, then a competitive tennis player, who would go on to become captain of the British Davis Cup team.

"I marveled at the physique and power of this amazing woman, who was a stronger version of [Louise] Brough," Barrett recalled in an interview. "I thought that was a man playing at first, but of course it wasn't."[82]

Althea was warmly applauded as she left the court, and later in the press. But even *American Lawn Tennis* magazine nodded to the British woman's attractive appearance, as was common in the day, in its description of the match. "The good-looking English girl was within a point of a love set before the American rallied to win the next two games. . . . Miss Gibson's superior service, which rivals Louse Brough's, and a volleying arm that stretches out almost too far to be fair in women's tennis, turned the scales in the well-fought third set," the magazine wrote.[83]

The Associated Press was equally enthused, saying, "Although the tall Negro girl is unseeded, she convinced the British experts that she has the equipment to rank high in the world within another year or two. She received warm applause as she left the court."[84]

In the third round, Althea faced a far more formidable opponent in Beverly Baker, a blond Californian as famous for her ambidextrous hitting style as her vivacious romantic life, who was seeded fifth in the women's singles. Baker's unusual technique used two forehand strokes, one hit with her right hand and one with her left, as she shifted her racket from one hand to the other mid-play. Sticking close to the baseline, always her comfort zone, Baker pounded her passing shots out of Althea's reach as she followed her serve to the net and easily took the first set 6–1. In the second set, Althea tried to lure Baker to the net with a series of drop shots, but she committed so many errors that Baker easily closed out the match 6–3. The unimpressive match took less than one hour.

And so it was that the Harlem girl's much-trumpeted debut at the world pinnacle of tennis ended with a whimper. But while Althea had not played her best, many felt she had performed well given the challenging circumstances facing her at Wimbledon.

Tennis historian Richard Hillway, coauthor of *The Birth of Lawn Tennis*, says he was not at all surprised by Althea's defeat. Baker, he said, "was simply a better player than Althea in the early 1950s. . . . To me, it was so obvious that Baker would win. Baker had all the shots, and so I considered it great practice for Althea. What [Gibson] should have thought afterward is, 'Now I know what I am up against. Now I know how to practice.' I see it as the beginning of her rise."[85]

The outcome of her performance in the remaining matches did not do a great deal to boost Althea's record. In the women's doubles, she was compelled to withdraw when her partner, the French Nelly Adamson, failed to show. Althea and her mixed doubles partner, Narendra Nath of India, made it to the third round, where they were defeated by Frank Sedgman and Doris Hart, 6–8. 6–8. The takeaway for many was that given another year or two of practice, Althea would be back. As Frank Rostron of the *London Daily Express* concluded, "Miss Baker's fierce barrage of ambidextrous fore-arm drives from either flank exposed the immaturity of the long-limbed Althea's game. . . . But inexperienced Althea will benefit from this first Wimbledon visit."[86]

Althea publicly agreed, telling reporters that she had gained valuable experience and planned to do better the next time. She had very much enjoyed her time in London and all of the largely positive attention she received from both the press and the crowds. What was apparent in the wake of her performance, however, was that she was not yet equipped to defeat world-class players. Althea had a volcanic serve and a stunning athletic ability, to be sure. But her game was erratic, and her trademark aggression at times undercut her performance. Perhaps more important, although she had achieved something enormous in integrating both Forest Hills and Wimbledon, the loss of both tournaments had seriously undermined her confidence. Confronted with the additional stressors of financial insecurity and the perennial media scrutiny, Althea was left in a state of uncertainty that would periodically undermine her tennis in the years to come.

With two more tournaments still ahead of her, she prepared to head to

Germany, but before she left London, she had one more thing to do. Sugar Ray, who was soon to square off with British champion Randy Turpin, was still in the city. Worn down by Wimbledon whiteness, Althea had been thrilled to see her Harlem hero and his enormous entourage pull into Piccadilly with all guns blazing, as always, in an eighteen-foot flamingo-pink Cadillac followed by two Rolls-Royces, two more Cadillacs, and a twenty-foot coach. A grinning Sugar Ray, who had helped finance Althea's Wimbledon expenses, jumped out of the car and onto the sidewalk, where Althea planted an enormous kiss on his cheek before dozens of photographers.[87]

The boxer, wary of sampling the unfamiliar British cuisine before his big fight, was having his wife cook his dinner each night at their hotel. So, on her way out of town, Althea, eager to contribute to his nourishing diet, hand-delivered a batch of steaks she had remaining from a stockpile that had sustained her through her Wimbledon experience. As it turned out, Harlem wasn't really so far away after all.[88]

6

"The Biggest Flop"

One of Althea's first stops after she returned to Tallahassee following her Wimbledon debut in 1951 was at a graying clapboard building crowned by a miniature cupola a few blocks off campus. After a demanding summer overseas, she did not immediately return to tennis or her beloved flickers or any of her other usual pastimes. Instead, she headed straight to St. Michael & All Angels Church, an Episcopalian house of worship originally established with the help of a former enslaved person, to which a persuasive priest frequently enticed FAMC freshmen with the promise of a home-cooked meal or an evening of games.[1] As the fall took hold, and the leaves became touched with a hint of rust, Althea showed up at the church with increasing regularity.

"She sat very quietly, mostly by herself, her hands folded in her lap," recalled Dr. Robert Smith, a retired FAMC sociology professor whose class Althea attended. "She always sat in a middle row, or to the rear. She was not the kind of person to sit in a front row seat."[2]

That humble young woman in the trim dress was not a person that either the students on the FAMC campus or the players on the national tennis circuit would have recognized. The Althea they knew would likely have commanded a center seat in the front row, or might well have bribed them into letting her take their place in that front row. In the fall of 1951, however, Althea was confronting a collision of roiling issues that undermined her confidence and threatened to derail her tennis career. Her unlikely appearance at St. Michael was less an act of faith than one of desperation, as she faced a critical turning point in her life. The real question looming before her was what her priority should be, her schooling or her tennis career. Just as confounding was the question of who among her ever-widening band of advisers, her doctor mentors or the cadre of ATA officials who seemed determined to call the shots, she should listen to. The doctors were on the academic side of the line, while the ATA leaders, not surprisingly, stressed tennis above all. Althea's performance during the tournament season just past, which she regarded as mediocre at best, further clouded her thinking. The St. Michael church arose as a steady mooring in the otherwise turbulent seas lapping around her that fall.

To much of the tennis world, Althea's showing in the previous months demonstrated how very far she had come in the sport to which she had dedicated so much of her young adulthood. She may not have won Wimbledon, but she easily won the women's singles at the Dortmund International tennis tournament in Dortmund, Germany, afterward. To Althea, however, the past season made clear just how far she had to go. She was disappointed in her performance on the British grass courts earlier in the year, and even more so in her second appearance at Forest Hills a couple of months afterward, where she was soundly defeated by the sixteen-year-old rising star Maureen Connolly. Also, as she moved into the international tennis arena, the widespread press emphasis on the color of her skin reinforced the enormous burden of race that weighed heavily on her, leaving her more ambivalent than ever. Being the lone Black player at the most demanding level of competition, with the press scrutinizing her every move, right down to her choice of tennis outfit, was overwhelming. Nor did she have a single soul mate on the white tennis circuit in whom she could confide, or the team support that Jackie Robinson and so many others in this class of firsts had enjoyed. The other, and perhaps more significant, aspect of Robinson that she lacked was obvious personal appeal, a crucial component of winning over the daily press. So moody, unpredictable, and downright full of herself did Althea appear at times that some reporters threw up their hands. Stacking her up against male athletes of the day, one writer dubbed her "Jackie Robinson without charm," while another dismissed her as "Ted Williams without his skills."[3] Faced with such derision, Althea was uncertain if she could meet the challenge of breaking into white tennis, or if she even wanted to try.

Back at school, there was still more to contend with. As ever, Althea grappled with a perennial shortage of money and the pressure to complete her college degree. Making matters worse, she had two incomplete courses to make up as a result of her long period away from school in the first half of the year. If she didn't devote more time to her coursework, she would never graduate. But if she didn't practice long hours and travel the circuit, she wouldn't be able to compete. For a twenty-four-year-old with virtually no financial or familial support, despite her network of parental substitutes, it was immobilizing. So, when Father David Brooks, the amiable Black St. Michael's priest, reached out his hand to her, she seized it.

"On the first day of the semester, Father Brooks would go up on campus and shake the freshmen's hands and say, 'Welcome. Why, I bet you miss your mother's cooking, don't you? Why don't you come on down to the church on Friday night. I can guarantee you a meal and a night of games,'" recounted Rev. Hugh Chapman, the rector of St. Michael & All Angels Church. "He never took no for an answer. He had a great love of people, was deeply involved in civil rights, and was a well-liked counselor to both students and faculty on campus."[4]

Althea was largely a newcomer to organized religion. Few members of her extended family had much association with it, and she rarely attended church during her childhood. One of her earliest mentors who propelled her toward sports was Rev. Marsden Burnell, the coach of the Mysterious Girls basketball team in Harlem on which she played in the late 1940s. Her first real exposure to the interior of a house of faith had apparently come a decade later, when she began spending time with the Darben family, who were all enthusiastic members of the Baptist church where they regularly took Althea on Sundays. Now she was turning to a church popular among other students in an effort to find answers to the intractable issues that loomed over her life and tennis career.

To be sure, there were plenty of interested parties hovering about Althea, ranging from the overeager ATA administrators to her more discerning doctor mentors and some FAMC administrators. As she matured, though, Althea was increasingly aware of the hard truth that she had confronted

as a young girl on the streets of Harlem, which was that she was funda-
mentally alone. As she came to realize that some of the acclaim engulfing
her had as much to do with the interests of Black tennis as it did with her
own personal accomplishment or well-being, she turned to the God that
had anchored so many in the Black community for so long. In later years,
Althea did not talk a great deal about her faith, but she remained a regular churchgoer. Asked by a reporter in her post-tennis years why she had
routinely observed a moment of silence before her matches, she admitted,
"I pray."[5]

In January 1952, Althea wrote to Eaton that she was discontent and
wanted a different environment. Increasingly, she believed that there was
not enough interest in her tennis at FAMC to provide her with the training and experience she so very much needed. As a result, she felt her tennis was being negatively impacted. She then introduced something wholly
new to their conversation, which was God. A few months earlier, she revealed, she had joined the Episcopal church. With God's help, she added,
she hoped to develop other aspects of herself beyond tennis. With a closing
inquiry about Eaton's golf game, she signed off.[6]

Ten months later, Althea was baptized at the altar of the St. Michael &
All Angels Church, and the following day she was confirmed along with
three other women. From that day on, Althea was a regular in the church's
hard-backed wooden pews on Sundays, briefly removed from the competition and stress that had dominated her life on campus just a few blocks
away. In later years she revealed to a reporter that, at one point in her
career, she was so frustrated with tennis that she almost gave up the sport
entirely, until she consulted with a minister and decided to reenter competition. Given the timing of her embrace of the St. Michael church and the
anguish reflected in her letters to Eaton at the same time, it is highly likely
that it was Father Brooks, who was also FAMC's Episcopal chaplain, with
whom Althea consulted.

There was more to Althea's uncertainty than her performance at Wimbledon and the handful of European tournaments that followed. She had
also not done her best at some of the fall tournaments held on American
soil. While the quality of her game had grown more consistent, and she
had learned, from watching other players, the benefits of diversifying her

strokes, she had shown a repeated tendency to come out of the box with a strong showing only to wilt in the face of a determined opponent, which many observers attributed to a lack of self-confidence. Althea also found herself at the center of a complex debate in the Black community regarding the possible consequences of the integration of tennis. If she, like Reginald Weir and eventually others among the most talented Black players, migrated entirely to the white USLTA competitions, the ATA would soon be decimated. It was the same dilemma that would arise with the integration of other aspects of American life, ranging from sports to education and beyond, as the Black community struggled to retain its ethnic identity and the quality of its own institutions. Increasingly, the question of whose interests prevailed, Althea's or that of Black tennis in general, was coming into play.

The subject was one of constant discussion in the Black press throughout the decade. Ever since Althea had come onto the ATA scene in the 1940s, Black sportswriters had watched her development with keen interest and had overwhelmingly applauded her advance to Forest Hills. In the years immediately following her 1950 debut, however, they grew impatient. Although Althea was ranked eleventh in 1951 by the USLTA, some reporters and columnists were chafing by midyear at the slow pace of her ascent on the national tennis scene. In May, Alvin Moses of the Black newspaper *Atlanta Daily World* quoted a recent magazine as saying, "Now that gangling Althea Gibson has 'arrived' in white company, there are those who suspect that she'll never again reach the heights that she attained in the 1950 Nationals at Forest Hills." Althea, the story continued, "has a tendency to wilt under fire. Her strokes become erratic in the clutch, and her general court tactics do not help create the impression that she knows what she's doing."[7]

Even Sam Lacy, who had been extolling Althea's potential since 1944, began to quietly grumble. In a September 1951 column, he quoted her description of all that she had learned during the past summer's competition abroad and her newfound appreciation for the importance of mastering a variety of strokes rather than just one or two. Lacy was still not happy with the results, concluding, "Experimentation has played havoc with Althea's tennis. . . . She is not as good as she was at this time last year."[8]

The role of "First Negro" was clearly growing increasingly complex.

Over the next four years, Althea would grapple with her life's direction, struggling to decide whether to continue in the role of racial pioneer or, instead, embrace the more relaxed pace of a singing career or a job as a tennis coach. She would come perilously close to quitting the sport at which she so excelled, but for a wholly unexpected invitation—ironically, one born of the racial turmoil beginning to churn hotly across the nation in the mid-1950s—that would determine the course of her life.

In the meantime, her "first" status continued to offer perks. In August, Althea was fêted at a lavish reception in the Peacock Lounge at the Waldorf Astoria hotel in Manhattan, where she was welcomed back home by New York City mayor Vincent Impellitteri and presented with awards from prominent supporters, including William H. Hastie, the first Black person to serve as governor of the U.S. Virgin Islands and a judge on the U.S. Circuit Court of Appeals. Photographers captured Althea, dressed in an elegant white suit, at the ATA-sponsored event, her beaming parents and sister Mildred at her side.

Three months later, glasses were again raised for Althea when Bethune-Cookman College, now University, proclaimed an "Althea Gibson Day," complete with a parade that escorted her from the local train station to the Daytona Beach campus for a series of celebratory events. Althea addressed a packed auditorium, where she was showered with gifts and presented with a trophy by Mary McLeod Bethune, a prominent civil rights leader and the college's first president.[9]

Althea's subsequent performance that fall, however, did not quite live up to either of those billings. In the aftermath of Wimbledon, she had been buoyed by victories at both the Essex Championships in Frinton-on-Sea, England, and the Dortmund tournament in Germany, where she defeated former Czechoslovakian champion Hannah Kozeluh 6–3, 6–2. Back in the United States, she scored a resounding triumph at the ATA National Championships at Wilberforce, Ohio, cruising easily through five rounds in which she lost only a single game out of a total of sixty, thus claiming the women's singles title for the fifth time at the end of a long, brutally hot day. In mixed doubles, however, she and Dr. Johnson, the reigning titleholders and first seed, fumbled and lost in the semifinals after Althea double-faulted at match point following a fiercely battled three-set match against Quentin Vaughan and Nana Davis, Althea's longtime ATA foe. Davis and Vaughan, scheduled to be married the following month, clasped sweaty hands as the stunned audience roared at the upset in the gathering dusk.[10] Althea and Johnson attributed her error to the strain of an accelerated schedule; the ATA had permitted her to play multiple matches in a day, so she could leave the tournament a day early to make it to Forest Hills on time. As Johnson explained it, "She has been playing too much tennis under this rush schedule."[11]

Part of the strain may also have stemmed from a flare-up between the ATA and Althea after she briefly considered committing an act of minor betrayal—skipping the ATA event to practice on grass courts in New York in preparation for her appearance at Forest Hills. Althea ran the idea by both Eaton and Johnson, but the two men responded with differing advice. Johnson encouraged her to skip the ATA tournament, reasoning that the additional grass experience would only benefit her performance at Forest Hills and therefore the ATA. Eaton disagreed, urging her to remember those who had so contributed to her progress. In the end, Althea remained loyal to the ATA tournament, but somewhere along the way, Baker got wind of her considering skipping the ATA event, and he angrily put his foot down.

James Booker, writing for the *Baltimore Afro-American*, reported that the angry ATA brass had drawn a hard line and declared that if Althea did not play in the Black tournament, she would not appear at Forest Hills at all.[12] Asked about the threat when she arrived at the Wilberforce tournament, she declared, "I don't know what all the talk's about—I'm here to play tennis at Wilberforce." But that wasn't the end of the incident. On the same day, Bertram Baker told the paper that the ATA had "ruled that Miss Gibson's tennis program would be outlined by Mr. Baker's office." Asked about this, Althea demurred. "Nobody told me anything about running my tennis program. It's the first I've heard of it."[13]

Further roiling the racial waters at the ATA tournament was the appearance of a contingent of eleven white tennis players. Although the organization's leadership had expressly invited the white group in the interest of integration as embraced in its founding charter, not all those attending were in agreement. Early on, some Black players vocally expressed their unhappiness, declaring that the event was an "all-Negro tournament," according to a story in the *Pittsburgh Courier*. In an echo of Althea's own painful experience at Forest Hills a year earlier, the grumbling got even louder as challenger Norman Appel, a white attorney from Dayton, appeared to be headed to victory in the semifinals against Carl Williams in the men's singles. "Most depressing was the few malcontents in the stands who failed to appreciate the significance of the play of whites in the tournament, and the splendid thing being done by the ATA. They applauded errors made by Appel and voiced their desire that Williams should win."[14]

Although Appel won the round, George Stewart, one of the ATA's most powerful players, defeated him in the men's singles final. However, the integration of tennis, clearly, was not going to be easy, despite the optimistic headlines that appeared in some newspapers at the tournament's end, such as that which ran in the *Pittsburgh Courier*: "ATA Passes Democracy Test at Annual Tournament."[15]

Days later, Althea, likely anticipating similar flak from the opposite direction, squared her shoulders and strode back onto the court, this time on the green velvet lawns of Forest Hills. She won the first two rounds and made it to the quarterfinals, where she confronted the daunting California wunderkind Maureen Connolly. Two years later, in 1953, Connolly would become the first woman to win a calendar Grand Slam—achieving victory in all four major tournaments during the same calendar year—at just eighteen years old, and she would ultimately take a total of nine Grand Slam singles titles. Connolly, whose petite stature belied her powerful forehand and backhand, which had earned her the nickname "Little Mo," in reference to the immense firepower of the battleship USS *Missouri*, known as "Big Mo," was a force to reckon with. Connolly's skills had been expertly honed by legendary instructor Eleanor "Teach" Tennant, coach to such champions as Alice Marble and Bobby Riggs, who had ingrained in the young champion the strategic importance of hating her opponents.[16] Althea had lost to Connolly just several weeks earlier, at the Eastern Grass Court Championships, and did so again at Forest Hills. Although the crowd got excited when Althea managed to pull neck-and-neck at 4–4 in the second set with her aggressive net assault, Connolly overwhelmed her with a series of pounding returns and won 6–2, 6–4.[17] The *Baltimore Afro-American*, which was not impressed by Althea's performance, pointed out that anytime Althea won a point, "it was primarily due to the fact the youthful Maureen had maneuvered herself out of position. Rarely did Miss Gibson score by virtue of her own strategy."[18]

Althea made it to the quarterfinals in the mixed doubles with Don Candy of Australia, but notably, she did not play in the women's doubles. In fact, her appearance in women's doubles was inconsistent throughout her entire career. In all of the nine years she competed in the U.S. National Championships, she played singles and mixed doubles each time, but played women's doubles only twice in the last two years of her career. At some of the smaller tournaments on the circuit, she played women's and mixed doubles, just as she did in each of her four appearances at Wimbledon. At the ATA national tournaments, however, it appears she did not play women's doubles once in her entire eleven years of play, likely in part because she focused her energy on the mixed doubles competition that she won seven times with her partner Dr. Johnson.

Althea appears to have steered clear of other doubles matches for a variety of reasons, one of the main ones being race. In fact, she did not blend well with the women's tennis group as much because of her remote nature and apparent arrogance as because of the color of her skin and her humble background. According to several women who played the circuit, the tall Black newcomer was generally kept at a good arm's length by most of the other players. She was often not invited to impromptu meals or social events and was subtly circumvented even in the locker room. On the tournament circuit, players would routinely pin up weekly stories about the goings-on a bulletin board or wall, using nicknames for the players involved, like "Broughie" for Louise Brough or "the Head" for Dottie Head Knode. Althea was neither mentioned in these postings nor given a nickname that would have folded her into the women's elite tennis sorority.[19] For the veteran women players, many of whom had come in contact with Black people only when they were being waited on or when passing them on the street, it was too much to absorb. Impassive, Althea feigned not to notice any of it. Why even try to find a doubles partner among the entrenched and at times overtly unfriendly members of the women's crowd at Forest Hills?

Angela Buxton, who won the women's doubles with Althea at both Wimbledon and the French Championships in 1956 and became her life-long friend, well remembers the way Althea was dodged, and not just on the doubles front. As Buxton describes it, "To tell you the truth, no one would speak to her in those days let alone play with her. . . . To get down to the nitty-gritty, it was because she was Black. And she wasn't educated. Her parents weren't educated. She was completely isolated. I was, too, because I am Jewish."[20]

Despite Buxton's relatively privileged upbringing, she and Althea found common ground in part because of their lifelong experience with discrimination and social ostracism. They did not, however, talk a great deal about it. It was no accident that it was another Jewish woman whom Althea found as a doubles partner, Gladys Heldman, who played the circuit for a few years before founding *World Tennis* magazine in 1953 and becoming a fierce advocate for women's tennis. Heldman was thrilled to have "Big Al," as Althea had been dubbed in her early tennis days, for her doubles partner and sometimes invited her out for dinner, according to Heldman's daughter.

"The prejudice was so grim that many of the best white women players shunned [Althea] socially and refused to play doubles with her," Julie Heldman wrote in her autobiography, *Driven: A Daughter's Odyssey*. "Mom hated those players' ugly prejudice, and she was happy to befriend Althea. Grateful, Althea chose Mom as her doubles partner several times, even though Mom was ranked much lower than 'Big Al.' Mom told us that the grass court clubs were the most prejudiced. She said one tournament shut its doors permanently rather than invite Althea."[21]

Race alone, however, didn't explain Althea's spotty participation in women's doubles, given her absence from those matches in the Black ATA tournaments. Another likely reason, according to both men and women who played doubles with her, was that she was famously domineering and not the easiest person to partner with on the court. In the 1950s, men generally dominated mixed doubles pairings and routinely served first. Not so with Althea, who more than once informed a stunned partner that "Big Althea will go first."[22]

Neale Fraser, an Australian champion player who was ranked No. 1 in the world in 1959, remembers Althea declaring that she would take the first serve when the two of them played together at Wimbledon in 1957, a particularly notable turf claim given that the left-handed Fraser had one of the best serves of the era. Sometimes when a ball streaked down the middle line or even on Fraser's side, Althea would shout, "Mine," before lunging for the kill. "I think we had a clash of M-I-N-E-S, not M-I-N-D-S," recalled Fraser, in his late eighties, who served as captain of the Australian Davis Cup for over two decades. "Althea was not prone to taking advice from a younger Australian. She had won the singles that day. She was on a high. All I can say is that she wished to play her part."

Fraser, twenty-three when he was paired with Althea, says that given Althea's win in the singles, she would likely have had her pick of a number of male partners with a higher ranking than he, who had lost three previous Wimbledon mixed doubles events. As he puts it, "I was second kettle, third kettle off the rank. You know, others must have turned her down. But there was no chance of me turning down a Wimbledon champion."[23]

Richard Hillway, the tennis historian, suggests that Althea may also have opted not to play women's doubles because many of the women were simply not up to her level of play, especially in the ATA. Her goal, he points out, "was to be a champion, not to make friends. It is also true that many of the female players at the highest level had long-standing doubles partners, such as Louise Brough and Margaret duPont, and Doris Hart and Shirley Fry, from whom they were not about to stray."

Hillway also suspects that Althea may have been simply saving her energy.

"Perhaps Althea felt that entering three divisions in a single tournament was just too much. She might have become too tired to win the singles, her real prize. This would have been especially true in the ATA tournaments, where she sometimes had to play at least three or four matches in the same day, because she kept winning," he said. "In any case, it is undeniable that Althea Gibson did regularly avoid women's doubles in the most significant tournaments."[24]

When she returned to Tallahassee in the fall of 1951, Althea tried to get back into the swing of things. Because of her busy spring travel schedule during her college years, "the Gib" found herself struggling each fall to catch up with what had been happening during her absence. In her junior and senior years, she had taken up babysitting for the children of some of the school's coaches, in order to make some money, and that also took her away from student social life. Lucille Alexander, a classmate in the same dorm, remembers that, in between tournaments, Althea sometimes wandered into her room looking to talk.

"She'd come to your room and sit on your bed and ask about what was going on," recalled Alexander, a nursing student at the time. "She wanted to know what had happened while she was away."

Althea also turned up frequently at mail call, when packages from students' homes, often containing yummy snacks, were delivered. The ever-hungry Althea, explained Alexander, "always knew whose mama sent what cake, cookies or whatever. I don't know how she knew, but she did. She always knew those people because I don't think Althea was ever fooled."[25]

That fall, Althea took predominantly physical education courses and a lightweight course in folk and tap dancing that she thought might ease her academic burden. She apparently enjoyed it so much that when she worked as an assistant teacher at Tallahassee's Bond Elementary School in her senior year, she managed to raise enough money to buy tap shoes for all the children in her class, so that she could teach them to dance. She also borrowed a handful of tennis rackets and balls from faculty and staff. When the children were not permitted to play on the few public courts that allowed Black players, Althea, according to her teacher supervisor, Eva Mannings, led a parade of children and their tennis rackets into the nearby woods to play.

"She'd say, 'Who wants to play tennis?'" recalled Mannings. "About ten kids would head into the woods with her, and they'd all come back *oooooh-weeeeeee* about tennis. They all loved it."[26]

In the early months of 1952, Althea's priorities vacillated wildly between tennis and her academics. One month after she wrote Eaton in January saying she wanted to leave campus in order to focus on tennis, she wrote again saying that she was thinking of quitting tennis in order to concentrate on her courses. Althea had asked Coach Gaither to tell Bertram Baker that she did not want to play in the National Indoors in the early spring for that reason. But Baker had telephoned Gaither immediately to insist that she play in order to maintain her national ranking of No. 11.

As a result, Althea wrote to Eaton, she was training around the clock to improve her strength.[27]

In the end, Althea played in four tournaments that spring, not as many as Baker might have wished, but more than she would have liked, and she missed out on much of campus life. When photos were taken that spring for the 1952 yearbook, the *Rattler*, of the Rattlers Net Squad, FAMC's tennis team, and of the women's basketball team, Althea was absent. Presumably, she was either away at a tournament or engaged in a brutal daily practice regimen as she prepared to make her fourth appearance in the high-profile National Indoor Championships. As the *Tallahassee Democrat* reported under the headline "Althea Gibson Sharpening Game," Althea was training with one of Florida's male champion players in the FAMC gym, "in two three hours daily sessions."[28]

It wasn't enough. Althea played better than she had two years before, when she made it to the finals in the tournament, but was nonetheless beaten 6–4, 6–4 in the semifinals in her fourth defeat at the hands of Nancy Chaffee Kiner, now married to Pittsburgh Pirates outfielder Ralph Kiner. Despite her loss in front of one of the largest crowds the indoor tournament had drawn in years, observers noted that Althea's game was overall more consistent and that her forehand had notably improved. Afterward, she claimed to have discovered a vulnerability in Kiner's game and predicted, "I think I can defeat her if we meet again."[29] Althea, or "Al," as *Baltimore Afro-American* columnist James Hicks had begun referring to her, also approached the net and playfully congratulated Kiner, asking jokingly, "Why don't you retire so I can win your crown?"[30]

Meanwhile, Althea's continued inability to break through to a higher level of the game and bring down players such as Kiner or Beverly Baker, who had married a man named John Fleitz and taken his last name, was prompting growing impatience in Black circles. Julius J. Adams, a columnist, director of the Global News Syndicate, and the former managing editor of the *New York Amsterdam News*, and often called the dean of the Black fourth estate, wrote that Althea was actually a better player than Chaffee, but that she suffered a "psychological handicap" that left her lacking the will to win or the championship spirit essential for victory. It appeared during the match, Adams wrote, "that she didn't possess the drive to rise to the occasion when a little extra effort might have meant victory. She looked as if she felt she was destined to defeat and was simply playing out her script." In conclusion, he wrote, "She just lacks, it seems, the champion's heart."[31]

The remainder of the spring of 1952 didn't go much better. Althea did not win any of the several tournaments in which she played over the following two months in Jamaica and Miami, and she was on the road for weeks at a time, away from her studies. Bertram Baker, who seemed to have taken control of her schedule, appeared unmoved by Althea's desire to finish her college education, so determined was he to propel her ever higher on the tennis ladder. In March, he wrote FAMC president Gore, whom he now deferentially addressed as "Dr." in his letters, rather than "Mr.," as he had before, to ask if Althea could play against Maureen Connolly in an exhibition match sponsored by the Chicago Tennis Patrons Association that May.[32] Gore, who had already turned down a request by the Pan American Tennis Association to have Althea play in Mexico City the previous fall, saying she had taken too many leaves of absence, apparently agreed. Althea played the match and even managed to take the second set off Connolly, who was unsteady on the hardwood floors of the Chicago Arena, but Althea ultimately lost 6–1, 4–6, 6–1.[33]

By the end of the spring, Baker apparently began to listen to his star player, or at least to recognize from her string of losses that the combined pressure of school and tennis had become too much to bear. At the end of May, he wrote to Slazenger, the London manufacturer that had sponsored her previous year's tour, to say that she would not be competing at Wimbledon this year. Given that she had only one year left before graduation, Althea, he explained, did not want to have to seek special permission again to take her examinations early.[34]

Althea had hoped to remain at school for the summer, but unable to secure a summer scholarship, she returned to the Eatons' to practice and play the circuit. Things began to brighten, at least briefly. One of her first destinations was Hamilton, Bermuda, where she had been invited to participate in the Black Somers Isle Lawn Tennis Association's first International Tennis Tournament. Not only did she sweep easily to victory in both the women's singles and mixed doubles competitions, but she trounced the country's male champions in exhibition matches as well.

164 • ALTHEA

That clean sweep turned out to be only one of many pleasures she enjoyed on her first visit to the Bermuda archipelago, which observed strict racial divisions as rigid as those in the United States. Starting on the night of her arrival, she was fêted with sightseeing events, a moonlight picnic, deep-sea fishing, and a parade of parties. At a Leopards Club luncheon, Althea thrilled the crowd when she rose to the microphone and sang three songs, including "Don't Take Your Love from Me."[35] Clearly enjoying herself, she extended her stay for two weeks, during which she went on a shopping spree for Eaton, buying him three pairs of white linen shorts. From her room in the elegant Imperial Hotel, she wrote him a buoyant letter, exclaiming that she was being given royal treatment and planned on taking a leisurely boat ride home, as she had never taken such a trip. Perhaps he would like her to buy him something else?[36]

On her return to the United States, the year resumed its disheartening course. Although she won some of the smaller tournaments and ATA events in which she played, she was unable to conquer the leading women of the day. Connolly, Brough, and Hart reigned supreme, a fact reinforced by Althea's disappointing showing at the U.S. Nationals. Facing the solemn Hart, the second seed, in the third round, Althea roared to a 5–3 lead in the first set, repeatedly rushing the net before faltering in the face of a more skillful opponent. Unable to hold on to her lead, the Associated Press reported, "Althea came completely apart, piled up error upon error and won only one more game."[37] She lost the first set 7–5 and, unable to sustain her opening assault, petered out in the second set, which she lost 6–1. As several observers pointed out, her performance was remarkably similar to that of 1950, when she had the formidable Louise Brough hard against the ropes only to collapse before losing the match when it resumed the following day. That afternoon, she was also eliminated from the mixed doubles in the second round, bowing yet again to the persistent Hart and her partner, Frank Sedgman.[38]

Hart, who was defeated in the finals by Connolly, took some satisfaction in beating Althea, whom she considered an ungracious loser. In one of their earliest encounters at the National Clay Court Championships in 1950, a time when Althea was still ragged around the edges, Althea approached her opponent after Hart had beaten her 6–2, 6–3, and expressed astonishment that she had won.

"She said to Hart, 'How come you beat me? I'm a much better player than you. I hit the ball harder. I move better. How come you beat me?'" Angela Buxton recalls Hart telling her. "Now, you don't say that to an opponent who's just beaten you. You may think it, but you certainly don't say it." Hart, infuriated, nonetheless remained characteristically cool. "She just smiled and walked away," added Buxton. "But she never liked [Althea] because of that. She was never her favorite person."[39]

Hart later said that Althea made similar unsportsmanlike remarks to other opponents. Such comments, she told an interviewer, "annoyed us as players. She was the only one I came in contact with who said those things. . . . I'd just bite my tongue and leave it at that."[40]

Despite Althea's losses, Black tennis in general was gaining traction on a couple of other fronts. In August, the heavy doors of the West Side Tennis Club creaked open a few inches wider to admit two Black men who were the first to compete in the men's singles of the U.S. Nationals. One was Reggie Weir, the first Black man to play in a USLTA tournament in 1948, and now on the outs with the ATA for drifting from its control. The other was wiry George Stewart, the Panamanian southpaw and ATA champion known for his heavy topspin. Both of them were ousted in the first round, although the aging Weir fought a riveting four-set battle against his opponent, one of the longest at the tournament.[41]

There was another bright light rising on the Black tennis horizon at the time, in the form of a sturdy, pigtailed thirteen-year-old whose story was not unlike Althea's. Her name was Lorraine Williams, and she was one of eight children being raised by her widowed mother in the shadow of the Prairie Tennis Club on the South Side of Chicago, one of the oldest African American tennis clubs in the nation. Lacking the funds to buy her athletically gifted daughter a racket, Williams's mother carved one for her out of used plywood, and by 1952 the girl had won nine trophies, four of them in tournaments against adults.[42] Like Althea, Williams had been mentored by a doctor. Two years earlier, a local dentist with a passion for tennis headed to the Prairie club to catch a glimpse of Althea, but as it turned out, Althea didn't make it. When he saw the little southpaw Williams return a couple of drop shots and smash an overhead, he forgot all about the older tennis star, or so said the story that splashed across the sports pages and the covers of the Black magazines that year.

Dr. W. G. Ewell, a Chicago dentist, and his wife were sorry not to see Althea, wrote the *Chicago Defender* in the spring of 1952. "But they may have seen something better. A lefthanded moppet romped back and forth across the court. . . . Her game was clever and she showed amazing poise. Dr. and Mrs. Ewell forgot about Althea."[43]

Even some of Althea's staunchest defenders, including tennis champion Mary Hardwick Hare, a close friend of Alice Marble who, along with her husband, avidly lobbied for more diversity in the sport, were dazzled by little Williams and predicted she could be a world champion, possibly greater than Althea. After Hare saw Williams play at the River Forest Tennis Club outside Chicago, she offered to coach her, just as she had done with Althea two years earlier. "She could be another Althea Gibson, or better," Hare said of Williams. "If she is given a chance to develop her natural talent while she is a child, she can go far."[44]

If Lorraine Williams was the rising Black female tennis star in early 1953, Althea was the descending one. Althea's game had improved over the past year, as her backhand strengthened, and she depended less exclusively on her formidable serve. But while her national ranking rose to an impressive No. 7 in 1953, she had yet to win a major national tournament or conquer any among the troupe of wavy-haired white women who dominated the national tennis scene. Support for Althea was fading, and she knew it. On the first day of the year, *Jet* magazine released its appraisal of the past year in sports. How did Althea Gibson stack up? One of the "biggest flops," declared writer A. S. "Doc" Young, a disciple of the *Chicago Defender*'s legendary senior sports columnist Fay Young, who six years earlier had taken sharp issue with Althea's rude behavior in his column. Doc Young, no relation to Fay Young, dubbed George Brown the other biggest flop. Brown was a UCLA student and the world's foremost broad jumper, who turned out to be a world-class disappointment when he fouled out at the 1952 Olympic Games in Helsinki. Now he and Althea, whom Doc

Young dismissively described as a "woman tennis player," had been tossed into the same sinking boat.

For more than a century, Black newspapers had assumed the task not just of reporting the news, but of working for positive social change by advocating for the causes and people they thought worthy. In the field of sports in particular, reporters and columnists had taken on the dual tasks of lobbying for integration and the equal treatment of Black athletes while also offering advice and counsel to those whom they thought worthy, people who were otherwise largely ignored by the white press. Nor did they hesitate to offer harsh criticism when they thought it necessary.

Althea's case was no exception. As Jennifer H. Lansbury lays out in detail in her book, the Black press had closely monitored Althea's rise from her early ATA tournaments to her groundbreaking first appearances at Forest Hills and Wimbledon. But the years that followed were disappointing ones, as "she managed to win everything in the ATA and nothing in the USLTA. She had been only a point away from beating a U.S. National champion in the late summer of 1950, but since then she could not even make it to the finals. During these barren years, black sportswriters reported her victories in the ATA but remained graciously silent over her struggles in the USLTA. They praised, advised, and encouraged, but they did not give up on her."[45]

Still, they didn't always make it easy for her. In the first week of the New Year, one Speaking of Sports column in the *New York Amsterdam News* summed up the feeling about Althea in some quarters: "One of the big questions to be answered during 1953 is the direction to be taken by Althea Gibson along the glory road. There is considerable speculation as to whether the lanky racquet swinger is over the hill or whether she just needs consistent campaigning on the big time wheel to make her realize her full potentiality."[46]

Others were far less patient. Cal Jacox, sports columnist for the *New Journal and Guide* in Norfolk, Virginia, suggested tartly that Althea justify her advance in the national rankings "by coming down to earth and concentrating on her tennis."[47] Still others, who had long chafed at Althea's sometimes impatient attitude toward the press, were even more critical.

The forthright Evelyn Cunningham, a journalist for the *Pittsburgh Courier* as famed for her towering height as for her dyed red hair, did not hold back in a piece titled "Things I'll Remember About Famous People." Of Althea, she would remember "the icicles that drip off the great tennis star. Sportswriters wax steadily about the girl's cool demeanor on the court, her stolid confidence. But she's impenetrable even in the street, on the campus, in the house. A real, cool kiddy."[48]

Althea, clearly, was developing a bit of a reputation among some members of the press. Part of the problem was that, in the early years of her tennis career in particular, she had become accustomed to doing things her own way, when and how she wanted to, just as she had as a child on the streets, and she resented having to explain herself to a curious group of reporters. In particular, she shirked from the inevitable questions that she felt pressed her into a Jackie Robinson kind of "First Negro" champion mold, with which she was distinctly uneasy. It was hard enough as a lone woman breaking the barrier for herself, much less for an entire race, excruciating at times when she sensed the hostile stares that bore into her back as she headed out onto the manicured country club lawns where, not so long ago, only white athletes had been permitted to play. The press by and large considered her posture selfish, and many reporters didn't hesitate to say so. As the years went on and her public image became increasingly high profile, Althea's relationship with the media would grow steadily more conflicted.

Rosemary Darben remembers trying to persuade Althea to be friendlier to some members of the press in the early 1950s, as her name repeatedly cropped up in the sports headlines. More than once, Rosemary recalled, Althea "would be yelling at a reporter trying to talk to her. I'd say, 'Be cool. You can't do that.' She'd say to a reporter, 'It's none of your business, blah, blah, blah.' And I would tell her, 'That's not the way you deal with a reporter because they're going to go right out and say you're rude and this and that.'"[49]

As Althea began to play in more prominent tournaments, Rosemary says she didn't quite grasp how significant her role in racial politics was becoming. When she did realize it, she recoiled from both her role and the press's escalating interest in her. "She didn't want to do it," Rosemary said of the media's request for interviews. "She thought people were prying into her life. And I said, 'They're not prying into you. You're the first!' I was more or less her conscience. I would fight her. I'd say, 'They're not prying into you, Althea. They just want to know about you.'"[50]

The *Jet* magazine barb was more than a rogue line in an entertainment magazine. Rather, it reflected a growing perception in the sporting world that Althea was plateauing or, perhaps, worse. It was pivotal enough that it prompted one man to come forward and entreat her to let him change her game, vowing that he could not only get her back on track, but also launch her to the pinnacle of the sport. His name was Sydney Llewellyn, but he was best known in the Black community as "Mr. T," or "Mr. Tennis." Althea had met Llewellyn back in 1946, when she was rising on the ATA circuit, but it was not until after the *Jet* magazine piece appeared that he began to coach her in earnest and gradually assume a steadily more influential role in her life.

A native of Jamaica, where he'd been introduced to the sport as a ball boy, Llewellyn had come to the United States at the age of nineteen and made his mark as a tap dancer in Harlem's dance halls before a friend suggested that he demonstrate his footwork at the Cosmopolitan Club. Llewellyn wound up being coached by Fred Johnson, but he later rejected virtually all that Johnson had taught him and developed his own philosophy of tennis, which he called "The Theory of Correct Returns." As authoritative as he was loquacious, Llewellyn was also a sugar-tongued ladies' man who regularly got his nails done by the girls on Amsterdam Avenue. He drove a cab by day and frequented the city's finest nightclubs by night, decked out in his trademark safari jacket and broad-brimmed hat. With an eye ever alert for a business opportunity, Llewellyn was a man who knew how to make connections. If a young lady ever needed help making a friend, or a gentleman hoped to find a companion on those glittering ballroom floors, Llewellyn was ready to lend a hand.

"Llewellyn tried to play the system as best he could," said Marvin Dent, a former student of his who became a tennis and life coach in New Jersey. "I don't think he fashioned himself as a pimp, but he had a pimp philosophy. 'Hustle. Take care of your people that worked for you and with you, and understand the war you are involved in.' That is how he said a Black man would survive. You had to have a core of young women who would do your bidding for you. Althea presented another kind of talent, and he used that. He benefited from her ability. He couldn't use her like the other women, so he used the other talents that she had."[51]

Before his coaching practice took off, Llewellyn pursued a host of other ventures, each of which merited a different hat. There was the safari hat for the nightclub hunting scene, a sporting cap for playing the numbers, and a plaid tam-o'-shanter under which he proffered worldly advice at his favorite bar. During one period when he was particularly hard up for cash, he pretended to be a French painter, poised on a street corner with palette and brush before a canvas, a beret perched jauntily on his head, as the change rained down into a bucket at his feet.[52]

By the early 1950s, Llewellyn had become an inspirational tennis coach and was working with some of the best young Black players in the city, such as Bill Davis; he eventually added Art Carrington, a rising ATA player who became a tennis teacher and historian, and Arthur Ashe to his student list. Llewellyn was a mediocre player himself, but he had a unique understanding of the motion of a tennis ball in relation to the human body, and of the interplay of the two. At heart, he was a philosopher, both on court and off. Strategy and finesse, he maintained, were far more important than force. His "Theory of Correct Returns" held that for every point played, there was a single correct return, a single shot with the highest potential for success, that was to be calculated on the basis of a select list of variables. Things to take into account, according to Llewellyn's theory, were the "angle of the shot, your readiness to hit the ball, early preparation and anticipation, and weight transfer and follow thru [sic]. Of course, your opponents [sic] weaknesses are paramount to any strategy, and should be considered first."[53]

He employed other strategies as well. Ever an enthusiastic dancer, "a hoofer," as they are sometimes called, Llewellyn spent hours studying the footwork of prominent boxers like Joe Louis and Sugar Ray Robinson on film, which he shared with his students. Preparedness was his mantra. Don't just get ready for the next shot, he constantly told his students, *stay ready!* For years, he worked on developing a device called the "Equiform Drill Master," an elastic cable designed to help players develop an equilibrium that would produce their ideal stroke, that never made it to market.

Binding all his tactics together, Llewellyn offered a spiritual soup of self-help salted with Jesus Christ. To become a good tennis player, he counseled his students, they needed to shed any emotional baggage that might interfere with the purity of their performance and pare themselves down to their spiritual essence. The best way to do that, he maintained, was to read the Bible, particularly the Book of Ecclesiastes, along with the writings of George Washington Carver, Dr. Johnson's hero Rudyard Kipling, and assorted poets.[54]

Never shy about talking with the media about his star pupil, Llewellyn often discussed what he described as Althea's "personality problem." In an interview in mid-1956, he told a wire reporter that "She pulls herself into a shell. She's not communicative and she's given to spells of deep depression. She has never seen tennis as a career."[55] His own prescription was that she bone up on the Bible and Dale Carnegie's *How to Win Friends and Influence People*.[56] After training sessions on the public courts in upper Harlem known as "the Jungle," Llewellyn would invite his students to return to his nearby apartment, where they would discuss theory and play chess well into the evening.

"It helps to be spiritual," he said in a 1984 film interview. "I have to get this over to my student that they can find themselves, because without a good attitude, you can never be a champion. This game, this tennis game, I find it doesn't matter who you were or what you are when you start playing tennis. If you gonna get good at tennis, it's gonna be when you divest yourself of all nonsense and get real spiritual."[57]

Althea, in Llewellyn's opinion, had a long way to go in that department, regardless of her recent attachment to the Episcopal Church. At the ATA tournaments in the late 1940s, he had seen her increasingly cocksure as she vanquished one opponent after the next, and then watched her stride off the court ever triumphant, and it had irked him.

"We were on a collision course, her and I," Llewellyn said with a grin. "She came in, and she used to have a little entourage with her. She played for her audience, and she'd leave. Now, she had everything but humility, obviously."[58]

Despite their mutual reservations, Lewellyn and Althea recognized that they could be of strategic help to each other, and in the early 1950s, she agreed to take him on as her coach. Llewellyn was a stern taskmaster and drilled his new student in his tennis philosophy while requiring her to spend up to five days a week serving hundreds of balls a day while aiming for a single spot, until she was able to nail the target precisely.[59] When fall rolled around, Althea had to return to Tallahassee and her life in the South, bringing their sessions to a temporary halt, but it was the beginning of a coaching relationship that would eventually take her game to a new level. She didn't make it easy, though. Although she had technically accepted Llewellyn as her coach, he later told the *Baltimore Afro-American*'s Sam Lacy that she remained characteristically aloof and indifferent to his suggestions for several years before fully accepting his counsel.[60]

Some of those in Black tennis circles at the time did not like Llewellyn and were convinced that all his talk about spirituality was simply an effort to shield his perennial hustle. More particularly, they worried that he was exploiting Althea's talents for his own financial benefit. Llewellyn, in fact, made no secret of the fact that he saw her as having enormous financial potential. "I see her," he declared in the 1956 AP interview, "as million-dollar box office material and I have tried to help her." Some, like Bob Ryland, the prominent ATA player whom Alice Marble had consulted with about Althea over a decade earlier, thought Llewellyn's real goal was to help himself. Ryland, who would become the first Black professional in the sport and who often practiced with Althea, describes Llewellyn as a "pimp" and a "shyster." In an interview, he explained that Llewellyn "rubbed a lot of people the wrong way. He thought he was up there. He would spend anything she made, every penny. . . . That's the way he was, a pimp. He takes money from women, had women. I felt sorry for Althea, though, in a way. She had no out, no independence. She was stuck with him."[61]

In the opening days of 1953, as Althea's career seemed stalled, Llewellyn was back at her door again. With a copy of *Jet* magazine held tightly in his hand, he pleaded with her to let him help. Impressed by his earnestness, she allowed him to change her grip from the Continental, favored by the one-armed Johnson at the Cosmopolitan Club, to the Eastern, considered more suitable for the kind of fast, flat shots she hit. At the time, there was an ongoing discussion about grips in tennis magazines, and the growing consensus among some was that the Eastern grip, which moved the player's hand slightly to the right of the Continental, allowed for greater flexibility and topspin.[62] As Althea put it in her autobiography: "He made me stop using the old-fashioned Continental grip, which allows you to hit both forehand and backhand with the same grip and which naturally enough was favored by Fred Johnson because he only had one arm. Syd also taught me a more limber stroke that enabled me to obtain a maximum use of my wrist in bringing the racket into contact with the ball . . . Syd did a lot for me. The ATA seemed to have lost interest in me, and I can't say I blamed them much."[63]

The ATA had not lost interest in Althea, but its officers were unhappy about the declining number of their tournaments she was playing in and the extent to which the twenty-five-year-old college senior had begun to assert her independence. At the start of 1953, she informed Baker that she did not want to play in the National Indoor that year, to ensure that she would graduate from college in the spring. Nor did she return to Wimbledon or play in any other tournaments that season, focusing instead on her school-work and applying for jobs teaching women's physical education. With the help of Jake Gaither, she attracted the interest of Lincoln University, a well-regarded HBCU in Jefferson City, Missouri, which invited her out for an interview. Some in her inner circle urged her not to accept a position so far away from the East Coast, where most of the major tournaments were located. But the increasingly independent-minded Althea ignored this advice and, a few months later, accepted the teaching position at Lincoln as well as the unlikely job as coach for the men's tennis team.

On the first day of June, Althea at long last graduated from FAMC. None of her family members were present that day in Tallahassee, apparently unable to afford the cost of travel. Eaton and his wife were there, however, beaming as they watched the young woman whom they had nurtured for seven years receive her diploma. In that crowning moment of their role as foster parents, Eaton later wrote, "We were as proud of Althea when she walked down the aisle in her black cap and gown as if she were our own daughter."[64] In photographs from that day, Althea beams into the camera on a brilliant sunny day, her diploma clasped in her hands.

Within days, Althea was back in Lynchburg and had resumed her life on the tennis circuit, where she paid the price for her months of absence. One of her first 1953 tournaments was the National Clay Court Championships, in

Chicago in July, where she advanced to the finals against the indomitable Little Mo. Since they last met, just over one year before at an exhibition match in the same city, Connolly had racked up a stunning list of achievements, including Wimbledon and the 1952 U.S. Championships. Already in 1953, she had won both the Australian and French Opens, had recently won Wimbledon, and in two months she would claim the U.S. Championship title again, becoming the first woman to win the Grand Slam, all four majors, in a single calendar year. That Althea managed to win eight games from Little Mo, in what would be Connolly's most triumphant year, with a final score of 6–4, 6–4, was notable. The match lasted fifty-eight minutes. It was also the high point of Althea's summer performance. One week later, she squared off once again with Louise Brough, in the semifinals in the Pennsylvania and Eastern States Championships, and again appeared to lose her nerve as the elder woman took charge. As *The New York Times*'s Danzig described it, Althea "made costly errors with little provocation" and lost the match 7–5, 6–1.[65]

Some in the Black press threw up their collective hands in despair.

"When is a champion not a champion? When he lacks a fighting heart. This would seem to describe Althea Gibson," wrote Olive A. Adams, of the *New Journal and Guide*. "What is the cause of her inability to make the final hurdle. . . . She plays well, but when facing the final test, she 'blows up.' She plays badly, and fumbles as she never does at any other time."[66]

Meanwhile, the rising young star Lorraine Williams seemed to have exactly what it took to be a champion. In August, Williams earned a place in tennis history when she, and not Althea Gibson, became the first Black player to claim a USLTA national tennis championship; she won the girls' fifteen-and-under competition in Kalamazoo, Michigan. Reporters gushed over the tennis darling's triumph, and many predicted that she would surely go farther than Althea. At the same time, several noted that Williams, like a handful of other Black players, was following in the footsteps of Reginald Weir and had twice skipped the ATA National Championships in order to compete in white tournaments. It was a harbinger of the complex future of Black tennis. The ATA expected loyalty from the Black players it boosted and had supported financially, and it demanded participation in its tournaments. Others felt it increasingly crucial that they should be exposed to the higher level of white competition if they were going to be genuine contenders. Of Little Lorraine, Joe Bostic of the *New York Amsterdam News* wrote, "While she hardly has the natural physical makeup of La Gibson, she may go further in the game because she has been getting the seasoning of high caliber opposition so much earlier in her career. It is a proven tennis axiom that to play top level tennis you must compete against top level opponents."[67]

Back on Black turf, Althea was victorious. To no one's surprise, she easily won the ATA national tournament at Bethune-Cookman College, defeating Mary Etta Fine 6–1, 6–1 without breaking a sweat and securing her seventh consecutive women's crown. So, too, she and Johnson comfortably won the mixed doubles for the fifth time. Meanwhile, George Stewart retained his crown, winning his third-consecutive men's championship title. But two weeks later, storm clouds gathered again.

Next on the calendar was the U.S. National Championships tournament, where the number of Black players had doubled to a total of six over the previous year. Stewart was playing again, while Weir was not. Newcomers included Oscar Johnson; Ubert Vincent; Ivy Ramsey, a female Jamaican tennis star who had recently begun playing in ATA tournaments; and Gerard Alleyne, a veteran ATA player. And, of course, Althea.[68]

In her fourth bid for the women's title, Althea wound up facing Connolly in the quarterfinals and commenced with her aggressive style of attack. But just a few points into the first set, one of the two linespeople at the baseline, a woman, called a series of foot faults against Althea that visibly unnerved her and ultimately derailed her game. From 2–2 in the first set, Althea went on to lose eight successive games. *The New York Times*'s Danzig reported that the five foot faults called on her in the third game "undoubtedly affected Miss Gibson's concentration and were responsible in part for the fact that her groundstrokes went completely out of control and she failed regularly with her volley until the match was beyond saving." In all, ten foot faults were called in the opening set and five in the second set, "until the gallery cried out in protest."[69] Althea went downhill fast. At the end of the second set, she committed several volleying errors and double-faulted twice, leaving Connolly to take the match 6–2, 6–3. Capping an otherwise feeble showing, Althea and Oscar Johnson were defeated in the mixed doubles by Connolly and Lew Hoad in the second round. In a post-match interview with the *Baltimore Afro-American*, Althea attributed her poor performance against Connolly largely to the wind, but the collective pressures of the past couple of years and her less-than-stellar summer performances had clearly taken an enormous toll.

"It may be true that the foul calls upset me a little, but they didn't bother me any more than the high wind," Althea said. "The wind got into my service and threw it off. And when I couldn't control my service, I guess it stands to reason that the rest of my game had to suffer."[70]

Observers were divided over whether the foot fault calls were merited and whether racism had played a part in the incident. Gayle Talbot of the Associated Press said he didn't think the calls impacted the outcome. But Hamilton Chambers, veteran writer for *American Lawn Tennis* magazine, told the *Baltimore Afro-American* that such fouls were often seen as unintentional and were overlooked in other matches, suggesting that Althea had been singled out. "I think she might at least have been warned about her error," said Chambers. If they had not happened, he added, "I'm reasonably sure she'd have taken Miss Connolly."[71]

The fiercely competitive Connolly, who went on to win the tournament, remembered the match in her autobiography as "a nightmare" punctuated by boos and catcalls aimed at the lineswoman. Frustrated that Althea kept committing faults, even after the judge told her what she was doing wrong, Connolly recalled that she snapped at Althea as they changed sides, saying, "'Althea, either play or default. I have never seen worse sportsmanship.' Hardly had I said this before I realized that Althea was under tremendous strain, and I was sorry I said it."[72]

Days after the tournament ended, Althea got behind the wheel of her Oldsmobile and began the two-day drive to Jefferson City, Missouri, and her first full-time job. If she had any second thoughts about her decision to put some distance between herself and the relentlessly high pressure of the competitive tennis world in order to pursue a career on a midwestern college campus, the churlish press likely only strengthened her resolve. While admonishing the high-handed ATA for its failure to cultivate more tennis talent beyond its predictable standbys or to develop a more robust calendar of tournaments, columnist Marion Jackson of the *Atlanta Daily*

Althea at age 17 in 1944. *(Bob Davis)*

Althea and Sydney Llewellyn at the Shady Rest Golf and Country Club in New Jersey in 1950. *(Bob Davis)*

George Stewart, Ora Washington, Dr. Robert Johnson, and Althea, mixed doubles finalists at the 1947 A.T.A. championships at Tuskegee Institute, Alabama. *(Tuskegee University Archives, Tuskegee University)*

(Clockwise from top-left) Althea and Dr. Robert "Whirlwind" Johnson in the 1940s. *(Robert Johnson Family)*; Fred Johnson, Althea's one-armed coach at the Cosmopolitan Club in the 1940s. *(Shutterstock Editorial)*; Althea and mentor Dr. Hubert Eaton Sr., in Wilmington, North Carolina, 1946. *(*Wilmington Star-News-USA Today *Network)*; Nana Davis congratulates Althea, who defeated her 6-0, 6-0, in the 1949 Eastern Tennis Championships women's singles. *(AFRO American Newspapers Archive)*

On an indoor court in New York in 1950. *(Gordon Parks © The Gordon Parks Foundation)*

Althea at Florida A&M College in the 1950s. *(Althea Gibson Collection and Exhibit, Meek-Eaton Southeastern Regional Black Archives Research Center and Museum, Florida A&M University)*

Preparing for a forehand in New York in 1950. *(Gordon Parks © The Gordon Parks Foundation)*

Althea addresses a meeting of New Homemakers of America at Florida A&M College, 1951. *(Althea Gibson Collection and Exhibit, Meek-Eaton Southeastern Regional Black Archives Research Center and Museum, Florida A&M University)*

FAMCEE's womens' basketball team in 1950. *(Althea Gibson Collection and Exhibit, Meek-Eaton Southeastern Regional Black Archives Research Center and Museum, Florida A&M University)*

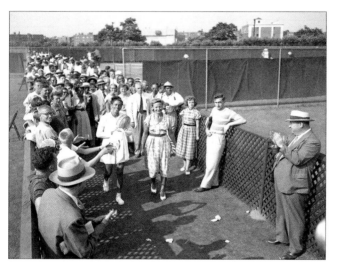

Walking with Alice Marble at Forest Hills on the day she broke the color barrier in tennis in 1950. *(*New York Daily News Archive, *via Getty Images)*

Althea's supporters from the Cosmopolitan Club on the eve of her 1950 match. From Left to Right: Dr. Hubert Eaton, Arthur Francis, Althea Gibson, Rhoda Smith, Bertram Baker, Buddy Walker, and Fred Johnson. *(Layne's Studio, Photographs and Prints Division, Schomburg Center for Research in Black Culture, The New York Public Library)*

Althea wipes off the sweat after her groundbreaking match with Louise Brough at Forest Hills in 1950. Although Althea lost, she broke the color barrier, becoming the first African American to play in a Grand Slam tournament. *(Associated Press)*

Poised for a backhand in the summer of 1951 during her first European tournaments. The press commented often on her androgynous appearance. *(Agence France-Presse)*

Althea kisses middleweight champ and friend Sugar Ray Robinson in London after losing in the third round of her first appearance at Wimbledon in 1951. *(Bettmann, via Getty Images)*

Despite a few years of poor performance, Althea is invited to join a U.S. State Department—sponsored international Goodwill Tour that began in 1955. Boarding a BOAC liner in London on their way to India, the four players are, from bottom left, clockwise: Karol Fageros, Hamilton Richardson, Robert Perry, and Althea Gibson. *(PA Images, via Getty Images)*

After a triumphant several-months-long swing across Europe, Althea beamed at photographers days before the French National tournament. There she won her first Grand Slam against archrival Angela Mortimer. *(AFRO American Newspapers Archives)*

Althea made a rapid climb to the top tier of women's tennis, and by the end of 1956 was ranked No. 2. by the USLTA. Her sometimes cool demeanor nonetheless often kept others at a distance. *(Paul Popper,* World Tennis Magazine Archives, *International Tennis Hall of Fame)*

Practicing with her friend and coach Sydney Llewellyn in New York in 1957. In the mid-1950s Llewellyn came to have increasing influence over Althea. *(D.D. & E.P. Schroeder,* World Tennis Magazine Archives, *International Tennis Hall of Fame)*

Following their 1956 wins, Angela met Althea at the airport on her return to London for the Wimbledon tournament each summer. Due to an injured wrist, Angela was unable to compete. (World Tennis Magazine Archives, *International Tennis Hall of Fame*)

On July 6, 1957, Althea won both the Wimbledon women's singles and doubles matches, the first Black person to do so. On that sweltering day, Queen Elizabeth II presented trophies to Althea and her opponent, Darlene Hard. *(Associated Press)*

Althea is greeted by her mother, Annie Gibson, at Idlewild Airport in New York shortly after her 1957 Wimbledon wins. (The New York Times: *Redux)*

Annie Gibson pours milk for her daughter while her father, Daniel, looks on after her return from Wimbledon in 1957. *(Carl T. Gossett Jr.,* The New York Times*: Redux)*

Althea is swarmed by children in her Harlem neighborhood on her return from Wimbledon in 1957. *(Carl T. Gossett Jr., The New York Times: Redux)*

Althea is feted by 100,000 New Yorkers attending a ticker-tape parade up Broadway on July 11, 1957. She was the second African American to receive such a tribute after Jesse Owens and the first woman of color to do so. *(Associated Press)*

Althea stuns the audience at the 1957 Wimbledon Ball when she takes the microphone and sings. *(AELTC-Michael Cole, LeRoye Productions, World Tennis Magazine Archive, International Tennis Hall of Fame)*

World as much as thumbed his nose at Althea's tailpipe as she churned her way westward.

"For a bit of enlightenment, let us state, that Miss Gibson's days in tennis are numbered," he grumbled. As a faculty member, he added, "She'll be isolated in Jefferson City, Mo., which is off the beaten path of press and public. The regency which she has enjoyed on the Eastern sports pages will sure come to an end. Doomsday is certain for Miss Gibson's tennis aspirations."[73]

Jefferson City may have been considered off the beaten path by some, but in the fall of 1953, it felt a lot like the same well-worn path winding through the Jim Crow South that Althea had traveled for the past seven years. At the time, a rigid duo of state laws mandated separation of the races in Missouri: one banned interracial marriage, and another mandated segregated schools. With the U.S. Supreme Court's sweeping ruling of 1954 calling for the integration of public schools, the ground would begin to shift, but segregation was nonetheless the accepted local practice when Althea pulled into the "Show-Me State," a nickname coined to reflect the purportedly no-nonsense, stalwart nature of its people.

In the capital city, where nonwhites accounted for about 11 percent of the 25,099 residents, Black and white people lived largely separate lives, much as they did in the South. The city's restaurants and hotels were segregated, as were its two movie theaters, the Capitol and the State, while certain neighborhoods were limited to whites. Black businesses were largely confined to a two-block neighborhood at the base of the campus, known as "the Foot." Months before Althea arrived, a student committee at Lincoln launched a boycott of the theaters, asking in one of its releases, "Why pay 50c for segregation whose 'best buddy' is discrimination?" In rural areas, where Black people could get food only "to go," divisions were even more extreme.[74]

Lincoln students and faculty, such as Althea, who dared to drive outside the city knew to chart their route with care, so they might avoid the scores of towns peppering the state that did not want Black people within their borders after nightfall, even if they did not have actual "sundown" laws on the books. In one incident reported in the student paper, the *Lincoln Clarion*, two students heading north on a spring day in 1954 encountered car trouble about four miles outside the small city of Lancaster, which required Black people to leave town at sunset. The students pushed their car to a service station, but, unable to fix the car, the attendant pushed it into a Lancaster station. As night fell, the students were ordered out of town, and so, they muscled their still-disabled car to a roadside beyond the town's border. In the morning, the attendant from the station in Lancaster appeared, pushed the car back into the city, and repaired it. As the students left, the attendant informed them "that most of the younger residents of Lancaster had never seen a Negro in real life."[75]

Lincoln University, however, was a haven in the heartland, commonly referred to as the "Black Harvard of the Midwest." Founded in 1866, just months after the end of the Civil War, it was the realization of a dream nurtured by members of the Sixty-Second and Sixty-Fifth Colored Infantry, some of them former slaves, determined that an educational facility be established in their home state. With the soldiers' dream in mind, W. E. B. Du Bois, the prominent Black author and civil rights leader, once described Lincoln as having "perhaps the most romantic beginning of all the black colleges."[76] By the mid-1950s, it had emerged as one of the nation's most prestigious HBCUs. Having raised faculty salaries early in the century and embarked on an aggressive building program, the school had attracted a talented cadre of teachers with advanced degrees as well as accomplished writers and poets. Lincoln's status was further enhanced with the establishment of highly regarded schools of law and journalism and its publication of *The Midwest Journal*, an esteemed magazine of research and creative writing.[77]

Divisions in the city not only fell along racial lines, but also simmered over class distinctions separating Black residents in town from those on the leafy Lincoln campus. The university community was a prideful one, and many of its members steered clear of the working-class enclaves like "the Foot." Gary R. Kremer, executive director of the State Historical Society of Missouri and a former Lincoln professor, explains it this way: "Prior to racial integration, there was a real dress code on campus, and students and faculty dressed very well. You could say that Blacks on campus defined who they were by defining who they were not. They were professional and elitist, and they did not want to be confused with the Black working class. That created a lot of tension with Blacks in town."[78]

With the blessing of an enhanced scholarship program, Lincoln, like many other institutions of higher education in the nation, began to actively recruit athletes for the first time in 1950. Once settled into her position as physical education teacher and coach of the men's tennis team, Althea again found herself something of an anomaly. At the time, there were virtually no women, either Black or white, coaching men's teams anywhere in the country. Casting her even more outside the mainstream, her highly competitive nature and her androgynous style of dress surely raised concerned eyebrows on campus. At a time when homosexual orientation was widely reviled in some quarters, just being a physical education professional or coach could make a woman the subject of speculation. Women, of any color, in physical education were routinely scrutinized for any signs of traits or behaviors considered "abnormal" at the time.[79]

Althea, whose masculine appearance had long ago posited her under that cloud on the tennis circuit, was no exception. *Jet* magazine blatantly called the question publicly in a 1954 summer issue, with a story titled "The Truth About Women Athletes." The piece examined the femininity of three female sports heroines: Althea, baseball star Toni Stone, and boxing champion Gloria Thompson. *Jet* magazine had a perennial interest in sexual topics, and in the mid-1950s, it routinely published such stories as "Women Who Fall for Lesbians," "Is There Hope for Homosexuals," and "The Sex Habits of Negro Women."[80] In the "Truth" story, the magazine appeared to put to rest any question that Stone or Thompson might be a lesbian with glimpses of their personal style. While the married Stone wore a ladylike pink flowered dress and exhibited an abundance of feminine charm during a public appearance, Thompson refused to wear slacks in public and delighted in rare perfumes. No need to worry about masculine inclinations with these two, the magazine concluded.

About Althea, *Jet* seemed uncertain. Since breaking the color barrier four years earlier, *Jet* noted, "Gibson has been the subject of more teacup gossip than any woman sports personality in recent years," adding that she had been "criticized for wearing trousers and having female friends."

But *Jet* did not appear to come to the same reassuring assessment that it had with the other two female athletes about which it wrote. Althea, it concluded, had a "voluptuous, eye-appealing figure and she has plenty of female friends of both races."[81] Although the photo caption concluded that she had outgrown her "tomboy" stage, the magazine's assessment was not exactly a resounding affirmation of her heterosexuality.

Nor did Althea do anything to assuage any suspicions about her orientation. When she wasn't coaching or teaching, and was lacking the distractions available on the streets of Manhattan, she turned to playing bridge and singing her beloved ballads in school productions. The bulk of her energy, however, was funneled into sport. She played tennis, Ping-Pong, and badminton and was an outfielder and pitcher on the faculty softball team, its lone woman. Barred from playing on the men's faculty basketball team—the men said she might get hurt—she was permitted to practice with the student varsity players, and "she outshot everybody on the team."[82] Looking at her, Dwight Green, the football coach at the time, had the same difficulty that Dr. Eaton had experienced years earlier in determining Althea's gender.

"You had to look two or three times at Althea in order to convince yourself that she was a girl," Green told Ted Poston of the *New York Post*. "She played all things so well. You couldn't tell she was a girl by her pitching or by the way she shagged balls."[83]

All of which, as it turned out, did not interfere with her dating life in the slightest. One of the highlights of her years at Lincoln was a handsome military man fresh back from the battlefields of Korea who had recently joined the Lincoln faculty as a professor of military science and tactics and who served as commander of the campus ROTC program. Capt. Dova L. Jones, fifteen years her senior, had a substantial résumé and had done postgraduate work in mathematics in Chicago and completed officers' training school at Fort Belvoir, Virginia, before serving in World War II.[84]

Jones was also an avid card player, and he and Althea sometimes participated in tournaments hosted by the Pla-Mor Duplicate Bridge Club. Otherwise, they struggled to find entertainment in sleepy Jefferson City, where they used to "put out the lights and pull in the sidewalks at nine o'clock," as Althea described it in her autobiography. She fell head over heels in love with Jones and thoroughly enjoyed what she called "a wingding of a time" with him, one she "wouldn't have missed . . . for the world." She added, "Being in love, and being loved by somebody, was something brand new to me."[85]

The second part of that sentence was not entirely true. The devoted Will Darben, who'd pursued Althea for several years, had proposed to her weeks before she left for Missouri. Although deeply fond of the piano-playing engineer, Althea turned him down in order to focus exclusively on her career. But despite her rebuff, the two of them became even closer friends in the years that followed rather than fully breaking up. Even when she was traveling the globe, Althea always stayed in touch with Will, and their relationship became an irreplaceable emotional constant in her sometimes turbulent life.

Althea did not play in any tournaments during the academic months of her first year at Lincoln. Unburdened by the multiple stressors that bore down on her on the tennis circuit, she began to rethink her commitment to the sport. Despite being ranked No. 7 that year, she began to seriously question whether she would ever be a major contender on the national tennis scene. Fueling her discontent was her inability to save any money playing amateur tennis, not that her small Lincoln salary was much of an improvement. Turning to her perennial passion for music, she began taking singing lessons and, according to *Jet* magazine, was offered a singing job with Count Basie's band in the spring. Later in the year, after she resumed tennis in midsummer, *Jet* explained her losses in the early rounds of several tournaments by saying she was "hitting the night club circuits and tooting her saxophone in jam sessions."[86]

Her Lincoln boyfriend had another idea. Why not join the Women's Army Corps (WAC), Jones suggested, referring to an auxiliary branch of the U.S. Army created during World War II and later integrated into the male units of the army to form a single military operation. When Jones addressed the senior Lincoln women on the merits of service that spring, Althea listened with mounting interest. If she joined the WAC, not only would she have a larger income and a stable employer, but she might also be able to stay with her beloved captain, either at Lincoln or at a military posting. Eager to try something new, she applied that spring to become a second lieutenant in the WAC for a two-year stint. It was likely difficult for her to explain her decision to either Eaton or Johnson, as it would mean taking an enormous step back from the sport she had pursued under their tutelage for so long.

As she awaited the army's response that summer of 1954, her attempt to enlist apparently got stalled by a request for medical information made by the U.S. surgeon general. Althea apparently did not immediately provide the information, according to a September 1955 letter from the Department of the Army that suggested that she obtain another physical due to the lapse of time since the initial request was made.[87] The issue may have stemmed from the information written on Althea's birth certificate back in 1927, which gave her name as "Alger" and appeared to identify her as male. Just three months after she submitted her papers to the WAC, her father successfully applied for corrections to be made to that document back in South Carolina. In June 1954, his name on the certificate was changed from "Duas" to "Daniel" and his daughter's was changed from "Alger" to "Althea." In addition, her gender was apparently changed from boy to girl. Whether the amended form was turned over to the army is unclear, as is the impact the matter might have had on Althea's interest in joining.[88]

The matter of the birth certificate might well have thrust Althea into the crosshairs of an ongoing State Department purge of homosexuals and lesbians in the federal government at the time, a campaign that reflected American society's rising animus toward same-sex unions. In a spin-off of the ongoing effort to purge Communists from the government's ranks, homosexuals and other "perverts" had become widely reviled across all social lines in the years after World War II. In 1953, the newly elected president, Dwight Eisenhower, issued an executive order banning homosexuals and lesbians from federal employment. Two years later, Althea was required to undergo a national security check, presumably intended in part to make sure she was neither a Communist nor a lesbian. Her confusing birth certificate may have raised some eyebrows, particularly regarding that second category. In the spring of 1955, she wrote to Eaton and informed him that she was confident that her record was clean of any of the sort of subversive activities for which she was to be investigated. With that, she also asked him if he would provide one of the five character references the army was requesting.[89] By the fall of 1955, the issue had become moot, as Althea was swept up by events relating to her tennis career.

While negotiations with the army continued, Althea returned to the tennis court, playing mostly in USLTA tournaments. Once again, her absence from competitive play during the academic season showed. Although she won the women's singles at the New York State Women's Tennis Championships in Pelham Manor, New York, against Isabel Troccole, things went downhill fast. One week later, she returned to the National Clay Court tournament in Chicago and, despite being the third seed, was trounced in the first round 6–1, 6–0 by relative newcomer Lois Felix, whom many had regarded as merely a warm-up opponent for Althea. At the Pennsylvania and Eastern States tournament, she was again beaten by a relatively unknown young player, named Janet Hopps. A junior at Seattle University, Hopps was the No. 1–ranked player in the Pacific Northwest and wasn't even aware that she was playing a nationally ranked competitor. It was a stunning win for the athletic brunette in the final match of the day under the nighttime lights of the Merion Cricket Club, one that would swiftly elevate the younger girl's name before the public eye. As it turned out, Hopps and Althea had many things in common and would encounter one another repeatedly in the years to come. Afterward, Althea scored her now-predictable victories at the ATA Nationals in the women's division and mixed doubles with Dr. Johnson toward the end of the summer in Daytona Beach, Florida.

The season ended with her fifth appearance at the U.S. National Championships, where, again, she did poorly, defeated in the first round. Matched against the lanky Californian Helen Perez, who was ranked No. 6, Althea worked hard during the first two sets, keeping her opponent on the run with a series of lobs, just as Llewellyn had advised. After each woman took a set, Althea seemed to have her eye trained on victory when she abruptly lost her service in the third set and appeared to lose her confidence as well. In a pattern that was becoming all too familiar, she petered out on the third set, missing several forehand shots, and the match went to Perez 6–3, 3–6, 6–3.[90]

It was a notable year at West Side, due largely to a prominent absence. Just one month earlier, not long after winning a third straight Wimbledon title, reigning champion Little Mo was seriously injured when the horse she was riding was frightened by a passing concrete mixer and she was thrown to the ground, badly breaking her right leg. Her retirement the following year marked the end of a remarkable career on court. Connolly remained on the periphery of the tennis scene, working as a newspaper correspondent and as a representative of the Wilson Sporting Goods Company for some years. But, as with Althea, the fact that her stunning achievement came before the current era of professional tennis—the Open Era—flooded the sport with cash meant that her name would be largely lost to history.

The U.S. Championships were also notable in 1954 because of the number of Black players on the draw, although none of them did particularly well. Of the five Black players participating, only George Stewart advanced beyond the first round.[91] Eaton, making his first and only appearance in the Nationals, was so grossly outmatched in his pairing against defending champion Cincinnati's Tony Trabert, the world's No. 1 player in 1953, that he managed to take only a single game in three sets.[92] While some observers questioned whether the pairing of Eaton against the star Trabert might have been a deliberate move by the USLTA, others took the outcome as proof that Black players were not yet ready to compete on the championship level. On a larger scale, the Black players' poor performances further fueled the simmering resentment among Black sportswriters against the ATA for what they considered to be its failure to produce a younger crop of able players and its refusal to bow to widespread integration of the sport. In its post-tournament assessment, the *New York Amsterdam News* pointed out that "Miss Gibson is more or less past her peak." So far, there was no one primed to take her place. The up-and-coming women's star Lorraine Williams, the paper pointedly noted, would not be doing so through the ATA when it came time for her to play at Forest Hills.[93]

The ATA, however, wasn't about to surrender its control of Black tennis, or of luminaries like Althea, without a fight, one that would ultimately pit integrationists like Weir and Johnson hard against the organization's brass. Johnson's relentless efforts on behalf of his Junior Development Program, which he launched in 1951, posited him in direct opposition to the ATA and Baker, whom he'd mockingly nicknamed "the Boss." Their disagreement over Johnson's plan to establish a separate junior tournament along the lines of the USLTA's program mushroomed into a fierce letter-writing battle that would rage for years. Toward the end of 1955, Johnson accused Baker of trying "to kill our program," and he threatened to hold an integrated junior tournament that would not require the ATA's sanction. Baker hurled back a biting response in early 1956, in which he dismissed Johnson's threat as the product of "a childish and irresponsible mind."[94] He went on to disparage the Black players who, he said, had deserted the ATA—Lorraine Williams, Oscar Johnson, and Reginald Weir—while praising Althea for having never missed an ATA tournament, despite the encouragement by some that she do so. It was Baker, after all, who had threatened to keep Althea out of Forest Hills in 1951 if she failed to appear at the ATA tournament in Wilberforce.[95]

Their disagreement, which was at heart a clash over how integration should best be achieved, raged on for close to two years. In his caustic 1956 letter, Baker concluded with the observation that "We welcome integration, but believe me, the Negro will always have to make good on his own and with his own people thus demonstrating racial pride, self respect and integrity. These qualities are the passport to integration."[96]

Meanwhile, as her second year of teaching back in Jefferson City progressed throughout the fall of 1954, Althea found herself unhappier than ever. Her "wingding" relationship was winding down, partly because Jones felt that the age difference between them was too great, but also because Althea found it harder to give up tennis than she had imagined. After all the hard work she, and others, had put into it, "Tennis," she wrote, "still had that big a hold on me."[97]

The other factor constantly gnawing at her was the chronic segregation she was colliding with in Jefferson City, which was just as relentless and punishing as it had been in Tallahassee and Wilmington. She and another physical education teacher had tried to find a place to take some of their students bowling. The first alley manager flat-out said no. The second one permitted them to use the lanes, but only if they were out by early afternoon, when regulars started to show up. Even that arrangement fell apart after white patrons began complaining about the Black students, who were subsequently forced to leave. By the spring of her second year, 1955, Althea had had it. When the semester ended, she packed up her Oldsmobile, tossed her tennis rackets on top of her luggage, and headed back east.

Living once again with the Darbens and going to Harlem to see friends and family, Althea encountered strong resistance to her plan to join the WACs, and on multiple fronts. Time and again, Rosemary urged her to change her mind, while insisting that Althea's big day in tennis was just around the corner. One afternoon, the two of them were driving around Montclair when Althea announced that she wanted to stop at the post office to send a follow-up letter of inquiry to the WAC. As Althea pulled up in front of the postal building with her letter, Rosemary threw up her hands and shouted, "Stop the car! Don't go in there," she recalled. "Your day is going to come. Don't put that letter in the mailbox. . . . You're going to lose your life when you go into the army because you're going to be nothing. You will be swallowed up."[98] For once, Althea listened, and she did not mail the letter.

Llewellyn was even more adamant. Sitting outside the Harlem tennis court complex, the two of them argued for hours, but Althea remained stubbornly committed to her plan. "If I was any good, I'd be the champ now. But I'm just not good enough. I'm probably never going to be," she told him. "And I'm sick of having people support me, taking up collections for me, and buying me clothes and airplane tickets and every damn thing I eat or wear. I want to take care of myself for a change. In the army, I can do it."[99]

Llewellyn reluctantly agreed to write one of the character references in support of Althea's application, but his larger strategy was to divert her by getting her back on the tennis court. In a way he never could have foreseen, it worked. Althea began the season with a handful of wins at moderate-size tournaments, including the New York State Championships and the Rose Taubele Memorial Tournament in Throggs Neck, New York. At her next stop, at the Pennsylvania and Eastern States tournament in Haverford, Pennsylvania, she shone in a bruising battle in blistering heat against Louise Brough, fresh back from her fourth Wimbledon win. In a riveting finals match before a capacity crowd of 2,500, Althea claimed the lead to take the first set 6–1 and proceeded to pocket two games in the second set with a series of powerful cross-court backhands. Just when it seemed clear that the Wimbledon champion was going down, Brough astonishingly pulled forward and managed to win six successive games. For the first time, Althea appeared to falter as she missed three volleys and then lost her service. Although she ultimately lost to Brough 1–6, 6–2, 6–1, in what was their third encounter since 1950, observers were stunned by Althea's dazzling play during what was described by one paper as "a brilliant one hour and fifteen minutes of action."[100] Even the normally measured Danzig of *The New York Times* was stirred. "Miss Gibson's tennis today was the best this observer has seen her play since that match of five years ago. . . . From both the baseline and the net she had such command of her racquet that she seemed infallible."[101] Her new grip, and Llewellyn's Theory of Correct Returns, it seemed, were paying off, at least sometimes.

Two weeks later, Althea walked onto the grass courts at West Side with her ninth consecutive ATA win in hand. The standards for admittance to the exclusive club were surely as rigorous as they were when she made her debut there, but the appearance of things was definitely beginning to change. On the well-tended courts, a record-breaking eight Black players were competing, including Robert Ryland and Billy Davis, both ATA powerhouses, as well as sixteen-year-old Lorraine Williams, making her debut appearance at the exclusive club. What's more, the trim courts were hosting Black ball boys chasing errant shots for the first time in the tournament's history. It wasn't Connolly or Brough on the other side of the net from Althea, but a player almost as challenging. Her quarterfinals opponent was Beverly Baker Fleitz, the masterful player with the ambidextrous forehand who had trounced Althea in her only Wimbledon appearance and who had recently won the women's doubles at the French Open. Daunted, Althea resorted to her old pattern, starting out strongly and then losing steam as Fleitz's passing shots streaked by her. In the end, Althea lost 6–2, 6–2, but the day was not without promise.

In between her matches, she had been approached by a solemn-faced Renville McMann, suited vice president of the USLTA; graduate of Harvard University, the Choate School, and the U.S. Naval Radio School; and a titan in the tennis world. He asked her for a moment of her time, and over the next two minutes, the mild-mannered executive outlined an offer that would radically alter the course of Althea's life, just as a pair of Black doctors had done nine years earlier. This time, however, the proposal laid on the table had little to do with tennis.

7

Black Ambassadors in Short Pants

The boy's name was Timothy L. Hudson. He was twelve years old when his mutilated body was found lying on a Mississippi dirt road in the fall of 1955, his head crushed and several bones broken. Neighbors said the Black boy had been lynched after he became friendly with a white farm girl.

The man's name was George Wesley Lee. The fifty-one-year-old died months earlier after his face was sprayed three times with buckshot while he was driving his car and he careened into a house. It was widely reported that Lee, cofounder of the local NAACP chapter and a Baptist minister, had been assassinated after he successfully registered nearly all ninety Black residents of Belzoni, Mississippi, to vote.

Neither of their names would become the subject of international furor like that of Emmett Till, the fourteen-year-old Black boy who was brutally murdered in the sweltering summer of 1955 after he was accused of whistling at a white woman in a grocery store. Till, a Chicagoan who was visiting relatives in Mississippi, was kidnapped, shot in the head, and drowned in a river a few days after the incident. A half a century later the woman in the store would confess that she had fabricated much of her story and the young Till had not made any advance on her.[1]

These three Black males, who died within a few months and a few miles of one another, were swept up in a crescendo of racial violence that surged in the aftermath of the 1954 Supreme Court decision *Brown v. Board of Education*, which mandated an end to school segregation. That

tide of hate, spearheaded by southern whites opposed to integration, became an incendiary issue in the ongoing propaganda battle between the
U.S. government and the Soviet Union during the Cold War as the Communist press trumpeted such incidents as evidence of the failure of American democracy and the hypocrisy of its leaders.

Describing the lynching of a young Negro couple in bloody detail, for
example, the Soviet newspaper *Red Star* declared in June 1957, "This is how
16,000,000 Negroes live today, in servitude to the White citizens, in terror
of lynching, the electric chair and the revolvers of policemen and sheriffs.
This is a terrible aspect of American life. The American press, crowing about
its 'freedom,' rarely publishes facts about the cruel treatment of Negroes."[2]

So damaging were such allegations to the country's global reputation
that President Eisenhower declared early in his presidency that bigotry and
discrimination were "spiritual acts of treason."[3] Even some members of the
Black press took the government's side in rejecting the more extreme forms
of Communist propaganda. As one prominent Black columnist put it, cases
of racial violence had become "the natural type of grist for the Red propaganda mill which has played up the murder and oppression of Negroes in
the Deep South. And unwittingly, or perhaps knowingly, the South has
given the Communist plenty to whoop it up in Asia with the Emmett Till
slaying, the murder of Rev. George Lee . . ."[4]

In the late summer of 1955, only weeks after Till's murder, the U.S.
State Department launched a new chapter in its ongoing response to Soviet accusations. Its title might have been "Althea Gibson."

A few years earlier, the U.S. government had ramped up its own red-
white-and-blue propaganda mill with a series of overseas cultural goodwill
tours designed to shine a positive light on capitalist democracy and the
opportunities available to the United States' most successful Black citizens. The tours featured both white and Black intellectuals, performers,
musicians, and athletes. Days after the Till murder, which electrified the
headlines in the Communist media, Althea's name shot to the top of the
list for a tour. What better proof of the fair treatment and opportunities for
advancement experienced by Black citizens in America could there be than
the Harlem-born Althea, the talented Black player who not only had risen
from the bleakest poverty to compete at the highest level of white tennis,

but also consistently downplayed talk of racism in her homeland. Her own words blithely affirmed the government's inaccurate position.

"Colour bar? I have never met it in tennis," she said to the press on her first visit to Wimbledon, casually dismissing the several years that she had been barred from white competition because of the color of her skin.[5] A few years later, she continued to maintain that she had never met with discrimination on the court, because "Tennis just isn't that kind of game."[6]

If some among the Black community were dismayed at her words, American officials were delighted. They weren't the only ones. The Egyptian government, which was negotiating a visit by Althea in 1958, noted in a cable to the U.S. government, "In addition [to] tennis prowess, Gibson superbly refutes racial bias propaganda of Soviets in all contacts."[7]

In the waning days of August, the International Educational Exchange Service, an arm of the U.S. State Department dedicated to strengthening relations with other countries through a variety of educational programs, and an integral facet of the nation's fast-growing international public relations operation, invited Althea to participate in a four-person tennis tour of Southeast Asia. Countries on the agenda included newly independent Burma, Ceylon, and India, which, like many dark-skinned nations of the day, viewed Black Americans' plight as akin to their own bitter struggle with British colonialism. If the United States was segregating and lynching its own Black citizens, as was being vividly documented on the front pages of America's newspapers, how could people of similar color in other countries be expected to be treated any differently? Which race did Americans really hate the most, U.S. representatives abroad were often asked. Why did the Americans tolerate the lynching of "Negroes"? And how could Americans support the liberation of people of color globally when it treated its own Black citizens so poorly?[8] As incidents of racial violence such as Till's murder dominated the news in the 1950s, America's global image took a steady battering. Racial strife in the United States fast became a popular target of Communist attack.

Following World War II, when many Black American soldiers returned from the front to face discrimination and abuse on their own home soil, the government had dispatched a series of speakers of color overseas to counter the country's racist image. The aim was to demonstrate the many racial milestones that had been achieved in American society. In 1948, for example, President Truman abolished segregation in the U.S. Army. Two years later, diplomat Ralph Bunche became the first Black person to be awarded the Nobel Peace Prize. Most dramatically, school segregation was ruled unconstitutional in 1954, thus proving that American democracy was working to correct any racist practices. Integration was well under way, and barriers to the Black man in social and economic life were steadily tumbling. Or so the official party line went.

With the end of segregation in baseball and football in the late 1940s and the accomplishments of Black athletes such as sprinter Jesse Owens, heavyweight champion Joe Louis, and Olympic champion runner Mal Whitfield, sports were increasingly put forth as a showplace for American racial progress. Variously dubbed "brown ambassadors" and "ambassadors in short pants," these three champions, and scores more, were dispatched to refute Communist critics. Never mind that advances in the athletic arena generally did not translate into other aspects of Black life, such as greater economic opportunity or the end of Jim Crow separatism. The nation's Black athletes were nonetheless presented as symbols of democracy's evolution. Unlike the increasingly strained world of political discourse, sports provided an arena of apparent common international interest, one that both the U.S. and Soviet governments exploited for their own ends. For that reason, the State Department funded the vast majority of the dark-skinned ambassadors it dispatched overseas. In the early 1950s, as Damion L. Thomas wrote in *Globetrotting: African American Athletes and Cold War Politics*, "Sports became a crucial Cold War weapon that deployed the notions of strength and cultural, political, and economic superiority over the Soviet Union. Projecting an image of racial equality became critical in this endeavor."[9]

Renville McMann, the trim USLTA vice president and former president of the West Side Tennis Club, mentioned none of this when he pulled Althea Gibson aside on the club patio on a warm September afternoon in 1955 to present her with an invitation. It was McMann who told her of the U.S. State Department's proposal to send her on a goodwill tour of Southeast Asia. In fact, he added, the plan specifically called for her to be included.

Althea was stunned.

"Are you kidding?" she exclaimed.[10]

As she would later describe it, she "wasn't exactly the ambassador type." But she was also well aware that Till's lynching had ravaged world opinion of the United States and galvanized the civil rights movement in America. Years later, U.S. congressman John Lewis, a Georgia native and a principal figure in the civil rights movement of the 1960s, would liken the impact of Till's violent death on his own life to that of George Floyd on a younger generation. Althea correctly concluded that the teenager's killing had triggered her inclusion on the trip. That, she later wrote, "was the main reason why I, a colored girl, was invited to help represent our country in Southeast Asia. I certainly wasn't picked because I was a champion; at the time I was champion of nothing and unlikely ever to be."[11]

The invitation stopped Althea in her tracks, abruptly arresting her momentum toward a career in the army. Here was an opportunity that was hard to turn down. It offered travel, tennis of a high level, and the possibility that "the biggest flop," as *Jet* had dubbed her two years before, might have a shot at restoring her public reputation. Best of all, the federal government was going to give each participating player $750 in traveler's checks, to cover expenses, and would pay for all their plane tickets.

After only a second's consideration, Althea accepted McMann's offer. As it turned out, the trip would provide a life-altering experience on multiple fronts. Her interaction with the other players, coupled with the resoundingly affirmative response she encountered from audiences around the world, instilled in her a self-confidence and sureness that no amount of psychotherapy or trophies could have provided. As she traveled from the pagodas of Rangoon, Burma (now known as Yangon, Myanmar), to the mangrove forests of Karachi, Pakistan, she would learn not only how to believe in herself, but how to win at the game of tennis.

McMann laid out some of the details of the trip and described Althea's two male traveling companions, both of them white. One was Hamilton "Ham" Richardson, a chisel-featured Rhodes Scholar who was then studying at Oxford University. Ranked No. 3 in men's tennis in the United States, Richardson had recently been named one of the nation's "Ten Outstanding Young Men" by the national Junior Chamber of Commerce and had the added media appeal of being a diabetic. The press jumped at every chance to gush about how well he coped with his insulin injections, sometimes even at courtside, and occasional mid-tournament hospitalizations. Even the State Department profile introducing him for the tour described his best victory as an eighty-three-game match that took four hours despite his "suffering from insulin reaction, cramps and fatigue."[12] Added to all of this, Richardson was as famously modest as he was generous, a well-mannered man as befitted his Louisiana upbringing.

The second man on the tour, who had a somewhat less glittering reputation, was Bob Perry, a recent UCLA graduate ranked No. 4 in men's singles in Southern California and a member of the U.S. Davis Cup team. The mild-mannered blond, aged twenty-two, was to begin a tour with the U.S. Army as a second lieutenant at the end of the goodwill tour.

The other woman to go on the tour, McMann explained, had yet to be chosen, or so he said. Althea suspected that the State Department was not identifying the woman until they were confident that she would be agreeable to making the tour with a Black woman, and she was probably right. She soon found out that her travel mate was to be Karol Fageros of Miami, an ebullient woman known as much for her cascading blond curls and sculpted dark eyebrows as for her tennis game. Routinely featured in tennis publications in cleavage-revealing outfits or shimmering evening gowns, Fageros would be temporarily banned from Wimbledon competition after having worn gold lamé underpants at the French Championships. Often referred to as "the Golden Goddess," Fageros was nonetheless a considerable player on the rise. In 1954, she won the Canadian Tennis Championships and made it to the finals in numerous tournaments, earning herself a ranking of No.18 among American women players.[13]

Althea was thrilled when she heard the news, for she admired Fageros, who was one of few women on the circuit who went out of her way to be friendly. The two of them forged a unique bond in part because of their difficult childhoods, and several years after the trip, they again toured together as professionals.

This was hardly the first group of tennis players to be selected for an overseas tour, nor were they the first choice of players for this particular tour, with the exception of Richardson. In 1954, Congress approved a $5 million package to fund cultural exchanges featuring a wide variety of spokespeople, including musicians, writers, artists, and athletes. But increasingly, athletes came to be seen as the preferred emissaries. Sports not only provided a cultural bridge that few other activities were able to establish as effectively, but also masked the tours' political dimensions. Given the language differences, the athletes hardly needed even to speak. As Damion Thomas pointed out, "As propaganda vehicles, the visual images of the African American athletes and white athletes working together and the material condition of the Black athletes made it unnecessary and, in many cases, undesirable for the athletes to verbally address the social condition of blacks in the United States."[14]

From 1954 to 1963, more than sixty groups of American athletes were dispatched overseas to play exhibition matches and conduct clinics for foreign citizens. Among the most popular emissaries were the Harlem Globetrotters, the exhibition basketball team famous for their comedic stunts, who embarked on an immensely popular series of world tours endorsed by the State Department beginning in 1951. From the U.S. government's perspective, the value of the Globetrotters' trip was twofold. Not only did the entertaining Globetrotters convey the symbolic message that Black athletes had ample opportunities to succeed within the democratic American system, but the government did not fund most of the team's trips in order to demonstrate that capitalism, too, was fully able to improve the state of dark-skinned peoples.[15] Instead, the State Department would "facilitate" the team's trips, and would help them raise funds while publicly praising the team's numerous engagements abroad. The message, in short, was that the Black basketball players were fully able to support themselves without government subsidies.[16]

Other athletes of color sent overseas who were subsidized by the State Department included Black hurdler Harrison Dillard and Korean American Sammy Lee, a two-time Olympic high-diving champion. Weeks after Althea was invited on the tour, Jesse Owens, known as "the fastest man in the world," went on one of the most celebrated goodwill tours, to India and the Far East, to talk about his work with underprivileged children. The idea behind the trip, wrote *The New York Times*, "is to make friends for the United States."[17]

The State Department maintained that the Black athletes were not sent overseas solely because of the color of their skin, but also because of their outstanding ability in their sport. Some Black Americans, however, questioned such explanations and criticized the traveling emissaries for defending overseas a government that subjected them to discrimination and even murder back home. Chief among these critics was Paul Robeson, the acclaimed actor and singer who by the early 1950s had become a harsh critic of American democracy and an outspoken champion of civil rights. Robeson denounced what he called the State Department's "global advertising campaign to deny the obvious" and wrote that "Negro spokesmen who have set out to calm the clamor of world humanity against racism in America have done a grievous disservice to both their people and their country."[18] Earl Brown, New York City councilman and newspaper columnist, put it more bluntly in a column lauding Louis "Satchmo" Armstrong for refusing to perform behind the Iron Curtain on behalf of the American government. The U.S. government, he wrote, had been paying Negro entertainers and athletes "to play the roles of ambassadorial Uncle Toms for years. They are supposed to show their well-fed, well-groomed faces behind the Iron Curtain as living proof that everyone is free and equal in the U.S., and the color bar is a myth. But it took Satchmo to blow the whistle and let the world know that he doesn't go in for this kind of stuff."[19]

Robeson's activist support for the Soviet Union put him at the margins of Black America. However, even the more centrist magazine *Ebony* took harsh issue with the State Department emissaries. The "dark diplomats in short pants" were undisputedly popular overseas, the magazine editorialized while Althea was on tour, but their efforts merely masked the racial problems churning in the United States. The "brown ambassador," the magazine concluded, "is most certainly America's finest answer to our critics on race. By the same token, the state of anarchy that exists in the South today cannot easily be explained away by lecturers or offset by physical feats. . . . The Negro athlete will have to run mighty fast to outdistance news wires bearing stories of hate and intolerance. . . . To distract foreign attention from our civil rights shortcomings, Negro entertainers will have to sing like Caruso, dance like Nijinsky and play the role of a Pagliacci."[20]

Nor did the Communist media miss the fact that some of the most prominent of America's brown ambassadors who extolled the fair treatment of "Negroes" overseas were met with harsh discrimination on their return back home. Sammy Lee faced overt housing discrimination after his return, while the once-celebrated Jesse Owens had such a hard time finding employment that he wound up pumping gas and racing on foot against horses to make some money. Invited to a celebratory dinner in his honor at the Waldorf Astoria in Chicago on his return from the 1936 Olympics, Owens was required to take the freight elevator.[21]

Nowhere was the hypocrisy of a State Department emissary's public image abroad and private experience at home more glaring than in the experience of Edith Sampson, an attorney who, in 1950, became the first Black American appointed as a delegate to the United Nations and with whom Althea was often linked as a barrier-breaking "First Negro" woman. Sampson, whom some Black leaders criticized for her apologist stance overseas, visited over a dozen capitals around the world without racial incident in the fall of 1949, only to be refused entry at a restaurant in a Washington, D.C., hotel upon her return because of her race. Without a trace of irony, Sampson blithely dismissed the incident, later saying, "I've been colored a long time. If I stopped eating every time something like this happened, I'd be as thin as a rail."[22]

Althea, who was all too accustomed to being barred at the door during her years in the South, might have said something similar. Far from seeing the proposed Southeast Asia trip as casting her as an "ambassadorial Uncle Tom," she saw opportunity. Apparently unbeknownst to her, she had come under consideration for a world tour shortly after she made international headlines during her first appearance at Wimbledon, in the summer of 1951. Weeks later, the Ceylon Lawn Tennis Association, in present-day Sri Lanka, wrote the State Department and asked if some of the country's top players could come compete in the Asian tennis championships the following year. The CLTA asked for several men by name and some of the best female players, but Althea was the only woman they requested by name.[23] Although no tour came about, the All India Lawn Tennis Association made a similar request four years later for top American players to visit their country, and both the USLTA and the State Department got to work recruiting players.[24]

In the opening days of 1955, Harold E. Howland, a representative of the specialists division of the International Educational Exchange Service and a staunch defender of the goodwill tours, had sent letters to Richardson; Tony Trabert, then ranked the No. 1 male player in the world, and William Talbert, the current captain of the U.S. Davis Cup team, who had been ranked No. 3 in the world in 1949, suggesting the possibility of a spring tennis tour in Southeast Asia. Howland stressed the abundant goodwill that such a tour could generate, saying, "That we win that goodwill today in that strategic area of the world is of prime urgency." If Talbert went, Howland added, he would "in all truth—be serving in the front ranks of our people, promoting essential foreign policy objectives of this country."[25] For varying reasons, the trip with Talbert failed to materialize, just as Althea's earlier tour had. By the end of August, the Till murder and several others in the South had changed political calculations such that Althea's name had floated to the top of Howland's list.

When she agreed to go on the tour, Althea became the only female tennis ambassador of color at the time, garnering herself one more "First Negro" title. And yet, the thumbnail State Department biography of her dispatched to officials in the cities the tour was to visit—which included Rangoon, Burma; Calcutta, India; Colombo, Sri Lanka; Dacca (now Dhaka), Bangladesh; Lahore and Karachi, Pakistan; and New Delhi, India—offered no hint of any kind that she was Black. As some observed it, this omission was no accident. Ashley N. Brown, assistant professor of history at the University of Wisconsin–Madison, maintains in her dissertation, "The Match of Her Life: Althea Gibson, Icon and Instrument of Integration," that there was a conscious strategy to separate Althea "from anything and anyone that was black" in order to hold her up as "proof of a progressive, integrated America."[26] There was no mention of Harlem, her American Tennis Association record, the fact that she had broken the nation's color barrier in the sport, or of any of her Black mentors.

So confident was the State Department in the players it had selected for the tour that none of them was coached about a specific message to convey or advised on how to achieve the goodwill so desired. In a letter sent to each of the players, Howland simply suggested that they look at their visits as one of "assistance" to the youth in the given country, rather than one of competition. He added, "So, patting some youngsters on the shoulders, conducting clinics to help their players, paying tribute . . . all this will add up to tremendous goodwill for the U.S."[27] During a meeting in New York before the players took off, Althea was pulled aside and counseled that she would likely be asked many questions about Black life in the United States. It was up to her how to respond. At the same time, she was also advised to "remember that I was representing my country." Not surprisingly, Althea was quizzed numerous times on the subject of the Black experience in America during the tour, and her responses were predictably benign.

"I always said, 'Well, we've got a problem, as all countries and all states and all individuals have, but it's a problem that certainly can be solved and that I firmly believe will be solved . . .' But I didn't see any point in going too deeply into the matter."[28]

Althea didn't want to dig too deeply into the matter because she well knew that to do so might easily disqualify her for the tour. For her, the trip was a singular opportunity that promised to give her high-profile visibility and the chance to compete against some of the nation's most talented players, which she sorely needed. While she enjoyed the attention showered on her on the trip, she was not about to engage in controversial conversations about race that might imperil it all. Nor was it in her nature to do so. Although her calculation might be regarded as having been driven by self-interest, it could just as easily be seen as a shrewd strategy that ultimately benefited many other people of color. Althea managed not only to pave the way for a subsequent generation of Black tennis players, but also to serve as an inspiration for many others.

However her stance was regarded, one thing that clearly mattered on the tour was appearance. Just the sight of the integrated team playing together and attending elegant cocktail parties and dinners overseas conveyed the message that Black and white people interacted well together in America. Althea's neat and smart appearance in particular was a testament to prosperity and good manners. Gone were the days of butch pants and boxy T-shirts, both now replaced by tailored patterned dresses, sophisticated leather purses, and monogrammed luggage. The doctors had done their job well. Just in case, Eaton wrote to Althea days before her departure with a reminder of the critical importance of her bearing: "Althea, when you make this Goodwill Tour remember that you are representing the United States. Take dresses with you and not slacks and try to put forth a special effort to be at your best at all times not only with regards to your dress, but with regards to your conduct in every way."[29]

At the end of November, Althea, Perry, and Fageros flew from New York to London, where they met up with Richardson, who was still on his Rhodes Scholarship at Oxford University. On the very afternoon that Althea sat down on a connecting plane to Rangoon, on December 1, 1955, seamstress Rosa Parks settled into a seat in the "colored" section of a bus in Montgomery, Alabama, on the other side of the world, and refused to get up when the driver ordered her to surrender her seat to a white passenger after the seats reserved for whites had filled up. While Althea crisscrossed the Indian subcontinent as a representative of the possibilities available to Black people in America, Parks's defiance triggered a yearlong bus boycott in opposition to segregated seating that became a landmark event in the fight for civil rights. It would be easy to point to such contrasting behavior and suggest that Althea took the easy route or was less courageous than the celebrated Parks, but that would be an unfair assessment of the two women. Althea's barrier smashing was in some ways just as critical as the seminal boycott, but her form of pioneering needed to be consistent with her nature, which meant doing it on her own, one step at a time, without speeches or raised fists. Somewhere during her journey through Southeast Asia, she began to understand this, and it was this realization, in part, that enabled her to return impassioned to the battlefield of white tennis when the goodwill tour was over.

Althea could not have helped but hear about Parks's defiant act when she landed in the Burmese capital, where accounts of the incident likely appeared on the same newsstands beside newspapers carrying stories excitedly heralding her arrival. "Althea Gibson Will Start Off a Firm Favorite for National Tennis Title," the *Times of India* headline exclaimed. The story, not unlike her State Department biography, described Althea largely in the context of white tennis luminaries, saying she "owes her career" to Alice Marble and was a pupil of Jean Hoxie's, even though she spent barely a week in Hoxie's Michigan home. While the story included Althea's victory in the ATA singles championships, it made no mention of the many Black coaches and institutions that had been her principal supporters. Althea, the story went on, "strides the court with a free and reckless ease. Her cannon-ball first service zooms with power and drive equal to any male's. So do her fluent cross-court drives."[30]

The mission in Rangoon was to perform exhibition matches for local audiences while practicing for the National Lawn Tennis Championships in India, while it would also conveniently generate goodwill for the United States. To the players' surprise, they found America's chief Cold War foe had beaten them there by a few days and was already pounding the Communist drums a few doors down from their hotel rooms. Not only were Soviet premier Nikolai Bulganin and Communist Party head Nikita Khrushchev, along with some one hundred aides, staying in the Strand Hotel with them, but at one of the athletes' first events, a Moscow-based soccer team called the Locomotivs was trouncing the locals on an adjacent field.[31] As soon as the Soviets realized that the Americans were next to them, Perry recalls, they dispatched a camera crew to photograph the tennis stars in action, apparently to gain some pointers on the game. At the time, tennis was a popular sport in Burma, although the level of tennis ability in the country was low. This popularity was partly because American Dale A. Lewis, tennis coach at the University of Indiana, had been the first coach sent abroad by the State Department under the Fulbright program in order to establish the National Junior Tennis Program in Burma. Tennis was still a novelty when Althea and the others arrived. Many of the Americans' events, sometimes played on courts in remote field settings, were packed with curious attendees. One of the first questions the touring stars were met with when they came off the court, invariably directed at Althea, was about race.

"The kids wanted us to talk to them immediately. That is what it was all about. They just didn't see Black people playing tennis, so [Althea] was the star of the show," Perry said in an interview. "The question was 'What's it like to be Black playing in a white man's game?' . . . The other thing the kids wanted to know was 'How could I get to the United States and go to college through tennis or through any means.' . . . These kids didn't have a lot of money."[32]

On the first day of their exhibition matches, the seats at Rangoon's Aung San Stadium were packed with tennis fans, who enthusiastically applauded each of the players. The Rangoon newspaper the *Nation* described the separate two-set matches between Fageros and Althea and Richardson and Perry: "Long rallies, tremendous top-spins, fast-dropping cross-court shots and devastating placements were witnessed in all the games."[33]

After the disparaging treatment she'd encountered in the Black newspapers back home in recent years, Althea was thrilled by the positive press coverage she received in Burma, but there was far more at play that buoyed her confidence. For starters, she had money in her pocket, and not just the $750 the State Department had given each of the four players to cover their room and board during the six-week tour. What's more, the group also had access to a $10,000 discretionary fund that had been given to Richardson, whom the State Department had appointed captain of the team, for use in emergencies or for medical expenses. The foursome jokingly called it "the Captain's Fund." Perhaps more important, Althea and the three other players got along well and mixed easily during a packed schedule of tournaments, cocktail parties, and elaborate dinners. On the flight over, Althea and Fageros decided to share a room, as did their male counterparts, in order to save money. Decades later, the Omaha-born Perry admitted that he was initially concerned about potential friction among the group, given that Fageros and Richardson were both from southern states ruled by Jim Crow, but as it turned out, the group got along exceedingly well.

"I didn't know how they'd get along, but they got along just fine," said Perry.[34]

This is not to say they didn't have to get accustomed to one another's habits. During their first days in Rangoon, for example, Fageros got a lesson in the challenging task of taming a Black woman's hair. Suspecting that local hairstylists would not be equipped to straighten her hair, Althea had come prepared: in her bag was a curling iron, a pressing comb, a jar of Dixie Peach Pomade hair grease, and an old soup can minus its top that she filled with flammable mentholated spirits and ignited in order to heat the flattening comb. As Althea got to work, the flaxen-haired Fageros was mesmerized, having apparently never witnessed such a procedure. But when Althea coated her hair with grease and dangled the comb over the flaming can, Fageros began to shriek in amusement. Althea moved her operation to the bathroom for some privacy, and when a giggling Fageros kept peeking in the door, Althea said jokingly, "Don't laugh at me, honey.

I can't help it. Us colored girls don't have hair like yours, that's all. This is what we got to do for it."[35]

During their daily public tennis matches, the other players in the tour became aware of one more aspect of Althea's game. As exceptional an athlete as she was, she didn't really grasp the larger concepts of strategy or how to close out a match, largely because of her lack of experience at high levels of the game. Despite the efforts of some of her coaches to get her to think more strategically, Althea continued to hit the ball as forcefully as she could as often as she could, with little thought to exploiting her opponent's weaknesses or timing her assaults at the net. Althea, Richardson said, "played every point the same. She just hit the ball as hard as she could and went for her shots. And some went in, and people clapped—but too many of [the shots] didn't go in, and her opponents eventually beat her."[36]

All three of the other players worked with Althea on her game strategy, but it was Richardson who really took on the task of teaching her the subtleties of the game. The twenty-two-year-old had won two NCAA singles championships, in 1953 and 1954, and had reached the U.S. National semifinals, where he was beaten by the indomitable Vic Seixas in 1954. He would rise to No. 1 in the United States in 1956 and was known for his strong all-around game and lethal backhand as well as his calm and courageous demeanor. In a 1960 profile, *World Tennis* magazine, which wrote frequently about the handsome southerner, said, "Ham is a solid man, a good man to have on your side."[37] Richardson was very much on Althea's side in Rangoon and beyond. On the sweltering Asian courts, he showed her how to time her strokes to her advantage, how to know when to attack, and when to bide her time. He demonstrated how some points were more strategically important than others, such as when a player had the advantage, and how to exploit them.

"What Ham told her was that she needed practice and she needed confidence in her game," Perry recalled. "She was much better after that first month. . . . The big thing she learned was how to close out matches. You've got to have the confidence to play out the big points, and she was gaining in that, too."[38]

Further adding to Althea's sense of well-being was an array of lavish parties and meetings with dignitaries at which she was invariably center stage. On a few occasions, she claimed the microphone and crooned some of her favorite songs, impressing both the foreigners and her own playing partners. At a culminating banquet given in their honor by the All Burma Lawn Tennis Association Perry and Richardson were presented with blue silk *longyis*, a cloth worn by Burmese men, while Fageros and Althea received elegant silk parasols—although Althea was too ill from indigestion to receive hers in person. So successful was their first stopover on the tour that William Hussey, attaché to the U.S. embassy in Rangoon, referred to it in a letter to his friend Henry "Harry" Hopman, the talented Australian tennis player who would be the captain of the Davis Cup for more than two decades. Hussey wrote excitedly, "What a big success their visit in the various troubled areas out here was in the 'cold war' being waged daily between the Western powers and the Russian bloc. As far as Burma is concerned we feel their exhibitions in Rangoon and Mandalay won their weight in gold as far as goodwill is concerned (a poor sentence but the idea is there)."[39]

Before the group took off for New Delhi, Althea wrote to Rosemary Darben, saying that the schedule was grueling but wonderful, while describing her adventures and listing the many pagodas she had visited. Being there, she said, "seeing how the people live in this part of the world is an education in itself." She sent her love to "Mom, Pop and Will and all of the family. I will try and send a card from each place I visit. Sending a letter from these parts is so expensive. Love, Althea."[40]

On arriving in India, the players were ready for some real competition from the ranking players there. Some of the world's best from Europe and Asia had assembled for the National Lawn Tennis Championships, held at the elegant, white-columned Gymkhana Club in New Delhi, which, despite having dropped the word *Imperial* from its name after India won independence, carried a distinctly regal air. Althea, flush with the acclaim she was receiving, and Richardson both did well before packed audiences, who continued to besiege the dark-skinned American with questions.

"I was obviously the principal attraction of the group," Althea later wrote. "I was played up everywhere we went. Because I was a Negro, the Asians not only were particularly interested in me, they also were especially proud of me. . . . I can testify that they loved Karol, [Fageros] who not only played fine tennis but also looked like a Hollywood movie star, but they unquestionably got a special kick out of me because of my color."[41]

On their second day in New Delhi, the team ran into their British counterparts in the airy lobby of the commanding Imperial Hotel, another architectural creation of the colonial era, replete with a palatial tea lawn and potted palms in the high-ceilinged lobby. The group included Roger Becker, John Barrett, Pat Ward, and a chatty blonde in a stylish scalloped white tennis dress—the very same Angela Buxton who had watched Althea in awe on the Queen's Club courts as a young girl four years earlier. Not surprisingly, Althea barely remembered Buxton. But when Ward fell ill shortly after the American group arrived, Buxton began to hit regularly with Fageros and Althea, and the threesome spent many hours together. By the tour's end, Buxton and Althea, who discovered they had a great deal in common, had cemented a bond that would endure throughout their lives.

For Buxton, her growing friendship with Althea was a direct hearkening back to her childhood in South Africa, where she had been expressly forbidden to have a dark-skinned playmate of any kind. That experience, she recalled, "stuck in my memory for ages. I was five. So, when I came to Althea, nobody told me I couldn't talk to her, or play with her, or speak to her. Nothing. I *could*. And I embraced that with two hands."[42]

Since that day four years earlier, when she trailed Althea in the hope of getting an autograph, Buxton had matured significantly. Her fledgling tennis game had developed steadily, and she was now not only ranked No. 4 in the United Kingdom, but also was a member of the prestigious women's Wightman Cup team, created as a counterpart to the men's Davis Cup. Hers had been a circuitous route, similar to Althea's in more recent years. Bankrolled by her wealthy father, who owned a profitable movie theater chain, Buxton had been shunned by tennis clubs in both the United States and England due to her religious faith, but she had managed to develop a reasonably competitive if unexciting game. Frustrated after a couple of disastrous matches, she was on the brink of quitting in 1953 when she came under the wing of a maverick sports reporter and amateur tennis player named Jimmy Jones. Like Sydney Llewellyn, Jones had his own singular theory, one he called "Pattern Tennis," which held that tennis adhered to a series of formations and routines that reflected a player's nature. One pattern, for example, called for a short ball to be hit to the opponent's forehand, then long to the backhand, followed by an assault at the net. Another pattern involved two forehands, one short and one long, then a long shot to the backhand. It was an unconventional and methodical style of play that might have straitjacketed some players, but it worked for Buxton, just as Llewellyn's "Theory of Correct Returns" had helped make Althea's game more predictable. In 1955, Buxton made it to the quarterfinals at Wimbledon, her best showing ever, although she was soundly defeated by Beverly Baker Fleitz, the powerhouse who had trumped Althea there four years earlier.

A keenly determined woman, Buxton had a taste for couture and a brusque manner that kept her at arm's length from many of the more reserved British women players in their circumspect whites and buttoned collars. Inclined to elegant tennis dresses featuring lace bodices and satin trim designed by the premier tennis wear designer Teddy Tinling, Buxton was a talented clothing designer herself and worked at the popular sportswear emporium in Piccadilly Circus, called Lillywhites, a name Althea found highly amusing. Most days, her bemused teammates watched from the fan-cooled patio as a dripping Buxton zealously practiced her tennis under the blistering midday sun while they sipped their gin and tonics.

"She was obsessive," recalled tennis historian John Barrett, her teammate and mixed doubles partner. "I mean, she had an aggressive outlook. She had to be, to achieve what she achieved."[43]

Buxton paid no mind to the observations of her teammates.

"Water off a duck's back," she declared with a broad smile years later. "I was in a different time frame, and the court surface was different, and everything was different. I needed to get used to it, and if they didn't, that was their problem. . . . They disapproved of me, everything about me, all the time. My lifestyle. The clothes I wore. It didn't endear me to them, but it just made me all the more serious about what I was doing."[44]

That dismissive attitude was something she and Althea both displayed not infrequently and would ultimately bring them closer. While some of the women tennis players, particularly those on the British side of the fence, were occasionally put off by Althea's at-times overly confident bearing, Buxton considered it inspiring. Of Althea, she said, "Even when she wasn't the top of the tree, she always pretended to be, the way she swayed around and threw herself around. I liked that about her. The other girls weren't like that at all. . . . No, in England we are brought up to keep that sort of thing under wraps."[45]

Toward the end of the New Delhi tournament, Althea did better than any on the American team. In the semifinals, she easily beat Buxton 6–3, 6–4, while Perry and Richardson were both ousted in the same round. In the end, the men's singles title was won by Swedish star Sven Davidson, and Althea took the women's title after easily defeating Japan's leading woman, Sachiko Kamo—who, like Maureen Connolly, was also nicknamed "Little Mo." One news story described the encounter as a one-sided affair in which Althea easily dominated. Kamo, the story continued, "had no answer to Miss Gibson's powerful services and all-court game . . . and the Japanese girl's defence crumbled before her volleys."[46] The British mixed doubles team of Barrett and Buxton easily defeated Perry and Fageros 6–3, 6–3.

The next stop on the program, the Fifth Asian Lawn Tennis Championships, in Calcutta, was much the same story. Althea played slightly less well, displaying poor ground strokes, and lost a set to both Buxton in the semifinals and Kamo in the finals. Once again, though, she won the women's singles contest, as *World Tennis* reported, "by her mere presence in the forecourt, from whence she volleyed and smashed to gain the upper hand."[47] Althea and Richardson also prevailed easily over Buxton and Barrett 6–1, 6–3, to win the mixed doubles. Describing the match in a letter to tennis friends, William Hussey wrote, "Althea was the best man on the court in that match and just couldn't miss."[48]

After a grueling overnight train ride, during which all four of the Americans found themselves bunking in a single car, the team arrived in Dacca, a burgeoning metropolis then under Pakistani rule. Althea continued her winning streak. With Fageros indisposed by illness, as they all were at one point or another, the other three players participated in a series of exhibition matches against locals in which they were all victorious. With no local women available to play, Althea was matched against local men's champion Mohamed Ali, whom she soundly beat, and was ceremoniously presented with a tiger skin rug. The headline in the newspaper *Dawn* solemnly proclaimed, "American Woman Beats Man."[49] But that wasn't Althea's only triumph on behalf of womanhood that day. Later in the evening, she managed to trounce both Richardson and Perry at a game of pool, a historic milestone for the women of Pakistan, whose lives were strictly governed by purdah customs. It was reportedly the first time in the country's history that a woman had been witnessed inside a poolroom, much less emerging the victor.[50]

As the remainder of the tour unfurled through Ceylon to Bangkok and Karachi at the start of 1956 with a series of highly celebrated exhibition matches and more lavish banquets, Althea was confronted with the dilemma of what she might do next. Like the other players, she had a first-class return ticket home but no plan for what she might do once back in the United States. Richardson was returning to Oxford, while Perry was heading to a tournament in New Zealand, and Fageros intended to reunite with a boyfriend in Germany. Althea's own plans for joining the army were on hold, as was her relationship with Will Darben. Before Buxton had departed from Calcutta, she strongly urged her new friend to keep her ticket and travel the European tennis circuit for a few months, in preparation for the French Open and maybe even Wimbledon. Besides, the two of them could meet in Paris for the French Indoor tournament in February and hit some nightclubs and movie houses.

"I said, 'If I were you, I'd hang on to it and try my luck, if you've nothing better to do, on these smaller tournaments,'" Buxton recalled. "'You're a great pull at the gate because they've never seen anybody like you. If they see you there, a Black player, they'll go to have a look at you because you're unusual. And if that doesn't work out, you can use your ticket home anytime.' She said, 'Good thinking.' And I said, 'If it does work out, you can play Wimbledon again, and you can stay with us this time.'"[51]

Althea did just what Buxton suggested. A week later, she cashed in her ticket and embarked by herself on an extended goodwill journey that would take her through the heart of Europe for six months. Buoyed by the acclaim she had received on multiple fronts in Asia, and with her game at peak performance, Althea proceeded to win the women's singles in thirteen out of seventeen tournaments. She even played the women's doubles regularly, racking up another eight wins. The only woman to beat her during her victorious run leading up to Wimbledon was a British woman named Angela Mortimer. A solemn player who had become the first woman of her country to win a Grand Slam tournament since World War II by taking the French National title in June 1955, Mortimer was now ranked No. 4 in the world. Inclined to poor health and partially deaf since her early twenties, she was a fiercely determined baseline player who thrived when confronted with an aggressive competitor, precisely one such as Althea. In later years, Mortimer would confess that her hearing difficulties actually worked to her advantage on the court. Undistracted by any sound, she played within a sort of insulated cocoon, which allowed for laser-like focus on the ball, but it also cost her socially. As Mortimer was reluctant to explain her deafness, some around her, by her own account, interpreted her remoteness as arrogance or snobbishness.[52] Some British reporters mocked her stern affect, calling her "Miss Poker Face from Torquay."[53] Although she maintained a deliberate distance from Buxton and Althea, who were both far too aggressive for her refined British sensibilities, she was in fact a bit of a loner on the tennis circuit as well.

In a six-month period, Mortimer, who later married tennis historian John Barrett, trumped Althea in Mexico City, Stockholm, Cairo, and Alexandria. The stage for their rivalry was set at the Pan American Tennis Tournament in Mexico City, where Mortimer struggled with the altitude and looked askance at the appearance of her opponent in the semifinals. As she later noted in her autobiography, *My Waiting Game*, "I was playing against a tall darkie girl from America. She wasn't well known then, but she played a powerful game. Her name was Althea Gibson."[54] The first set of the nearly two-hour match was a fierce battle of thirty games, which Mortimer ultimately took 16–14. After a long drink of orange juice, Althea wilted and appeared to have given up, easily surrendering the second set 6–1. In Cairo five months later, things got even worse. Although Althea defeated Mortimer in both doubles and mixed doubles in Egypt championships, she appeared wholly overwhelmed in the singles competition, which she lost to her determined opponent 6–0, 6–1.

It would take Althea months to turn back the Mortimer tide, but her spirits were not totally flattened. Perry recalls meeting up with her at the Alexandria Lawn Tennis Championships at the end of March, where the two of them had been paired in the mixed doubles competition. At the start of their first match, the two pairs of players flipped a coin to see who would serve first, as was the tradition, and the Perry-Althea duo won the toss. Although the man invariably served first in such situations, Althea promptly declared otherwise.

"Big Althea will serve first," she announced without hesitation. Perry paused, but then he smiled. "I was kind of laughing to myself. Of course, she served. I knew then that Althea had gotten her confidence together."[55]

Althea's triumphant march across Europe was a cumulative achievement closely watched by the press, earning her headlines both in the United States and across the Continent. She moved from Stockholm to Cologne, from Paris to Nice to Cannes. Cairo led to Alexandria and then Monte Carlo, Palermo, Naples, Genoa, Florence, Rome, and finally Paris again. Despite her success, Althea found it a difficult journey, often traveling alone, anxious about money, and ever in the eye of the news photographers' cameras. As soon as she left Alexandria, she wrote, "I was painfully lonesome . . . I hungered to be with somebody. No matter how hard I tried to think of myself as just another person, I was constantly being confronted with proof that I wasn't, that I was a special sort of person—a Negro with a certain amount of international significance. It was pleasant to think about but very hard to live with. . . . It was a strain, always trying to say and do the right thing, so that I wouldn't give people the wrong idea of what Negroes are like."[56]

Traveling the southern European coastline, particularly in Italy, had its advantages. The cities were far smaller and notably more relaxed than the bustling capitals, where prices were exorbitant and a room could be hard for a single Black woman to secure. In Monte Carlo, for example, Althea performed with a couple of white tennis players at a waterfront nightclub and mixed easily. Jenny Hoad, wife of champion Lew Hoad, who also competed against Althea, recalls Althea performing at several venues on the circuit "where a number of players were involved doing silly things, anyone could play or do an act."[57] Similarly, in Sweden, she borrowed a guitar at a party and strummed out a few ballads with a band of other players, a moment captured in a photograph that appeared in *World Tennis* magazine that spring. Other than those venues, however, Althea remained well outside the tribe of white women players who often bunked and dined in pairs. The loneliness took a psychic toll.

Aching for personal connection, Althea wrote regularly to her closest supporters back home, including Eaton, the Darbens, and her mother. Of all her family members, she appears to have stayed in closest touch with her sister Mildred and their mother. When she flew back to New York, it was her mother who most often greeted her as she came off the plane. In the event that she was anywhere near their home, she almost always stayed at the Darbens', partly because there was more space there, but also because of her deepening relationships with both Rosemary and Will. When reporters wanted more detail about the rising young tennis player in the headlines, the Gibsons cooperated and posed for the cameras with their daughter, their faces in broad smiles. In fact, Althea's parents reportedly had virtually no understanding of the sport their daughter was playing, and by the early summer of 1956, they had yet to attend a single one of her matches. A *Life* magazine profile of her shortly after she appeared at Wimbledon for the second time ran a photo of her parents, who were described as being "proud of her fame but are puzzled by it. They have never seen her play."[58]

Althea also sent Eaton a series of cheerful postcards from overseas, often including her itinerary, and more personal notes to Rosemary describing the exotic foods she was eating and the various cities she was visiting. In almost every letter, she sent love to the Darben family and made a flirtatious mention of Will. From her snow-covered hotel in Stockholm, she wrote longingly of how she wished Rosemary and Will were with her, suggesting that Rosemary "tell William to drink an extra Martini and think of me. (Still love that boy.) How much headway are you making with your romance? Have you given in yet?"[59]

Llewellyn was also a regular on Althea's correspondence list. She frequently wrote to him asking for pointers on how she might have played better in a given match. In Stockholm, for example, she had won the first set from her rival Mortimer, only to crumble under the stress as she often had in the past and lose the last two sets. Llewellyn's advice was to turn to God and also to count her pennies. He wrote, "To be a champion one must get close to God. Most people call on God when they are in dire circumstances, but God is forever with you and all consistent Champions know and feel his presence. Without making any sign of the cross or any other obvious motion . . . I suggest that when you find yourself ahead of a good rival, ask God in silent prayer to help you to maintain the same attitude towards the ball that you had when you first came on the court."

Llewellyn, who would gradually take over management of Althea's financial affairs while she was on the road, also weighed in with monetary advice. Players were required to abide by the strict rules of the USLTA regarding compensation if they wanted to retain their amateur status. While they could accept financial support, including lodging and meals, from the clubs hosting tournaments in which they were playing or from their own sponsoring organization, they were limited to a strict fifteen-dollar per diem in expenses while traveling, as mandated by the International Lawn Tennis Federation. Under a 1954 USLTA rule change, players were permitted to represent sporting goods companies and accept gifts of company equipment but were prohibited from playing for pay. The reality was that many of the best players received financial support from clubs under the table and accepted gifts of tennis rackets, clothing, and other items from manufacturers, all of which at least some members of the USLTA were surely aware. So was Llewellyn. He noted pointedly in his letter to Althea that while she was clearly "having a nice time in these fabulous places" in Europe, she should remember her friends back home who had kept her from joining the army—namely, him. He suggested that she "remember also your obligation to yourself to return with some money, so be thrifty."[60]

In March, Althea received a letter from her mother that had trailed her from London, through two cities in Egypt, and appears to have found her in Palermo, Italy. In her letter, Annie Gibson reminded her daughter of the family's chronic financial needs, expressing concern about the expenses of the family car and an insurance policy. Unable to pay for either, she was perhaps hoping that Althea would send her some money. She promised to send a shoebox full of her daughter's mail the following week, and concluded, "All the kids sends their love. So take care of yourself and don't do any worrying. I want you to keep up the good work. Love, Mother."[61]

Although lonely, Althea was benefiting from the kind of constant competition she'd been unable to engage in either during college or after.

Heeding the lessons she had learned from both Llewellyn and Richardson, she had become a more strategic player and was less prone to her old tendency of lunging for the kill shot only to follow it with a feeble return. That she was often playing against world-class competitors helped her raise the level of her game. By the time she arrived at the Paris Indoor International Tennis Tournament in February 1956, she was in peak competitive form. She was also very ready to hit the town with her buddy Angela Buxton.

During the week they were in the French capital, the two women visited many of the city's famous nightclubs and movie houses, all the while snapping photographs of each other mugging playfully for the camera. As they sipped lattes in the elegant cafés on the Avenue des Champs-Élysées, Buxton noticed that in the aftermath of her highly successful Asia tour, Althea was taking better care of herself, drinking less and going to bed earlier. She was also, Buxton noted, eating healthier foods and acting more like a professional, all of which impacted her performance on the hardwood courts of the Stade Pierre de Coubertin, where they were both rising slowly up the ladder in the French Indoor tournament. There, for the first time, they played together as a doubles team, adding a new and complex dimension to their relationship. Like many who came before her, Buxton found that playing doubles with Althea was not for the meek.

"She was very intimidating. She didn't really play doubles. She played singles on a doubles court," Buxton explained. "She had this very statuesque way of walking. If I were to miss a return of serve, she would look at me like I was daft."[62]

Their first foray onto the court as a team couldn't have turned out better. Althea and Buxton easily won the women's doubles title and were photographed gleefully clutching their trophies. The following day, the friends encountered each other from opposite sides of the court and battled their way through a fierce contest for the women's singles crown. Although Buxton exhibited her notorious determination and led briefly in the second set, she was no match for Althea's volcanic serves and superior passing shots, and she lost to her friend 6–2, 8–6. Buxton gained some retribution later in the day when she and Torsten Johansson of Sweden beat Althea and Californian Hugh Stewart in three sets.

Althea drew additional press scrutiny at the indoor tournament, where she earned the distinction of being the first Black American woman to win a major tournament in France. One newspaper cartoon depicted her as a highly menacing figure at net, her racket raised over her head, back arched, and eyes bulging. The cartoon also exaggerated her features, giving her enlarged lips and a mass of tightly coiled hair. Amused, Althea, sent a copy of the image to Rosemary Darben, on which she penned, "Why don't that ball hurry up and get here . . . dig that hair style." In an accompanying letter, she wrote, "When I first saw it, I thought to myself that the cartoonist had no conception of the Negroid features. I can imagine that his idea was that all Negroes had big lips and wide eyes. Anyway, this one is good for a few giggles. (smile)." At the end of the letter, which was written on Valentine's Day, she included a note to Will, apparently prodding him to write her by saying, "Will; you can't imagine how much I am looking forward to your serious letter. (smile). I hope you think of me when you write your first song on your new piano. Love you, Al."[63]

Back in Montclair, Ro and Will and the rest of the family were keeping a hawk's eye on newspaper accounts of Althea's European journey and were well aware of her successes. Will wrote her back soon afterward, exclaiming, "Darling, Al, . . . I have been thinking about you—missing you and hardly being able to wait until you get back home." Will updated her on his life and wondered if she could find any good cigarette holders the two of them could use. He was hopeful, he added, that he might be able to come see her play at Wimbledon in a few months. If he could make it, he added, he would "come Hell or High H_2O . . . Darling—keep up the good work and keep on winning because you know that I am definitely in your corner 100%. . . . Please Baby—remember—always—I love you, 'Will.'"[64]

Flush with their success, Althea and Buxton departed from Paris and headed their separate ways, vowing to meet next at the French Championships in three months. Buxton returned to London, while Althea continued her lone sojourn through the South of France, down to Egypt, and back up to Monte Carlo. With the exception of her twin losses to Angela Mortimer in Egypt, she continued on her winning streak, amassing one victory after another, but within a couple of months the old loneliness was beginning to gnaw at her once again. By the time she strode onto the courts of the international tournament at the Monte Carlo Country Club, the bejeweled resort on the French Riviera synonymous with opulence and the whitest of privilege, she had wrapped herself in a defensive cocoon once again. One British player remembered feeling diminished just watching Althea walk across the court, let alone losing to her as she did. Fending off Althea's serve, the player recalls, was "like being in a thunderstorm. Not a wet shower or rain. A thunderstorm." But it was her presence that was far more daunting.

"She walked on the court as if she owned Monte Carlo. I don't know of any other woman that did that," she sighed. "I think some days she really did own Monte Carlo. . . . Althea was in charge. I was the servant."

By the time she returned to Paris in May, Althea had amassed so many titles on a five-city circuit through the south of Italy that the tennis press was touting her, along with the handsome blond Australian Lew Hoad, dubbed the unbeatable "Truck Driver," as unconquerable champions. Just twenty-one, Hoad was the fast-rising emperor of the international tennis circuit, once described by the British tennis correspondent Lance Tingay as "a brute with an iron wrist."[65] Describing their singles victories in Rome that spring, the Associated Press declared that "Two cannonball servers— Lew Hoad of Australia and Althea Gibson of New York City—smashed through the Rome International Tennis Tournament looking like major threats for this year's Wimbledon Championships. . . . They both said they thought they had a good chance at Wimbledon and opponents they waded through here agreed with them emphatically."[66]

Althea's success was celebrated as effusively in Montclair and on Harlem's 143rd Street as it was in both the Black and white press. Her international tour, Cal Jacox of the *New Journal and Guide* predicted, "has returned her to the forefront as a prospect to keep an eye on."[67] *World Tennis* magazine, slightly more cautious, praised Althea as "unquestionably very talented," but noted that she had yet to prove herself against the world's best women players. "It will be interesting to see what happens when the top American contingent arrives and whether she will have it quite as much her own way as she hopes."[68] Whatever came next, though, in the eyes of many, Althea had accomplished her mission and resoundingly dispatched the intended message to the Communist parts of the world. On May 13,

1956, *The New York Times* published an editorial called "A Good Envoy," which glowingly described Althea as "a credit to the game and in this case an unusually good envoy for her country. . . . She is part and parcel of the real America that works for what it gets and plays hard and well to win. We are happy in her success and proud of her."[69]

It was time for the streamlined Althea to try her hand once again at one of the major international tournaments, and that meant the French National Championships, next on the calendar. It was not the highest ranked of the four Grand Slams. That honor went to Wimbledon, the oldest and most prestigious of the international tournaments, and easily the stuffiest of the lot. Nor was the French tournament the most popular among some of the ranking players, because the turgid clay courts at the Roland Garros Stadium in Paris slowed the ball considerably and prolonged the matches to such an extent that players were still exhausted by the time they had to compete at Wimbledon several weeks later. In some ways, however, that made Roland Garros the greater athletic challenge, for it was not the players of sheer power who excelled on the gritty red clay, but those of strategic ingenuity and perseverance. In his book *Game, Set and Deadline: A Tennis Odyssey*, Rex Bellamy boiled the difference down to this: "The quick-footed, violent cut-and-thrust that prospers at Wimbledon and Flushing Meadow [*sic*] is not good enough for Paris. Rallies last longer. The ball cannot be put away easily. So matches become a prolonged series of tactical manoeuvres containing every trick in the book; every variation of pace and length, spin, angle, and trajectory."[70]

Not surprisingly, tennis in Paris also offered the most sensuous experience of the four big tournaments, far from the straitlaced strawberries and cream and frosted glasses of Pimm's that are de rigueur at Wimbledon or the trademark Tudor style and starched cotton shirts at Forest Hills. In Paris, there was the heady aroma of espresso and unfiltered Gauloises cigarettes and a plunging neckline or three. There was also the infamous French audience, a highly expressive and partisan group inclined to loud emotional outbursts and a not-infrequent obscenity. If Wimbledon was a punctual serving of high tea, Roland Garros was a seven-course feast topped off with a vintage champagne and unfurled by *Le Premier Chef*. Some of the top-ranked American players skipped the event, particularly serve-and-volley players who found the languid surface and heat too grueling, but not all did. That spring, some of the first-tier women players were on the Roland Garros draw, including American Darlene Hard, Zsuzsa "Suzy" Körmöczy of Hungary, and Shirley Bloomer. Angela Buxton would be there, and so would the formidable Angela Mortimer.

Buxton and Althea greeted each other at the Parisian stadium like long-lost friends. Neither of them had arranged a doubles partner in advance. Watching the two women hug enthusiastically in a hallway, Jimmy Jones realized how close the pair had become, and over dinner that night, a doubles partnership was sealed with his blessing. Over the next two weeks, the two advanced on the roster in both singles and doubles, and somewhat to their mutual surprise, they found themselves pitted against each other in the women's semifinal. Far more surprising was the reception Althea received when she walked out of the tunnel and onto Center Court for the first time, a stark contrast with all her earlier matches, which had been played on smaller, more remote courts. It started with a few disparaging whistles and catcalls. Then the booing began, first a rogue voice here and there and then a collective thrum percolating ever higher into the stands. Althea, bewildered, looked around her as some among the eight thousand spectators began to jeer provocatively.

"She soon learned how Parisians earned their reputation as the world's most critical tennis students," wrote the United Press reporter covering the event. "The 27-year-old New York girl was so upset by the rapid succession of applause, boos and whistles that she lost control of her strokes at the start."[71]

Just what triggered the unfriendly reception was unclear. Some observers attributed it to European partisanship; Buxton wasn't French, but she was closer to being European than not. Others felt the raucous response was distinctly anti-Althea, whom the French may have found overconfident and whose game they considered too aggressive. Was Althea's color also a factor contributing to the churning of the largely white audience, which had never before witnessed a Black person compete in such a setting, much less come close to the coveted title? Or was it all just a classic display of European emotional excess? Only three days earlier, Lew Hoad had been unsettled by an unfriendly gallery and the antics of a couple of

Italian players who flamboyantly surrendered points in protest of a linesman's calls.

Whatever its origin, the crowd's response so rattled Althea that she lost the first set 2–6 to Buxton, who clung to her predictable baseline game. Althea recovered swiftly, regained control of her serve, and took the second set 6–0. She was holding her lead into the third set when unexpected trouble erupted. As she unfurled a powerful serve, one of her bra straps abruptly broke. Buxton rushed to her friend and ushered her off the court to help repair the strap in the ladies' dressing room while the audience, unaware of what the problem was, erupted in a storm of catcalls and hoots. The pair returned only to disappear yet again—apparently the rogue strap was not adequately fixed—to the consternation of both the crowd and the linesman.

"What the hell is going on?" Buxton recalls the linesman shouting at them.[72]

In the chaos that followed their second return from the locker room, the linesman advised Buxton that she should bring a code violation against Althea for leaving the court before the end of the match, which was strictly forbidden. That Buxton had left the court herself appeared not to matter. For a brief moment, the highly competitive Buxton had the semifinals match within her grasp, a Grand Slam final in her sights. All she had to do was agree. But more compelling was her sense of solidarity with Althea and their shared experience of exactly the kind of animosity that was playing out right there on the court. Buxton said no.

"I could have said, 'All right, you can go and change,'" she recalled. "In most cases, nine and a half out of ten, you'd just stay there and wait for her to return. She might have been disqualified. I would sit there and wait for her in most cases. But because she was my friend, I wanted to make her feel more comfortable and go with her."[73]

By the time play resumed, the whole tenor of the match had shifted, and Buxton's strong initial showing had deflated. In the aftermath, some witnesses acidly suggested that Althea had lied about the strap in order to shift the momentum of the match to her advantage, as indeed it had. Another less-than-friendly observer described Buxton's decision not to call a violation as "the lone magnanimous gesture in Angela's entire career."[74] Buxton and Althea ignored it all.

As the crowd continued to boil over the incident, the two women resumed play, and Althea easily surged to a 4–1 lead. Buxton switched her
strategy and began rushing the net, unsettling Althea, which enabled
Buxton to pull into a 5–4 lead. When the crowd exulted over Buxton's
advance, a flustered Althea double-faulted and hit several balls into the net
before she hurled her racket to the ground in exasperation. The linesman
glared darkly. Deliberately calming herself, Althea regained her lead and,
finally, claimed the match with a relentless volley that Buxton could barely
return.

There was little time to process the victory. Two days later, Althea was
faced with a finals contest against her perennial foe Angela Mortimer, the
only woman who had beaten her in tournament play over the past seven
months. Mortimer was her nemesis, or what the press had dubbed her "jinx."
She was also the defending champion, which anointed the British favorite as
a crowd favorite as well. Peter Wilson, the blunt-speaking star sportswriter
for the London *Daily Mirror* newspaper, praised the rise of "the tall rangy
Negress" heading into the French finals in a story that ran on the same day,
headlined "The Girl Globe-Trotter from Harlem." But he also predicted that
she would surely lose. "I do not for one moment expect her to win," he wrote
of Althea. "And even less do I think that she will come anywhere near to
eventual triumph at Wimbledon. Her game is not good enough."[75]

Wilson got it wrong. The first set, he observed, "was over like a thun-
derclap in eighteen minutes." Mortimer didn't win a single game. But the
British player, as was her habit, began to claw her way back in the second
set, switching from lobs to a series of angled shots intended to keep Althea from her preferred net position. It worked. With a series of brilliant
serves, Mortimer inched forward to take the lead until the score was 9–8.
Unnerved, Althea double-faulted, and as the capacity crowd of 12,500
broke into whistles and hoots, she belted a ball petulantly into the stands
in exasperation. Finally, she pulled herself together. Her face expressionless, Althea bore down and, as Wilson put it, "raced up to the net like a
black windmill with all its sails whirling and bludgeon-smashed her way
to match point." Hurling an unreturnable ace down the center line, Althea
took the set 12–10, shattering the jinx that had been hanging over her for
months and seizing the first Grand Slam victory of her tennis career. With

that, she became the first Black player to win one of the world's celebrated quartet of tennis tournaments. As the *Daily Mirror* headline put it, using Wilson's singular wording, it was a "Triumph for the Black Windmill."[76] So delighted was Althea that she leaped over the net and threw her arms around an astonished Mortimer. Her victory easily overshadowed Hoad's win over Sven Davidson of Sweden in the men's final, which had been universally expected.

All that was left to complete Althea's sweep was the women's doubles match, in which she and Buxton were paired against Americans Darlene Hard and Dorothy Knode in the finals. Despite losing a ragged first set, the duo slipped into a groove in the second, with Buxton stepping up her groundstroke attack and Althea using her vast wingspan to capture anything rogue. They claimed the second set 8–6 and sailed through the third set to a 6–1 victory that Althea sealed with a blistering overhead smash. Bookmakers and columnists on both sides of the Atlantic promptly declared Althea the Wimbledon women's favorite. That she lost the mixed doubles with Tony Vincent barely registered.

That night, Althea and Buxton and a few others landed in a Saint-Germain-des-Prés nightclub for an impromptu celebration and some classic blues songs. Affirming their friendship and their doubles triumph, the two women boisterously toasted each other with a string of Coca-Colas capped with a single shot of brandy. It would definitely not be their last.[77] Somewhere else in the City of Light on that glittering night, Lew Hoad was celebrating both his triumph in the men's singles and his newfound status as the world's supreme amateur player. Hoad and Althea, about as unalike as two human beings could be, were nonetheless destined to cross paths at the highest level of their sport repeatedly in the coming year.

Deep in the cavernous State Department building back in Washington, D.C., there were likely a few other glasses being raised. Althea had not only done it, but she'd spun out a stunning string of victories on behalf of her country in a resounding affirmation of democratic promise for the world to see. In America, a Black woman, even one from the humblest of beginnings, could rise to the loftiest perch of the whitest of sports. In a corner of the department's sprawling public relations department, a dark-haired press officer who was also a talented cartoonist began etching out a black-and-white sketch of Althea that would eventually be the lead image on a U.S. Information Service sports information packet featuring American athletic heroes. "Althea Gibson of New York City," the headline would proclaim, "A Leading World Tennis Player." The brochure would be distributed free of charge to newspapers, magazines, and radio stations around the world.[78]

The scrawny urchin from Harlem had blossomed into a leading world tennis player, the brochure proclaimed, and become a global symbol of America's self-proclaimed racial progress. That the same world-famous American athlete was required to sit in the back of a public bus back home and was barred from many hotels and restaurants because of the color of her skin was not mentioned.

8

Small Fry, Big Fry

Two weeks after her groundbreaking triumph in the French Championships in Paris, Althea pulled up in front of the low-slung clapboard Redland Green Tennis Club in Bristol, England, a sprawling city a couple of hours west of London still recovering from heavy bombing by the German Luftwaffe in World War II.

Despite a soaking rain that day, she should have been soaring atop the world.

Not only had she amassed a succession of twelve singles trophies in fifteen tournaments during her six-month tour across Europe, but she had just scored a pair of sterling victories at the Northern Lawn Tennis Championships, in Manchester, defeating both Shirley Fry, the No. 1 women's player in the United States, and the legendary Louise Brough, now four-time Wimbledon winner. The London bookies were giddy with excitement. More than a few columnists pegged Althea as the women's favorite in the Wimbledon Championships, which was only weeks away. Lance Tingay, tennis correspondent for the *London Daily Telegraph*, dubbed her the best American player which, he wrote, "is the same as the best in the world."[1] The Black *Pittsburgh Courier* put it a bit more vividly, calling Althea "hot as an exploded A-bomb."[2] Tossing a cinematic cherry on top, the weather gods washed out an entire day of the Manchester tournament with relentless rain that postponed play, freeing Althea to spend the afternoon sitting happily in the darkened back row of the "flickers," escorted by Buxton's brother, who managed the city's cinema chain for his father.

When play finally got under way at the West of England Lawn Tennis Championships in Bristol, however, Althea was hardly feeling on top of the world. She was instead hovering emotionally closer to the South Pole than the North. Drenched by the lingering British rain, the courts were a grassy soup, and Althea got off to a poor start in the semifinal playing against Jenny Hoad. A talented but not-quite-first-string player, Hoad surged into a 4–1 lead before Althea got her bearings and took the set. As she lunged for a lob in the second set, though, a distracted Althea dove headlong into the muck, splattering mud across her white shorts and shirt. Looking down disgustedly at her filthy clothing, she scowled and hurled her racquet into the stands.

The mud was the least of it. In Bristol, her third stop on the circuit outside London, a Black tennis player, much less a keenly competitive one regarded by some as the world's best, was practically unheard of. With a rising number of immigrants from the West Indies flooding the country in response to a labor shortage in the mid-1950s, England was grappling with a surging tide of hostility toward the dark-skinned newcomers, who were often lumped together as "the coloured invasion." Signs proclaiming, "No Dogs, No Blacks, No Irish" were not uncommon on the doors of shops and hotels; those that did serve people of color demanded exorbitant prices. Immigrants referred to the higher charge as "the colour tax." One pamphlet, titled *Don't Blame the Blacks*, published by the Afro–West Indian Union in 1956, described how the letters KBW (meaning "Keep Britain White") were being whitewashed on walls throughout the country. The pamphlet also referred to sensational anti-immigration stories headlined "Stop Them Now" and to reports of "crackpots trying to form a Ku Klux Klan organization in Britain."[3] One South African male player on the grass court circuit, who had cut his teeth on his country's racial chasm that culminated in apartheid, refused to give Althea the dignity of even saying her name out loud when they encountered each other.

After just over a week in the country, Althea was fuming at the averted eyes in the ladies' rooms of the exclusive tennis clubs where she was competing and the backs turned against her on certain city streets. Even without the racial real estate surcharge, prices in London and the surrounding suburbs were significantly higher than the waterfront cafés of southern Italy, where she had spent so many weeks, and her wallet was hurting even more than usual. Making matters worse, she was exhausted from near-weekly tennis tournaments over the past half year, during which she had lost close to fifteen pounds. Nor did the steady drumbeat of pre-Wimbledon anticipation playing out in Black broadsheets and the British tabloids—"Althea's Favored for Tennis Title, Looms as champion of world," exulted the *Baltimore Afro-American*—do much to help her state of mind.[4]

Althea won the match against Hoad, or, as one wire story put it, "Negress Beats Mrs. Hoad," and, in the end, claimed the Bristol women's singles title in a final match against Australian Daphne Seeney.[5] She and Seeney then tore through the women's doubles ranks to take the final title. Despite her string of triumphs, though, Althea was not in good mental shape for the critical Wimbledon challenge ahead. Years later, she would say that she was overeager: "I wanted to win so badly that I pressed. I tried too hard."[6] In truth, however, there were other factors sabotaging her game, including financial anxiety, sheer overwork, and the grinding Jim Crow–like humiliations she was encountering in England. By the time she stepped on to Wimbledon's grass courts, the old insecurities spawned on the Harlem asphalt were gnawing at her once again, threatening to derail the glorious run of the previous months.

Jenny Hoad, who had attended several of the same tournaments in Italy as Althea, noticed a change in Althea's manner immediately after arriving in England. "It was okay in Monte Carlo and in Rome, but I felt she was a little uncomfortable in England. I just don't think she felt accepted, and she didn't seem happy. I heard she could not go into the dressing room facilities in some places and had to change in the car park. . . . People in England were not wild about her. She was so different being the only coloured lady on the tour. She must have felt, at times, very lonely."[7]

"Lonely" was putting it mildly. Althea, in fact, felt distinctly unwanted, even reviled in some parts of suburban England, the brilliant flame of her tennis stardom all but extinguished by the crowd's reaction to the darkness of her skin. Arriving in the capital city two days after the Bristol tournament, she was worn down, her defenses at a low. When Ralph Hewins, a reporter for the *Daily Mail*, cornered her a few days before her second appearance at the fabled Wimbledon tournament, Althea uncharacteristically let her hair down and gave what may have been the most candid—and brutally honest—interview of her life.

The two-part series, titled "Harlem to Wimbledon," was launched with an introductory paragraph that described Althea as "The FIRST Negress to break the colour bar, which does not officially exist but none the less has kept her people out of big-time lawn tennis. . . . But she often seemed a Cinderella-alone, sad, and serious until she got on to the courts." Althea reinforced that image, saying in the interview, "After ten years of it I am still a poor Negress: as poor as when I was picked off the back streets of Harlem. . . . I am much richer in knowledge and experience. But I have no money. I have no apartment or even a room of my own anywhere in America. . . . I have no clothes beyond those with which I travel around. . . . I haven't been able to help my mother and father and the rest of the family. They are still poor. Very poor."[8]

On the second day of the series, Althea opened the door—just a tiny crack of light—to the reality that Black players were treated differently from whites. While she herself had not experienced any "trouble" because of her race, she admitted to Hewins that, at times, she had been made to feel "uncomfortable . . . felt perhaps wrongly that she didn't somehow belong: that she was different." She insisted that she did not want "to say too much about my inner thoughts for publication as I am one of those people who don't like to be invaded." But she allowed that she saw herself as a sort of "ambassadress for my people. . . . I seek to prove by my own performance that we are equals of anybody. It's wrong that we should so often get that feeling of not belonging and uncomfortableness."[9]

So memorable was the interview that, in later years, Althea would attempt to explain her comments in her autobiography, saying that she had been feeling sorry for herself at the time. Some might argue she had abundant reason to do so. From the very beginning of her tennis career, Althea had deliberately steered clear of being an advocate for or a vocal defender of her race, knowing that to do so would add substantial weight to the already large burden she was carrying as a lone Black woman defying the status quo. But the State Department tour had taken a toll. Despite the success she had enjoyed, representing a country that was riven with racial divisions while witnessing the discriminatory treatment of people of color in parts of England could not have been easy. Althea would rarely speak openly about her personal feelings on the subject of race, or even acknowledge the multiple instances of racism that she personally encountered, until much later in her career. But, exhausted, and facing the enormous challenge of Wimbledon just ahead, she spoke her mind. Her words triggered a reaction that stunned her.

The Lawn Tennis Association in Great Britain was furious at her comments, not because of their substance, but because it apparently believed she had written one of the stories herself, given that it was told in the first person; if she had been paid to do so, she was in violation of her amateur status. The association immediately slapped a gag order on her and sternly advised her not to speak to the press without its permission. "Negress Warned," the *Sydney Morning Herald* headline exclaimed the following day.[10] That Althea had simply relayed her observations to a reporter, as an explanatory headline made clear, seemed not to matter. Thus admonished, Althea avoided the press in the days to come, hovering in the ladies' room in between matches, which likely frustrated her even more.

With the LTA's punishing words hovering over her, Althea approached the ivy-draped tennis mecca of Wimbledon on Church Road with a mixture of anticipation and anxiety. At the time, American players still dominated the women's game, as they had since the aftermath of World War II. But much had changed even since Althea made her first appearance there in 1951, as some of the leading women retired or struggled to hold their place. Maureen Connolly, the determined doyenne of the first half of the decade and the first woman to win a singles Grand Slam in a calendar year, in 1953, had officially retired in early 1955 after her horseback riding accident. Doris Hart, the first woman to win a career Grand Slam in all events, known as a boxed set, had abandoned her amateur status and gone professional later in the same year. Louise Brough and Margaret duPont, reigning doubles queens, were both aging, and their tennis had begun to show it. Althea and Fry, just two months apart in age, belonged to the next generation of women players, followed by the slightly younger Beverly Baker Fleitz, who had soundly beaten Althea in her first Wimbledon appearance with her unparalleled ambidextrous forehands. As they headed into the seventieth staging of the Wimbledon Championships, their seedings reflected the changing landscape. Not surprisingly, Brough, the title defender, was No. 1 on the list, followed by Fleitz, Britain's Angela Mortimer, Althea at No. 4, Fry, and then Angela Buxton. On the men's side, the sometimes-moody Hoad, who was launching his fifth attempt to win the men's crown, was ranked No. 1, followed by his Australian Davis Cup partner and lifelong friend Ken Rosewall as No. 2, Swedish Sven Davidson as No. 3, and Ham Richardson in the No. 6 position. The seedings aside, Althea Gibson was the name on most everyone's lips, and the popular favorite to win.[11]

Shirley Fry, fresh back from a one-year semiretirement, was the other woman to watch. The longtime doubles partner of Doris Hart, with whom she had won eleven Grand Slam titles, the unflappable Fry had persevered in the sport for a decade without making headway on the Grand Slam singles front since the 1951 French Championships. To describe Fry as tenacious hardly did her justice. By 1956, she had played Wimbledon seven times without winning a title, and the U.S. Championships a whopping fifteen times. A consistent baseline player known as one of the fastest women on the court, Fry was shy in nature, content to play a waiting game both on the court and in life. After years of playing at the side of the dominant Hart, she was also famously self-deprecating. With nearly a decade on tour under her belt, Fry walked away from tennis in the fall of 1954 and worked briefly as a reporter in St. Petersburg, Florida, only to return to the tennis circuit several months later and find that her game was stronger than ever. This was to be her last try at the big time, and she knew it.[12]

On the British front, it was Buxton, somewhat surprisingly, who came to dominate the headlines. Part of her celebrity was due to the fact she had just won the women's final at the London lawn tennis tournament at Queen's Club. Part of it was also that she had played stunning tennis against Shirley Fry at the nationally coveted Wightman Cup matches and had almost won, but for a controversial line call at match point in the third set by a linesman who was said to have dozed off. Both players and many observers thought the ball was out, but the linesman called it in.[13]

Buxton may not have been the most naturally skilled player, but she was easily among the most determined and vastly improved players on the court, and many admired her fighting spirit. Maureen Connolly, who worked as a reporter for the *Daily Mail* following her accident, observed that although in the past Buxton had played with robot-like stiffness, she had now "found the beauty and the rhythm of smooth, flowing strokes. Her racket glides through the air in one continuous motion. . . . Her volleying has also improved 100 percent."[14] The *Daily Sketch* put it a bit more bluntly, exclaiming in a headline, "The Girl They Said Was Useless Can Make Wimbledon History, It's Angela's Big Chance to Wear the Crown."[15] The Wightman defeat was galling, and the British were quick to rally around their underdog, nicknamed "Miss Determination." The tabloids also found the blue-eyed, smartly dressed Lillywhites salesgirl far easier to like than the "other Angela," meaning Angela Mortimer, who was the epitome of conservative reserve.

For the media, the fair-haired Jewish underdog and the proud "First Negress," as Althea was so often called in the headlines overseas, made an irresistible duo. That Harry Buxton, Angela's wealthy father, and a man with high-profile Hollywood friends, had promised his daughter, only half in jest a year earlier, a gift of the Bognor Regis Pier, which he leased in a popular resort area, if she won Wimbledon, made the story all the more alluring. Some columnists even predicted that the pair had a good shot at taking the women's doubles title. In the days leading up to the Championships, photographers and reporters flocked to the Buxtons' two-bedroom apartment on Rossmore Court, not far from the bustling Paddington Goods Station where Althea had been welcomed with open arms. Buxton's mother, Violet, moved into the single bedroom so that the two young friends could bunk together, and she took delight in occasionally tossing the press morsels of information or arranging a photo op. Years later, Buxton would recall fondly the three Wimbledon fortnights during which she and Althea roomed together, as she had had difficulty making close friends with whom she had much in common, and particularly ones who shared her passion for tennis. "I was delighted that there was somebody like that, because I hadn't found anybody like that. . . . Even to this day I have difficulty."[16]

The two young women each kept to her own routine for part of the day. Althea, who promptly took to calling Violet "Mom," adding yet another name to her collection of maternal figures, stayed up late into the night sipping her cherished glass of gin and smoking cigarettes while watching movies on the "telly." In the morning, while Violet whipped up a big breakfast for "my girls," as she affectionately called them, Althea would lounge in the bathtub singing show tunes while Buxton hummed along in the next room. "I used to leave the door open so I could hear her," Buxton recalled. "It was quite good."[17] Buxton would rise much earlier, and three days a week she headed across the street, to Regent's Park, to run timed wind sprints, bending down every twenty yards or so to grab a handful of small rocks she had laid along a chalked line, as her coach Jimmy Jones had instructed her to do. The idea was to improve her agility, which it did.

By late morning, the two players came together. Althea, American to her core, had convinced the public transportation–minded Buxton that they each needed a rental car to drive out to Wimbledon, because of their varying playing schedules. Side by side, they picked up their cars at the Blue Star Garage next door and headed to Queen's Club for a practice session on the wooden courts, before continuing to Wimbledon. On Sundays, they ambled across the street to Harry Morgan's Deli for a special dinner of "salt beef," or corned beef, sandwiches. On weekend evenings, there were nightclubs to visit—sometimes Buxton managed to take the microphone— and late-night discussions about sex. That, as Buxton recalled with a broad smile, "was one of Althea's favorite topics." Althea, Buxton remembered, "loved sex. She would talk to me about the enjoyment of it. I'd never had sex in those days. I was only twenty. My mother never spoke about it, so she was my entrance into the sex world. . . . She could see she had an interested audience in me, so she carried on."[18]

All their comings and goings invariably attracted the attention of at least one neighbor, who complained about such offensive racial mixing to the building's real estate manager. Late one morning, Violet, cooking utensils still in hand, hurried from the kitchen to answer a knock at the door and found the manager standing outside.

"Have you got a Black person staying there?" he barked. "We've had a resident complain that you have."

"Yes, we have," Violet answered.

"How long is she going to be staying there?" queried the manager. "She wants to know."

Violet Buxton, well accustomed to discrimination from her days in South Africa as well as London in the 1950s, was not easily cowed. She laid her utensils down and took a step forward so that her face was directly in front of the manager's. "Whoever it was who complained and said that to you, send them here tomorrow at two p.m. I've got a free hour, and I'll deal with them then," she said firmly. And then she turned around and slammed the door. Nobody ever showed up.[19]

Despite such incidents, and her comments to the *Daily Mail* a week earlier about Black athletes being made to feel unwelcome, Althea held back from even acknowledging the role of race as the event grew closer. On the day before her foray onto the Wimbledon courts as the first Negro to be the favored women's player, she proclaimed most adamantly her unwillingness to be identified as a Negro tennis player. Never, she maintained in an interview with *The New York Times*, had she experienced any discrimination in her long climb up the ranks of the tennis ladder. She added, "I am just another tennis player, not a Negro tennis player. Of course, I am a Negro—everybody knows that—but you don't say somebody is a white tennis player, do you?"[20]

Llewellyn, who wrote her almost weekly during the buildup to Wimbledon, encouraged her downplaying of race. In a letter addressed to "Al," which he sent days before her first match, he said that his reading of the media hubbub engulfing her only proved to him "that you are there on the eve of one of the greatest contest[s] in the world today not because you are a negro, but because you are an American, true you are one of the many millions of colored Americans in the United States but your being there is proof of a working democracy that exists here; a democracy where anyone of merit can get an opportunity." In apparent reference to profiles that described her as aloof and less than communicative, he concluded, "Don't let any of the nonsense they write in the papers upset you. We talked about that and decided the best thing is to be cool; remember?"[21]

Not surprisingly, some in the Black press sharply disapproved of Althea's reluctance to champion her race, a difference that would become increasingly fraught in coming years. Shortly after the *Times* interview appeared, the *Pittsburgh Courier* published an editorial, titled "Orchids to Althea," that firmly admonished her. Any victories she might achieve, the piece declared, would affect opinion about others of her race. The athletes at Wimbledon, it continued, were not just tennis players, but *American* tennis players. "And whether Miss Gibson likes it or not, she will be an American Negro tennis player as long as she wields a racquet. Whether she wants to be identified as a Negro tennis player or not, she will be, and her victories will reflect credit upon all other Negroes. We therefore commend her for her past success and hope she goes all the way at Wimbledon."[22]

At the start, it appeared that she might. The second day of the tournament, when the women's play began, was dubbed "Ladies' Day." By the end of the first round, all ten of the American women in the draw had easily won their first matches before an audience of twenty-two thousand, as had all the top-ranked men. Defending champion Brough destroyed a sixteen-year-old South African opponent, while Fry won plaudits for her triumph against Belgian competitor Christiane Mercelis. Althea also won easily against German player Edda Buding 6–4, 6–2, employing a series of feints and unreachable drop shots that complemented her formidable power game. Critics also noted, however, that her game was flawed by several elementary errors that seemed to stem from nervousness. It was Buxton who injected an element of excitement into the proceedings, boosting British hopes that, at long last, one of their own might triumph over an American, with her resounding defeat of the French player Suzanne Le Besnerais. Her performance, her first ever on Centre Court, prompted one reporter to declare that "Miss Buxton, above any other English player, has the stuff of latent greatness."[23]

It wasn't until the third round that Althea ran into difficulty. Playing on Centre Court and battling a whipping wind, she struggled to find her groove and lost the first set to British player Anne Shilcock. She recovered her rhythm in the next set, and her forceful play seemed to overcome her opponent, who committed several overhead errors and wilted in the final points of the third set. Despite Althea's masterful play, the crowd remained coolly unenthusiastic, prompting veteran *Daily Mirror* columnist Peter Wilson to point out that Althea was the first colored player "to 'invade' a game which is riddled with snobbery—even if your skin is the same colour as the majority of the other players." The audience's indifference, he added, was not born of British nationalism, as many claimed. "It's easy to say that they only applaud the player who is leading. But it doesn't happen to be true. It's easy to say that they applauded because it was an English girl leading against an American. But that, too, I fear, is not quite accurate. The colour bar dies hard in any sport." In the end, Wilson concluded, "And when Althea, serving like a dream and volleying like a nightmare (for her opponent) won the last two sets, I wished that white palms could have waved a little less languidly."[24]

Those pale palms never picked up the pace for Althea. Part of the crowd's discomfort with her likely stemmed from her much-commented-on angular appearance, her unflattering shorts and boxy shirt, and even the unladylike way she held her body. At the start of the tournament, the *New York World–Telegram* ran a pair of photos of her, one that showed her as a grinning teenage girl, the other as a mature player crouched in masculine aggression awaiting a serve from her male opponent. "Yes, the Same Gal," the headline announced. The cutline under the second photo observed, "You can see the 'man's stance' and service power to Althea Gibson's game."[25] Whether it was that or her disconcerting inconsistency and cool demeanor, or something entirely different, the crowd remained unmoved. Even when she felled her fourth opponent, Pat Hird of England, the audience appeared put off by Althea's erratic performance in the match. What kind of player raced through the first set 6–0, then lost the next four straight games due to her own errors, only to blast forward with a six-game winning streak? By the time she took her place on Centre Court in the quarterfinals against Fry, the indifference had curdled into something quite different, something harsher. If Althea Gibson actually won, if a poor Black girl managed to claim the ultimate prize in the sport, what were the implications for the future of the game, or for British sports overall, some wondered.

Scottie Hall, of the London *Sunday Graphic* newspaper, called it for what it was. "It was an unspoken, unexpressed but anti-Gibson atmosphere. It's part of my job to smell atmosphere. Halfway through the Gibson-Fry match, I found myself sniffing hard. I didn't like the smell. . . . This was when I glanced at the face of an American tennis reporter. It was tense, strained. And this was when I conveniently remembered that Yankee voice rising from the hubbub of the press bar at lunchtime: 'So Joe Louis became a champ. And what happened? Nigger boxers came out from under every stone. Same thing if Gibson walks away from here with a tennis pot.'"[26]

The first set, which Althea won 6–4, was a showcase of her athletic artistry—or, as the *Times* put it, "The way Miss Gibson planned the rallies was fascinating. She was like a spider spinning a dark web. The variety of her game, with spin and chop or flat drive, time after time landed her the final coup."[27] Althea delivered her trademark serve with topspin, followed by searing volleys directed at alternate sides of the backcourt. Fry had difficulty with the returns, while her own serve remained flat and often landed in the net. Althea, it seemed, was on her way.

In the second set, however, the energy of the game shifted. Fry, one of the most seasoned players on the circuit, picked up the pace of the play, and now it was Althea struggling with returns. At 3–2, Althea abruptly double-faulted and lost a critical point. As several observers later noted, it appeared that her determination began to wane. Fry, serving softly in order to reduce any benefit of generated speed and delivering precise backhands that were impossible to return from Althea's preferred net position, took the second set 6–3. As the third set got under way, Fry was hitting the ball with deadly precision and deliberately opted for a strategy that both Connolly and Fleitz had successfully employed against Althea: attacking her inconsistent backhand. It didn't help that Althea shifted from her attacking net game and now hovered at the baseline in an effort to retrieve Fry's bullet-like returns. She strained to dodge the assault, launching one lob and then another, and chopped her returns, but the tide was clearly turning in Fry's direction. The hushed spectators were transfixed as Althea inched forward in the final game, only to have Fry take the set 6–4. It was, clearly, shaping up to be Shirley Fry's tournament and, perhaps, even her year.

The *Sunday Graphic*'s Hall also saw something else.

"Shame on the Centre Court! . . . I accuse the Wimbledon crowd of showing bias against Miss Gibson," he wrote. "I say it was this bias that helped to rob Miss Gibson of a quarter-final round victory over fellow American, Shirley Fry."[28]

Whatever the elements that led to Althea's loss, she took her defeat stoically. Slowly, she lifted her arm in a solemn salute to the umpire and then, languidly, pulled on her cardigan. Only when the two players bowed to the Royal Box, did she smile briefly. As the two women turned away, the *Guardian* concluded, "There seemed to be a strange emotion in the applause as the players walked off. It was as though everyone was conscious that this was no ordinary victory and no ordinary defeat."[29]

In the aftermath, both women were gracious. At a press conference, Althea showed none of the venom over her loss that she had sometimes displayed in the past. She had learned, she said with a straight face, that "I can beat small fry in small tournaments better than I can [beat] big Fry at Wimbledon."[30] For her part, the ever-humble Fry declared, "I should not have won. . . . But she got scared . . . she hung back, through nerves, I guess. I feel sorry for her because I know how it feels."[31]

Meanwhile, Buxton was plowing through the competition under the prayerful gaze of thousands of Londoners and the watchful eyes of her parents. On each of her play days, Harry Buxton would pull up on Church Road in his secondhand Rolls-Royce with Buxton's boyfriend of the hour at his side and flash a fistful of cash, in lieu of the requested credential, to gain admittance. At night, Buxton, who was a poet at heart, penciled poems at her kitchen table describing the day's highlights. After Angela Buxton's fourth-round victory, she enjoyed an astonishing stroke of luck in getting a walkover in the quarterfinals when Fleitz withdrew, announcing that she didn't have the flu, as had been widely reported, but was pregnant and could no longer continue in the tournament. Now just a single match stood between Buxton and the Wimbledon finals. That night at the kitchen table, Violet excitedly penned the opening lines of a lengthy poem that she would eventually address "To Angela, Wimbledon 1956 June."[32]

> *Then two days of rest & Tuesday came*
> *We thought perhaps Fleitz was playing a game*
> *But it wasn't the flu that she had at all*
> *She was just a little bit pregnant, that's all*

Buxton and Althea had also been gliding steadily through their doubles matches toward the semifinals, and they now faced the formidable duo of

Fry and Brough. Each of the two, Fry and Brough, had been a partner in one of the most successful women's doubles pairings of the early 1950s, albeit not with each other. During the series of pre-Wimbledon grass court warm-ups, the same two partnerships had met in the finals at the Queen's Club tournament. Althea and Buxton bombed in their match against the Brough-Fry duo, largely because of erratic play by Buxton. Althea was visibly infuriated, and the two of them stalked off the court not speaking.

Jimmy Jones was quick to the scene, and in a blunt cafeteria discussion, he stressed to both of them, his gaze fixed primarily on Althea, the importance of supportive teamwork on the court. Somehow, his words made a difference. The fiercely independent Althea was able to let down her rigid defenses and embrace a partnership with Buxton. This was, after all, her "Angie," as she fondly called Buxton. After their next practice match, Althea, by then nearly in tears, hurried over to her partner, hugged her, and uncharacteristically apologized. With the two friends now working together, their games began to coordinate. Jones helped them develop a way to privately communicate strategy during a match, and by the time they faced Brough and Fry on Centre Court at Wimbledon, they were primed. As usual, Althea dominated, pounding serves into the corners and angling lobs out of reach, but now she was doing so *with* Buxton, who set up the plays for Althea to drive home. Surprising nearly everyone who expected the Brough-Fry pair to be invincible, Althea and Buxton pulled it off. With a 7–5, 6–4 win, they now faced a Wimbledon final together. That night, Violet returned to the kitchen table.

> *Then for the doubles against Brough & Fry*
> *It looked as though it might be a very close tie*
> *But the girls pulled it off & now they could see*
> *They were in the finals on Saturday—Gee!!!*

First, though, came the all-important singles semifinals. At long last, Fry managed to beat the aging queen Brough, whose legendary twist serve, a staple of her game, had visibly deteriorated. When Buxton trounced British player Pat Ward, the grand finale was cast. The American Fry would square off with the British Buxton, anointing Buxton the first woman of her nationality to make it to a Wimbledon final since 1939, when Alice Marble beat Kay Stammers. Buxton, not surprisingly, was thrilled, as were the tabloids.

"Whoopee! I'm in the Final," trumpeted the headline in the *Evening News*, over a photograph of a joyous Buxton leaping into the air, her arms outstretched. "Victory Out of a Bucket . . ." the headline continued, in reference to her training regimen of sprinting between the strategically positioned stones she toted in a bucket.[33]

"Angela Is Out for Revenge," declared the *News Chronicle*, citing the recent Wightman Cup competition in which many felt the linesman had unfairly denied Buxton a victory.[34]

The match lasted a miserable fifty-two minutes. Buxton, nearly immobilized by the expectations of the fourteen thousand spectators in the Centre Court stands and the blank page in the British tennis history book yawning before her, fell, missed several easy shots, and began to sweat profusely as Fry's returns sailed past her. And then she began to cry. Midway through the first set, it was painfully clear that the hard-hitting Fry was going to win, and the audience fell largely silent for the remainder of play. Afterward, some critics dubbed it the worst women's final ever. Violet put it slightly more delicately.

> *I kept crossing my fingers with all my might.*
> *But nothing—just nothing—seemed to go quite right*
> *I knew she was nervous, though it didn't show*
> *Just the perspiration seemed to flow & flow*

Buxton lost 6–3, 6–1, leaving an American once again holding the cherished Championship trophy. Days before the tournament, the mayor of St. Petersburg, Florida, at the time had sent Fry a telegram promising her the city's downtown pier, in a humorous response to Harry Buxton's vow to give his daughter a seaside pier if she won Wimbledon. Less than an hour after her Wimbledon victory, Fry telegrammed the mayor to say she was "Coming soon to collect my pier."[35]

To many veterans of the international grass court circuit, Fry's win and likely retirement to follow signaled the beginning of the end of a glorious era of high-performance women's tennis that had dominated Wimbledon beginning with Helen Wills Moody's win in 1938. Buxton, however, had little time to anguish over her own dismal outcome. Within hours, she was due back on the court for the women's doubles final against a pair of young Australian girls, Daphne Seeney and Fay Muller, a relatively inexperienced duo who had nonetheless made it almost to the finish line without losing a set. Buxton headed to the ladies' room, took a hot bath, and pulled on her new Lillywhites tennis dress with the dropped waistline and lime-green piping before heading back to Centre Court with Althea at her side.

If Buxton was anxious, Seeney and Muller were even more so, despite their brand-new matching Teddy Tinling outfits with flared skirts and snug bodices. In the opening set, Seeney was so laser-like in her focus on an impending serve that she failed to notice Muller gesticulating wildly at her back. Then she heard the tittering in the audience. The wind had blown Seeney's dress up over her rear end, revealing to the thousands in the audience, including the Duke and Duchess of Kent, seated in the Royal Box, the elaborate ruffled panties à la Gussie Moran she was wearing underneath. Seeney, a poor country girl from the Australian bush, who had already been beaten badly by Althea at Bristol the previous month, froze.

"I don't think I hit a ball over the net for the next five minutes," she recalled.[36]

The Australians lost the first set 6–1. Although they pulled it together in the second set, and even managed to turn the tide at five crucial points to pull into the lead from behind by aggressively rushing the net, Althea and Buxton claimed it at the end 8–6. The two victorious women—partners, flatmates, and now Wimbledon champions for the first time—threw their arms around one another and headed to the Royal Box to accept their victory cup. Several of the rural newspapers gave scant attention to the triumph of the American Negress and the British Jew, but Buxton long remembered one that did.

"The headline," she said, was "'Minorities Win.'"[37]

Violet would never forget a moment of any of it.

But win it they did—the second set 8–6,
They had to use every one of their tricks
The Australians jumped & twisted & curled
But it didn't stop our girls from being champions of the world.

As impressive as the women's doubles performance had been, it did not quite win top billing among the excitable crowd. The best of the finals, by many accounts, was the mixed doubles, an all-American standoff that pitted Fry and Vic Seixas, three-time previous winner with Doris Hart, against Althea and forty-two-year-old Gardnar Mulloy, veteran doubles champion, who was ranked No. 6 in the world by *American Lawn Tennis* magazine in 1947. Althea and Mulloy had won the mixed doubles final at Queen's Club just a couple of weeks before, and Mulloy wanted nothing more than to win the Wimbledon title with her as well, as Seixas recalls it. He wanted it so badly, in fact, that he was willing to abide by a strategy wholly unconventional at the time and deferred repeatedly to his very dominant female partner. Even when balls hurtled down Centre Court, shots customarily taken by the male player, he hung back. During the first set, the tactic worked, as Mulloy repeatedly set up shots for Althea. They took the set. The second went to Fry and Seixas, now getting used to playing with Hart's former partner. As the third set inched along with the score neck-and-neck, the crowd bubbled with excitement. On match point, Fry rammed the ball straight down the center of the court. Neither Althea nor Mulloy, seemingly frozen in indecision, went for it, and they lost the last set 5–7.

"I don't think Gar ever forgot that his entire life," recalled Seixas, now in his nineties. "Gar was willing to let Althea take any balls she wanted because she was so aggressive. He didn't care about anything but winning. . . . He really thought they were a cinch to win the tournament."[38]

If Mulloy was irked at Althea, he never revealed it. In fact, he became something of a defender of his Wimbledon partner and later described her as a good friend. A few weeks after Wimbledon, he was talking with a handful of lawyers in his native Miami when one of them unexpectedly asked, "How come you played doubles with that nigger?" Mulloy later recounted. "I looked him straight in the eyes and said, 'Oh, I didn't know she was a nigger. I thought she was a brilliant tennis player.'"[39]

Two months later, Mulloy and Althea were cheered at the posh Denver Country Club when they won the mixed doubles against Shirley Bloomer and Hugh Stewart during the Colorado State Championships. That night, however, Althea encountered exactly the opposite reaction when she strolled into the club's elegant ballroom to attend "The Tennis Ball" with Mulloy and his wife. Not only did some members begin muttering unhappily about her presence, but Mulloy was cornered "by several slightly inebriated members who wanted me to discreetly escort Althea from the premises. I was livid," Mulloy wrote in his memoir, *As It Was*. Unfazed, he did exactly the opposite, coaxing Althea into taking the stage as he urged the band to play "Moon Over Miami." As she obligingly began to sing, club members calmed down, apparently finding it more acceptable for the dark-skinned woman who was the first seed at their tournament to be performing *for* them rather than dancing *with* them, as Mulloy noted years later.[40]

Even that disturbing incident did not impel her to speak out. Days later, Althea, who could not have been unaware of the racist churning in the ballroom, once again maintained that she had never experienced any bad treatment related to her skin color. Never, she declared in an interview with the International News Service, had she experienced discrimination during her years playing big-time tennis. "Tennis," she said, "just isn't that kind of game."[41]

Althea was deeply disappointed by her loss at Wimbledon, as were many who had cheered her along during the many months of anticipation beforehand. *The New York Times* ran an editorial afterward that encouraged her to take heart from her impressive overall record overseas. Titled "Miss Gibson's Loss," the piece concluded, "A record such as Miss Gibson made this year suggests a tenacity, courage and skill that must be reckoned with another day. There will be other Wimbledons, and some perhaps that will not end this way."[42] Indeed, Althea was already declaring her intent to return the following year, as was the man of the hour, Lew Hoad. The powerful young Australian had just won the Wimbledon men's singles in a thundering four-set contest against Ken Rosewall, his tennis soul mate and the other half of what was often referred to as the "Whiz Kids" combo. The win by Hoad, who had claimed the Australian and French championships earlier in the year, brought him one step closer to becoming only the second man ever to claim a Grand Slam since American Don Budge did so in 1938. Already he was chafing for the American tournament just two months away, where he would encounter Althea once again. For the moment, however, it was time for Althea to finally go home.

Neither Althea nor Buxton had achieved the tennis heights for which they yearned, but they shared the gleaming silver Wimbledon doubles championship trophy. Just as important, they were a partnership now, one that had deepened each of them on an emotional level and that would last a lifetime. Following their victory, they attended the ceremonial Wimbledon Ball together and made one more stop at their favorite Berkeley Square nightclub on their way home. In a final London foray, Buxton personally arranged for Althea to have a singing audition and make a test recording with Buxton's friend, the recording star Jerry Wayne. Despite discouragement by Llewellyn, who felt singing was a distraction from her all-important tennis career—he often told her she couldn't sing her way out of a bathtub—Althea was intrigued by the prospect of a performing career, and the London recording session only enhanced her hopes.

Althea had accomplished another, somewhat less-talked-about milestone on her journey. As one of the first Black women to represent the United States overseas, she had put herself forward as an accomplished, highly talented person who spoke positively of her country, just as government officials had intended. Not, she would admit in later years, that it had been easy. Having so often downplayed the role of race, she found that it had impacted virtually every aspect of her trip, beginning with the very reason she was selected to be a part of it. "Being considered an adjunct of U.S. State Department policy, as had been the case off and on during our Southeast Asia tour, was bad enough. . . . Having to contend with crowds hostile to me because of my color, with newspapermen demanding twice as much of me as they did of anybody else simply because my color made me more newsworthy, and even with powerful governments seeking to use me as an instrument of national policy because of my color, seemed to me to be more than anybody should have to bear."[43]

Nor did the role of race dissipate on her return back home. Althea landed at Idlewild Airport in Queens, New York, at 6:30 a.m., after an eighteen-hour flight on a Pan Am Clipper from London, exhausted but ebullient. She had been gone for eight months, much of it traveling in Europe. Awaiting her at the airport were her parents, New York City mayor Robert F. Wagner, a delegation of the American Tennis Association headed by Assemblyman Bertram Baker, and a gaggle of reporters and photographers. In the back of the crowd stood a beaming Rosemary and Will Darben, whom the press described as "a good-looking twenty-nine-year-old Jerseyite wearing a fashionable three-button suit and pink-tabbed shirt." When Althea appeared to grow weary after making a few comments, a protective Will escorted her to a waiting car, prompting newspapers to speculate excitedly about their relationship. "Althea Loses Heart to Jersey Engineer," exclaimed the *New York Amsterdam News*. Darben downplayed any possible nuptials in the offing, saying, "There are a few things to be worked out yet."[44]

A few hours later, a grinning Althea arrived at City Hall to receive Mayor Wagner's formal congratulations. Renville McMann, now the USLTA's president, attended the event, explaining that he had deliberately stayed in the background so as not to upstage the ATA. "It was their show," said a spokesman for the national organization. Althea made no apologies for her Wimbledon loss, but said she felt she might have played too much tennis leading up to the tournament. Far from planning to take a break, however, she announced a grueling schedule to start in just a few days, one that would take her from the Chicago Clay Court Tournament to competitions in Pennsylvania and South Orange, New Jersey. The trip would culminate in a September return to Forest Hills, her seventh appearance there, where she would surely face Fry again. She would try, she added, "to take a week's rest in there somewhere. . . . I don't want to be stale for the Nationals. I think I may have over-tennised myself before Wimbledon."[45] As she spoke, her father sat outside the building on a park bench, reluctant to come inside, as he did not have a proper jacket. At the urging of a friend, he reluctantly borrowed a jacket from a Harlem radio announcer and approached the podium to shake Mayor Wagner's hand. Quizzed by a reporter, the elder Gibson said, "I can't tell you how proud

Althea has made me and her mother," before retreating to a bench in the back of the room.[46] High-level ceremonial functions, clearly, were not in his comfort zone, nor in that of Althea's mother, who did not attend.

While the brief ceremony was an acknowledgment of all that Althea had achieved, it fell far short of an honorary parade up Broadway of the sort that had greeted Jesse Owens on his return to the city after winning four gold medals at the 1936 Olympics and other celebrated heroes. Nor was there any mention of the proposed parade for her that had originated in the Black press, bounced around City Hall, and then ricocheted through the White House, ultimately dying in the backyard of the ATA. Althea must surely have known of it, but she never made any public mention of the matter. Nonetheless, the incident was a telling reflection of the ambivalence with which American culture, and its loftiest politicians, continued to regard high-achieving Black citizens, even in the face of the incremental civil rights progress in the 1950s.

The parade proposal had been first suggested by the *New York Amsterdam News* in an editorial entitled "We Make a Motion," long before Althea stepped onto the Wimbledon grass. Although Althea's career had benefited enormously from the tour, the piece stressed that she was like many other Black citizens who had performed admirably overseas and allowed themselves to serve as a propaganda tool in the Cold War against Communism. "Armed with only her brown skin and her tennis racket, Althea . . . has brought honor and glory to this nation while doing so—even under the most adverse circumstances. . . . We feel that New York should applaud her in the true New York tradition. And that means with a ticker tape parade up Broadway! . . . We proudly make the motion. We feel certain that New Yorkers will second it."[47]

Except that those in key positions of power didn't. At first, City Hall tried to dodge the idea, saying that such honors were reserved for foreign heads of state. The *Amsterdam News*, however, quickly pointed out that the city had given the ticker tape treatment to such figures as Gertrude Ederle, who swam across the English Channel; Charles Lindbergh, who flew solo across the Atlantic; and others.[48] Bertram Baker, the ATA's all-powerful executive secretary, initially supported the idea of a reception for Althea upon her return and wrote not only to Mayor Wagner, but also to President Eisenhower, suggesting as much. But somewhere amid the flurry of memos about "the Negro tennis player" that passed between the White House and City Hall, the idea foundered, and it was decided that no parade could be had without *all* the American players at Wimbledon on board. It was to be an example of "practical democracy." Just days before Althea returned, both the parade and reception were ruled out, and even Baker backed off the idea. Instead, Althea was given a brief welcome at City Hall and photographed with Mayor Wagner and Baker. Furious at not being included, many in the city's Black community who had toiled for years on Althea's behalf charged Baker with hijacking her glory for himself.[49] In the end, Black city councilman Earl Brown proposed a resolution congratulating Althea on her Wimbledon performance, but even that was watered down by the city council to include Shirley Fry.[50]

The Black press was incensed.

"So what do you have to do to earn a motorcade up Broadway?" stormed *New York Amsterdam News* columnist Jesse H. Walker. "Nobody at City Hall, nor any of the other Americans who played at Wimbledon . . . can best what Miss Gibson accomplished during the past nine months. And I mean they can not best her politically or sportwise. To my mind, City Hall goofed. Althea should have had her parade."[51]

Even some in the White House disapproved of the outcome. In a memo to cabinet secretary Maxwell Rabb, Jacob Seidenberg, director of the President's Committee on Government Contracts, which worked against discrimination, noted the negative reaction among the Black press and proposed that a reception for Althea be hosted by either the White House or the new National Physical Fitness Commission.[52] That didn't go anywhere, either. Ann Whitman, Eisenhower's personal secretary, consulted with both the president and Vice President Nixon's staff and concluded that there were too many obstacles to the committee's doing anything, according to her letter to Rabb. As for the president reaching out to Althea at such a late date, she added that it "smacks of politicking too much. If she wins at Forest Hills, maybe." The symbolism of the situation, however, was hardly lost on anyone. At the end of her letter, Whitman noted the absence of any dark skin at high-security levels in the White House. "Incidentally," she wrote, "why don't we in our own front yard have some Negro White House police, and Negro Secret Servicemen?"[53]

Baker's waffling on the matter apparently reignited Whirlwind Johnson's long-simmering rage over the ATA's failure to support his Junior Development Program in general and over what he considered to be Baker's arrogant behavior in particular. Days after Althea arrived back on American soil, Johnson fired off an open letter to Baker and ATA president Sylvester Smith, charging that Baker's "egotism" was causing a decline of the ATA and demanding that he resign from the organization. Baker, whom Johnson continued to deride with the nickname "the Boss," promptly responded in kind through a reporter, growling, "Tell him to go to Hell."[54]

The incident also reflected the extent to which the Black press had, at least for the moment, rallied behind Althea again. After the years of disappointment, followed by a period of relative disinterest in her when she faded from tennis during her Lincoln University days, reporters now stood bullishly on her side, even defending her against occasional critics. During the second week of Wimbledon, for example, the *Chicago Defender* wrote that the gossip in the ladies' room was that Althea was no longer the naïve, unspoiled girl who had played there in 1951, but had turned into a "sulky tight-lipped, moody Miss So-and-So only interested in her Mission—a ruthless title-chasing mission. In other words, they are saying Althea is a snob who wants nobody's company but her own." But the unidentified writer vehemently disagreed with this characterization. "My answer to that is 'Tripe! Rubbish!' and 'Phooey!'" Althea, the column continued, had simply matured and was, in fact, "one of the most dignified girls I've ever seen." Despite Althea's own downplaying of her race, the writer even dubbed her as a kind of racial apostle. "You can take it from me that she looks upon herself as an evangelist whose skill with the tennis racket, and her sincerity, is breaking the colour barriers."[55]

In a measure of just how committed to her the Black press had become, Fay Young, who had publicly admonished her for rudeness in his *Chicago Defender* column nine years earlier, now empathized with her burden. "Funny person—that Althea. Doesn't talk about herself. Doesn't seek publicity. . . . We believe she is misunderstood," he wrote upon her return from London. Citing her string of overseas wins, he concluded, "We all are with her—win or lose."[56]

Ebony magazine took it to an even higher level of breathlessness. In a four-page spread headlined "Althea Has Finally Arrived," the magazine ticked off her achievements from Paris through Manchester and on to Wimbledon, concluding that, "in her chosen sport, she is about as good as they come." She had even made important connections among "the smart set." Often playing before galleries composed of snobbish people who deny any trace of racial prejudice, Althea had nonetheless managed to grow "wealthy in fame and acclaim. . . . Occasionally, she may smash a racquet to the court in disgust; but her poise runs to such depths that she can be trusted with a goodwill ambassadorship."[57]

Buoyed by such support, Althea set her sights on the next challenge before her, which was America's premier tournament at Forest Hills, only two months away. The only problem was that she headed into the preceding practice tournaments just a little too soon. Ten days after she landed in the United States, she stood across from Shirley Fry in the finals of the National Clay Court Tournament in Chicago, at the River Forest Tennis Club. She did not do well. Part of the problem was that she was still exhausted and twenty pounds underweight. Part of it was that she had injured her wrist in a match over the weekend. Perhaps most daunting of all, she was playing against *Shirley* again, and everyone knew, after all, that it was shaping up to be Shirley Fry's year.

Althea launched into her now-predictable pattern from the outset, taking a 5–2 lead in the first set, then abruptly disintegrating. Fry won the next eight games in a row, further unnerving Althea, who struggled to return the relentless drives coming at her, fumbled her own backhands, and lost 7–5, 6–1. One of the many observers deeply disappointed at Althea's performance was Mary Hardwick Hare, the former highly ranked British tennis player who had supported her years earlier. Of the match, Hare wrote in *World Tennis*, "This was one of the saddest matches I have ever witnessed in a national final. I hope Althea will learn a lot from it. The human body needs rest and relaxation; after six months of continuous traveling and tournament play she is mentally and physically exhausted."[58]

Althea heard her. After a bit of rest, she returned to the court refreshed and fully recovered from her eight months overseas. First, she felled doyenne Margaret duPont, at that time, holder of fourteen women's singles and doubles U.S. National titles, a six-time Wimbledon champion, and perennial doubles partner and friend of Louise Brough in the women's Pennsylvania and Eastern States Championships in Haverford, Pennsylvania. Several observers had noted in recent months that the aging duPont, famed for her masterful overheads and dazzling twist serve, was "not the player she was a few years back," as *The New York Times* put it.[59] Still, the 6–1, 6–4 victory was more clearly a reflection of the superior game executed by Althea, who earned her first grass court title on American soil in record time before an awestruck audience of 2,700.

Althea's spirits, already at a high ebb, were further boosted when Buxton arrived in the United States and joined her on the Eastern Grass Court Championships in South Orange, New Jersey. On one of the days leading up to the championships, they joined Rosemary Darben in nearby Montclair for an evening at the "flickers" followed by a visit to a favorite nightclub. On the first day of play at the tournament, the two of them easily won their first round, but that night, Buxton's right wrist began to swell alarmingly. By the next morning, it was twice its normal size, and at an emergency doctor's visit, she learned that she had tenosynovitis, a chronic inflammation that made it impossible for her to continue to play. Crestfallen, her arm in a cast, Buxton said goodbye to her friend and headed back to London, consoled only by the notion that they would surely meet at Wimbledon the following year.

Days later, Althea easily brought down her longtime nemesis Brough in the Eastern finals at the Orange Lawn Tennis Club. So obvious was the outcome of the match from the start that it generated only a smattering of applause. Brough double-faulted repeatedly and made a host of errors, enabling Althea to easily take the match 6–1, 6–3. By its end, two things had become abundantly clear. First, the generation of women players who had so dominated the game in the postwar years were fading before a younger cadre; and second, Althea was likely to be a formidable contender at Forest Hills.

Now on the brink of her return to the West Side Tennis Club, Althea had two events to attend, both linked to her past. One was a luncheon in her honor hosted by the U.S. Paddle Tennis Association in Manhattan, at which some of her closest supporters, including Karol Fageros and Bobby Riggs, celebrated her beginnings in that sport on a Harlem street corner more than a decade earlier.[60] There was also her annual appearance at the annual ATA tournament in Wilberforce, Ohio, where she won against Nana Davis, the same sturdy competitor who had defeated her in 1942 at her first big tournament, the semifinals at Lincoln University. At the time, Davis had called Althea "a very crude creature" when she refused to shake hands after the match and instead rushed into the stands to pummel someone she thought had been laughing at her. To the disappointment of many, including her doctor benefactors, who were both present at Wilberforce, her 1956 match would be Althea's last appearance at an ATA tournament. The organization's tennis prodigy had graduated to the premier rank of white tournament tennis and, unlike some Black athletes, who used their high profile to take a political stand during the tumultuous civil rights era ahead, she declined to act as an advocate for the Black chapter of the sport. In the years to come, many among the Black press would come to resent her deeply for her decision.

Althea and Fry both arrived at the Diamond Jubilee Seventy-Fifth National Championships at Forest Hills in high spirits, never mind that they both shared the distinction of having been defeated there on multiple occasions. For Althea, the No. 2 seed, it was her seventh try at the coveted American trophy, her first having been her history-making match, and defeat, against Brough in 1950. In none of those attempts had she made it beyond the quarterfinals. Fry, the No. 1 seed, had Althea beaten even in that category. The Ohio-born player had been the youngest female competitor ever to play at Forest Hills when she first appeared there as a fourteen-year-old in 1941, and she had returned a stunning fifteen consecutive years without success. This time around, Fry's sixteenth attempt, they both tore through the early rounds of competition. Althea easily dispensed with Nell Hopman, wife of Harry Hopman; her pal Karol Fageros; and three others, until she stood across from Fry in the final round on a windy but brilliant afternoon before a crowd of thirteen thousand excited spectators. Anticipation was at a fevered peak not only because Althea was the first Black player to make it to the finals of the American championship, but also because, as soon as the women's event was over, Lew Hoad would take the court in the final chapter of his determined bid to win the world's second male Grand Slam.

At the start, anything seemed possible in the Althea-Fry duel. Both employed their trademark strategies, with Althea rushing the net and Fry commanding her unyielding backcourt position. Within a few games, however, a jittery Althea began to crumble, netting fifteen balls and making twenty-seven errors. In the second set, Fry pressed even harder, and her bullet-like ground strokes repeatedly sailed past Althea at the net, just as they had at Wimbledon. Further unnerved by frequent foot fault calls, Althea found her vulnerable backhand caving, and even her usually powerful serves were frequently off the mark. She was beating herself, and both players knew it. In the second set, she flailed at the baseline and made another twenty-three errors before Fry won 6–3, 6–4. It was over in just fifty-two minutes. Althea had won every set at the tournament except for the two she lost to Fry. But, of course, those two, as she wrote in her biography, "were the ones that counted."[61] Shirley Fry's year was wrapping up nicely.

A couple of hours later, Hoad saw his vision of a historic Grand Slam record implode when his pal and Davis Cup teammate Ken Rosewall bested him in a stunning assault of line drives and drop shots that left viewers, and Hoad himself, astonished. Dubbing the masterful young Australian men as "possibly the two most accomplished 21-year-old finalists in the tournament's history," *The New York Times*'s Danzig described the match as "a madcap, lightning-fast duel."[62] For Hoad, the defeat meant that his dream of glory, and the possibility of turning professional, would have to wait for another year. The slender Rosewall, on the other hand, would accept a pro contract from Jack Kramer several months later for $55,000 for the first year, plus 20 percent of the gate over $350,000, thus becoming the latest male champion to migrate from amateur tennis to the relentless promoter's moneymaking stable. Others, almost all of them men, would soon follow.

In the aftermath, many mulled over the why of Althea's poor performance. Was it the Fry jinx playing itself out again? Or, as the *Boston Herald* suggested, maybe Althea just didn't have the stuff of a big-time champion after all, as some had been muttering for a while. In his usual blunt fashion,

Sydney Llewellyn explained that Althea simply wanted the win too badly. So badly did she hunger for the victory, he explained to *Time* magazine, that "it was like living in a pressure cabin. When the day came, she was a nervous wreck, and Fry beat her like a mother beats a child."[63] Increasingly sought after by the press to explain the sometimes-remote Althea, Llewellyn suggested that her problem stemmed from long-standing psychological issues. Althea, he told *Sport* magazine, "has been a mixed-up girl all her life. As a tennis player, she has the finest equipment of any woman who ever lived. As an individual, she has personality problems so deep and enveloping that they are constantly interfering with her career. But I think she is cutting loose from them." None of them, he hastily added, had anything to do with race. "She has been treated magnificently by everybody."[64]

Milton Gross, a *New York Post* sports columnist who had followed Althea since her debut at West Side, however, stepped back and took quite a different view. Althea wasn't beaten in a mere hour, he suggested, but by the staggering burden of her race and the seventy-five years it had taken a Black player to make it to the Nationals singles final. So nervous had Althea been, Gross pointed out, that she didn't hold service until the seventh game in the first set, and she clung to the baseline rather than play her normal attacking game. Fry and Althea each carried a racket in her hand, Gross noted, "but Althea also carried the weight of the years and of her race. It gave her caution when it should have given her daring. It gave her concern when it should have given her comfort. . . . She was the first Negro to reach the final and it was too much for her."[65]

Althea was keenly disappointed with her performance, as she had been with the outcome at Wimbledon, but she was not at all defeated. On the contrary, she took heart at the improvement in her game over the year and publicly expressed confidence that, with Llewellyn at her side, she would triumph in the year to come. Far from collapsing, she promptly hit the road and ricocheted from tournaments in Toronto to Denver to Mexico, during which the world tennis rankings were released. Fry, not surprisingly, won the No. 1 position, with Althea right behind her at No. 2, followed by Brough and then Angela Mortimer, in fourth place, according to one set of rankings. In perhaps an equally significant indication of the stature she had acquired over the course of her world tour, Althea appeared on the cover of the November issue of *World Tennis* magazine, which featured a photo of her smiling warmly, her arm resting on a pile of tennis rackets. The cutline beneath a far more severe, some might even have said arrogant, picture of her inside explained that she had "made one of the fastest climbs to the top in women's tennis history. After four years of knocking at the door, she suddenly consolidated her game and clearly earned the No. 2 spot."[66] Toward the end of her North American trip, she received an invitation from the Australian Lawn Tennis Association to travel with Fry to Australia and compete in their biggest tournaments, which she eagerly accepted. One reason for her eagerness was that she couldn't stand to let Fry's multiple victories over her stand, but she also liked Fry and was looking forward to traveling with her. First, however, she headed east to see her family and, perhaps more important, the Darbens.

Given her relentless pace, she and Will Darben had seen each other rarely even during the month she had been back on American soil. Still, both of them were thrilled to be reunited even for a short period, and they apparently discussed marriage, even if Althea continued to keep the reality of an actual wedding at bay. Within days of Althea's departure for Sydney, Darben launched a series of passionate, near-weekly letters that would follow her overseas for the next three months. In his first letter, he announced that he had dutifully washed her beloved car, which she had left in his care, and had visited her mother. "You see, darling—I do love you and will never be satisfied until you are completely mine!" He described a second job he had recently taken on, explaining, "You know I have to get a ring for you—so all the money I make comes in quite handy." Concluding with a warm hello to Fry, he signed off, "Well, darling—you know I love you—I want you—and I miss you. So please write soon . . . I love you. 'Will.' P.S. How do the monkeys kiss?????" This was followed by a series of *X*s. "Those are kisses!!!!!"[67]

One week later, on Thanksgiving Day, he wrote again. Rosemary, he explained, had cooked an elaborate dinner for the whole family, while he had mixed the martinis, and they all had made a toast to Althea. "I wished that you could have been there to have one with us," he wrote. Telling her that he had again talked to her family, he concluded, "Darling—I know that you are lonely there . . . but you know how time flies so be patient. I love you and that alone will keep us together even though so far apart."[68]

Given the tone of Darben's frequent letters, it appears that Althea was writing him back in a similar manner and was equally smitten, given the tone of his responses. She apparently did not include copies of her own letters along with the many others than she saved. Their relationship, however, did not rule out other men in her life altogether. During the more than one year since she had left Lincoln University, Althea had apparently stayed in touch with Capt. Dova Jones, the man with whom she had a "wingding" of a good time, and she had seen him somewhere during her fall travels across the country. In a September letter to her, Jones wrote to say how much he had enjoyed their recent visit. He wrote, "The evening was perfect, which goes without saying. Wish that we had been able to have more time together. . . . You must write me as often as you find time. Always, Dova Lee."[69]

By the time she landed on the other side of the world—a journey requiring stops in San Francisco, Honolulu, the Fiji Islands, and Canton, now called Guangzhou, before arriving in Sydney—Althea didn't have time to think about either of her suitors. She and Fry were immediately swept up in the five biggest tournaments in Australia, with Althea taking three titles and Fry winning two. For Althea, there was a degree of solace in the fact that she was able to overcome what some were calling her "Shirley complex" and beat the big Fry, the world's No. 1 female player, as she did in both Sydney and Adelaide.

The match that earned them the biggest headlines was an explosive encounter at the Victoria Women's Tennis Tournament in Melbourne. Furious after losing three match points in intermittent rain and livid at a linesman who called her on twenty-one foot faults, Althea smashed a ball into the stands, where it streaked within inches of the head of Australian prime minister Robert Menzies and the former president of the Lawn Tennis Association of Australia. At first, tournament officials had merely warned Althea that she was stepping over the service line, but as she repeatedly continued to do so, they began calling the faults. Incensed, Althea screamed, "Why don't you stop this and let's get on with the game?" Some of the eight thousand spectators in the stands were on her side and shouted, "Give her a go, you mugs, give her a go at it!" and "Wake up . . .

Change the umpire." With multiple breaks for the rain, the marathon match stretched close to three hours, with one of three sets going to sixteen games. In the end, Fry was the victor at 4–6, 9–7, and 8–6.[70]

One wire story describing the match exclaimed in its headline, "Prime Minister Victim of Near-Assault," but even that didn't begin to compare with the excitement that arose on a totally different front back at their hotel.[71] The following afternoon, while they were resting after a match, Shirley received a phone call from a man she had met back in the United States who was working in the Sydney office of an advertisement agency. The man, Karl Irvin, wanted to take her out for dinner, and Fry halfheartedly agreed. But on her return that night, she was ecstatic, already half in love with him. Shirley Fry, the girl ever known for her willingness to wait, to hold back both in life and on the baseline, was going to wait no more. Within two weeks, she had decided to get married. Having informed her parents back in Ohio that she was staying in Australia, she was soon hard at work finalizing the details for her wedding. Shirley Fry's year was ending with an explosion of passion, champagne, and confetti.

When the final wisps of shredded paper fell to the ground, Althea Gibson was left standing on her own. After beating Althea in the Australian National Tournament in Melbourne in the first month of 1957, Fry would retire, and her name would be added to the growing list of dominant women players of the past decade who had done the same or moved on.

Althea was unable to attend the wedding, as she was already committed to a return trip to Ceylon the following month, on behalf of the State Department. As she packed up her belongings and prepared to travel, she received a letter that Llewellyn had written on the first day of the New Year. He admonished her, briefly, for the foot fault debacle, saying, "You see, Champ, it's not enough that you win—but you must win with class. To achieve this class you have to work or practice at intervals—in all due respect to your abundance of talent." But the real purpose of his letter was something much more important. The goal now, he advised her, was to step boldly forward in what was already looking like a promising new year.

"Stay in there, Champ, and give them hell in 57. Your year. Love—The Coach."[72]

Turned out, The Coach was right.

9

At Last, at Last

As 1957 got under way, Althea Gibson had a single radical goal, and that was *not* to play tennis, at least not in the grinding and competitive way she had been in recent months. After a long year of weekly competition and sometimes more, shuttling across international borders and anxiously tallying up the spare change at the bottom of her purse, she was bone weary and still below her normal weight. She was also smarter.

Althea resolved to focus her sights on the big one, to channel all her being into a roughly 130-by-70-square-foot patch of immaculate grass turf on the far side of the ocean a half hour southwest of London. The Wimbledon women's singles tournament of 1957 was where she would finally conquer the world. She wouldn't play the southern spring circuit or even defend her title at the French Open. She would rest and practice with Llewellyn and play only on turf. In her spare time, she would mix a few martinis with Darben and read Dale Carnegie's *How to Win Friends and Influence People*, as Llewellyn had suggested.

In the spring, she got a call from Harold Lebair, chairman of the USLTA's international play committee, informing her that she had been selected as their No. 1 player for Wimbledon, meaning that all her expenses would be paid. Althea was still ranked the nation's No. 2 by the USLTA, behind Fry, who had retired, and just ahead of Brough. Ecstatic, Althea promptly wrote Eaton to inform him of the news, thanking him for all he had done for her and marveling at the distance they had traveled together.¹ Now all she had to do was stay focused.

The media, starved for fodder about the would-be tennis queen, made that difficult. Without her tournament play to scrutinize, reporters began to poke around their second-most-favorite subject of interest when it came to Althea Gibson: her love life. That spring, even before she returned from her Ceylon trip, the *New York Amsterdam News* declared that Althea was going to announce her engagement as soon as she got back. Weeks later, speculation swirled hotly around Darben, to whose home Althea had returned after her overseas run. In mid-March, the *Baltimore Afro-American* scored a lengthy interview in the Darbens' Montclair living room during which Althea repeatedly dodged questions about rumors of her impending marriage to Will Darben, saying, "I have no comment." Darben, described in the article as "a quiet, handsome aviation plant employee who answered the doorbell and made me welcome," sat silently at her side throughout the interview, his eyes locked on the television, a smile tugging at his lips. Althea continued: "'All I plan to do is to rest and prepare for the Wimbledon matches,' she kept repeating like a woman possessed."²

Next, *World Tennis* declared the wedding a fact, announcing in its May 1957 issue that the couple would be married "sometime in the near future." The item ran inches below a photograph of Althea practicing on the wooden court boards at Nick's Armory in New York as Llewellyn hunched at her feet and analyzed her footwork.³

While questions about Althea's sexuality perennially percolated in the media—her "mannish" style of dress and bearing were stock items in many profiles that ran of her during her steady rise up the tennis ladder—she had in fact become ever more deeply involved with Darben. During the months she had been traveling overseas, the two had been in frequent contact by both letter and phone and were now in deep discussion about the details of their wedding. According to their written exchange, Althea had suggested a small and intimate nuptial event, and the ever-accommodating Darben was all for it. Before she returned to Ceylon on a State Department tour at the end of January, Darben wrote to her, saying, "Now darling, about our wedding plans: we can do exactly as we wanted. That is—we can either get married away and very Quiet or in the city—fairly Quiet. You know how you want things—so any way you want will be OK with me. The only catch is that I do want to marry you and very soon." At the end, he added, "Always remember—you are all I want ever in the world—I mean it Baby. Love You Always, Will."[4]

For Althea, all the press speculation about her impending nuptials was part of a convergence of cultural expectations that had plagued her for years and would engulf her in the months ahead. Everyone, it seemed, wanted something of her. She may have lost to Fry in the major tournaments of the previous year, but over the course of her global travels, her game had improved on many fronts, and with it, so had her confidence. As the prognostications about her performances to come grew tremulous with excitement, Althea approached the pinnacle of women's tennis. While her star rose ever higher, she would be besieged by the demands of others. Black people wanted her to speak out on the escalating civil rights issues of the day. White people wanted her to persuade the rest of the world, and the Soviet Union in particular, that the United States' record on race wasn't as horrific as it seemed. America's conservative culture of all hues wanted her to be heterosexual, ideally married, and clad in something willowier than her boxy shorts—a pastel dress perhaps, and some matching pumps with kitten heels. The press, of course, wanted her to unbutton and talk about how she felt about it all.

Althea wasn't having it. The longtime loner had learned on her tour that the only way to achieve what she wanted on the court was to shut out the noise, to ignore the catcalls and jeers from the stands, the turned backs in the dressing room, and the icy stares at the front desk. Althea was going to do it for herself, and by herself, because that is what she'd had to do to survive since she was a child. Right or wrong, it was the only way she could do it.

It wasn't going to be easy. As Althea was defending her single's title at the Asian Championships in Ceylon, President Eisenhower dashed the hopes of many Black people back home early in 1957 when he refused multiple pleas to travel to the violence-torn American South and make a speech on behalf of civil rights. One month earlier, Rev. Martin Luther King Jr., the Montgomery minister and activist who had emerged as a national figure after leading a yearlong boycott of the city's segregated bus system, had requested, along with other leaders, that the president visit and urge southerners to abide by recent Supreme Court decisions calling for desegregation. Ike declined to speak. In the absence of a national voice protesting the spiraling racial violence in the South, King and other civil rights figures organized a Prayer Pilgrimage for Freedom to Washington, D.C., that would draw close to twenty-five thousand demonstrators from across the nation at the Lincoln Memorial. Held on the third anniversary of the 1954 *Brown v. Board of Education* decision, the assembly marked the first time King addressed a national audience, an event that would position him at the forefront of the emerging civil rights movement. Althea could hardly have been unaware of the event. Days before the Washington, D.C., gathering, King had addressed a rally of thousands of marchers in front of the Theresa Hotel in Harlem, not far from the Gibson family apartment. In the coming months, the passionate fervor that characterized the pilgrimage would surge throughout the nation and eventually lap across Althea's own trajectory.

Days prior to the Harlem rally, Althea was fêted at an ATA-sponsored bon voyage event held at the Birdland Jazz Club in New York as she prepared to head off to Wimbledon. She was toasted by Sammy Davis Jr. and other notables, while she herself crooned "I'll Be Seeing You" before a crowd that included the USLTA's Renville McMann and the ATA's Bertram Baker. Darben, described as Althea's fiancé, was photographed sitting somberly at one of the tables by *World Tennis* magazine, but he was notably absent from the small group that escorted Althea to Idlewild Airport not long afterward.[5] Instead, it was Syd Llewellyn behind the wheel, along with bandleader Buddy Walker and Althea. Edna Mae Robinson, longtime friend and supporter, showed up to say farewell and slipped twenty dollars in Althea's pocket for spending money. In the weeks to come, it would be the voluble Llewellyn—not Will Darben—who often addressed the press and explained the sometimes-remote Althea to hungry reporters. As she boarded the Pan American Stratocruiser, Althea held her three rackets, one Harry C. Lee and two Slazengers, close to her chest as usual. So worked up was the press about her and the possibilities that lay ahead that her mere landing at Heathrow Airport in London hours later merited attention. Even *The New York Times* noted the arrival of the women's singles favorite, with a single-sentence paragraph headlined "Miss Gibson Reaches London."[6]

Awaiting her at the gate was a beaming Angela Buxton, dressed in the finest from Lillywhites, her blond hair artfully coiffed, a boxy white purse hanging from her forearm. Sidelined by her wrist injury, Buxton was now writing for several sports publications and would be reporting on the Wimbledon Championships from the sidelines. Touting a new beau on her other arm, Buxton was eager to show her old doubles partner her first new car, a hot-pink Morris Minor convertible with the name "Agatha III" written in maroon-colored Old English script on the back. Buxton had owned two previous Agathas, both of them bicycles, named for a favorite nun who had been her teacher during her South Africa days. Before heading into the city to Buxton's apartment on Rossmore Court, where Althea would again stay for the duration of the Championships, the two friends posed arm in arm for a photo.

Snapped in the airport parking lot, the picture is a study of contrasts. Angela is dressed in flowing white from her elegant ribbed sweater to her knee-length wool skirt and arched spike pumps. Her studied affect is accentuated by oversize white pearl earrings and a pair of designer sunglasses clasped languidly in her hand. Althea is a collection of dark angles. She wears a stiff black leather knee-length coat and flat brown leather lace-up shoes. She stands flatfooted, her tennis rackets secured under her right arm, as though ready to race to the end of a tennis court. And yet, the dark and light are bound by the women's shared delight at their reunion. It was an exhilarating moment for them both, and the media was devouring every morsel. In the same issue that it announced Althea's nuptials, *World Tennis* magazine displayed a pair of photographs of "lovely Angela Buxton" modeling her designer creations, including a Lillywhite tennis dress featuring ribbed panties and a matching bodice and a pair of dainty white leather tennis slippers embroidered with crossed tennis rackets.[7]

There was little time to catch up. No sooner did Althea drop her bags at Buxton's Paddington flat than the two women hurried off in opposite directions. Buxton was due at work, while Althea headed toward Surbiton, about an hour south of London, where she would launch her tour at the Surrey Grass Court Tournament, the first of four pre-Wimbledon tournaments in which she was to play. Althea won the singles finals in the first three tournaments and took the doubles with Darlene Hard at Queen's Club. Like a number of other high-profile players, she chose not to play the Queen's singles matches, in order to conserve her strength for the big one right around the corner. Beckenham, the third of the grass court events, was Althea's strongest showing, for she managed to defeat both Hard and one of the hottest items on the London tennis circuit, a short-haired sixteen-year-old schoolgirl named Christine Truman. The round-faced Essex teenager, who, at five feet, eleven inches topped even Althea, was a powerful player and the reigning British junior champion, despite a chronic vision problem in her left eye that had been discovered in her childhood years. Although unseeded in the lineup at Wimbledon, where she was making her debut, Truman was the subject of a deep-seated nationwide hope that maybe, just maybe, after twenty straight years of American domination, a British woman could finally reclaim the Venus Rosewater Dish, the trophy in the Wimbledon women's competition. The Beckenham encounter did not bode well for Londoners, though, as Althea easily beat the youngster 6–0, 6–3 despite a spill in the second set that left her knee gashed and bloody.

The press continued to build up the hype in the days before Wimbledon, incited by several intriguing elements. First on most everyone's list of likely winners were the top seeds, defending champion Hoad and Althea. The giant killer Hoad had recovered from arm and back injuries earlier in the season and was primed to become only the second man to win consecutive Wimbledon singles titles since the days of Don Budge. Reporters and players alike obsessed over the looming question of whether a victory would bring the mercurial Hoad one step closer to the $125,000 offer that professional promoter Jack Kramer had laid down a couple of months earlier. Like Hoad, Althea was easily the favorite among bookies and pundits. Her most serious challenger was thought to be the thirty-four-year-old Brough, four-time Wimbledon champion and the second seed. But age and anxiety had visibly undermined the older woman's game, leaving Shirley Bloomer, Britain's No. 1 player and the French Open women's champion in 1957, the next most serious threat. There was also Angela Mortimer to consider, the "other Angela" who had beaten Althea several times in the beginning of 1956 and who was now emerging from a yearlong struggle with health issues. The bigger threat to both front-runners Althea and Hoad, as many saw it, was Althea and Hoad themselves, for both were inclined to self-sabotaging behavior when under stress. As the *Daily Mail* put it succinctly a few days before play began, "THE ONLY PEOPLE WHO WILL BEAT MISS GIBSON AND LEW HOAD AT WIMBLEDON ARE THEMSELVES. THEY ARE, WITHOUT DOUBT, THE BEST PLAYERS."[8]

Compounding the anticipation was the fact that, for the first time, Queen Elizabeth II was going to pay a visit to the All England Club and was expected to present the trophy to the women's winner. That, coupled with the possibility that one of the new crop of British women players might at long last reverse the American domination of the women's event that had prevailed since World War II, surely merited a whopping extra helping of strawberries and cream. Anything, it seemed, could happen. No doubt, the club's thirty thousand seats would be jammed for the full two-week event given that over a half million dollars, the equivalent of $4.6 million today, in advance bookings had been made and lines were already beginning to form outside the gates a day before the tournament began.[9]

Some in the Black press angled to get a read on Althea's state of mind as she stood on the brink of possible world triumph, but few probed as deeply as *Baltimore Afro-American* columnist Sam Lacy, who had followed her for years. His lengthy story, titled "Has Althea Gibson Conquered Herself?," which ran several days after play began, opened with the observation that "Althea Gibson is an enigma at the crossroads. A mystery to the experts in the field of sports, a puzzle to her closest friends, Althea this week seeks the answer to her own inexplicable personality." Lacy mused over Althea's trajectory in an effort to understand her erratic moods and lack of self-control on the court. Lacy, who apparently shared a certain discomfort with Althea's less-than-feminine ways, believed that her issues stemmed from her chaotic childhood, and he suspected that her domination of boys' sports as a child had ultimately worked against her. Later in life, he wrote, "the "'tomboy' finds herself victimized by complexes. Miss Gibson is no exception. Her frustrations have made of her an introvert. She has a way of going into her hard shell and refusing to come out of it."

Both Lacy and Llewellyn, who was interviewed for the story, were insistent that race had played no part in Althea's personality problems. "It is not that at all," Lacy wrote. "Miss Gibson would be Miss Gibson if she were Nordic, Chinese or Afghanistani. It is her makeup to be moody, indifferent, sometimes arrogant." Llewellyn heartily concurred, saying, "I know, and she has often said, everybody has been magnificent in their treatment of her."[10]

It is difficult to imagine, however, that the throbbing drumbeat of race that dominated the coverage of Althea's Wimbledon play, particularly in the British tabloids, could not have had an impact or slashed at her sense of self. In those stories, she wasn't "just another tennis player," as she had explained herself to *The New York Times* on the eve of Wimbledon play the year before. She wasn't even just a "Negro tennis player," as she had said she was not. She was a "Negress," a "Negro," the "coloured favorite," and "the long-limbed ebony opponent"—all terms used to describe her in the British coverage of the opening days of the 1957 Championships. She was the "brown, lean Althea Gibson" with "supple brown muscles." In fact, she wasn't just a "colored" person, she was *the* dark-skinned representative of the entire colored race. She was the girl on whose "dusky shoulders" an entire people's prestige balanced. "Hers is no solitary battle but one which, successfully ended, must bring pride and perhaps hope to millions of under-privileged oppressed folk who share her colour." She was "the Negro girl from Harlem, fighting with missionary zeal for the honor of the coloured peoples." In a story headlined "Althea Beats Her Bogy—and Fans," Clifford Webb of the *Daily Herald* summed up the formidable elements confronting Althea as she strode on to Centre Court for her first match this way: "Imagine you're a coloured girl fighting for a place in sports history. . . . Your first match in the toughest two weeks of your life is about to begin . . . and 14,000 fans crowded in tiers around you are urging on your underdog opponent."[11]

Angela Buxton was equally blunt in a *Daily Sketch* column headlined "Althea Can Beat the Colour Bar." In the piece, she catalogued the many racial slights Althea had endured over the years that she, Buxton, believed had left a racial chip on Althea's shoulder, "which has always seemed to stand in her way." While Althea might not run into any direct colour bar trouble at the All England Club this time round, Buxton assured her that "the feeling will be there nevertheless, just as it always has been." Nonetheless, she urged her friend to stare it down and keep on fighting, concluding her column in all capital letters, "GO TO IT, GIRL! KNOCK THAT 'BROWN' CHIP OFF YOUR SHOULDER. YOU CAN DO IT THIS TIME!"[12]

Buxton was without a doubt a genuine friend of Althea's, one who perhaps wished the best outcome for her more fervently than anyone in the Wimbledon stadium. And yet, her column borders on the naïve. To reduce a lifetime of racial offense and discrimination such as that which Althea had experienced, never mind the weighty legacy of enslavement that also bore on her psyche, to a little brown chip on the shoulder approached the level of insult. The notion that Althea could simply brush away that annoying chip, could blithely toss a lifetime of injury into the rarefied Wimbledon air, was a failure of understanding. As Althea prepared to make a stand on Centre Court before the eyes of the world, it seems likely that she simply tossed her friend's glib words on the pile of racial commentary mounting in the press.

Nor did the British crowd make it any easier. No sooner did an unsmiling Althea drive a ball into the net in the first game of her first match than many among the thousands packed into the stands erupt into cheers, just as Clifford Webb had predicted. They did not want the colored girl to win, as some saw it. Whether it was because of the tone of her skin, or the crowd's nationalistic partisanship for her European opponent, Hungarian Suzy Körmöczy, or something else, it was to become the subject of much debate in the days and weeks to follow. British pundits by and large attributed the jeering and eruption of applause prompted by some of Althea's errors to a long-standing British sporting tradition of backing the underdog or simply enthusiasm for players close to their hearts. In a story headlined "Centre Court Bias Upsets Americans," *Daily Express* veteran reporter Frank Rostron conceded that the crowd had reached "the unpardonable stage" in applauding errors by Althea, whom he described as "Harlem's globe-trotting invader." All that clapping was simply support for underdog Körmöczy, he continued, and was "nothing personal," certainly nothing racist.

"While chiding the ignoramuses, who kept applauding Miss Gibson's misses, I hasten to assure Althea's countrymen that this was just the old story of the British crowd cheering the underdog," Rostron wrote.[13]

Some Americans disagreed. At the end of the tournament, the *Pittsburgh Courier* chalked up the two weeks of jeering and catcalls that Althea had endured at Wimbledon to "British color prejudice . . . there seemed to be thousands who did not want a colored girl to win." The paper ran an unflattering cartoon of Althea that had appeared in a British newspaper; it showed a thick-lipped Althea clasping the hand of a white player at the net. Her seemingly southern-tinged words in the overhead bubble read, "Do I shake hands with the 17,000 spectators? Ah sure was playin' against all of them too." The overhead caption summed it up: "IT'S ALTHEA v THE REST."[14]

Even without the voluble crowd, it was a difficult start for Althea, who had scored a bye in the first round. Beset by nerves and seemingly flustered by Körmöczy's persistent retrieval of some of her hardest-angled shots, Althea struggled mightily to best her petite opponent. Time and again, as warm rain began to descend on the grass court, her searing forehands missed their mark and soared over the baseline. In the end, Althea pulled it off and won 6–4, 6–4, but it was the hardest match she played in the tournament. In the men's play the previous day, meanwhile, the big news was that the Ham Richardson, Althea's amiable partner from her State Department tour and America's No. 1 male player, was routed by Chilean player Luis Ayala in less than one hour. Hoad, meanwhile, had beaten his French opponent with ease and appeared to be well over his injuries.

With the temperature rising steadily in the ivy-draped tennis center, dubbed the "ivied oven" by one paper, Althea cruised through her next three matches in the coming days, as both her confidence and her standing among the bookies mounted. By the tournament's midpoint, the only real surprise in what was turning out to be a fairly mediocre display of women's tennis was the stunning performance by Britain's teenage Truman, who had beaten Shirley Bloomer in a shocking fourth-round upset. Truman, whose rocketing forehand drive was already being compared to that of Maureen Connolly, scored another impressive victory in the quarterfinal against American Betty Rosenquest Pratt, America's No. 5 female player, as the crowd leapt to its feet and roared in approval for several minutes. As the round-faced girl mopped her face wearily with a small blue towel, few cheered more excitedly than Truman's parents and four of her five siblings, who were packed into a row together. Having made it to the semifinals, the freckle-faced schoolgirl confronted none other than the formidable No. 1 seed, the all-around favorite, Althea Gibson.

"I'm looking forward to it," a smiling Truman told reporters. "What have I got to lose?"[15]

On the day of the match, reporters flocked to Centre Court, while untold thousands of British women turned on the telly with their afternoon tea in the hope that the nation's tennis sweetheart might reclaim the national championship title at long last. Utterly unfazed, Althea declared coolly before their encounter, "I'll gobble her up."[16] Ears pricked up at the comment. When Truman walked onto the court that afternoon, a tennis ball rolled slowly in front of her. Bending down to pick it up, she found a newspaper headline of Althea's prediction taped to the ball—an attempt at a joke from a friend, of sorts, who was sitting in the stands.[17]

Althea, indeed, devoured Truman whole. As thousands looked on, she sent her young opponent flailing around the court from the first point pretty much to the last and never let up. It all came to an end in less than forty minutes at 6–1, 6–1, a score that told the story of the match. "It Was Murder on the Centre Court," as the *Daily Telegraph* summed it up.[18] Althea was in complete control from the first shot. Patiently, she waited for Truman to come to the net before unleashing a series of kill shots. As the *Times* put it, Althea was, "weaving her web around her gasping opponent like a spider. . . . She seemed to be everywhere at once, gliding about silently, effortlessly, and seemingly at half pace, which is always the illusion given by a fine player. Miss Gibson is that."[19] Although Truman lunged and ran as best she could, she could neither pass Althea at the net nor return her succession of deadly kick serves. The second set was slightly closer, as Althea double-faulted twice and Truman steadied herself, but Althea swiftly closed out the match with a serve that Truman belted far off the court. Smiling, Althea slowly approached the net and amiably reached out a hand to her young opponent.

"She said, 'You'll get here one day,'" Truman recalled in an interview. "You know, she was always very nice to me."[20]

Althea's win delivered her to the door of the Wimbledon women's finals, across from opponent Darlene Hard. Here were two American women, as far apart in background and appearance as they could possibly be, one a moody dark-haired easterner, the other a squat ponytailed college girl from the West Coast nearly a decade younger. They were also friends. Hard, who had learned tennis on the public courts of Southern California from her mother, was as amiable as she was approachable, and she clearly relished playing with Althea. Over the past year, Althea and the "chunky California waitress," as Hard was routinely referred to in the tabloids, had become a formidable doubles team, winning four tournaments, most recently at Queen's Club weeks before. At Wimbledon, they were the first seed of the women's doubles and had made their way with relative ease to the finals, where they faced Mary Hawton and Thelma Long of Australia.

The ebullient Hard was known for playing somewhat erratic tennis, regarded by some as a reflection of her carefree personality. On her good days, she was as forceful as any woman on the court, with her flat serve and deliberate backhand, and easily outran her competitors. On her off days, she chronically double-faulted, and her play veered from wild shots to unreturnable winners. Over the past year, Althea had beaten her four times, most recently in a fierce three-set battle at Beckenham during which Hard double-faulted six times and Althea did so at set point. Hard, however, had been playing extraordinarily well at Wimbledon so far, exhibiting a more mature game of measured strategy and control. Earlier in the day, she had disposed of American Dorothy Knode in a decisive, if unexciting, semifinal contest that lasted only forty-three minutes. She had even sent aging queen Brough packing in the quarterfinals, perhaps the biggest win of Hard's career to date. The crowd, moved by the significance of Brough's defeat, gave her a heartfelt ovation as she walked despondently off the court.

And then it was time for the finish. On the second-to-last day of the tournament, Lew Hoad had retained his men's singles title in a dazzling performance, defeating his fellow Australian Ashley Cooper in a mere fifty-six minutes. "Hurricane" Hoad's performance, as *The New York Times* described it, "must rank as one of the fiercest hitting rampages in tennis history."[21] Afterward, Hoad repeated his plan to remain an amateur until the end of the year. On the last day, all the remaining rivalries that had played out over the past two weeks would come to an end, including the women's singles final and the doubles and mixed doubles finals.

Althea was more than ready for what lay ahead. After a boisterous press conference on her defeat of Truman, and a quick shower, she headed back to the city in her small rented Austin. So confident was Althea in her ability to win the championships in those final days that she had bought herself a stunning floral-print strapless gown with a festive bow tucked under the bustline, which Angela had helped her pick out at, of course, Lillywhites, to wear at the celebratory ball. Althea had also spent days penning a three-and-a-half-page victory speech in green ink on onionskin paper for the event. That evening, she laid out her clothes for the following day: a brand-new pair of creamy-white pleated tennis shorts made for her by designer Teddy Tinling and a crisp white Fred Perry shirt. Her tennis shoes, freshly cleaned by a clubhouse assistant, were ready to go. At dinnertime, she headed out with a pair of friends from the ATA circuit to her favorite London restaurant, an elegant French bistro called Le Couple, where she feasted on filet mignon broiled in butter and a glass of sherry. Althea had come a long way from the days when she toured the American South in the backseat of Dr. Johnson's packed green Buick and had a gun stuck in her face at a gas station because of the color of her skin.

The day of the finals dawned blistering hot, with the mercury headed north of ninety degrees by late morning. Warming up on a remote court, Althea happened to notice Queen Elizabeth having lunch on the clubhouse porch, which reminded her to take with her the instructions she had been given for the curtsy protocol before the Royal Box. Shortly after 1 p.m., Althea and Hard headed into the ivy-covered inferno as a crowd of seventeen thousand spectators fanning themselves with their programs seemed to hold its collective breath in the blistering heat. Althea and Hard, sporting a Tinling dress with blue trim, both clasped bouquets of red, white, and blue flowers, representing their American citizenship, as they walked slowly onto the court and paused to curtsy before the Queen in the Royal Box.

It was not a good final, as the pundits would later declare. So sluggish was the match that one reporter would call it "almost pathetic," while a *World Tennis* writer dubbed it "the worst women's final ever remembered."[22] In fact, it was painfully slow, with more games won as a result of player error than any brilliant shots. Not a single rally in the entire match lasted longer than five strokes. Neither of the players was in top form. While Althea was in calm control throughout, she was clearly playing with uncharacteristic caution. Meanwhile, Hard, limp from the heat, her face etched with anxiety, seemed unmoored from the start, tossing her ribboned blond ponytail nervously as she was repeatedly overwhelmed by her opponent's high-kicking second serves. In the first four games, she managed to win only four points. On the brink of taking the seventh game at love–40, with two games now in her pocket and a pair of advantage points in her favor, Hard flubbed her return. And with that failure, wrote Stanley Doust, former Australian Wimbledon finalist and a longtime tennis correspondent, "Miss Hard was never again in the picture."[23]

Althea took the first set 6–3 in under twenty-five minutes. In the second set, she picked up the pace, while Hard appeared to wilt completely after losing her first service game, her usual effervescence squashed. Althea continued to rush the net while maintaining her laser-like focus, pausing only to glare with harnessed irritation at the perspiring linesman making repeated calls of foot faults. Nor did she allow the crowd's annoying habit of clapping at her mistakes, just as they had done in some of both her and Lew Hoad's earlier matches, to distract her. Hard struggled fitfully onward, at times dropping her head in her hands in despair. In a few memorable instances, she even paused to applaud Althea's shots ripping by her. Armed with a new set of balls in the final game, Althea delivered a series of searing serves and triumphantly took the set without surrendering a single point. The match was over at 6–3, 6–2 in fifty minutes. With that final shot, not only was one woman's epic undertaking of more than fifteen years accomplished, but a page in the history of the African American struggle for parity had irrevocably been turned.

A beaming Althea rushed up to the net and threw her arm around Hard as the crowd erupted in exuberant applause that rang through the tennis complex. The two drenched players were escorted to the trophy table near the umpire's chair, while a thick green carpet was unfurled for Queen

Elizabeth and three of her attendants. One by one, the players again curt-sied for the monarch, who was clad demurely in a rose and white silk dress, a beribboned pink hat, and white gloves, before Althea approached her.[24] As the crowd looked on, seemingly more riveted by the ceremony than it had been by the sluggish match, the Queen presented Althea with the Venus Rosewater Dish, the silver salver engraved with the names of all the previous Wimbledon champions.

"At last, at last," Althea exclaimed.

"My congratulations," the Queen said to her. "It must have been terri-bly hot out there."

"Yes, Your Majesty," said Althea, "but I hope it wasn't as hot in your box. At least, I was able to stir up a breeze."[25]

Althea, the first Wimbledon winner to be presented with a trophy by the Queen, teared up as she curtsied, and then stepped back so that Hard could come forward to accept her trophy as the camera flashes erupted. The press followed up with an explosion of superlatives and a succession of more photographs back in the club pressroom.

"Althea Gibson fulfilled her destiny at Wimbledon today and became the first member of her race to rule the world of tennis," declared *The New York Times*. The *Baltimore Afro-American* headline announced simply, "Althea Is Crowned." The *Evening News* put it slightly differently, saying, "QUEEN SEES COLOURED GIRL WIN WIMBLEDON CROWN." And then there was the *Sunday Pictorial* headline: "ALTHEA—BUT SO DULL!"[26]

Some among the Black press put it in even more cosmic terms. Her win, thundered Sam Lacy, "is the greatest triumph a colored athlete has accomplished in my time. . . . Althea, on Saturday, beat the world at ten-nis."[27] Others wasted no time in raising the question of whether Althea would use her status to help other Black people, just as she had been helped by so many. As P. L. Prattis of the *Pittsburgh Courier* wrote, "Faith in Al-thea has paid off. But what now—now that the door is open? Jackie Rob-inson walked through the doors of organized baseball due to the efforts of others, and kept the doors open for scores of others. What will Queen Al-thea do?"[28] To Gordon B. Hancock, a prominent professor and columnist for the *Norfolk Journal and Guide*, writing for the Associated Negro Press, Althea's triumph symbolized the journey of the entire race. "We might have been foiled in Reconstruction days, and we may be foiled in the Year of Our Lord 1957," he wrote, "but if we keep on coming back for another round, one day the Negro race will be worthy of the heart and stamina of Althea Gibson. Long live Althea Gibson, Negro!"[29] One can only imagine how that ringing statement struck Althea, she who had resoundingly declared on the eve of her Wimbledon appearance the previous year that the one thing she was *not* was a Negro tennis player, but simply a tennis player just like anyone else. Now she was being trumpeted as not only a Negro player, but a heroine forging the way for the entire Negro race. The cymbals would grow ever louder before they subsided.

Back in the dressing room, Althea found a pile of telegrams from around the world, with many from those who had known her since childhood. "Congratulations. Edna cried with joy. I knew you'd do it," wrote Sugar Ray. From the Williston High School in Wilmington, North Carolina, there were hearty congratulations from all the students and staff. The governor of New York, Averell Harriman, sent his congratulations "to a fellow New Yorker on winning the Wimbledon Championship. We are all very proud of you."[30]

The day was far from over. Less than two hours later, Althea and Hard were back on Centre Court, this time as partners, playing the women's doubles against the Australian team of Hawton and Long. In a match as sluggish as the women's singles, the Americans easily won the title 6–2, 6–1. By then, Althea was near her energy's end, and the mixed doubles sapped the last bit she had. With Hard now on the opposite side of the court, paired with Mervyn Rose of Australia, Althea and Neale Fraser struggled, but the triple crown was not to be Althea's that day; they lost the mixed doubles 4–6, 5–7. By far the bigger excitement of the day was the men's doubles, which featured a sensational conquest of the top-seeded team of Hoad and Fraser by the unseeded seniors forty-three-year-old Gar Mulloy and thirty-three-year-old Californian Budge Patty. The contest went on for four grueling, action-packed sets before the younger men were routed, making Mulloy the oldest man in Wimbledon history to win a title.

The Wimbledon Ball took place that night at the iconic Grosvenor House hotel, in the heart of the Victoria district and just a short walk from Buckingham Palace. As Althea alighted from the car that evening dressed in her Lillywhites frock with a choker of pearls around her neck and accompanied by one of her ATA friends, a surge of cheering and clapping erupted, following her through the hotel lobby and into the ornate ballroom, where she was seated at the head table in between Lew Hoad, the men's champion, and the Duke of Devonshire, the master of ceremonies. Buxton and her boyfriend sat at a nearby table. It was Althea's night from the start. She began her three-and-a-half-page handwritten speech with an approximation of the words uttered by Winston Churchill in 1940 shortly after the French sought an armistice, saying, "This is my finest hour. This is the hour I will remember always as the crowning conclusion to a long and wonderful journey." She went on to thank many on the long list of those who had contributed to her victory, including Drs. Johnson and Eaton, Fred Johnson, Syd Llewellyn, and the USLTA and ATA, and she joked about her long-running quarrel with Buxton over the ideal temperature for the morning milk they routinely shared.[31]

Afterward, a beaming Althea and the square-jawed Hoad, the king and queen of the ball, spun around the ballroom floor in "the Winners' Waltz." Giddy with her triumph, Althea allowed herself to be talked into taking the microphone, and in her deep contralto, she crooned two of her favorite tunes, "If I Loved You" and "Around the World." In doing so, she attained yet another "first" in apparently becoming the first Wimbledon champion to perform before the crowd attending the ball. She wrapped up the evening with Buxton and a few others at the swank Astor Club, where she belted out yet a few more tunes before heading back to Rossmore Court at dawn. Remembering the momentous day later, she said, "Shaking hands with the Queen of England was a long way from being forced to sit in the colored section of the bus going into downtown Wilmington, North Carolina."[32]

And yet, in her historic speech at the ball, and in all her remarks to the press that day and in subsequent days to come, Althea apparently never made mention of race or alluded to the larger historic significance of her win. Despite the jubilation in the Black press, she was not going to be a racial heroine, even at her moment of ultimate triumph. Others, however, were keenly conscious of the fact that a Black woman had just won the Wimbledon classic and they were deeply hopeful that it would never happen again. Gathered at the one of the elaborate cocktail parties held in the city preceding the ball, a handful of tennis officials were overheard reassuring one another that Althea's win was just a fluke, surely not something that would recur.

"They were murmuring, 'Well, there won't be another one like this,'" recalled Lew Hoad's wife, Jenny, who attended a couple of the parties with her husband. "They thought Blacks weren't athletic enough. . . . It was a freak thing that she had managed to be that good or have the opportunity to become that good."[33]

While the consternation of some was whispered under the cover of a private event, others were far less circumspect in expressing their unhappiness over "the Black girl's" triumph. Hours after photos of Althea dancing arm in arm with Hoad appeared on the front pages of the London tabloids, the bags of hate mail began to show up at the door of the Hoads' hotel room. Some of the letters expressed anger at Althea's win, but most raged that Hoad had dared dance with a Black woman.

"Afterward, Lew got a lot of angry mail accusing him of dancing with a Black woman," Jenny Hoad recalled. "There were just hundreds of letters from people who accused him of breaking the rules, saying, 'You have no right to dance with coloured people.' It was shocking and wrong and sinful. . . . We didn't even read most of them. We just threw the letters away."[34]

Althea, meanwhile, was flying back to a lavish welcome in New York. Somewhere along the way, she received word that her dance partner Hoad was also headed to New York. Despite his post-Wimbledon pronouncement that he would remain an amateur, he had accepted Jack Kramer's offer of $125,000 to go professional and, within days, was to appear at the West Side Tennis Club to play his first pro match. Around the same time that Althea's Pan Am Clipper was landing at Idlewild Airport, the fast-moving Kramer was telling reporters that he was considering adding Althea and Maureen Connolly to his pro tour next, saying, "There's a lot of interest in Althea right now. I'm sure she would be a good draw."[35] But, for the moment, it was time for Althea to relish her victory on home turf. Talk of tennis and big money could wait.

The airport was packed. In addition to the three people who had escorted her there weeks before, there was now her mother and two of her siblings;

Will Darben; her first coach, Fred Johnson, in an overcoat and broad-brimmed white hat; and a bevy of city officials and reporters. Clad in a willowy white skirt, four carefully wrapped tennis rackets tucked under her left arm, Althea called out to her mother as soon as her feet hit the tarmac. "Hi, ya, sweetie pie!"[36] Then, tucked in a gleaming black Cadillac led by a police escort and followed by several accompanying cars, Althea headed to a breakfast celebration at the Brooklyn home of ATA secretary Bertram Baker. Raising his glass high in the air, Baker beamed at the crowd of Black officials and activists gathered in his dining room. "He gave a toast to the new queen of tennis and drank 'high balls' of Old Grand Dad whiskey and ginger ale as he slapped backs and made the most of the moment. Gibson sat next to him at the dining room table, with Baker's family . . . friends and members of the community," recalled Ron Howell, Baker's grandson, in his biography of Baker, entitled *Boss of Black Brooklyn: The Life and Times of Bertram L. Baker.* Howell, who was also at the table in 1957, recalled that Baker, his eye ever on the larger political agenda, used the moment to nod to the gradual advances that Black citizens were making across the country. It would turn out to be one of remarkably few acknowledgments of the racial dimension of Althea's victory, either on that day or the next.[37]

Forty-eight hours later, Althea was lavishly fêted with a ticker tape parade up Broadway—the very procession the *New York Amsterdam News* had lobbied unsuccessfully for the previous year—led by a cavalcade of military divisions, band units, and Coast Guard members. This time, the city was fully prepared to honor its tennis star, who was the first and remains the only lone Black woman to be given an elaborate procession up the Canyon of Heroes from the Battery to City Hall, where the mayor and a gaggle of officials awaited her.[38] Perched on the high back of a cream-colored Chrysler Imperial convertible, Althea waved ecstatically to a crowd of nearly one hundred thousand well-wishers churning on the sidewalk and hanging from office windows overhead. Beside her were Manhattan borough president Hulan E. Jack, a native of St. Lucia in the West Indies and the first Black person to hold his position, and Richard Patterson, commissioner of the Department of Commerce and Public Events. Dressed as though the State Department had handpicked her outfit, in a red-and-blue-checked silk dress borrowed from Rosemary Darben, a white orchid pinned to her front, Althea blew a succession of kisses through the gentle downpour of confetti, exclaiming, "It's amazing, it's wonderful."[39]

At City Hall, she was received by Mayor Robert Wagner, who later presented her with the city's medallion, as her beaming parents looked on, saying, "If we had more wonderful people like you, the world would be a better place." A beaming Althea told the assembled crowd that her victory had been achieved largely with the help of their encouragement. "With God's help," she added, "I hope to wear this crown that I have attained with honor and dignity."[40] Forty-eight hours later, Ed Sullivan, host of the popular television entertainment program that bore his name, would repeat her words to her during a short on-air interview during which she again gave thanks to the many people who had helped her along her way. It would not be their last encounter.

After the City Hall presentation, Althea was the guest of honor at a luncheon in the Palm Room of the swank Waldorf Astoria hotel that was also attended by her family and friends, including Jackie Robinson and Bobby Riggs. Neither Mayor Wagner nor the two men of color who spoke at the lunch that day, Bertram Baker and Hulan Jack, directly referenced Althea's color or the racial significance of her achievement. Even Jack, a "First Negro" himself, who had fought for years against all forms of racial discrimination, couched Althea's achievement as a triumph of American democracy, rather than race, as had the USLTA's president, Renville H. McMann, who also spoke. Althea's achievement, Jack said, "has added strength and meaning to the Star-Spangled Banner and is as truly American as the stars and stripes." It showed, he concluded, in what was apparently an oblique reference to race, that democracy valued human achievement in its "vigorous crusade toward full equal opportunity."[41]

The day concluded with a visit to Althea's childhood home on 143rd Street in Harlem, where a balloon-filled block party was held in her honor beneath a "Welcome Home" banner strung across the street. Among the scores of letters she received was one she particularly treasured, from President Dwight Eisenhower. Millions of Americans, he wrote, would surely join him "in felicitations on your outstanding victory at Wimbledon last week. Recognizing the odds you faced, we have applauded your courage, persistence and application."[42] Eisenhower also indicated that Althea was welcome to come visit him in the White House when she was next in Washington, D.C., according to the accounts of several Black newspapers. The administration, though, apparently remained ambivalent about the Black tennis champion, and it was unclear if an actual invitation would be extended.

Vice President Richard Nixon also sent a letter of congratulations, saying, "You have proved that the ultimate goal can be reached."[43] Nixon was a curious choice to pen such a letter, given that he had a spotty congressional voting record on civil rights in the early 1950s. In the fall of 1952, he had also come under criticism for having signed a restrictive covenant with the purchase of a new house in Washington, D.C., which said the land could not be conveyed to any "persons of Negro blood or extraction . . . or person of the Semitic race, blood or origin." Although Nixon worked to improve his record on civil rights in subsequent years, he and his wife came under a vicious anti-American attack in Venezuela several months after he made a ceremonial appearance at Forest Hills. Still enraged over the latest civil rights explosion in the United States to make international headlines, some among the jeering crowd repeatedly shouted the words "Little Rock, Little Rock."[44]

The *New York Times*, which had run daily stories not only about the parade, but also about Althea's visit to her family's Harlem apartment and her parents' reactions to her triumph, capped its coverage with an editorial noting the larger significance of her victory. According to the editorial, titled "A Party for Miss Gibson," it wasn't just that Althea was the first Black player to achieve the Wimbledon prize, but that, like any human being from disadvantaged circumstances, she had overcome great difficulty to do so. The significance of her win, it concluded, reflected the fact that the "social atmosphere of our country is changing" and the nation was becoming one of "diminished discrimination and of greater opportunity."[45]

What the editorial didn't mention was that this change was encountering fierce and, at times, bloody resistance in parts of America, particularly in the South. In the summer of 1957, that resistance centered on the proposed Civil Rights Act of 1957, a federal bill designed to safeguard Black Americans' right to vote, which had been severely eroded by discriminatory state laws following the Supreme Court's decision of *Brown*

v. Board of Education three years earlier. As Althea was making her celebratory voyage up Broadway, the U.S. Congress was riven in debate over
the bill, which would culminate in an extraordinary filibuster by southern
Democrats. Georgia senator Richard Russell, the leader of the southern
opposition and an avid proponent of segregation, likened the bill to efforts
by extremists in Reconstruction days to "put black heels on white necks"
and predicted bloodshed in the months to come.[46]

Although Althea predictably made no comment on the subject, some
in the Black press used her as an example to counter southerners' claims
that Black people failed to measure up and were therefore not fit to vote.
As the Black weekly the *Michigan Chronicle* put it, "Althea Gibson can represent the United States at Wimbledon, compete with the best in the world
at Forest Hills, yet men stand on the floor of the Senate of the United
States and fight to keep Negro Americans from voting in elections in their
own country." Althea was not once quoted in the story, which was nonetheless headlined "Althea Gibson Answers Senator Russell." Whether she
liked it or not, Althea's triumphs were being used to dramatize the formidable powers of one Black woman and, with them, the potential of her race
as a whole. The very name "Althea Gibson" was becoming a potent symbol
in an escalating social crisis.[47]

Even the most formidable Black woman, however, could only do so
much. Just one day after Althea's triumphant parade, which prompted
New Yorkers both Black and white to rejoice in the social advance it signified, the illusion of racial progress she had come to symbolize crumbled
around her very feet. The following morning, she boarded a plane to Chicago, where she was to compete in the Clay Court Championships, held,
as in past years, at the tony River Forest Tennis Club. When she tried to
secure a hotel room in the surrounding neighborhood, she was refused
lodging for the same reason that untold numbers of children were barred
from schools throughout the American South and their parents were refused
access to the voting booth: because of the color of her skin. The only place
where she managed to find a room was twelve miles away. As Quentin Reynolds later wrote for *The Saturday Review*, "Midnight had come for Cinder-
ella, not in some small Mississippi town, but in liberal Greater Chicago."[48]

The hotels' rejection was just the beginning. Next, the elegant Pump

Room of the Ambassador East Hotel refused to accept reservations for a luncheon in her honor for the same reason. Despite laws prohibiting discrimination in some northern cities, segregated hotels were not uncommon at the time. Althea's refusal to speak up about the incident contributed to a firestorm of rage against her by the Black press, which erupted in the aftermath of the Chicago tournament. Her reasoning may have stemmed from more than her usual reluctance to address issues of race. She was also still smarting from the gag order slapped on her by Wimbledon officials the previous summer after she gave a revealing interview to the *Daily Mail* in London. Admonished, she'd been cautious about talking to the press ever since. With a Wimbledon win under her belt, she was even more reluctant to champion her role as "First Negro," much less that of "First Negro Barred." In a way, she had good reason. On the eve of the high-profile Chicago tournament, with the Forest Hills championships just weeks ahead, it seems more than likely that she was loath to incite the anger of tournament officials by publicly challenging the city's prominent hoteliers on the subject of race or anything else for that matter. A celebrated Wimbledon champion speaking out, particularly at a time when the nation was roiled in debate over the Civil Rights Act, would have garnered front-page attention. She did not need a replay of the earlier Wimbledon press incident. Whatever her reasons, however, the Black press was not happy with her.

Serrell Hillman, a reporter for *Time* magazine who spent close to a week with Althea in Chicago before she would open up to him, noted of the hotel incident, "Officials and newsmen burned with rage, but Althea hardly noticed it."[49]

From a tennis perspective, Chicago couldn't have gone better. It was a replay of Wimbledon in several aspects. Squared off in the finals against Darlene Hard in a brutal summer heat, Althea repeated her London performance to take the match by the same overall score, only reversed, at 6–2, 6–3. Although Hard put up a somewhat stronger performance than she had at Wimbledon, she double-faulted repeatedly and was unable to keep pace with Althea's blazing serve and strategic placement. For Althea, the win was a pair of firsts: not only was the title her first USLTA championship, but she was the "First Negro" to win the Chicago tournament. As with Wimbledon, she and Hard went on to mow down the opposition in the women's doubles, overwhelming Karol Fageros and Jeanne Arth in the finals to take the match 6–3, 6–0.

Althea's performance, however, was by far the lesser story to come out of Chicago's Black papers. A much louder and more tumultuous tale competed with the news as reporters vented long-simmering anger at Althea's evasive behavior and aloofness. Although the Black press had lobbied hard for her during her career and had remained loyal to her even during her stagnant years in the early 1950s, some were infuriated by her reluctance to champion the Black cause as her star rose. Althea's conduct in Chicago only made it worse. Perhaps overwhelmed by the avalanche of post-Wimbledon attention engulfing her, she was more evasive with reporters than ever. She refused some requests for interviews, repeatedly postponed a planned meeting with a New York magazine reporter, and brushed by dozens of photographers without pausing. When one reporter managed to engage her briefly to ask her the cliché question she had most come to dread—how did she like to be compared to Jackie Robinson?—Althea retorted, "No, I don't consider myself to be a representative of my people. I am thinking of me and nobody else."[50] When reporters got wind of the fact that Althea had remained mute when turned away from Chicago's finest hotels, their rage ignited. What resulted was something that the *New York Post*'s Ted Poston dubbed "the most virulent attack ever aimed at any Negro athlete by the same sections of the press which had done so much to establish her early reputation."[51]

Russ Cowans, reporter for the *Chicago Defender* and one of those unable to get an interview with Althea, fumed, in a column titled "She Should Be Told," that Althea was "as ungracious as a stubborn jackass" and "the most arrogant athlete it has been my displeasure to meet." In a related story, he detailed how she had not only blown him off, but also had given the brush-off to many other reporters who "were just trying to do a job they had been assigned" and had flatly refused to allow her photograph to be taken. He suggested that instead of a trophy, the British queen should have given Althea "a few words of advice on graciousness. In this great quality the Wimbledon champion is seriously lacking."[52]

Wendell Smith of the *Pittsburgh Courier* answered the question posed in the headline to his own story, "Has Net Queen Althea Gibson Gone

High Hat?" by saying that the queen of tennis "has become so obsessed with herself and her court skill that she apparently speaks only to kings and queens." If Althea never returns to Chicago, he concluded, "she will never be missed." Leo Fischer of the *Chicago American* snapped, "Someone ought to tell Althea Gibson that graciousness is as much a quality of a real champion as the ability to play a game well." Two months later, as word of the negative press engulfing Althea spread ever wider beyond Black readers, *World Tennis* ran Fischer's column verbatim in its pages.[53] Even Eaton got wind of it all. Over in Virginia, his friend Thomas Young, of the *Norfolk Journal and Guide*, heard about the skirmish and wrote to Eaton urging him to advise Althea to be more patient with the press, lest she get a reputation for being arrogant.[54] Ironically, in all the press hubbub about her failings, it almost got lost among some of the Black press that Althea was the first Black player, female or male, to win the Chicago title.

Althea's avoidance of the press was problematic, to be sure. Her aversion to taking a public stand on race, however, was complicated. It had to do with more than her personal inclination to go it alone or even with her perception of what would best advance the cause of Black people in the United States. There was also the very real factor of the cultural expectations of women at the time and of Black women in particular. If Althea was culturally not "permitted" to be a lesbian, if she was ideally to be heterosexual and married, she was also expected to be politically chaste, at least in the middle-class white world. In her book *A Spectacular Leap*, an examination of Black women athletes in twentieth-century America, historian Jennifer H. Lansbury points out that in her response to the community's desire for a race hero, Althea was equally bound by 1950s ideals of womanhood. As she emerged as a champion in American society, "middle-class femininity made it virtually impossible for her to live up to such expectations and assume the hero-like status of a Jackie Robinson. In the culture of 1950s America, it would have been inappropriate for a woman, particularly a woman of the elite, white amateur tennis world, to 'make a fuss' in a public setting. Perhaps Gibson understood such limitations."[55]

Meanwhile, Althea took yet another step that annoyed some among the Black press. Just a week after the Chicago tournament, the ATA announced that for the first time in a decade, Althea would not defend her

ATA singles championship title, but would instead play in the USLTA women's doubles championships in Boston. Althea, in short, would not be playing Black tennis anymore. Instead, she and Darlene Hard would play an exhibition match a few days before the ATA Championships, at Central State College in Wilberforce. The decision was a poignant juncture in both her career and the ATA's history. Althea had come into her own within the Black tennis organization, beginning when she was a rough-edged teenager, and had amassed a record ten national ATA singles titles, surpassing even Ora Washington. The truth was that, by 1957, she had outgrown the ATA and any continued appearances by her there would have been ceremonial at best. Her decision provoked the predictable sniping from some columnists, while others rallied to her defense. Compelling Althea to play in the Black championships, Atlanta columnist Marion Jackson wrote, would have been "farcical." Her decision not to play, he explained, "is no snub. It is a realistic view of what any fairminded *[sic]* person would admit. Miss Gibson is like Alexander The Great—who cried because he had no more worlds to conquer." Jackson also stood with Althea on her larger refusal to champion the whole of the Black race, pointing out that "Althea is the race's only personality on the international tennis circuit. There are still racial difficulties she has faced with the compelling silence that Branch Rickey imposed upon Jackie Robinson. She can not speak out. Won't her detractors realize this?"[56]

As the press turmoil over Althea's passive stance continued to boil, her tennis career continued its upward arc. In yet another nod to her national standing, Althea, along with Darlene Hard and three other players, was selected to be a member of the American Wightman Cup team in its annual exhibition match against Britain. Her selection, needless to say, earned her yet another "First Negro" title to add to her ever-mounting pile of such distinctions. Althea had been furious when she was not chosen the year before, and some, like columnist Sam Lacy, speculated openly that racism was a factor. Team officials, however, maintained that their selection was based on the 1955 national rankings, which had put Althea at No. 8, taking her out of the running. No sooner did she arrive in Sewickley, Pennsylvania, where the matches were to take place, than the press turmoil that had erupted in Chicago threatened to spill over anew. Asked for an interview by a Pittsburgh reporter, Althea suggested that he get permission from her team's captain, apparently still mindful of her run-in with Wimbledon officials and the need to do things by the book. Stung by a reporter's accusation in the following day's paper that she was becoming "big-headed," Althea stopped to meet with other members of the press in the elegant Edgeworth Country Club, where the matches were being held. Although a couple of the reporters commented snarkily on the lavish setting where they met the Harlem player, Althea was nonetheless given a chance to present her side of the matter.

"I am amazed at these stories about my treatment of the press," she told the *Baltimore Afro-American*. "I have always treated reporters with the greatest respect, but I don't stop every time they bark."

Althea described several incidents that had apparently occurred in Pennsylvania in which she felt reporters had made unfair demands on her. The first occurred right after a match when she was parched and headed for some water when a reporter stopped her and asked to talk. When Althea asked him to wait while she got a drink, "he became peeved and wrote that I was becoming impossible." The second incident happened when she was again coming off the court: a photographer grabbed her by the arm and demanded that she allow him to take her photograph. As Althea explained it, "No gentleman would have snatched me the way he did. Yet, when I refused his command he seemed to think I had committed one of the worst sins in the world." Althea likened her experience to that of Sugar Ray Robinson, who also grappled with the press. In his case, she said, "they cut him to bits. It seems when a person gets to be a champion or reaches some high station, that's when they start chopping away." Going forward, she insisted, she was going to do what she thought right, and if she got angry, "I'm going out on the tennis court and take it out on whoever's across the net."[57]

In the current moment, that turned out to be the opposing team members of the Wightman Cup contest. Before play began, she proudly tried on her fitted cream-colored Wightman Cup blazer, emblazoned with an American shield above a pair of crossed tennis rackets, in front of a mirror while some of her teammates looked on. Now officially the best women's amateur player in the world, Althea would treasure the jacket and wear it to special occasions for the rest of her life. After she died, her estate put it up for auction, selling it for $3,000. Back on court, Althea once again easily beat the British teenager Christine Truman 6–4, 6–2, repeatedly changing the pace of her shots and winning the match in a mere thirty-five minutes. Together, she and Hard took the women's doubles. In the end, the American women's team won the coveted cup for the twenty-first time in a row with a 6–1 victory, to which Althea contributed three points. Britain's other rising teenage star, eighteen-year-old Ann Haydon, scored her country's single point in a fierce contest against Hard, making her the one to watch in the future.

Ahead lay what could be described as the biggest challenge of all, the U.S. National Championships. While lacking the international prestige of Wimbledon, the Forest Hills tournament was the centerpiece of American tennis and one that had particular meaning for Althea. Not only was it just a half hour's drive from her childhood home in Harlem, but it was also where she had made her first appearance in a national white tournament, back in 1950. The event not only brought her full circle to the tony suburban West Side Tennis Club, but also would ultimately pit her against the very same formidable opponent, tennis queen Louise Brough, the world's No. 1 player in 1955. It was Brough who had just narrowly beaten her in their now-legendary match seven years earlier.

Neither of them was the same woman she had been, or even the same player. Brough, now thirty-four, was slower, far less inclined to run after lobs she once easily nailed, and her powerhouse net game was notably less forceful. Nonetheless, she was still the classic blond Brough, still a considerable tennis powerhouse, and ranked No. 3 in the United States, right behind Althea at No. 2. Althea was also older. As many in the press had noted of late, she was no longer the same tempestuous, erratic athlete she had once been, prone to roar out of the starting box only to lose steam in the face of hard-core opposition. Her previous year's loss to Fry was yesterday's news. Althea had not lost a single tournament since losing to Fry in Australia at the start of the year. A vastly more seasoned player now, with both Wimbledon and the Wightman Cup under her belt, she was a visibly more confident competitor, and both she and her opponents knew it. "New Person, Althea Gibson Fears Nobody," declared the headline on one wire story.[58]

If anyone doubted who was the hands-down favorite heading into the Women's Seventy-First National Championships, they needed only to glance at a nearby newsstand. There, on the cover of *Time* magazine, Althea's knowing face at once emerged from and dominated a clay court. Next to it, she beamed, girlish and expectant, from the cover of *Sports Illustrated*. She was only the second Black woman to appear on the cover of *Time*, following singer Marian Anderson, who was on the cover in 1946, and the first to appear on the cover of *Sports Illustrated*. The sports magazine raised the question of whether Althea would be able to stake a claim to true superiority in her time when she appeared at Forest Hills. "Few doubt she can, and will," wrote William F. Talbert, captain of the U.S. Davis Cup team, who had played against Althea more than once.[59] *Time* put it more bluntly: "Next week, a lanky jumping jack of a girl who grew up in the slums of Harlem will play tennis. She may not belong to any of the clubs that run the tournament, but this year the tournament belongs to her."[60]

Those who remained uncertain—and some surely did—could confirm the media's enthusiasm with the outcome of the Essex County Club tournament in Manchester, Massachusetts, the week before. Althea defeated Brough in the singles for the Essex title, and Althea and Hard also scored the women's doubles against the reigning U.S. champions, Brough and duPont. The singles, however, was no shoe-in. Althea had to battle hard in the first set, and it was not until she pulled ahead in the sixteenth game that she appeared to have it under control, after which she surged smoothly forward to take the match 9–7, 6–4. So great a draw had Althea become by then that the Essex tournament, considered a rehearsal for Forest Hills, broke all attendance records. It was Althea's third defeat of Brough in a singles match, and for her supporters, it seemed to bode well.

Despite their loss at the Essex tournament, Brough and duPont, however, were hardly out. Shortly afterward, the seemingly indefatigable pair of veterans felled Althea and Hard in straight sets at the USLTA's National Doubles Championships at the Longwood Cricket Club in Brookline, Massachusetts, thus "snapping the victory string" out of the younger women's winning streak, during which they had claimed thirty-seven matches in nine tournaments, as *The New York Times* pointed out.[61] The loss, however, was offset by the news, announced on the same day, that Althea had been seeded first in the National Championship singles, with

Brough taking second place. In the men's singles, Ashley Cooper, Australian wunderkind, was seeded first. At long last, the door to the American tennis pinnacle had swung wide open for Althea, and she was more than ready to walk through it. She celebrated the achievement at a thirtieth birthday party given in her honor at the Longwood club by Hazel Hotchkiss Wightman, founder of the Wightman Cup and a former tennis champion sometimes referred to as the "First Lady of Tennis" for her passionate devotion to the sport. Wightman, who often hosted players at her home and had invited Althea to stay with her previously, supported Althea publicly for years.

Buoyed by her unblemished record and the confidence of the press, Althea headed into the tournament with perceptible calm. Unlike her previous seven appearances at the West Side Tennis Club, conditions were different from the start. Instead of staying at the home of her old Cosmopolitan Club mentor, Rhoda Smith, as she usually did during the Forest Hills tournament, she booked a room for the week at the Vanderbilt Hotel on Park Avenue in Manhattan, where many other players stayed. Like the Wimbledon veteran she now was, she even had a private car take her to the tournament, rather than navigate the crowded subway as she had in the past.

Her opening match against her longtime friend Karol Fageros, of lace panties fame, proved surprisingly competitive. The stunning Fageros, now ranked No. 8 in the country and clad in a Teddy Tinling creation, played what was probably her best tennis ever, putting Althea to the test, with a fierce forehand setting up a series of prolonged rallies. Although Althea was never in real danger of losing, their energetic and fast-paced match kept the audience of six thousand riveted until Althea closed it out 6–4, 6–4. From there, she had smooth sailing through her next four opponents. At the same time, Brough was steadily mowing down the other side of the draw as the two women inched ever closer toward the finals. The only real surprise in the women's singles, other than Fageros's excellent performance, was Darlene Hard's rather poor one. Despite her generally excellent showing over the past year, the erratic Hard wilted in the semifinals against Brough, playing almost as timidly as she had at Wimbledon a couple of months earlier. Brough's 6–2, 6–4 defeat of her younger opponent in a mere forty minutes prompted some commentators to wonder if the aging blond champion just might have a shot at regaining the national women's title she had won back in 1947 after all.

On the day of the finals—a day that Althea had kept in her unwavering sights for seven years since she first squared off with Brough in 1950, through tennis ups and downs, a series of plateaus, and a couple of personal crises—Althea started out at a leisurely pace. First, she had her hair done by a special Harlem hairdresser, a friend of Llewellyn's who had opened up the shop especially for such a big-name client. Llewellyn met her there, and the two of them returned to the Vanderbilt Hotel, where they had breakfast with Tommy Giangrande, the vice president of Harry C. Lee & Company. The sporting goods company had supported Althea since her early days and had long paid her a monthly seventy-five dollars to promote their products, as was permitted under USLTA rules. Llewellyn, increasingly appearing by Althea's side in public, would watch the match with the dignitaries from the club's VIP box, while Will Darben, yet again reduced to second string, would watch from elsewhere. Although Althea had both her Wimbledon victory and the front-runner's status to bolster her confidence, she would later admit to having some serious nerves heading into her eighth bid for the national title. So would Brough.

It was another less-than-thrilling match. While not as disappointing as Wimbledon had been, it was well below the abilities of two such world champions. Althea, her face as stonily impassive as ever, dug in from the start. She managed to break through Brough's service at the outset and take the first six points, but then she double-faulted and saw her own service broken. Both women played cautiously during the rest of the set, as Althea was tagged with multiple foot faults and Brough hovered at the baseline rather than confront Althea's rocketing passing shots. In the second set, Althea lost the first game, but then she slipped into her groove, and the match was as good as over. Adopting the same spider-like strategy she had employed at Wimbledon, Althea deftly wove a web around Brough, lobbing the ball high into the air and then hurtling to the net. Deliberately suspending the tension, she leisurely bounced the ball, bounced it again, and then one more time, before unleashing the full firepower of her service. Brough persevered courageously, but after committing several errors in the second game, she sagged and appeared to accept her fate. Althea blasted her way to a win of 6–3, 6–2, bringing to an end her tumultuous eight-year quest and laying claim to the loftiest tennis title in America.

Althea Gibson, the onetime Harlem dropout, had conquered the indomitable white tennis kingdom to become the first Black woman to win the U.S. National Championships tournament, capping a year of sustained conquest. Hours earlier, Malcolm Anderson, a relative unknown from the cattle country outside Brisbane, stunned the crowd with an astonishing three-set win over Ashley Cooper, the crowd favorite and a fellow countryman, to become the first unseeded player to win the men's final in recent memory. It was a day that would go down in the tennis history books in capital letters.

A dripping Althea shook hands boisterously with her longtime nemesis Brough, her personal tennis odyssey now having come full circle. After stealing a quick glance over at a beaming Llewellyn, she headed to the marquee. Vice President Richard M. Nixon presented the trophies to the winners, Althea's spilling over with red roses and white gladioli, before he stepped aside from the microphone to make way for her. Althea was now not only the "First Negro" to win the U.S. Championships, but the first to win a major national title in the United States. She had not lost a single set in the women's singles. Hours later, she took the mixed doubles with Kurt Nielsen of Denmark.

Her expression at once exhausted and ebullient, Althea stared into the churning sea of television cameras and photographers before her and began: "Words cannot express how I feel. I thank God for giving me the ability and opportunity to play in the matches. . . . It was a thrill to have won at Wimbledon, but it was a climax to win here before so many of my friends and well-wishers."[62] The resounding applause that followed was believed to be the biggest ovation in the arena's history.[63] It was an exuberant sound that State Department officials and the occupant of the White House surely hoped would be heard around the world and help to muffle the persistent criticism of the country's ongoing racial difficulties.

In the press conference that followed, where the parties on both sides of the podium were more at ease with one another than they had been in months, Althea spoke as much about her hopes for her financial future as she did about tennis. She did not, she emphasized, have plans to go pro.

Still, she sorely needed to earn some money, partly to pay an assistant for helping her respond to her thousands of fan letters. She also had to think about paying for the stamps to send them, she added, only partially in jest. In a wry nod to the moneyed crowd at West Side, *The New York Times* noted that Althea's consciousness of the cost of stamps "may never have been put into so many words out at Forest Hills before. But the girl from West 143rd Street, is a frank person."[64] What she really wanted to do, Althea concluded, was to pursue a singing career, and for that, she needed to return to her voice lessons.

Not surprisingly, Althea made no mention of the events unfolding more than a thousand miles to the southwest that had dominated both national and global attention. On the very day that she achieved her national title, the Arkansas state government was defying President Eisenhower over the court-ordered racial integration of the school system there, in what would become one of the most incendiary civil rights conflicts of the era. One week earlier, in response to the 1954 Supreme Court ruling ending segregation in the nation's schools, the Arkansas governor had called out the National Guard to block nine Black students—the "Little Rock Nine"—from entering the white high school in the state capital of Little Rock, as hundreds of enraged white citizens threatened violence. His action was the culmination of angry resistance to the court order that had percolated throughout the southern states for three years and had garnered mounting attention from the nation's critics abroad. Just hours after Althea's win, Arkansas governor Orval Faubus had gone on television and further inflamed tensions with the declaration that he had no intention of retreating from his position, thus slamming the door on compromise with the federal government. Faubus insisted that he was not violating the federal court order by keeping the National Guardsmen on alert but was doing so only to prevent violence.

The following day, September 9, the front pages of a few Black newspapers struggled to accommodate the burgeoning news events. "Faubus on TV: Troops Remain," trumpeted one *Chicago Defender* headline, pushing Althea's win to the bottom of the page, under the headline "Althea Tries Again, Wins National," the story running on page 22. The *New York Amsterdam News*, which did not run an edition until five days after the match, splashed three news stories about the Little Rock standoff—one describing how its own reporter was attacked by the white crowds there—on its front page, with a story about Althea at the bottom. Headlined "Althea Wants: 1. Apt., 2. Pro Singing Career," the story presented a somewhat-curious contrast of the Black tennis conqueror's personal desires with the racial crisis tearing at the American social fabric.[65]

So closely did some of the press coverage link the two events that it seemed to beg Althea to comment. "An Offset for Our Faubuses," declared the headline in the white-owned *Tallahassee Democrat* over an editorial that heralded Althea's win as "a demonstration of non-discrimination on the tennis courts." The *Star Tribune* of Minneapolis also nodded to the correspondence of events, writing that Althea's victory represented distinct progress in the face of the goings-on in Arkansas, in an editorial titled "Althea and Arkansas."[66]

Althea said nothing on the subject that was riveting the world's attention, but other high-profile Black people did. As the Little Rock standoff boiled in the coming weeks, and garnered increasing international outrage, a number of Black entertainers publicly objected to the federal government's inaction. It began with trumpet player Louis Armstrong, who stunned many with the announcement that he would bow out of a planned State Department goodwill trip to the Soviet Union because "the way they are treating my people in the South, the Government can go to hell." President Eisenhower, Satchmo added, had "no guts" and had allowed Governor Faubus to control the federal government. "It's getting almost so bad a colored man hasn't got any country."[67] Armstrong's remarks raised a few eyebrows, given that he himself had been harshly criticized for performing before segregated audiences in the Midwest just two months earlier. His trip to Russia had been long in the works, and the trumpeter had delighted U.S. State Department officials when he vowed that he would "fracture them cats" on his trip.[68] While few, if any, national figures went as far as Armstrong in their condemnation, several, such as Jackie Robinson and singers Lena Horne and Eartha Kitt, publicly endorsed his position. "Armstrong," said Kitt, "is absolutely right. We shouldn't go to Russia preaching things we are not." Eisenhower, she added, "is a man without a soul."[69]

As world condemnation of the Little Rock situation spread, the U.S. government finally took a stand. At the end of September, a federal judge began legal proceedings to force Faubus's hand, while President Eisenhower, despite hundreds of furious white citizens rioting in protest, dispatched twelve hundred members of the U.S. Army's 101st Airborne Division to supervise the integration of the school by the nine Black students. Overshadowed by the Arkansas furor was the fact that, earlier in the month, Eisenhower had signed the Civil Rights Bill of 1957, a piece of legislation that triggered a similar conflict between state and federal powers. Although originally designed to protect the much-diminished voting rights of non-white Americans, the final bill was a watered-down version more in line with Eisenhower's gradualist approach to integration. The president made no comment on the signing of the landmark bill, nor was there any ceremony to mark the enactment of the first civil rights legislation to become official since the Reconstruction era. Legal challenges to persisting segregation continued throughout the year as increasing numbers of Black citizens, as well as white ones, raised their voices in protest. Althea, however, did just the opposite.

In a determined effort to neutralize the global condemnation that the Little Rock crisis had triggered, the U.S. Information Agency (USIA), an independent body within the executive branch tasked with promoting national interests abroad and combating Communist propaganda, got to work. Its policies were executed overseas through the posts of the U.S. Information Service, or USIS. As Alvin A. Snyder, then the USIA's director of television and film service, described it, the agency worked tirelessly to counter negative Soviet propaganda and further its positive spin about American democracy, particularly regarding the subject of race. "Whatever worked was fair game," Snyder wrote in his book, *Warriors of Disinformation: How Lies, Videotape, and the USIA Won the Cold War.* "The U.S. government ran a full-service public relations organization, the largest in the world, about the size of the twenty biggest U.S. commercial PR firms combined."[70] One of the USIA's pet projects in the 1950s was the production of a series of films that were distributed overseas celebrating the accomplishments of successful Black citizens, including diplomat Ralph Bunche and athletes Wilma Rudolph and Althea Gibson. In a paper titled "'Negro

Stars' and the USIA's Portrait of Democracy," author Melinda Schwenk detailed how the filmmakers deliberately focused on Black stars enjoying the public embrace of American society and an elevated social status as a result of their achievements. The message was that American democracy, in short, was working for Black people.

Althea Gibson fit the bill perfectly. The USIA's ten-minute film about Althea, titled *Althea Gibson: Tennis Champion*, was commissioned at the height of the Little Rock crisis and immediately after she had won both Wimbledon and Forest Hills. Althea is shown being congratulated by Vice President Nixon, celebrated in the ticker tape parade in New York City, and walking arm in arm with white players. She is shown only in news footage in the film, while an unseen male narrator describes her decade of hard work on the tennis court without once referring to any obstacles raised by her race. In the government's version of Althea's life, it turned out that race had been no impediment at all. It was, of course, a self-serving myth. There is no indication that Althea opposed the making of the film or refused in any way to cooperate with the filmmakers.

"Instead, the U.S.I.A. appropriated the worldwide acclaim that Gibson had achieved for her tennis tournament wins to show American democracy in a positive light," Schwenk wrote.[71]

At the same time, Althea was also being celebrated on the covers of multiple American magazines during the latter part of 1957. While some of those stories allowed that she had experienced some difficulties on her journey, their saccharine message was that she had managed to put all her problems behind her in her remarkable rise to the top. In August, *Jet* magazine featured a cover photo, accompanying an article titled "How Althea Gibson Conquered Herself," that showed her racing cross court while focused on an incoming shot.[72] Two months later, the ever-upbeat *Ebony* featured on its cover a very American Althea smiling beatifically at the camera, a pair of rackets sheathed in patriotic red, white, and blue nestled against her pleated white tennis skirt. The headline over the sympathetic story inside declared that "Althea Is Probably Sports' Most Misunderstood Star."[73] In the same month, she appeared again on the cover of *World Tennis* magazine, this time clasping her U.S. Nationals trophy, her head inclined amiably toward the white Australian Mal Anderson, winner of the men's singles, at her side.[74]

Not all of what appeared in American magazines, however, was so up-beat. In November, a *Look* magazine cover story struck a bleaker note. The story emphasized all that Althea did *not* have and enumerated some of the criticisms that had been lodged against her. Althea not only had no place to display her many trophies, but she had no home of her own. Over the past decade, she had "lived in other people's houses, the homes of various benefactors, some of whom she called 'Mom' and 'Dad.' Althea over the years has had to be beholden to many different people, for everything from lessons in tennis to instructions in manners." Gratitude, nonetheless, did not come easy to her, the story continued, "and for a person like Althea, who has a champ's tenacity and necessary arrogance, it is close to unbearable." There were those who accused her of being a prima donna, while some of her benefactors indicated "that she isn't living up to her obligations to her race." Perhaps she and Will Darben would someday set up house, the story concluded. The photograph of the two of them pensively packing her trophies into boxes, however, suggested otherwise. The photo caption noted that Althea had made clear that she didn't want to get married while she was still playing tennis.[75]

All the media attention generated a degree of racist backlash, just as the photos of Althea dancing with the handsome white Hoad at the Wimbledon Ball had done. One reader of *Time* magazine's August cover story complained, "We have enough trouble with these people without paying for a magazine which carries such news. You will ruin your magazine if you continue to run such articles. Don't do it again." Another reader wrote in the same issue that he "couldn't stand your Althea Gibson cover around the house."[76] While there were also some positive letters, the racial objections would continue unabated while Althea remained high profile in the media.

President Eisenhower's White House also had lingering ambivalence about Althea's success, dating back to her wins in 1956. Despite the president's July letter congratulating her on her Wimbledon win, the invitation he had mentioned to her to visit the White House never materialized, as some among the Black press had predicted. Quizzed by columnist Sam

Lacy on the subject later in the fall, Althea said, "I have never received an invitation to the White House."[77]

Having hardened herself to such slights over the years, Althea paid little mind. The larger truth was that 1957 was a pivotal year for Black athletes. It began shortly after Jackie Robinson's announcement that he was going to retire from baseball in order to take an executive position with the Chock Full o' Nuts restaurant chain, a move that clashed with the Brooklyn Dodgers' plan to trade him to their archrival, the New York Giants, for $30,000. Black sports figures otherwise gained significant ground particularly on the football field, where all but one team in the National Football League now claimed a Black player. On the basketball court, center Bill Russell, who was drafted in the final days of 1956, was instrumental in helping the Boston Celtics achieve a record number of championships and would go on to become one of the greatest players of all times. Equally notable, and with tremendous ramifications for Althea personally, as she mulled future athletic undertakings, Charlie Sifford became the first Black to win a major golf tournament after a riveting sudden-death playoff in the Long Beach Open golf tournament in Long Beach, California.

As with all those players, Althea won the acclaim of being a "first"—in her case, on multiple fronts—but the title did not do much to help the state of her bank account. Now thirty years old, she faced a difficult future without a single viable prospect for supporting herself yet on the horizon. By then, she was living in a one-room apartment on Central Park West, likely paid for with the monthly seventy-five dollars she earned from Harry C. Lee & Company. The apartment, which Buxton had photographed in detail on one of her visits to the city, had a console television and a corner table laden with some of Althea's favorite trophies, a couple of striped armchairs, a convertible bed, and not much else. Although modest, it was relatively luxurious compared to the cramped Harlem walk-up she had grown up in several miles to the north.

It was also some distance from the place she had called home for half a dozen years, the Darben household in Montclair, New Jersey. Althea had distanced herself not just from the house, but also from the warm embrace of her loving beau, Will Darben. Although she was deeply attached to Darben, she was clearly not ready for marriage, and children were not an option. Now that she was the world champion women's tennis player, and one of the biggest Black celebrities in the country, the possibilities appeared to loom large before her. And that propelled her increasingly in the direction of Sydney Llewellyn, with whom she was spending greater amounts of time. Llewellyn, sensing Althea's mounting bankable potential, was ever ready to offer advice on court and off and had begun to handle some of her personal financial affairs. Although Althea was seriously considering formally breaking up with the soft-spoken Darben, she would later write that she had "no doubt that whatever twist my fate should take in the future, the crazy darling would go on loving me."[78] She was right.

The only trouble was that the financial offers were not exactly rolling in. Althea was clearly interested in turning professional, but no invitation to do so was yet forthcoming. Maureen Connolly, viewed as the most likely player able to take Althea on, had indicated that her injuries made it impossible for her to return to tournament tennis. With several of the other dominant women's champions, such as Doris Hart and Shirley Fry, having moved on, there were no other obvious competitors. Partly because of this, promoter Jack Kramer backed off the interest he had expressed in Connolly and Althea back in July, saying that he now wanted to see Althea win another round of Wimbledon and Forest Hills the following year. Kramer was moving cautiously on the women's front, mindful of promoter Bobby Riggs's attempt to launch such an effort back in 1950, using the tantalizing team of "Gorgeous Gussie" Moran and Pauline Betz, the No. 1 woman player in the world in 1946. That venture had collapsed midway through a ninety-city tour, despite the highly touted leopard fur shorts and gold-banded panties the women sometimes wore. The truth was that while an increasing number of top male tennis players were turning professional and signing contracts starting at $100,000, there was no market for a women's tour as of yet. It would take years before women objected to their second-class status and demanded the respect they deserved. With few other options at hand, Althea continued to play on the amateur circuit while focusing increasing amounts of time on her beloved singing.

That fall, she got serious about it. Llewellyn had long opposed her singing, variously telling her she couldn't sing her way out of a paper bag or a bathtub, but over time Althea managed to convince him otherwise. As the trees bordering Central Park outside her window began to turn a seasonal blend of orange and scarlet, he agreed to introduce her to his friend Dr. James S. Kennedy, a professor of speech at Long Island University and a trailblazer in a host of creative disciplines. Known as "Mr. Speech," Kennedy strove to improve communication in both the written and spoken word and spent years in Africa exploring theater and culture. An actor, director, and producer, he founded one of the first multicultural acting troupes in New York City and would ultimately produce more than one hundred songs and plays. While still an undergraduate at New York University, Kennedy worked as a manager at the popular Harlem nightclub Smalls Paradise and was a regular at several other of New York's hottest hangouts. His close friends included some of the big names in Black culture at the time, such as James Baldwin and Muhammad Ali. In later years, he taught actors Denzel Washington and Jimmy Smits, of *L.A. Law* and *NYPD Blue* fame, as undergraduates.

When Althea walked into his office that fall, Kennedy put her through a series of voice tests and agreed to meet with her three times a week, something they would continue to do for close to two years. He not only focused on her singing, but also taught her how to develop the muscles in her diaphragm to bring more strength to her voice projection. More important, he urged her not just to sing the words of a song, but to delve into memories of her personal life experience to add feeling to her performance. Janie Sykes-Kennedy, his wife, who met Althea and Llewellyn a few times with him over dinner at popular Black hangouts like the Red Rooster and Jock's Place in Harlem in the late 1950s, remembers Althea talking effusively about what she was learning from her coach.

"He taught her things she had never thought about," said Sykes-Kennedy, now in her eighties. "He taught her not just how to use her voice, but to delve into areas of her own experience, to work with sense memory to bring meaning and feeling to her singing. You take from your life experience. . . . I just remember her being very excited. Her voice was opening up, and she was developing the confidence she needed."[79]

While working hard to develop her voice, Althea continued to travel the tennis circuit, affirming her dominance of women's tennis. That fall, she twice beat Brough again, first at the Pacific Southwest tournament in

Los Angeles and again at the Pacific Coast tennis tournament in Berkeley a week later. In both instances, Althea simply overpowered Brough, defeating her in under one hour in the second tournament. In December, Althea was officially dubbed the nation's No. 1 women's tennis player by the USLTA, followed by Brough and then Dorothy Head Knode. In January, she would receive the ultimate athletic honor by being crowned the Associated Press's Female Athlete of the Year in 1957 by an overwhelming vote of sportswriters and broadcasters. It was yet another notch on the "First Negro" belt. Althea was the first Black woman to win the award, which had previously gone to Alice Marble and Maureen Connolly.

And yet, for all her astounding success and worldwide recognition, Althea, the athlete who had outperformed some of the most talented sportswomen of the day, had barely any more money in her pocket than on the day she strode into the Cosmopolitan Club in her tattered blue jeans clasping her secondhand tennis racket. A couple of players of her caliber had negotiated contracts after they turned professional, including Maureen Connolly, who served on the advisory board for Wilson Sporting Goods and for whom one of the company's series of "Autograph" rackets was named. Doris Hart also signed a deal, with Spalding, and had a racket design named after her. While Althea would be named to the Harry C. Lee advisory board after she went professional, there were few new offers coming her way after her wins. Whether it was the color of her skin, her gender, or her much-discussed temperament, or likely a combination of all three that stood in her way, the press took note. "Is Althea Gibson Really Broke?" questioned the *Pittsburgh Courier* that fall. "Tennis great Althea Gibson will probably go down in history as the greatest and brokest woman tennis champ. Rumored to be flat broke (she's had none of the usual fabulous 'please turn pro' offers ordinarily showered upon tennis greats), Althea has turned to school teaching for bread and butter."[80]

As 1957 drew to a close, it wasn't actually teaching, but singing that Althea believed more adamantly than ever would be the key to a secure financial future. In November, she was invited to sing at a testimonial birthday dinner at the luxurious Waldorf Astoria in New York on behalf of legendary blues composer W. C. Handy, known as "the Father of the Blues." Althea sang a couple of tunes at the high-profile event, one of them a duet side by side with the wheelchair-bound composer, who was turning eighty-four years old. The lavish evening, sponsored by the American Society of Composers, Authors and Publishers, drew entertainers such as Milton Berle, Lena Horne, and Tallulah Bankhead. Scattered among the crowd were also a number of entertainment industry executives, including a man named Henry Onorati, vice president of Dot Records. Intrigued by Althea's performance, Onorati asked if she would be interested in making some test recordings at his studio, to see if she might be suitable to record a long-playing album. Althea leapt at the offer.

Onorati wasn't the only one listening to Althea croon in her floral print dress and pearl choker. Seated at one of the front-row tables was a trimly dressed man named Ed Sullivan, the former sports and entertainment reporter now best known for his television show, which featured a broad assortment of performers and show business talent. Just a few months ago, Althea had done a televised interview with Sullivan on his program. A white Catholic who had been born in Harlem some thirty blocks from Althea's childhood home, Sullivan had a unique appreciation for Black performers and regularly welcomed them onto the stage next to him.[81] Having experienced his own share of discrimination due to his religion, Sullivan was such an early and avid backer of Black entertainers and athletes that a Black comic once popped an Afro wig on Sullivan's head while he was on-camera and dubbed him an "honorary Negro." Not surprisingly, Sullivan's warm relations with talented Black performers onstage elicited volumes of furious and racist mail from viewers; his sponsors were even angrier. Once, after Sullivan kissed Black performer Pearl Bailey on the cheek and shook Nat "King" Cole's hand, for instance, his sponsor Ford's Lincoln dealers was enraged. Others adamantly insisted that he invite fewer dark-skinned stars on to the show. Sullivan never blinked. Not only did he defy pressure from some of his sponsors to limit the number of Black acts on his show, but he once had a Ford executive tossed out of his theater for his racist views. Race, however, was but one of the show's aspects. Mostly, Ed Sullivan was a stern-faced kingmaker who hungered for talent of any color, and he liked what he heard of Althea Gibson that night. He didn't do anything right away, but "Big Al" was now on the Great Stone Face's radar.

10

Am I Somebody?

It was the last leg of the 1958 Sunshine Circuit, the spring stretch of tennis tournaments that launched in Colombia and culminated amid the bank of art deco towers that flanked Miami Beach. Heartened by the balmy tropical breeze, Althea swung a sharp left off Route 1 and onto the scenic Venetian Causeway, which spans Biscayne Bay.

In a way, she was making a hero's return to the Good Neighbor tennis tournament in Flamingo Park. Back in 1951, Althea, then a college sophomore, had made history as the "First Negro" to play not only in the popular Miami event, but in any major tennis tournament in the Deep South. Unfazed by some of the disapproving faces in the audience, she had trounced her opponents straight through to the finals in both the singles and mixed doubles matches and was enthusiastically welcomed by the tournament director. Never mind that at least one competitor had refused to participate because of Althea's color. Now Big Al was back, cruising past the bridge's latticed gridwork, the greatest female tennis player in the world with three Grand Slam singles titles under her belt. The official No. 1 female tennis player in America was warming up to repeat her past year's triumphant performances.

And then it happened. Just one mile from the causeway's end, a toll guard flagged Althea to a stop. Tournament officials may have enthusiastically welcomed the star player to their event, but Miami Beach remained a locale famously unfriendly to Black people. Since passage of Ordinance

457 in 1936, those working in seasonal or tourism-related jobs on Miami Beach were required to register and carry an identification card. Although the law did not specify Black workers, reporters and residents of color maintained that the ordinance was frequently employed to harass Black people and discourage them from visiting. The toll guard, apparently not recognizing Althea, nor believing her story, adamantly refused to let her pass.

"She was beyond upset, she was beside herself," recalled Janet Hopps Adkisson, a rising Seattle tennis player who had become friendly with Althea during their time on the Sunshine Circuit. "Here she was the champion of the world, and some dummy at the gate refused to let her pass. She had to call tournament officials on the phone and explain what was happening. By the time she got through and started to play tennis, she was just not herself."[1]

As Althea stood on the sunbaked clay court across from the fourth-seeded Hopps in the semifinals of the Good Neighbor tournament shortly afterward, her mood was dark. Although she had managed to win her first three rounds with little effort, she was a wreck by the time the semifinals got under way and the larger implications of what had happened on the causeway sank in. Part of her emotional state may have been triggered by the fact that she now faced a friend and confidante on the other side of the net. Part of it may have been that word of the incident at the tollbooth was being quietly whispered among some of the other players. The truth of it was a darkly bitter one, something that would take a few years to fully sink its ragged teeth into Althea's skin. She may have been the subject of international acclaim and an incomparable athlete, but on some level, she was still just an anonymous Black girl who got stopped at the gate, barred from the white world beyond.

Althea tore into the match, delivering a couple of unreturnable serves across the net and hurtled to a 5–1 lead. She and Hopps were familiar with each other's game, as they had competed a half-dozen times before the Sunshine Circuit; Hopps had even managed to defeat Althea in an astonishing first encounter when the former was just nineteen years old. Now nearly twenty-four and the ninth-ranked female player in the United States, Hopps had again beaten Althea in one of their four singles matches so far in the Caribbean this spring. Hopps knew better than to deploy her own power game against Althea's. Instead, she dropped a succession of shallow shots into the forecourt—a strategy she called "dinkus"—making it almost impossible for Althea to lob returns or launch her overhead game. As Hopps claimed one game and then the next, word that the world champion was teetering began to circulate among the crowd, and reporters began to gather at courtside to see what was going on. Already anxious, her customary game mask more taut than usual, Althea began to slip. After Hopps won the first set 8–6, Althea retreated to the baseline, double-faulted repeatedly, and committed numerous errors. Althea, as Hopps Adkisson later described it, "had had it. I think she must have just said to herself, 'That's it. I'm outta here.' And I didn't want her to do that. . . . I think I won the first set legitimately, and she gave me the second one. . . . I didn't want that."[2]

After Hopps took the second set 6–2, Althea stormed off the court, ignoring one reporter's questions and responding brusquely to another. "I didn't feel good. Anybody could have beaten me today. She just beat me period."[3]

The following day, Althea went on to win doubles with her partner, the dazzling Brazilian teenager Maria Bueno, against Hopps and Martha Hernández of Mexico. But the press was already speculating about the ability of the world's No. 1 female player to reclaim her Grand Slam titles in the months to come. Not only had Althea twice lost to Hopps, but she had also lost a tournament in San Juan to Beverly Baker Fleitz. Althea, back on steady footing some days later, dismissed her losses and expressed confidence that she would hold on to her titles. "These tournaments don't mean anything. They were just a test. It's Wimbledon that counts, and I definitely think I'll win it again this year."[4]

The turbulent Miami tournament was nonetheless a harbinger of the complicated few years that lay ahead. As her multiple losses to Hopps attested, a younger generation of tennis players, which also included Bueno and England's Christine Truman, were nipping at her heels. That, coupled with ever-increasing debate over the pros and cons of professional tennis raging in the media, increasingly compelled Althea to contemplate her unhappy financial situation. Was Jack Kramer going to make good on his stated intent to invite her into the play-for-pay ranks? Should she go out on a limb and launch a professional women's tennis tour of her own? How could she pursue the singing career she had dreamed of and had been training for in earnest? And what about sweet Will Darben, ever eager to tie the knot with his globetrotting beloved? Had she made a mistake in not marrying him earlier? Further roiling the mix, race was cropping up increasingly, just as it had in Miami. Big Al, who had managed to effectively downplay the role her color had played in her career for years, now found herself compelled to acknowledge and sometimes even confront it—except for those times, of course, when she chose not to.

Pete Wilson of the *Daily Mirror* in London, who had followed Althea's every Wimbledon appearance over the years, picked up on her apparent vulnerability and noted it with some empathy. In a column headlined "Songbird Althea Flops on Tennis 'Hit' Parade," Wilson declared, "Now there is some ray of hope for our up-and-coming youngsters, for the Gibson Girl has already been beaten three times this year." The story suggested that Althea's Caribbean losses were in part attributable to her focus on singing. Wilson revealed that Althea had signed up for two appearances on *The Ed Sullivan Show* in coming months and was working on a commercial recording. But Althea, Wilson pointed out, was still Althea, "as prickly as a dusky cactus." Asked by another reporter what impact it might have on her lawn tennis career if she made a good showing on television, Althea replied brusquely, "What do you mean, '*if*'? This is a big chance for me. I fully intend to make a hit."[5]

Singing had been her dream ever since she won second place in Harlem's Apollo Theater amateur show back in 1943. Although the theater manager had awarded her a mere ten dollars rather than a week's engagement on the Apollo stage as had been promised beforehand, she had long ached for more. With the cherished saxophone given to her by Sugar Ray Robinson slung about her neck and a tune invariably on her lips, she'd played her way with the high school band in Wilmington, North Carolina; crooned at night with a local five-piece band while working at Lincoln University; and belted out the blues in a succession of nightclubs stretching from the Italian coast through London's Piccadilly Circus and back down into the heart of the Caribbean during the Sunshine Circuit. By the late spring of 1958, the months of coaching by Mr. Speech had helped mature Althea's deep contralto and instill it with an appealing throaty quality.

Indeed, her test recordings for Dot Records, initiated in the weeks after her performance at W. C. Handy's birthday party the previous year, were so successful that she had happily signed a contract several months later.

Althea's debut album, *Althea Gibson Sings*, featured a mix of a dozen popular ballads, including "I Can't Give You Anything but Love," "Don't Say No," and what would become her trademark song, "So Much to Live For," written by Professor Kennedy. On the hot copper-toned album cover, a newly minted Althea appears with heavily processed hair as uncharacteristic as the generous application of makeup she sports. During the same week of the album's May release, Althea made her first live appearance on *The Ed Sullivan Show*. Dressed in a shimmering floor-length gown set off by elbow-length white silk gloves and faux diamond earrings, selected with help from Sugar Ray's wife, Edna Mae, Althea gave an earnest and somewhat languid performance of her title song, earning a generous round of applause. She also received sincere congratulations from Sullivan, who presented her with the Mildred "Babe" Didrikson Zaharias Courage Award, an enormous silver trophy given to the outstanding female athlete of the year. What it did not garner her were glowing media reviews.

In a brief appraisal of her singing debut, columnist Bill Lane of the Black newspaper the *Michigan Chronicle* observed, "Miss Gibson is an exceptional tennis player. Now, as a singer, we feel, Miss Gibson continues to be a good tennis player."[6] John Shanley of the New York Times News Service put it a little more bluntly, saying that Althea's delivery "of a rather saccharine ballad called 'So Much to Live For' was much less exciting than her achievements at Forest Hills, Wimbledon, and other tennis arenas."[7] And then there was the *Philadelphia Inquirer*, which sniffed that "as a tennis player, she has much, much more on the ball."[8] Even longtime supporter Lacy of the *Baltimore Afro-American* found little good to say about Althea's performance, concluding that she did "an acceptable job."[9]

Nor did her album fare any better. By the end of November, a whopping 1,230 records had been sold, while a separate single of her singing "Around the World" sold only thirty records. Three months after the album was released, Dot declined to renew its option with Althea. She believed the album had suffered from poor recording conditions, as she would later write.

Not only did she have a chest cold at the time the record was made, but the entire recording session was compressed into a single, highly stressful day. But, in the end, the result was what it was. As Althea wrote in her second book, *So Much to Live For*, published in 1968, "The record did not live up to my expectations. In fact, it sank beneath a sea of indifference."[10]

Days after her appearance on *The Ed Sullivan Show*, Althea sought to put the experience behind her by turning her attention back to tennis. With her rackets bundled under her arm, she boarded an overnight flight to England, where she would defend her titles in the grass court tournaments leading up to Wimbledon. Six hours after she landed, she handily locked up her first win at the Surrey Lawn Tennis Championships in Surbiton in a mere twenty-nine minutes. It appeared a good omen, but it was a misleading one. Although Althea easily defended three of her grass tournament titles, including devastating defeats of two up-and-coming young players, America's nineteen-year-old Mimi Arnold and eighteen-year-old Bueno, she stumbled in the Wightman Cup tournament that followed.

At the start, the odds were heavily in the American team's favor. The American women had won the tournament twenty-one times in a row since 1930, not counting the World War II years, during which it was not played. Fans on both sides of the pond had no doubt that the all-powerful Althea would not lose a single one of her matches. Even Peter Wilson, the *Daily Mirror* columnist and irrepressible British booster, who had put the odds of a British win at eleven to ten, conceded wins to the Americans in the two singles matches that would be played by "the talented Negress Althea Gibson" in his column on the day the tournament began.[11] It was also true, though, that the British team boasted some fresh young blood, particularly the towering Christine Truman, who had been lifting weights and running sprints since she was savaged by Althea at Wimbledon in the semifinals the previous year. With the nineteen-year-old lefty Ann Haydon a powerful addition to the team, the British cadre was considered to be in significantly better fighting condition than those of previous years. Given the potential, even the merest breath of possibility that an upset might occur was enough to jam the stands beyond capacity at Wimbledon's Centre Court. In the midst of the crowd were thousands of ponytailed girls in their school uniforms with eyes glued to their idol, the teenage Truman with her short-cropped hair and trim ladies' purse ever at her side.

Althea lived up to her promise in the first of the tournament's seven matches, easily beating Shirley Bloomer, the determined British woman who had given her a challenge more than once in the past, by a score of 6–3, 6–4. Although Althea made an inordinate number of errors, she deftly wielded her serve to keep Bloomer racing to the corners of the court while she commandeered the net. Truman did just as well in her match, coming from behind in two sets to beat her opponent, the veteran American Dottie Knode. Displaying a steadier, more reliable game than she had the year before, the expressionless Truman wore down the older Knode with a series of overhead smashes and scorching forehands to take the match 6–4, 6–4. Following a prolonged tea break, Truman masterminded a second and even more impressive win with her partner Bloomer by taking the tournament's first doubles match against Karol Fageros and a visibly weary Knode in just forty minutes. School blazer seams were stretched to their limit as the young girls in the stands leapt into the air, shrieking and writhing with excitement. With a score of 2–1 in Britain's favor at the end of the day, hope for a reversal of the pattern that had prevailed for twenty-eight years surged across the nation as the tabloids bowed to the young queen of the day. "CHRISTINE—YOU'RE JUST SMASHING!" exclaimed the *Daily Herald*. "CHRISTINE CONQUERS WIMBLEDON WOBBLE," shouted the *Daily Mirror*. Expectations unfurled on the front pages across the country the following morning. "Britain, whisper it gently," advised the *Times* of London, "may to-day win the Wightman Cup for the first time since 1930."[12]

On the second and final day of the event, Knode won the opening singles match, bringing the overall score to a dead heat, at 2–2, and setting the stage for the most anticipated encounter of the tournament. On one side was the thirty-year-old global queen of tennis, Althea Gibson. On the other side was Christine Truman, the seventeen-year-old moonfaced high-schooler who was virtually blind in her left eye. How could the school blazers possibly maintain their high hopes? Three times Althea and Truman had met on the court in 1957, and three times Althea had won handily. Truman never took a single set. Fans under either flag largely presumed an Althea win was a foregone conclusion. As the staid *Times* put it succinctly, "To expect Miss Truman to defeat Miss Gibson would be to expect anarchy."[13] But the towering British girl had a secret up her sleeve: she was wearing her lucky tennis dress that day, a tailored white outfit covered with tiny embroidered tennis rackets, made just for her by none other than Ted Tinling.

The tennis dress performed its magic, and then some. Truman started out bravely but unevenly, double-faulting once and flubbing an easy volley before losing the first set 6–2 in nineteen minutes. The teenager, however, learned something invaluable during that first set. Over the past month she had returned thousands of practice serves to her coach, knowing full well that she would very likely be squaring off against Althea's laser-shot service, her most powerful weapon. As the second set began, all that practice began to pay off. Now Truman knew that she could in fact return Althea's serve.

"Althea knew it, too," Truman recalled. "She knew that she could no longer control me with her serve, and that unsettled her. That was the turning point."[14]

Truman surged into the lead in the second set, prompting Althea to recoil and fight back "with the venom of a striking snake," as the *Daily Mirror*'s Peter Wilson put it in his account in *World Tennis*. At the conclusion of a fierce battle of hammering backhands and strategic lobs, Truman took the second set, and the earth shifted ever so slightly. On they raged, first one in the lead and then the other; a winning forehand by Truman, an angle shot in return from Althea and then a cross-court backhand by Truman. As the players battled furiously for each point, inching ahead shot by killer shot, game by game, the mesmerized onlookers were oblivious to all but the court before them. "In the mounting tension, I don't really recommend trying to smoke your ball-point and make extra notes with your cigarette!" wrote Wilson. Truman then hammered a series of smashes so forceful that it launched her to match point, as every Brit and school blazer in the audience emptied their seats and hurled hats and programs in the air.

"You suddenly realized that you'd forgotten to breathe for the last minute," Wilson wrote in frenzied excitement. "Christine served—a fault and . . . another. Where are the stretcher bearers? Get me the oxygen. . . .

A brief rally, a backhand volley hooked out—AND CHRISTINE HAD WON! It was one of the most amazing women's victories I had witnessed in the 30 years I've been attending tennis matches."[15] The match had lasted sixty-six minutes.

Althea, who was hardly playing her best and lost 2–6, 6–3, 6–4, was none-theless magnanimous. She walked briskly to the net and took the younger girl's hand with a broad smile. "She was very gracious," Truman recalled. "She didn't come up with an excuse, like they all do now, with an ice pack on their neck or saying they haven't played for a month because they were injured or that sort of a thing. She simply said, 'You were too good for me today, Christine.' So, I look back and think, that was a good win for me. I actually beat Althea."[16]

Although the rest was an anticlimax, it demonstrated again that change was not just in the offing but had firmly taken hold. The next upset came with a match that pitted British teenager Ann Haydon against America's "Little Mimi" Arnold, as the press liked to call the sturdy California girl. Haydon won relatively easily, bringing the game count to 4–2 and thus ensuring that the British would at long last claim the coveted Wightman Cup. In the final match of the day, which had no substantive bearing on the outcome, Althea again made a misstep. As she and Hopps squared off in their first game against their British opponents, Althea surprised her partner by telling her to take the first serve and then move to the left court. She advised the younger girl that she planned to poach any return to the right court, but as the return came back, Althea failed to make her move, and the ball sailed off court.

"She looked at me and said, 'Oh, my God, I forgot,'" recalled Hopps. "She had just been beaten by Truman, and she was still reeling from that. She just forgot. It made me look like a dummy, though."[17]

Althea's error appeared to thrust her back into the moment, and she and Hopps comfortably won their match. Althea, however, was deeply disappointed by her loss to Truman. She later attributed it, and some of her losses in the Caribbean, to the fact that she had been experimenting with backcourt play in an effort to sharpen her ground strokes, thus ceding the net to her opponents. But the truth was that Althea was distracted. Unbeknownst to any but her tiny inner circle, she was preparing to take a sabbatical from amateur tennis immediately after playing Forest Hills that fall. It was time to finally explore some moneymaking possibilities, and it was that which preoccupied her during the summer of 1958 more than anything else.

Althea had little experience in handling contracts or managing money, having never dealt much with either, and she realized that she needed guidance as she considered the professional realm. The one person she knew with a perennial interest in money, both the making of it and the spending of it, was Syd Llewellyn. Llewellyn had street savvy about financial matters, if not exactly an accountant's acumen or a Jack Kramer's cunning. Equally important, he had the gift of gab and could negotiate with the shrewdest of deal makers, something Althea was also going to need. If Llewellyn was going to assume greater authority over her affairs than he already had, though, and Althea was going to be hitting the road on a quite different kind of circuit in his company, she needed to make some adjustments.

Days after she arrived in London to prepare for Wimbledon, she made a surprising public announcement. Her relationship with her longtime boyfriend, Will Darben, was finished. As columnist A. S. "Doc" Young put it, "her longtime romance with that New Jerseyite had gone kaput!"[18] Althea had discussed the matter with Hopps a number of times in previous months as the two traveled the circuit, sitting side by side on airplanes and playing gin rummy in waiting rooms. Hopps had much in common with her traveling companion. Not only had she been a tomboy much like Althea, and was one of five children, but she also liked to sing show tunes. Althea had shown her new friend how to do Sugar Ray's agility drills in the locker room, while Hopps had taught Althea how to swim and do the jackknife. Although Althea almost never talked with Hopps about race, just as she had sidestepped the topic with other close, white female friends like Fageros and Angela Buxton, the two women shared their feelings about their love lives.

"Once, we were on a plane talking about the future, and I said, 'Eventually I want to be married and have children,'" recalled Hopps Adkisson. "Althea said, 'Oh, I never want to have children.' That surprised me, but, then, knowing her background and her life, it really didn't surprise me. I just kinda shut up. I mean, I went on to have seven children."[19]

Althea had clearly felt comfortable putting the doe-eyed Darben and his marriage proposal on hold, again. Part of it was her aversion to the limitations of matrimony. But she was also keenly aware that her long periods of absence, which were likely to remain constant in the next chapter of her career, might take a toll on their relationship. As she explained to *Jet* magazine a couple of months later, in a story titled "What Winning at Tennis Cost Althea Gibson," "Most fellows I know want their women around most of the time, where they can see and talk to them. In my case I'm never in one place long enough."[20] She turned instead to Llewellyn, a man who served many of her immediate needs, who doubled as dancer, coach, psycho-spiritual guru, and now her evolving financial manager. Despite speculation that they might be lovers, the relationship was a platonic one. In addition to regular coaching sessions in New York, Llewellyn had been writing to her steadily while she was on the road, advising her simultaneously to remain humble to God and to "stay mean and don't let up."[21]

As he assumed increasing control over Althea's financial affairs, including paying her rent and having her car repaired while she traveled, his letters were a blend of housekeeping details and advice on tennis strategy. In one letter following her loss to Truman in the Wightman Cup, he advised her never to criticize another player. Instead, he counseled, she should only praise them, for in doing so, "you put the pressure on them, and that's where you want it."[22] As she headed into Wimbledon in the summer of 1958, Llewellyn's counsel was ringing in her ears. The two of them, she would later write, agreed that she was done with the experiment in backcourt play that had tarnished her performance earlier in the year. "There was no doubt in our minds that I would stick religiously to my tried and true serve-and-run-to-the-net tactics at Wimbledon."[23]

Landing in London, Althea found Buxton waiting once again to collect her old doubles partner and ferry her back to Rossmore Court, where the warm British milk they had so often joked about was waiting. During the nearly one year since they had seen each other, things had changed quite a bit. Having retired from tennis the previous year as a result of her tenosynovitis, Buxton had focused her energy on becoming a dress designer. She had fashioned several outfits she hoped Althea would wear both at Wimbledon and a few of the social events they would attend together.

Althea is celebrated in Harlem on her return to New York in 1957. *(Genevieve Naylor)*

Althea and her father, Daniel, on a street near their apartment on 143rd Street in Harlem. *(Genevieve Naylor)*

Angela and Althea win the 1956 Wimbledon women's doubles title and are presented their trophy by Princess Mariana, Duchess of Kent. Bound in part by their outsider status, the two players became lifelong friends. *(S&G/PA Images, via Getty Images)*

"It's Althea v The Rest," *The Pittsburgh Courier*, July 13, 1957.

The players are received at an event in India in 1956. (*Homai Vyarawalla, HV Archive, via the Alkazi Collection of Photography*)

The Gibson Girl, as the press often called her, is presented her trophy for winning the 1957 U.S. Nationals women's singles by Vice President Richard Nixon. Australian Mal Anderson, right, won the men's singles title. (*Bettmann, via Getty images*)

On the brink of defeating Darlene Hard at the U.S. National Championships in New York, Sept. 7, 1958. (*Allyn Baum, The New York Times: Redux*)

Coach Llewellyn presents Althea with a birthday present. Llewellyn would eventually become Althea's second husband. *(Genevieve Naylor, Library of Congress Prints & Photographs Division,* Look *magazine collection)*

Angela greets her friend at Heathrow Airport in 1958. Althea would win the women's singles at both Wimbledon and the U.S. National Championships back home in that year. *(*World Tennis Magazine Archives, *International Tennis Hall of Fame)*

The album *Althea Gibson Sings* was released by Dot Records in 1958. It did not do well. *(Cecil Williams Photography and Universal Music Enterprises)*

New York City mayor Robert Wagner is presented with a copy of Althea's first album at a reception in her honor after her second Wimbledon win. *(*World Tennis Magazine Archives, *International Tennis Hall of Fame)*

In her film acting debut, Althea appeared as a servant in the 1959 Civil War movie *The Horse Soldiers* with stars John Wayne and William Holden. Several Black columnists criticized her for wearing a kerchief. *(Bettmann, via Getty Images)*

Karol Fageros and Althea sign up with Abe Saperstein, owner of the Harlem Globetrotters, a pro basketball team, to play in a series of exhibition games in 1960. *(Harry Harris, Associated Press)*

Althea and Karol Fageros pose before their debut match with the Harlem Globetrotters at Madison Square Garden on New Year's Eve in 1959. *(Marty Lederhandler, Associated Press)*

The Ward Baking Company hired Althea to promote its Tip Top bread and serve as a community relations representative in 1960. The job lasted five years. *(The New Pittsburgh Courier)*

The Tip Top Toasters basketball team plays at a 1961 benefit for the Harlem YMCA at the Renaissance Casino. *(Harlem YMCA: University of Minnesota Libraries)*

Will Darben and Althea in the mid-1960s. *(Rosemary Darben)*

Rosemary Darben with her brother, Will. *(Frances Gray collection)*

Althea and Will. *(Frances Gray collection)*

Record-breaking athletes Althea Gibson and Jackie Robinson play in the 1962 North-South Tournament in Miami Springs. Althea would go on to be the first Black member of the LPGA. *(AP Images)*

Lining up a putt at the Pleasant Valley Country Club in Sutton, Massachusetts, in 1966. *(AP Images/Bill Chaplis)*

The eighth annual Miller Lite Arthur Ashe Tennis Classic at Flushing Meadows, New York. From Left to Right: Charlie Kapp, Miller Brewing Company eastern regional manager; Earl "The Pearl" Monroe, former New York Knicks basketball player; Arthur Ashe, captain of America's Davis Cup team; Althea Gibson; and Larry Waters, Miller supervisor of special events. *(New Journal & Guide, Photographs & Prints Division, via the Schomburg Center for Research in Black Culture, The New York Public Library.)*

Angela Buxton, Carol Gaither, and Althea Gibson in the 1990s. *(Don Felder)*

Sunny Billie outside Sunny's store in Silver, South Carolina. *(Sally H. Jacobs)*

More than fifteen years after she died, a sculpture of Althea was installed at the Billie Jean King National Tennis Center in Queens in 2019. *(Jeenah Moon,* The New York Times: Redux*)*

The Wimbledon women's champ was Buxton's first big-name customer. Another change was that Buxton's mother, Violet, had moved out and now lived in an apartment across town, leaving the two young women on their own. One day, a week before the Championships began, Buxton answered the doorbell to find a handsome man in an American military uniform complete with brass buttons and a chest full of ribbons at the door, likely Cpt. Dova L. Jones, whom Althea had fallen in love with in Lincoln. The man, who sported a mustache and identified himself as a captain, politely asked for Althea. Buxton called into the apartment, and Althea came running to the door, threw her arms around the man, and led him to her bedroom, where they stayed for several days with the door closed. Buxton, on the other side of the door, did what she could to accommodate.

"I thought to myself, *Well, whatever is going on in there they need to eat,*" Buxton recalled with a grin decades later. "So, I used to provide trays of food and put them outside the door on the floor. And it would just disappear." Decades later, when the nature of talk about high-profile personalities had become more probing, Buxton was frequently asked if she thought Althea was a lesbian. "Well, I nearly died laughing at that," she said. As Buxton saw it, what she had viewed during those few days in the summer of 1958 "said it all, really."[24]

After the inevitable weeks of buildup and speculation, the Seventy-Second Wimbledon Championships got under way in the fourth week of June with a pulse notably feebler than usual. Part of it was that some among the crop of American women players, such as Doris Hart, who had reigned for close to a decade, had retired. But weighing far more heavily was the exodus of some of the bigger-name male champions, such as Lew Hoad and Ken Rosewall, to the professional ranks, bringing down the overall level of play. As former player turned columnist Tony Mottram morosely wrote in the *Belfast Telegraph*, as the ranks of professional tennis expand, "the level at Wimbledon steadily deteriorates. . . . The voracious appetite of the fast-growing professional game has swallowed up all the big names in men's tennis, and even in women's play we now have the lowest standard since the war."[25] Many others even mournfully predicted the fabled tournament's end.

At the same time, several factors kept interest in the women's singles event high, despite a relentless cold rain that plagued nearly the entire tournament. For starters, the talented incoming generation of young British women players, including the teenagers Truman and Haydon, had already inflamed expectations with their dramatic wins at the Wightman encounter. Adding to the anticipation was the unpredictable hard hitter Bueno, who had recently aced the women's singles in the Italian Championships. There was also the presence of the controversial promoter Jack Kramer, who had already plucked some of the Championships' male titans for his pro tour and would be closely watching the event with an eye to possibly nabbing a female player or two. Adding zest to the staid backdrop of the British tennis tradition was the looming and ever-fascinating question of the glamorous Karol Fageros's underpants. The blond vixen Fageros, seeded No. 8, had been warned that she would be barred from Wimbledon's green velvet lawns if she dared to appear in the same gold lamé panties edged with black lace that she had worn months earlier at the French Open. Wimbledon officials had declared that her gold panties would be too distracting to be worn during the tournament. The rules, after all, said that players must wear white and only white.

Outraged, "Gorgeous Gussie" Moran, the first to reveal distracting undergarments at Wimbledon in 1949, declared their warning "dictatorial. It's czaristic. It's a blow at democracy and freedom."[26] Although Fageros had been reinstated for the Championships after agreeing to cover her bottom in white lace, there was no telling what the Miami seductress, as the press sometimes referred to her, might actually show up wearing under her tennis dress. Last but not least, there was the remote possibility that the reigning queen, Althea, just might be vulnerable to an upset, given what had happened weeks earlier, never mind that the betting was firmly on her side two to one.

The opening day of the women's singles, called Ladies' Day, proved columnist Mottram prescient. Three of the top female players—Althea, Truman, and Bueno—all knocked out their opponents in heavily one-sided, somewhat predictable contests lasting less than thirty minutes. Bored by reports of equally unexciting performances in the men's singles the previous day, Kramer promptly announced that he would not be signing on anyone new from the Championships, including Althea. "They are just not good enough," he reportedly said.[27]

More chaos followed after the beloved Truman, seeded No. 2 and the great hope of the British crowd, went down in a sizzling Centre Court battle that pitted the towering teenager against the diminutive American Mimi Arnold, who was almost one foot shorter—a contest invariably likened to that of David versus Goliath. In the most notable upset of the tournament so far, the idolized Truman lost 10–8, 6–3 to her determined American opponent in under one hour. The headline writers could barely control themselves. "'I'VE NO EXCUSE' ADMITS CARELESS CHRISTINE. Mimi the midget a master planner," trilled the tabloid *The People*.[28]

Althea, meanwhile, moved steadily forward, swatting away each of her opponents and losing only a single set to the persistent British fighter Shirley Bloomer Brasher. In the semifinal, she crushed Ann Haydon 6–2, 6–0 in a little under forty minutes. As the London *Times* put it, the numbers "tell the bare story of two characters in different worlds. Miss Gibson, lissome and loose limbed, took charge of the whole green stage. She was the lead; she spoke all the lines; largely she even answered her own cues."[29] It would take the young Haydon years to recover from the onslaught. "I got killed. . . . I didn't want to play on that court for a long time. . . . I wanted to dig a hole and bury myself," Haydon recalled in an interview more than a half century later."[30] Meanwhile, on a court somewhat removed, Karol Fageros—who had obligingly worn the agreed-upon white nylon panties, but had cleverly managed to conceal her gold lamé underneath them—was ousted in the third round.

While attention was focused largely on the big-name competitors, another British player, as earnest as she was unseeded, had been toiling patiently up the other side of the ladder, leaving a trail of vanquished victims in her wake. Neither the fans nor the pundits had taken much note. Her name was Angela Mortimer, the same determined woman who had beaten Althea—whom Mortimer refers to in her autobiography as "a tall darkie girl from America"—in four successive matches before losing to her in the French Open in 1956.[31] For a time, Mortimer had been ranked Britain's No. 1 female player. But then she had disappeared for two years as she grappled with a virus she had contracted in Egypt as well as with nagging anxiety. Experts predicted that the country's top female was finished. Indeed, as Mortimer inched her way back into the game at the start of 1958, she ranked low enough that she failed to make the Wightman Cup team, despite having won the Australian Open that year. But suddenly, like a rogue tennis ball returned from the heavens, Mortimer landed in the Wimbledon finals for the first time in her tennis career, the first unseeded player in twenty years to reach the women's final.

After Mortimer routed Hungary's Zsuzsa "Suzy" Körmöczy in the semifinals, British fans had an entirely new and unlikely heroine to lionize, and the national press dutifully fanned the patriotic flames.

"OUTCAST ANGELA IS BRITAIN'S ACE," roared the *Daily Express.* "FORGOTTEN ANGELA IS IN THE FINAL," exclaimed the *Daily Mirror* headline. The story beneath described how the twenty-six-year-old blond, "Unheralded, unsung-and 'unseeded'—Angela Mortimer, the 'forgotten girl of British lawn tennis' yesterday reached the final of the women's singles at Wimbledon in just thirty-one minutes of relentless, ruthless, ravaging play."[32]

The forgotten girl roared back into memory on the emerald grass of Centre Court. Minutes after she met Althea before a crowd of fourteen thousand, she broke the American's serve and tucked one game under her belt. Then she had two. Mortimer was still the rock-solid baseline player she had been before; it was Althea who had changed. She, too, had become much more consistent, had grown out of her unpredictable ways, and remained just as relentless at the net. But Althea seemed taken aback by Mortimer's assault. Early on, she double-faulted and was rapped for a foot fault before she managed to claim the third game at love. Then came another double fault, two foot faults, and yet another double fault, which, astonishingly, put Mortimer in the lead at 4–2. All told, the green-suited linesman called eleven foot faults on Althea in the first set alone, which teetered briefly at 5–4, a set point for Mortimer. A roar went through the stadium, prompting the umpire to call for silence.[33]

Althea finally asserted control, aiming a blazing forehand shot across the court and into the far corner as she began to inch her way out of trouble. Visibly tiring, Mortimer sank two serves into the net, and the first set went to Althea 8–6. Again, Mortimer took the lead in the second set, but this time she could not sustain it. Despite two more calls of foot faults, Althea managed to claim the next six straight games as her British opponent wilted, thus winning the final set at 6–2. With that, she retained not only her Wimbledon crown but her status as the premier woman tennis player in the world. This time she accepted the iconic Wimbledon silver plate from the Duchess of Kent at mid-court.

The day was not over, though. Hours later, Althea was back on Centre Court with her partner, Maria Bueno, winning the doubles final. The triple crown, however, was not to be hers. Although she and her partner in the mixed doubles, Kurt Nielsen of Denmark, got off to a strong start despite a descending rainy gloom, they could not pull it off. But two titles, claimed in two successive years, was still more than enough for a serious celebration. That night, Althea, dressed in an attractive sleeveless white sheath, took the first dance with the male champion, Australia's Ashley Cooper, who had soundly beaten Neale Fraser, his neighbor from across the Yarra River back home, in four sets. Later, Althea hit the town with Buxton in what would come to be one of their final London nights out for a long time.

In the hours after her triumphant performance, an exhausted Althea told the press that she planned on returning the following year, "God willing!"[34] The truth was quite otherwise. Althea had more tennis ahead in 1958, with Forest Hills just two months away, but she was far more focused on determining what her next steps would be after she quit the amateur game. That summer, she was on the cusp of thirty-one, and she knew she had to market her triumphs as swiftly as possible, before the next tennis queen came along. In eight years of playing the amateur circuit, she had earned so little money that she had never once had to file a tax return, as *Jet* magazine reported that summer. It was time to turn a new financial page, and not just because 1958 marked her debut as a taxpayer. What, though, would be the title of her next chapter?

While debate over the professionalization of tennis continued to percolate hotly on the circuit and in the tennis press, race once again loomed to block Althea's progress. Over the years, she had managed to maneuver around or ignore the thorny subject time and again throughout her rise, often deftly sidestepping an angry Black press. Now, as she faced the

American marketplace of the 1950s, she was confronted head-on with a culture at war with itself and riven by racial disparities.

The year 1958, like much of the 1950s, saw fitful progress marred by episodic setbacks on the civil rights front. As Althea prepared for the quarterfinals at Wimbledon, the Bethel Baptist Church of Birmingham, Alabama, led by a popular pastor active in trying to desegregate the city, was bombed for the second time. Despite multiple rulings by the U.S. Supreme Court upholding desegregation, the subject of school integration continued to rage hotly across the country and particularly in the South. In the aftermath of a tumultuous first year of desegregation at Little Rock High School in Arkansas that concluded with the summer of 1958, Arkansas governor Orval Faubus closed all the state's public high schools to both Black and white students, rather than allow integration to proceed in the fall in what became known as "the Lost Year." Several hundred miles to the southeast, in Alabama, a young judge named George Wallace ran for governor with the support of the NAACP and lost by a landslide. Four years later, in 1962, recast as an ardent Jim Crow supporter and chanting the motto "Segregation now, segregation tomorrow, segregation forever," Wallace would win a crushing victory. Toward the end of 1958, the Rev. Martin Luther King Jr., who was fast emerging as the face of the civil rights movement, was viciously stabbed in the chest with a letter opener by a mentally ill Black woman as he signed copies of his book in a Harlem bookstore. While not a reflection of racial hostility, the incident was a sharp reminder of King's perennial vulnerability amid the steadily escalating social tensions.

Well aware that more than a few doors would remain closed to her as a Black woman, Althea forged ahead. One thing she knew was that she needed to carve out a public identity apart from tennis, one that focused on her singing and the unlikely saga of her life. She had already taken steps toward the latter and had signed a contract with Harper & Brothers to write her autobiography, with the help of Ed Fitzgerald, the editor of *Sport* magazine. As Althea put feelers out in search of opportunities during the week, she spent weekends at Fitzgerald's home working on the book.[35] By midsummer, *The Saturday Evening Post* had bought first publication rights and committed to run excerpts from the book in a three-part series to begin in August. In return, Althea received what *New York Post* columnist Milton Gross called "a substantial sum."[36]

The odds facing Althea were considerable. Few among the media grasped—or took the time to fully consider—Althea's situation more thoughtfully than columnist Gross, who had closely followed her career, at times more sympathetically than the Black press. Not long after she won Wimbledon for the second time, Gross penned a poignant column, pointing out how little reward Althea had gained in becoming the best tennis player in the world and how little control she had over even her own future. For the most likely professional offer, she had to wait for a nod not just from Jack Kramer but also from Maureen Connolly, considered the only player good enough to challenge her. "It is a peculiar position in which Althea finds herself," Gross wrote.

Nor could she breathe a word of her interest in making money, lest the USLTA strip her of her amateur status and banish her from the court. Instead, Gross continued, giving voice to the same thoughts that surely plagued Althea, "Althea now must sit by idly while the wheels move and she waits to learn whether she plays as a pro and sings on the side or spends her time singing and continues to play amateur tennis on the side." While she waits, he concluded, she sits in an apartment nearly empty of furniture, only a handful of outfits in her closet and her bank account empty. What, he asked, had she really gained from sixteen years of working at tennis? "She's Althea Gibson, a woman of history, and there should be a reward for one who can win against all the odds. It should be something more substantial than a silver platter or another trophy that can be placed on a mantle [*sic*] in an apartment which needs furnishing more than it needs decorating."[37]

Since no one was exactly pursuing her, Althea, now a blossoming if necessarily closeted entrepreneur in the making, turned to the market-place of the public. One week after she returned to New York, she was fêted at a July reception in her honor at Gracie Mansion, the mayor's residence. As hundreds of guests looked on, New York City mayor Robert Wagner read a proclamation declaring the day "Tennis Day" in her honor and lauded her achievements. Clad in the same white sheath she had worn to the Wimbledon Ball and a pair of translucent white gloves complete with faux petals at the wrist, Althea used the moment to present the mayor with a copy of her record album, a moment captured by several news photographers. The USIA also seized the opportunity and included the photo of Wagner standing side by side with Althea and her parents in its August media packet to be sent around the world as yet another shining example of the success of Black people and their fair treatment in the United States. "New York Hails Althea Gibson, World Tennis Queen," exclaimed the headline over the press release.[38]

During the following month, Althea's public profile rose steadily. First, she was featured on the cover of *Jet* magazine, with an empathetic story inside its pages extolling all that she had sacrificed for her tennis career, including both love and money.[39] Next, she appeared as the mystery guest on the popular CBS television game show *What's My Line?*, just hours after she staved off a ferocious challenge from California teenager Sally Moore to retain her title as champion of the Eastern Grass Court Championships in South Orange, New Jersey. Althea used her appearance on the show, during which blindfolded celebrity panelists, including television star Arlene Francis and publishing czar Bennett Cerf, attempted to guess her identity, to talk up her album and hoped-for singing career. The panel collectively noted her many accomplishments, while Francis exclaimed that she was "practically our best tennis player." Asked about her new album, Althea, dressed in the same white sheath she had worn at her last two public appearances, grew solemn. "I hope it's doing well," she said somberly.[40]

Toward the end of August, she got another opportunity to boost her budding second career when she made her second in-person appearance on *The Ed Sullivan Show*. Just three months after her debut on the show, Althea appeared far more relaxed in a sequined bodice and artfully styled hair. Although her rendition of "I Should Care" was smoother and more melodic than her previous singing performance, critics remained less than thrilled. "Whoever is picking her costumes isn't doing right by our champion," grumbled one *Boston Globe* writer. "The sequin-topped dress and the gloves didn't do a thing for her."[41]

At the end of her performance, the show's guest host, following in the lead of the ever-supportive Ed Sullivan, displayed a copy of *The Saturday*

Evening Post, which had published the first of the three-part excerpt of Althea's autobiography that was to be released in the fall and wished her well in the upcoming U.S. National Tournament at West Side.

"Thank you, I need it," Althea responded emphatically.[42]

Althea was likely referring to the previous day's surprising development, when she and her doubles partner, Maria Bueno, lost the National doubles at the Longwood Cricket Club in Boston to Darlene Hard and Jeanne Arth in three hard-fought sets. The victorious duo was the first unseeded pair in memory to win the national women's doubles crown, which remained the lone national title that eluded Althea. One week later, however, Althea silenced those who were questioning her ability to stave off the upcoming younger generation of players with a triumphant performance at Forest Hills, one that was particularly gratifying for her personally.

Despite a persistent virus, Althea cruised easily through the early rounds until the quarterfinals, where she met the British Christine Truman yet again, the same teenager who had surprisingly beaten her in the Wightman Cup months earlier. Once again, Truman forged into the lead in the first set, but Althea persevered to win 11–9, and by the second set, she was in full control throughout, winning 6–1. In the semifinals, Althea encountered her toughest match of the tournament, faced with the powerful Beverly Baker Fleitz, who had beaten her several times, most recently in Puerto Rico the previous spring. This time was different. Now a veteran of her opponent's rapid-fire game and hurried approach, Althea deliberately slowed the pace and managed to throw Fleitz off her stride from the start, winning the match 6–4, 6–2. By virtually all assessments, Althea had given her best performance of the year, exhibiting masterful control of the ball and committing few of the foot faults that had so plagued her of late.

Fittingly, she was once again paired in the final against Darlene Hard, the buoyant former waitress whom she had both competed against and paired with frequently over the years. It was Hard whom Althea had defeated to take her first Wimbledon victory the previous year. Hard was now in top shape, however, racing across the court and driving returns so hard to Althea's backhand from the net that she took the first set 3–6. Althea picked up her pace and managed to take the second set 6–1.

As the third set began, Hard resumed racing to the net, and Althea, beginning to panic, looked to Llewellyn sitting in the stands. As Althea described the moment in an interview a quarter of a century later, "I looked over at the coach, just glanced, and he, you know, I guess this is done between coach and player, he gave me one signal, and I proceeded to obey that signal, and started putting a shot on Darlene that surprised her, and that shot was a lob." That tip—a hand Llewellyn inconspicuously put to his chest—turned the tide of the set. Time and again, Althea floated the ball high into the air with such precision that it landed squarely on the baseline, quickly exhausting Hard and ultimately enabling Althea to win the third set 6–2. Sixty years later, Serena Williams was slapped with a code violation for apparently doing pretty much the same thing in taking a signal from her coach, triggering an on-court imbroglio between her and the referee. At the time that Williams's coach apparently made the gesture in 2018, doing so was specifically prohibited by the 2018 Grand Slam rule book. In 1958, however, the tennis rule books were silent on the subject of coaching during a match and Althea again won the women's singles championship. In doing so, she became only the third woman after Helen Wills and Maureen Connolly to win both Wimbledon and the U.S. Championships in two consecutive years.[43]

Afterward, Althea and men's champion Ashley Cooper, winner of the men's singles championship, who had shared the winners' podium with her at Wimbledon, were presented with trophies by Secretary of State John Foster Dulles, who smilingly grasped one of Althea's fingers, which had been injured during a fall in the third set. Minutes later, at an impromptu news conference arranged by Llewellyn, Althea announced a piece of personal news: she was going to take a yearlong break to focus on her singing and the release of her autobiography, which she was permitted to do without jeopardizing her amateur status. "I'll keep practicing and keep in touch, but no more competition at least until 1960," she said to the stunned crowd.

And professional tennis?

"Well, I'd listen if Jack Kramer made an offer," Althea responded.[44]

Althea's announcement wasn't the only thing heralding big changes in the amateur tennis world. Just two months earlier, a skinny fourteen-year-old

Black boy became the first of his race to win the Maryland State Junior Tennis Championships in Baltimore, which he had integrated along with a few other boys the previous year. His name was Arthur Ashe. A ninety-seven-pound sophomore from Richmond, Virginia, he had long regarded Althea as his idol and absorbed accounts of virtually all her tournaments with fascination. Like Althea, he was both a student of Dr. Robert Johnson's, easily the doctor's most promising player at the time, and similarly determined to be evaluated on the basis of his tennis and not his race. In the coming years, Althea and Ashe would come to know each other well, teaming up to play mixed doubles in the 1973 U.S. Open and sponsoring an annual benefit / tennis tournament. Not only did the two players come from vastly different backgrounds and have contrasting temperaments, but Althea deeply resented the large amounts of money Ashe earned in the Open Era of tennis, which began in 1968, and remained forever out of her reach. It was not, however, something she held against him personally, and the two found common ground in a number of undertakings, largely sponsored by Ashe, to encourage greater participation in tennis by Black juniors, just as Dr. Johnson had done before them.

As she left Forest Hills after announcing her news and headed to Harlem to celebrate at a crowded table at the Ebony Lounge, Althea knew she was on the brink of challenging terrain. Just as women's matches had often been relegated to remote courts at the country club and coverage of them invariably subordinated to men's matches in the newspapers, so women clearly had inferior status to men in the professional sphere. Although eager to try her hand at activities other than tennis, Althea was well aware of some of the roadblocks her female predecessors had encountered.

There were those who had made tentative inroads. Alice Marble, a leading women's player in the 1930s and Althea's outspoken champion, was one of the first to break into the commercial world by making public appearances and writing a magazine column. In the early 1940s, the Wilson Sporting Goods Company signed her up, along with Mary Hardwick and Pauline Betz, to serve on its advisory staff.[45] Then came "Gorgeous Gussie" Moran and her golden underpants. In 1951, Moran was working for Springs Cotton Mills Fabrics, her image appearing in advertisements as she exited a sleek black car with her patterned underpants visible through a diaphanous red dress. Moran, as the ad explained it, had been so excited to go shopping for the company's new cotton sheets that she had forgotten to wear her slip. After their celebrated wins in the 1950s, Maureen Connolly joined the Wilson advisory board, while Doris Hart signed with Spalding. Hart also landed a job as a teaching professional in Florida after her retirement in 1955. Althea still had her monthly seventy-five-dollar contract with Harry C. Lee & Company, and in 1959, both she and Fageros joined the company's advisory board and endorsed one of its rackets. But none of the large sports interests was rushing to sign her up, even after her string of major victories in the late 1950s.

Women who pursued professional tennis tours didn't fare much better. Toward the end of 1958, Kramer had lured some of the world's greatest male amateurs under his pro tent with contracts of $100,000 and more. Women who embarked on tours, as Mary Jo Festle points out in her book *Playing Nice: Politics and Apologies in Women's Sports*, either had to drive enormous distances to secure audiences or engage in novelty exhibitions that involved wearing costumes. The display of gold-trimmed underpants was also always popular. At the end of any tour, which rarely lasted longer than one year, the women were prohibited from returning to the amateur ranks. Instead, "they dropped from the limelight. In the long run it did not pay off—in fact, from 1959 to 1967 no women toured as professionals. Lack of opportunities combined with gender prescriptions to insure that a female tennis player could only go so far."[46]

Althea's own hopes for an invitation from Kramer had fizzled even as she nailed her second win at Forest Hills, which he had insisted she do in order to be considered. In the closing moments of the finals match, as Althea repeatedly lobbed Hard to the baseline, Kramer told a reporter bluntly that, on the pro tour, "There is no demand for the girls," despite having publicly expressed interest in Althea repeatedly in the past. "They don't pull in enough at the gate to make it worthwhile. All they'd do is cut the take for Pancho Gonzales and the other boys."[47]

As a Black woman, Althea faced a double whammy. In the opening pages of her second book, *So Much to Live For*, published in 1968, she bluntly acknowledged that private clubs were unlikely to hire her as a pro. "It was here that the barrier of race slammed in front of my face," she wrote. As for the larger sporting companies, they weren't particularly interested in her as a sponsor, either. "In short," she lamented, "I had surprisingly few irons in the fire when it came to exploiting my tennis abilities in the professional field. But that doesn't mean there weren't other fires to put my irons into."⁴⁸

Althea approached the next chapter of her career with much the same determination she had exhibited when she walked onto the tennis court some fifteen years earlier. Why, she half-jokingly told reporters, she might even turn her hand to another sport, such as golf, which would be a "wonderful" game to go along with her singing.⁴⁹ Over the summer, she had formed Althea Gibson Enterprises, staffed by Llewellyn and an attorney, and with a new batch of stationery bearing the company name positioned on her desk, she began scouting for offers. The USLTA, however, was still the boss. Acceptance of any offer during her year of "semiretirement" would require the board's approval if she wanted to retain her amateur status.

One of the first proposals to come her way, astonishingly, was a possible role in a Hollywood movie with none other than John Wayne and William Holden in the male leads. A "flickers" addict since her childhood days, Althea was beside herself with excitement, and not just because the job came with a sizable paycheck. The movie, called *The Horse Soldiers*, directed by John Ford, was a Civil War saga depicting a Union cavalry unit making an expedition into Confederate territory to cut off a supply depot in Mississippi. Althea's role was that of a servant girl to a blond Southern belle and called for such period details as the wearing of a kerchief on her head and the uttering of obsequious terms of address such as "Yassuh" and Yassm." Even Althea objected to the servile language, which, she later wrote, was "offensive and unnecessary." She was "determined not to utter lines that reflected so negatively and distortedly the character of a colored woman. I felt that my own dignity and the dignity of the American Negro were on the line." The producers relented, and the offensive lines were deleted.⁵⁰

Then there was another racial hurdle. Weeks later, Althea learned that she was to be segregated from the rest of the cast during filming in New Orleans, where state law outlawed public interaction between Black and white people involving personal and social contacts. Althea refused to travel to Louisiana, and Ford agreed to have her half-dozen scenes shot in Holly-wood, while a double was used down south.[51] So thrilled was Althea to be on set in Hollywood that she often showed up early in the morning, even when she wasn't involved in the scene under way, just to observe the action. With her character shot dead by Confederate gunfire midway through the film, Althea delighted in socializing with the cast and even got a chance to attend a cocktail party with her idol Gregory Peck.

The release of the film, which appeared in cinemas in the summer of 1959, was a somewhat less positive experience. Some reviews were encouraging, like that in the Black *Philadelphia Tribune*, which said of Althea, "she has the talent plus that certain something which enables her to convey to the audience the point she is trying to put across." Others assumed a more neutral position on what they regarded as a mediocre film. *Time* magazine, for example, wrote succinctly, "For those who like tennis there is Althea Gibson, women's national champion, who plays a slave." But there were numerous others who took issue not only with her performance, but with the fact that she played the role of a kerchiefed servant girl at all. *The Reporter* magazine expressed its disappointment succinctly: "Miss Gibson should stick to her own racket."[52]

Articulating the feeling of a number of Black journalists, A. S. "Doc" Young, senior Black columnist for the *Los Angeles Sentinel*, who had weighed in on Althea both pro and con over the years, took her to task most fervently in a column that harshly opposed Black star athletes taking slave roles of any kind for Hollywood. Summarizing the observations of a writer for the Associated Negro Press, Young wrote, "Althea Gibson demeaned herself, and the Negro race, when she played a handkerchief-headed slave girl in 'The Horse Soldiers.'" Hollywood moguls' use, he warned, "of outstanding Negroes in degrading roles may be a part of a plot to maintain the old racial status—nothing." The *Chicago Defender*, meanwhile, noted that when the film debuted in Shreveport, Louisiana, in the heart of Dixie, there was "Nothing, as you'd expect for Althea Gibson, the greatest tennis player in the world now gone Hollywood." Her role was lamented even at the NAACP's fiftieth annual convention in New York City, where Dr. Charles Wesley, president of Central State College in Ohio, objected sharply to the stereotypes to which Black people were often reduced. That the great tennis star Althea Gibson, he declared to the thousands attending, had been cast as a housemaid in the film was "a sad commentary on a brilliant career."[53]

The release of Althea's autobiography in the fall of 1958 triggered similarly divergent responses. The book, called *I Always Wanted to Be Somebody*, tells a largely unflinching story of her grueling journey from the harsh streets of Harlem to the pinnacle of world tennis. The advertisements splashed across the nation's newspapers touted her story with such slogans as "From Harlem slums to Forest Hills fame!" In the book, Althea candidly expresses her unwillingness to campaign on behalf of the "Negro" race or to speak publicly about her experience with racial discrimination. On the contrary, she writes, "I am not a racially conscious person. I don't want to be. I see myself as just an individual . . . I'm a tennis player, not a Negro tennis player. I have never set myself up as a champion of the Negro race. Someone once wrote that the difference between me and Jackie Robinson is that he thrived in his role as a Negro battling for equality whereas I shy away from it. That man read me correctly."

Nor did she hesitate to call out the Black press for its criticism of her. The "regular American newspapers and magazines," she wrote, presumably meaning the white press, had been good to her. In saying so, she conveniently overlooked the large amounts of ink that had been spilled in criticizing her unfeminine ways, haughty attitude, and "mannish" style of hitting the tennis ball. As for Black writers, she continued, "I am uncomfortably close to being Public Enemy No. 1 to some sections of the Negro press. I have, they have said, an unbecoming attitude; they say I'm bigheaded, uppity, ungrateful." The reason for that, she added, "is that they resent my refusal to turn my tennis achievements into a rousing crusade for racial equality, brass band, seventy-six trombones, and all. I won't do it . . . I want my success to speak for itself as an advertisement for my race."[54]

Reviews of the book, not surprisingly, were all over the map. Impressed by her story, Allison Danzig, *The New York Times* veteran sportswriter who had covered many of Althea's matches, declared that she had been a "somebody," even in her Harlem days of thieving and playing hooky. "She was an individual with a drive to be herself, live her life as she pleased, at all costs, and intolerant of checkreins, even by her father." Despite all the adversity she had faced, he added, "Never did she compromise in being herself. Not even the diatribes of her own Negro press, furious with her for not being more militant . . . could budge her." Even distant publications, such as the *Leicester Evening News* in England, took complimentary note of the book. "It is at times a moving narrative, spiced with laughter and just a tinge of ego, but always warm, frank and human." Although the Black newspaper the *Chicago Defender* took a swipe at the casual language in the first part of the book, saying, "You'll wonder if she finished grade school," it declared in its headline that the book was "Light, Entertaining and Informative."[55]

One of the readers who was most inspired by her book was an athletic Los Angeles teenager with a crown of dark hair who had been keeping a hawk's gaze on Althea's performance for more than a year. Even before Billie Jean Moffitt, as she was then known, watched Althea easily win both the singles and doubles matches at the Pacific Southwest Championships at the Los Angeles Tennis Club the year before, she'd been deeply inspired by the older woman's athletic prowess and her ability to overcome the odds stacked against her. When Althea published her autobiography, the thirteen-year-old Moffitt read the book ten times and tucked it into her bed next to her tennis racket at night.

"I knew if she had gone through what she had gone through and changed the world by example, then maybe I had a chance too," Billie Jean King wrote in her 2021 autobiography, *All In*.[56]

Nonetheless, more than a few among the Black press were again incensed. That Althea had chosen Edward E. Fitzgerald, the white editor of *Sport* magazine, to edit her life story, rather than one of the many Black journalists who had covered her for years, surely did not help. Leading the pack of her critics was P. L. Prattis, a *Pittsburgh Courier* columnist, who declared, "I wish I could shrug Miss Gibson off as easily as she shrugs me off. Will somebody please tell me what Althea Gibson is if she is not a NEGRO TENNIS PLAYER?" What particularly infuriated Prattis was Althea's failure to recognize that the countless Negroes who had helped her reach the pinnacle of success had done so "because she is a NEGRO TENNIS PLAYER. It may annoy her to be reminded of the fact, but she'll never be able to get away from it." In a parting shot, Prattis, whose column appeared shortly after *The Horse Soldiers* was released, noted that the film's producers had cast Althea in the role of a menial Black. "The whites," he concluded, "know what she is if she doesn't."[57] Others were angered by Althea's comment that she didn't care if she couldn't stay at hotels or attend events in the segregated South, as there were ample other places in the world where she could. "That kind of talk," raged a columnist for the *Philadelphia Tribune*, "aside from being nonsense, shows a spirit of selfishness which is one of the chief reasons for the slow progress Negroes are making toward the goal of full citizenship rights."[58]

Adding to the cacophony were angry white readers who were upset that *The Saturday Evening Post* had run a three-part excerpt of the book accompanied by photographs of Althea interacting with white people. The first excerpt, wrote one New Yorker, "will set the Negro people back 100 years. I hope it does as much for SEP circulation." A woman from the South declared it was a "disgrace" to run a photo of Althea and Lew Hoad dancing at the Wimbledon Ball in 1957. "I wish you would be a little more considerate of your white southern readers."[59]

Tennis, somewhat ironically, provided Althea with some distraction from the controversy generated by her film and book debuts. Early in 1959, she embarked on another State Department–sponsored goodwill tour, this time of five Latin American countries. Months after she returned from the highly successful tour, she landed a two-year gig as a correspondent covering the two weeks of Wimbledon play for the *London Evening Standard*. Althea did not actually write about the tournament, but sat courtside and channeled her observations to a reporter, as was the long-standing tradition. Richard Evans, then a twenty-one-year-old novice reporter on his first day of the tennis beat, was assigned to work with Althea during her second year on the job. "And that changed my life, because I was told to go introduce myself to Althea on Centre Court at two p.m.," recalled Evans, who went on to cover tennis for more than half a century, first as a BBC commentator and later at the Tennis Channel. So well did the two get along that, at the fortnight's end, the white Evans invited Althea to attend the Wimbledon Ball with him at Grosvenor House. As the two of them twirled across the dance floor that night, many of the stodgy Wimbledon crowd looked on disapprovingly, just as they had in years past.

"I was only partially aware," Evans said. "You know you come down this big staircase into the Grand Ballroom, and I suppose we must have caused quite a stir."[60]

Days before Althea returned to the United States, racial trouble was brewing anew back home and would soon engulf her. It began when the coach at the West Side Tennis Club invited the teenage son of Dr. Ralph J. Bunche, the United Nations Undersecretary for Special Political Affairs, a Nobel Peace Prize winner, and one of the highest-profile Black men in the country at the time, to join the club, apparently unaware that the light-skinned boy was Black. Shortly afterward, Bunche was matter-of-factly notified in a phone call with the club's president that, in fact, neither he nor his son could become members of the club, which excluded both Jews and Black people. The incident erupted into a highly public firestorm, leading to the resignation of the club's president, an outpouring of protest by many of the club's own members in support of Bunche, and demands by congressmen and city leaders that the club be barred from hosting international matches unless it ended its discriminatory policies. Bunche and his family were ultimately invited to apply for club membership but they declined.

Althea, questioned by reporters while still in London, said she was stunned at the news. "How ridiculous. Are we living in the twentieth century or not?"[61] But upon landing at Idlewild Airport in New York several days later, she struck a more conciliatory tone. Asked if she would accept an invitation to play at the club, she said, "As long as they treat me as a person and a guest, I'll play."[62]

The response from the Black press came fast and furious.

"I'm so mad at Althea Gibson I could break one of her best tennis rackets over her head," roared James Hicks, the same columnist and top editor for the *New York Amsterdam News* who had relentlessly, and unsuccessfully, lobbied City Hall into giving her a ticker tape parade three years earlier. "Althea's book says she wants to be somebody. I say Althea has a long long way to go!" Reactions among some Black tennis leaders, as reported in an *Baltimore Afro-American* story by Sam Lacy, varied. Professor Arthur Chippey, secretary of the ATA, said it was "unfortunate" that Althea had failed to realize that "there is more at stake than her own personal pleasure." He added, "I have reason to believe that Althea now prefers to divorce herself from the race." Dr. Hubert Eaton sided with Althea, saying that he felt withdrawing from the offending club's tournaments would bring little gain and "may hamper our younger players." In his column the following week, Lacy expressed his own thoughts on the matter, mirroring just how low opinion of Althea had sunk among many in the Black press since her year's sabbatical began. "It is not surprising," Lacy wrote, "that Althea would have been willing to sacrifice her dignity in order to further her personal ambitions." His conclusion? Her book was aptly titled. "She calls it 'I Wanted to Be Somebody.' . . . She might have added 'even if wearing a bandana.'"[63]

The furor over the Bunche incident compounded the discord between Althea and the Black press, not to mention some in the larger Black community, but as a news event, it was soon displaced by a different kind of headline. Rumor had it that Althea was maneuvering to start a pro tour of her own, in direct competition with Jack Kramer's crew. The *Daily Mirror* of London even reported that she had offered $150,000 to Peruvian tennis champion Alex Olmedo and was angling for other male pros. Other newspapers reported that she was organizing a national "all-girlie pro net troupe, a la Jack Kramer," that would include Darlene Hard and Karol Fageros, complete with parades and fashion shows and—watch out, Kramer—gold lamé underpants. Maria Bueno and Christine Truman had turned her down, the gossip had it, but others were interested. Some columnists exulted in the chatter, bemoaning how dull women's tennis had become as a result of Althea's departure and with the absence of any other high-profile female players. As Gene Roswell of the *New York Post* put it in his column, reporters may not have particularly liked Althea, but "with Althea around, things were always popping. . . . Honest, and we never thought it possible, we miss her on the tennis beat."[64]

Althea had indeed put out feelers to gauge possible interest in a women's tour to take place in South America and had sounded out several women, including Fageros, Bueno, Hard, and Janet Hopps. Hard and Hopps discussed the possibility with a USLTA representative and were told that Althea and Llewellyn had neither lined up any tournaments nor had the financial backing to do so. The fact was that "there was nothing. It was just kind of something they were trying to put together. . . . If you turned pro then, you wouldn't be in the USLTA, and we weren't ready for that."[65]

Althea, however, was more than ready. She had taken to responding to any inquiries about her possible interest in pro tennis by saying, "A girl has to eat." In October, she announced at a press conference at the tony 21 Club in Manhattan that she and the "Golden Goddess," Karol Fageros, were going pro. The two of them had signed a contract for a twelve-week national tour as a warm-up act for the Harlem Globetrotters, the Black exhibition basketball team geared more to entertainment than competition and often accompanied by vaudeville and comedy acts. Now the show, founded and managed by the irrepressible Abe Saperstein, would also include tennis.

Although Fageros had been ranked No. 5 by the USLTA in 1957, she was clearly far outmatched by Althea, the world's best female player. But she would bring her much-celebrated curves and shimmering panties to the ninety-some appearances to be made, while Althea would bring the celebrity athletic exhibition. Both would bring their red lipstick. If it was a bit of a comedown for Althea after Wimbledon's fabled Centre Court and the international circuit, the tour was praised as a brazenly lucrative deal all around. Fageros was to be paid $30,000, while Althea would receive up to $100,000, likely making her the highest-paid female athlete in history.[66]

As for Abe Saperstein, the rotund white owner and promotor of the Harlem Globetrotters, who had signed many high-profile Black basketball players such as Wilt "the Stilt" Chamberlain and Reece "Goose" Tatum at top dollar, the profits were potentially immense. Where others had balked at the combination of Althea's prickly temperament, her color, and secretly, even her appearance, Saperstein charged ahead.

"Abe, long a reaper in the colored sports vineyard, knew what the score was." wrote Dan Burley of the *Daily Defender*. "Where others hemmed and hawed, Saperstein recognized Althea for what she is: a Negro girl worth a potential million through expert exploitation and exposure and Saperstein is master there. There was no big problem. Althea was sitting around waiting to be signed by somebody."[67]

While Althea made clear that she intended to continue with her professional singing career, and perhaps even launch into golf, she leaped wholeheartedly into her role as an accompaniment to the Globetrotters. So did Fageros, who had become one of Althea's closest friends on the tennis circuit after their State Department goodwill tour. The two women—the Miami-born blond and the dark-haired Harlem combatant—could not have been more different, but each had survived a difficult childhood as well as an abusive father, and they found much in common. While Althea coordinated the paperwork for the trip, Fageros replenished her supply of underpants and ordered forty-four glimmering new pairs at a cost of twenty-five dollars apiece, for a total of over $1,100. And so, together, "with Karol's bottom sheathed in gold lamé and mine in conventional white linen, we began barnstorming the country," Althea wrote in her second memoir.[68]

The tour was immensely popular. One of the things that made it highly appealing to Althea was that her fellow athletes were in at least one regard vastly unlike those with whom she had played tennis. "The fact that they were Negroes made my tour a little easier to bear, for it was comforting to have people with me with whom I could completely drop my guard from time to time," she wrote.[69] The new tour debuted on New Year's Eve at Madison Square Garden, where a crowd of nearly ten thousand screaming fans saw Althea easily defeat Fageros as the heavily made-up women raced around the polished wooden basketball court. Their headline appearance was followed by a basketball exhibition, a Japanese bicycle ballet, and a sibling balancing act. In the weeks to come, the show was an ever-bigger hit as it moved across the country, drawing capacity crowds from the Chicago Stadium in Illinois to the Sports Arena in Los Angeles. Popular though it was, the tour nonetheless turned out to be much harder than either of the tennis players had anticipated.

As it turned out, Althea and Fageros did not travel with the Globetrotters but, for the most part, drove themselves across the country in a station wagon with a U-Haul trailer, along with Llewellyn; Billy Davis, the talented ATA player from New York; and an assistant. Often traveling hundreds of miles a day to make their evening appearance, they had virtually no time for socializing and certainly none for the flickers. Adding to the stress, the erratic lighting, screaming fans, and inconsistent basketball court conditions made playing tennis very difficult. There were flimsy portable nets, ill-trained local ball boys, and yawning overhead spaces into which the tennis ball sometimes disappeared. There were also endless newspaper photo shoots of the two women, who were required to grin into a mirror together as they simultaneously applied their rocket-red lipstick in advance of a match. And then there were the cold stares and slammed doors to contend with.

The racial hostility that would plague them throughout the South began at their very first road stop, in Dallas. Fageros approached the front desk of the Shamrock Hilton, where Saperstein had rented them a penthouse to launch the tour in high style. The desk clerk eyed the two women closely before exclaiming, "Oh, Miss Fageros, we're so excited to have you. This is a wonderful experience. But I'm terribly sorry, Miss Gibson, we cannot put you up here." Fageros was staring at the man in shock and humiliation, uncertain about what to do, when Llewellyn stepped forward and suggested that he and Althea find another hotel. Years later, Fageros would write of the moment in her unpublished autobiography, "Heaven Will Have to Wait, "It really irked me. Here was Althea Gibson, the No. One tennis player in the world, being treated disdainfully because she was black. I felt so bad for her."

It was hardly the last of it. Weeks later, Althea and Llewellyn were refused rooms at a hotel in Charleston, West Virginia. The pair had called ahead to confirm that the hotel had vacancies but were refused admittance when they showed up in person. Prompted by the incident to take a stand on the matter, the local branch of the NAACP declared one month later that it was prepared to file a $100,000 lawsuit on behalf of any Black person who was denied a room at a hotel where they had a confirmed reservation.

Hotels were not the only places where the tennis players collided with the steel doors of segregation. In some parts of the South where they traveled, Black people were not just isolated in separate seating areas at restaurants, but were barred from entering the establishment at all. Fageros would go inside and buy take-out meals, which she, Althea, Llewellyn, and the rest would eat in the car. The Miami-born Fageros, although herself a child of the South, was nonetheless stunned. Althea and the rest, she wrote, "were totally mistreated on most of the tour by hotel and restaurant owners, not because they were being malicious but merely because that's how things were. Ugly."[70]

Althea describes her months traveling with the Globetrotters in some detail in her second memoir, but she makes no mention of the punishing racism that she and the others experienced on the road. On the contrary, she writes in awe of the magnificence and splendor of the vast stretches of the American heartland they traveled across. "It was nothing less than a blessing to tour through my county, and at times I would catch myself humming the opening stanzas of "America the Beautiful": '*O beautiful for spacious skies, For amber waves of grain . . .*'"[71]

At the tour's end in the spring of 1960, Althea felt so flush with the $80,000 she had grossed that she put a down payment on a ten-room house in Queens for her family and began to consider launching her own tour with a basketball team or two. When Saperstein invited her and Fageros to extend their contract with an overseas tour, Althea declined, confident that she could profit more from going out on her own with Llewellyn. That fall, Althea Gibson Enterprises launched a tour with Fageros and two exhibition basketball teams, the Harlem Ambassadors and the New York Skyscrapers, and headed west. Newspaper advertisements excitedly heralded their arrival in almost every city. As the *Kansas City Star* put it:

"BIG!! Double Bill!!! ALL NEW-ALL IN PERSON.
Tennis.
The Great ALTHEA GIBSON World's Champion
VS.
KAROL FAGEROS "Golden Goddess of Tennis"
Basketball
Harlem Ambassadors (New Tricks) vs. New York Skyscrapers[72]

What followed was a series of half-empty gymnasiums, unsold tickets, and returned checks. So dismal was the turnout that the tour was canceled after three months. Althea was left nearly $25,000 the poorer, her reputation tarnished. "I was, in effect, ruined," she wrote.[73]

And so was Fageros. Promised $25,000 for the four-month tour, Fageros, who had not signed a written contract with Althea, never saw a penny. Making matters much worse, on one of the final days of the tour, their chartered bus carrying the Skyscrapers and Fageros collided with a

truck on an Ohio turnpike and Fageros wound up in the hospital with broken ribs. Her tennis career at an end, her body racked with pain, and her
friendship with Althea shattered, she got on a plane back to Miami saying
to herself, "Just get me out of New York. Get me home. . . . Please, God,
stop the hurting."[74]

The tour's failure prompted Althea to take a cold, hard look at her situation. Despite her status as the greatest female tennis player in the world,
her crashing of the racial barrier to the lily-white world of tennis, nothing
really had changed at all. She remained as poor as she had been when she
began, just as the *New York Post*'s Milton Gross had pointed out more than
a year earlier. As she reflected on the experience of other prominent tennis
players, "I saw that white tennis players, some of whom I had thrashed on
the court, *were* picking up offers and invitations. Suddenly, it dawned on
me that my triumphs had not destroyed the racial barriers once and for
all, as I had—perhaps naively—hoped. Or, if I did destroy them, they had
been erected behind me again."[75]

In her despondency, Althea turned to the one person who had remained
her most steadfast supporter, seemingly no matter what: Will Darben. Although she had turned down his marriage proposal in 1953 and had publicly announced their breakup two years ago, the ever-loyal Darben, her
rock, was still there. Through it all, the two had stayed in touch, and Althea
had become deeply dependent on Darben, who, she wrote, was not unlike
"a vital organ whose existence keeps you alive but which you usually take for
granted."[76] With the embers of their romance rekindled by the end of a tumultuous 1960, the pair announced their engagement at a Christmas party
in Althea's apartment, where she proudly displayed a one-carat diamond
engagement ring. Four months later, Althea broke the engagement off.
"It's unfortunate, but it's just one of those things," she told the *Pittsburgh
Courier*.[77] This time she didn't blame the demands of her highly successful career, but just the opposite. As she described it matter-of-factly in her
memoir, "When Will asked me again to marry him, I very coyly, very fem-
ininely said no. From the 'You just love me because I'm a star' argument,' I
moved to the opposite pole with the 'You just feel sorry for me, I've got to
prove I'm worthy' argument." Once again, Will Darben was put on hold.[78]

Instead, Althea decided to devote herself to a little white orb pocked with tiny dimples, better known as a golf ball. It was a sport that she had learned to play back in her college days at FAMC, when she had even managed to beat the school's golf coach. As she pondered possible paths to improve her fortunes, she remembered that Gene Roswell, the *New York Post* columnist, had observed that she had the muscle and coordination for most any sport, as well as "the cold aplomb for golf."[79] Throughout 1960, Althea began to visit the links periodically and had even toted her clubs with her in the back of the U-Haul on the Globetrotters' tour. Having won a one-year $25,000 contract with the Ward Baking Company as a community relations representative, she was soon traveling widely across the country. Her role consisted largely of media presentations and appearances at women's and school events, which concluded with a singing of her theme song, "So Much to Live For." By the time Althea began making these public appearances, she had significantly upgraded her wardrobe and general appearance and often sported a mink wrap and elegant dress. Once-oft-heard comparisons likening her strokes or bearing to that of a man were now rarely uttered. As an Associated Press story describing her appearance at an elegant luncheon at the Waldorf Astoria in New York at which her new job was announced put it, "The girl from the sidewalks of New York arrived for her reception about a half-hour late—wearing a new hair-do, a devil-red flowered chiffon dress, a silver mink stole and black pumps with a rose petal adornment. She was accompanied by her attorney, her personal manager and other members of Althea Gibson Enterprises."[80]

As a company representative, Althea also hawked Ward's Tip Top Bread products in a series of newspaper advertisements featuring her beaming over a plump loaf of bread or gently folding a slice of softest white to demonstrate its freshness. Although she was clearly hired as much for her color as her prominent media profile, she made it abundantly clear from the start that she would continue to avoid making public statements on behalf of her race. "I won't be a soap-box orator for racial equality," she declared in the fall of 1960, saying that she did not consider doing so to be in good taste. Instead, she added, she felt she could "do more good by serving as an example to others."[81] She was similarly mute when the Ward Baking Company and two other bakeries became the subject of a NAACP-sponsored boycott for failing "to employ one Negro salesman, even though they all enjoy a sizable market in the Negro community."[82] The boycott was launched in the same year that Ward declined to renew Althea's contract in 1965. Needless to say, her passive relationship with Ward was one more thing that irked the Black community.

While she toured the country on behalf of the Ward Baking Company in the early 1960s, Llewellyn, her coach turned manager, frequently went with her. In her downtime, she headed to the golf course. That golf remained as exclusively white as tennis had been when she began knocking on the door of the USLTA and that it expressly restricted its members to "whites only" seemed not to faze her. The PGA's bylaw, written in 1943, specifically limited its membership to "Professional golfers of the Caucasian race, over the age of eighteen years, residing in North or South America."[83]

In many respects, golf was an even more unlikely sport for Althea than tennis had been. Not only was it a relatively slow and solitary sport, especially for one who thrived on rapid-paced combat against an opponent, but it was regarded as even more the province of a rarefied and exclusive white elite. If Black people had been unwelcome on the lush green grass courts of the country's tony country clubs, they were even more personae non gratae on the emerald carpet of the front nine. Although John Shippen, who was of African American and Native American descent, competed in the second U.S. Open in 1896, despite a threatened protest walkout by white players, no other Black American was permitted to play in the tournament until Ted Rhodes did so in 1948. Even after World War II, when the desegregation of sports began to accelerate on multiple fronts, golf remained staunchly unyielding to people of color. While white people continued to resist Black participation in some sports, even after racial barriers had been broken, "nowhere was this resistance more complete than in golf where the maintenance of a system of overt and institutional racism prevailed for many decades after initial race barriers were removed," as Marvin P. Dawkins, University of Miami professor of sociology, wrote in his 2004 paper, "Race Relations and the Sport of Golf: The African American Golf Legacy."[84]

Some would contend that it remained that way well into the twenty-first century. In the more than seventy years since the founding of the LPGA in 1950, only eight Black women have been granted full-time membership on the tour, according to the LPGA.[85] In 2021, there were only two Black play-ers with LPGA tour status, Mariah Stackhouse and Cheyenne Woods. At the same time, Asian women came to dominate the sport. In that year, more than sixty of the LPGA's roughly two hundred active players were Asian and many of the organization's strongest performers were Korean. The reason for this is a subject of some speculation. Inbee Park, the legendary South Ko-rean four times ranked the No. 1 player in the world since 2013, explained it like this: "It's in our blood. I think maybe we have dominant blood." Others attribute the Asian players' success in the sport to cultural factors, including the absence of social safety nets, the primacy placed on hard work, and the active presence of corporate sponsorships. Religion, too, is believed to play a role. As Su-Lin Tan, a well-known journalist for the *South China Morning Post*, puts it, "Hard work is an age-old Asian value. Some say it comes from Confucius' teachings. I say it is driven by population: there are so many people in Asia but limited school and work opportunities."[86]

Nor have Black men fared much better than women at gaining en-trance to the cloistered realm of the fairway, despite the much-heralded performance of Tiger Woods, who is a mix of Black, Asian, Native Amer-ican, and Caucasian. During the first fifteen years of this century, Woods was the only male of color on the PGA Tour, with the exception of Joe Bramlett, who was also a member in 2011, until he lost his card. In 2021, the organization had a total of four African American players. While the National Golf Foundation said in the same year that the number of non-Caucasian golfers was up by more than 6 percent, it declined to say how many of those were Black.[87]

For Black players in the twentieth century, the doors remained firmly shut. Barred from participation in mainstream tournaments, Black golfers followed the example of other Black athletes, such as those in tennis and baseball, and formed a separate organization, the United Golfers Asso-ciation, in 1925. Nearly a quarter of a century later, Ted Rhodes and two other Black players brought a lawsuit challenging the PGA's discrimina-tory practices, which resulted in an agreement that the organization would reevaluate the offending clause. The PGA, founded in 1916, nonetheless continued to dodge change. More challenges from Black players followed. Heavyweight boxing champ Joe Louis, for example, an avid golf fan who was a student of Rhodes's, raised such a media ruckus about the PGA exclusion that he was permitted to participate in a PGA tournament as an amateur in 1952. Still, it would take nearly another decade before the organization lifted its racially restrictive bylaw in 1961, partly due to public pressure from Jackie Robinson.

Black women, not surprisingly, hit the fairways even later than men and were barred from membership even in the Black UGA until 1939. Many of them were effective advocates in the push for desegregation, forming individual clubs that lobbied and petitioned against racial barriers at the nation's exclusive clubs. Easily the most prominent among them was Ann Moore Gregory, a talented athlete who became the first Black woman to enter an event sponsored by the United States Golf Association, the sport's amateur governing organization. She surmounted that barrier in September 1956, four months after Althea won her first Grand Slam in Paris. Considered the best African American female golfer in the country at the time, Gregory steadfastly declined to go professional, but she served as a bold inspiration for many younger women. One of those was Althea, whom Gregory occasionally advised and against whom she once competed, in an exhibition match that pitted her and Joe Louis against Jackie Robinson and Althea in Chicago in the summer of 1962.

Another for whom Gregory stood as a model was Renee Powell, the daughter of the founder of the Clearview Golf Club in East Canton, Ohio, the first golf course in the country built, owned, and operated by an African American. By 1960, Powell had won dozens of junior trophies and was well on her way to being one of the best Black women golfers in the sport. That year, she traveled to Boston to participate in a UGA tournament and was stunned to find herself paired with one of her childhood heroes, Althea Gibson.[88] Almost as surprising was how Althea, nineteen years Powell's senior, was playing. Wedged awkwardly beneath some trees in a relentless rain as she tried to hit the ball, Althea motioned her caddy to hold the limbs back to improve her swing, a violation of golf regulations. Minutes later, she moved onto the green as the caddy held an umbrella over her head. Other players, taking note, called to Althea, "Hey, you can't do that," Powell recalled.

"I thought to myself, *Oh, my gosh, she needs to learn the rules*," exclaimed

Powell. "She kept making these mistakes one after the other. Althea just did not know."[89]

Althea may have toppled the race barrier to tennis and scaled the international heights of that sport, but the obstacles facing her as she broached the new sport of golf were daunting. How could she afford coaching, which she definitely needed? While the potential earnings in golf were better than in tennis, the average take was only a few thousand dollars, and that was before the weekly expenses of room and board while on the road. Of the seventy-three women on the LPGA tour in 1970, less than one quarter of them made $10,000 or more.[90] Just as important, what country club would allow a Black woman to compete or even practice? Even if Althea could afford the dues, which she couldn't, no club owner was likely to welcome her.

But then, out of the blue there came one who did.

His name was Jerry Volpe, the onetime owner and pro at the Englewood Country Club in northern New Jersey and a huge fan of Althea's. Impressed by Althea's formidable strength and perseverance, Volpe declared to a reporter at the end of 1959, "That girl hits just like a man. She has a big easy swing and wonderful hands. With practice, I don't see how she can miss."[91] Volpe welcomed Althea onto the club's property, where she spent endless hours driving in the morning and evening and playing up to thirty-six holes in between. Impressed at her determination, Volpe made her an honorary member in late 1960, a major step toward surmounting the barrier at the professional level of the sport. In addition to giving her ongoing pro guidance, he sat her down and had her watch slow-motion films of the best pros, as she peppered him with questions. Afterward, she headed back out to practice on her own. As she strode across the emerald lawns in her Bermuda shorts and golf cleats, her heavy golf bag slung over her back, the other players' eyebrows rose in astonishment, just as they had on the municipal courses.

"I got some funny looks, I can tell you, as I signed in on the course waiting lists and took my place on the practice tee or putting green among the white males," Althea later wrote. "But stares were nothing new to me."[92]

Some of the eyes watching were those of reporters, curious about the world's greatest female tennis player's new choice of sport. Althea, according to the consensus view, had a powerful long drive thanks to her formidable strength, but her short game was lackluster. So, too, her putting was erratic. Her skills as a golfer, clearly, were still evolving.

"Althea has great potential," Betsy Rawls, four-time U.S. Women's Open champion, said diplomatically.[93]

Gene Roswell of the *New York Post* agreed. "People who have played golf with Althea are impressed with her potential, her awesome drives (260 yards, at times) and her attitude. Her score, they say, is around 90."[94]

Inspired by those who had come before her, and confident that she had a natural inclination for the sport, Althea cast her lot with golf. After a year of practice, she entered her first competitions in 1961, the Harlem YMCA tournament in New Jersey and the Green Ladies Tournament in Philadelphia, both of them for Black players. Althea scored a 95 in the Harlem Y tournament and took second place. By the end of the year, she had cut nine strokes off her score, bringing her average down to the low 80s, and came in third in the Black UGA tournament. Of greater significance on the nation's golf record that year, the PGA finally eliminated its "Caucasian-only" clause.[95] In early 1962, Althea won the UGA's National North and South Tournament in Miami by twenty-six strokes and was admitted as a full member at the Englewood Club, now able to represent the club in local tournaments. The Ward Baking Company, impressed at their representative's mounting success on the fairways, made things a bit easier by renewing her contract and allowing her the flexibility to practice golf while on the road.

Major media began playing closer attention. Following her win in Miami, *The New York Times* dispatched its golf editor, Lincoln A. Werden, known fittingly as "Linc," and a classic *Times* gentleman from his balding head to his mannered suit, to interview her. His story was headlined "View of the Fairway: An Analysis of Stumbling Blocks in Althea Gibson's Path to Golf Crown."[96] Three months later, the paper covered her debut as a New Jersey Metropolitan District golfer in a professional celebrity tournament in Plainfield, New Jersey, in the summer of 1962. Althea, the story noted, "showed flashes of brilliance as well as a tendency to hook and pull the ball." She also went over par by seventeen strokes.[97]

Having played her last Black tournament in the early summer of 1963, the nearly thirty-six-year-old Althea then took a historic step forward.

In July of that year, the girl from Harlem often criticized for not taking a more aggressive stand on behalf of her race broke the color barrier in America for the second time in her life, becoming the first Black woman to apply for membership in the all-white Ladies Professional Golf Association. Being the "First Negro" in professional golf was not going to be easy. With the final passage of the landmark Civil Rights Act of 1964 outlawing discrimination based on race just months away, the vast majority of clubs in the South steadfastly refused to accept Althea's entry application. By coincidence, the last of four tournaments in which she needed to place among the top 80 percent in order to get her official LPGA playing card was to be held at the Beaumont Country Club in Texas in the summer of 1964. Although the club permitted her to play, it refused to let her use its facilities or have a meal there. Althea, as usual, didn't blink. Not only did she play well enough to become an official member of the LPGA, but she did so at a place that barred her from using the bathroom.

"Un-showered I may have been when I left that place, but I was so enthralled with my triumph that I just didn't care a hang," she later wrote in her autobiography.[98]

Lest anyone doubt that Althea would be a memorable presence on the golf course in the years to come, she adopted one small fashion adjustment that made this abundantly clear. While other female golfers often appeared with their frosted hair permed or tucked into a dainty pastel visor, Althea, in her early forays on the fairway, often sported a plaid tam-o'-shanter with an enormous pom-pom atop. The tam-o'-shanter, for those not up on Scottish headgear, is a flat bonnet once worn by infantry units during World War I. Althea was ready for battle, just in case.

11

Great Ugga Mugga!

The caravan was ready to roll. The cars were fully gassed and lined up bumper to shimmering bumper. Each of the drivers had the address of a common destination and a trunkful of golf clubs and shorts stowed in the back. Most important, they had their colored Ping-Pong paddles by their sides.

The drivers, a group of women who were about to log up to a couple of hundred miles a day en route to a succession of golf tournaments, were members of the fledgling Ladies Professional Golf Association. Day after day, their half-dozen cars trailed one another on the roadways, stopping for meals and pulling up simultaneously at inexpensive motels as dusk began to fall. In an era long before cell phones, their Ping-Pong paddles served as a vital method of communication between cars. Raise one out the window or wave it over the car's roof, and the other drivers would immediately get the message. A red paddle meant it was time to stop for gas. A yellow paddle signaled a bathroom stop, and a green one indicated that it was time to eat. If a police cruiser was seen, headlights were flashed or turn signals flickered.

In 1963, thirty-five-year-old Althea Gibson got herself some paddles and wheeled her Coupe de Ville into the procession.[1] That some among the players group, many of whom were from the Deep South, squirmed at the admission of the first Black player into their organization was inevitable. But the thirteen founding members of the LPGA, who had broken a crucial barrier to women's participation in competitive sports when they formed the organization in 1950, were committed to gender equity as a prime raison d'être. Race was put aside for the good of the cause. Althea was nothing if not an intrepid and pioneering sister, and they not only welcomed her in a way the tennis world never had, but some even liked her. That her celebrated accomplishments and international recognition boosted ticket sales and drew a curious press didn't hurt matters. The group needed as much attention and support as it could drum up in order to stay on the road. When tournament directors in the South threatened to close the door to Althea because of her color, as happened not infrequently, the entire group sometimes refused to play.[2]

"We took care of each other no matter what," recalled Marlene Hagge Vossler, now in her late eighties, and one of the LPGA founders, who often roomed with Althea on tour. "That's what we were fighting for, equality as women. So, we decided that we wouldn't play any tournaments in towns where they wouldn't let her in the clubhouse and she had to change her shoes in the car. As badly as we needed tournaments at that point, we said, 'No, this is not going to happen.' . . . We were all in favor of that."[3]

After grueling days on the fairway or the highway, the women gathered in the evenings at their hotel, and after a season on tour, they well knew one another's spouses, parents, and, in some cases, pets. They ate in small groups in restaurants, roomed in pairs, and to Althea's delight, played poker on rainy afternoons and days off. As in tennis, so close did many of them become that they often referred to one another by nicknames. Kathy Whitworth, one of the fastest-rising players on the tour and eventual three-time president of the LPGA, was "Whit." Gloria Ehret, who won the 1966 LPGA Championship, was "Zip." One night, nearly a dozen of them gathered in one of their hotel rooms and wound up watching *The Horse Soldiers*, the 1959 film in which Althea appeared with John Wayne and William Holden. About halfway through the movie, Althea is tossed from her horse and lands on the ground, where she mutters something that sounds like "Great ugga mugga!"—at least, that's what some of the women *heard*. And so it was that Althea, who had never gotten deep enough inside the inner circle of pro tennis to earn a nickname from her peers, was affectionately referred to as "Ugga Mugga" on the golf course.[4]

"If you'd pass her, you'd just say, 'Ugga Mugga, what's going on?'" said Gloria Ehret, now in her early eighties. "She was just part of us."[5]

Although golf offered a far more positive social experience than what Althea had encountered in the realm of tennis, the sport itself turned out to be far more difficult for her to master. Not only was she a late starter, but the finesse required in the short game often eluded her. As a golfer, Althea never approached anything near the heights she had reached on the tennis court. In all her years on the golf tour, she never won a single tournament, and she struggled constantly to make ends meet. In her best year, 1967, she competed in twenty-five events and won a total of $5,567.50, or about $44,000 in today's currency. With a scoring average of 75.82, she ranked No. 19. Between 1963 and 1971, she played in 148 tournaments and earned a total of $19,727—not exactly the financial return one might have hoped for after nearly a decade of hard work. In fact, the amount didn't even come close to covering her expenses.[6]

Althea clearly enjoyed the challenge of a new sport and strove to improve her game during the decade and a half that she played competitively. In the years immediately following her tennis career, her name continued to be a draw, earning her regular headlines, while her job at the Ward Baking Company kept her bank account in the black. As time passed, however, it became clear that she was not going to earn a lucrative position on one of the sports companies' advisory staffs or gain a product endorsement, as some other female golfers were getting in the early 1960s. Althea did sign a contract with Dunlop at the end of 1963, to represent its sports division, according to press accounts, but the deal was apparently good only for the following year. It had also become clear that she was never going to reap the financial rewards that some white tennis players were, particularly after the Open Era in tennis got under way in 1968, transforming the sport. Major sponsors continued to elude her in large part because of her race and, in the case of golf, because she did not excel. Instead, she struggled to come up with the weekly $250 it cost her to stay on the road. Golf, in the end, was one of a series of disappointing undertakings that characterized her post-tennis years, leaving her increasingly bitter.

By 1969, Althea's golf game had begun to falter, and her ranking dropped to No. 26, her annual winnings totaling a mere $1,925.[7] Although she had matured over the years, and she maintained the well-mannered demeanor on the golf course that Dr. Johnson had instilled in her so many years earlier, she was beginning to boil internally. As the nation churned in the aftermath of Martin Luther King Jr.'s assassination, and as civil rights began to dominate the center of the political stage, she increasingly railed against the impediment that race had been in her own career. As the *New York Post*'s Gene Roswell noted in his column in the summer of 1969, "Althea Gibson is a slow burn. . . . Right now the steam is beginning to come out of her ears and somebody better watch out." Two paragraphs later, Althea unleashed.

When she left tennis a world champion and turned to golf, she said, "I was a big name in sports. You'd think some sporting goods company would have signed me, but to this day I still haven't got an association with any firm. . . . When I first went on the tour, my name drew. The first few holes, I really had a gallery. Then I'd make a few bloopers and, whooee, suddenly where was everybody?"

Her still-developing ability, she concluded, wasn't the reason she lacked a substantive contract. "I think it's color," she declared. "Because I'm black. I don't mean it's hurt me in golf itself, the competitive end and my associations with the girls and other people in the game, but only in the commercial aspects."[8]

The game of golf started out for Althea on a much more promising note, despite the inevitable bumps in her learning curve. Determined as ever, she golfed relentlessly, steadily racking up the miles on her car, as her scoring average declined from an 82 in 1963 to 77 in 1964 and 1965.[9] Often driving alone in the caravan, she scrupulously avoided tournaments in the South because, she explained to *The New York Times*, "I don't want to go where I'm not wanted. I'm trying to be a good golfer. I have enough problems as it is."[10]

In the fall of 1964, she made headlines when she claimed a one-stroke lead in the $11,000 Thunderbirds Ladies' Open at the Arizona Biltmore Golf Club in Phoenix, with a three-under-par 69, including four birdies and an eagle. It was the best round she had played to date, but her triumph didn't last long. The following day, she was disqualified for turning in an incorrect score card, and Mickey Wright, who was one of the most talented and strongest-hitting players of the day, took her place in the rankings. Seven months later, playing in the Dallas Civitan Open, she had a 303 and claimed winnings of $107.50. One of her strongest showings that year was at the Lady Carling Open in Baltimore, with a final score of 228 for 54 holes. She won $200. Although her progress was slow, it was happening.

"Ex-Net Queen Althea Gibson Just Hopes to Finish Higher," declared the headline in the *Baltimore Evening Sun*. As Althea told the paper, "My game feels as if it may be beginning to jell. I'm not saying this is the year I win a tournament, but this may be the year I start finishing a little higher."[11]

Discrimination continued to haunt her on the tour, where "some ugly scenes" developed, Althea would later write in her autobiography. Despite the support of her fellow LPGA members, she rarely talked to them about those ugly scenes and never asked them to assist her in the face of such prejudice, which she feared might compromise their standing in some way.[12] Instead, it was an unexpected combatant who came to her defense in her golf years. He was a short man with a crown of blond hair and the appearance of a college fraternity brother who nonetheless burned with a keen sense of justice. His name was Lenny Wirtz. The LPGA's tournament director since 1961, the Cincinnati-born Wirtz had officiated at NCAA basketball games for years and was accustomed to being around Black athletes. Wirtz was determined to make the still-struggling LPGA tour a success, and he needed his players to be taken seriously. He would, for instance, require them to dress up and attend weekly social events in order to appeal to sponsors. But he was equally determined to ensure that Althea be treated fairly.

When sponsors refused to allow her to attend receptions or other events, Wirtz was said to have refused to participate himself. More than once, when a motel pretended not to have Althea's reservation on file, Wirtz would glare at the manager, his barely five-foot-five stature ablaze with outrage, and exclaim, "Wait a minute! *Just* a minute." When members of the women's group learned early on that a couple of tournament directors had refused to allow Althea to participate in an event, they headed to Wirtz's office.[13]

"We were all furious when we heard that Althea couldn't play. We said, 'No way,'" recalled Gloria Ehret. "We went to Lenny and we told him, 'If

Althea doesn't play, we all don't play.' I don't know who it was who delivered the message, but it was definitely 100 percent."[14]

Wirtz heard them. One by one, he approached the tournament directors and sponsors and, in a few cases, he was able to talk them into changing their position. But in several instances, according to players, an event had to be canceled or moved to an alternate location where Althea would be welcomed. Althea recalled one of those events in particular in her memoir, noting that, at the time, the LPGA was so struggling that it could ill afford to walk away from a tournament on its roster. "Nevertheless, gallant Lenny Wirtz, five foot five, snatched Princess Althea, five foot ten and a half, from the teeth of the dragon and has my eternal gratitude for his moving display of courage."[15]

Althea's own less-than-confrontational posture on the subject did not go unnoticed. As Wirtz was standing up to racist directors on her behalf, angry civil rights demonstrations were escalating on the streets of America, and rising numbers of Black militants, such as the Black Panthers, were loudly challenging the pacifist elements of the movement who aligned themselves more with Dr. King's teachings. LPGA officials were keenly aware that Althea could easily have raised a public alarm about the racist exclusion she was encountering on the tour. After all, she remained a high-profile public figure, one once touted by the U.S. State Department, who routinely drew a healthy knot of curious reporters on the LPGA trail. If she had opted to hoist such a flag, it could easily have damaged the reputation of the organization and perhaps even undermined its very existence. So, when the LPGA's board quietly sat down with her to suggest a conciliatory stance be adopted with sponsors, and she agreed, they breathed more easily. Never mind that some critics, largely among the Black press, who remained irked with Althea, would later describe her refusal to call out discriminatory practices as selfish.

"She definitely could have really raised a ruckus, and rightfully so. I mean, she certainly had a right to do that," said Kathy Whitworth, a Texan who later became the first woman to reach career earnings of $1 million on the tour in 1981. "She understood that if she did contest this, and she could have called the NAACP, we could have had a real mess. . . . She could have raised a lot of negativity. But we didn't want to destroy the whole tour until we had a chance to see if we could work this out. And she agreed to that, as it turned out."[16]

Equally important, the players always did their part to support Althea on the road. When she was barred from a hosting clubhouse and compelled to change her shoes in her car, a couple of other players changed shoes in their cars beside her. If motel operators refused to honor her reservation, they spoke up or offered to share their room. Marlene Hagge Vossler, for one, described just such a late night in Columbus, Ohio, when she found Althea standing silently in front of a disgruntled hotel clerk. "The guy said, 'We don't have you down here,'" Vossler recalled. "I knew what was happening, so I made a funny face at her and said, 'Wait for me. I'll handle it.' I finished checking in, and I said, 'Come with me.' She stayed with me in my room. We ended up rooming together for a couple of years."[17]

In 1967, a second Black woman joined Althea on the LPGA tour. Unlike Althea, Renee Powell had been playing golf for almost her entire life, ever since her father, the first Black man to design, build, and operate a golf course in the United States, had handed her a putter when she was three years old. Powell rose steadily through the ranks of the Black United Golfers Association in the 1960s and was so gifted that *Ebony* magazine predicted early on that she would become "the Althea Gibson of golf."[18] Although nearly two decades younger than Althea, Powell nonetheless knew all too well the racist ways of golf, having been barred from numerous tournaments because of her color since the time she was a child in Ohio.[19]

After Powell joined the LPGA, race became a more present issue, and vanishing hotel reservations were only the start. Restaurants refused to serve her, while country club security guards routinely barraged her with questions at the locker room door as white players sailed past her. In the South, her phone erupted with obscene calls that left her quaking. Then came death threats so chilling that Powell routinely stacked furniture and other items against her hotel room door so that if anybody tried to come in, "at least I would wake up."

Powell, who eventually took over as the manager of her family's Clearview Golf Club in East Canton, Ohio, was named the first at-large member of the PGA board of directors in 2019 and is a strong supporter of the LPGA. She remembered warmly the closeness of tour members in the

1960s, saying, "It was like one big family. People would caravan. You stay in the same hotels. You just knew everyone and their parents, their siblings, their jobs. . . . People were concerned about each other." Nonetheless, Powell said she rarely confided in the members of that cozy group, other than her roommate, about the racial threats and abuse she was routinely subjected to. Part of the reason for this was because the one time she went to Lenny Wirtz—the same person who had squared off with tournament directors in defense of Althea—and told him about the threats she was receiving on the tour, he told her he could not help her.

"I went to Lenny because it really bothered me, and I can remember Lenny said, 'There's nothing we can do.' And I'm thinking, *Oh my God, there's nothing we can do,*" said Powell.

For various reasons, Powell decided not to pursue or discuss the harassment she was experiencing. As she saw it, "The more you dwell on the negative things, the harder it would be. Golf is such a mental game, if you think about things like that, or think about fear or whatever, and you are competing, and no one else has to think about that, well, you try and get away from as many negative things as you can. . . . [Players on tour] didn't know what I was going through."[20]

Althea endured her own share of racist insults on tour, and they were likely even worse than those Powell had faced, given the earlier time in which she started. Those insults came not only in the form of institutional bars, such as those leveled by country club administrators or hotel clerks, but from random people. Time and again, Althea opened her mail in southern states to be met with hostile or racist language.

"Suggest in future you confine your playing to Nortern [*sic*] cities. Colored not wanted in this locale," wrote Al Watson of St. Petersburg, Florida, in an April 6, 1964, letter.[21]

Two years later, she received another typed letter, addressed to the Sunset Country Club, in St. Petersburg, Florida, signed by Herb Raver and Marvin Jackson. It read, "Go home, nigger. We don't need you or your kind here."[22]

Althea kept both letters for the rest of her life, and they eventually wound up buried in a trunk of her belongings in a New Jersey storage unit. But she never confided in Powell about such happenings on the golf tour;

nor did Powell share her experience of such racial hatred. Part of the reason that both chose to remain largely silent about race was that neither of them wanted to be distracted from the competition at hand. A hardened veteran of the nation's ongoing racial strife, Althea regarded the hurdles on the tour much as Powell did—as a distraction. The best strategy to deal with them, Althea wrote in her memoir, "is simply to be a winner."[23]

There was also the fact that Powell and Althea were coming from quite different worlds. Not only were they a generation apart, but Powell knew most of the LPGA players by the time she joined the tour, having competed against them as a junior. She was also a far more experienced player. Althea was the newcomer, struggling to learn the rules. Powell was earning a salary as a staff member of the Wilson Sporting Goods Company, while Althea was barely making it into the money at all. Still, each likely had a pretty good idea of what the other was going through as they crisscrossed the country. In a 1971 *Ebony* feature pairing the two women, Powell said she avoided southern tournaments, where she had experienced trouble, adding that, "Althea went through more of that than I did." Althea, by then playing fewer tournaments, acknowledged that she had been barred from locker rooms and dining rooms on the tour, saying with a smile, "I don't know if they thought I was going to eat the grass. . . . All I wanted to do was hit the ball off it."[24] Long after both women had retired, they remained friendly. Powell regularly telephoned Althea right up until her friend's death, calling to her through the answering machine when she did not pick up. "Hey, Ugga Mugga, it's Renee," Powell would typically say. "Pretty soon she'd pick up the phone."[25]

Of greater apparent concern to Althea than race in her early years playing golf was her ongoing financial struggle. To her disappointment, the Ward Baking Company terminated her contract of five years in 1965, as Althea had become too absorbed with her golf schedule to manage all the far-flung public appearances on its behalf as she had in the past. At one point, lacking a single source of funds to pay for her gas bills or even for her meals after Ward stopped paying her, she panicked. But, just as had happened in tennis, community members acted to provide some critical backing. First, a jewelry store owner agreed to back her for $300 a month for the remaining season. Then a pair of Black doctor friends committed to supporting her in 1967 and 1968. With the addition of occasional financial gifts from friends, she was able to relax and focus on her game.

Through all the anxiety and stress of those early years on the tour, one person remained solidly at her side, the same person from whom she had twice walked away in the past, the same person whom she delighted in beating at whist and checkers. Will Darben was nothing if not a loyal man. By the end of 1965, Althea, perhaps made calmer by her improving golf performance and her stabler financial situation, decided at long last to commit to her ever-patient, unwaveringly devoted boyfriend. They agreed over the phone that they would be married in a private ceremony in Nevada, where Althea was next scheduled to compete.

On October 17, 1965, the couple was married before friends in Las Vegas. Days later, Althea bent over her clubs in a Phoenix tournament, keenly aware that her doting spouse was watching her. "Although Will had watched me play in many matches, I felt almost childishly nervous to know that my *husband* was in the gallery that day!" she wrote in her memoir.[26] In the months to come, when they were sometimes separated for weeks at a time, she on the road playing golf and he at his job as a production analyst at the Bendix Aviation Corporation, Althea kept her marriage license tucked into her wallet, next to her player's card, twin symbols of the stability of her current phase of life. Now there was a breadwinner in the family, and blessedly, it wasn't Althea.

Although they had known each other for almost fifteen years, Althea and Darben delighted in their union like newfound lovers. Together, they mixed their trademark martinis, posed for photographs looking longingly into each other's eyes, and danced the Twist with friends late into the night after dinners barbecued on the brick grill out back. Even their long-running love of music was invigorated by their union. Althea bought her new husband the first piano he'd ever had and would join him on the saxophone while crooning some of her favorite ballads. The burnished tennis trophies that once crowded her Central Park apartment now lined the mantel over their fireplace in the cherished Pleasant Way home in Montclair where they had first met and which Darben had inherited from his mother.

Invigorated by her newfound marital contentment, Althea returned to the golf course full steam. In 1966, her scoring average dropped to 77.53

while her year-end earnings nearly doubled, to $2,737. That summer, she achieved a personal best with a record-breaking six-under-par 68 in the opening round of the Lady Carling Eastern Open in Sutton, Massachusetts. The next day, however, her game grew erratic, and her score leapt to 88 after she got a two-stroke penalty for slow play, a tendency she often exhibited as she deliberated over her strokes. In the final round, she finished with an 80 and tied for twenty-fourth place with an overall score of 236.[27]

Now that she was a married woman, Althea found being on the road more grueling than ever. In September 1966, she penned her new husband a heartfelt letter intended to shore both of them up during what was apparently a two-month separation.

"Darling," she wrote on her pale blue stationery, her Central Park address scratched out. "Knowing that I will always love you and you will always love me should give us the strength to cope with the absence until November. Be good baby. . . . Believe me, I miss and love you more as each day passes. Always, 'Girl'"[28]

The following year, the best of her golf career, Althea set a new one-round record at the Venice Open golf tournament in Venice, Florida, again scoring a 68. This time, her play remained consistent throughout the tournament, and she tied for fifth place. One of her best showings that year came at the Pacific Ladies Golf Classic in Eugene, Oregon, where she tied for third place.

In the years that followed, however, both Althea's performance and her participation declined—and with them, the media attention waned. The novelty of her presence was wearing off just as the likelihood that she would not reach the top ranks of the sport was becoming apparent. In 1968, her earnings ranking dropped from twenty-third to forty-second, while her cash take was slashed by half, to $2,339.50. The Black press, keeping an eye on her less-than-stellar performance, didn't hold back. As the *New York Amsterdam News* put it in one midyear column, "Althea Gibson, who can drive a golf ball further than most guys you know is having a cold time on the women's tour. She seldom has more than one good round during any tournament—and seldom that. What gives, Althea?"[29]

Althea might have answered that part of the reason was, despite her hardworking husband, she continued to need to earn a paycheck. In 1970, she took a job as a special sports consultant with the Essex County Park Commission in New Jersey, which soon evolved into the more consuming position as supervisor of women's and girls' activities. Her primary motive in taking the job was financial, but it is likely that she, too, saw the writing on the fairway. She had started too late to become a top-ranked golfer and was never going to achieve her dream of matching the achievement of the legendary athlete Babe Didrikson Zaharias, who had successfully made the transition from other sports to become a golf champion in her thirties. By the end of 1970, Althea had participated in only seven golf events the entire year, although, ironically, she achieved her career best at a tournament in Columbus, Ohio, where she wound up in a sudden-death playoff with two other women. As her fellow players cheered loudly from the sidelines, Althea tied for second place with 216 and took home $2,032.[30]

By contrast, her plateau on the golf course coincided with the escalating success of a young Black man from Richmond, Virginia, the same slender player who had admired Althea ever since he walked onto Dr. Johnson's hard-packed court at age ten. In 1963, a decade after coming under Johnson's wing, Arthur Ashe was a twenty-year-old junior at UCLA when he became the first Black player to be named to the U.S. Davis Cup tennis team, a prestigious international men's team not unlike the women's Wightman Cup that was originally played between the United States and Britain and now includes scores of countries. In 1968, Ashe's name exploded across the front pages of the nation's newspapers when he became the first Black man, and the second Black person after Althea, to win the U.S. Open, the new name of the U.S. National Championships, in a marathon five-set win over Dutchman Tom Okker. Although 1968 was also the first year of the long-awaited Open Era in tennis, enabling amateurs to compete against professionals in Grand Slam and other events and to earn money, Ashe was unable to accept the $14,000 prize money because of his amateur status on the Davis Cup team. Nonetheless, it was a transformative day in the tennis world on both racial and professional fronts, described by *The New York Times* as "the most significant event in the game's history in this country."[31] Neither that story nor many of the others about the event mentioned Althea Gibson, the first Black person of any gender to win the tournament just eleven years earlier.

Ashe's win signaled a turning of the page in tennis history that gently nudged Althea's own accomplishments toward the rear of the nation's collective memory. To this day, many incorrectly believe that Arthur Ashe was the first Black person to win a Grand Slam tournament. Why Althea is often eclipsed in this context appears to have as much to do with gender as it does with money. In the 1960s, women's sports were universally regarded as lesser than men's, such that Althea's achievement has often been subordinated to Ashe's. At the same time, the introduction of cash prizes into the game of tennis added a gripping new dimension, and even status, to the sport, which likely contributed to the perceived greater significance of Ashe's win. That the reigning tennis fathers were far more comfortable with the well-educated and much-mannered Ashe, compared to the roughshod Althea and her assertive ways, surely contributed further to the diminishment of her accomplishment.

Nearly four months after his Forest Hills win, Ashe led America's Davis Cup team to victory for the first time since 1963. Named the country's No. 1 amateur player at the end of the year, "King Arthur," as the media often referred to him, had attained a potentially powerful international platform. All he had to do was use it. Several months earlier, he had taken a tentative but much-noticed step in that direction by issuing a moderate summons to political activism. Steeped in the conservative teachings of both Dr. Johnson and the U.S. Military Academy at West Point, where he worked as a data processing instructor, the famously unflappable Ashe had remained at some distance from the civil rights furor gaining momentum across the nation toward the end of the 1960s. But in the spring of 1968, perhaps compelled as much by the words of Rev. Martin Luther King Jr. as by the rabid segregationist George Wallace's bid for the U.S. presidency, Ashe agreed to speak at a Washington, D.C., church about the responsibilities of Black athletes in the civil rights era. His speech was hardly revolutionary. Nonetheless, Ashe's call to his athletic peers to "make a commitment to his or her community and attempt to transform it" in the manner of Jackie Robinson and Bill Russell was interpreted by the media as a clear indication of his rising political consciousness. He received a standing ovation. Raymond Arsenault, Ashe's biographer, describes the speech as a "major milestone" in Ashe's life, one that launched him on the path toward his singular brand of political activism in the years to come. "For one of the first times in his life, he was playing the role of a rebel."[32]

Not surprisingly, Ashe made no mention in that speech of Althea, the athlete whom he had much admired in his childhood and who had pried open the doors to the sport of tennis for their race and for him. Although Althea spoke far more openly, and at times even angrily, about how discrimination had impacted her career in the years after she left amateur tennis, she would never take up arms in the racial turmoil of the day. Divided by an age difference of nearly sixteen years and vastly different life experiences, Ashe and Althea never became political soul mates or even particularly close friends. Althea deeply resented not only that Ashe made so much money in the sport while she struggled even to get by, but also that he was routinely mistaken as the first Black player to break the color barrier in the sport. It was not something she held personally against him, however, and the two players greatly respected each other.

"She didn't blame Arthur for it. She really blamed the tennis community for it, because Arthur never undervalued Althea's contributions," recalled Bob Davis, an ATA champion in the 1960s and a friend of both Althea and Ashe. "But the tennis community tended to slide over her contributions and go right to him because he was a personality, he was media-friendly, he was articulate, and he came along during the civil rights era. . . . I don't think they ever addressed the way the world treated them differently. It was just, if they were both invited to a place, they would both show up. They both appreciated each other. They enjoyed being with each other. They enjoyed sharing the spotlight."[33]

And they did so frequently. During the 1970s and '80s, the two were linked on countless tennis platforms, occasionally playing together, often appearing at charities and benefits, always seeking to encourage greater Black participation in their sport. In 1971, the apolitical Althea even dipped her foot in the swirling political waters and lent her name to a group of athletes seeking to support American soldiers being held prisoner or missing in action in Indochina, led by a committee on which Ashe sat. In the 1980s, she served as a director of Ashe's Black Tennis & Sports Foundation, which provided support for disadvantaged Black junior athletes and was also a part of his celebrity tennis tournament, Artists and Athletes Against Apartheid, among many other causes. Their names would inevitably be forever linked in the tennis history books as the two most successful players to walk off the Lynchburg, Virginia, tennis court of Dr. Johnson, who died in 1971 at age seventy-two.

Not that Althea was entirely done with tennis herself. Toward the end of the tumultuous year of 1968, Althea, then forty-one, returned to her first sport, drawn largely by the prospect of potential prize earnings made freshly available with the dawning of the Open Era. Two days before Ashe claimed his first Grand Slam title in the U.S. Open at the West Side Tennis Club, Althea, who was attending the two-week event, announced that she was preparing to make a tennis comeback. Her plan, she announced to reporters, was to combine her two sports, playing golf early in the year and then switching to tennis. "I still have it," she declared. "As long as I've got the big serve, I'm all right."[34]

Her first appearance came at the Oakland Pro Invitational in February 1969, an event sponsored by Larry King, the husband of one of her greatest fans, the rising star Billie Jean King. The event, to be played by four men and four women, would be Althea's first since she retired nine years earlier, and would pit her against far younger female professionals, including King and Britain's Ann Haydon, who now bore the married last name of Jones. Althea made no secret of the fact that she hoped her appearance would result in a pro contract, enabling her to make one more appearance at Wimbledon, which was then finally open to professionals. Although she practiced nearly five hours a day leading up to the match, she was easily defeated by Jones 6–2, 7–5, whom she had obliterated in the Wimbledon semifinals in 1958. The passing of nearly a decade had clearly made a difference. While Althea had difficulty returning service, though, she nonetheless said she was "reasonably well pleased with my game. My serves were good and the volley was fairly strong."[35]

In the coming years, Althea played in a number of high-profile tournaments but never came even close to repeating her performance of past years. In 1970, she paired with Australian Judy Tegart Dalton in the Marlboro Open in South Orange, New Jersey, and won the first round before being defeated in the quarterfinals. She twice returned to the U.S. Open, playing mixed doubles, first in 1972, with fifty-eight-year-old Gar Mulloy, and was defeated in the first round, although they managed to take one set. The following year, she paired with Arthur Ashe, at her request, only to be crushed by Marita Redonda and Jean-Baptiste Chanfreau in back-to-back sets 6–2, 6–2. Ashe, who was also defeated in the singles, by seventeen-year-old rising Swedish star Björn Borg, lamented in his diary that "This was the worst day of the year. . . . Jesus, I feel like an old man. I'm thirty years old and teeny-boppers are upsetting me."[36]

Due to a misplaced chair that broke the toe of Australian pro player Kerry Melville, Althea was back again on center court in 1974. Because of the injury, Melville was forced to withdraw from the S&H Green Stamps Classic in Fort Lauderdale, Florida, and Althea was asked to substitute in an exhibition match against Chris Evert. Almost three decades younger than Althea, Evert routed her opponent 6–1, 6–2, but many in the crowd enthusiastically rooted for "Big Mama," as Althea had jokingly nicknamed herself before the match got under way. "I really thought I could beat her," Althea exclaimed as she walked off the court. "Maybe she'll give me a rematch on my home turf."[37]

Althea was disappointed with her attempted comeback, not just because of her performance but because she still wasn't making any money. Other women in the sport, however, were starting to do quite well. After a long and hard-fought battle by a group of female tennis players, the Women's Tennis Association was created in June 1973, the same year the U.S. Open offered equal prize money to men and women for the first time. Just months earlier, the Women's International Tennis Federation and the ATA jointly announced that promising Black female tennis players would be welcome to compete on the women's Virginia Slims Circuit. Then, in 1976, Chris Evert, then the world's No. 1 player, became the first female athlete to reach more than $1 million in career earnings.

Althea was clearly pleased by such developments and even took the podium at the WITF/ATA announcement to say so. At the same time, it must also have been galling for her to see the money begin to flow even to those who had achieved far less than she had. Althea had long hungered to return to professional tennis, drawn in large part by the rising financial awards, but she balked at the requirement that she needed to qualify to do so, saying that her status as a former champion should suffice. Tournament officials refused to budge on the issue. As the financial rewards of pro tennis mushroomed over the years, so, too, did Althea's rage over earning virtually nothing during her years on the circuit. While other retired tennis players were increasingly sought out to provide televised commentary or colorful background, Althea's phone remained conspicuously silent.

Nor was her job with the Essex County Park Commission exactly making her rich. Only two years into the job, she resigned in 1972 and launched a series of undertakings that she believed would improve her financial standing while enabling her to keep her racket in play. First, she landed a job as program director and head pro at the Valley View Racquet Club in Northvale, New Jersey. Althea not only ran clinics and provided hourly instruction at the six-court indoor club, but she had a 5 percent interest in the business. Far more central to her bid for financial success was an enigmatic local businessman named Gil Fuller, whose legendary skill at arranging jazz compositions was matched only by his personal charisma.

Fuller, a stocky Newark native and an accomplished musician, had had a hand in the development of numerous modern American jazz and bebop arrangements as well as the musical scores of a large number of films. A well-known composer and arranger, he had established an orchestral framework for many of the improvisational harmonies of the 1940s into the 1960s that were performed by the likes of Ella Fitzgerald, Ray Charles, and Sarah Vaughan. His most successful connection was with the legendary trumpeter and composer Dizzy Gillespie, for whom he worked as an arranger and band manager while running a music publishing business on the side. By the 1970s, he had rebranded himself as a developer-cum-consultant and was a familiar, if somewhat inscrutable, figure on the New Jersey business scene.[38]

In 1970, Althea retained the smooth-talking Fuller as her business and personal adviser. Far from earning her much money, however, the connection turned out to be a chronic drain on her meager financial resources. Over the next decade, she and Fuller would engage in a succession of undertakings, including a documentary about her life, called *The Black Queen of Tennis*; the development of a downtown hotel in Newark, New Jersey; and the establishment of a sports management and equipment firm designed to create opportunities for talented urban youth. Every one of them would fail, while investors in the proposed film ultimately brought a lawsuit against Fuller, and eventually Althea, for misrepresenting the project. In the end, a court judgment found against the defendants for $6,159 in March of 1980.[39]

George Kanzler, a retired music critic for the *Star Ledger* of New Jersey, who worked briefly for Fuller, remembered him as a man who "had all these big ideas. He was a smooth talker and knew all the right things to say. We all drank the Kool-Aid and thought he was going to do all this stuff. But nothing ever seemed to get done."[40]

Of all the Fuller-inspired projects, the film appeared to have the most promise. It was to be a one-hour documentary about Althea's life, highlighting her challenging upbringing and culminating in her tennis triumphs. In 1974, Althea signed papers designating Fuller as her personal manager and attorney in handling an investors' partnership called Geocine Films Incorporated Angels Group I, which would finance the film. With the project expected to cost $85,000 to produce, Althea agreed to put up a staggering $52,500 on its completion.[41] By the middle of 1975, a host of notables had apparently been filmed as part of the undertaking, including Bob Hope, New Jersey governor Brendan Byrne, Bill Cosby, and members of the Kennedy family, some of whom had played tennis with Althea. In August of that year, Althea wrote to her friend Pearl Bailey, a prominent actress and singer at the time, and asked if she would consider narrating the film for $1,500. Furthermore, Althea offered an additional $5,000 plus 5 percent of the net proceeds if she was able to place the film with a major network. Althea sought to appeal to Bailey in her letter, saying, "I know this isn't the biggest deal of the century for you, but for me, and young black girls coming up in tennis, its value is immeasurable as an inspirational goal for a better future. Please give me a call as soon as it is convenient. . . . In the meantime, I'll keep on drinking Yoo-Hoo chocolate drink and eating Paramount chickens . . . direct from your kitchen. (smile.) Love, Althea."[42]

In the end, the film was not produced, but Althea nonetheless hung in with Fuller. Two years after the film project was initiated, she partnered with him and several other sizable names in an even more ambitious project to purchase the old Military Park Hotel in downtown Newark and turn it into a major television, film, and recording studio. Under the name

"Starcity Broadcasting Corporation of New York," the principal group, including Althea, Dizzy Gillespie, and Yankees coach Elston Howard, purchased the property for $100,000 and committed to putting $1.5 million into the tired building. As with *The Black Queen of Tennis*, however, the project went nowhere. After several years, Starcity, of which Fuller was vice president, defaulted on the property, and the hotel was returned to the city.[43]

"He just disappeared. He folded up his tent and left," Kanzler said of Fuller. "It was a mystery."[44]

Althea's failed dealings with Fuller had greater consequences than those that impacted her slender bank account, which were considerable. They also had a corrosive effect on her already flagging marriage. Althea was on the road—a lot. In addition to her coaching job at the Valley View Raquet Club, she had also taken on a position as national director of Pepsi-Cola's Mobile Tennis Program, which involved running a series of tennis instruction sessions for inner-city children around the country. There were also continuing golf and tennis exhibitions on her calendar, all of which left diminishing time for her husband. Will Darben had been wary of Gil Fuller's smooth-talking ways from the start and had repeatedly urged Althea to steer clear of him. Stubborn as usual, though, Althea ignored him and continued with her somewhat quixotic plans. As she crisscrossed the country on her various missions, Darben sometimes accompanied her, forever trailing his still-famous wife, but just as often he stayed behind. By the early 1970s, some in the couple's inner circle believed that both Althea and Darben, worn down by her long absences, were seeking emotional solace from others.

"I don't think they fell out of love, but Althea was called on so much here and there that she sort of got away from being married to Will," Rosemary Darben explained. "William began to think that he was more or less being neglected. . . . He just said that she was gone all the time."[45]

Will Darben's accommodating nature might have enabled him to endure the perennial role of second fiddle, but when he was repeatedly referred to as "Mr. Gibson" during interviews, even he drew the line. As Sandra Terry, Darben's niece, recalled it, "I don't think he was comfortable being 'Mr. Gibson.' He was kind of in her shadow, and I don't think most men can do that."[46]

Althea disagreed that her taxing schedule contributed to her separation from Darben, although she much preferred not to talk about it at all. Pressed on the subject by a reporter for the New York *Daily News* in 1974, she shrugged and said, "With understanding and sincere concern, a couple can make it no matter what their careers are or where they have to go. . . . We just didn't make it, that's all, and we didn't have any children, thank goodness."[47]

In 1972, Darben and Althea separated, and four years later their divorce was finalized. It was hardly the end of their relationship, however, which had begun more than two decades earlier. The pair remained in close touch, often talking over the phone as Althea continued her travels and golf appearances. Darben even continued to serve as her escort on some of her golf trips, amiably carrying her luggage and helping to make arrangements, unperturbed when she introduced him as her "ex-husband." Not only did they stay in touch by phone, but in their later years, they began to spend regular time together watching TV sports and eating out.

Althea was also distracted from her marriage by the occasional tennis matches at what was then the New Jersey governor's mansion, known as "Morven," in Princeton, New Jersey. Governor Brendan T. Byrne, an avid tennis enthusiast, first invited her to play after he met her at a ceremony honoring Black athletes in the summer of 1974. That *The New York Times* had written a glowing column about her one month earlier likely also piqued Bryne's interest. Headlined "Althea Revisited," the story declared that "the years have been unusually kind to Althea Gibson." Her tennis game, the piece continued, "is little changed from the banner years: slashing backhand, searing forehand, crisp volley, thundering overhead, and the huge, punishing service that hammers tiny depressions into a clay or grass court."[48]

Althea's game, though, had changed radically in one notable respect, at least when she was playing with political celebrities such as Byrne. Gone was the ruthless tennis warrior brutally battering her opponents and hellbent on victory. The retooled Althea not only complimented the governor's game across the court, she was downright nice as well. She even let him tie the abbreviated match they played at 2–2. "It was Althea's charitable heart," Byrne explained to reporters after the match. He presented Althea with a plaque making her the honorary pro at the so-called Morven

Bath and Tennis Club, before the two of them paired together in a doubles match against state senator Stephen Wiley and Assemblyman Gordon MacInnes. Enthused about the tennis pairing, Byrne invited Althea to play in several charitable events in the coming months. So taken with Althea was Byrne that he next invited her to play golf. In the summer of 1975, she participated in a celebrity tournament to benefit the Garden State Arts Center, along with Byrne, comedian Bob Hope, and Salvatore Bontempo, chairman of the New Jersey Highway Authority. Althea, it seemed, was developing some unexpected political friends. The next thing she knew, she received an entirely different kind of invitation.

That fall, Byrne nominated his sometime tennis partner to be New Jersey's new athletic commissioner, which would make her the first woman to hold the post. Although well aware of the nomination, Althea declared that she was "flabbergasted" by the announcement. "What can I say? I'll have to think about it first," she told the press.[49] She was approved by the state senate and accepted the part-time, $7,000-a-year post, which was then largely limited to the regulation of boxing and wrestling. Althea was learning the political game fast: a year later, she scratched back and appeared at a fund-raiser that invited Democrats to meet local political candidates over cocktails and to "Play Tennis with Althea Gibson."[50]

The appointment marked the beginning of a several-year stint on the New Jersey political scene for Althea, which, like so many other things, would lead to more disappointment than not. Politics, it turned out, didn't suit her much better than golf. At the start, she leapt into the athletic post with enthusiasm, declaring even at her swearing-in that she hoped to expand the functions of the post and establish the state as a preeminent athletic center in the country. High on her list of proposals was the construction of new athletic facilities that would give the state an identity apart from the neighboring powerhouses of New York and Pennsylvania. Her hair now fashionably shorn, and clad often in a trendy pantsuit, Althea repeatedly presented her ideas to Byrne, with Gil Fuller still at her side serving as an adviser, but she made little progress.

At the start of 1977, little over one year on the job, Althea resigned from the athletic commission, saying she was tired of battling the entrenched political machine. As she explained to reporters, she had hoped to "make the commissioner's job a viable post, but it seemed everything I wanted to do was knocked down. I found I didn't have a voice. Fighting the bureaucracy is a tough task for someone not used to it," she said.[51]

In a letter to her friend Byrne, she explained her decision, saying, "I have concluded that the true value of my work is being impaired by past and present policies and practices, over which I have no voice or control. . . . Unfortunately, I learned too late about the workings of bureaucracies. Needless to say, I'll be on hand for a game of tennis with you when your schedule permits."[52]

Byrne responded promptly, writing to wish her well in future endeavors. "You have brought new excitement to this position. You have approached your task with the same dedication and energy that you have demonstrated throughout your illustrious athletic career."[53]

Althea, however, was not done with politics. In recent years, she had developed a taste for the power game, and three months after she resigned from the athletic commission, she leaped onto the campaign trail to run for the state senate seat held by Democrat Sen. Frank J. Dodd. Her platform was clear cut: promote sports and stimulate economic development. Tickled by the unexpected development, the national press took note of her move. "'Jackie Robinson of Tennis' Moves to Political Arena," exclaimed the headline over a Los Angeles Times–Washington Post News Service story. "Tennis great Gibson for state senate," announced the UPI, while *The New York Times* ran a lengthy column on the item beneath a photo of a beaming Althea in wide-rimmed glasses.[54]

Althea had signed on with mayoral candidate Tom Cooke Jr. and Congressman James J. Florio, who was running for governor. Together they composed a breakaway slate to challenge the establishment Essex County Democratic Committee. Saying that she hoped to use a senate seat to further the goals she had articulated while athletic commissioner, she joined the race with a level of gusto that even she didn't expect.

"I have always wanted to do things that were beneficial to the public. But politics. I guess I was mildly surprised at my decision," she said in an interview with the *Washington Post*. "I thought about what I had read about crooked politicians, the kind not concerned with people, but then I finally thought, maybe this was my chance to do something for a number of people."[55]

Althea campaigned like she was angling to wrap up the tail end of the third set on Centre Court. She raised a glass of champagne at a campaign breakfast at the Holiday Inn and waved to supporters at the Doddtown ShopRite in East Orange. She embarked on brisk walking tours of Hackensack, shaking hands with well-wishers who came out to greet the tennis legend and handing out campaign brochures pledging more jobs and tax equity. Sporting a multicolored dashiki and bell bottom pants, she staged an outdoor concert with a boisterous R&B band. Yet it all amounted to nothing. In the end, neither Althea nor her Black primary opponent, Assemblyman Eldridge Hawkins, was able to capitalize on the large Black constituency in the district, and Dodd easily retained the nomination.

By the late 1970s, Althea's golf career wasn't faring much better than her political one. Now in her early fifties, she was competing against women half her age and younger, and the hundreds of miles she continued to log on her car each week were taking a toll. After her second-place showing in the Len Immke Buick Open in 1970—the best of her golf career—her play in subsequent years was spotty. In 1972, she played in only three tournaments. Throughout the decade, her score fluctuated from the mid-70s into the 80s. In the summer of 1977, she played her last LPGA tournament, the three-day Wheeling Ladies' Classic in West Virginia, and came in near the last, with a score of 243. It was the fourth and final tournament she competed in that year, at the end of which she wound up with a grand total of $186 for the year.[56] By the middle of 1978, she'd failed to qualify in thirteen tournaments and was now struggling with her long game. Even Althea conceded that she was flagging.

"I'm not doing so good scoring-wise, mainly because I've had troubles off the tee," she grumbled to a reporter for the *State Journal-Register* in Springfield, Illinois. "It's one of those slumps athletes get into—I guess it's my turn. I'm encouraged in that I know I can still hit the ball well, but my alignment and keeping the ball in the fairway are problems."[57]

Such problems made it impossible for Althea to regain her player's card after 1977. It was a bleak moment in her golf career, one profoundly discouraging to a world-class athlete who had invested fifteen years in the sport and had never won a single tournament. Nonetheless, she played on, appearing at occasional tournaments but never making the cut. In 1980, she attempted a return, attending the LPGA Tour Q-School, one of a series of qualifying tournaments that enable professional players to seek membership in the tour, but failed to advance. A decade later, in the fall of 1990, Althea gave it one last try, participating with 195 other women in a qualifying tournament in Venice, Florida. Then sixty-three, she again played poorly, shooting twin rounds of 86. Not only did she fail to make the cut, but she finished dead last. "I don't want to talk about it," she snapped at a *Sports Illustrated* reporter. "I'm mad at my game."[58] Althea never managed to regain her card, although she continued to play in benefits and exhibition events.

By the start of the 1980s, with both her athletic careers seemingly behind her, Althea turned her attention elsewhere. In 1980, she accepted a short-term appointment as manager of the Department of Neighborhood Facilities in East Orange, New Jersey, which gave her the responsibility of overseeing community recreational facilities. Still burning with the competitive spirit, Althea couldn't resist offering coaching advice when she happened upon young people, whether on the tennis or basketball court or in the bowling alley. Victoria Lewis, supervisor of women's and girls' activities in the recreation department, worked closely with Althea and remembers her as being "very, very, very into her sport. Even when she came down to the courts for an event, she'd be like, 'You're not going to win playing like that.' And then she'd give tips. People were about having fun, but that wasn't for her," said Lewis. "She'd be serious, serious. It sort of spruced the thing up. People got for real."[59]

It was an unexpected call from an old friend that ignited Althea's competitive spirit even more. Angela Buxton and Althea had drifted apart since Althea's triumph at Wimbledon in 1958. Each year, Buxton called her old pal on the phone—it was always Buxton who made the call, given that it was she who could afford the long-distance connection—and they reminisced, promising to visit each other soon. Shortly after the two went their separate ways in the late 1950s, Buxton had gotten married to a man named Donald Silk, an attorney and, later, president of the Zionist

Federation of Great Britain. Although they had three children, the couple was grossly mismatched and divorced eleven years later. To distract herself from her unhappy marriage, Buxton had returned to tennis and was soon running a flourishing tennis academy in Hampstead Garden Suburb, in northern London. She was also romantically involved with Jimmy Jones, her old tennis coach from her days on the tour. It was Jones who had counseled the aggressive Althea back in 1956 to accommodate Buxton during a match and had vastly improved the doubles partners' performance on Wimbledon's Centre Court.

In the fall of 1980, Buxton and Jones took an impromptu trip across the ocean for a romantic weekend in Manhattan to attend the U.S. Open at the new tennis facility in Flushing Meadows. When they landed, Buxton picked up the phone, called Althea, and the following day, the two women met at the tennis stadium outside the office of the USTA, which had dropped the "L" for Lawn from its name in 1975. Like other former players, they were given prime seats on Center Court, where they could see the best matches and where the fans could see them. They did the exact same thing every year that followed for the next decade. Sometimes, when Buxton was in town for a while, she'd also rent a car and go visit Althea in East Orange, and they'd head out for dinner.

"We would meet there at the USTA office because they knew Althea and they knew me. It was never a problem. We were always on time," Buxton said of their meetings in Flushing Meadows. "Then we would get something to eat, chat away, and watch some tennis. I think that would be about it, because she would then go home in her car, and I'd have a car to go back to Manhattan. . . . Oh, I looked forward to it."[60]

Like Buxton, Althea also had a new partner at the time. Hers, too, was a man she had known for years and who had worked as her tennis coach, Syd Llewellyn. Over the past two decades, the authoritative Llewellyn, sixteen years her senior, had served many roles in Althea's life, from coach to press agent to business manager. By the early 1980s, the two were spending increasing amounts of time together, fueling concern among Althea's closer friends who had never fully trusted his intentions. While some of Llewellyn's students considered him inspirational, Althea's team largely regarded him as a self-interested manipulator, one predominantly motivated by a desire to exploit Althea's fame and profit from her business undertakings. Some among them would likely not have been reassured by Llewellyn's comments to the *New York Amsterdam News* reporter who queried several men in 1976 about whether they preferred an independent woman or just the opposite. Llewellyn's response: "Here's my answer: It's a sad house where the hen crows louder than the rooster. A woman must have intelligence, and a willingness to make a man feel like a man in her presence at all times."[61]

With his rakish safari hat and glib manner, Llewellyn could not have been more unlike the mild Will Darben. In 1983, many among Althea's friends and family were stunned, some would even have said dismayed, to hear that she had married Llewellyn in a Maryland courthouse that spring. Virtually no one thought it was a union of love. On the contrary, Althea had apparently agreed to the marriage as a sort of payback to Llewellyn, who, she felt, had been critical to her accomplishments on the tennis court. It was he, after all, who changed her grip way back in the early 1950s and talked her out of joining the military. In the summer of 1984, Wimbledon was hosting a lavish celebration of one hundred years of women's tennis, to which all the surviving champions and their spouses were invited, with all expenses paid. There was also the 1984 Summer Olympics in Los Angeles looming on the calendar, to which Althea also had an all-expenses-paid invitation. By marrying Llewellyn, she secured him free trips to both events, complete with all the trimmings. Marriage would also enable them to file a single tax return, which provided financial savings, however small. Neither of them hesitated to admit to friends that both these things were the practical impetus for their union.

"She was quite open about it. I mean, it was no secret," recalled Buxton. "She said, 'I just married him for the trips. We're really not sharing living quarters. I'm staying in my place, and he's staying in his place. After the Olympic Games, we'll see.'"[62]

Arriving in London in the summer of 1984, Althea and Llewellyn checked into a five-star hotel and toured the city while awaiting their appearance on Centre Court. One morning, the pair had their Wimbledon chauffeur deliver them unannounced at the doorway of Buxton's tennis center. Buxton was just about to take a group of women onto the court for a class when Llewellyn stepped forward and announced that he would teach them instead. As Llewellyn led the surprised players onto the court, Buxton and Althea sat down to watch.

"Did he seem forward? Well, to us in England, all Americans are forward," Buxton said, laughing.[63]

If Buxton had some mixed feelings about the union, Marvin Dent, the longtime former student of Llewellyn's, with whom he had once shared the same Harlem manicurist, decidedly did not. In the summer of 1985, Dent, then the director of the national tennis program in Côte d'Ivoire, on the coast of West Africa, invited the couple to preside over a national junior tennis tournament at the Intercontinental Hotel. As he socialized with them and several other American friends attending the event, Dent was impressed by the closeness of the couple's relationship. While he saw no sign of romantic attraction between the two, he was struck by their obvious mutual respect for each other. Althea, he recalled, clearly looked up to Llewellyn, while he exhibited a strong sense of responsibility for her. In a way, each seemed to serve a useful purpose for the other.

"My notion at the time was that they were both trying to take advantage of whatever name recognition they had to benefit each other. They had both kind of fell on hard times," said Dent. "I thought they had great admiration and appreciation for what each brought to the table. I'm not sure I would associate love in a romantic sense with the relationship. I thought it was a marriage of convenience. And it was fine with me, because I adored them both."[64]

The union did not last long. Only a couple of years into the marriage, Althea apparently grew to distrust Llewellyn just as her friends had. In part, she was suspicious of his handling of her precarious finances, but she also suspected him of having affairs, according to *Born to Win*, an authorized biography of Althea published in 2004. Once, when she was undergoing testing at a hospital for a stomach disorder, she hid her purse behind an overhead ceiling panel in her room and refused to allow Llewellyn to take it home with him, infuriating him. In another incident, he allegedly struck her in the face, according to *Born*. Although Althea apparently did nothing at the time, the marriage came to an abrupt end in 1988. Not long afterward, Althea made her way down Washington Street to Will Darben's apartment, and pretty soon, they were parked in front of his television set together and meeting every Wednesday for lunch at the Harris Diner. Usually, they feasted on the diner's legendary Dagwood sandwiches, daunting towers of blended meats and cheeses. At times, they even discussed possibly remarrying, but for the moment, friendship seemed to fit just fine.

With two failed marriages behind her and a dormant athletic career, Althea faced a bleak future with a slowly diminishing circle of supporters. Many of the friends and fans who had been closest to her over the past two decades were gone, such as her mentor Dr. Johnson. Although she had not been much in touch with him in the years before he died, the practical lessons he had instilled in her as a young woman had served as a behavioral bulwark for her throughout her life, and his death left a void. Will Darben once again became central to her orbit, but she had been distant from his sister, Rosemary, once one of her most cherished confidantes, ever since the couple got divorced a decade earlier. As for Karol Fageros, one of her closest friends on the tennis circuit, they hadn't spoken since the collapse of their failed tennis tour back in 1960 and Fageros's injury in the bus crash. Now, even Llewellyn, her coach and adviser of nearly three decades, was gone from her life. Her family circle was also diminishing. Her father had passed away back in 1967. Although her mother was still living with various family members in the house in Queens, New York, Althea had bought for them, Annie Gibson was contemplating a move to Petersburg, Virginia, where one of her closest friends lived. Of all her family members, Althea was closest to her mother and her sister Millie. But by the early 1990s, even they had moved out of her range, having decamped several hours to the south.

After her breakup with Llewellyn, Althea continued to live in the same modest two-bedroom apartment on the bottom floor of a brick duplex about fifteen minutes northwest of Newark. Although she didn't particularly like living alone, neither did she yearn to find another spouse. A couple of years before she married Llewellyn, when she was living on her own, Althea purchased a pair of guns, a .22 pistol and a .38-caliber handgun. Although she did so partly for self-protection, Althea not surprisingly discovered a competitive aspect to gun ownership and enjoyed going to a nearby shooting range with a couple of police officer friends.

In the years after her divorce from Llewellyn, Althea developed a some-what different kind of social circle, one composed largely of a group of women she'd been introduced to back in the 1970s, while working for the Essex County Park Commission. At the heart of the group was a woman named Frances Clayton Gray, the administrator of a local nonprofit who also ran a restaurant called Around the Corner. Gray, who also had roots in South Carolina, had attended a number of social events hosted by Al-thea and Darben when they were a couple and remained friendly with both of them. Gray and several members of the group had female partners, but they openly welcomed Althea and Darben, who by then had apparently assumed an arm's-length, asexual relationship. When Althea found her-self unmoored from either personal or professional attachments in the late 1980s, Gray offered both her and Darben work in her restaurant. Darben toiled in the kitchen, while Althea helped organize the restaurant's school delivery network.

Nearing sixty, Althea had little interest in retiring, not that she could have afforded to. Bored by the restaurant work, she reached out to some of her old contacts in state government, and within a couple of months, she had added two entries to her résumé. First, she was appointed to the three-member State Athletic Control Board, a body newly created to monitor and promote New Jersey's boxing industry. More to her liking, she was called on to serve as a special assistant to the commissioner of the state's Department of Community Affairs, Leonard S. Coleman Jr., a former college football standout who had been raised in Montclair and a close family friend of the Darbens. Coleman, who was also Black, had run into Althea a few times around town in recent months, and he was one of the ones she had called when she began casting about for work. When his office launched a Senior Games program in 1987, it came up with the idea of an opening event pit-ting her against the flamboyant player turned hustler Bobby Riggs, then sixty-nine. It was to be a silver-haired version of the notorious gender battle of 1973, known as the Battle of the Sexes, in which Riggs was crushed by Billie Jean King in three sets.

This time around, the Y chromosome won. Evoking memories of her cannon-like forehand of days past, Althea managed to deliver a number of shots into the far court, positioning them so artfully that Riggs didn't even bother to try to return them. Riggs countered by dinking several shots over the net, which a gusting wind obligingly sent in a different direction and out of Althea's reach. Midway through the match, Althea, who had recently had a bout with the flu and was still on medication, ran out of steam, and Riggs easily won the contest 5–3. Althea, of course, did not take it well.

"She was boiling mad," Coleman recalled. "She came off the court and she said, 'Commissioner, I want the same match next year. I was sick and I couldn't train. I want to take him on next year.' She was very upset. I said fine."

Althea may have lost on court, but she was a hands-down winner in her work as an envoy to seniors, extolling the benefits of physical exercise on behalf of Coleman's department. Crisscrossing the state addressing conferences and groups of elders and therapists, Althea told engaging tales of her personal experiences, made jokes, and listened to seniors' tribulations, all the while urging her audiences to keep moving. Coleman's office was deluged with calls seeking to engage her. By 1988, Althea was working as a spokeswoman for the Governor's Council on Physical Fitness and Sports. Two years later, she was named employee of the month by the Department of Community Affairs and was extolled as "our very own superstar" in the department's newsletter. While her salary was not huge, Althea had found a secure and comfortable perch.

"Word got out that I was sending Althea Gibson to these engagements and we were swamped. They loved her and she loved them," said Coleman. "She had a car and a steady income. We would do a lot of fun things. . . . She was not Centre Court, Wimbledon, but she was center stage in a bunch of small venues."[65]

In fact, Althea made an appearance on the real Centre Court at Wimbledon around the same time. Back in the summer of 1980, she had coached a tennis camp at the Sportsmen's Tennis Club in Dorchester, Massachusetts, outside Boston, along with several Black tennis pros, where she encountered a handful of talented young Black female athletes. Among them were Zina Garrison and Leslie Allen, both of whom would go on to become world-ranked players in part because of Althea's inspirational words during that week. Allen, then twenty-three, remembers Althea watching the group practice and then standing tall over a table at which the up-and-coming players were sitting. After asking each of them what their individual goals were, she proceeded to explain to them, one by one, how they should aim even higher.

Eyeing Allen's towering height and long limbs, for example, Althea explained, "'With your wing-span'—and she put her arm out to the left and right, and her arms were as long as mine—she said, 'You need to think about winning the WTA Tour tournament,'" recalled Allen, who went on to be ranked No. 17 in the world the following year. "I was like, Okay, a few-time Wimbledon/U.S. Open champion thinks I can win the WTA Tournament. Oh, I need to change everything. I need to up my game. I need to set my sights higher. . . . It was just [being] embraced by the beauty of Black girl magic."[66]

Zina Garrison, the youngest of the group at sixteen, was even more deeply affected by her sessions with Althea. The older champion not only pushed Garrison to her physical limits, but told her bluntly that she would always have to work harder than white players on the tour. Even if she did so, Garrison later recalled Althea's advising her, "I'd probably find myself in a situation where being the best wasn't good enough."[67]

Struck by Althea's words, Garrison went home and decided to quit tennis. Althea had made it sound like being a champion was "almost unreachable unless you do something different. And I couldn't be just the average next Black girl that's playing," said Garrison. "I had to go beyond and beyond if I wanted to make myself a champ."[68]

And that's exactly what she did. After two weeks, Garrison returned to tennis, resolved to commit herself even more fiercely to the sport—and her performance steadily improved. By 1983, she reached the semifinals of the Australian Open and was ranked No. 10 in the world. In 1985, she was a semifinalist at Wimbledon, and three years later she won the mixed doubles there with partner and fellow Texan Sherwood Stewart. Although she grappled with being perennially labeled "the next Althea Gibson," she nonetheless became Althea's friend in later years. When Garrison made it to the women's singles final at Wimbledon in 1990, the first Black woman to do so since Althea's last victory there thirty-two years earlier, Althea was sitting in the Royal Box wearing the same tracksuit she had worn when she visited Garrison's morning practice. After the practice, the two women visited the locker room, where Althea showed Garrison the bathroom stall she had used before one of her final matches and the corner space where she had sat and pulled herself together before going on court. Garrison ultimately lost to Martina Navratilova in straight sets, 6–4, 6–1, but the match would be the highlight of her career.[69]

Althea enjoyed a relatively contented period during the early 1990s, but as with many aspects of her post-tennis life, that, too, came to a sudden and bitter ending. On the last day of June 1992, she was abruptly laid off along with thousands of other government workers as the result of budget cuts made by the Republican legislature that trimmed $167,000 from the Governor's Council budget. In addition to Althea, Harry Carson, the celebrated former New York Giants linebacker, who was the council's director and her boss, also lost his job. Althea, the legendary queen of tennis, who had broken the color barrier in the sport, was given a single day to pack up her things and leave her office. Devastated, she drove slowly home, her belongings crammed into a box at her side.

All her life, Althea had worried about money and struggled to ensure that she had enough to pay for her basic needs. Now, at age sixty-four, Althea found the fears that had plagued her for decades were materializing. With just a few thousand dollars in her savings account, barely enough to pay for a couple of months' rent and her several medications, she didn't have a single prospect for earning more. Making matters worse, she had suffered a stroke at the beginning of the year while at a public speaking engagement, and her gait remained slightly delayed. Despite her friendship with Darben, Althea had neither a permanent partner nor children to help bear the burden of it all. When she returned to her apartment after being laid off on that summer afternoon, she slowly locked the door behind her. And then she took the phone off the hook.

"She was despondent because she was let go before she was ready to retire," said Frances Gray. "She had made some investments with her own private money that didn't pan out."[70]

In the months to come, the situation only got worse. Althea withdrew into a sealed shell of isolation, consenting to contact with only a handful of her old friends. Every now and then, when a caller was particularly persistent or said something through the answering machine that piqued her curiosity, she'd pick up. More often than not, the many callers wound up with only the machine. Only Fran Gray and, every now and then, Angela Buxton were permitted to come inside. Parked in front of her beloved television set with its split screen, Althea spent the afternoons alternating between *Perry Mason* and ABC's *Wide World of Sports*. With decidedly mixed feelings, she watched the Williams sisters streak across the tennis court, their winnings steadily mounting. In the mornings, the young man who lived upstairs delivered a bag from McDonald's containing her beloved pancakes and bacon to her front door.

Every now and then, Althea got into her car and carefully drove the several miles of side streets from East Orange to Montclair. With her hat pulled low over her face, so that no one would recognize her, she'd park in front of the two-story yellow clapboard house at 69 Pleasant Way, the Darben family's former home, the same one she'd been taken into back in the early 1950s. Sitting in the car, sometimes for an hour or more, she'd recall her favorite memories of all the boisterous outdoor barbecues she'd shared there, the chaotic touch football games, the frosted martinis, and, always, Will's earnest brown eyes.

Looking out from inside the old Darben family home, Victor L. White, the current resident, recognized Althea under her hat. A generation younger than the elderly woman hunched over her steering wheel, White had grown up down the block and had known all the residents of the house he eventually purchased. Sometimes he'd stroll outside to Althea's car and quietly ask if she wanted to come in the house.

"She'd say, 'No, baby, I'm just sitting here,'" White recalled. "And then we'd get to talking. She wasn't really sad exactly, she was just coming back. She'd say, 'This is where my happy days were. This is where my whole life started.' But, you know, by then, all of that was gone."[71]

12

Not the Gibson Grandstand

Angela Buxton was standing in the small kitchen of her airy Pompano Beach, Florida, condominium frying onions, an apron bearing the seal of her beloved British flag secured comfortably around her waist, when the phone in the next room rang. Although reluctant to interrupt her Sabbath cooking, Buxton, at age sixty, was busier than ever with tennis writing assignments, her three adult children, and the handful of former tennis students who still checked in every now and again. She never missed a call if she could help it. When she picked up the phone on that March afternoon in 1995, she was stunned to hear the voice of her old tennis friend up north in New Jersey.

"Angie, baby. Althea here," said the voice. Buxton knew immediately that there was something terribly wrong. In all the nearly forty years that the two women had been friends since winning the 1956 French Open doubles championship together, Althea had almost never called Buxton. It was invariably Buxton who initiated the annual call to Althea to arrange their visit together to the U.S. Open each summer. If Althea was calling *her*, she was undoubtedly in serious trouble.

"Just phoned up to say goodbye," Althea said.

"Oh, so where are you going?" asked Buxton.

"I'm going to commit suicide," Althea said matter-of-factly.

"I beg your pardon!?" Buxton exclaimed. "Look, I've got something cooking. It's Friday, and you know I always do my cooking on a Friday.

I've got some onions frying in the kitchen. Let me go and turn the light off, and I'll phone you back."[1]

The two women hung up. As she dropped the phone in its cradle, Althea settled back in her black leather La-Z-Boy recliner and fixed her gaze on the forty-eight-inch split-screen television in front of her. As usual, the lights were dim in the two-story apartment in the boxy brick building complex with iron grilles on the doors and windows in which she had lived alone for close to two decades since her divorce. In addition to the stroke she had suffered in 1992, Althea had had two cerebral aneurysms in subsequent years. Her weight had dwindled from the robust 150 pounds she carried during her competitive tennis years to about 100 pounds. Now so frail that she could barely walk without her cane, she almost never left her apartment. When she did, it was usually to go to McDonald's to pick up her cherished breakfast when the young man who lived above her was unable to do so.

Even if she might have wanted a more lavish meal, she couldn't have afforded it. Since being laid off from her government job three years before, she had exhausted her meager few thousand dollars in savings and had only her Social Security check to sustain herself.

Having deliberately withdrawn from public view years ago, the onetime groundbreaking tennis champion who had routinely crisscrossed the globe for years and whose crashing of racial barriers had earned her a place in the nation's history books had grown so deeply depressed that she grudgingly permitted only a handful of people to see her. On the day she telephoned Buxton, Althea barely had enough money to pay for her pancakes, much less anything else.

"I've got no money," Althea sighed when Buxton called her back. "I've run out of money completely. I've no money for food, for rent, for my medications, nothing. So, I think I'm just going to end it. I'm going to kill myself."

"Now, you just *wait* a minute," Buxton declared. And then they got down to it.[2]

That Althea had called Buxton was no accident. At the time, practically the only people whom Althea permitted into her apartment were her friend Frances Gray, whose friends called her Fran, and Gray's girlfriend, Carol Gaither. The two women took care of Althea and brought her daily meals, while Gray fielded most all her communications with the outside world. There were many others whom Althea might have called. Her telephone, in fact, rang periodically with calls from numerous friends and acquaintances who might have provided help. For the most part, she never picked up. Every now and then, though, she couldn't resist one of the entreaties wafting out of her answering machine, and just as the caller was about to give up, Althea would grab the receiver.

Few were more persuasive than David Dinkins, a Harlem tennis pal from the 1940s and the former mayor of New York City. "Champ, hey, Champ," Dinkins would call out, using his favorite nickname for her. "Pick up!" Then there was Renee Powell, the only other Black player on the LPGA in the late 1960s. "Hey, Ugga Mugga, it's Renee," Powell would sing into the phone, using the lady golfers' nickname for their towering colleague. "It's me!" Also hard to resist was Billie Jean King, one of the most accomplished tennis players in history and a fan of Althea's since childhood, who telephoned Althea as persistently as she had once slammed her forehands into the backcourt. Worn down by Althea's unresponsiveness, King once concluded her phone message, "I'm just thinking about you. I hope I can come and see you someday. I hope you'll let us . . ."[3] The "us" included Zina Garrison, the second Black female tennis player after Althea to make it to a Grand Slam final, in 1990, who also called regularly. Eventually, both King and Garrison were permitted to visit. Even Sam Lacy, the veteran sports columnist for the *Baltimore Afro-American* who had covered Althea throughout her entire career, phoned "Al" regularly and every now and then, sometimes he even got an answer. The sole person whose calls Althea always answered was Will Darben, her beloved ex-husband, who was suffering his own health issues in a high-rise building nearby.

Althea might have turned to any one of those callers at this profoundly vulnerable moment, but it was Buxton's number she dialed. Buxton, after all, was the person with whom she had first tasted a major victory, on a Parisian tennis court in 1956, as the two outcasts achieved what no one thought remotely possible. It was Buxton who had done the even more unthinkable that year, forgoing a shot at a Grand Slam singles title in France to help her friend when Althea's bra strap snapped on court and she risked being hit with a code violation. In the years that followed, Buxton had not only welcomed Althea into her London home time and again, but also had remained loyal to her in ways no one else ever had. What's more, she was a doer who had the connections and the perseverance to make things happen. She also had money.

"I said, 'What does it cost you to live, you know, the items you just mentioned. About?'" said Buxton. "And she said, 'About fifteen hundred dollars a month.' I said, 'I'll send you that.'"[4]

The ever-determined Buxton, however, had no intention of leaving it at that. Several weeks later, she got in touch with Bud Collins, the legendary *Boston Globe* sports columnist as famed for his vividly colored custom pants as his eloquent tennis analysis. Long a fan of Althea's, Collins put out word of her alarming condition to a circle of his well-heeled tennis friends, including Chris Evert and Martina Navratilova. Exactly what happened after that is unclear. Although many of Collins's friends reportedly wrote Althea generous checks, the funds were apparently diverted somewhere along the way, according to Buxton, either by one of the tennis organizations involved or by someone with access to Althea's personal affairs. Buxton claims that Althea received almost nothing.

Buxton continued to send her a monthly check of $1,500, and in the spring of 1996, she made another attempt at fundraising for Althea. This time, she approached Paul S. Fein, a longtime friend and freelance writer for a host of tennis magazines, and asked for help.[5] On July 18, 1996, Fein's open letter to the tennis community appeared in *Tennis Week* magazine. It began, "I call upon tennis lovers and all men and women of good will and compassion to help Althea Gibson before it is too late." Althea, the letter continued, was financially destitute, a physically shrunken version of her old self and deeply dispirited. "She may not last much longer," Fein wrote. In conclusion, he urged readers to send money to her personal mailbox in East Orange. Althea was told nothing of this.[6]

The envelopes began to show up within days. Within a week, Althea's mailbox was so jam-packed with mail that she had to get the building handyman to help her pry it open. Inside were letters and cards, easily numbering in the hundreds, springing from nearly every corner of her life and stretching around the world. They ranged from small, personal messages wishing her well to sweeping commendations for her bold and historic achievements. There were big checks from big names, including $10,000 from the USTA, $5,000 from Billie Jean King, and $2,500 from entertainer Bette Midler. There were smaller checks for $50 and $25 from less-famous fans, accompanied by heartfelt handwritten notes of admiration. A California insurance salesman who had been a ball boy in one of Althea's Wilberforce, Ohio, matches sent $150 with a five-page letter saying, "I'll always remember that summer day in August when you shined like a bright star." The members of the tennis teams at five Texas and Oklahoma colleges and universities opted to forgo tournament prizes and instead pooled the value of those awards to send Althea a check for $410. "We appreciate what you did for tennis!" their card read. There were children who broke open their piggy banks and sent along a few crumpled dollar bills, like Omari and Sigele Winbush of College Park, Georgia, who pulled together $12. Omari's handwritten letter concluded, "I hope things get better for you." There were even moving letters from remote parts of the Indian subcontinent where Althea had visited on her goodwill tour of decades before.[7]

Among the pile of correspondence from those years, which Althea would treasure for the rest of her life, was a note from Shirley Fry, one of her fiercest tennis foes in the 1950s and later a close friend. Fry had called her old partner from her Connecticut home as soon as she read Fein's letter and followed up with a note saying, "Your voice sounded strong, but the fatigue of the battle showed through." Fry grew nostalgic as she continued: "We will always have our memories—my last grand slam being with you in Australia—we did have a fun trip. Aren't we lucky to have traveled so much and reached the top of a sport we love."[8]

Althea, not surprisingly, guessed immediately who was behind the outpouring of money and well-wishes flooding her postbox. Once again, she picked up the telephone and dialed Buxton, who by then was back home in England.

"Angie, baby," Althea said when Buxton picked up. "A very strange thing has happened. I was down at the PO box today, and there are so many things inside, it's blocked. You can't get in. I had to get the man to unblock it and unlock it. . . . Was this something that possibly has to do with you? Sounds like you."

"Me!?" Buxton declared in mock surprise. "I'm sitting here minding my own business here in Cheshire in England. How could it be something to do with me?"[9]

Buxton finally confessed. This time around, she decided to take steps to make sure that Althea received all the funds intended for her. In the weeks before the U.S. Open, she flew across the Atlantic and set up a card table in Althea's apartment, where the two of them began cataloguing the checks rolling in. On each envelope, one of them penciled the amount of money that had been sent, and the other filed the check away until the next trip to the bank, where it would be deposited. Althea also wrote a personal note to each of the donors. Far from declining in number in the months after Fein's letter appeared, the donations continued to crowd Althea's mailbox until the end of 1997. Fein's letter had triggered a surge of press accounts of Althea's predicament that prompted even more fundraising drives and individual gifts.

"I started getting phone calls, lots of messages," Fein recalled in an interview. "The thing was, nobody knew about [her situation]. They were shocked."[10]

Next came a fall column in *The New York Times* headlined "Althea Gibson's Long Days," which described her as being "nearly destitute" and suffering from a "terminal disease" that had not been disclosed. The *Times* story spread word of Althea's condition to an ever-broader swath of readers, extending far beyond the tennis crowd, and more than a few reached into their pockets. At her old alma mater, now Florida A&M University, the school president donated $1,000 and sent out a public appeal to employees and alumnae to contribute. "Tennis Legend Faces Greatest Challenge," declared a *Tallahassee Democrat* headline over a story about the fundraising drive. In Marina del Rey, California, William Hayling, Althea's longtime gynecologist and friend, and her lifelong tennis buddy Billy Davis staged a benefit that raised $25,000. Several months later, the USTA's Eastern Section sponsored a black-tie tribute to Althea that included a live auction and entertainment that raised about $30,000. A *Newsday* reporter writing about the event noted that the amount was "Not enough to make up for the never-offered shoe contracts and soda commercial accolades, but the strength of Gibson's accomplishments will provide her name with glory for years to come."[11]

As the envelopes continued to pile up, Fran Gray pulled up a third chair at the card table in Althea's apartment in order to help count the checks, at least according to Buxton. It was an awkward time at best for Buxton and Gray—the two women closest to Althea in her declining years, who have now both passed away—as they were increasingly jealous of the other's closeness to Althea. As Althea deteriorated, Gray gained greater control over almost all aspects of her life. Among Althea's friends and the few family members who remained in contact with her, Gray was regarded as a formidable gatekeeper and virtually the only person who could talk Althea into allowing a personal visitation. Even the powerful USTA nodded to Gray's role and abided by her decision on who could and could not see Althea. Buxton, for her part, was a far more widely recognized persona and was considered by some to be Althea's most devoted friend. Not surprisingly, the two women's accounts of what happened during this period vary widely.

Buxton maintained that the results of the combined fundraising efforts generated a total of $1 million. Some of that, she also said, mysteriously disappeared from Althea's checking account just as she says the funds raised in the previous year's drive had. In later years, Buxton would claim that Gray had siphoned off a substantial portion of the donations.[12] Gray, however, insisted that the incoming checks totaled only about $150,000. All that, she maintained, went into Althea's checking account except for about $40,000, which was given to the Althea Gibson Foundation, a nonprofit organization Gray had cofounded with Althea in 1998 to help urban youth develop skills in tennis and golf.[13] Gray was the organization's executive director until it disbanded fifteen years later. What's more, she said that neither she nor Buxton helped tabulate the donations to Althea, but that Althea did so herself, with the help of their friend Carol Gaither. Whatever the amount that ultimately ended up in her bank account, both Gray and Buxton agreed that the influx of money and adoring mail significantly improved Althea's spirits—at least for a while.

"As she got the letters from all over the world, children, piggy bank money, she began to say. 'People do love me, people do care about me,'" said Gray. "Her mood changed."[14]

No longer in chronic financial straits, Althea began to spend a little.

First, she had some major dental work done that she had put off for many years. Next, she purchased an enormous television and moved her hospital bed and belongings downstairs, so she no longer had to maneuver the stairs, which had become increasingly difficult. An aficionado of elegant cars all her life, she splurged and bought a sleek silver Cadillac, which she merrily drove to the bank.

"That car, of course, was the apple of her eye," recalled Buxton. "She'd lean out the window and wave to me."[15]

With Althea's spirits significantly improved, Buxton returned to Florida and her journalistic pursuits. She continued, however, to fly north periodically to visit Althea, and in the coming years, her ailing friend was never far from her mind. It was in part Buxton's connection to Althea that enabled her to wangle a 1997 meeting with Richard Williams and his fast-rising tennis-playing daughters, Venus and Serena, who lived in Palm Beach, less than an hour's drive from Buxton's Pompano Beach condo. A longtime admirer of Althea's, Williams invited Buxton to come practice and watch his daughters, both of whom considered the ailing tennis champion a model. A lanky six foot, two inches with stunning speed and a commanding serve, the seventeen-year-old Venus had already been compared publicly to Althea more than once. When Buxton spontaneously offered to call her long-ago doubles partner on her mobile phone from the Williamses' court after the girls' session, according to Buxton's account, Richard Williams eagerly agreed.

As soon as Buxton got Althea on the line, she briefly explained the reason for the call and handed the phone to Venus. Clearly nervous, the teenager spoke hesitantly, but soon she and Althea were in rapt conversation that lasted for several minutes. Serena, a year younger and apparently uninterested, or too nervous to talk with Althea, sat at a distance from the court playing with a cat.[16] As Buxton described the conversation in a story she wrote for *Tennis* magazine a few months later, Althea advised Venus, "Play aggressively and with spirit. . . . Since you'll be the underdog, you'll have nothing to lose. The crowds will love you. But most of all, be who you are and let your racquet do the talking."[17]

The young Williams sisters were as intrigued by the tennis trailblazer as she was by them, although they never met in person. In high school,

Serena did a project on Althea and faxed her a list of questions.[18] Two years after the phone conversation between Venus and Althea, the Williams sisters produced a newsletter in connection with Black History Month, and Althea was displayed on the back cover. On at least one occasion, Althea called Zina Garrison before one of Venus's matches with some tips for her to pass along. When Venus won her first Grand Slam singles title, at Wimbledon in 2000, becoming only the third Black woman to do so after Serena won the U.S. Open women's title the previous year, Althea wrote her a congratulatory telegram. "You are now in the history books forever. I gladly pass the torch to you and Serena," she wrote. "I know that you two will carry it well because you and your sister have been prepared for this day by your parents. Congratulations on your magnificent victory. Althea Gibson."[19]

Althea clearly took pleasure in the Williams sisters' ascent, but it was a short-lived emotion. In the nearly four decades that had passed since Althea was crowned the queen of the women's tennis hierarchy, the sport of tennis had changed radically. As lightweight graphite rackets replaced the more cumbersome wooden ones, the game had become steadily faster and more power-driven. At the same time, there was a shift in court surfaces, from the fast grass on which Althea had played to the hard surfaces used at today's U.S. Open and Australian Open, which are somewhat slower. Of far greater impact, the prize money, once nearly nonexistent, soared into the millions during the final years of Althea's life. In 2000, nineteen-year-old Serena Williams won just over $1 million in prize money, while Venus, just over a year older, won more than $2 million.[20] For Althea, who had been unable to win prize money of any substance or profit in any way from the sport of tennis, the sisters' triumph was at once thrilling and deeply embittering. Althea Gibson was not only yesterday's news as far as some fans were concerned, she'd faded into the recycling bin long ago.

Thanks to Buxton's fundraising efforts, Althea had her basic expenses covered, which lifted her out of her suicidal trough. Just a few months after the fundraising campaign began, however, an event that Althea had long dreaded came to pass. On September 13, 1995, Will Darben died, leaving her in a state of grief from which she would never fully recover. Two years older than Althea, Will had struggled with diabetes for the better part of his adult life, and his condition had worsened over the past two years. With his passing, Althea had lost her ex-husband, fellow sports fan, dinner companion, and soul mate. Without him at her side to watch the Wimbledon warm-ups or the next *Perry Mason* episode, Althea would sit alone in front of her television set for the rest of her life. Her depression plunged her ever deeper into a darkness within which only the faintest glimpses of light were visible.

"Sometimes you can slowly die in ways no coroner can ascertain," wrote the *Tampa Bay Times*'s Darrell Fry in a 1998 column entitled "We Didn't Do Enough for Althea." "Doctors say Gibson is severely depressed, but in essence she suffers from a broken spirit brought on by a long bout with life."[21]

At times, she sought solace in a shot or two of gin. Althea had always liked her drink, especially back in the days when Will would whip up a pitcher of his famous frosted martinis for a group of neighbors. Buxton had often marveled at how her doubles partner could indulge in a glass of gin and a few cigarettes on the eve of a major tournament and still come out the victor the next day. By the late 1990s, though, Althea was drinking by herself, and both Gray and Gaither were worried. They had more than a little reason to be. In early 1987, Althea had lost her driver's license due to drunk driving and was required to go through an alcohol education program.[22] Just as concerning, she still had the two guns, a .22 pistol and a .38 revolver in her home, left over from earlier days of shooting practice. Gray periodically hid the weapons in the laundry basket on the second floor of Althea's apartment, just to keep them out of her reach. One day, Althea noticed that the guns were missing.

"Fran, you took my guns out of here," she said irritably to Gray.

"No, I didn't take your guns," Gray responded. "They're still in here."

"I don't believe you," Althea retorted.

"You want to see a gun," Gray responded.

"Yes, go get it," Althea said.[23]

Gray went upstairs and retrieved one of the guns from the laundry basket and brought it downstairs. When the opportunity arose, Gray would hide the guns again, but it wasn't long before Althea began demanding that they be returned to her.

Once Althea had closed the door of her apartment to the outside world, there were few other people permitted inside who might have taken a stand against the guns, or any other matter bearing on her well-being. Althea wouldn't let it happen. At age seventy, she was a shrunken version of her former self. Her skirts hung loosely over her spindly legs, and her hair was streaked with gray. Determined that she be remembered as the towering athletic powerhouse she once was, Althea adamantly refused to allow herself to be seen by other than a select few. The few included Zina Garrison, who dropped in for a visit several times during Althea's final years, usually when she was en route to the U.S. Open, and occasionally Billie Jean King. Althea made them work for it.

"[Zina] and I kept saying, 'We've got to go see Althea. . . . She's got to let us see her,'" King said. "I'd call Fran. 'Fran. Get her to see us.' You know, Zina would do the same. Finally, Althea says, 'You guys can come out to the house.'"[24]

King and Garrison made a final visit to Althea together just weeks before she died. Perched on a sofa in between piles of fashion and golf magazines in Althea's home, Garrison listened raptly as the two veteran tennis players swapped stories of days long past.

"Little things would come up, like how [Althea] couldn't come to the front door and playing with Alice Marble," recalled Garrison. "I was in awe, to be honest, just sitting there listening to those two champs talk."[25]

On the rare occasions that Althea left her home, she generally needed some kind of assistance. Sometimes she consented to being pushed in a wheelchair, when her steps were particularly wobbly. Without it, she needed some form of support. Never a diligent follower of doctor's orders, she nonetheless always took with her the cane she had been advised to use for stability. Althea, however, never allowed the cane to actually touch the ground but simply clasped it to her side, to the amusement of Gray and Gaither.

One day in 2001, as she was heading out of McDonald's, a familiar-looking man with a broad smile approached her and held out his hand. His name was Roger Terry, and he was one of Will Darben's nephews who had grown up going to parties and throwing a football behind the Darbens' home with his "Aunt Althea," as he fondly called her, and Aunt Rosemary.

A lieutenant with the Montclair Police Department at the time, Terry was at once delighted to see her and stunned to see how frail the once vibrant and athletic woman he remembered had become.

"First of all, I didn't recognize her," Terry said. "She looked almost like a homeless person. She looked that bad. Shoddy clothes, a big coat, and she had lost a lot of weight, a lot of weight. And she had a hat pulled over. As I got close, I said, 'Aunt Althea? . . . How are you doing? It's good to see you.'"

The two chatted amiably for a few minutes. As they parted, Terry told her that if she ever needed anything, to call him. "Please, please come on over and have some dinner. I would love you to come have dinner at my house." Terry added, "But I never heard anything from her. It was the last time I saw her."[26]

In her final years, Althea was not only unavailable to many of her old friends and the few surviving family members with whom she had stayed in touch, she was also glaringly absent from almost all of the many events honoring her achievements. When the Intercollegiate Tennis Association launched a Women's Collegiate Tennis Hall of Fame at the College of William & Mary, in Williamsburg, Virginia, in 1995 and named her as one of its first class of entries, Althea was nowhere to be found. Nor was she present when American Express launched a 1999 advertising campaign featuring tennis champion cardholders such as Althea, the Williams sisters, and John McEnroe on New York City billboards and subways, in an effort to appeal to a more diversified audience during the U.S. Open. When she was inducted into the International Scholar-Athlete Hall of Fame at the University of Rhode Island in 2001, Althea was a no-show. And when General Mills honored her by putting her image on millions of boxes of its Wheaties cereal in part of its "Breakfast of Champions" series in 2001, she skipped the Newark ceremony at which the box design was unveiled. Often, Frances Gray appeared in her stead.

On the occasion of the Wheaties ceremony, for example, Gray reassured the press in saying of Althea, "Her health is failing, but she is aware of everything. She's very sharp."[27]

In early 1997, Althea surrendered substantially more control over her affairs. That spring, she granted Gray and Carol Gaither joint power of attorney status, enabling them to handle any and all of her financial matters.

When Althea told her old tennis partner what she had done, Buxton was alarmed, but she could see little alternative. "She had nobody else, and I was too far away," she said. "I did say to Althea, I would take that power of attorney back, if I were you."[28] Others close to Althea, including a couple of Darben family relatives, were similarly concerned. Given Althea's poor health and spotty memory after her first stroke, it seemed she could easily be taken advantage of.

By the start of the next decade, Gaither had become ill with cancer. By then, Gray alone had come to serve not only as Althea's official spokesperson, but as her primary lifeline to the outside world and main source of food and medication. Gray was also still cofounder and executive director of the Althea Gibson Foundation, which was the recipient of some of Althea's later earnings from the American Express and Wheaties campaigns, among others. In 2001, a single fundraising dinner on behalf of the organization reportedly raised more than $100,000 for scholarships and junior development programs.[29]

It was Gray who also ruled on appeals for personal visits to Althea and on the scores of requests for press interviews that rolled in around the time of any induction or ceremony—mostly, she turned them down, as Althea apparently wished her to. Even some principals of the USTA found their attempted overtures to Althea stopped short by Gray. Alan Schwartz, president of the organization starting in 2003 and a longtime board member, said it was well known that "if you wanted to get to [Althea,] you had to do it through Fran Gray. And at this point, Althea was a recluse," But Gray, he added, turned out to be a "roadblock."

Schwartz recalls that David Dinkins, a USTA director at large at the time and former New York City mayor, suggested several times that the board do something for the ailing tennis champion. But when Dinkins approached Gray, said Schwartz, things fell apart. "Something happened between Dinkins and Fran Gray where it got blocked there. I don't remember whether he had come back and said, 'Didn't have a good meeting with Fran Gray.' He would have said it much more diplomatically. But I didn't enjoy the success I'd hoped on that. There's no question that he had brought it up."[30]

Years later, some of the concerns about Gray erupted in a legal dispute over Althea's estate. Although it contained little of value other than the rights to her autobiography, the three women left in control—Gray; Rosemary Darben, Althea's close friend and former sister-in-law; and Althea's younger sister Lillian Chisholm—could not come to an agreement over how the estate should be administered. After a prolonged court battle, in 2017, both Chisholm and Darben were removed as co-administrators and co-executrix, respectively, of Althea's estate, leaving Gray as the sole executrix.[31]

It was Gray whom Althea's upstairs neighbor telephoned in South Carolina on the last Friday of September in 2003 to tell her that Althea was having trouble breathing. Gray, who was visiting relatives in Charleston for a couple of days, caught the first plane home the next morning and drove directly to the East Orange General Hospital where Althea had been rushed the night before. As soon as she entered the intensive care unit, Althea began groping at the oxygen mask strapped to her face and begged Gray to get someone to remove it. But she was really saying something much more.

"She didn't like it, and she kept saying, 'Fran, make them take it off. It stinks. Let what's happening, happen,'" Gray said. "She was fully mentally aware, but she was ready to die. She said it all of the time."

Once Althea calmed down, Gray decided to go to the Wendy's directly across the street from the hospital for some food. When she asked Althea if she wanted something, Althea said, "Yes. Bring me a Frosty," Gray said. As she was returning carrying her dinner and the frozen drink, though, Gray had a change of mind. "I said, *You know what? Why am I taking a Frosty in here to her? She shouldn't have a Frosty, too much sugar,* I'm thinking. So I sat there, and I ate whatever it was and drank the Frosty. Then I went upstairs."

Back in Althea's room, Gray found Althea struggling for breath as one of the doctors again tried to place an oxygen mask on her face. Again, Althea begged him to stop. "She kept saying, 'Fran, make him stop. It stinks.' And it did, because I could smell it. . . . I wasn't sitting too far away from the bed. 'Fran, make him take it off. Make him take it off.' And that's what troubled me. I couldn't stay. It was a bit much for me . . . and I was tired. I said, 'Well, I'm going to go home, Gipper,'" recalled Gray, using a nickname that Althea was called by a few of her friends for reasons that no one seems to remember.[32]

The next morning, shortly after six o'clock, Gray's phone rang. Althea had died just minutes earlier. Her death certificate listed the cause of death as septicemia and septic shock, most likely caused by a chronic urinary tract infection she had battled for some time. The following day, newspapers across the country carried notice of the seventy-six-year-old tennis champion's passing. While every one of those obituaries listed her many historic achievements, in the eyes of some, Althea was still a wild child spawned by the poorest slums. As *The New York Times* put it, "Althea Gibson, the gangly Harlem street urchin who parlayed an asphalt championship in paddle tennis into an unlikely reign as queen of the lawns of Wimbledon and Forest Hills, died Sunday."[33]

There was only one thing that Althea had asked for regarding her funeral, and that was that it be as much like Will Darben's as possible. Unlike with Will, though, Althea's body lay in state at the Newark Museum on the day before her burial. With the exception of a few small details, everything else about her funeral service was exactly as Will's had been. Dressed all in white from her crisp tennis blazer to her tennis shoes, Althea's body was laid in her casket beneath the vaunted arches of the Trinity and St. Philip's Cathedral in Newark, where she and Will had attended services together many a Sunday in years past. By the time the two-hour service began, the attending crowd of family members, friends, news reporters, and numerous tennis celebrities had grown so large that it spilled onto the street outside. Standing near Althea's casket, which was flanked by both the USTA and ATA flags, her old friend David Dinkins noted the universal resonance of her accomplishments.

"A lot of folks stood on the shoulders of Althea Gibson," Dinkins said. "I'm not just talking about Black folks, but many others who were inspired by what she achieved."[34]

Among those in attendance were several Black players who had stood on her shoulders, such as Zina Garrison, Kyle Copeland, Leslie Allen, and Katrina Adams, who served as president of the USTA board from 2015 to 2018 and was the first Black person to occupy the position. Garrison, who grappled with the comparisons the press persistently made between her own career and that of Althea's during her early years in tennis, explained that she had learned in part from Althea herself that she was not a carbon copy at all, but a highly talented player in her own right. "I, for so long, was going to be the next Althea Gibson," Garrison said. "Althea Gibson, thank you for the chance for me to be me."[35]

The other speakers included Newark mayor Sharpe James, FAMU president Dr. Fred Gainous, and the USTA's president, Schwartz. Introduced to Althea when he was fifteen years old by pioneering Black tennis player Reggie Weir, Schwartz says he apologized to Althea for what he considered to be the multiple failings of the USTA. Althea, he began, "once said she was lucky to have tennis. I think she had it backwards. Tennis was lucky to have Althea."[36] The founder and chairman of the Tennis Corporation of America and a longtime USTA board member, Schwartz said later that he regretted that the USTA had not done more to help Althea during the years she was destitute and struggling with poor health. Reflecting on her life, he added, he began to fully realize other things the organization had failed to do for Althea, like admitting her into white tournaments earlier on and increasing the diversity of the sport.

"Maybe it was the easy thing to bring up because it was a mea culpa, too," Schwartz, an honorary pallbearer at her funeral, later said. "I knew my theme. My theme was to apologize, and she had it coming. We had never done it, it was a little late, but it was appropriate to do it out loud in my position as president."[37]

After the service, a procession of cars and stretch limousines, led by a dozen uniformed police officers on motorcycles, slowly traveled the several miles from Newark to the Rosedale Cemetery in Orange, New Jersey, where her ashes were to be buried next to Will. Scores of sidewalk viewers, some aware of the celebrity passing by, others drawn out of their shops and apartments by the sheer spectacle, crowded the route. The couple's shared rectangular granite headstone, fittingly, was within sight of the Darbens' old home on Pleasant Way, where Althea and Will had once entertained and performed duos on the saxophone and piano. Althea's name comes first on the stone, followed by a brief list of the Grand Slam tournaments she won, and accentuated by a small tennis racket to the left. Will's full

name, William Alexander Darben, comes next, followed by the words
"the love of her life."

That headstone, tucked amid a row of similar stones in the New Jersey
suburb, would stand as one of the most meaningful memorials to Althea
Gibson's life for years to come. As it turned out, the neglect and indifference that colored much of her post-tennis life did not end with her death.
Unlike some other high-profile barrier breakers like Joe Louis, Jackie Robinson, and Arthur Ashe, Althea received few official tributes of significant
national magnitude for many decades. Not that there was nothing done in
her name. She was, to be sure, inducted into a great number of sports and
women's halls of fame beginning in the 1980s. There are also a half-dozen
tennis courts and complexes, largely along the East Coast, that bear her
name. There is a bronze statue of her stepping deep into a backhand at the
Branch Brook Park in Newark and a monument dedicated to her in Soverel
Park in East Orange, New Jersey. So, too, she has received recognition
abroad. In 1998, the International Tennis Federation initiated a women's
senior event called the Althea Gibson Cup, for players seventy and over,
for which the USTA donated the winner's trophy. The French were among
the first to dedicate a sizable structure to Althea, when a gymnasium in
Paris's 12th Arrondissement was named "Gymnase Althéa Gibson" for
her in 2016, sixty years after she became the first Black woman to win the
French Championship, as the Grand Slam tournament in Paris was then
called. At the time the Paris Council voted on the project, city councilor
Nicolas Bonnet articulated a poignant truth that few others had been bold
enough to utter. Gibson, he said, "is practically unknown to the general
public and to Parisians."[38]

The truth is that Althea Gibson is not much better known in the
United States than she is on the boulevards of Paris. In some respect, her
anonymity is not exceptional. Many of the greatest record-setting tennis
players in the world, including Americans Don Budge, Maureen Connolly,
and Helen Wills, who won thirty-one Grand Slam titles in the 1920s and
'30s and is considered by some to have been the greatest female player in
history, are virtually unknown to today's tennis fans. It was not until prize
money entered the game with the Open Era in 1968 that achievement on
the tennis court captured the attention of the general public outside rarefied

tennis circles. Like many other superior tennis players, Althea was simply born too early to reap the profits that her tremendous skill and hard work warranted. Unlike those other players, however, she had faced the enormous additional barrier of being a Black woman—which makes her achievements all the more remarkable and, some would argue, worthy of enshrinement.

For Althea, the timing of it all could hardly have been more painful. Just as she was exiting her sport, plum professional contracts worth hundreds of thousands of dollars were being bandied about, dangled just years beyond her reach. In the wake of her retirement Ashe, the Williams sisters, Coco Gauff, and others followed in her footsteps and pocketed millions, while she slipped ever deeper into an impoverished abyss.

On her last visit to the U.S. Open, in the late 1980s, Althea headed to one of the private dining rooms at the tennis center with an old friend, only to find herself brusquely dismissed, according to *Born to Win*. Staffers did not recognize the eleven-time Grand Slam winner whose face had graced most every major magazine cover in the late 1950s; nor did they apparently believe her story. Rejected at the heart of the nation's premier tennis turf, Althea strode out in bitter humiliation. She never returned.[39]

Nor have the executive powers of the USTA treated her much better than its restaurant staff. In the six decades since Althea retired from tennis in order to make a living, the organization has done painfully little to recognize her. On the opening night of the 2007 U.S. Open, fifty years after Althea became the first Black player to win the National Championship, the USTA honored her achievement with a ceremony that included nearly two dozen prominent Black women and first-round matches played on the Arthur Ashe Stadium court by Venus and Serena Williams—both of which they won. Aretha Franklin sang, and veteran sportscaster Dick Enberg paid homage, while New York City mayor Michael Bloomberg and Billie Jean King unveiled a commemorative plaque dedicated to Althea that would be added to a display of dozens of other singles champions at the tennis center's U.S. Open Court of Champions.[40]

And yet, to many, it was far from enough. When it has come to christening the major structures of the nation's dominant tennis complex, Althea's name has almost never even made it onto the long list. When the

USTA named its elaborate new Center Court stadium in Flushing Meadows in 1997, it chose the name of Arthur Ashe, the second Black player to win a Grand Slam, not Althea Gibson, who was the first to do so. When it renamed its national tennis complex in 2006, it chose the name of Billie Jean King, one of the best-known female tennis players in the world, not Althea Gibson. There are those who argue, with some merit, that Ashe and King were not just tremendous tennis players, but also passionate activists who labored tirelessly for social change far beyond the limits of their particular sport. For that reason, the thinking goes, it was appropriate that the national tennis structures be named for them rather than for the far-more-reticent Althea Gibson. What is less often mentioned is the fact that both Ashe and King more than likely had powerful political forces and leaders lobbying behind the scenes on their behalf in both those cases. Althea, a lone wolf throughout her entire career, did not.

At the same time, there have been other structures that might have been named for her. Some have publicly suggested that the Grandstand, the third stadium at the national tennis center, in addition to the Arthur Ashe and Louis Armstrong Stadiums, is the most likely candidate. As *The New York Times* put it in a 2001 column, with two stadiums named for out-of-towners, Ashe and Armstrong, "why not rename the Grandstand for a native daughter whose efforts were heroic and historic: Althea Gibson? Repeat after me—The Gibson Grandstand."[41]

Two years after that column appeared and just over a week before Althea's death, a formal proposal calling for the Grandstand to be named after Althea was put forth by David Oats, the president of the Flushing Meadows–Corona Park World's Fair Association. Oats wrote to USTA president Schwartz that doing so would be "a fitting tribute to this true American hero." Several others, like David Dinkins and tennis champion Pam Shriver, publicly agreed. Two days after Althea died, Schwartz wrote back that he agreed that Althea should indeed receive recognition, "but it may or may not be in naming the Grandstand court after her."[42]

It never happened. Another fifteen years passed after Oats made his proposal, and nothing was done to honor Althea. Dinkins, a USTA director-at-large for over a decade, says he raised the topic behind closed doors time and again, but it went nowhere. Billie Jean King says she personally appealed to the USTA presidents over the course of twenty-five years and asked repeatedly that something of lasting significance be done for Althea. Finally, toward the end of 2017, King made a personal appeal before the entire board on behalf of Althea. Within the hour, the board, then under the leadership of Katrina Adams, voted unanimously to take some kind of action to recognize Althea Gibson. Never mind that some USTA officials and news stories later publicizing the board's decision, unfailingly described Althea as "the Jackie Robinson of tennis," the hackneyed cliché that had dogged her throughout her entire tennis career and which she wholeheartedly detested. Reporters and tennis big wheels had repeated the irritating platitude for so long that it might have been jarring if they had called her something more accurate or original.

What the board ultimately approved was not, however, a tennis complex or a stadium. It was to be a statue of Althea that would be positioned in the shadow of the Arthur Ashe Stadium, deep within the Billie Jean King National Tennis Center, in Queens, New York. The statue, unveiled in the summer of 2019, is composed of five granite blocks, from the loftiest of which Althea's face and left shoulder emerge. As sculptor Eric Goulder conceived of the structure, it is the face at the threshold of imminent life-altering change. It is the youthful face of a twenty-three-year-old Althea, minutes away from becoming the first Black person to step onto the tennis court to compete against a white player in a Grand Slam tournament, a deep breath away from planting an irreversible foothold on turf that had forever been denied to people of color. The man high in the stands who shouts a racial slur at Althea during the match knows that she is but a step away from changing forever the national order of things.

Althea's expression is inscrutable, neither smiling nor frowning. She is looking directly into her own future as it is about to unfold before her. It is almost as though she is wondering if the short-lived glory that lies ahead will be worth all the pain and humiliation that follows. But Big Al doesn't let fear stop her, not ever. She steps calmly onto the court and raises her racket in readiness.

Acknowledgments

For someone often described as a temperamental loner, Althea Gibson had an awful lot of friends. There are an even larger number of people who were touched or inspired in some way by her often difficult journey. This book would not have come about without the patience and ongoing support of a great many of them.

When I started out on this project in 2018, I headed directly to Althea's closest friends, Rosemary Darben and Angela Buxton. Rosemary, or "Ro" as she was called, was a fellow tennis player on the Black ATA circuit and the sister of the man who would eventually become Althea's first husband. Angela, a British player who had experienced discrimination since childhood due to her Jewish faith, was Althea's doubles partner and lifelong friend. I spent days with each of them and returned periodically with ever more questions. Ro, whose family home in Montclair, New Jersey, became Althea's own home for much of the 1950s, pulled up a virtual chair for me at the family dinner table where Althea had delighted in new foods and family rituals. It was Ro who regularly counseled a self-protective Althea to be kinder to the eager reporters on her trail and helped to divert her from abandoning tennis mid-career in order to enlist in the Women's Army Corps. Angela, whose London flat Althea shared during all but the first of her Wimbledon appearances, took me on a tour of their favorite spots in her native city and spent days with me in her Pompano Beach condo and in New York regaling me with stories about their adventures together as well as the colorful personalities on the women's tennis circuit.

Fran Gray, a friend who fulfilled many roles in Althea's life, took longer to win over, but in the end she signed on with enthusiasm. It was due to her efforts and those of her grandniece Michelle Curry that Althea's personal papers were preserved in a pair of storage units in New Jersey. Those papers included letters from Althea's two husbands and several friends, numerous personal documents, as well as records of her business undertakings in her post-tennis years, none of which had been made public before. Gray, who coauthored Althea's authorized biography, *Born to Win*, shared not only the painful details of Althea's final years but those of the final hours shortly before she died. It was Curry who later unlocked the storage unit in Trenton, New Jersey, for me that was packed to the roof with Althea's suitcases, tennis rackets, boxes full of papers, and her treasured pair of guns. Over the course of a few days Curry also shared with me dozens more of Althea's letters that years earlier she had tossed in a plastic bag in her basement in hopes of keeping the mice at bay. Together, those materials provide a unique window on the life of this very private, at times seemingly aloof woman.

I am very grateful to both Curry and Don Felder, Althea's cousin, who helped me sort through the materials in Curry's basement. Felder, a close cultivator of family history, not only provided me with numerous additional documents but over the years has shared many thoughtful observations about family personalities and relationships. Thanks to Felder who led me up the narrow stairs to the Gibsons' 143rd Street apartment in Harlem, I was able to look down on the long-ago play street where paddle sports all began for Althea.

The two people most instrumental in Althea's accomplishments were a pair of doctors who alternately took her into their homes for three years and honed both her tennis and social skills. Their names were Dr. Hubert A. Eaton of Wilmington, North Carolina, and Dr. Robert "Whirlwind" Johnson, of Lynchburg, Virginia, known among his pupils as "Dr. J." While both of them have passed away, many of their children and students contributed generously to this book. I am very grateful to Bobby Johnson III, Lange Johnson, Carolyn "Waltee" Johnson Moore, Geraldine Bennett Wood, Elmer Reid Jr., Helen Mundy Witt, Frank Bondurant, and the late Ethel Reid

Miller. One of the highlights of my reporting was standing on Dr. J's old tennis court in Lynchburg and listening to his former student, Elmer Reid Jr., belt out the song that Dr. J's students composed and often sang in the back seat of his commanding green Buick when heading to a tournament. The song, based on the spiritual "Good News! (Chariot's A-Comin')," goes like this: "Good news, Whirlwind's comin', / Good news, Whirlwind's comin', / Good news, we're gonna take all the trophies home!" And indeed they did.

On the Wilmington front, I am grateful to Hubert Eaton Jr., Lendward Simpson, and the exceptionally helpful staff at the University of North Carolina–Wilmington, Randall Library Special Collections.

The highlights of Althea's tennis career occurred at the twin tennis meccas of the All England Lawn Tennis Club (AELTC), better known as Wimbledon, and the West Side Tennis Club in Forest Hills, New York, where what is now called the U.S. Open was held for many years. My huge thanks to Robert McNicol, Wimbledon librarian and keeper of the enormous green books of British newspaper clippings that occupy the library's lower level, who assisted me on multiple fronts. Thanks also to Beatrice Hunt, West Side archivist and longtime club member who also went out of her way repeatedly to find documents and contacts for me. I am indebted to the many tennis players who competed with and against Althea at those venues who took time to meet or speak with me, including Jenny Staley Hoad, Christine Truman Janes, Ann Haydon Jones, Neale Fraser, John Barrett, Janet Hopps Adkisson, Shirley Bloomer Brasher, and the late Daphne Seeney Fancutt and Gordon Forbes.

Others to whom I am deeply grateful include Katrina Adams, Bob Davis, Bob Perry, Kristin Short, Karol Fageros's daughter, Zina Garrison, Leslie Allen, Harold "Sunny" Billie, Elgin Klugh, Don Gobbie, Warren F. Kimball, Gary Cogar, Herb Boyd, Jennifer H. Lansbury, Marvin Dent, and Sam Penceal. More than a few who contributed significantly to this book have passed away, among them David Dinkins, Billy Davis, and Bob Ryland. I was greatly assisted by the staff at the Clarendon County Archives and History Center in Manning, South Carolina; the International Tennis Hall of Fame; the New York Public Library's Schomburg Center for Research in Black Culture; the American Tennis Association; the City of East Orange, New Jersey; the Women's Tennis Association; the Ladies Professional Golf Association; the Black Tennis Hall of Fame; and the United States Tennis Association.

I am singularly appreciative to international tennis historian Richard A. Hillway. Richard is, among many other things, the coauthor of the seminal *The Birth of Lawn Tennis: From the Origin of the Game to the First Championship at Wimbledon,* author of over one hundred tennis articles, and the founder of the Colorado Tennis Hall of Fame. But perhaps one of his most honorable titles was bestowed upon him by Arthur A. Carrington Jr., a former player and ace Black tennis historian, who crowned him "the tennis cat." What he means is that Hillway, unlike most historians of the sport, is an expert in both white *and* Black tennis. From the day I met him on a hot summer afternoon in the Wimbledon library basement, Hillway was of incomparable and steady assistance on multiple fronts. Thank you, Richard!

I would like to acknowledge several publications and histories that were instrumental in my understanding of Althea and the period in which she played. First is Althea's biography, *Born to Win,* written by Frances Clayton Gray and Yanick Rice Lamb; followed by *The Match: Althea Gibson and a Portrait of a Friendship,* by Bruce Schoenfeld, the story of Althea and Angela Buxton's unlikely friendship; and *Whirlwind: The Godfather of Black Tennis,* a biography of Dr. Robert Walter Johnson by Doug Smith. I am particularly indebted to the digital history *Breaking the Barriers: The ATA and Black Tennis Pioneers,* originally created by the International Tennis Hall of Fame, as well as Art Carrington's invaluable history, *Black Tennis: An Archival Collection, 1890–1962.* Both of those histories introduced me to the many talented and colorful personalities in Black tennis and the challenging period in American history during which they evolved. I am also very appreciative of the work of Ashley Nicole Brown, whose dissertation, *The Match of her Life: Althea Gibson, Icon and Instrument of Integration,* and other academic works present a thoughtful and detailed examination of Althea and the period in which she rose.

Last but definitely not least, I want to applaud my personal team. I bow first and foremost to Debbie Bloom, archivist and researcher extraordinaire of the Dead Librarian LLC, who stuck with me from the musty Clarendon County deed books where research on this book began to the interminable endnotes at its conclusion. Debbie is the kind of researcher that every author might wish for, an investigator who goes far beyond the call of duty and who many times over knew what I was looking for before I knew myself.

I am deeply indebted to my assistants Flaviana Sandoval, who hung in remotely throughout despite relocation to Colombia, South America, and Jonathan Chang for their hard work and perseverance. A monumental thank-you to my partner Ray Levy, tennis devotee and player extraordinaire who nearly seven decades ago watched Althea on the court at the Forest Hills club in New York and gave me the idea for this book. These pages were immeasurably improved by the readings of my wonderful friends, writers Larry Tye, Eileen McNamara, and Sarah Wesson. I am saddened beyond measure that my extraordinary and inspiring agent Jill Kneerim, who passed away in the spring of 2022, is not alive to see this project come to its conclusion. Finally, a stand-alone thank-you to Michael Flamini, my very wonderful editor at St. Martin's Press who had the vision to see what my idea could become and who heard me throughout. I am also very appreciative of the unfailing efforts of Hannah Phillips, Claire Cheek, and the entire team at St. Martin's.

As I approached the end of my in-person research for this book in early 2020, the COVID-19 virus emerged and began its deadly creep around the world. As someone particularly susceptible to the disease, I withdrew to the third-floor office in my home outside of Boston and got to work writing. Over the course of the next two years both of my children, Streett and Shi Shi, and our yoga-loving dog, Noah, along with my incredible circle of friends, supported me and listened to my numerous tales of the peaks and valleys that occurred along the way. I thank you all deeply for sharing with me what has been a fascinating and illuminating journey with Althea.

Interviews

All interviews were conducted with the author unless stated otherwise.

Aaron, Roxanne. September 20, 2020.

Adams, Katrina. June 20, 2018.

Adkisson, Janet Hopps. June 14, 2019; August 27, 2019; January 30, 2021.

Alexander, Lucille. April 18, 2020, interview by Aurelia Alexander.

Allen, Leslie. July 8, 2021.

Barnes, Althemese. October 25, 2019.

Barrett, John. July 2, 2019.

Berryman, Joseph. March 4, 2020.

Bertrand McFadden, Evelyn. April 14, 2019.

Billie, Sunny. April 7, 2019.

Bloomer-Brasher, Shirley. Interview by her daughter, Kate Sabisky, February 8, 2020.

Bloss, Margaret Varner. November 19, 2019.

Bondurant, Frank. September 10, 2019.

Buxton, Angela. December 6, 2018; February 19, 2019; February 20, 2019; July 15, 2019; January 21, 2020; August 25, 2021.

Carrington, Arthur A. Jr. August 10, 2018.

Chalmers, Alan. July 17, 2021.

Chapman, Hugh. July 23, 2020.

Cheatham, Mark. January 12, 2021.

Coleman, Leonard. March 29, 2021.

Curry, Michelle. April 19, 2021.

Curtis, Richard. February 12, 2020.

Darben, Rosemary. January 4, 2019; July 18, 2020.

Davis, Bob. February 18, 2019, August 6, 2019; April 11, 2021.

Davis, Sheila Meek. October 18, 2019.

Davis, Wilbert. January 17, 2019.

Davis, Zack. June 4, 2019.

Dent, Marvin. February 20, 2020; March 30, 2020.

Dinkins, David. June 19, 2018.

Eaton, Hubert Jr. August 21, 2018; April 7, 2020.

Ehret, Gloria. March 15, 2021.

Elam, Sallie. June 26, 2018.

Evans, Richard. July 4, 2019.

Fein, Paul. July 27, 2021.

Felder, Don. April 26, May 17, July 30, 2019, September 8, 2020, April 16, 2021.

Fitzmartin, Raymond. April 18, 2019.

Forbes, Gordon. July 4, 2019.

Ford, Clinita A. December 5, 2019.

Fraser, Neale. July 4, 2019.

Garrison, Zina. July 7, 2021.

Giangrande, Michael. February 18, 2022.

Giberga, Jane Sughrue. April 25, 2019.

Gobbie, Donn. April 15, 2021.

Godwin, John L. April 3, 2020.

Goulder, Eric. August 5, 2121.

Gray, Frances C. April 17, 2017, March 4, 2019.

Grundy, Pamela. January 10, 2020.

Hare, Julianne. November 14, 2019.

Harper, Rose. March 15, 2021.

Hartley, Brodes Jr. (Col.). October 9, 2019.

Haydon-Jones, Ann. July 4, 2019.

Heldman, Julie. July 13, 2020.

Hillway, Richard A. July 4, 2019, July 12, 2020.

Hine, William. December 15, 2019.

Hoad, Jennifer Staley. February 22, 2019.

Howell, Ron. June 14, 2019.

Hunt, Beatrice. April 18, 2019.

Hurt, Patricia. January 18, 2022.

Huss, Sally Moore. December 6, 2019.

Hutcherson, Carl Jr. February 25, 2020.

Jackson, Eddie. December 16, 2019.

Jackson, O'Neal Jr. "Bossman". October 24, 2019.

James, Agnes Washington. April 26, 2019.

Janes, Christine Truman. July 5, 2019.

Johnson, Audrey McFadden. January 24, 2019.

Johnson, Lange. June 26, 2018.

Johnson, Robert III. August 15, 2018, September 15, 2018.

Jones, Sam. January 2, 2020.

Jordan, Denise. July 29, 2021.

Kanzler, George. April 13, 2021.

Kennedy, Henry. September 11, 2018.

Kennedy, Terri. September 19, 2019.

Kimball, Warren. February 17, 2020.

King, Billie Jean. August 19, 2019.

Klugh, Elgin. April 27, 2021.

Kremer, Gary R. August 11, 2020.

Kukla, Barbara. March 24, 2021.

Lacy, Tim. April 30, 2021.

Lansbury, Jennifer H. January 27, 2020, February 5, 2021.

Laurant, Darrell. March 4, 2020.

Ledes, Christine Schott. December 15, 2019.

Lewis, Victoria. March 23, 2021.

Mannings, Eva. September 25, 2019.

Martin, Edwina. September 15, 2019.

McElveen, Elizabeth Swilley. October 1, 2019, June 6, 2020.

Miller, Ethel Reid. Feb 13, 2020.

Mitchell, Tommy. October 22, 2019.

Moore, Carolyn "Waltee" Johnson. January 3, 2020.

Mosley, Charles. December 20, 2019.

Penceal, Sam. June 15, 2018, August 26, 2019.

Perry, Robert. January 11, 2019, October 4, 2019.

Pinn, Vivian. March 8, 2020.

Powell, Renee. February 28, 2021.

Reid, Elmer. January 17, 2020.

Russell, Nina Melodi. September 9, 2019.

Ryland, Robert. May 16, 2019.

Schleicher, Barret. April 18, 2019.

Schwartz, Alan. July 27, 2021.

Seeney-Fancutt, Daphne. February 26, 2019

Seixas, Vic. June 17, 2019.

Short, Dale. May 30, 2020.

Simpson, Lendward. August 20, 2018.

Smith, Doug. August 10, 2019.

Smith, Eva Clack. October 12, 2019.

Smith, Robert. July 21, 2020.

Speller, Islah. September 6, 2020.

Spencer-Hester, Shaun. January 15, 2020.

Spork, Shirley G. March 12, 2021.

Sykes-Kennedy, Janie. September 26, 2019.

Terry, Roger. January 8, 2019, March 29, 2021.

Terry, Sandra. June 24, 2020.

Thomas, Damion. September 30, 2021.

Todd, Bertha. August 21, 2018.

Tookes, Darryl. September 12, 2019.

Tribble, Ralph Jr. August 28, 2019.

Tyson, Timothy. April 30, 2020.

Vossler, Marlene Hagge. March 22, 2021.

Washington, Eleanor Clark. April 11, 2019.

White, Charles "Trickshot." November 6, 2019.

White, Victor L. April 2, 2021.

Whitworth, Kathy. March 19, 2021, March 21, 2021.

Williams, Reggie, Jan. 18, 2020.

Witt, Helen Mundy. Interview by Jocelyn Grzeszczak. May 13, 2019.

Wood, Geraldine Bennett. January 13, 2020.

Wyatt, James (Col.). December 23, 2019.

Selected Bibliography

Anderson, Daniel. *The Culture of Sports in the Harlem Renaissance.* Jefferson, NC: McFarland & Company, 2017.

Arsenault, Raymond. *Arthur Ashe: A Life.* New York: Simon & Schuster Paperbacks, 2019.

Ashe, Arthur Jr. *A Hard Road to Glory: A History of the African-American Athlete, 1919–1945.* New York: Warner Books, 1988.

———. *A Hard Road to Glory: A History of the African-American Athlete since 1946.* New York: Amistad Press, 1993.

———. *A Hard Road to Glory: The African-American Athlete in Basketball.* New York: Amistad Press, 1993.

Ashe, Arthur Jr., and Arnold Rampersad. *Days of Grace: A Memoir.* New York: Ballantine Books, 1993.

Barnes, Althemese, and Ann Roberts. *Tallahassee Florida.* Black America Series. Charleston, SC: Arcadia Publishing, 2000.

Barrett, John. *Wimbledon: The Official History.* 4th ed. London: Vision Sports Publishing, 2014.

Bellamy, Rex. *Game, Set, and Deadline: A Tennis Odyssey.* London: Kingswood Press, 1986.

Black Champions. Interviews with Althea Gibson and Sydney Llewellyn, October 21, 1984, William Miles Collection, Washington University Libraries, Department of Special Collections.

Blue, Adrianne. *Grace Under Pressure: The Emergence of Women in Sport.* London: Sidgwick & Jackson, 1987.

Bowles, Jerry G. *A Thousand Sundays: The Story of the Ed Sullivan Show.* New York: G.P. Putnam's Sons, 1980.

Boyd, Herb, and Ray Robinson. *Pound for Pound: A Biography of Sugar Ray Robinson.* New York: Amistad, 2006.

Boyd, Herb, ed. *The Harlem Reader.* New York: Three Rivers Press, 2003.

Brandt, Nat. *Harlem at War: The Black Experience in WWII.* Syracuse, NY: The John Ben Snow Foundation, 1997.

Breaking the Barriers: The ATA and Black Tennis Pioneers. International Tennis Hall of Fame and Museum, 2020. https://breakingbarriers.tennisfame.com.

Brown, Ashley. "Swinging for the State Department: American Women Tennis Players in Diplomatic Goodwill Tours, 1941–59." *Journal of Sport History* 42, no. 3 (2015). https://doi.org/10.5406/jsporthistory.42.3.0289.

———. "'Uncomplimentary Things': Tennis Player Althea Gibson, Sexism, Homophobia, and Anti-Queerness in the Black Media." *Journal of African American History* 106, no. 2 (2021): 249–77. https://doi.org/10.1086/713677.

Brown, Ashley Nicole. "The Match of Her Life: Althea Gibson, Icon and Instrument of Integration." PhD diss., George Washington University, 2017.

Brown, Claude. *Manchild in the Promised Land.* New York: Macmillan Company, 1965.

Caldwell, Dale G., and Nancy Gill McShea. *Tennis in New York: The History of the Most Influential Sport in the Most Influential City in the World.* Mamaroneck, NY: Intelligent Influence Publishing Group, 2011.

Caro, Robert A. *The Power Broker: Robert Moses and the Fall of New York.* New York: Vintage Books, 1974.

Carrington, Arthur A. *Black Tennis: An Archival Collection, 1890–1962.* Amherst, MA: Arthur Carrington, 2009.

Clark, Sylvia H. *Shadows of the Past: An Illustrated History of Clarendon County, SC.* Virginia Beach: Donning Co. Publishers, 2005.

Cohen, Shari. "The Lasting Legacy of *An American Dilemma.*" Carnegie Results (Fall 2004): 1–26. https://www.carnegie.org/publications/lasting-legacy-american-dilemma/.

Collins, Bud, and Anita Ruthling Klaussen. *The Bud Collins History of Tennis: An Authoritative Encyclopedia and Record Book.* 3rd ed. Washington, DC: New Chapter Press, 2016.

Connolly, Maureen, and Tom Gwynne. *Forehand Drive.* London: Macgibbon & Kee, 1957.

Danzig, Allison, and Peter Schwed. *The Fireside Book of Tennis.* New York: Simon & Schuster, 1972.

Dawkins, Marvin P. "Race Relations and the Sport of Golf: The African American Golf Legacy." *Western Journal of Black History* 28, no. 1 (2004): 327–31.

Dawkins, Marvin P., and Graham Charles Kinloch. *African American Golfers During the Jim Crow Era.* Westport, CT: Praeger, 2000.

De Laine, Marguirite, F. S. Corbett, and Cecil J. Williams. *Clarendon County.* Images of America Series. Charleston, SC: Arcadia Publishing, 2002.

D'Emilio, John, and Estelle B. Freedman. *Intimate Matters: A History of Sexuality in America.* 2nd ed. Chicago, IL: University of Chicago Press, 1998.

Du Bois, William E. B. *The Souls of Black Folks.* Print on demand, CreateSpace, 2013.

Dudziak, Mary L. *Cold War Civil Rights: Race and the Image of American Democracy.* Princeton, NJ: Princeton University Press, 2002.

Eaton, Hubert A. *Every Man Should Try.* Wilmington, NC: Bonaparte Press, 1984.

Edgar, Walter B. *South Carolina: A History.* Columbia: University of South Carolina Press, 1998.

Evans, Richard. *The Roving Eye: A Reporter's Love Affair with Paris, Politics and Sport*. New York: Clink Street Publishing, 2017.

Everitt, Robert T., and Richard A. Hillway. *The Birth of Lawn Tennis: From the Origins of the Game to the First Championship at Wimbledon*. Surrey: Vision Sports Publishing, 2018.

Eyman, Scott. *Print the Legend: The Life and Times of John Ford*. New York: Simon & Schuster, 2015.

Federal Writers Project. *The WPA Guide to New York City: The Federal Writers Project Guide to 1930s New York; a Comprehensive Guide to the Five Boroughs of the Metropolis Manhattan, Brooklyn, the Bronx, Queens, and Richmond*. New York: New Press, 1992.

Festle, Mary Jo. "Jackie Robinson Without the Charm: The Challenges of Being Althea Gibson." In *Out of the Shadows: A Biographical History of African American Athletes*, edited by David Kenneth Wiggins, 187–205. Fayetteville: University of Arkansas Press, 2006.

———. *Playing Nice: Politics and Apologies in Women's Sports*. New York: Columbia University Press, 1996.

Fisher, Rudolph. *The Walls of Jericho*. Ann Arbor: University of Michigan Press, 2010.

Fitzgerald, Ed. *A Nickel an Inch: A Memoir*. New York: Atheneum, 1985.

Forstall, Richard L. *Population of States and Counties of the United States: 1790 to 1990: From the Twenty-One Decennial Censuses*. Population Division, Bureau of the Census, U.S. Department of Commerce, Washington, DC, 1996.

Garrison, Zina, and Doug Smith. *Zina: My Life in Women's Tennis*. Berkeley, CA: Frog, 2001.

Gaster, Sanford. "Historical Changes in Children's Access to U.S. Cities: A Critical Review." *Children's Environments* 9, no. 2 (April 1992): 23–36.

Gates, Henry Louis Jr., and Evelyn Brooks Higginbotham. *African American National Biography*. Oxford, UK: Oxford University Press, 2013.

Gibson, Althea. *I Always Wanted to Be Somebody*. Edited by Ed Fitzgerald. New York: Harper & Row Publishers, 1958.

Gibson, Althea, and Richard Curtis. *So Much to Live For*. New York: Putnam, 1968.

Gobbie, Donn Thomas. "Gladys Heldman and the Original Nine: The Visionaries Who Pioneered the Women's Professional Tennis Circuit," 2015. https://docs.lib.purdue.edu/cgi/viewcontent.cgi?article=2629&context=open_access_dissertations.

Godwin, John L. *Black Wilmington and the North Carolina Way: Portrait of a Community in the Era of Civil Rights Protest*. Lanham, MD: University Press of America, 2000.

Gray, Frances Clayton, and Yanick Rice Lamb. *Born to Win: The Authorized Biography of Althea Gibson*. Hoboken, NJ: John Wiley and Sons, 2004.

Green, Ben. *Spinning the Globe: The Rise, Fall, and Return to Greatness of the Harlem Globetrotters*. New York: Amistad, 2006.

Greenberg, Cheryl Lynn. *"Or Does It Explode?": Black Harlem in the Great Depression*. New York: Oxford University Press, 1997.

Greenfield, Josh. "Althea Against the World." In *Sport, Sport, Sport; True Stories of Athletes and Great Human Beings*, ed. John L. Pratt, 63–74. New York: Franklin Watts, 1960.

Grundy, Pamela. "Ora Washington: The First Black Female Athletic Star." In *Out of the*

Shadows: A Biographical History of African American Athletes, edited by David Kenneth Wiggins, 90–91. Fayetteville: University of Arkansas Press, 2006.

Hare, Julianne. *Tallahassee: A Capital City History*. The Making of America Series. Charleston, SC: Arcadia Publishing, 2002.

Harris, Cecil, and Larryette Kyle-DeBose. *Charging the Net: A History of Blacks in Tennis from Althea Gibson and Arthur Ashe to the Williams Sisters*. Chicago, IL: Ivan R. Dee, 2007.

Heldman, Julie. *Driven: A Daughter's Odyssey*. Julie Heldman, 2018.

Hillway, Richard A. *The Origins & Formative Years of Lawn Tennis: The Historian's Essential Guide*. Belston, UK: John Price, 2021.

Hobbs, Tameka Bradley. *Democracy Abroad, Lynching at Home: Racial Violence in Florida*. Gainesville: University Press of Florida, 2016.

Holland, Antonio Frederick. *The Soldiers' Dream Continued: A Pictorial History of Lincoln University of Missouri*. Jefferson City, MO: Lincoln University, 1991.

Howell, Ron. *Boss of Black Brooklyn: The Life and Times of Bertram L. Baker*. New York: Empire State Editions, 2019.

Jones, Ann. *A Game to Love*. London: S. Paul, 1971.

Kimball, Warren F. *The United States Tennis Association: Raising the Game*. Lincoln: University of Nebraska Press, 2017.

King, Billie Jean. *All In: An Autobiography*. New York: Alfred A. Knopf, 2021.

Kluger, Richard. *Simple Justice: The History of* Brown v. Board of Education *and Black America's Struggle for Equality*. New York: Alfred A. Knopf, 2004.

Lanker, Brian. *I Dream a World: Portraits of Black Women Who Changed America*. New York: Stewart, Tabori and Chang, 1999.

Lansbury, Jennifer H. *A Spectacular Leap: Black Women Athletes in Twentieth-Century America*. Fayetteville: University of Arkansas Press, 2014.

Laurant, Darrell. *Inspiration Street: Two City Blocks That Helped Change America*. Lynchburg, VA: Blackwell Press, 2016.

Laville, Helen, and Scott Lucas. "The American Way: Edith Sampson, the NAACP, and African American Identity in the Cold War." *Diplomatic History* 20, no. 4 (1996). https://doi.org/10.1111/j.1467-7709.1996.tb00287.x.

Lawson, R. Alan, and Mark T. Williams. *Longwood Covered Courts and the Rise of American Tennis*. Boston, MA: Longwood Covered Courts, 2013.

Lovejoy, Owen. *The Negro Children of New York*. New York: Children's Aid Society, 1932.

Lovett, Bobby L. *America's Historically Black Colleges and Universities: A Narrative History from the Nineteenth Century into the Twenty-First Century*. Macon, GA: Mercer University Press, 2018.

Major, Clarence, ed. *Juba to Jive: Dictionary of Afro-American Slang*. New York: Penguin Books, 1994.

Marble, Alice, and Dale Leatherman. *Courting Danger: My Adventures in World-Class Tennis, Golden-Age Hollywood, and High-Stakes Spying*. New York: St. Martin's Press, 1991.

Marshall, Albert P. *Soldiers' Dream: A Centennial History of Lincoln University of Missouri*.

Lincoln University Book Collection. Jefferson City, MO: Lincoln University, 1966. https://bluetigercommons.lincolnu.edu/lu_history_book/2/.

McDaniel, Pete. *Uneven Lies: The Heroic Story of African-Americans in Golf.* Greenwich, CT: American Golfer, 2000.

McPhee, John. *Levels of the Game.* New York: Farrar, Straus and Giroux, 1969.

Miller, Michael S. "Activism in the Harlem Renaissance." *Gay and Lesbian Review,* 2008. https://glreview.org/article/article-701/.

Minton, Robert. *Forest Hills: An Illustrated History.* Philadelphia, PA: Lippincott, 1975.

Moody, Anne. *Coming of Age in Mississippi: The Classic Autobiography of Growing Up Poor and Black in the Rural South.* New York: Bantam Doubleday Dell Publishers, 1976.

Mortimer, Angela. *My Waiting Game.* London: F. Muller, 1962.

Mulloy, Gardnar P. *As It Was: Reminiscences from a Man for All Seasons.* Flexigroup, 2009.

Nachman, Gerald. *Right Here on Our Stage Tonight!: Ed Sullivan's America.* Berkeley: University of California Press, 2009.

Complete Report of Mayor La Guardia's Commission on the Harlem Riot of March 19, 1935. New York: Arno Press, 1969.

Neyland, Leedell W., and John W. Riley. *Florida Agricultural and Mechanical University: A Centennial History (1887–1987).* FAMU Digital Resource Center. Tallahassee: Florida A&M University Foundation, 1987. http://purl.flvc.org/famu/fd/AMDT3319211.

Osgood, Kenneth Alan. *Total Cold War: Eisenhower's Secret Propaganda Battle at Home and Abroad.* Lawrence: University Press of Kansas, 2006.

Osofsky, Gilbert. *Harlem, the Making of a Ghetto: Negro New York, 1890–1930.* Chicago, IL: Ivan R. Dee, 1996.

Parks, Arnold G. *Lincoln University, 1920–1970.* Charleston, SC: Arcadia Publishing, 2007.

Powe, Oswald George, and Afro–West Indian Union. *Don't Blame the Blacks.* Nottingham, UK: O. G. Powe, 1956.

Rabby, Glenda Alice. *The Pain and the Promise: The Struggle for Civil Rights in Tallahassee, Florida.* Athens: University of Georgia Press, 2016.

Rhoden, William C. *$40 Million Slaves: The Rise, Fall, and Redemption of the Black Athlete.* New York: Three Rivers Press, 2006.

Riess, Steven A. *City Games: The Evolution of American Urban Society and the Rise of Sports.* Urbana: University of Illinois Press, 1989.

Roberts, George W. *The Population of Jamaica.* Cambridge, UK: Cambridge University Press, 2013.

Robeson, Paul. *Here I Stand.* Boston, MA: Beacon Press, 1988.

Rose, Chanelle N. "Tourism and the Hispanicization of Race in Jim Crow Miami, 1945–1965." *Journal of Social History* 45, no. 3 (April 2012): 735–56. https://doi.org/10.1093/jsh/shr087.

Schoenfeld, Bruce. *The Match: Althea Gibson and Angela Buxton.* New York: Amistad, 2005.

Schwarz, A. B. Christa. *Gay Voices of the Harlem Renaissance.* Bloomington: Indiana University Press, 2003.

Schwenck, Melinda M. "Negro Stars and the USIA's Portrait of Democracy." *Race, Gender and Class* 8, no. 4 (2001): 116–39.

Sinnette, Calvin H. *Forbidden Fairways: African Americans and the Game of Golf.* Chelsea, MI: Sleeping Bear Press, 1998.

Smith, Doug. *Whirlwind: The Godfather of Black Tennis: The Life and Times of Dr. Robert Walter Johnson.* Washington, DC: Blue Eagle, 2004.

Snyder, Alvin A. *Warriors of Disinformation: American Propaganda, Soviet Lies, and the Winning of the Cold War: An Insider's Account.* New York: Arcade Publishers, 1995.

Thomas, Damion L. *Globetrotting: African American Athletes and Cold War Politics.* Urbana: University of Illinois Press, 2017.

Tinling, Teddy, and Rod Humphries. *Love and Faults: Personalities Who Have Changed the History of Tennis in My Lifetime.* New York: Crown, 1979.

Todd, Bertha Boykin. *My Restless Journey.* Ed. Rhonda Bellamy. Wilmington, NC: The Ageless Foundation, 2010.

Tolnay, Stewart Emory, and E. M. Beck. *A Festival of Violence: An Analysis of Southern Lynchings, 1882–1930.* Urbana: University of Illinois Press, 1995.

Trinkley, Michael, Nicole Southerland, and Sarah Fick. *Reconnaissance Cultural Resources Survey of Cantey Bay Plantation, Clarendon County, South Carolina.* Columbia, SC: Chicora Foundation, 2008.

Van Vechten, Carl. *Nigger Heaven.* Chicago: University of Illinois Press, 2000.

Verbrugge, Martha H. *Active Bodies: A History of Women's Physical Education in Twentieth-Century America.* New York: Oxford University Press, 2017.

Warner, Lee H. *Free Men in an Age of Servitude: Three Generations of a Black Family.* Lexington: University Press of Kentucky, 1992.

Watson, Steven. *The Harlem Renaissance: Hub of African-American Culture, 1920–1930.* New York: Pantheon Books, 1996.

Weintraub, Robert. *The Divine Miss Marble: A Life of Tennis, Fame, and Mystery.* New York: Dutton, 2021.

Wiggins, David Kenneth, ed. *Out of the Shadows: A Biographical History of African American Athletes.* Fayetteville: University of Arkansas Press, 2006.

Wilkerson, Isabel. *Caste: The Origins of Our Discontents.* New York: Random House, 2020.

———. *The Warmth of Other Suns: The Epic Story of America's Great Migration.* New York: Vintage Books, 2011.

Witt, Helen Mundy. *As Memories Ebb and Flow.* Self-published. Charleston, SC: CreateSpace, 2016.

Wood, Sidney, and David Wood. *The Wimbledon Final That Never Was . . . And Other Tennis Tales from a Bygone Era.* Chicago, IL: New Chapter Press, 2011.

Zhang, Junfu. "Black-White Relations: The American Dilemma." *Perspectives,* February 2000.

Notes

1. The Promised Land

1. Ted Poston, "Althea Gibson," *New York Post Daily Magazine*, Aug. 27, 1957.
2. Ted Poston, "Althea Gibson," *New York Post Daily Magazine*, Aug. 26, 1957.
3. Poston, "Althea Gibson," Aug. 27, 1957
4. Poston, "Althea Gibson," Aug. 26, 1957.
5. Poston, "Althea Gibson," Aug. 27, 1957.
6. Ed Hughes, *Brooklyn Eagle*, July 30, 1940, reprinted in the American Tennis Association's 1941 annual report, 17.
7. Dan Burley, "Budge Praises McDaniel as a Fine Prospect," *New York Amsterdam News*, Aug. 3, 1940.
8. Warren F. Kimball, *The United States Tennis Association: Raising the Game* (Lincoln: University of Nebraska Press, 2017), 122.
9. Althea Gibson, *I Always Wanted to Be Somebody* (New York: Harper & Row, 1958), 29.
10. Gibson, *Somebody*, 32. Several newspaper accounts describing the outcome of the tournament vary, with some saying that Irwin won and others saying that Althea won. Nina Melodi Russell, Irwin's daughter, said in a September 9, 2019, interview that her mother told her that it was a difficult match and that she lost to Althea. In addition, Fred Johnson's May 25, 1963, obituary in the *New York Amsterdam News* says that Althea won the match.
11. Gibson, *Somebody*, 33.
12. Sumter County, SC, probate case file no. 122, pkg. 4, Benjamin Walker, 1849, "South Carolina, U.S., Wills and Probate Records, 1670–1980," image 31–48, Jan. 25, 1849; Tiller's age, U.S. Census 1900, Clarendon County, SC.
13. The year of January's recorded date of birth varies widely. On his death certificate, it is 1848; on his tombstone at the Mount Zero Missionary Baptist Church Cemetery in Manning, South Carolina, it is 1842; and on the Calvary Township, South Carolina, 1900 census, it is 1849. Certificate of Death, State of South Carolina, Clarendon County, File No. 0539.
14. Thelmer Bethune interview with Kisha Turner, Summerton, SC, July 6, 1995, in *Behind the Veil: Documenting African-American Life in the Jim Crow South*, Digital Collection, John

Hope Franklin Research Center, Duke University Libraries, https://repository.duke.edu/dc/behindtheveil/btvct09125.

15. Last will of January Gibson, Jan. 17, 1928, apartment No. 74, package no. 22, State of South Carolina, County of Clarendon. January Gibson's grandson Thelmer Bethune said in a 1995 interview that his grandfather had 465 acres, so, at one time, January's holdings may have been larger than what was reflected in his will.

16. Sylvia H. Clark, *Shadows of the Past: An Illustrated History of Clarendon County, South Carolina* (Virginia Beach: Donning Company Publishers, 2005), 82.

17. Daniel Gibson apparently worked on multiple parcels of land. Althea writes in *Somebody* (3) that her father sharecropped with her uncle. Daniel told reporter Ted Poston that he worked his father-in-law's land, Ted Poston, "Althea Gibson," *New York Post Daily Magazine*, Aug. 26, 1957.

18. Agnes Washington James, in-person interview with author, Apr. 26, 2019.

19. History of the Mount Zero Missionary Baptist Church from the Mount Zero Missionary Baptist Church, Manning, SC; WPA Survey of State and Local Historical Records: 1936, South Carolina Historical Records Survey; Church records from the Black River Association, Clarendon County Archive.

20. Walter B. Edgar, *South Carolina: A History* (Columbia: University of South Carolina Press, 1998), 490.

21. Illiteracy rates come from the 1930 U.S. Census, vol. 3, part 2, table 13, "Composition of the Population by Counties," 789.

22. January Gibson's obituary in the *Palmetto Leader*, Feb. 4, 1928, says he was the father of eight living children at the time of his death, while his headstone states that he had eleven children.

23. "The Colored People of Clarendon at Work," *Manning Times*, July 12, 1905.

24. Clark, *Shadows of the Past*, 173; "Notice," *Manning Times*, Dec. 5, 1906.

25. Clark, *Shadows of the Past*, 149–51. On Althea's cousin signing petition: Thelmer Bethune interview.

26. Frances Clayton Gray and Yanick Rice Lamb, *Born to Win: The Authorized Biography of Althea Gibson* (Hoboken, NJ: John Wiley and Sons, 2004), 2.

27. James A. Burchard, "Althea Gibson's Story—From Harlem to Wimbledon," *New York World Telegram*, June 23, 1956.

28. Edgar, *South Carolina*, 485.

29. Reconnaissance Cultural Resources Survey of Cantey Bay Plantation, Clarendon County, SC, conducted by Chicora Foundation, Columbia, SC, May 26, 2008, 29.

30. Richard Kluger, *Simple Justice: The History of Brown v. Board of Education and Black America's Struggle for Equality* (New York: First Vantage Books Edition, 2004), 4.

31. Sunny Billie, in-person interview with author, Apr. 7, 2019.

32. "New Migration Hits Far South, Families Leaving Storm Belt of Florida and South Carolina," *Baltimore Afro-American*, Nov. 24, 1928.

33. South Carolina Department of Health and Environmental Control, original birth certificate #028999, correction June 29, 1954.

34. Gibson, *Somebody*, 4.

35. Claude Brown, *Manchild in the Promised Land* (New York: Macmillan and Company, 1965), vii.

36. James, in-person interview with author.

37. Gibson, *Somebody*, 5.

2. The Cosmo Club

1. Althea Gibson, *I Wanted to Be Somebody* (New York: Harper & Row, 1958), 29.
2. Gibson, *Somebody*, 10.
3. Gibson, *Somebody*, 10.
4. Gibson, *Somebody*, 9.
5. Angela Buxton, *Althea & Angela*, Figaro Films, Sept. 12, 2013, 6:52.
6. Owen Lovejoy, *The Negro Children of New York* (New York: Children's Aid Society, 1932), 5.
7. Claude Brown, *Manchild in the Promised Land* (New York: Macmillan and Company, 1965), 21.
8. Gibson, *Somebody*, 13; definition of an "ace boon coon" from Clarence Major, *Juba to Jive: A Dictionary of African-American Slang* (New York: Penguin Books, 1994), 1.
9. Richard L. Forstall, *Population of States and Counties of the United States: 1790–1990*, Population Division, Bureau of the Census, U.S. Department of Commerce, Washington, DC, 1996.
10. James Weldon Johnson to Carl Van Vechten, March 6, 1927, James Weldon Johnson Memorial Collection, Beinecke Rare Book and Manuscript Library, Yale University, New Haven, CT.
11. Rudolph Fisher, *The Walls of Jericho* (Ann Arbor, MI: University of Michigan Press, 2010), 298–299.
12. Daniel Anderson, *The Culture of Sports in the Harlem Renaissance* (Jefferson, NC: McFarland & Company, 2017), 9.
13. Anderson, *Culture of Sports*, 4, 14.
14. Jack London, "Jack London Describes the Fight and Jack Johnson's Golden Smile," *San Francisco Call*, Dec. 27, 1908.
15. W. E. B. Du Bois, "The Prize Fighter," *The Crisis* 8 (Aug. 1914): 181.
16. C. Gerald Fraser, "Ed Smalls, Whose Club Brought the Famous to Harlem, Is Dead," *The New York Times*, Oct. 18, 1974.
17. Gibson, *Somebody*, 5.
18. Gibson, *Somebody*, 6.
19. Gibson, *Somebody*, 5.
20. Eleanor Clark Washington, phone interview with author, Apr. 17, 2019.
21. Christopher Buck, "Harlem Renaissance," The American Mosaic: The African American Experience, ABC-CLIO, 2021, https://bahai-library.com/pdf/b/buck_america-mosaic_harlem_renaissance.pdf.
22. Gilbert Osofsky, *Harlem, the Making of a Ghetto: Negro New York, 1890–1930* (Chicago, IL: Ivan R. Dee, 1996), 128–29.
23. Federal Writers Project, *New York City Guide* (New York: Random House, 1939), 258.
24. Osofsky, *Harlem*, 141.
25. Alain Locke, "Harlem: Dark Weather Vane," *Survey Graphic* 25 no. 8 (1936): 457.
26. *The Complete Report of Mayor La Guardia's Commission on the Harlem Riot of March 19, 1935* (New York: Arno Press, 43) [hereafter "Mayor La Guardia's Commission, *Complete Report on Harlem Riot*"].
27. Mayor La Guardia's Commission, *Complete Report on Harlem Riot*, 127.
28. Brown, *Manchild in the Promised Land*, 19.
29. Brown, *Manchild in the Promised Land*, 428.

30. Federal Writers Project, *New York City Guide*, 258.

31. Gibson, *Somebody*, 8.

32. Gibson, *Somebody*, 11.

33. On playing the dozens, Poston, "Althea Gibson," Aug. 26, 1957. "Playing the dozens" is an elaborate verbal rhyming game once played by Black males on street corners in which the participants insulted one another's relatives, especially their mothers. The first one to succumb to emotion or anger lost. *Baltimore Sun*, Sept. 11, 1994; Major, *Juba to Jive*, 138.

34. Gibson, *Somebody*, 34.

35. "That Gibson Girl," *Time*, Aug. 26, 1957.

36. Ruthie Stein, "A Wimbledon Star's New Challenge," *San Francisco Chronicle*, Nov. 15, 1984.

37. Gibson, *Somebody*, 19.

38. Steven A. Riess, *City Games: The Evolution of American Urban Society and the Rise of Sports* (Urbana: University of Illinois Press, 1989), 148.

39. Colonial Park was renamed Jackie Robinson Park by the New York City Department of Parks and Recreation in 1978. "Jackie Robinson Park," History, New York City Department of Parks and Recreation, website, n.d., https://www.nycgovparks.org/parks/jackie-robinson -park_manhattan/history.

40. Robert Caro, *The Power Broker* (New York: Alfred A. Knopf, 1974), 514.

41. "Back Lot Playgrounds for City Children," *The New York Times*, Oct. 28, 1917.

42. Sanford Gaster, "Historical Changes in Children's Access to U.S. Cities: A Critical Review," *Children's Environments* 9, no. 2 (1992): 30.

43. Ted Poston, "Althea Gibson," *New York Post Daily Magazine*, Aug. 26, 1957.

44. Poston, "Althea Gibson," Aug. 27, 1957.

45. Michael Giangrande, phone interview with author, Feb. 18, 2022.

46. Mayor La Guardia's Commission, *Complete Report on Harlem Riot*, 86.

47. Mayor La Guardia's Commission, *Complete Report on Harlem Riot*, 84.

48. Mayor La Guardia's Commission, *Complete Report on Harlem Riot*, 2.

49. Mayor La Guardia's Commission, *Complete Report on Harlem Riot*, 6.

50. Gibson, *Somebody*, 19.

51. Gibson, *Somebody*, 20.

52. Gibson, *Somebody*, 20.

53. Gibson, *Somebody*, 25.

54. Ashley L. Landers, Domenica H. Carrese, and Robin Spath, "A Decade in Review of Trends in Social Work Literature: The Link between Poverty and Child Maltreatment in the United States," *Child Welfare* 97 (2019), 65–96.

55. Gibson, *Somebody*, 21.

56. Billy Davis, phone interview with author, Jan. 17, 2019.

57. Selections of the prints created for the *Darktown* series can be seen at http://www.booktryst .com/2011/02/dark-side-of-currier-ives.html. "Breaking the Barriers: The ATA and Black Tennis Pioneers" was an exhibition created by the International Tennis Hall of Fame and Museum, Newport, Rhode Island, for the 2007 U.S. Open. It was expanded and digitized for the museum's website in 2020 (https://breakingbarriers.tennisfame.com).

58. Mary Jo Festle, "Jackie Robinson Without the Charm," in David Kenneth Wiggins, ed., *Out of the Shadows: A Biographical History of African American Athletes* (Fayetteville: University of Arkansas Press, 2006), 193.

59. "Moss Explains Ban on Negroes in Tennis," *The New York Times*, Dec. 28, 1929.

60. Three books that provide detailed histories of the early years of Black tennis, among others, are Henry Louis Gates Jr. and Evelyn Higginbotham, *The African American National Biography* (Oxford, UK: Oxford University Press, 2008); Arthur R. Ashe Jr., *A Hard Road to Glory: A History of the African-American Athlete Since 1946* (New York: Amistad, 1988); and Kimball, *The United States Tennis Association.*

61. "Breaking the Barriers," 2020, https://breakingbarriers.tennisfame.com.

62. Ed R. Harris, "Points and Errors," *Philadelphia Tribune*, Sept. 6, 1934; Pamela Grundy, "Ora Washington: The First Black Female Athletic Star," in *Out of the Shadows*, ed. Wiggins, 90–91.

63. Michael S. Miller, "Activism in the Harlem Renaissance," *Gay and Lesbian Review* (January/February 2008): 30.

64. A. B. Christa Schwartz, *Gay Voices of the Harlem Renaissance* (Bloomington: Indiana University Press, 2003), 16–19; Ashley Brown, "'Uncomplimentary Things': Tennis Player Althea Gibson, Sexism, Homophobia, and Anti-Queerness in the Black Media," *Journal of African American History* 106, no. 2 (2021): 257–58.

65. Jennifer H. Lansbury, *A Spectacular Leap: Women Athletes in Twentieth-Century America* (Fayetteville: University of Arkansas Press, 2014), 5.

66. Robert Ryland, in-person interview with author, May 16, 2019.

67. Photograph, "Miss Rhoda Smith," *Pittsburgh Courier*, Sept. 23, 1933.

68. Poston, "Althea Gibson," Aug. 27, 1957.

69. On the nickname "Mama," M. J. Sleet, "Althea Beats Rhoda Smith, But Was Sorry," *New York Amsterdam News*, Aug. 12, 1950. On the purchase of coat and underwear, see Betty Granger, *New York Amsterdam News*, July 21, 1956. On making a tennis outfit, see Lester Granger, *New York Amsterdam News*, Sept. 23, 1961.

70. The "Inside Tennis" series was launched by the *New York Age*, but various versions of it were carried in several other Black newspapers. This quote was in the Final Day series in both the *Chicago Defender* (May 11, 1940) and the *New York Age* (May 4, 1940).

71. Shari Cohen, "The Lasting Legacy of *An American Dilemma*," Carnegie Results (Fall 2004): 1–26, https://www.carnegie.org/publications/lasting-legacy-american-dilemma/; Junfu Zhang, "Black-White Relations: The American Dilemma," *Perspectives* (Feb. 2000), https://oycf.org/black-white-relations-the-american-dilemma/.

72. Sam Lacy, "Looking 'Em Over," *Baltimore Afro-American*, Aug. 19, 1944.

73. "Democracy in Action," *Baltimore Afro-American*, Aug. 26, 1944.

74. Gibson, *Somebody*, 31.

75. Lacy, "Looking 'Em Over."

76. Ryland, in-person interview with author May 16, 2019.

3. The Doctors

1. Lula Jones Garrett, "3,000 Fans Add Color to ATA Tennis Tournament," *Baltimore Afro-American*, Aug. 31, 1946.

2. Garrett, "3,000 Fans."

3. Althea Gibson, *I Wanted to Be Somebody* (New York: Harper & Row, 1958), 36–37.

4. Ted Poston, "Althea Gibson," *New York Post Daily Magazine*, Aug. 28, 1957.

5. James Murdock, "Lynchburg Negro Surgeon Played Major Role in Althea's Victory," *Lynchburg Advance*, July 11, 1957.

6. Carolyn "Waltee" Johnson Moore, phone interview with author, Jan. 3, 2020.

7. Lula Jones Garrett, "Net Stars Rebel, Set Up Own Body as Rebuke to 'Autocratic' ATA Group," *Baltimore Afro-American*, Aug. 31, 1946.

8. Warren F. Kimball, *The United States Tennis Association: Raising the Game* (Lincoln: University of Nebraska Press, 2017), 267, 269, 271, and 270.

9. Gibson, *Somebody*, 38.

10. Gibson, *Somebody*, 39. Althea Gibson writes that it was she who wrote to Eaton and accepted the offer. Hubert A. Eaton, *Every Man Should Try* (Wilmington, NC: Bonaparte Press, 1984), 28. Dr. Eaton writes that Gibson's mother wrote the letter approving the plan, saying, "God bless you for your help with my child."

11. Timothy B. Tyson, "The Ghosts of 1898, Wilmington's Race Riot, and the Rise of White Supremacy," *Raleigh News and Observer*, Nov. 17, 2006.

12. Hubert A. Eaton, *Every Man Should Try*. (Wilmington, NC: Bonaparte Press, 1984), 21.

13. Tyson, "The Ghosts of 1898."

14. John L. Godwin, *Black Wilmington and the North Carolina Way: Portrait of a Community in the Era of Civil Rights Protest* (Lanham, MD: University Press of America, 2000), 43.

15. Bertha Todd, in-person interview with author, Aug. 21, 2018.

16. Eaton, *Every Man Should Try*, 28.

17. Eaton, *Every Man Should Try*, x. Eaton was also instrumental in desegregating a number of other local institutions, including the local library, the golf course, and the institution that would become the University of North Carolina–Wilmington. In his autobiography, Eaton noted that he had filed so many complaints about racism from the 1950s through the 1970s with the U.S. Department of Justice that the Federal Bureau of Investigation had a 324-page file on him.

18. Eaton, *Every Man Should Try*, 25.

19. Garrett, "3,000 Fans."

20. "That Gibson Girl," *Time*, Aug. 26, 1957, 5.

21. Gibson, *Somebody*, 44.

22. Eaton, *Every Man Should Try*, 29.

23. Eaton, *Every Man Should Try*, 29.

24. Talk by Althea Gibson, March 14, 1959, RG306, 306-EN-T-T-2367, Production Library Audio Recordings, 1999–2005, National Archives at College Park, College Park, MD.

25. Gibson, *Somebody*, 48.

26. Hubert Eaton Jr., in-person interview with author, Aug. 21, 2018.

27. Gibson, *Somebody*, 46.

28. Eaton Jr., in-person interview with author.

29. Eaton Jr., phone interview with author, Apr. 7, 2020.

30. Eaton, *Every Man Should Try*, 31–32.

31. Gibson, *Somebody*, 45.

32. *New Journal and Guide*, May 30, 1942, June 27, 1942, and Nov. 14, 1942. The case file on record is at the Campbell County Circuit Court, Rustburg, VA. Johnson's statement appears in Exhibit No. 7. The indictment record appears in Law Order Book #7, page 377, and the verdicts are on pages 399 and 404.

33. *New Journal and Guide*, Nov. 21, 1964; *Baltimore Afro-American*, Nov. 28, 1964; and *Pittsburgh Courier*, Nov. 28, 1964.

34. Eaton, *Every Man Should Try*, 162.

35. Doug Smith, *Whirlwind: The Godfather of Black Tennis: The Life and Times of Dr. Robert Walter Johnson* (Washington, DC: Blue Eagle Publishing, 2004), 52.

36. Bobby Johnson III, phone interview with author, Aug. 15, 2018.

37. Mike Hudson, "Court of Dreams," *Roanoke Times*, Jan. 6, 2002.

38. Geraldine Bennett Wood, in-person interview with author, Jan. 13, 2020.

39. Elmer Reid, in-person interview with author, Jan. 13, 2020.

40. John McPhee, *Levels of the Game* (New York: Farrar, Straus and Giroux, 1969), 29.

41. Sallie Elam, phone interview with author, June 26, 2018.

42. Henry Kennedy, phone interview with author, Sept. 11, 2018.

43. Bob Davis, in-person interview with author, Feb. 18, 2019.

44. Smith, *Whirlwind*, xiii.

45. Johnson III, in-person interview with author Sept. 17, 2018.

46. Lendward Simpson, in-person interview with author, Aug. 20, 2018.

47. Carolyn "Waltee" Johnson Moore, in-person interview with author, January 13, 2020.

48. Gibson, *Somebody*, 50.

49. "Tennis Title to Stewart," *The New York Times*, Aug. 24, 1947.

50. Benjamin Hill, "Walker's Interests Were Far and Wide," Minor League Baseball, Feb. 18, 2008, https://www.milb.com/news/moses-fleetwood-walker-was-baseball-renaissance-man -303457114.

51. Gibson, *Somebody*, 50.

52. Fay Young, "Through the Years," *Chicago Defender*, Aug. 30, 1947.

53. McPhee, *Levels of the Game*, 38.

54. Lula Jones Garrett, "Lynchburg Tennis Sponsors Score as Champion Hosts," *Baltimore Afro-American*, Sept. 13, 1947.

55. Harold Rosenthal, "U.S.L.T.A. Lifts Racial Barrier," *American Lawn Tennis*, May 1948, 10.

56. Joe Bostic, "Weir Very Easy for Bill Talbert," *New York Amsterdam News*, March 20, 1948.

57. Allison Danzig, "Negro to Compete for First Time in a National Tennis Tournament," *The New York Times*, March 9, 1948.

58. Arthur Ashe, *A Hard Road to Glory: A History of the African American Athlete Since 1946* (New York: Warner Books, vol. 3, 1988), 145.

59. "Vivacious Althea Gibson to Defend Her National Women's Title This Week," *Pittsburgh Courier*, Aug. 21, 1948.

60. Joe Bostic, "The Scoreboard," *New York Amsterdam News*, Aug. 28, 1948.

61. Johnson III, in-person interview with author, Sept. 17, 2018.

62. Helen Mundy Witt, *As Memories Ebb and Flow* (Charleston, SC: Self-published, 2016), 18.

63. "Negress Stars in Eastern," *American Lawn Tennis*, Apr. 1949, 29.

64. "Tennis Star Enters USLTA Net Tourney," *New Journal and Guide*, March 26, 1949.

65. "Gibson, Weir in Nationals," *New York Amsterdam News*, March 19, 1949.

66. "Althea Gibson in Tennis Quarter-Finals," *Baltimore Afro-American*, March 26, 1949.

67. "Althea Gibson, Dr. Reggie Weir Defeated in Indoor Tennis Meet," *Atlanta Daily World*, March 30, 1949.

68. Gibson, *Somebody*, 55.

69. Dan Burley, "The Lowdown on Our Tennis Hopes," *New York Age*, Apr. 16, 1949.

4. "First Negro"

1. Florida A&M College, *College Student Handbook, 1950–1951* (Tallahassee: Florida A&M College), 16, 19–25.

2. "Women Tennis Star Enrolled at State A&M," *Tampa Tribune*, June 18, 1949.

3. Marion E. Jackson, "Sports of the World," *Atlanta Daily World*, July 1, 1949.

4. Gerald Ensley, "Florida A&M's Gaither Was True Football Success Story," *Chicago Tribune*, Feb. 27, 1994.

5. Charles "Trickshot" White, phone interview with author, Nov. 6, 2019.

6. White, interview with author.

7. Elizabeth Swilley McElveen, phone interview with author, Oct. 1, 2019.

8. Eva Clack Smith, phone interview with author, Oct. 12, 2019.

9. Associated Press, "'Irregularities' Given in State Auditor Report," *Tallahassee Democrat*, March 14, 1950; Leedell W. Neyland, *Florida Agricultural and Mechanical University: A Centennial History, 1887–1987* (Tallahassee: The Florida A&M Foundation, 1987), 185–87.

10. "Students Hear Dr. Gore at Fla. A. and M.," *Atlanta Daily World*, Apr. 11, 1950.

11. Stewart Emory Tolnay and E. M. Beck, *A Festival of Violence: An Analysis of Southern Lynchings, 1882–1930* (Urbana: University of Illinois Press, 1995), 38.

12. Althemese Barnes, in-person interview with author, Oct. 25, 2019.

13. Julianne Hare, phone interview with author, Nov. 14, 2019.

14. John Schelble, "Conversations with Carrie: A Personal History" (unpublished manuscript, 2011), 29.

15. Associated Press, "Sheriff Blasts Rape Decision," *Tampa Times*, Apr. 11, 1951.

16. "Florida Sheriff Cleared," *The New York Times,* Nov. 15, 1952.

17. Department of Justice, "Harry T. Moore, Harriette V. Moore—Notice to Close File," July 13, 2011, https://www.justice.gov/crt/case-document/harry-t-moore-harriette-v-moore -notice-close-file.

18. Amanda Holpuch, "Four Black Men Wrongly Charged with Rape Are Exonerated 72 Years Later," *The New York Times*, Nov. 22, 2021.

19. Althea Gibson, *I Wanted to Be Somebody* (New York: Harper & Row, 1958), 59.

20. "Rain Halts National Tennis Finals," *Baltimore Afro-American*, Sept. 3, 1949.

21. The caption of a FAMC photo reads, "Althea Gibson, college tennis star, is shown addressing a meeting of New Homemaker Girls of Florida A&M College. 1951," Althea Gibson Collection and Exhibit, Meek-Eaton Black Archives Research Center and Museum, Florida A&M University.

22. McElveen, phone interview with author, Oct. 1, 2019.

23. Col. Brodes Hartley, phone interview with author, Oct. 9, 2019.

24. Col. James Wyatt, phone interview with author, Dec. 23, 2019.

25. Edwina Martin, in-person interview with author, Sept. 15, 2019.

26. Helen Mundy Witt, in-person interview with Jocelyn Grzeszczak, May 13, 2019.

27. Althea Gibson to Hubert Eaton, Oct. 4, 1949, Dr. Hubert A. Eaton Sr. Papers, Randall Library, University of North Carolina, Wilmington [hereafter "Dr. Hubert A. Eaton Sr. Papers"].

28. Official transcript of Althea Gibson, Registrar's Office, Florida A&M University, Tallahassee; Althea Gibson to Hubert Eaton, Feb. 10, 1950, Dr. Hubert A. Eaton Sr. Papers.

29. Don McNeill, "Cops Indoor Tennis Title," *Hartford Courant*, March 26, 1950.

30. Gibson, *Somebody*, 61.

31. Gibson, *Somebody*, 61.

32. Hubert Eaton to Althea Gibson, Apr. 6, 1950, Dr. Hubert A. Eaton Sr. Papers.

33. James L. Hicks, "Althea Gibson Earns Bid to U.S. Tennis Nationals," *Baltimore Afro-American*, Apr. 1, 1950.

34. James L. Hicks, "Big Town," *Baltimore Afro-American*, Apr. 15, 1950.

35. "Brawn Helps, Too," *Chicago Defender*, Apr. 8, 1950.
36. Chestine Everett, "Althea Gibson Looks Forward to Bid to Compete in National This Summer," *Chicago Defender*, June 17, 1950.
37. "New Tennis Threat," *Life*, Apr. 3, 1950.
38. Ted Poston, "Althea Gibson," *New York Post Daily Magazine*, Aug. 30, 1957.
39. "The New Gibson Girl," *Sports Illustrated,* July 2, 1956, 19.
40. Charles Hare to Althea Gibson, May 4, 1950, Frances Gray collection.
41. Mary Hardwick to Althea Gibson, June 22, 1950, Frances Gray collection.
42. Arthur Francis to Althea Gibson, Apr. 18, 1950, Frances Gray collection.
43. Arthur Francis to Althea Gibson, May 11, 1950, Frances Gray collection.
44. "Alice Marble, 77, Top U.S. Tennis Star of 1930s," *The New York Times*, Dec. 14, 1990.
45. Robert Weintraub, *The Divine Miss Marble* (New York: Dutton, 2021), 298–311. This book, the most recent biography of Marble, raises such questions but does not answer them definitively.
46. Bill Dwyre, "Tennis Player Created an Uproar with Her Short Skirt," *Los Angeles Times*, Jan. 18, 2013. Although Moran was almost universally referred to in the media as "Gorgeous Gussie," she preferred that her name be spelled "Gussy," which is how Marble spelled it.
47. Lena Williams, "Gussie Moran, a Tennis Star Who Wore a Daring Wimbledon Outfit, Dies at 89," *The New York Times*, Jan. 19, 2013.
48. Alice Marble, "A Vital Issue," *American Lawn Tennis*, July 1950.
49. Howard Cohn, "The Gibson Story," *American Lawn Tennis*, July 1950.
50. "Justice on the Court," *Baltimore Afro-American*, July 15, 1950.
51. Cal Jacox, "In the World of Sports, a New Voice Seeks Fair Play in Tennis," *New Journal and Guide*, July 22, 1950.
52. "Justice and the Courts (Tennis)," *Life*, July 17, 1950.
53. "Ladies & Gentleman . . . ," *Time*, July 17, 1950.
54. "Althea Gets Backing for Entering USLTA Tourney," *Alabama Tribune*, July 28, 1950.
55. "Alice Marble Asks for End to Tennis Ban," *Cleveland Call and Post*, July 15, 1950.
56. "The New Gibson Girl," 19.
57. "The New Gibson Girl," 19.
58. "Sarah Palfrey" (online biographical profile). International Tennis Hall of Fame and Museum, n.d., https://www.tennisfame.com/hall-of-famers/inductees/sarah-palfrey.
59. Allison Danzig and Peter Schwed, *The Fireside Book of Tennis* (New York: Simon & Schuster, 1972), 326.
60. Sarah Palfrey, "A Champion Looks at Althea Gibson," *Ebony*, Nov. 1950.
61. "Althea Gibson Defeated in Clay Courts Quarterfinals, 6–2, 6–3," *Chicago Defender*, July 29, 1950.
62. Frances Clayton Gray and Yanick Rice Lamb, *Born to Win: The Authorized Biography of Althea Gibson* (Hoboken, NJ: John Wiley and Sons, 2004), 55.
63. Sarah Palfrey, "A Champion Looks to Althea Gibson," *Ebony*, Nov. 1950.
64. "Expert Advice," *New York Herald Tribune*, photograph, July 31, 1950.
65. "Miss Gibson Conquers Mrs. Johnson as Eastern Grass Court Tennis Starts," *The New York Times*, Aug. 1, 1950.
66. "Flam's Stirring Rally Halts Brown in Eastern Grass Court Tennis," *The New York Times*, Aug. 2, 1950.
67. Poston, "Althea Gibson," Aug. 30, 1957.

68. "Fans Cheer Althea Gibson Despite Loss," *Chicago Defender*, Aug. 12, 1950.

69. Associated Press, "Althea Gibson Temporarily Down, Needs Only Experience to Go Far," *Boston Globe*, Aug. 2, 1950.

70. The record is unclear on the exact year Althea first stayed at the Darbens' home. In her autobiography Gibson writes that it was in 1951 (*Somebody*, 78). Ted Poston (*New York Post Daily Magazine*, Aug. 29, 1957) says she first moved in in 1950. In an in-person interview on January 4, 2019, Rosemary Darben said she thought it was around 1950. Althea met Rosemary in the 1940s, and it seems most likely that it was not until she first played the Eastern Grass Court Championships in 1950 that the ATA would have suggested that Althea stay with the Darbens, so 1950 seems the most likely year.

71. Rosemary Darben, in-person interview with author, Jan. 4, 2019.

72. Darben, in-person interview with author, Jan. 4, 2019.

73. Sandra Terry, phone interview with author, June 24, 2020.

74. Darben, in-person interview with author, Jan. 4, 2019.

75. Terry, phone interview with author, June 24, 2020.

76. M. J. Sleet, "Althea Beats Rhoda Smith, but Was Sorry," *New York Amsterdam News*, Aug. 12, 1950.

77. "Negro Woman's Entry Received by Net Group," *Baltimore Sun*, Aug. 16, 1950.

78. Kimball, *The United States Tennis Association*, 123.

79. Warren F. Kimball, in-person interview with author, Feb. 17, 2020.

80. Sidney Wood and David Wood, *The Wimbledon Final That Never Was and Other Tennis Tales from a Bygone Era* (New York: New Chapter Press, 2011), 84.

81. "Althea Gibson Awaits Forest Hills Bid," *Baltimore Afro-American*, Aug. 26, 1950.

82. "Title Tennis Admits First Negro, a Girl," *The New York Times*, Aug. 22, 1950.

83. United Press/*Hartfrord Courant*, "Negro Player Hails Entry into Women's Tennis Tournament," Aug. 23, 1950.

84. Arthur Ashe, *A Hard Road to Glory: A History of the African American Athlete Since 1946* (New York: Warner Books, vol. 3, 1988), 149.

85. Marion E. Jackson. "A Sports Editorial: Althea Gibson, Pawn or Trailblazer?" *Atlanta Daily World*, Aug. 29, 1950.

86. "Round Table Discussion: The Negro in American Sport," *Negro History Bulletin* 24, no. 2 (1960): 28.

5. The Other Gibson Girl

1. Robert Minton, *Forest Hills: An Illustrated History* (Philadelphia, PA: Lippincott, 1975), 16.

2. "New Tennis Threat," *Life*, Apr. 3, 1950.

3. Lester Rodney, "Miss Gibson Plays at Forest Hills," *Daily Worker*, Aug. 24, 1950.

4. Lacy, "From A to Z with Sam Lacy," *Baltimore Afro-American*, Sept. 9, 1950; on use of flashbulbs: Poston, "Althea Gibson," Aug. 30, 1957.

5. Milton Gross, "By the Gross," *New York Post*, Aug. 29, 1950.

6. Allison Danzig, "McNeill Upsets McGregor in First Round of U.S. Tennis Tourney," *The New York Times*, Aug. 29, 1950.

7. Richard Goldstein, "Louise Brough Clapp, Tennis Champion at Midcentury, Dies at 90," *The New York Times*, Feb. 5, 2014.

8. Ted Poston, "Althea Gibson," *New York Post Daily Magazine,* Aug. 30, 1957.

9. "The New Gibson Girl," *Sports Illustrated*, July 2, 1956, 63.

10. Allison Danzig, "Miss Gibson Game from Victory Over Louise Brough as Rain Stops Match," *The New York Times*, Aug. 30, 1950.

11. Minton, *Forest Hills*, 175.

12. Sam Lacy, "From A to Z," *Baltimore Afro-American*, Sept. 9, 1950, 17.

13. Barret Schleicher, in-person interview with author, Apr. 18, 2019.

14. Danzig, "Miss Gibson Game from Victory," Aug. 30, 1950.

15. Ray Arsenault, *Arthur Ashe: A Life* (New York: Simon & Schuster, 2019), 33; Cecil Harris and Larryette Kyle-DeBose, *Charging the Net: A History of Blacks in Tennis from Althea Gibson and Arthur Ashe to the Williams Sisters* (Chicago, IL: Ivan R. Dee, 2007), 57.

16. Althea Gibson, *I Wanted to Be Somebody* (New York: Harper & Row, 1958), 72; Poston, "Althea Gibson," Aug. 30, 1957, 2; W. C. Heinz, "The Powerhouse" (New York) *Daily News*, Sept. 1, 1950; Eaton, *Every Man Should Try*, 35.

17. Schleicher, interview with author, Apr. 18, 2019.

18. Gibson, *Somebody*, 73.

19. Howard Sigmand, "Althea Gibson's Amazing Tennis Thrills America," *New Journal and Guide*, Sept. 2, 1950.

20. M. J. Sleet, "Althea Did a Splendid Job," *New York Amsterdam News*, Sept. 2, 1950.

21. "Fine Achievement," *New York Herald Tribune*, reprinted in the *Montreal Gazette*, Sept. 2, 1950.

22. Hubert A. Eaton, *Every Man Should Try*. (Wilmington, NC: Bonaparte Press, 1984), 36.

23. James Edmund Boyack, "Handles Self Well in Women's Nat'l," *Pittsburgh Courier*, Sept. 9, 1950.

24. Al Moses, "Beating the Gun," *Atlanta Daily World*, Sept. 12, 1950.

25. Ed Fitzgerald, "Little Mo vs Althea Gibson," *The American Weekly*, May 4, 1958.

26. Alice Marble, "An Open Letter to Althea Gibson," As I See It, *American Lawn Tennis*, Nov. 1950.

27. Althea Gibson, "Dear Miss Marble," *American Lawn Tennis*, Feb. 1951.

28. On the plan: Gibson, *Somebody*, 76; Jennifer H. Lansbury, *A Spectacular Leap: Women Athletes in Twentieth-Century America* (Fayetteville: University of Arkansas Press, 2014), 96; Bertram Baker to Jake Gaither, March 29, 1951, Dr. Hubert A. Eaton Sr. Papers; on Hoxie: Fred Kovaleski, "Tennis in Hamtramck," *World Tennis*, Apr. 1954, 54.

29. Talk by Althea Gibson, March 14, 1959, RG306, 306-EN-T-T-2367, Production Library Audio Recordings, 1999–2005, National Archives at College Park, College Park, MD.

30. E. R. Shipp, "Ebony—40—Viewed as More than a Magazine," *The New York Times*, Dec. 6, 1985.

31. "Althea Got Early Training in Harlem," *Ebony*, Nov. 1950.

32. "She's In," *Pittsburgh Courier*, Sept. 2, 1950; "Pace-Setting Women," *Pittsburgh Courier*, June 16, 1951.

33. Helen Laville and Scott Lucas, "The American Way: Edith Sampson, the NAACP, and African American Identity in the Cold War," *Diplomatic History* 20, no. 4 (1996): 565; "Ambassadors of Goodwill," *Ebony*, Apr. 1956.

34. "Star Gallery of 1950," *Baltimore Afro-American*, Jan. 6, 1951.

35. Alva Ramsey, "Althea Gibson's Inclusion Makes Sporting History," *Daily Gleaner*, Feb. 1, 1951; "Visitors Presented to the Governor," *Daily Gleaner*, Feb. 5, 1951.

36. Alva Ramsey, "American Players Advance as Carib Tennis Tourney Starts," *Daily Gleaner*, Feb. 6, 1951.

37. Alva Ramsey, "Caribbean Lawn Tennis Tourney," *Daily Gleaner*, Feb. 13, 1951.

38. George W. Roberts, *The Population of Jamaica* (Cambridge, UK: Cambridge University Press, 1957), 64.

39. Vere Johns, "Althea Gibson," *Daily Gleaner*, Feb. 9, 1951.

40. Roy Lawrence, "Althea Gibson," *Daily Gleaner*, Feb. 14, 1951.

41. Calvin News Service, "'Wild Style' Costs Althea Two Crowns," *Baltimore Afro-American*, March 17, 1951.

42. Chanelle N. Rose, "The Hidden History of Crime, Corruption, and States," *Journal of Social History* 45, no. 3 (April 2012): 741–42.

43. Nneka M. Okona, "Beaches That Are Havens for Black Vacationers Now Used to Be Our Only Problems," *Washington Post*, June 19, 2018.

44. Sam Lacy, "From A to Z," *Baltimore Afro-American*, Apr. 7, 1951.

45. Gibson, *Somebody*, 76.

46. Don Murray, "Mulloy's Age Tells in Finale," *Miami Herald*, Apr. 2, 1951; Pat Robinson, "Miss Althea Gibson Wins Women's Singles Title in Good Neighbor Tourney in Miami," *Alabama Tribune*, Apr. 6, 1951.

47. Sam Lacy, "From A to Z."

48. Marion E. Jackson, "Sports of the World," *Atlanta Daily World*, Apr. 8, 1951.

49. Bertram Baker to Jake Gaither, March 29, 1951, Dr. Hubert A. Eaton Sr. Papers.

50. Jake Gaither to Bertram Baker, Apr. 7, 1951, Dr. Hubert A. Eaton Sr. Papers.

51. Lansbury, *A Spectacular Leap*, 97.

52. Lansbury, *A Spectacular Leap*, 97.

53. Lansbury, *A Spectacular Leap*, 97.

54. Jennifer H. Lansbury, phone interview with author, Jan. 27, 2020.

55. Lansbury, *A Spectacular Leap*, 97.

56. Alice Marble to Bill Tilden, Apr. 9, 1951, Richard Hillway collection.

57. "Gaither's Biggest Battle Was Saving Althea Gibson," *Ebony*, Nov. 1, 1960, 168.

58. Marion E. Jackson, "Sports of the World," *Atlanta Daily World*, Apr. 15, 1951.

59. "To Compete in Wimbledon: Althea Reported to Be Leaving Fla. A&M," *New York Amsterdam News*, Apr. 28, 1951.

60. "Althea Refutes Previous Report of Leaving College," *New York Amsterdam News*, May 5, 1951.

61. Associated Negro Press, "Althea Won't Quit Famcee," *Pittsburgh Courier*, May 5, 1951.

62. Simone Briggs, "Meet Bertrand Milbourne Clark: The Sporting Polymath Who Became Wimbledon's First Black Participant in 1924," *The Telegraph*, Nov. 8, 2019.

63. Elizabeth Swilley McElveen, phone interview with author, June 6, 2020.

64. Joe Bostic, "The Scoreboard," *New York Amsterdam News*, March 3, 1951.

65. Joe Bostic, "The Scoreboard," *New York Amsterdam News*, Apr. 14, 1951.

66. George Puscas, "Althea Praised for Net Game," *Detroit Free Press*, May 25, 1951.

67. Sam Lacy, "Althea Gibson on Way to Wimbledon," *Baltimore Afro-American*, June 9, 1951.

68. "Tennis Girl from Harlem to Wimbledon," *Daily Herald*, June 4, 1951.

69. "Like 'Sugar Ray,'" *Belfast Telegraph*, June 5, 1951.

70. Adrienne Blue, *Grace Under Pressure: The Emergence of Women in Sport* (London: Sidgwick & Jackson, 1987), 28.

71. Associated Press, "Miss Hart Checks Miss Gibson at Net," *The New York Times*, June 9, 1951; "Doris Hart" (online biographical profile), International Tennis Hall of Fame, https://www.tennisfame.com/hall-of-famers/inductees/doris-hart.

72. National Newspapers Publishers Association, "Miss Rosenquest Defeats Miss Gibson in Semi-Finals at Kent," *New Journal and Guide*, June 23, 1951.

73. Angela Buxton, phone interview with author, Dec. 6, 2018.

74. Associated Press, "Wimbledon Infiltrated Ralph Lauren," *Star Phoenix*, June 17, 2016; John Parsons, "Wimbledon Drops the Royal Box Curtsey," *Daily Telegraph*, Apr. 30, 2003.

75. "Refrigerated Tennis Balls at Wimbledon," *Northern Whig*, June 25, 1930; Richard Howells, "The Unbelievable Journey of a Wimbledon Tennis Ball," *Forbes*, July 9, 2015.

76. John McPhee, "The Lawns of Wimbledon," *The New Yorker*, June 22, 1968.

77. Ollie Stewart, "Wimbledon Notebook," *Baltimore Afro-American*, July 7, 1951.

78. John Barrett, *Wimbledon: The Official History* (London: Vision Sports Publishing, 2013), 176.

79. United Press/*Courier Post*, "Sugar Ray Wary of British Food," *Courier Post*, July 7, 1951, 13; Denzil Batchelor, "The Different Gibson Girl," *Picture Post*, June 30, 1951.

80. Gray and Lamb, *Born to Win*, 74.

81. Stanley Doust, "Pat Ward Takes Set from Althea," *Daily Mail*, June 27, 1951.

82. John Barrett, in-person interview with author, July 2, 2019.

83. Neville Deed, "Americans Win at Wimbledon," *American Lawn Tennis*, Aug. 1951.

84. Associated Press, "Miss Gibson Victor at Wimbledon Net," *The New York Times*, June 27, 1951.

85. Richard Hillway, phone interview with author, July 12, 2020.

86. Frank Rostron, "Beverly Power-Drives Sweep Althea Out," *London Daily Express*, June 30, 1951.

87. Ron Burton, "Althea Gibson and Sugar Ray Meet in London," *New Journal and Guide*, July 14, 1951.

88. United Press/*Courier Post*, "Sugar Ray Wary of British Food."

6. "The Biggest Flop"

1. Lee H. Warner, *Free Men in the Age of Servitude: Three Generations of a Black Family* (Lexington: University Press of Kentucky, 1992), 137; Althemese Barnes, interview with author.

2. Robert Smith, phone interview with author, July 21, 2020.

3. Josh Greenfield, "Althea Against the World," in *Sport, Sport, Sport: True Stories of Great Athletes and Human Beings*, ed. John L. Pratt (New York: Franklin Watts, 1960), 64.

4. Hugh Chapman, phone interview with author, July 23, 2020.

5. "Today's Stars Are Highly Intelligent Persons Who Praise God and Pass Up Paths of Sin," *Ebony*, Apr. 1959.

6. Althea Gibson to Hubert Eaton, Jan. 12, 1952, Dr. Hubert A. Eaton Sr. Papers.

7. Alvin Moses, "Beating the Gun," *Atlanta Daily World*, May 30, 1951.

8. Sam Lacy, "From A to Z," *Baltimore Afro-American*, Sept. 1, 1951, 15.

9. Frances Clayton Gray and Yanick Rice Lamb, *Born to Win: The Authorized Biography of Althea Gibson* (Hoboken, NJ: John Wiley and Sons, 2004), 76; "Bethune Cats Close Season November 24th," *Alabama Tribune*, Nov. 23, 1951.

10. Biddy Wood, "'Love Set' on Tennis Court to Climax in Fall Wedding," *Baltimore Afro-American*, Sept. 8, 1951.

11. Biddy Wood, "Stewart, Gibson Win ATA Titles," *Baltimore Afro-American*, Sept. 1, 1951.

12. James Booker, "Big Town," *Baltimore Afro-American*, Aug. 25, 1951.

13. "ATA Sidelights," *Baltimore Afro-American*, Sept. 1, 1951.

14. Al Dunmore, "ATA Passes Democracy Test at Annual Tournament, Some Fans Disapprove of 11 White Entrants," *Pittsburgh Courier*, September 8, 1951.

15. Dunmore, ATA Passes Democracy Test at Annual Tournament," *PIttsburgh Courier*, September 8, 1951.

16. Maureen Connolly and Tom Gwynne, *Forehand Drive* (London: Macgibbon & Kee, 1957), 27.

17. Allison Danzig, "Sedgman and Mulloy Gain Tennis Quarter-Finals," *The New York Times*, Aug. 30, 1951.

18. "Althea Gibson Beaten in Forest Hills Play," *Baltimore Afro-American*, Sept. 8, 1951.

19. Bruce Schoenfeld, *The Match: Althea Gibson and Angela Buxton* (New York: Amistad, 2005), 122.

20. Angela Buxton, in-person interview with author, Jan. 29, 2019.

21. Julie Heldman, *Driven: A Daughter's Odyssey* (self-published, 2018), 132.

22. Bob Perry, phone interview with author, Jan. 11, 2019.

23. Neale Fraser, phone interview with author, July 4, 2019.

24. Richard Hillway, email to author, July 19, 2020.

25. Lucille Alexander, interview with Aurelia Alexander, Apr. 18, 2020, in author's possession.

26. Eva Mannings, in-person interview with author, Sept. 25, 2019.

27. Althea Gibson to Hubert Eaton, Feb. 4, 1952, Dr. Hubert A. Eaton Sr. Papers.

28. "Althea Gibson Sharpening Game," *Tallahassee Democrat*, Feb. 11, 1952.

29. James L. Hicks, "3 Bow in National Indoor Net Play," *Baltimore Afro-American*, March 1, 1952.

30. James L. Hicks, "Big Town," *Baltimore Afro-American*, March 8, 1952.

31. Julius Adams, "Straight Ahead," *Alabama Citizen*, March 8, 1952.

32. Bertram Baker to George Gore, March 22, 1952, Dr. Hubert A. Eaton Sr. Papers.

33. Nelson Fisher, "Second Glance," *San Diego Union*, May 20, 1952.

34. Jennifer H. Lansbury, *A Spectacular Leap: Women Athletes in Twentieth-Century America* (Fayetteville: University of Arkansas Press, 2014), 5; Bertram Baker to M. V. S. Smith, May 24, 1952, Dr. Hubert A. Eaton Sr. Papers.

35. "Famous Tennis Star Reveals Other Talents at Leopards Club Luncheon," *Bermuda Recorder*, July 12, 1952; "Althea Gibson Thrills Fans at Bermuda Tourney," *Cleveland Call and Post*, Aug. 9, 1952.

36. Althea Gibson to Hubert Eaton, July 8, 1952, Dr. Hubert A. Eaton Sr. Papers.

37. "Favorites Gain in Tennis Meet," *Orlando Sentinel*, Sept. 4, 1952.

38. "Althea Bows in Nationals," *Baltimore Afro-American*, Sept. 13, 1952.

39. Buxton, in-person interview with author, Feb. 19, 2019.

40. Gray and Lamb, *Born to Win*, 77.

41. Al Dunmore, "They Wink at the Age Limit," *Pittsburgh Courier*, Sept. 20, 1952.

42. "Girl Tennis Star," *Ebony*, June 1952.

43. Chuck Davis, "Little Lorraine's Racquet Prowess Is Causing Quite a Racket in Tennis," *Chicago Defender*, Apr. 12, 1952.

44. "Girl Tennis Star."

45. Lansbury, *A Spectacular Leap*, 101.

46. "Speaking of Sports," *New York Amsterdam News*, Jan. 3, 1953.

47. Cal Jacox, "From the Pressbox," *New Journal and Guide*, Jan. 10, 1953.

48. Evelyn Cunningham, The Women, "Things I'll Remember About Famous People," *Pittsburgh Courier*, Aug. 16, 1952.

49. Rosemary Darben, in-person interview with author, Jan. 4, 2019.

50. Darben, in-person interview with author, Jan. 4, 2019.

51. Marvin Dent, phone interview with author, Feb. 20, 2020.

52. Zach Davis, phone interview with author, June 4, 2019.

53. Sydney Llewellyn, "Theory of Correct Returns," unpublished manuscript from the personal collection of Billy Davis.

54. Sydney Llewellyn, interview by Miles Educational Film Productions for *Black Champions*, Oct. 21, 1984, Film and Media Archive, William Miles Collection, Washington University Libraries [hereafter "Llewellyn, interview for *Black Champions*"].

55. Associated Press, "Miss Gibson Nearly Quit Tennis," *Des Moines Register*, June 7, 1956.

56. Sam Lacy, "Has Althea Gibson Conquered Herself?," *Baltimore Afro-American*, June 29, 1957.

57. Llewellyn, interview for *Black Champions*.

58. Llewellyn, interview for *Black Champions*.

59. Althea Gibson, interview by Miles Educational Film Productions for *Black Champions*, Oct. 21, 1984, Film and Media Archive, William Miles Collection, Washington University Libraries, 20:27 [hereafter "Gibson, interview for *Black Champions*"].

60. Lacy, "Has Althea Gibson Conquered Herself?"

61. Robert Ryland, interview with author, May 16, 2019.

62. Eddie Moylan, "Don't Change Your Grip," *World Tennis Magazine*, Apr. 1955; Billy Talbert, "The Volley," *World Tennis Magazine*, Aug. 1956.

63. Althea Gibson, *I Wanted to Be Somebody* (New York: Harper & Row, 1958), 81.

64. Hubert A. Eaton, *Every Man Should Try.* (Wilmington, NC: Bonaparte Press, 1984), 34.

65. Allison Danzig, "Seixas and Trabert Reach Final of Pennsylvania Tennis Tourney," *The New York Times*, July 26, 1953.

66. Olive A. Adams, "Failure in Finals Nips Althea Gibson Bid for Net Titles," *New Journal and Guide*, Aug. 1, 1953.

67. Joe Bostic, "The Scoreboard," *New York Amsterdam News*, Aug. 1, 1953; Malcolm Poindexter Jr., "Sports I-View," *Philadelphia Tribune*, Aug. 11, 1953.

68. Gerard Alleyne's name is spelled variously in the media. On his Social Security card, it is spelled "Gerard Alleyne."

69. Allison Danzig, "Nielsen Is Ousted," *The New York Times*, Sept. 6, 1953.

70. "Foul Calls Help Defeat Althea at Forest Hills," *Baltimore Afro-American*, Sept. 12, 1953.

71. "Foul Calls Help Defeat Althea at Forest Hills," Sept 12, 1953.

72. Maureen Connelly and Thomas Gwynne, *Forehand Drive*.

73. Marion E. Jackson, "Sports of the World," *Atlanta Daily World*, Aug. 27, 1953.

74. "Student Committee Decides on Boycott," *Lincoln Clarion*, Feb. 27, 1953; on "food to go": "Picture of Denial," *St. Louis Post Dispatch*, Jan. 19, 1961; on segregation: Jenny Smith, "Cole County History: The Foot Has Rich History in Capital City," *News Tribune*, June 8, 2019, https://www.newstribune.com/news/2019/jun/08/The-Foot-has-rich-history-in-Capital-City/.

75. "Town Maintains Anti-Negro Law," *Lincoln Clarion*, March 5, 1954.

76. Albert Marshall, *Soldiers' Dream: A Centennial History of Lincoln University of Missouri* (Jefferson City, MO: Lincoln University, 1989), 1; Antonio F. Holland with Timothy R. Roberts and Dennis White, *Soldiers' Dream Continued: A Pictorial History of Lincoln University of Missouri* (Jefferson City, MO: Lincoln University, 1991), 1, https://bluetigercommons.lincolnu.edu/lu_history_book/1/.

77. Holland with Roberts and White, *Soldiers' Dream Continued*, 21–26.

78. Gary R. Kremer, phone interview with author, Aug. 11, 2020.

79. Martha Verbrugge, *Active Bodies, A History of Women's Physical Education in Twentieth Century America* (New York: Oxford University Press, 2017), 7, 181; Martha Verbrugge, email to author, July 27, 2020.

80. "Women Who Fall for Lesbians," *Jet*, Feb. 25, 1954; "Is There Hope for Homosexuals," *Jet*, Aug. 7, 1952; "The Sex Habits of Negro Women," *Jet*, Jan. 10, 1952.

81. "The Truth About Women Athletes," *Jet*, Aug. 5, 1954.

82. Ted Poston, "Althea Gibson," *New York Post Daily Magazine*, Aug. 30, 1957.

83. Poston, "Dwight Reed Now Top Man at Lincoln," *The Michigan Chronicle*, May 7, 1955, 23. Poston incorrectly identified Lincoln's football coach as Dwight Green. In fact, the name of the coach during Gibson's years at Lincoln was Dwight T. Reed.

84. "Capt. Dova Jones Is New PMS and T," *Lincoln Clarion*, Dec. 11, 1953.

85. Gibson, *Somebody*, 85, 81, 82. Althea does not identify Dova Jones by name in her autobiography, but there is good reason to believe that she is referring to him. Jones was the head of the ROTC at the time Althea was at Lincoln, and he wrote her letters after she left Lincoln. Gary R. Kremer, executive director of the State Historical Society of Missouri, said in an interview August 11, 2020 that he was told by another faculty member that Althea was in love with Dova Jones.

86. "New York Beat," *Jet*, Apr. 8, 1954; "New York Beat," *Jet*, Aug. 26, 1954.

87. Lt. Col. Emily Gorman, deputy director, Women's Army Corps, to Althea Gibson, Sept. 26, 1955, Frances Gray collection.

88. State of South Carolina Board of Health, Certificate of Birth number 28999 (August 25, 1927, altered June 29, 1954), Althea Gibson, Bureau of Vital Statistics, Clarendon, Don Felder collection.

89. Althea Gibson to Hubert Eaton, March 27, 1955, Hubert A. Eaton Sr. Papers.

90. Allison Danzig, "Hoad Wins in National Tennis After First-Set Loss to Schwartz," *The New York Times*, Aug. 30, 1954.

91. C. Gerald Fraser, "Althea Gibson Loses Tourney to Perez," *New York Amsterdam News*, Sept. 4, 1954.

92. Danzig, "Hoad Wins in National Tennis After First-Set Loss to Schwartz."

93. Fraser, "Althea Gibson Loses Tourney to Perez," 7.

94. Lansbury, *A Spectacular Leap*, 98.

95. Althea had in fact missed some ATA tournaments as her participation in white competitions increased.

96. Lansbury, *A Spectacular Leap*, 99.

97. Gibson, *Somebody*, 83.

98. Darben, in-person interview with author, Jan. 4, 2019.

99. Gibson, *Somebody*, 86.

100. W. Rollo Wilson, "Althea Bows Out in Finals of Eastern Championships," *Pittsburgh Courier*, July 30, 1955.

101. Allison Danzig, "Tennis Title Goes to Louise Brough," *The New York Times*, July 24, 1955.

7. Black Ambassadors in Short Pants

1. Shelia Weller, "How Author Timothy Tyson Found the Woman at the Center of the Emmett Till Case," *Vanity Fair*, Jan. 26, 2017.

2. *Krasnaya Zvezda*, June 9, 1957. Translation published in *The Current Digest of the Soviet Press* 9, no. 23: 11, reprinted with the permission of East View Press.

3. "Racial Hate Is 'Spiritual Act of Treason,'" *Baltimore Sun*, Feb. 20, 1953.

4. Marion E. Jackson, "Sports of the World," *Atlanta Daily World*, Dec. 27, 1955.

5. "Tennis Girl, from Harlem to Wimbledon," *Daily Herald*, June 4, 1951.

6. "Althea Eyes '57 Win at Forest Hills Meet," *New Journal and Guide*, Sept. 22, 1956.

7. Raymond Arthur Hare, American Ambassador to Egypt, to John Foster Dulles, Jan. 30, 1958, RG59, State Department Decimal File, 032 Gibson, Althea 1–3058, National Archives, College Park, MD; U.S. Embassy in Colombo to the Secretary of State, Dec. 12, 1956, RG59, State Department Decimal File, 032 Gibson, Althea 1–3058, National Archives, College Park, MD.

8. Damion L. Thomas, *Globetrotting: African American Athletes and Cold War Politics* (Urbana: University of Illinois Press, 2012), 81–83. Thomas gives examples of such questions asked in the early 1950s.

9. Thomas, *Globetrotting: African American Athletes*, 79.

10. Althea Gibson, *I Wanted to Be Somebody* (New York: Harper & Row, 1958), 89.

11. Gibson, *Somebody*, 101.

12. John Foster Dulles, U.S. Secretary of State, Instruction #2176, re the American Specialists Program, to the U.S. embassies in Calcutta, Colombo, Dacca, Lahore, Karachi, New Delhi, and Rangoon, Oct. 21, 1955, RG59, State Department Decimal File, 1955–1959, 511.903/10–2155, National Archives, College Park, MD [hereafter "Dulles re. American Specialist Program"]; Richard Goldstein, "Ham Richardson, 73, a Star in Tennis Despite Diabetes, Is Dead," *The New York Times*, Nov. 8, 2006.

13. Dulles re. American Specialists Program.

14. Thomas, *Globetrotting: African American Athletes*, 91.

15. Thomas, *Globetrotting: African American Athletes*, 48.

16. Fabien Archambault, "Harlem Globetrotter Tours in Europe During the Second Half of the Twentieth Century," Digital Encyclopedia of European History, 2020, https://ehne .fr/en/encyclopedia/themes/material-civilization/european-sports-circulations/harlem -globetrotter-tours-in-europe-during-second-half-twentieth-century.

17. "Ex-'Fastest Man' a Speedy U.S. Aide," *The New York Times*, Oct. 5, 1955.

18. Paul Robeson, *Here I Stand* (Boston, MA: Beacon Press, 1988), 82.

19. Earl Brown, "'Satchmo' Blows Hot," *New York Amsterdam News*, Sept. 28, 1957.

20. "Ambassadors of Goodwill," *Ebony*, Apr. 1, 1956; *Pagliacci* is an Italian opera whose main character is a clown who smiles despite his broken heart.

21. Veronica Chambers, "Remembering Jesse Owens," *Parade Magazine*, Feb. 21, 2016.

22. Helen Laville and Scott Lucas, "The American Way: Edith Sampson, the NAACP, and African American Identity in the Cold War," *Diplomatic History* 20, no. 4 (1996): 565.

23. Argus Trendler, Colombo Embassy Public Affairs Officer, to Department of State, Aug. 7, 1951, RG 59, State Department Decimal File, 1950–1954, 890.4533/8–751, National Archives, College Park, MD.

24. Thomas E. Flanagan, Country Public Affairs Officer, to Harold E. Howland, U.S. Specialists Program, Jan. 13, 1955, RG59, State Department Decimal File, 1955–1959, 891.453/2–2855, National Archives, College Park, MD.

25. Harold E. Howland, Specialists Division, to William Talbert, Jan. 10, 1955, RG59, State Department Decimal File, 1950–1954, 511.903/1–1055, National Archives, College Park, MD.

26. Ashley Brown, "The Match of Her Life: Althea Gibson, Icon and Instrument of Integration" (Ph.D. diss. George Washington University, 2017), 340.

27. Harold E. Howland, Specialists Division, to Althea Gibson, Oct. 20, 1955, RG59, State Department Decimal File, 1950–1954, 511.903/10–2055, National Archives, College Park, MD.

28. Gibson, *Somebody*, 102.
29. Ashley Brown, "Swinging for the State Department: American Women Tennis Players in Diplomatic Goodwill Tours, 1941–59," *Journal of Sport History* 42, no. 3 (2015): 300.
30. "Althea Gibson Will Start Off a Firm Favorite for National Tennis Title," *Times of India*, Dec. 1, 1955.
31. William Hussey, U.S. Embassy Attaché, to Ham Richardson, Nov. 22, 1955, Richard Hillway collection.
32. Bob Perry, in-person interview with author, Oct. 4, 2019.
33. "US Tennis Stars Give Exhibition," *The Nation*, Dec. 5, 1955.
34. Perry, in-person interview with author, Oct. 4, 2019.
35. Gibson, *Somebody*, 92.
36. Bruce Schoenfeld, *The Match: Althea Gibson and Angela Buxton* (New York: Amistad, 2005), 140.
37. "Ham Richardson, Sportsman and Scholar, Wins Marlboro Award," *World Tennis*, March 1960.
38. Perry, phone interview with author, Jan. 11, 2019.
39. William B. Hussey to Harry Hopman, Feb. 22, 1956, Richard A. Hillway collection.
40. Althea Gibson to Rosemary Darben, Dec. 10, 1955, Rosemary Darben collection.
41. Gibson, *Somebody*, 102.
42. Angela Buxton, in-person interview with author, July 15, 2019.
43. John Barrett, in-person interview with author, July 2, 2019.
44. Buxton, in-person interview with author, Feb. 19, 2019.
45. Buxton, in-person interview with author, Feb. 20, 2019.
46. "Davidson Conquers Nielsen in Great Singles Final: Women's Title for Althea Gibson, Jap Girl Swamped," *Times of India*, Dec. 19, 1955.
47. S. J. Matthews, "Kurt Nielsen Wins Calcutta Championships," *World Tennis*, March 1956.
48. William Hussey to Beverly and John Fleitz, Feb. 19, 1956, Richard Hillway collection.
49. "American Woman Beats Man," *Dawn*, Jan. 3, 1956.
50. Talk by Althea Gibson, March 14, 1959, RG306, 306-EN-T-T-2367, Production Library Audio Recordings, 1999–2005, National Archives at College Park, MD.
51. Buxton, in-person interview with author, Feb. 19, 2019.
52. Angela Mortimer, *My Waiting Game* (London: F. Muller, 1962), 56.
53. Clifford Webb, "Exit Angela - and 'History' Final," *Daily Herald*, May 25, 1956.
54. Mortimer, *My Waiting Game*, 61.
55. Perry, phone interview with author, Jan. 11, 2019.
56. Gibson, *Somebody*, 105.
57. Jenny Hoad, phone interview with author, Feb. 22, 2019.
58. "Althea's Odyssey," *Life*, July 2, 1956.
59. Althea Gibson to Rosemary Darben, Jan. 21, 1956, Rosemary Darben collection.
60. Sydney Llewellyn to Althea Gibson, Feb. 6, 1956, Frances Gray collection.
61. Annie Gibson to Althea Gibson, March 11, 1956, Frances Gray collection.
62. Buxton, in-person interview with author, Feb. 19, 2019.
63. Althea Gibson to Rosemary Darben, Feb. 14, 1956, Rosemary Darben collection.
64. Will Darben to Althea Gibson, Apr. 17, 1956, Frances Gray collection.
65. Mike Lupica, "Fate Kept Hoad from Being One of Greatest," *New York Daily News*, July 3, 1979.
66. Associated Press, "Hoad Captures Rome Net Title," *Alabama Journal*, May 9, 1956.

67. Cal Jacox, "Althea's Successful Tour," "From the Press Box," *New Journal and Guide*, May 5, 1956.

68. Gloria Butler, "The Italian Championships, Lewis Hoad and Althea Gibson Win Singles Titles," *World Tennis*, July 1956.

69. "A Good Envoy," *The New York Times*, May 13, 1956.

70. Rex Bellamy, *Game, Set, and Deadline: A Tennis Odyssey* (London: Kingswood Press, 1986), 11. In 1956, the U.S. Open was played at Forest Hills and not Flushing Meadows.

71. United Press, "Althea Gibson Rallies to Beat Angela Buxton and Gain French Tennis Final," *The New York Times*, May 25, 1956.

72. Buxton, in-person interview with author, Feb. 19, 2019.

73. Buxton, in-person interview with author, Feb. 19, 2019.

74. Schoenfeld, *The Match*, 166.

75. Peter Wilson, "The Girl Globe-trotter from Harlem," *Daily Mirror*, May 26, 1956.

76. Peter Wilson, "Triumph for the Black Windmill," *Daily Mirror*, May 28, 1956.

77. "Althea in Paris," *Sports Illustrated*, June 4, 1956, 20.

78. "Feature Packets with Recurring Subjects, 1953–59," U.S. Information Agency, Nov. 1956, RG306, Entry 1003, Box 26, National Archives, College Park, MD.

8. Small Fry, Big Fry

1. Associated Press/*The New York Times*, "Miss Gibson Is Hailed, British Writers Rate U.S. Star World's Top Tennis Player," June 12, 1956.

2. "Althea Gibson's Net Stock Zooms Higher," *Pittsburgh Courier*, June 16, 1956.

3. Oswald George Powe and Afro–West Indian Union, *Don't Blame the Blacks* (Nottingham, UK: O. G. Powe, 1956), 1.

4. "Althea's Favored for Tennis Title," *Baltimore Afro-American*, June 23, 1956.

5. "Negress Beats Mrs. Hoad," *Canberra Times*, June 15, 1956.

6. Althea Gibson, *I Wanted to Be Somebody* (New York: Harper & Row, 1958), 112.

7. Jenny Hoad, phone interview with author, Feb. 22, 2019.

8. Ralph Hewins, "Harlem to Wimbledon, Althea Gibson," *Daily Mail*, June 18, 1956.

9. Ralph Hewins, "Harlem to Wimbledon, Why She Aims to Reach the Top," *Daily Mail*, June 19, 1956.

10. "Negress Warned," *Sydney Morning Herald*, June 21, 1956.

11. "Wimbledon Tennis Tournament Opens Tomorrow with Women in Spotlight," *The New York Times*, June 24, 1956; "Seedings for Wimbledon, Hoad and Rosewall First Two Twice," *Guardian*, June 20, 1956.

12. "Triumph of Tenacity, Shirley Fry," *The New York Times*, Sept. 10, 1956; Darrell Fry, "The Story of Whirley Shirley: Shirley Fry Won Wimbledon and St. Petersburg's Heart," *St. Petersburg Times*, July 3, 1989; "Shirley Fry," profile, International Tennis Hall of Fame, https://www.tennisfame.com/hall-of-famers/inductees/shirley-fry.

13. "American Women Ahead," *Guardian*, June 16, 1956; Fred Tupper, "American Excels, Miss Fry Halts Angela Buxton and Shares a Doubles Title," *The New York Times*, July 8, 1956.

14. Maureen Connolly, "It's So Very Easy from the Top," *Daily Mail*, June 25, 1956.

15. Laurie Pignon, "The Girl They Said Was Useless Can Make Wimbledon History, It's Angela's Big Chance to Wear the Crown," *Daily Sketch*, July 4, 1956.

16. Angela Buxton, in-person interview with author, Feb. 19, 2019.

17. Buxton, in-person interview with author, Feb. 20, 2019.

18. Buxton, in-person interview with author, Feb. 19, 2019.

19. Buxton, in-person interview with author, Feb. 19, 2019.

20. Kennett Love, "Althea Is at Home Abroad on Tennis Court: Miss Gibson's Tour Has Brought Her World Acclaim," *The New York Times*, June 24, 1956.

21. Sydney Llewellyn to Althea Gibson, June 20, 1956, Frances Gray collection.

22. "Orchids to Althea," *Pittsburgh Courier*, July 7, 1956.

23. Gerald Walter, "Wightman Cup Four Win for Britain," *News Chronicle*, June 27, 1956.

24. Peter Wilson, "'Names' Flop," *Daily Mirror*, June 29, 1956.

25. James A. Burchard, "Althea Gibson's Story," *New York World Telegram*, June 23, 1956.

26. Scottie Hall, as quoted in "Triumphing Over Prejudice," by Jon Henderson and Matthew O'Donnell, *Guardian*, July 8, 2001.

27. "Miss Buxton or Miss Ward in Singles Final," (London) *Times*, July 4, 1956.

28. Gibson, *Somebody*, 114–15.

29. "Miss Brough's Hard Struggle, British Player in Women's Final," *Guardian*, July 4, 1956.

30. Laurie Pignon, The Girl They Said Was Useless Can Make Wimbledon History, "It's Angela's Big Chance to Wear the Crown," *Daily Sketch*, July 4, 1956.

31. Gibson, *Somebody*, 114.

32. Violet Buxton, "To Angela, Wimbledon 1956 June." All verses quoted provided by Angela Buxton.

33. Diana Narracott, "Whoopee! I'm in the Final," *Evening News*, July 6, 1956.

34. Gerard Walter, "Angela Is Out for Revenge," *News Chronicle*, July 6, 1956.

35. Fry, "The Story of Whirley Shirley."

36. Daphne Seeney-Fancutt, interview with author, Feb. 26, 2019.

37. Buxton, in-person interview with author, Feb. 19, 2019; Henderson and O'Donnell, "Triumphing over Prejudice."

38. Vic Seixas, phone interview with author, June 17, 2019.

39. Gardnar Mulloy, *As It Was* (U.S.: Flexigroup, 2009), 204; Michelle Kaufman, "A Beacon of Change," *Miami Herald*, Aug. 26, 2007.

40. Mulloy, *As It Was*, 204.

41. "Althea Eyes '57 Win at Forest Hills Meet," *New Journal and Guide*, Sept. 22, 1956.

42. "Miss Gibson's Loss," *The New York Times*, July 5, 1956.

43. Gibson, *Somebody*, 118.

44. Clyde Reid, "Althea Loses Heart to Jersey Engineer," *New York Amsterdam News*, July 21, 1956.

45. "Althea Returns from Tennis Tour," *The New York Times*, July 12, 1956.

46. Reid, "Althea Loses Heart to Jersey Engineer."

47. "We Make a Motion," *New York Amsterdam News*, June 9, 1956.

48. James L. Hicks, "Another Angle, Althea Gibson," *New York Amsterdam News*, July 18, 1959.

49. Malcolm Poindexter, "Sports-I-View," *Philadelphia Tribune*, Aug. 7, 1956.

50. "Squabbling Council Hails Tennis Stars," *The New York Times*, July 11, 1956.

51. Jesse H. Walker, "City Hall Goofed," *New York Amsterdam News*, July 21, 1956.

52. Jacob Seidenberg to Maxwell Rabb, July 19, 1956. Box 117, Dwight D. Eisenhower Library, Abilene, KS.

53. Ann Whitman to Maxwell Rabb, 1956, General File 121, Box 745, Dwight D. Eisenhower Library, Abilene, KS.

54. "Tennis, a 'Nice' Game, Brings Rough Rhubarbs," *New York Amsterdam News*, July 28, 1956; Robert Johnson to Bertram Baker, March 23, 1956, Jennifer H. Lansbury collection.

55. "Althea Gibson Not as Talkative Now as She Was on 1951 Net Tour," *Chicago Defender*, July 7, 1956.

56. Fay Young, Fay Says, column, *Chicago Defender*, July 14, 1956.

57. "Althea Has Finally Arrived," *Ebony*, Aug. 1, 1956.

58. Mary Hardwick, "The Women's Singles," *World Tennis*, Sept. 1956.

59. Allison Danzig, "Miss Gibson Gains Merion Laurels," *The New York Times*, July 29, 1956.

60. "Around the World," *World Tennis*, Oct. 1956.

61. Gibson, *Somebody*, 119.

62. Allison Danzig, "Rosewall Defeats Hoad, Miss Fry Beats Miss Gibson for U.S. Tennis Titles," *The New York Times*, Sept. 10, 1956.

63. Serrell Hillman, "Sport: That Gibson Girl," *Time*, Aug. 26, 1957.

64. Gussie Moran, "Can Althea Gibson Make It?" *Sport*, Oct. 1956.

65. Milton Gross, "Speaking Out," *New York Post*, Sept. 10, 1956.

66. Edward C. Potter, "The World's First Tens of 1956," *World Tennis*, Nov. 1956.

67. Will Darben to Althea Gibson, Nov. 13, 1956, Frances Gray collection.

68. Will Darben to Althea Gibson, Nov. 22, 1956, Frances Gray collection.

69. Dova L. Jones to Althea Gibson, Sept. 21, 1956, Frances Gray collection.

70. United Press, "Irate Miss Gibson Bows to Miss Fry," *The New York Times*, Dec. 16, 1956; "Gibson Gets 21 'Calls' in Singles Final," *Sydney Morning Herald*, Dec. 16, 1956.

71. United Press, "Fry Is Victor, Prime Minister Victim of Near-Assault," *Akron Beacon Journal*, Dec. 16, 1956.

72. Sydney Llewellyn to Althea Gibson, Jan. 1, 1957, Frances Gray collection.

9. At Last, at Last

1. Althea Gibson to Hubert Eaton, March 28, 1957, Dr. Hubert A. Eaton Sr. Papers.

2. Samuel A. Haynes, "Althea to Be a Bride? She's Mum," *Baltimore Afro-American*, March 16, 1957.

3. "Around the World," *World Tennis*, May 1957, 58.

4. Will Darben to Althea Gibson, Jan. 14, 1957, Frances Gray collection.

5. "Around the World," *World Tennis*, June 1957, 65.

6. "Miss Gibson Reaches London," *The New York Times*, May 25, 1957.

7. "Around the World," *World Tennis*, May 1957, 54.

8. Roy McKelvie, "Worried Althea Ought to Win, and Hoad Can Be Beaten Only by Himself," *Daily Mail*, June 24, 1957.

9. Fred Tupper, "Hoad Is Favored at Wimbledon Despite Mediocre 1957 Record," *The New York Times*, June 24, 1957.

10. Sam Lacy, "Has Althea Gibson Conquered Herself?" *Afro American*, June 29, 1957.

11. Laurie Pignon, "The Centre Court Could Be a Nightmare," *Daily Sketch*, June 23, 1957; C. M. Jones, "Hoad Calms Himself with Music," *Daily Mirror*, June 24, 1957; Frank Shaw, "The Line-up for a Royal Wimbledon," *The Tatler*, June 19, 1957; Clifford Webb, "Althea Beats Her Bogy—and Fans," *Daily Herald*, June 26, 1957.

12. Angela Buxton, "Althea Can Beat the Colour Bar," *Daily Sketch*, June 27, 1957.

13. Frank Rostron, "Centre Court Bias Upsets Americans," *Daily Express*, June 26, 1957.

14. "It's Althea v the Rest," *Pittsburgh Courier*, July 13, 1957.

15. Fred Tupper, "Britain's Miss Truman, 16, Joins 3 U.S. Women in Wimbledon Semi-finals," *The New York Times*, July 3, 1957.

16. "Sport: The Power Game," *Time*, July 15, 1957.

17. Christine Truman, in-person interview with author, July 5, 2019.

18. "It Was Murder on the Centre Court," *Daily Telegraph*, July 5, 1957.

19. "Miss Gibson and Miss Hard Progress to All-American Final," (London) *Times*, July 5, 1957.

20. Truman, phone interview with author, March 13, 2019.

21. Fred Tupper, "Hoad Disposes of Cooper in 56 Minutes to Retain Wimbledon Tennis Title," *The New York Times*, July 6, 1957.

22. Christopher Brasher, "Humidity, Veterans and Miss Gibson," *Observer*, July 7, 1957; Mary Hardwick, "Wimbledon Women," *World Tennis*, Aug. 1957.

23. Stanley Doust, "Harlem Girl Gains Tennis Crown and Her Life Ambition," *Sunday Dispatch*, July 7, 1957.

24. Fred Tupper, "Miss Hard Routed, Althea Gibson Becomes First Negro to Take Wimbledon Tennis," *The New York Times*, July 7, 1957.

25. Althea Gibson, *I Wanted to Be Somebody* (New York: Harper & Row, 1958), 134.

26. Tupper, "Miss Hard Routed"; "Althea Is Crowned," *Baltimore Afro-American*, July 13, 1957; "Queen Sees Colored Girls Win Wimbledon Crown," *Evening News*, July 6, 1957; Jack Peart, "Althea - but so Dull!" *Sunday Pictorial*, July 7, 1957.

27. Sam Lacy, "From A to Z," *Baltimore Afro-American*, July 13, 1957.

28. P. L. Prattis, "Horizon," *Pittsburgh Courier*, July 20, 1957.

29. Dean Gordon B. Hancock, "Between the Lines, Winning at Wimbledon," *Indianapolis Recorder*, July 27, 1957.

30. Gibson, *Somebody*, 135.

31. Gibson, *Somebody*, 137.

32. Gibson, *Somebody*, 139.

33. Jenny Hoad, interview with author, February 22, 2019.

34. Hoad, interview with author.

35. "Ladies' Attraction, Kramer Seeks Althea, 'Little Mo' for Tour," *Los Angeles Times*, July 11, 1957.

36. "'Queen Althea' Hailed by Harlem Neighbors," *The New York Times*, July 10, 1957.

37. Ron Howell, *Boss of Black Brooklyn: The Life and Times of Bertram L. Baker* (New York: Empire State Editions, 2019), 86; Ron Howell, phone interview with author, June 14, 2019.

38. Althea Gibson was the first and only lone woman to get a ticker-tape parade in New York, according to the Alliance for Downtown New York. In 2015 and 2019, two women's soccer teams, each of which appeared to include some women of color, were given parades, but New York City officials say they do not keep track of how people identify. See "The History of New York's Ticker-Tape Parades," Downtown Alliance, https://downtownny.com/ticker-tape-parades.

39. Frances Clayton Gray and Yanick Rice Lamb, *Born to Win: The Authorized Biography of Althea Gibson* (Hoboken, NJ: John Wiley and Sons, 2004), 101.

40. Edith Evans Asbury, "City Pays Tribute to Althea Gibson: Tennis Victor at Wimbledon," *The New York Times*, July 12, 1957.

41. New York City Municipal Archive, July 11, 1957, "Reception for Althea Gibson," WNYC Collection ID 73564, https://www.wnyc.org/story/reception-for-althea-gibson.

42. Dwight D. Eisenhower to Althea Gibson, July 10, 1957, Dwight D. Eisenhower Presidential Library, Abilene, KS.

43. Richard Nixon to Althea Gibson, July 10, 1957, Series 320, Box 287, Richard Nixon Presidential Library, Yorba Linda, CA.

44. Michael O'Neill, "Venezuela Mobs Attack Nixon, Wife; Angry Ike Demands He Be Protected," *Daily News*, May 14, 1958.

45. "A Party for Miss Gibson," *The New York Times*, July 12, 1957.

46. William S. White, "Russell Demands Civil Rights Issue Be Put to Nation," *The New York Times*, July 3, 1957.

47. "Althea Gibson Answers Senator Russell," *Michigan Chronicle*, July 13, 1957.

48. Quentin Reynolds, "Long Road to the Center Court," *The Saturday Review*, Nov. 29, 1958.

49. Serrell Hillman, "Sport: That Gibson Girl," *Time,* Aug. 26, 1957.

50. Wendell Smith, "Has Net Queen Althea Gibson Gone High Hat?," *Pittsburgh Courier*, July 27, 1957.

51. Ted Poston, "Althea Gibson," *New York Post Daily Magazine,* Aug. 30, 1957.

52. Russ J. Cowans, "Sports Writers Sour on Althea," *Chicago Defender*, July 27, 1957.

53. Smith, "Has Net Queen Althea Gibson Gone High Hat?"; Leo Fischer, "Some Constructive Advice to Althea and the White Sox," *Chicago American*, July 19, 1957; *World Tennis*, Sept. 1957, 64.

54. Thomas Young to Hubert Eaton, Aug. 6, 1957, Dr. Hubert A. Eaton Sr. Papers.

55. Jennifer H. Lansbury, *A Spectacular Leap: Women Athletes in Twentieth-Century America* (Fayetteville: University of Arkansas Press, 2014), 107.

56. Marion E. Jackson, "Sports of the World," *Atlanta Daily World*, Aug. 4, 1957.

57. "Miss Gibson Bitter in Cup Score," *Baltimore Afro-American*, Aug. 17, 1957; Bill Nunn Jr., "Change of Pace: Althea Gibson Speaks Her Mind," *Pittsburgh Courier*, Aug. 17, 1957.

58. Ed Corrigan, "New Person, Althea Gibson Fears Nobody," *Longview Daily News*, Sept. 4, 1957.

59. William F. Talbert, "A Year for the Newcomers," *Sports Illustrated*, Sept. 2, 1957, 31.

60. Hillman, "Sport: That Gibson Girl."

61. "Cooper-Fraser Take U.S. Title in Tennis Doubles at Brookline," "Sports of the World," *The New York Times*, Aug. 28, 1957.

62. Claude Harrison Jr., "Althea Makes Grand Sweep, Adds U.S. Nationals Title to Wimbledon Championship," *Philadelphia Tribune*, Sept. 10, 1957.

63. "At Forest Hills," *The New York Times*, Sept. 10, 1957.

64. Emma Harrison, "Althea, Pride of One West Side, Becomes the Queen of Another," *The New York Times*, Sept. 9, 1957.

65. "Althea Tries Again, Wins National," *Chicago Defender*, Sept. 9, 1957; "Althea Wants: 1. Apt., 2. Pro Singing Career," *New York Amsterdam News*, Sept. 14, 1957.

66. "What Others Think: An Offset for Our Faubuses," *Tallahassee Democrat*, Sept. 11, 1957; "Althea and Arkansas," *Star Tribune*, Sept. 10, 1957.

67. "Louis Armstrong, Barring Soviet Tour, Denounces Eisenhower and Gov. Faubus," *The New York Times*, Sept. 19, 1957.

68. Associated Press, "'U.S. Government Can Go To—': 'Satchmo' Calls Off Russian Trip," *Cincinnati Enquirer*, Sept. 19, 1957.

69. "Satch Blast Echoed by Top Performers: Nixes Tour, Raps Ike and Faubus," *Chicago Defender*, Sept. 28, 1957.

70. Alvin A. Snyder, *Warriors of Disinformation* (New York: Arcade Publishing, 1995), xi.

71. Melinda M. Schwenk, "'Negro Stars' and the USIA's Portrait of Democracy," *Race, Gender and Class* 8, no. 4 (2001): 125.

72. "How Althea Conquered Herself," *Jet*, Aug. 1, 1957.

73. "Althea Is Probably Sports' Most Misunderstood Star," *Ebony*, Oct. 1957.

74. *World Tennis*, October 1957.

75. "Althea Gibson: Tragic Success Story," *Look*, Nov. 12, 1957.

76. "Letters," *Time*, Sept. 9, 1957.

77. Sam Lacy, "From A to Z," *Baltimore Afro-American*, Nov. 30, 1957.

78. Althea Gibson and Richard Curtis, *So Much to Live For* (New York: Putman, 1968), 116.

79. Janie Sykes-Kennedy, phone interview with author, Sept. 26, 2019.

80. "Is Althea Gibson Really Broke?," *Pittsburgh Courier*, Nov. 23, 1957.

81. Gerald Nachman, *Right Here on Our Stage Tonight! Ed Sullivan's America* (Berkeley: University of California Press, 2009), 109.

10. Am I Somebody?

1. Janet Hopps Adkisson, phone interview with author, June 14, 2019.

2. Adkisson, in-person interview with author, Aug. 27, 2019.

3. Tommy Fitzgerald, "Althea Gibson Is Beaten by Janet Hopps in Upset," *Miami News*, Apr. 6, 1958.

4. Manny Berliner, "The Good Neighbor Championships," *World Tennis*, June 1958.

5. Peter Wilson, "Songbird Althea Flops on Tennis 'Hit' Parade," *Daily Mirror*, Apr. 23, 1958.

6. Bill Lane, "People, Places 'n' Situwayshuns," *Michigan Chronicle*, May 31, 1958.

7. John P. Shanley, "'Challenge' Again Proves Ideas Stimulating TV Fare," *Courier Journal*, New York Times News Service, May 26, 1958.

8. Harry Harris, "'Music Bingo'—Sour Note," *Philadelphia Inquirer*, May 30, 1958.

9. Sam Lacy, "Star Gazing," *Baltimore Afro-American*, June 14, 1958.

10. Althea Gibson and Richard Curtis, *So Much to Live For* (New York: Putman, 1968), 34.

11. Peter Wilson, "It's 11–10 on Victory for Britain," *Daily Mirror*, June 13, 1958.

12. Ted Stevens, "Christine—You're Just Smashing!," *Daily Herald*, June 14, 1958; Peter Wilson, "Christine Conquers Wimbledon Wobble," *Daily Mirror*, June 14, 1958; "Britain Lead 2–1 in the Wightman Cup," (London) *Times*, June 14, 1958.

13. "Britain Lead 2–1 in the Wightman Cup," (London) *Times*, June 14, 1958.

14. Christine Truman, in-person interview with author, July 5, 2019.

15. Peter Wilson, "England Regains Wightman Cup," *World Tennis*, Aug. 1958.

16. Truman, in-person interview with author, July 5, 2019.

17. Adkisson, phone interview with author, June 14, 2019.

18. A. S. "Doc" Young, "The Big Beat," *Los Angeles Sentinel*, July 3, 1958.

19. Adkisson, telephone interview with author, June 14, 2019.

20. "What Winning at Tennis Cost Althea Gibson," *Jet*, Aug. 7, 1958.

21. Sydney Llewellyn to Althea Gibson, Dec. 1, 1956, Frances Gray collection.

22. Sydney Llewellyn to Althea Gibson, June 18, 1958, Frances Gray collection.

23. Althea Gibson, *I Wanted to Be Somebody* (New York: Harper & Row, 1958), 173.

24. Angela Buxton, in-person interview with author, Feb. 19, 2019.

25. Tony Mottram, "It Looks Like Being a Lean Wimbledon," *Belfast Telegraph*, May 10, 1958.

26. Associated Press, "British Tennis Casts Solid Vote of 'No!' Against Gold Panties," *Chicago Daily Tribune*, May 22, 1958.

27. Ted Stevens, "Nothing Here for Me Says Kramer," *Daily Herald*, June 25, 1958.

28. "'I've No Excuse,' Admits Careless Christine," *The People*, June 29, 1958.

29. "Miss Mortimer to Meet Miss Gibson in Final," (London) *Times*, July 4, 1958.

30. Ann Haydon Jones, in-person interview with author, July 4, 2019.

31. Mortimer, Angela. *My Waiting Game*. (London: F. Muller, 1962), 81.

32. "Outcast Angela Is Britain's Ace," *Daily Express*, July 4, 1958; Peter Wilson, "Forgotten Angela Is in the Final," *Daily Mirror*, July 4, 1958.

33. Press accounts of the number of foot faults varied from Fred Tupper, "American Rallies," *The New York Times*, July 6, 1958, which reported nine in the first set, to *News of the World* (July 6, 1958), which reported eleven, and the *Sunday Dispatch* (July 6, 1958), which reported twelve. Gibson herself put the number at eleven in the first set (Gibson, *Somebody*, 174).

34. Associated Press, "Althea May Go for 3D Net Crown," *Sunday News*, July 6, 1958.

35. Ed Fitzgerald, *A Nickel an Inch* (New York: Atheneum, 1985), 95.

36. Milton Gross, "Speaking Out," *New York Daily Post*, July 8, 1958.

37. Gross, "Speaking Out," July 8, 1958.

38. U.S. Information Service, "New York Hails Althea Gibson, World Tennis Queen," United States Information Service, Women's Packet, Aug. 1958, RG59, Entry 1003, Box 24, National Archives at College Park, MD.

39. "What Winning at Tennis Cost Althea Gibson," *Jet* magazine cover, Aug. 7, 1958.

40. "What's My Line," Season 9, Episode 50, CBS, Mark Goodson–Bill Todman Productions, featuring Althea Gibson and George Sanders, aired Aug. 10, 1958, https://www.youtube.com/watch?v=BNa2zMLzZMo.

41. Elizabeth W. Driscoll, "Althea Scores Hit with TV Net Work," *Boston Globe*, Aug. 25, 1958.

42. *The Ed Sullivan Show*, Season 11, Episode 48, CBS, aired Aug. 24, 1958.

43. Richard A. Hillway, tennis historian and coauthor of *The Birth of Lawn Tennis*, and Nicole F. Markham, curator of collections at the International Tennis Hall of Fame, say that in Althea's day, the tennis rule books were silent on coaching. Althea Gibson interview for *Black Champions*; Frances Clayton Gray and Yanick Rice Lamb, *Born to Win: The Authorized Biography of Althea Gibson* (Hoboken, NJ: John Wiley and Sons, 2004), 111.

44. Steve Snider, "Althea Scores Tennis Little Slam," *Daily Defender*, Sept. 8, 1958.

45. Alice Marble and Dale Leatherman, *Courting Danger: My Adventures in World-Class Tennis, Golden-Age Hollywood, and High-Stakes Spying* (New York: St. Martin's Press, 1991), 206; Wilson Sporting Goods Company, *Wilson Tennis Information for Press, Radio, TV* (River Grove, IL: Wilson Sporting Goods Co.).

46. Mary Jo Festle, *Playing Nice: Politics and Apologies in Women's Sports* (New York: Columbia University Press, 1996), 67.

47. Gene Roswell, "Althea Hasn't a Thing to Gain in Tennis Now," *New York Post*, Sept. 8, 1958, 44.

48. Gibson and Curtis, *So Much to Live For*, 20–21.

49. Associated Negro Press, "Althea Might Try Golf Next," *Philadelphia Tribune*, Sept. 23, 1958.

50. Gibson and Curtis, *So Much to Live For*, 36.

51. "New York Beat," *Jet*, Nov. 13, 1958; Scott Eyman, *Print the Legend: The Life and Times of John Ford* (New York: Simon & Schuster, 2015), 467.

52. Darcy DeMille, "Columnist Hails Althea Gibson's Acting in 'Horse Soldiers,'" *Philadelphia Tribune*, July 21, 1959; "The New Pictures," *Time*, July 20, 1959; Jay Jacobs, "Strawberries and Lemons," *The Reporter*, July 9, 1959.

53. A. S. 'Doc' Young, "The Question of Slave Roles," *Los Angeles Sentinel*, Aug. 27, 1959; "Dixie

Accepts, Hails First Althea Gibson Pix 'Horse Soldiers'," *Chicago Defender*, June 27, 1959; Richard J. H. Johnson, "N.A.A.C.P. Scores Carolina Leader," *The New York Times*, July 18, 1959.

54. Gibson, *Somebody*, 158–59.

55. Allison Danzig, "Off the Court There Were Victories Too," *The New York Times*, Dec. 7, 1958; "From Harlem to Wimbledon," *Leicester Evening News*, June 13, 1959; Ernestine Cofield, "Althea's Book Is Light, Entertaining, Informative," *Chicago Defender*, Nov. 17, 1958.

56. Billie Jean King, *All In: An Autobiography* (New York: Alfred A. Knopf, 2021), 45.

57. P. L. Prattis, "Horizon," *Pittsburgh Courier*, Aug. 8, 1959.

58. "Miss Gibson Speaks," *Philadelphia Tribune*, Sept. 6, 1958.

59. Margaret Makin, letter to the editor, *Saturday Evening Post*, Sept. 27, 1958; (Mrs.) Wayne B. Vinson, letter to the editor, *Saturday Evening Post*, Sept. 27, 1958.

60. Richard Evans, in-person interview with author, July 4, 2019.

61. Associated Press, "Althea Gibson Is 'Stunned' by Tennis Club Color Line," *Baltimore Sun*, July 10, 1959.

62. Alice A. Dunnigan, "She'd Play at Club: Say Althea Spoke Too Fast on Dr. Bunche Controversy," *New Journal and Guide*, July 25, 1959.

63. James L. Hicks, "Althea Gibson," *New York Amsterdam News*, July 18, 1959; Sam Lacy, "Can Althea Play at Forest Hills? Many Answer 'No,'" *Baltimore Afro-American*, July 18, 1959; Sam Lacy, "A to Z," *Baltimore Afro-American*, July 25, 1959.

64. "Althea Is Ready for $$Pro Tour?" *Pittsburgh Courier*, Sept. 19, 1959; Gene Roswell, "Working Press," *New York Post*, Sept. 11, 1959.

65. Adkisson, interview with author, June 14, 2019.

66. There is no official record of salaries for female tennis players at the time. Press accounts said Gibson was either the highest-paid woman in the history of the sport (Jeanne Hoffman, "Althea Gibson Visions Lucrative Pro Career If Amateurs Hold Out," *Los Angeles Times*, Feb. 3, 1960) or the highest-paid woman athlete (United Press International, "$100 G's Pot for Althea!," *Daily Defender*, Oct. 20, 1959). Baseball star Ted Williams, by way of comparison, was paid $125,000 in 1959.

67. Dan Burley, "Saperstein and Althea," *Daily Defender*, Oct. 21, 1959.

68. Gibson and Curtis, *So Much to Live For*, 57.

69. Gibson and Curtis, *So Much to Live For*, 62.

70. Karol Fageros with Julie Murphy, "Memoirs of the Golden Goddess," *World Tennis*, March 1989, 88.

71. Gibson and Curtis, *So Much to Live For*, 64.

72. Althea Gibson Enterprises, "Althea Gibson vs. Karol Fageros," *Kansas City Star*, Nov. 2, 1960.

73. Gibson and Curtis, *So Much to Live For*, 79.

74. Karol Fageros recording of undated interviews for her autobiography, tape 5, side A.

75. Gibson and Curtis, *So Much to Live For*, 76.

76. Gibson and Curtis, *So Much to Live For*, 113.

77. "Still No Wedding—Althea," *Pittsburgh Courier*, Apr. 15, 1961.

78. Gibson and Curtis, *So Much to Live For*, 116.

79. Gene Roswell, "Working Press," *New York Post*, Oct. 30, 1959.

80. Will Grimsley, "Althea Gibson Wants Open Tennis Crown," *Clarion Ledger*, March 8, 1960.

81. "Althea Gibson Says: 'I Won't Be Orator for Racial Equality,'" *Baltimore Afro-American*, Oct. 22, 1960.

82. Gibson and Curtis, *So Much to Live For*, 140; "NAACP Boycotts Three Local Baking Firms," *Bay State Banner*, Oct. 16, 1965.

83. Todd Graff, "The Clause That Closed a Rule in the PGA of America's Constitution Kept African-Americans Out of the Country's Top Tournaments from 1943 to 1961," *Greensboro News and Record*, Apr. 21, 2001.

84. Marvin P. Dawkins, "Race Relations and the Sport of Golf: The African American Golf Legacy," *Western Journal of Black Studies* 28, no.1 (2004): 327–31.

85. Sana Noor Haq, "There's a Dearth of Black Players on the LPGA Tour. This Woman Wants to Change That," CNN, March 7, 2021, https://www.cnn.com/2021/03/06/golf/diversity-lpga-golf-women-cmd-spt-intl/index.html.

86. Tom Gorman, "LPGA's (Not So) Dirty Little Secret: Asian Dominance," *Pro Golf Weekly*, June 5, 2019, https://progolfweekly.com/lpgas-not-so-dirty-little-secret-asian-dominance/.

87. "African American PGA Tour Participation, 1961–Present," from Ryan Parsons of the Buffalo Agency, May 21, 2021. In February 2021, the four Black players were Joe Bramlett, Cameron Champ, Harold Varner III, and Tiger Woods.

88. Steve Eubanks, "Pioneeer Althea Gibson an Almost Forgotten Figure in Two Sports," LPGA, Feb. 19, 2020, https://www.lpga.com/news/2020/2020-pioneer-althea-gibson-an-almost-forgotten-figure-in-two-sports; Anya Alvarez, "At the Height of Her Tennis Career, Althea Gibson Turned to Golf," WBUR, Dec. 22, 2017, https://www.wbur.org/onlyagame/2017/12/22/althea-gibson-golf.

89. Renee Powell, phone interview with author, Feb. 28, 2021.

90. "Lady Pros Seek Golf Glory," *Ebony*, July 1971.

91. Gene Roswell, "Working Press," *New York Post*, Oct. 30, 1959.

92. Gibson and Curtis, *So Much to Live For*, 108.

93. Associated Press, "Althea Gibson Plans to Conquer Women Golfers; Amateur Her Goal," *Herald News*, Aug. 3, 1962.

94. Gene Roswell, "Golf Is Driving Althea Off the Tennis Court," *New York Post*, May 3, 1961.

95. Lincoln A. Werden, "Pro Golf Organization Ends Ban Against Nonwhites as Members," *The New York Times*, Nov. 10, 1961.

96. Lincoln A. Werden, "View of the Fairway," *The New York Times*, March 25, 1962.

97. Lincoln A. Werden, "Althea Gibson Draws Plaudits In Debut on Metropolitan Links," *The New York Times*, June 21, 1962.

98. Gibson and Curtis, *So Much to Live For*, 135.

11. Great Ugga Mugga!

1. At some point in the mid-1960s, the players switched from paddles to walkie-talkies. While none of the players interviewed were certain which Althea used when she started on the tour, it appears likely they were still using the Ping-Pong paddles.

2. Not all racist tournament directors were confronted. Sometimes Althea avoided going to tournaments in the South where she knew she would be turned away; Robert Lipsyte, "Althea Gibson: Golf Is Just Another Challenge," *The New York Times*, Aug. 23, 1964. LPGA officials in the early 1960s also occasionally asked Althea not to participate in certain southern tournaments where they had been told she would not be permitted, and Althea agreed to stay away; Rhonda Glenn, "Althea Gibson's Second Act," USGA Golf Museum, United States Golf Association, Feb. 9, 2018, https://www.usga.org/articles/2016/02/golf—althea-gibson-s-second-act.html.

3. Marlene Hagge Vossler, phone interview with author, March 22, 2021.

4. Renee Powell, interview with author, February 28, 2021.

5. Gloria Ehret, phone interview with author, March 15, 2021.

6. LPGA Communications Department, *The LPGA 1972 Player Guide* (Daytona Beach, FL: Ladies Professional Golf Association, 1972); LPGA Communications Department, *The LPGA 1968 Player Guide* (Daytona Beach, FL: Ladies Professional Golf Association, 1968); LPGA Communications Department, *The LPGA 1978 Player Guide* (Daytona Beach, FL: Ladies Professional Golf Association, 1978).

7. *LPGA 1972 Player Guide*, 45.

8. Gene Roswell, "The Pro Gets a Lesson," *New York Post*, July 23, 1969.

9. *The LPGA 1972 Player Guide*, 42.

10. Lipsyte, "Althea Gibson: Golf Is Just Another Challenge."

11. Ernie Accorsi, "Ex-Net Queen Althea Gibson Just Hopes to Finish Higher," *Evening Sun*, June 25, 1965.

12. Althea Gibson and Richard Curtis, *So Much to Live For* (New York: Putman, 1968), 136.

13. Frances Clayton Gray and Yanick Rice Lamb, *Born to Win: The Authorized Biography of Althea Gibson* (Hoboken, NJ: John Wiley and Sons, 2004), 155.

14. Gloria Ehret, interview with author, March 15, 2021.

15. Gibson and Curtis, *So Much to Live For*, 137.

16. Kathy Whitworth, phone interview with author, March 19, 2021.

17. Marlene Hagge Vossler, interview with author, March 22, 2021.

18. "Girl Golfing Marvel," *Ebony*, Aug. 1961.

19. Candace Mayeron, "Renee Powell Survives Pressures to Make Good on Pro Golf Tour," *The New York Times*, Sept. 23, 1976; Susan Fornoff, "When Golf Was Beyond Hard: An Interview with Trailblazer Renee Powell," LPGA Women's Network, Ladies Professional Golf Association, Aug. 4, 2020, https://lpgawomensnetwork.com/when-golf-was-beyond-hard-an-interview-with-trailblazer-renee-powell/.

20. Powell, interview with author, Feb. 28, 2021.

21. Al Watson to Althea Gibson, Apr. 6, 1964, Frances Gray collection.

22. Herb Raver and Marvin Jackson to Althea Gibson, March 14, 1966, Frances Gray collection.

23. Gibson and Curtis, *So Much to Live For*, 139.

24. "Lady Pros Seek Golf Glory," *Ebony*.

25. Powell, interview with author, Feb. 28, 2021.

26. Gibson and Curtis, *So Much to Live For*, 139.

27. "Miss Whitworth Wins With a 217, Cards Final 70 for Stroke Victory in Carling Golf," *The New York Times*, Aug. 8, 1966.

28. Althea Gibson to Will Darben, Sept. 27, 1966, Frances Gray collection.

29. Dick Edwards, "Sports Smidgens," *New York Amsterdam News*, June 29, 1968.

30. United Press International, "Mary Mills Wins Playoff on Second Hole," *Cincinnati Enquirer*, June 29, 1970.

31. Dave Anderson, "Significant Tennis Step," *The New York Times*, Sept. 11, 1968.

32. Arsenault, *Arthur Ashe, A Life*, 210. On data processing job: Peter Alfano, "Ashe Looks Back at a Year of Troubles and Triumph," *The New York Times*, Aug. 28, 1988.

33. Bob Davis, phone interview with author, Apr. 11, 2021.

34. "Althea Gibson Plans a Tennis Comeback," *The New York Times*, Sept. 8, 1968.

35. United Press International, "Althea Is Satisfied," *San Mateo Times*, Feb. 25, 1969.

36. Arsenault, *Arthur Ashe, A Life*, 316.
37. Ray Recchi, "Chris Wins, Kerry Weeps, Althea Wishes," *Fort Lauderdale News*, Feb. 11, 1974.
38. George Kanzler Jr., "Starcity Looks to Bridge Jersey's Communications Gap," *The Star-Ledger*, May 16, 1977.
39. Augustin Yap and Norma Yap vs. Gil Fuller, Marvin Mann, G.F.I Angels, Vanguard Sports, Ltd., and Geocine Films, Docket No. L-54367–77, Superior Court of New Jersey, Aug. 28, 1978, Frances Gray collection.
40. George Kanzler, phone interview with author, Apr. 13, 2021.
41. Geocine Films, Inc. and Althea Gibson, July 2, 1974, contract, Frances Gray collection.
42. Althea Gibson to Pearl Bailey, Aug. 22, 1975, Frances Gray collection.
43. Guy Sterling, "Military Park Hotel Sold to Developers," *Star Ledger*, Aug. 7, 1986.
44. Kanzler, interview with author, Apr. 13, 2021.
45. Rosemary Darben, in-person interview with author, Jan. 4, 2019.
46. Sandra Terry, phone interview with author June 24, 2020.
47. Kay Gilman, "Althea Gibson . . . Still Every Inch a Queen," *Daily News*, June 30, 1974.
48. "Althea Revisited," *The New York Times*, June 21, 1974.
49. Linda Lamendola, "Byrne Nominates Althea as Athletic Commissioner," *Star Ledger*, Sept. 19, 1975.
50. "Democratic Party," *The Item of Millburn and Short Hills*, Oct. 14, 1976.
51. "Althea Gibson Resigns as Sports Commissioner," *Trenton Evening Times*, Jan. 19, 1977.
52. Althea Gibson to Brendan Byrne, Jan. 3, 1977, Frances Gray collection.
53. Brendan Byrne to Althea Gibson, Jan. 6, 1977, Frances Gray collection.
54. Los Angeles Times–Washington Post News Service, "'Jackie Robinson of Tennis' Moves to Political Arena," *Albuquerque Journal*, June 5, 1977; United Press International, "Tennis Great Gibson for State Senate," *Jersey Journal*, Apr. 26, 1977; Robert Hanley, "Althea Gibson in Bid for Trenton Senate," *The New York Times*, Apr. 26, 1977.
55. Jacqueline Trescott, "Update: Althea Gibson was the Queen of Tennis, Now, it's politics that's lured her back into the public eye." *Washington Post*, June 5, 1977.
56. *LPGA 1978 Player Guide*, 108.
57. Larry Coffman, "Gibson Still an Exceptional Athlete at Middle Age," *State Journal-Register*, July 14, 1978.
58. "Teeing It Up," *Sports Illustrated*, Sept. 10, 1990, 48.
59. Victoria Lewis, phone interview with author, March 23, 2021.
60. Angela Buxton, in-person interview with author, Feb. 20, 2019.
61. Tex Harris, "Tex Harris' Roving Camera," *New York Amsterdam News*, Oct. 9, 1976.
62. Buxton, in-person interview with author, Feb. 20, 2019.
63. Buxton, in-person interview with author, Feb. 20, 2019.
64. Marvin Dent, phone interview with author, Feb. 20, 2020.
65. Leonard Coleman, phone interview with author, March 29, 2021.
66. Leslie Allen, phone interview with author, July 8, 2021.
67. Zina Garrison and Doug Smith, *Zina: My Life in Women's Tennis* (Berkeley, CA: Frog, Ltd., 2001), 80.
68. Zina Garrison, phone interview with author, July 7, 2021.
69. Garrison and Smith, *Zina*, 151.
70. Frances Gray, in-person interview with author, March 4, 2019.
71. Victor L. White, phone interview with author, Apr. 2, 2021.

12. Not the Gibson Grandstand

1. Angela Buxton, in-person interview with author, Feb. 19, 2019.

2. Buxton, in-person interview with author, Feb. 19, 2019.

3. Billie Jean King, phone interview with author, Aug. 19, 2019.

4. Buxton, in-person interview with author, Feb. 19, 2019.

5. Buxton, in-person interview with author, Feb. 19, 2019.

6. Paul Fein, letter to the editor, *Tennis Week*, July 18, 1996.

7. Letters, personal collection of Don Felder.

8. Shirley Fry Irvin to Althea Gibson, July 28, 1996, Frances Gray collection.

9. Buxton, in-person interview with author, Feb. 19, 2019.

10. Paul Fein, phone interview with author, July 27, 2021.

11. Ira Berkow, "Althea Gibson's Long Days," *The New York Times*, Nov. 19, 1996; "Tennis Legend Faces Greatest Challenge," *Tallahassee Democrat*, Dec. 4, 1996; Frances Clayton Gray and Yanick Rice Lamb, *Born to Win: The Authorized Biography of Althea Gibson* (Hoboken, NJ: John Wiley and Sons, 2004), 205; Stacy Y. China, "Helping Hands for a Tennis Legend," *Newsday*, May 25, 1997.

12. Buxton, in-person interview with author, Feb. 19, 2019.

13. Frances Gray, in-person interview with author, March 4, 2019.

14. Gray, in-person interview with author, March 4, 2019.

15. Buxton, in-person interview with author, Feb. 19, 2019.

16. Schoenfeld, *The Match*, 284; Buxton, in-person interview with author, Feb. 19, 2019.

17. Angela Buxton, "Advice from a Legend," *Tennis*, Aug. 1997.

18. Neil Amdur, "Serena Williams Has Tie to a Legend," *The New York Times*, Sept. 16, 1999; Bruce Schoenfeld, *The Match: Althea Gibson and Angela Buxton* (New York: Amistad, 2005), 284.

19. Telegram, Althea Gibson to Venus Williams, July 9, 2000, personal collection of Don Felder.

20. Fred Simonsson, "Venus Williams—Net Worth, Endorsements & Earnings (2022)," TennisPredict.com, Dec. 23, 2021, https://tennispredict.com/venus-williams-net-worth-2/; Fred Simonsson, "Serena Williams—Net Worth, Endorsements & Earnings (2022)," TennisPredict.com, Dec. 23, 2021, https://tennispredict.com/serena-williams-net-worth/.

21. Darrell Fry, "We Didn't Do Enough for Althea," *Tampa Bay Times*, Oct. 5, 1998.

22. Althea Gibson, restoration notice, New Jersey Division of Motor Vehicles, effective May 5, 1987, Frances Gray collection.

23. Gray, in-person interview with author, Apr. 17, 2019.

24. Billie Jean King, phone interview with author, Aug. 19, 2019.

25. Zina Garrison, phone interview with author, July 7, 2021.

26. Roger Terry, phone interview with author, March 29, 2021.

27. Associated Press, "Wheaties, Anyone? Tennis Legend Honored," *Hackensack Record*, Feb. 28, 2001.

28. Buxton, in-person interview with author, Feb. 19, 2019.

29. Neil Amdur, "Althea Gibson Congratulates the Sisters," *The New York Times*, Sept. 1, 2001.

30. Alan Schwartz, phone interview author, July 27, 2021.

31. Frances Gray said in an interview that she lost one of the two storage units in her care containing Althea Gibson's papers and personal items when she became ill and failed to pay rent on the unit.

32. Gray, in-person interview with author.
33. Robert McG. Thomas Jr., "Althea Gibson, First Black Wimbledon Champion, Dies at 76," *The New York Times*, Sept. 28, 2003.
34. Steve Strunsky, "Gibson Recalled as Color Barrier Breaking Athlete," *Daily Record*, Oct. 3, 2003.
35. Paul H. Johnson, "Requiem for a Champion," (Hackensack) *Record*, Oct. 3, 2003.
36. Howie Evans, "Family, Friends, Fans Say Goodbye to Althea Gibson," *New York Amsterdam News*, Oct. 9, 2003.
37. Schwartz, interview with author.
38. Yann Bouchez, "Paris Grateful with Althea Gibson," *Le Monde*, Nov. 10, 2016.
39. Frances Clayton Gray and Yanick Rice Lamb, *Born to Win: The Authorized Biography of Althea Gibson* (Hoboken, NJ: John Wiley and Sons, 2004), 207.
40. Bill Dwyre, "Delayed Honors," *Los Angeles Times*, Aug. 28, 2007.
41. Kathleen McElroy, "From A to Z: The Open," *The New York Times*, Aug. 26, 2001.
42. Sarah Shapiro, "To Honor a Marquee Player," *Newsday*, October 16, 2003.

Index